The Ruin of
J. Robert
Oppenheimer

Priscilla J. McMillan

The Ruin of
J. Robert
Oppenheimer

and the Birth
of the Modern
Arms Race

VIKING

VIKING

Published by the Penguin Group

Penguin Group (USA) Inc., 375 Hudson Street,
New York, New York 10014, U.S.A.
Penguin Group (Canada), 10 Alcorn Avenue,
Toronto, Ontario, Canada M4V 3B2
(a division of Pearson Penguin Canada Inc.)
Penguin Books Ltd, 80 Strand, London WC2R 0RL, England
Penguin Ireland, 25 St. Stephen's Green, Dublin 2, Ireland
(a division of Penguin Books Ltd)
Penguin Books Australia Ltd, 250 Camberwell Road, Camberwell,
Victoria 3124, Australia (a division of Pearson Australia Group Pty Ltd)
Penguin Books India Pvt Ltd, 11 Community Centre, Panchsheel Park,
New Delhi–110 017, India
Penguin Group (NZ), Cnr Airborne and Rosedale Roads, Albany,
Auckland 1310, New Zealand (a division of Pearson New Zealand Ltd)
Penguin Books (South Africa) (Pty) Ltd, 24 Sturdee Avenue,
Rosebank, Johannesburg 2196, South Africa

Penguin Books Ltd, Registered Offices: 80 Strand, London WC2R 0RL, England

First published in 2005 by Viking Penguin, a member of Penguin Group (USA) Inc.

1 3 5 7 9 10 8 6 4 2

Photograph credits appear on page 374.

LIBRARY OF CONGRESS CATALOGING-IN-PUBLICATION DATA
McMillan, Priscilla Johnson.
The ruin of J. Robert Oppenheimer / Priscilla J. McMillan.
p. cm.
Includes index.
ISBN 0-670-03422-3
1. Oppenheimer, J. Robert, 1904–1967. 2. Physicists—United States—Biography.
3. Manhattan Project (U.S.) 4. Atomic bomb—United States—History. 5. Nuclear physics—
United States—History—20th century. 6. Teller, Edward, 1908– I. Title.
QC16.062M36 2005
530'.092—dc22   2004066103

This book is printed on acid-free paper. ∞

Printed in the United States of America
Set in Adobe Garamond   Designed by Francesca Belanger

For Sam and Ethel Ballen

CONTENTS

The Ruin of
J. Robert
Oppenheimer

Introduction

ON THE MORNING of April 12, 1954, readers of the *New York Times* woke to startling news. The security clearance of the nation's best-known nuclear scientist, J. Robert Oppenheimer, had been suspended in the face of charges that he was a security risk.

The *Times*'s scoop created a sensation, for Oppenheimer was a national hero. He had been the leader of the Manhattan Project during World War II, and his name, more than that of any other American, was coupled with the building of the atomic bomb and the war's victorious end at Hiroshima and Nagasaki. After the war, as the government's number one adviser on atomic weapons, he had been privy to all its decisions about these weapons. If Oppenheimer was a security risk, did the United States have a single important secret left?

It was almost unthinkable that this man's loyalty should be in question. Except that as U.S. disagreement with the Soviet Union hardened into a state of permanent tension, the certainties that had sustained the American people during the war and the early years thereafter ebbed away, and so did some of the nation's confidence. After the defections of two people who had spied for the USSR (a Soviet code clerk in Canada named Igor Gouzenko in 1946 and a woman named Elizabeth Bentley from the U.S. Communist Party in 1948), Americans learned that key parts of the government—State, Treasury, and possibly even the White House—had been penetrated by Soviet agents. Then, in 1948, a rumpled-looking former writer for *Time* magazine named Whittaker Chambers rose in a crowded congressional committee room and, in an unforgettable televised confrontation, accused the irreproachable Alger Hiss, president of the

Carnegie Endowment for International Peace, of having handed U.S. government secrets to Russia years before, while he had been a State Department official. The confidence of Americans was shaken again in the late summer of 1949, when the Soviet Union tested its first atomic bomb, an event the CIA had not expected for at least two more years. Its atomic monopoly broken, the country learned in early 1950 that Hiss had been convicted on charges of perjury and that a serious-looking, bespectacled ex–Manhattan Project scientist named Klaus Fuchs had confessed in England to having passed atomic secrets to Russia.

After only four short years, the United States found itself shorn of its monopoly on the weapon that had given it a feeling of omnipotence, and learned that the key to its unrivaled ascendancy—the secrets of the atomic bomb—had been stolen. It was not long before ambitious politicians started to capitalize on the nation's new sense of vulnerability, and no accident that the most strident of those who tried to do so was a hard-drinking senator from the heartland of traditional isolationism. Within days of the Hiss conviction and the Fuchs confession, Joseph McCarthy stood up in Wheeling, West Virginia, and brandished a piece of paper purportedly containing the names of 205 "known" Communists who he claimed were working for the Department of State.

As McCarthy spoke, a debate that had been waged in secret about a possible next step in the arms race reached its decisive point, as President Harry Truman ordered the nation's scientists to find out whether a new weapon, the so-called hydrogen bomb, could be built in response to the Soviet success. Such a bomb would, if feasible, have a thousand times the explosive power of the atomic bomb. And, in subsequent directives, Truman made clear that the effort to build a hydrogen bomb was to be an all-out affair, and that everything about the program was to be held in utmost secrecy.

Robert Oppenheimer had been at the center of the debate over whether to try to build the hydrogen bomb. As chairman of the Atomic Energy Commission's General Advisory Committee, the group which, more than any other, made the government's decisions about atomic weapons, Oppenheimer had chaired the October 1949 meeting at which the GAC had voted 8 to 0 (a ninth GAC member was out of the country) against a crash program to develop the hydrogen bomb. Oppenheimer's committee had cited both technical and moral arguments. It had before it only one design for the weapon, and despite several years of research, it was not clear that it could ever be made to work. To launch a new stage of the arms race by committing the nation to build a weapon that had so far been proof against every effort at invention seemed to the committee members supremely irresponsible. Nor did they think it would be ethical. The new weapon, should it ever prove feasible, could be designed to carry unlimited destructive power. It would be a weapon not of warfare but, quite possibly, of genocide. As an answer to Russia's newfound possession of the atomic bomb it was, all too literally, overkill.

Oppenheimer agreed with the committee, but, contrary to accusations that were brought against him later, he had not led the GAC to its conclusions. He came to his view only in the last few days before the meeting, partly under the influence of Harvard president James B. Conant, a committee member for whom he had almost filial respect, and in the course of the meeting itself, as the consensus took shape. His feelings were less vehement than Conant's and he did not write the majority opinion, as he very often did. Nevertheless, the four-month behind-the-scenes debate over the hydrogen bomb earned him bitter foes. One was Lewis Strauss, a highly partisan Republican banker and businessman who was one of five AEC commissioners. Another was Edward Teller, the Hungarian-born scientist whom Oppenheimer had known well during the Manhattan Project years, and whom he had disappointed in 1943 by declining to make him head of Los Alamos's Theoretical Division. A brilliant administrator, Oppenheimer had kept Teller on the reservation throughout the war by allowing him to form a small group of his own. But Teller, already obsessed by the idea of the hydrogen bomb, nursed his resentments and concluded that Oppenheimer was motivated not by honest conviction but by ambition, not wanting *his* success, the atomic bomb, to be trumped by a bigger weapon.

The enmities Oppenheimer incurred during the H-bomb debate of 1949–50 became deeper afterward, for as part of his H-bomb decision, Truman also decreed that the very fact of the debate, plus everything that had been said in the course of it, was to remain supersecret. No one who had taken part was permitted even to describe the proceedings to anyone who did not have a "Q" clearance, a clearance to see top secret nuclear data. As a result Oppenheimer and the rest of the General Advisory Committee were not permitted to explain why they had reached their conclusions. Yet the GAC had urged that the American people be kept more fully informed about atomic matters, and its members were almost as disheartened by Truman's secrecy order as by the H-bomb decision itself. A few days after Truman's announcement Oppenheimer spoke on Mrs. Roosevelt's special television program against the excessive secrecy, but he was the last Q-cleared insider to do so. From then on, it was only the scientists who no longer had any official portfolio who spoke out publicly against the dangers of the thermonuclear bomb, men such as Hans Bethe of Cornell, Victor Weisskopf of MIT, retired AEC commissioner Robert Bacher, and Ralph Lapp, an expert on the effects of radiation. Oppenheimer was aware of their efforts and no doubt approved, but he had to maintain public silence. Much later, however, his early opposition to the crash program was metamorphosed into the charge that because his opposition had become known, it had discouraged other scientists and slowed down the program—all to the benefit of the Russians.

Following Truman's silencing decision, Oppenheimer took other stands that earned him enemies in high places. First, like Conant and most of the government's other scientific advisers, he opposed a pet project of the Air Force, the building of a nuclear-powered aircraft. Second, like Gordon Dean, chairman of the AEC, and nearly all his own colleagues on the General Advisory Committee, he defended the ongoing work of Los Alamos and opposed pressure from Teller and the Air Force to build a second nuclear weapons laboratory to compete with it, the laboratory that exists today in Livermore, California. After his and the GAC's defeat on this issue, Oppenheimer was forced off the GAC. Finally, he helped write the "Vista" report, a study commissioned by the Air Force in 1951, which urged that tactical nuclear weapons be made available to defend Western Europe against Soviet land armies if necessary. Instead of relying on a small number of thermonuclear bombs with which the Air Force could pulverize targets in the far-off USSR, "Vista" recommended that a large number of smaller bombs be spread among the services so that, if need be, war could be fought on the ground in Europe. The Air Force, a young and cocksure branch of the armed services, took umbrage at the notion of sharing the powerful new weapons with the other services and assumed once again that Oppenheimer was the villain.

A brilliant, charismatic man with the gift of seeing further into the future of nuclear weapons than anyone else, either then or later, Oppenheimer also had glaring vulnerabilities, chief among them the possibility that he had been a member of the Communist Party. Certainly, several of those closest to him had been: Jean Tatlock, a woman he cared about deeply, and Frank and Jackie Oppenheimer, Robert's brother and sister-in-law. Katherine Puening, whom Robert married in 1940, had belonged to the Party, as had one of her former husbands, Joe Dallet, who died a hero in the Spanish civil war. Communists and Communist sympathizers were numerous in Depression-era Berkeley, and some were physics students of Oppenheimer's who joined the Party believing him to be a member and who paid dearly for it afterward. Robert Oppenheimer himself made monthly contributions to the Party up to 1942 and, by his own admission, "belonged to nearly every fellow-traveling organization on the West Coast." But he denied that he had ever joined the Party, and the testimony of a number of close witnesses of his political activity bears him out.

Jean Tatlock was the daughter of a highly regarded professor of English literature at the University of California at Berkeley. By all accounts she was a beautiful woman, generous and warmhearted, in training to be a doctor. She and Robert Oppenheimer met in the spring of 1936 and by the fall of that year he began to court her. With the courtship, a change was observed in Oppenheimer. His lectures became simpler and more accessible. And he was happier, he said later, because he now felt more a part of his time and country. Much of this he owed to Jean, an on-again, off-again member of the Communist Party who introduced him to her activist friends in Berkeley.

At least twice, Oppenheimer was to say, he and Jean were "close enough to marriage to think of ourselves as engaged." He was anxious to marry her, but Jean, one friend said, "out of troubles of her own," refused to marry him. Robert and Jean broke up in the fall of 1939, after he had met Kitty Harrison, and a year later he and Kitty were married.[1]

In early 1943, before he left for Los Alamos, he had a telephone call from Jean that he failed to answer. Through a mutual friend he soon had a message that she was in distress and needed to see him. So in June of that year he found an excuse to go to San Francisco, where he saw Jean. The FBI followed him during every moment of the visit, and on one of the two evenings he spent with Jean, FBI agents in a car outside her apartment building observed that he spent the night. The night he spent with Jean Tatlock in 1943 was brought up at his hearing eleven years later, always as part of the charge that he was an adulterer who disregarded demands of security by spending the night with a known Communist. "Was that good security?" someone asked at the hearing. "No," he admitted.

Kitty Oppenheimer knew about the meeting in advance. Knew of it, didn't like it, and accepted it. But when Robert got into trouble over it at the hearing, his relatives were amused. "There were dark secrets in his life on Shasta Road," said his cousin, Hilde Stern Hein, years afterward. (Shasta Road was where he had lived as a bachelor.) "And one of them was that Jean was lesbian." The "secret" was evidently true, but we can only speculate about the role played by Jean's lesbianism in her feelings toward Robert and her decision not to marry him.[2]

Whether Oppenheimer joined the Communist Party in Berkeley during the late 1930s was a question scrutinized intently by the FBI and Army security. The issue has been revived from time to time, most recently when historian Gregg Herken unearthed the diary of Haakon Chevalier's first wife. She wrote that Haakon, a lecturer in Romance languages at the university, and Robert had belonged to a closed unit of the Party that met every other week or so during the academic year at the house of one or the other of them. In a letter to another historian in 1973, Chevalier, who had been a Party member and insisted that Robert had been as well, gave the names of four deceased friends who, he claimed, had belonged to their unit.[3]

Oppenheimer steadfastly denied that he had ever belonged to the Communist Party, and the U.S. government, despite its efforts, never proved that he had. But he conceded that he had been an active fellow traveler and had, through the Party, contributed to Spanish war relief and other causes favored by the Communists. At his home in Truro, Massachusetts, in 1985, Steve Nelson, head of the Party in San Francisco during the early 1940s, told the author, "Absolutely I would have known if he was in the Party, and I have no reason to deny it now that he is dead." If Oppenheimer had belonged to the Party, added the eighty-four-year-old Nelson, "I'd have been the one to collect his dues." Instead, the Party assigned Isaac "Doc" Folkoff, an older man who knew how to discuss "philosophical questions," to collect Robert's donations to the war in Spain.[4]

Nelson said that he first met Oppenheimer in 1939 at a fund-raiser in Berkeley. After they had made their speeches, Oppenheimer went up to Nelson to shake his hand. "I am going to marry a friend of yours," he said. The friend was Kitty, who had been married to Joe Dallet, a comrade of Nelson's in the Spanish war. In 1936 or so, Nelson, Dallet, and Kitty had spent a week together in Paris when the men were on their way to Spain; eight months later, it fell to Nelson to break the news to Kitty that Dallet had been killed. Later, Kitty lived briefly in New York City with Nelson and his wife, Margaret. "My association with Spain and with his wife's former husband made a bond that's a little hard to explain," Nelson said of his relationship with Oppenheimer. "I admired him. I respected him. He was an outstanding figure whom people, especially his students, looked on with awe. He was a figure with a glow. Why on earth should he have cared about the anti-Fascist cause?" Nelson thought it had something to do with Oppenheimer's exposure to anti-Semitism during his student years in Germany. But the question of asking him to join the Communist Party did not arise, Nelson claimed, in any discussion he took part in. "He's a good person, fine. He made contributions to the Party, fine. There are people who want to squeeze every drop out of a lemon. I didn't put the question to Robert. Our relationship was sensitive. I didn't want to be told no."

The Oppenheimers and Nelsons saw each other three or four times "on a personal basis," Nelson said, and other times at parties and fund-raisers. But in early 1943 Robert told Nelson he'd have to say good-bye. "I already suspected that it might be something special, maybe connected with the war effort, so I said nothing but good-bye and good luck." Robert left for Los Alamos, and they never saw each other again.[5]

Nelson's picture of Oppenheimer as close to the Party but not of it is echoed by Philip Farley, later a State Department adviser on arms control. As a graduate student in English at Berkeley, Farley saw Oppenheimer licking envelopes nights at the teachers' union, and remembered him as someone, unlike lowly graduate students such as himself, whom the Communists backed for office—Oppie was elected recording secretary—*because* he was a non-Party member who was a hero to others.[6]

Philip Morrison, a devoted student of Oppenheimer's, and David Hawkins, the Party's education director in the Bay Area, carefully distinguished their roles inside the Party from Oppenheimer's outside it. Morrison remembers lecturing on Marx, Engels, and Lenin at an old Loew's Theater in San Francisco as one of his assigned tasks, and he and Hawkins raised funds from individual donors as well. Oppenheimer donated funds but was never asked to solicit them. Years afterward, Hawkins observed that Oppenheimer was content to leave "a certain calculated ambiguity" about his relationship with the Party. Possibly it was a manifestation of his overall style of leaving things unsaid, a style which lent him an air of mystery but led others to wonder about his motives.[7]

Today, nearly seventy years later, does it matter whether Oppenheimer, along with other liberals who felt that the New Deal was not far enough left, actually belonged to the Communist Party? The Gray board, the government panel that in 1954 ruled on whether he should have a top-level security clearance, dismissed the possibility of his spying and called him "unusually discreet" with secrets of the atomic project. The question, then, is one of truthfulness. If Oppenheimer, despite his many denials, did in fact join the Party, even briefly, then he was carrying a terrible burden—both of membership and of dishonesty—during the hearings and throughout his postwar years as a government adviser.

Oppenheimer was not one to submit to the demands of Party discipline. And whether membership in what, in the parlance of the day, was called a "professional section" amounted to Party membership, as the Chevaliers claimed, may be a matter of definition. Given Oppenheimer's character and the years of scrutiny he weathered, it seems fair to assume that for a time he was, as he admitted, close to the Party, but that he did not belong to it.

Still, how could a man with so radical a record have been cleared for the Manhattan Project? The answer is that the country needed him. General Leslie R. Groves, director of the project for the Army, knew of his past connections but decided early on that Oppenheimer was the man to lead the effort and cleared him despite the objections of subordinates. Throughout the war Oppenheimer was subjected to closer surveillance than anybody else at Los Alamos: whenever he went outside the gates, he was driven in a government car by an Army security agent who listened in on his conversations. When Jean Tatlock in deep depression appealed to him and he went to her in Berkeley in 1943, FBI agents parked outside her apartment recorded the fact that he had spent the night.

After the war the surveillance continued. In the J. Edgar Hoover Building on Pennsylvania Avenue in Washington there are thousands of pages of transcripts of Oppenheimer's telephone conversations with his wife, Kitty, and others from 1946 on, all recorded by the FBI. And throughout this time he was advising the government on its policies about atomic weapons and, inevitably, its foreign policies as well. Oppenheimer knew he was being watched. Countless times, when he and Kitty were on a picnic or were stranded beside an airstrip somewhere, they and their two children would scour the ground for the four-leaf clovers they knew they would be needing someday. Although he expected lightning to strike, Oppenheimer did not trim his advice to the government. In the Acheson-Lilienthal plan, which he and his associate I. I. Rabi drafted at the end of 1945, he proposed international control of all fissionable materials although he was aware that this could—as it did—give rise to the charge that he wanted to give away the "secret" to the Russians. He opposed the H-bomb crash program although his position could—as it did—lead to the official charge that he had failed to advocate "the strongest offensive military posture for the United States." Beneath the debates, in minutes and letters that were classified for decades but are at long last available today, it is clear that he unfailingly took positions that he believed would optimize the nation's military posture.

Oppenheimer had other vulnerabilities besides his left-wing past. Ordinarily solicitous, even courtly, toward others, he also had a cruel streak. Sometimes, for no discernible reason, he would lash out at a student, a colleague, even a powerful official, with an acerbity bound to humiliate. This earned him enemies with power to retaliate and, just as much as his left-wing past or positions he had taken on major issues, paved the way to his downfall.

And there were questions about his character. While Oppenheimer did not trim his political advice in an effort to protect himself, in at least five instances he informed the government that he suspected a former student of being, or having once been, a Party member. And, spectacularly, by his own admission he had lied to Army security officials in 1943 in describing a feeler as to whether he might be willing to reveal atomic secrets to Russia—the so-called Chevalier affair.

Given these attributes, his enormous personal magnetism, his contempt for anyone he regarded as stupid or pompous or hypocritical, the fact that he was known to have lied on occasion, plus a delphic way of expressing himself that could make his pronouncements seem puzzling or double-edged, Oppenheimer was bound to become a point of anxiety to an administration which wanted to protect itself against charges that it was sheltering Communist spies. Thus, when a one-time congressional aide wrote a letter to FBI director

J. Edgar Hoover charging that Oppenheimer was "more probably than not" a spy for the Soviet Union, President Eisenhower quickly ordered that the scientist's clearances be suspended pending a hearing to determine whether he represented a danger to the nation's security.

Behind the scenes, the president was pursuing two related purposes. One was to break McCarthy's power; the other, to keep McCarthy as far as possible from the atomic energy program. As it happened, these purposes came together during the heartbreakingly beautiful Washington spring of 1954. After he had assaulted one government agency after another for alleged security lapses, McCarthy's unfriendly gaze had at last fallen upon Eisenhower's favorite institution, the U.S. Army. The commanding officer at Fort Monmouth, New Jersey, had inadvertently countenanced the promotion of a dentist named Irving Peress, who was charged by McCarthy with having been a Communist Party member. For this, McCarthy decided, the Army would have to pay. And so for the first ten days of May the secretary of the Army, Robert Stevens, occupied the witness stand in televised hearings before Congress that riveted the nation's attention. Each day after testifying, Stevens, whose career as a textile manufacturer had in no way prepared him for his ordeal, was driven back to the Pentagon to go over the testimony he had just given and be coached for his appearance the next day.

For three weeks that April and May, about the same time Stevens was suffering under the klieg lights on Capitol Hill, Oppenheimer was undergoing a comparable ordeal far out of public sight, in a dilapidated government building close by the Washington Monument. After he had testified each day and listened to the testimony of others, Oppenheimer, too, was driven across town, to the house of an attorney in Georgetown, to review the day's events and prepare for the next day's torment.

The ordeals the two men were undergoing were by no means symmetrical, for the Army secretary enjoyed the president's enthusiastic behind-the-scenes support, while the scientist endured just the opposite. The government placed obstacle after obstacle in the way of Oppenheimer's lawyers. They were denied access to documents they needed, witnesses for the defense were subjected to entrapment, and when his attorneys conferred with their client or with one another in person or by telephone, their conversations were recorded by the FBI and transmitted to the prosecution.

This wiretapping was illegal and would have caused a scandal had it been known at the time (it became public knowledge only after passage of the Freedom of Information Act more than twenty years later). In addition, nearly all the charges against Oppenheimer were wildly out of date. One accusation was that the scientist had continued to oppose the H-bomb program after it had become official policy and that his opposition had slowed down the program. Only a few days before the hearing began, however, the Atomic Energy Commission detonated a hydrogen bomb in the Pacific so powerful that it caused a diplomatic incident with Japan and gave rise to fears that thermonuclear explosions could no longer be controlled. Not only was the program successful, it was embarrassingly successful, and it had plainly outpaced that of the Russians.

Another of the accusations was that Oppenheimer had advocated the dispersal of small atomic weapons in Europe so that the West could fight a defensive war there as an alternative to mass bombing of civilians in the USSR. Testimony on this issue took up about a quarter of the transcript, yet by the time of the hearing in the spring of 1954, the measures Oppenheimer had advocated in 1951 were already the official policy of the administration that was conducting the prosecution. If Oppenheimer had committed heresy, it was the heresy of being right a year or two too soon.

During the hearing, Oppenheimer was not accused of ever having given away a government secret, nor did either of the panels that judged him find that he had done so. To the contrary, the court of first instance, the Gray board (so named after its chairman, former secretary of the Army Gordon Gray), concluded that the defendant had shown "extraordinary discretion in keeping to himself secrets," adding that had it been allowed to apply "mature common sense judgment" instead of the government's tangled security regulations, it would have cleared him. Nevertheless, citing his opposition to the

H-bomb crash program, it recommended by a vote of 2 to 1 that his clearance be withdrawn. Next, the five AEC commissioners, to whom Oppenheimer appealed the verdict, upheld the Gray board's decision by a vote of 4 to 1, this time on the entirely new ground that the scientist did not take the requirements of the security system seriously enough and that he had "defects of character" that made him a security risk.

By the conclusion of the parallel proceedings that spring, the public hearing on Capitol Hill and the secret one in the run-down building just off the Mall, Eisenhower's purposes had been achieved. In the course of the Army-McCarthy hearings the demagogic senator from Wisconsin overreached himself, and a few months later his colleagues voted to censure him, thereby ending his power. And, dominating the headlines as they did, the hearings over the Army drowned out the Oppenheimer hearing and stifled debate over the momentous questions that had led to it. As Stephen Ambrose, one of Eisenhower's biographers, pointed out, such was the furor over McCarthy that the president and Lewis Strauss got rid of Robert Oppenheimer without any public discussion of whether he had been right: whether it had been a breach of morality to build the H-bomb. The McCarthy hearings also distracted the public from fears stirred by the "Bravo" test in the Pacific that spring—the second U.S. thermonuclear test and one so enormous that it almost seemed out of control—and obscured the fact that thanks to Presidents Truman and Eisenhower, the United States was now embroiled in an all-out H-bomb race with the Russians.

But for the president, and the country, the hearing held in secret had its costs. Eisenhower respected Oppenheimer, shared his moral qualms about nuclear weapons, and knew that he was not disloyal. By allowing his officials to deceive him about Oppenheimer's alleged foot-dragging over the H-bomb and about methods used during the hearing, Eisenhower countenanced a travesty of justice that rankles in the American conscience to this day. Early in the year 2000, at a fiftieth-anniversary observance at the National Archives of McCarthy's West Virginia speech, no one—not a single member of Eisenhower's family or administration—took issue with the verdict of the historians in attendance that the Oppenheimer hearing was the single worst blot on Eisenhower's record in domestic affairs.

In writing this book, it was not my intention to write a parable for our time. But the story I tell is an old one, the story of what happens when some institution—a church, say, or a government—decides to rid itself of someone who has become anathema to it, or when it wants to change course without saying so openly.

Stories like this one do not take place in the open. Secrecy is at their heart, and so is the exclusive claim to orthodoxy. The people must be protected, whether from the taint of alien ideology or from the threat of military attack. The result is always the same. The fever passes, and most people never find out what was really at stake.

In the case of Robert Oppenheimer, the deviations from what we consider basic rules of our democracy were so egregious that even today, half a century later, the story still stirs our consciences and makes us wonder what it was all about. It was about many things. One of them was our government's decision to move to a new and deadlier level of the nuclear arms race without telling the American people. Not only was the hearing an extraordinary display of ingratitude toward a man to whom the nation owed much, but it resulted in the removal from public life of the one individual who might have helped restrain our catastrophic rush to overarmament.

This book is a look at the people and events that led to the destruction of J. Robert Oppenheimer.

There are stories like it today.

PART ONE

1945-1949

CHAPTER ONE

David Lilienthal's Vacation

FROM THE KITCHEN of his rented house on Martha's Vineyard, David Lilienthal watched on the early morning of September 19, 1949, as bluebirds flew in and out of a hole in the old knotted apple tree outside. A downy woodpecker was whacking away at the tree, along with a large flicker, a kingbird, and a pair of gray crested waxwings. The whirring sounds the birds made and the distant lapping noises of Nantucket Sound, these were nursing Helen and David Lilienthal back to life after a devastating spring and summer.

It had begun, if their current troubles could be said to have had so neat a beginning, back in May, when Republican senator Bourke Hickenlooper had demanded Lilienthal's resignation as chairman of the Atomic Energy Commission. Each day, said Hickenlooper, a member of the joint congressional committee on atomic energy, he had found new evidence of Lilienthal's "incredible mismanagement." For three months the hearings had dragged on, with Lilienthal on the witness stand day after sweltering summer day, with cameramen at his feet and glaring klieg lights in his eyes. Three months, and then Hickenlooper's Republican colleague Arthur Vandenberg had called David Lilienthal in and told him, almost casually, that the charges against him were being dropped.

Through it all, through banner newspaper headlines and nightly verbal attacks by the virulently right-wing radio commentator Fulton Lewis Jr., David and Helen Lilienthal had had over them the shadow of former secretary of defense James Forrestal, who had jumped to his death from a window of Bethesda Naval Hospital on May 22, the very day the attack on Lilienthal's "mismanagement" had begun.

Reminded in this abrupt and shocking way of what the pressures of public life could do to a man, Lilienthal felt grateful once again that he was able to count on the encouragement of his wife, Helen, and the staunch support of the president of the United States.[1]

On the Vineyard he had slept away some of his exhaustion. "I'm not a new man and never will be," Lilienthal wrote in his journal, "but I'm no longer acutely weary." It was time to think about the future. His term on the commission would be ending the following June. Nineteen years on government salaries, first as a founding director of the Tennessee Valley Authority and then as the first chairman of the AEC, had left him without much in the way of savings. He had just turned fifty, and with parents who needed help and a son and daughter who hoped to go to graduate school, he figured he had ten years left in which to put something by for his retirement. His three years at the AEC had been deeply disappointing to him in that the harnessing of atomic energy for peaceful purposes was still a long way down the road, and he knew the agency would never become what he had hoped—another TVA. On the other hand, in what the AEC had determined, to his regret, to be its main task, the commission had met its responsibility: the country had enough atomic weapons to ensure its safety for the foreseeable future.[2]

The AEC had been created in 1946, with five commissioners appointed by the president and answerable to both the White House and the Joint Committee on Atomic Energy of the House and Senate (JCAE). In addition to Lilienthal, the original commissioners were Robert Bacher, a nuclear physicist from Cornell who had worked on the Manhattan Project; Lewis Strauss and Sumner Pike, small-town boys who had been successful on Wall Street; and William Waymack, former editor of the Des Moines *Register* and *Tribune* and deputy chairman of the Federal Reserve Bank of Chicago. Because it had been created to manage atomic energy development for military as well as civilian purposes, the commission had had to take a tougher line on almost everything than Lilienthal would have liked. And of the five commissioners, the toughest had been Lewis Strauss, a strongly partisan Republican investment banker from New York. A dozen times, finding himself in a minority of one, Strauss had gone over the heads of the others to the White House, the newspapers, and even to highly placed friends such as Defense Secretary Forrestal. Strauss's habit of "shooting at one's brothers," as Lilienthal called it, had shattered the spirit of collegiality so important to Lilienthal's way of running things. He realized that he would no longer be able to lead in the way that suited him, by reconciling differences. He knew, moreover, that if he were to accept reappointment, there would probably be another ugly fight, like the one he had had with Democratic senator Kenneth McKellar of Tennessee on his confirmation in 1947 and the one he had just been through. "If we have another one," Helen told him, referring to the Hickenlooper hearings as they sat drinking coffee on the front stoop a day or two before, "*I'll* resign." Not that David Lilienthal looked with much enthusiasm on the prospect of a return to private life. For all that it cost him, the cameras and the headlines and the constant pressure to make decisions too portentous for any one man, he was in his metier as a public servant. The mere making of money held little appeal for him.

Driving home from dinner with friends in a heavy ground fog that evening of September 19, Lilienthal thought he recognized the man who, with his thumb up in a hitchhiker's gesture, was peering into the headlights. "It's Jim McCormack," he said quietly, as if he found this man every night squinting beside a goat field in dense fog. Had he parachuted in, or what?

Back at the house, the flame from the kerosene lantern made the rickety summer furniture wobble and dance as if in a Charles Addams drawing. Lilienthal gazed out the window at the Big Dipper as the visitor he called "General Jim" half apologized and half joked about being the messenger bearing bad news.

"Are you troubled?" Helen Lilienthal asked as they went to bed. "Oh, some, one of those things," her husband told her. He said he had to leave at seven the next morning, and would "probably be back by night." He did not believe it, of course, and at dawn he pumped enough water in the well to keep her supplied for two days. Before departing, he said good-bye to the birds, the slender, tufted things he had so enjoyed watching the day before. They were in a poplar tree now. Off they flew in a cloud, into the sunrise, swinging from side to side.

General Jim (Brigadier General James McCormack, director of the Division of Military Applications, AEC) filled Lilienthal in during the flight. On September 3, a weather reconnaissance plane on patrol from Japan to Alaska had picked up signs of radioactivity just east of the Kamchatka Peninsula, and more signs had been picked up during the next few days. No one in official Washington had expected the Russians to test an atomic device so soon—Secretary of State Dean Acheson had said it might occur as early as 1951 and General Leslie Groves, head of the Manhattan Project, had said it would take twenty years—and the news was bound to cause shock. William Webster, the defense secretary's deputy for atomic energy, had gone to see Lilienthal's deputy, AEC general manager Carroll Wilson, and suggested that a scientific panel be appointed to examine the evidence. Vannevar Bush, civilian director of the Manhattan Project during the war, was appointed chairman, with three Los Alamos veterans, Robert Oppenheimer, former commissioner Robert Bacher, and Admiral William S. Parsons, as members.[3]

That all of this had occurred while the chairman of the Atomic Energy Commission was allowed to rusticate in ignorance for nearly three weeks on Martha's Vineyard says worlds about the secrecy that suffused the enterprise, since no one had dared inform him by telephone or telegraph. But on Monday, September 19, at Air Force detection headquarters on G Street, the members of the Bush panel, General Hoyt Vandenberg and other high-ranking Air Force officers, a dozen scientists from various laboratories, and a small British mission gathered to question the scientists who had analyzed radioactive samples from the suspected test. Even here, however, secrecy imposed its restrictions: Oppenheimer's task of explaining what the Russians had done was the more difficult because he was not permitted to reveal how the panel had arrived at its conclusions. The assembled scientists and officers nonetheless accepted the panel's assessment that what it had seen was "consistent with the view that the origin of the fission products was the explosion of an atomic bomb" on August 29. The members of the Bush panel and the three commissioners on hand that afternoon hoped the news would be announced by the president before it leaked and before the Russians announced it. They decided to dispatch General McCormack to Martha's Vineyard to bring Lilienthal back so that he could persuade the president to announce the Soviet success without delay.[4]

When he arrived at his office on the morning of September 20, Lilienthal hoped to be told that the explosion had turned out to be something else. But Oppenheimer, looking "frantic," and a "deeply worried" Bacher assured him that the event they had feared since 1946 was upon them. Both of them urged that the news be made public right away.

Harry Truman was at his desk, reading the *Congressional Record,* when Lilienthal entered the Oval Office just before four in the afternoon. As the president joked about partisan goings-on in the Senate the day before, his mood seemed as serene as the garden outside, with the golden September sunlight streaming through it. As for this detection report—*he* raised the subject—he had known it would happen someday. Those captured German scientists had probably helped the Russians pull it off. But maybe it wasn't the real thing. Oh, yes, it was, Lilienthal assured him. The evidence had been persuasive even to the doubters. "Really?" asked the president. Still, he said, he was not going to announce it right away. The Russians had finally sent a *real* negotiator to the UN and the British were about to announce devaluation of the pound, and he wanted to let things simmer down. Another reason for silence was that announcing the test would reveal our detection capabilities to the Russians.

Lilienthal urged him to reconsider. Far from alarming the country, Truman's announcing—before it leaked—that the Russians had acquired the bomb would show that he was taking it in stride and that no one else need be upset either. And it would show that this was a president who leveled with the American people. Harry Truman heard his visitor out and accompanied him to the door, apparently still determined to take his time.

Back at commission headquarters, Lilienthal found his fellow commissioners upset by the delay. Oppenheimer was particularly unhappy, seeing it as one more case of the government's behaving as if there were some big secret when there was none, and missing the chance to bring the facts about atomic energy a little more into the open. Lilienthal agreed but, knowledgeable about the ways of government, pointed out that the decision was up to the president.

Go on back to the Vineyard, Lilienthal's secretary, Martha Jane Brown, urged him late that afternoon. Lilienthal stopped by the apartment of his friend and fellow commissioner Sumner Pike for whiskey and some talk before boarding the B-25. By 10:30 that night he was back with Helen by the fireplace on Martha's Vineyard, with the wind blowing outside, the limbs of dead apple trees dancing eerily in the firelight. The "Wuthering Heights touch again," he wrote in his journal before they went to bed.

A couple of days later Lilienthal was summoned to a neighbor's telephone on the Vineyard to take a call from acting AEC chairman Pike. The president had announced the Russian bomb that morning after all, and in the text Pike read aloud to him, Lilienthal recognized arguments he had made to President Truman three days before. The choice of words showed that the president still questioned whether the Russians really had done it—he termed it "an atomic explosion," not a full-fledged bomb test—but Lilienthal was pleased that his trip to Washington had had some effect.[5]

The General Advisory Committee of the Atomic Energy Commission happened to be meeting that day. The nine-man GAC was the tail that wagged the AEC dog, being composed of the country's wisest and most experienced nuclear scientists and engineers. Appointed by the president for fixed terms, the GAC members enjoyed an authority in nuclear affairs that no one in the Pentagon, White House, or AEC could match. The commission therefore looked to the GAC and its chairman, Robert Oppenheimer, for guidance on technical issues and much more.

Oppenheimer described the evidence that what the Russians had set off was really an atomic test. The first reaction of Glenn Seaborg, chemistry professor at the University of California and the committee's youngest member, was that the U.S. government's stringent secrecy policies had failed. Isidor Isaac Rabi, professor of physics at Columbia University, thought the Soviet bomb made war more likely. He wanted the government to take action, but he did not say what. Oppenheimer thought it too early to suggest changes in the weapons program, since it was the country's response, and not the Russian bomb, now called Joe One, that might make changes necessary. He agreed with Seaborg that if the committee were to make any response, it should be an expression of hope for a secrecy policy that made sense. When news came that the president had just announced the test—ahead of the inevitable leak or an announcement from Moscow—everyone was relieved.

Later that day Oppenheimer had a call from a former colleague, Edward Teller, in town for a meeting at the Pentagon. Teller wanted to know what *he* should do now that the Russians had tested a bomb. "Keep your shirt on," Oppenheimer told him.[6]

CHAPTER TWO

The Maneuvering Begins

NO SOONER HAD the Russian test been announced than intensive lobbying got under way, with the Joint Committee on Atomic Energy, chaired by the high-powered and ambitious senator Brien McMahon of Connecticut, taking the lead. At the end of September the JCAE's executive director, a twenty-nine-year-old veteran of World War II in Europe named William Borden, told the committee that development of a weapon a thousand times more powerful than the A-bomb, something so far unattainable called the hydrogen bomb, was the answer to the Soviet success. A few days after the president's announcement, McMahon asked General James McCormack how much the new bomb, providing it could be built at all, would "magnify the destructiveness" of the atomic bomb. McCormack replied in secret session that "if all the theory turned out," the bomb would be "infinite. You can have it any size up to the sun. . . . A million tons or more of . . . TNT."[1]

Across the ocean, a headline caught the eye of a wealthy American as he passed a newsstand in Florence, Italy. The American knew only a few words of Italian, but he grabbed the paper and puzzled out Truman's announcement. Then he sat up until three in the morning writing a letter to an old friend back in New York. The next day he carried the letter to the U.S. consul general and asked him to send it via diplomatic pouch.

The American who had spotted the president's announcement was a Wall Street investor named William Golden, and the friend to whom he sent his letter was AEC commissioner Lewis Strauss. The two men had been in the Navy together during World War II and remained friends afterward as they pursued lucrative careers in finance. After Strauss joined the commission, Golden signed on as his dollar-a-year assistant; in September 1949, he was vacationing with his wife in Europe. Years afterward Alice Strauss remembered her husband's receiving a secret message in New York that the Russians had exploded what appeared to be an atomic bomb. Dismayed and alarmed, he boarded the first flight to Washington and left her to catch up as best she could.[2]

As soon as he received Golden's letter Strauss penned a memorandum, which he read to the other commissioners on October 5. With our monopoly gone, he said, it was not enough for the United States to maintain an "arithmetical" lead in atomic weapons. Borrowing an expression from Golden, he said it was time for a "quantum jump." The only way to stay ahead was to make a commitment comparable "in talent and money . . . to that which produced the first atomic bomb." The GAC should be consulted not about whether, but about "how we can proceed with expedition."[3]

A determined man who left nothing to chance, Strauss next paid a call on Sidney Souers, another friend from naval intelligence during the war. Souers was a banker in St. Louis, Missouri, Truman's home state. Surprisingly, however, he and the president did not know each other, and it had been at Strauss's request that Souers had come to Washington to serve on an AEC security panel. Discreet and self-effacing, Souers soon won the president's trust and became executive secretary of the National Security Council (NSC). He was Strauss's man, and Strauss decided to use him as his conduit to the president. In doing so, Souers said later, Strauss had come "to the right place."[4]

Strauss asked his old acquaintance whether something called the hydrogen bomb had reached the president's attention, and if so, if Truman had made up his mind to build it.

Souers responded that as far as he knew, the president had never heard of such a bomb. "Can we build one?" he asked.

Strauss said yes.

"Then why in the world don't we build it?" Souers wanted to know.

Strauss replied that the president had not been told about the weapon because AEC chairman David Lilienthal was opposed to building it.

"See that it gets to the President," Souers said.

"I don't think I can since I'm almost alone in the Commission," said Strauss, adding that the GAC, too, was almost unanimously opposed to building the new bomb.

"That doesn't matter," said Souers. "You were appointed by the President. *You* bring it up, let your colleagues refute what you . . . recommend, and then the President can do what he thinks best."

"Check with the President, anyway," Strauss requested. "If you'll just tell me to go ahead, I'll accept that from you."

"I'll tell you right now," Souers said. "I know he would want it done."[5]

The next day Souers asked the president whether he had heard of something called the hydrogen bomb. "No," said the president, "but you tell Strauss to go to it and fast." Souers called Strauss and said nothing about talking to the president, merely that he had thought about the matter overnight, and told him to go ahead.

The memo Strauss read aloud at the commission on October 5 had its effect. Within days David Lilienthal asked Oppenheimer to call a meeting of the GAC to advise on "as broad a basis as possible" whether the atomic energy program "constitutes doing everything that it is reasonably possible for us to do for the common defense and security." Oppenheimer arranged a meeting for the final weekend of October, the earliest date at which two of his members, James Conant and Enrico Fermi, could be there.[6]

Meanwhile, a handful of scientists in Berkeley were horrified by the Soviet success. One was a tall, ruddy, intensely creative physicist named Luis Alvarez, and another was the chemist Wendell Latimer. They lost no time going to see Ernest Lawrence, director of the University of California's Radiation Laboratory, inventor of its cyclotron, and a scientist of enormous influence in political circles, who had had much to do with getting the Manhattan Project started back in 1942. Alvarez and Latimer found Lawrence worried that the Russians might already be working on the H-bomb and might succeed in building it first. The only thing to do, the three men agreed, was to get there before the Russians did. On their way to Washington for a scheduled visit, Lawrence and Alvarez decided to make a stop at Los Alamos to check with Edward Teller. On Friday, October 7, they spent a full day there talking to Teller, the Russian-born astrophysicist George Gamow, the Polish-born mathematician Stanislaw Ulam, and John Manley, the lab's associate director. Teller assured Lawrence and Alvarez, who had not done any research on the weapon, that the Super—Teller's proposed thermonuclear, or hydrogen, bomb—was feasible and, with an effort comparable to that of the Manhattan Project, could be built in about two years. Alvarez reported in his diary that the men they talked to at Los Alamos thought the Super would have a "good chance," provided there was plenty of an element called tritium—a big *if*—and provided the calculating machines at Princeton and Los Alamos could be geared up to perform the millions of mathematical calculations the project would require. Teller accompanied the visitors to their hotel in Albuquerque and stayed up half the night with them discussing how to obtain the needed supply of excess neutrons. Lawrence, in what the Hungarian took to be an exhortation to go on the stump campaigning for the H-bomb, showed Teller how to wash his shirts and hang them out to dry.[7]

At lunch three days later in Washington, Lawrence and Alvarez told Brien McMahon and California congressman Carl Hinshaw, a member of McMahon's committee, that current research on the Super was inadequate and that the "booster" test scheduled for 1951 was merely a "mincing step." According to Borden, they expressed "keen and even grave concern that Russia is giving top priority to development of the thermonuclear super-bomb. They pointed out that the Russian expert, Kapitsa, is one of the world's foremost authorities on the problems involved in light elements . . . and even went so far as to say that they fear Russia may be ahead of us. . . . They declared that for the first time in their experience they are actually fearful of America's losing a war unless immediate steps are taken on our own super-bomb project." Finally, they said that a Super could be developed in one and a half to two years if an all-out effort was mounted.[8]

Alvarez paid a visit to AEC headquarters in Washington, where he got the impression that Lilienthal felt "lukewarm" about the Super; Lilienthal wrote with disgust in his journal that Alvarez and Lawrence had come to see him, "drooling" over the H-bomb. We keep saying we have no other course, Lilienthal observed, when the real difficulty is that "we are not bright enough to see any other course."[9]

Lawrence and Alvarez were not the only ones who believed the Super was the answer. After the Soviet test, Teller went to Major General Roscoe Charles Wilson, deputy chief of the Air Force Special Weapons Group, to urge that Air Force higher-ups be briefed about the hydrogen bomb. Air Force chief of staff Hoyt Vandenberg appeared before the JCAE the day after he was briefed to plead for the weapon on the grounds that the United States had to beat Russia to the punch. General Omar N. Bradley, chairman of the Joint Chiefs of Staff, did not put it nearly so bluntly, but right after the session at which the two men testified McMahon wrote to Lilienthal that should the USSR achieve a thermonuclear bomb ahead of the United States, "the fatal consequences are obvious. . . . American efforts along this line should be as bold and urgent as our original atomic enterprise." He wanted to know whether the AEC was considering an all-out, Manhattan Project–type of effort.[10]

As busy as things were in Washington, Fuld Hall in Princeton was even busier. Fuld Hall was home of the Institute for Advanced Study, to which Robert Oppenheimer, scientific director of the atomic bomb project at Los Alamos during the war, had come as director in 1947. Of all Oppenheimer's responsibilities as adviser to the government, none meant as much to him as his chairmanship of the GAC, and during October 1949, nearly everyone in the country concerned in a high-level way with atomic energy came to Princeton to seek his counsel. The first was his close friend I. I. Rabi, and the next was another close friend, Admiral William "Deak" Parsons, the ranking military officer at Los Alamos during the war and a highly intelligent

Navy official, with whom Oppenheimer discussed everything. Then came the two top men at Los Alamos, Norris Bradbury, Oppenheimer's successor as director of the lab, and John Manley. Both men wanted a thorough review of what the laboratory was doing in light of the Russians' success. Since the Soviet test, they told Oppenheimer, scientists at the lab had been advocating everything from business as usual to an all-out program to develop the H-bomb. After the visit by the Los Alamos men, two representatives of the military side of things came, James McCormack and Robert LeBaron, of the Pentagon's Military Liaison Committee, and after them the physicists Hans Bethe and Edward Teller.

Back in 1942, Oppenheimer, aided mostly by Manley but by Teller and others as well, had scoured the country in search of talent for the Manhattan Project. The time was late, most scientists were already working on the war effort, and recruiting first-class men for a project too secret to be described had been a tough sell. But Oppenheimer had worked miracles of persuasion, and Los Alamos soon was staffed by young Americans trained during the 1930s at Berkeley, Caltech, the University of Chicago, Purdue, the University of Illinois, and East Coast universities, and by Europeans (Bethe and Teller among them) who had fled Hitler's anti-Semitism and might not have received U.S. citizenship in time to be cleared for other projects. Now Teller, perhaps in unconscious emulation of Oppenheimer's wartime effort, had embarked on a recruiting drive of his own. His first stop was Ithaca, New York, where his close friend Hans Bethe was professor of physics at Cornell.

Bethe later said that at this time he had been in "very great" internal conflict as to whether he should take part in an all-out effort to build a hydrogen bomb. He had attended the meeting at Le Conte Hall in Berkeley in the early summer of 1942, the first to consider basic thermonuclear reactions, and had taken a leading part in theoretical research during his many stints as consultant to Los Alamos since the war. Always, at the back of his mind, was the hope that he, or if not he then someone else, would succeed in proving the thermonuclear bomb impossible. Now Teller, anxious to persuade Bethe to head the theoretical effort, told him about some new ideas that might make at least one phase of the program more feasible technically than it had seemed before. Hearing about Teller's ideas in his living room, Bethe was impressed, but he still felt that building such a large bomb, and escalating the weapons race, would be a "terrible undertaking." He and his wife, Rose, discussed what he ought to do. "I was deeply troubled," he has said, and "Rose was very much against it."[11]

The two friends therefore converged on Oppenheimer's office in Fuld Hall to ask his opinion. Oppenheimer later remembered Bethe's saying, "I cannot see what we can do but build this, and I don't see that it can eventuate in anything but utter catastrophe. I cannot refuse . . . but if I go, it will be with a very heavy heart." According to Bethe, he and Teller found Oppenheimer "equally undecided and equally troubled about what should be done. I did not get from him the advice I was hoping to get" as to whether to join Teller in trying to build the bomb. When Teller presented his case, Oppenheimer did not argue for or against the bomb, but confined himself to the observation that one GAC member, James Conant, was very much against it. He pointed to a letter on his desk which he said he had just received from Conant and read part of it aloud. All Teller could remember later was that Conant had said that a crash program to develop the hydrogen bomb would be approved only "over my dead body." As for Oppenheimer, Teller remembered only his saying that if there were to be such a program, then the country should be told openly, without the hermetic secrecy that had shrouded the Manhattan Project. Bethe disagreed, and said that the fact that work was under way, and the outcome, should be kept secret. Memorably, Oppenheimer called the contest that would take place between the United States and Soviet Russia to build the bomb "a race between a piece of glass and a piece of onyx, [one] totally transparent and [the other] totally obscure."[12]

Prior to the visit, Teller had predicted that after seeing Oppenheimer, Bethe would decline to work on the bomb. But as they left Oppenheimer's office, Teller later recalled, Bethe told him, "You see, you can be quite satisfied. I am still coming."[13]

But during the weekend Bethe strolled around the Princeton campus with Victor Weisskopf, a theoretical physicist from Vienna with whom he had worked closely at Los Alamos. Weisskopf spoke in vivid terms about the costs of a thermonuclear war. He said that the world that survived would be "not worth preserving," a world in which "we would lose the things we were fighting for." Bethe later called the conversation "very long" and "very difficult . . . for both of us." Later that weekend, as Bethe, Weisskopf, and another close friend, the Czech-born physicist George Placzek, drove to La Guardia Airport, they went over it again, with both Weisskopf and Placzek urging Bethe in the strongest terms not to work on the bomb. All three speculated about the position Oppenheimer and the GAC were likely to take. After talking a full hour with Oppenheimer, Bethe said, he still did not know his opinion. So intense was the conversation that Weisskopf forgot his coat. He left it in Placzek's car and took Placzek's instead of his own, while Bethe missed his flight to Oak Ridge, Tennessee.[14]

A day or so later, Bethe called Teller to say that he had decided against working on the bomb. Then and later, Teller assumed it was Oppenheimer who had dissuaded him.

But Bethe was right—Oppenheimer had not made up his mind. Of all his colleagues on the GAC, Conant was the one Oppenheimer was closest to. Earlier that month he had stayed with the Conants during a meeting of the Harvard Board of Overseers in Cambridge. Of the visit he wrote to a colleague that he and Conant had had "a long and difficult discussion having, alas, nothing to do with Harvard." During their talk the two men apparently discussed whether the GAC should ask for a meeting with President Truman at the end of its late-October session. And on Friday, October 21, before he saw Bethe and Teller, Oppenheimer had penned his reply to Conant.[15]

"Dear Uncle Jim," he wrote, addressing Conant by his Los Alamos nickname. "We are exploring the possibilities for our talk with the President on October 30."

Oppenheimer continued:

On the technical side, . . . the super is not very different from
what it was when we first spoke of it more than seven years
ago—a weapon of unknown design, cost, deliverability and military value. But a very great change has taken place in the climate of opinion. On the one hand, two experienced promoters
have been at work, i.e., Ernest Lawrence and Edward Teller. The
project has long been dear to Teller's heart; and Ernest has convinced himself that we must learn from Operation Joe that the
Russians will soon do the super, and that we had better beat
them to it. . . .

What concerns me is really not the technical problem. I am
not sure the miserable thing will work, nor that it can be gotten
to a target except by ox cart. It seems likely to me even further to
worsen the unbalance of our present war plans. What does
worry me is that this thing appears to have caught the imagination, both of the congressional and of military people, as the answer to the problem posed by the Russian advance. It would be
folly to oppose the exploration of this weapon. We have always
known it had to be done; and it does have to be done, though it
appears to be singularly proof against any form of experimental
approach. But that we become committed to it as the way to save
the country and the peace appears to me full of dangers.

We will be faced with all this at our meeting; and anything
that we do or do not say to the President, will have to take it into
consideration. I shall feel far more secure if you have had an opportunity to think about it.

I still remember my visit with gratitude and affection.

Oppenheimer had already answered Conant when Bethe and
Teller visited him on October 21, but it was Conant's letter to him,
and not his reply, that he chose to read aloud. Bethe speculated long
afterward that Oppenheimer might already have made up his mind,
but, believing that as chairman of the GAC he ought to maintain
neutrality, he had let Conant's letter speak for him. But the fact is that

Oppenheimer still was uncertain. He testified at his 1954 security hearing that he had not yet made up his mind at the time he received Conant's letter, and in a 1957 interview he pointed out that the position he ultimately took was different from the one he had taken in his letter to Conant. It was Conant's arguments later, at the GAC meeting, that persuaded him.[16]

These were the discussions that were taking place as the GAC met to discuss the most important question that had ever come before it. The American people knew nothing except that Russia had tested the atomic bomb.

CHAPTER THREE

The Halloween Meeting

EACH TIME the General Advisory Committee met, the secretary, John Manley, flew to Washington a day or two early to prepare. Manley was a slight, able experimentalist who had helped Oppenheimer set up the Los Alamos laboratory early in the war and had stayed on afterward. As associate director of the laboratory and a trusted colleague of GAC chairman Oppenheimer, Manley was in a perfect position to shape the committee's agenda. This he did informally, drifting from desk to desk at AEC headquarters prior to each meeting, greeting everyone who felt like talking to him, typists to division heads, and asking what was on their minds. In this way he not only took the commission's pulse, he helped keep the advisory committee so well informed that it earned the reputation of running the commission. In late October 1949, Manley had more than the usual quantity of papers to prepare and distribute ahead of time.

He was setting out documents on the afternoon of Friday, October 28, when Robert Oppenheimer appeared in the conference room overlooking Constitution Avenue. Oppenheimer had with him someone Manley had not seen before, a slender, tall, rather dapper-looking man from the Department of State who turned out to be George Kennan, special adviser to Secretary of State Acheson. After Oppenheimer, other members of the GAC appeared: I. I. Rabi; Cyril Smith and Enrico Fermi from the University of Chicago; Oliver Buckley, head of Bell Labs in New Jersey; Hartley Rowe of the United Fruit Company; and Lee DuBridge, president of Caltech, who had been director of the radar project at MIT during the war. Two members did not appear that day: James Conant, who arrived from Boston the next morning, and Glenn Seaborg, the University of California chemist who was in Stockholm, being looked over by the Nobel Prize committee.

Kennan spoke informally to the committee that afternoon about conditions in the USSR, with a view to whether Stalin would want to embark on a new stage of the arms race so soon after the devastation of World War II. With its industry still in ruins, Kennan thought, the Soviet Union might be willing to enter an agreement to restrain nuclear weapons development, provided the United States did so as well. Kennan also believed that it would not take a huge stockpile of atomic weapons to deter the Russians from aggressive acts—a few bombs would suffice. Speaking after Kennan, Hans Bethe described the technical difficulties of igniting the Super weapon and suggested that the odds of building it were not good.[1]

On the morning of Saturday, October 29, the committee met, first with the five commissioners and other officials from the AEC, and then with Pentagon officers led by General Bradley and Air Force chief of staff General Lauris Norstad. Oppenheimer was seated at one end of the long rectangular table, with Manley behind him, taking notes. Manley was as impressed by General Bradley's homespun manner and obvious decency as he had been the previous day by Kennan's impassioned fluency and his knowledge of the Russians. But he noticed to his surprise that the generals seemed to be hearing about the hydrogen bomb for the first time. The meeting therefore devolved not into a discussion of whether the generals wanted a new, more powerful bomb, but of how, since the armies of Europe and the United States had been demobilized since the end of the war, Western Europe could be defended in the event of a Soviet attack. Manley got the impression that the two generals had not given much thought to other important questions. Would the United States, for example, respond to a Soviet attack on Europe by dropping an atomic bomb on Moscow? Norstad and Bradley did not even answer the question as to whether the armed services wanted more A-bombs. As for a hydrogen bomb, Bradley said nothing about its military usefulness, only that it might be of "psychological" value.[2]

The physicist Luis Alvarez was not a member of the GAC, but his enthusiasm for the H-bomb had prompted him to come all the way from Berkeley on his own. He stationed himself inside the entrance to the AEC to watch the generals and scientists come and go. Spotting him there at the lunch break, Oppenheimer invited Alvarez and Robert Serber, a former student now teaching at Berkeley, who had spoken before the committee on technical issues the day before, to join him at a restaurant nearby. Oppenheimer echoed Kennan's view that if the United States refrained from trying to build the Super, the Russians might do likewise. While he told his luncheon companions that negative views about the H-bomb had been expressed at the meeting on moral grounds, Oppenheimer did not say anything about the fact that in the course of discussion those views were coming to be his own. But Alvarez picked up on the tenor of Oppenheimer's remarks. Concluding, mistakenly, that he was leading the opposition and would carry the day, Alvarez gave up and flew back to California, convinced that "the program was dead."[3]

Like Oppenheimer, most GAC members had arrived with their minds not fully made up. A consensus was therefore reached only gradually, after lengthy soul-searching, in the course of which most of them changed their views. At one end of the spectrum, adamant in opposition to any effort to build an H-bomb, was James Conant who, as civilian director of the Manhattan Project in Washington during the war and Truman's original choice to be chairman of the AEC, was the senior person in the room.[4] An austere-looking New Englander whom Lilienthal described in his journal as "looking almost translucent, so grey," Conant said that mere discussion of the issue made him feel as if he were "seeing the same film, and a punk one, for the second time." Another member, Hartley Rowe, agreed—"we already built one Frankenstein." Lilienthal had the impression that Rabi was "completely on [the] other side." And Fermi gave a technical summary in which he concluded that the chances of building a deliverable thermonuclear weapon (as the H-bomb was called) were only "a little better than even."[5]

The meeting produced three documents. The main report, by

Oppenheimer and Manley, was signed by all eight members who were present. "We all hope that by one means or another the development of these weapons can be avoided. We are all reluctant to see the United States taking the initiative. . . . We are all agreed that it would be wrong at the present moment to commit ourselves to an all-out effort." Explaining that if the first problem, that of initiating an explosion, proved soluble, then deuterium, a gaseous isotope of hydrogen, could be added to the weapon to the point where "there is no limit to the explosive power of the bomb except that imposed by requirements of delivery." And if it could be delivered by ship and did not have to be dropped from the air, then, said the committee, "the weapon is from a technical point of view without limitations with regard to the damage it can inflict. . . . Its use therefore carries much further than the atomic bomb itself the policy of exterminating civilian populations." The committee recommended that, in deciding against development, the government make clear to the public the fact that the bomb would have no civilian uses and that it could be built to have unlimited destructive power.

The committee had before it only one H-bomb model, a concept invented by Edward Teller called the "Classical Super." While it had not so far proven mathematically feasible, the committee did not rule out the possibility that this or some other model might be achievable: "We believe that an imaginative and concerted attack on the problem has a better than even chance of producing the weapon within five years."

The report addressed itself also to Lilienthal's original question: was the AEC doing everything that could be done for the nation's defense? The answer, again, was no. The report urged a major effort to expand the supply of fissionable material and to adapt aircraft and weaponry to the use of smaller atomic weapons for limited, or tactical, purposes.

As against its unanimity on these issues, the committee admitted that it was divided as to the nature of its commitment not to develop the hydrogen weapon. "The majority feels that this should be an unqualified commitment. Others feel that it should be made conditional on the response of the Soviet government to a proposal to renounce such development." To the main report two appendices were added, a majority annex written by Conant and DuBridge and signed by six members, and a minority annex by Rabi and Fermi.

The majority annex read as follows:

We have been asked by the Commission whether or not they should immediately initiate an "all-out" effort to develop a weapon whose energy release is 100 to 1000 times greater and whose destructive power in terms of area of damage is 20 to 100 times greater than those of the present atomic bomb. We recommend strongly against such action.

We base our recommendation on our belief that the extreme dangers to mankind inherent in the proposal wholly outweigh any military advantage. . . . Let it be clearly realized that this is a super weapon; it is in a wholly different category from an atomic bomb. The reason for developing such super bombs would be to have the capacity to devastate a vast area with a single bomb. Its use would involve a decision to slaughter a vast number of civilians. We are alarmed as to the possible global effects of the radioactivity generated by the explosion of a few super bombs of conceivable magnitude. If super bombs will work at all, there is no inherent limit in the destructive power that may be attained with them. Therefore, a super bomb might become a weapon of genocide.

We believe a super bomb should never be produced [italics added]. Mankind would be far better off not to have a demonstration of the feasibility of such a weapon until the present climate of world opinion changes.

It is by no means certain that the weapon can be developed at all and by no means certain that the Russians will produce one within a decade. . . . Should they use the weapon against us, reprisals by our large stock of atomic bombs would be comparably effective to the use of a super.

In determining not to proceed to develop the super bomb, we see a unique opportunity of providing by example some limitations on the totality of war and thus of limiting the fear and arousing the hopes of mankind.

James B. Conant
Hartley Rowe
Cyril Stanley Smith
L. A. DuBridge
Oliver E. Buckley
J. R. Oppenheimer

The minority statement by Fermi and Rabi makes the moral case even more strongly:

Necessarily such a weapon goes far beyond any military objective and enters the range of very great natural catastrophes. By its very nature it cannot be confined to a military objective but becomes a weapon which in practical effect is almost one of genocide.

It is clear that the use of such a weapon cannot be justified on any ethical ground which gives a human being a certain individuality and dignity even if he happens to be a resident of an enemy country. It is evident to us that this would be the view of people in other countries. Its use would put the United States in a bad moral position relative to the peoples of the world.

Any postwar situation resulting from such a weapon would leave unresolvable enmities for generations. A desirable peace cannot come from such an inhuman application of force. The postwar problems would dwarf the problems which confront us at present. . . .

The fact that no limit exists to the destructiveness of this weapon makes its very existence and the knowledge of its construction a danger to humanity as a whole. *It is necessarily an evil thing considered in any light* [italics added].

For these reasons we believe it important for the President of the United States to tell the American public and the world that we think it wrong on fundamental ethical principles to initiate a program of development of such a weapon. At the same time it would be appropriate to invite the nations of the world to join us in a solemn pledge not to proceed. . . . If such a pledge were accepted even without control machinery, it appears highly probable that an advanced stage of development leading to a test could be detected by available physical means. Furthermore we have in our possession, in our stockpile of atomic bombs, the means for adequate "military" retaliation for the production or use of a Super.[6]

Despite their strong moral language, Fermi and Rabi were proposing a practical solution. Development of the hydrogen bomb would require testing, a fact that made possible a system of control. Since any test large enough to produce debris in the atmosphere could be detected by our aircraft, American scientists would be alerted to any Soviet thermonuclear test. Having continued its research into thermonuclear processes, the United States could then go ahead with a test program of its own. Fermi and Rabi were proposing a thermonuclear test ban that was self-enforcing and would not require an intrusive system of inspection.

As they said their good-byes on Sunday, the committee members felt they had accomplished something. One of them described the spirit of the meeting as "astonishingly harmonious," and Oppenheimer called it "a meeting of sensibilities." No one had dominated; no one had even tried to win any of the others to his point of view. A consensus had evolved, and the question had become "how much we were going to say and how strongly we were going to say it."[7]

John Manley was pleased by the outcome. The GAC, he felt, had reversed the momentum created by Teller and Lawrence and pointed the way to ending the arms race. Cyril Smith, a British-born specialist in metals physics, felt the same way. On the flight back to Chicago, he and Fermi, barred from discussing sensitive matters where others could overhear them, passed the time playing mathematical games. It occurred to Smith while they were playing that the proposals they had just fashioned might be the beginning of a revolution in man's relationship to the weapons he had created. Back in Washington, however, David Lilienthal was less hopeful. He had "terrible and deeply important things" on his mind, among them the differences in kind between the ordinary atomic bomb and the Super. The Super would have no civilian by-products, and its existence was certain to increase the risk of war. It was not enough to forgo development, as the GAC had suggested: before making decisions about the future of nuclear weaponry, Americans would have to rethink where "national security" really lay. It was not something that could be left to insiders; it would have to be entrusted to citizens *outside* the government.[8]

But how to do this, given the pervasive secrecy? Not a word about the GAC meeting had appeared in the newspapers. The members had agreed not to give their views in public until the AEC gave them the go-ahead, and the go-ahead never came. Apart from a handful of officials at the very top of government, no one knew the meeting had taken place, much less its reasoning or conclusions. And the tiny group that did hear of it greeted the GAC verdict with puzzlement verging on disbelief. The Russians had broken our monopoly on the A-bomb. They had proven themselves possessors of scientific talent and industrial resources beyond anything we had supposed. The way to protect ourselves—the only way—was to build a bigger and better weapon. Against this, as this group of officials saw it, the GAC was proposing unilateral disarmament.

Unlike the scientists who had built the atomic bomb, top U.S. officials had no experience with nuclear weapons. They did not understand that the thermonuclear bomb as conceived at that time was too large to serve as a military weapon and would destroy civilian populations. And in spite of the use of the word "genocide" in both the majority and minority annexes, these officials did not understand that a weapon that could be built to carry unlimited destructive power could wipe out much of life on earth.

Nor did they comprehend that in attempting to build an H-bomb—how, in our society, could such a fact be kept secret?—we would be inviting the Russians to compete with us in building a weapon to which we were more vulnerable than they. We were surrounded by oceans, with two heavily populated coasts against which large weapons could be launched by ship—warship, barge, or submarine—whereas if we wanted to deliver a bomb on Moscow, we would have to do it from the air and would be limited to the much smaller size and weight that an airplane could carry.

Finally, there was the problem that the scientists who wrote the GAC's recommendations, and the officials who knew of them, did not speak the same language. Physicists had tried for seven years to figure out how the H-bomb could be built, and had failed. When Oppenheimer stated, as he did in the main report, that "an imaginative and concerted attack . . . has a better than even chance" of producing a weapon within five years, he was saying that the technical outlook was not promising. Senators, statesmen, and generals looked at things differently. The lesson they had drawn from recent experience with radar and the atomic bomb was that if the government threw enough money at a scientific problem, the laws of nature would succumb. They overlooked the fact that those who were warning against the Super were virtually the only influential men in the country who knew at first hand what nuclear weapons could do.

When the war ended in 1945, no one had known what to do with the laboratory that produced the atomic bomb. Los Alamos had languished, more or less, until passage of the McMahon Act in 1946 placed the atomic energy enterprise in the hands of a new civilian agency, the AEC. During that period one man held the lab together, Norris Bradbury, the lean, intense, and capable Navy commander who had succeeded Robert Oppenheimer as director. On October 8, 1945, the day he took over, Bradbury promised the scientists, in an effort to keep them at Los Alamos, that investigation of the Super's feasibility was a major reason for the lab to continue. "Another Trinity," he declared, alluding to the A-bomb test at Alamogordo in July 1945, "might even be FUN." But before the Super could be built, a smaller, more powerful A-bomb had to be designed to serve as the trigger. The emphasis had to remain on fission.

After the Halloween meeting it fell to John Manley, who helped write the GAC's conclusions and passionately agreed with them, to inform the division heads at Los Alamos that the advisory committee was unanimously opposed to an all-out program to develop the Super. Chairman Brien McMahon of the JCAE, an avid proponent of more and bigger bombs, was due for a visit November 16 to assess the lab's willingness and capability to build them. Despite the super-secrecy surrounding the Halloween meeting, it had been decided that the scientists who would be briefing McMahon on the status of H-bomb research ought to be aware of the GAC's conclusions. Carroll Wilson had therefore taken the unusual step of having the documents flown to Los Alamos by courier, and Robert Oppenheimer had given Manley permission to explain why the GAC had come to the conclusions it had.[9]

The scientists' reactions to the GAC's opinion were mixed. The first man Manley talked to, Jerry Kellogg, leader of the Experimental Division, was fearful that the decision would mean suspension of the work his division was doing. Carson Mark, head of the Theoretical Division, was "on the fence," while Darol Froman, like Manley an associate director of the lab, was all in favor of the Super. He did not think the prospective new bomb was so very different from the A-bomb, or that the public would recoil when it learned of its enormous power. Only Alvin Graves, head of the Test Division, agreed with the GAC.

Manley knew that an on-again, off-again member of the lab, Edward Teller, had been obsessed for years by the idea of a thermonuclear bomb and had been waiting for some event that would precipitate an all-out effort to build it. He was also aware that the Hungarian hoped the Soviet A-bomb would be that event. When Manley explained the GAC's thinking—that it made no sense to counter the Russians by building a new, even deadlier weapon without first trying to end the arms race—he saw that Teller was not listening. Teller did not say much, however, except to comment that if the great brains on the GAC were so sure that agreement with the Russians was possible, why hadn't they suggested some means of going about it? Manley did not know the lengths to which Teller, who was not a member of the GAC and not in possession of a "Q" clearance, had gone to learn its recommendations. When Fermi and Cyril Smith had arrived home after the Halloween meeting, Teller had met their airplane in Chicago to try to pry the news out of Fermi. When Fermi did not tell him, he had flown to Washington to see McMahon. McMahon did not tell him outright, either, but let drop that the GAC opinion made him "feel sick." Teller had the information he wanted, and Manley's briefing in Los Alamos ten days later told him nothing he did not already know.

In planning the agenda for the senator's visit, Manley had decided not to permit the visit to turn into a policy debate. He instructed the scientists to resist discussion of larger questions or even of whether the Super bomb would be militarily useful. But prior to McMahon's arrival Teller and Froman telephoned Manley repeatedly to urge that the lab formally approve the so-called crash program. Manley responded that the lab had never before taken a stand on national policy and would have no business doing so now. It was the laboratory's job to make weapons, not to decide whether they ought to be made. Teller could talk policy with McMahon outside the formal sessions if he felt like it.

But from the moment of his arrival on the morning of Tuesday, November 16, it was obvious that McMahon was thinking only about policy. The Russians, he said, had a long record as an evil people who failed to keep their promises, force was the only language they understood, and the United States must remain as strong as possible. He considered the GAC position suicidal. During lunch at Fuller Lodge, the big log building that was the lab's social center, the senator and members of his party spoke so loudly that Manley was worried about security, the lab members at tables around them not being cleared to overhear conversations of such sensitivity. McMahon compared the United States and Russia to two neighbors, of whom one possessed a machine gun and the other was building one. What sense would it make for the neighbor with the gun to throw his weapon away? Robert LeBaron, deputy to the secretary of defense for atomic energy, conceded that the armed forces had not thought much about how the Super might be used or whether it would actually be more effective than the A-bomb, but he said that "the existence of a weapon always brought forth new ideas about how it could be used." Walking back to the Tech Building after lunch, LeBaron added that the Super would be ideal for a United Nations peacekeeping force. Manley was so appalled by the idea of using a weapon a thousand times more powerful than the one that had leveled Hiroshima to carry out UN peace-keeping missions that he remembered the remark for the rest of his life.[10]

During the formal sessions, when the lab members described their thermonuclear research so far, Manley found Teller's presentation more balanced than he had expected. Teller conceded that no one knew whether a thermonuclear reaction could be made to burn and added that even if the tests scheduled for 1951 in the Pacific were successful, they would not in themselves prove that the Super bomb could be built. In private conversation with McMahon, however, outside the hearing of Manley and the other physicists, Teller painted a different picture. He told McMahon that a program to build the Super had a better than even, perhaps a much better than even, chance of success, this in spite of the fact that Teller himself had been working on it for seven years with inconclusive results.

Years afterward, it seemed to Manley that McMahon's visit marked the beginning of a change in his own feelings toward Edward Teller. He had known Teller during the mid-1940s as a colleague who refused to work on the lab's project to end the war, the atomic bomb, focusing instead on a hypothetical hydrogen bomb. Now Manley wrote in his diary that prior to the visit by McMahon, "despite many tribulations of which Teller was the cause, I had mistakenly dismissed him as forgivably eccentric, but most imaginative in compensation; almost wholly impractical but possessed of a keen mind; unaccustomed to disciplined, concentrated creativity . . . but still a valued colleague. Now I began to see a distorted human being, petty, perhaps nearly paranoid in his hatred of the Russians, and jealous in personal relations."[11]

These characteristics may have been at work in Teller's misreading of the laboratory's mood on learning that the GAC, with which it had agreed until now on nearly everything, opposed a stepped-up program to build the hydrogen bomb. He wrote to a close friend, the renowned mathematician John von Neumann, that because of the committee's opinion, "the really fine and unanimous enthusiasm which was building up at Los Alamos is now checked, at least temporarily."[12]

Von Neumann had a letter from another close friend at Los Alamos, the dashing, dark-haired Polish mathematician Stanislaw Ulam. In a letter to von Neumann at the Institute for Advanced Study in Princeton, Ulam wrote that "everybody here is against the proposals of the GAC," and predicted accurately that the GAC's verdict would "merely mean a loss of time and not any final . . . negative." Ulam, who had lost nearly all his family in the Holocaust, was in no hurry to produce a weapon a thousand times more powerful than that which had wasted Hiroshima. But he was offended by the idea of intentionally sidestepping a possible discovery. To his French-born wife, Françoise, he wondered aloud whether Newton and Archimedes would have made their great discoveries if they had had to worry constantly about the consequences.[13]

Norris Bradbury and Carson Mark, who along with Ulam were to play critical roles in bringing into being the real H-bomb—not Teller's Super, which the lab had been working on without success—felt very much as Ulam did. Protesting that "one cannot tell scientists not to think," Bradbury said, "I'll be damned if I'll let those people tell me what *not* to do." And Mark, a Canadian mathematician who had learned physics on the job, later thought it was astonishing that the GAC had taken the possibility of an H-bomb seriously enough to make a recommendation, since there was no prospect at the time of building one. Nothing had changed except the fact that the Russians had tested an A-bomb. Mark hoped to be able to prove that a thermonuclear bomb was inconsistent with the laws of nature and could not be built. But he said later that he wished the GAC had phrased its recommendations in the words Oppenheimer had used in his October letter to Conant: "It would be folly to oppose the exploration of this weapon. We have always known it had to be done. . . . But that we become committed to it as the way to save the country and the peace appears to me full of dangers."[14]

CHAPTER FOUR

The Secret Debate

SINCE ITS BEGINNING IN 1947, the Atomic Energy Commission had dealt with major questions, but never one so portentous as whether to advise that the nation embark on an all-out effort to build a thermonuclear bomb. At a meeting of the GAC in early December 1949, Robert Oppenheimer gave members a chance to reconsider their earlier recommendations. Not only did everyone stand by his original opinion, but several went further and went on record with deeply thought-out statements of their own. No one felt more strongly than Lee DuBridge, who pointed out that the Super was not suited to the annihilation of military targets and would be solely a weapon of terror. DuBridge, like Fermi, noted that with its two long coasts, the United States was more vulnerable than the USSR to attack from the sea and, like Manley, said that in embarking on a Super program, the United States would be doing Russia's research for it: the Russians inevitably would learn what we were up to. Everyone agreed that the Super was needed for neither deterrence nor retaliation, since the U.S. atomic stockpile would be sufficient to deal the Soviet Union a devastating blow even if that country had the Super and we did not.[1]

The five commissioners met several times to consider the advisory committee's recommendations, arriving at a 3–2 split; David Lilienthal, Sumner Pike, and Henry DeWolf Smyth were in agreement with the GAC and opposed to Super development "at this time," while the other two, Lewis Strauss and Gordon Dean, favored a secret effort to reach agreement with the Russians and "if this fails, then proceed with the development." All agreed that the public should be informed. Smyth later shifted to a position closer to that of Strauss and Dean.

It fell to Lilienthal to inform the president that his colleagues had failed to reach agreement. Since Lilienthal was known for the gift of bringing men of opposing views together and was anxious to present the president with an unambiguous recommendation, his friends later wondered why he had not tried harder to obtain a consensus. Did he consider building the hydrogen bomb an issue of morality too fundamental to be compromised? Or was he simply tired, worn out by years in the job and by the humiliation of the Hickenlooper hearings the summer before?

Whatever the cause of his ineffectiveness this time, Lilienthal had no second thoughts about his decision to resign and went to the president to inform him. His spirits fell as he entered the Oval Office: what would it be like never to walk through that door again? When Harry Truman glanced up from his reading, Lilienthal noted the tired look in his eyes. But the president's grin reassured the AEC chairman—maybe the conversation would not be so painful after all. "I hate like the dickens to see you go," Truman said, adding that he, too, had a tough decision to make. Lilienthal observed that McMahon and his friends in Congress seemed to think that blowing up the world was our only recourse now that the Russians had the A-bomb. He was afraid they would try to blitz the president into a quick decision. "I don't blitz easily." Truman smiled.[2]

But those who were trying to blitz him were among the heaviest hitters in Washington, ambitious, determined men who were accustomed to getting their own way. And they had access to the Oval Office: McMahon as chair of the powerful congressional committee on atomic energy and a man who aspired to the presidency, Lewis Strauss as a friend of National Security Adviser Sidney Souers, and Defense Secretary Louis Johnson as a swashbuckling donor to the Democratic Party with presidential aspirations of his own. Strauss and McMahon had joined forces early in the fall and had been bombarding the president with strongly worded letters in which they demanded an all-out effort to build the hydrogen bomb. "Brien," the president had said to McMahon, "it's not an easy thing to order development of a weapon that will kill ten million people." But he added that he had read McMahon's letter several times, and this persuaded the senator that Truman would side with him in the end. "He has just got enough of Missouri common sense," McMahon told his committee. "I can go ahead on that."[3]

When Lilienthal told the secretary of state that he had decided to resign, Dean Acheson was sympathetic. "I don't understand how you have stood it as long as you have, living with this grim thing all the time." And after Lilienthal informed him that the theoretical outlook had improved to the point where physicists considered the chances of building the Super about even, Acheson seemed sorry to hear it. He was "somber enough when I began," Lilienthal wrote in his journal, "and after a few questions he was graver still. 'What a depressing world it is,' said Dean, looking quite gray."[4]

Dean and Alice Acheson frequently spent the weekend on their farm outside Washington. As he put his garden to bed on mellow afternoons that fall, the secretary thought about the horrifying weapon that might soon be a reality. After interminable hours testifying on Capitol Hill, Acheson had concluded that congressional opinion was a fairly accurate reflection of opinion in the country. Knowing that foreign as well as domestic policy is the art of the possible, he did not see how the president could survive a decision not to try to make the new bomb, and he said as much to Oppenheimer. But he was appalled by the prospect of the nation's impaling itself on a deadly new phase of the arms race, and he cast about for other options. In a meeting with his Policy Planning Staff he floated the idea of a one-and-a-half- to two-year moratorium on H-bomb development, accompanied by an effort to reach agreement with the Russians on a range of issues that included arms control. Only if this effort failed would the United States try to build the bomb. He and Lilienthal were close for a time to recommending that H-bomb possibilities be investigated, any decision to produce the weapon be deferred, and a far-reaching review of foreign and domestic policies begun forthwith.

But a poorly timed leak by a member of the Joint Committee on

Atomic Energy ratcheted up pressure on the president to make a quick decision. While scolding scientists for allegedly leaking secret information, Senator Edwin Johnson of Colorado announced on television that the president was trying to decide whether to try to build a weapon a thousand times more powerful than the atomic bomb. The administration collectively held its breath, hoping no one would notice Johnson's statement. And for nearly three weeks no one did, until the *Washington Post* on November 18 reported it in a front-page story. Harry Truman hit the ceiling. He called in his attorney general and JCAE chairman McMahon and ordered them to stop the leaks. He banned government employees, even scientific advisers, from speaking about the Super except inside a tiny circle. And he named a committee comprising the state and defense secretaries and the chairman of the AEC to advise him on whether to go ahead with a crash program. Truman's order cut off discussion inside the government and meant that, with Lilienthal and Defense Secretary Johnson at odds with each other on the issue at hand and loath even to be in the same room together, Acheson's opinion would be decisive.

Although by Christmas Acheson had concluded that it would probably be necessary to launch enough of a program to determine whether the bomb could be built, he continued to seek alternatives. He consulted the head of his Policy Planning Staff, George Kennan. Kennan, known within the department—although not to the general public—for helping conceive the Truman Doctrine and the Marshall Plan and as author of the policy of "containing" Russia, pointed out that U.S. policy was based on a willingness to make "first use" of nuclear weapons. Kennan, who had discussed the matter with Oppenheimer, recommended that until the policy of first use had been reconsidered—Kennan hoped it would be abandoned—the United States should refrain from any decision about the hydrogen bomb. Acheson was put off by what an aide called Kennan's "evangelical zeal" and admonished him, "If that is your view of the matter, I suggest you put on a monk's robe, put a tin cup in your hand, and go to the street corner and announce that the end of the world is nigh." Still, he sought Conant's opinion, and had a long talk with the chairman of the Joint Chiefs of Staff, General Omar Bradley, in an effort to find out what—apart from a psychological edge over the Russians—the Pentagon wanted the H-bomb *for*.[5]

While Acheson sought answers, proponents of the Super continued to proselytize. Strauss called Sidney Souers at the White House and warned darkly that "it may be later than we think." In early January, McMahon wrote the president twice on one day alone, accusing the AEC of leaks and again demanding a quick decision. And Secretary of Defense Louis Johnson gave the president a secret Pentagon report urging that determination of the bomb's feasibility be a matter of the highest priority. These and other developments caused Truman to worry that unless he acted quickly, Congress might usurp a decision he considered part of his prerogative as president.

At a press conference on January 19, he was asked for the first time about the Super.

> Q: Mr. President, are you considering direct negotiations with
> Russia on the hydrogen bomb?
> A: No.

A week later, asked about the Super again, he replied that he would have nothing to say until he had made his decision. The secrecy-minded president thereby casually declassified the fact that there *was* a decision to be made and increased the pressure on himself to make it quickly. Lilienthal called the admission "a major event" and a final setback in the effort to keep the decision from being railroaded through.[6]

Acheson had had a strenuous year. Early in 1949 he had become secretary of state, succeeding the revered General George Catlett Marshall. When China fell to the armies of Mao Tse-tung and was declared a people's republic in October, Marshall, Truman's former ambassador to China, was, together with the Truman administration, accused of having "lost" China to the Communists. In addition to its defeat in Asia, the administration was plagued by espionage scandals at home. Alger Hiss, a former State Department official who was suspected of having passed secrets to the Soviet Union, went on trial for perjury for a second time in November. The case was a particular embarrassment for the secretary of state because he knew Alger Hiss and was known to be close to Hiss's brother, Donald, Acheson's former law partner and trusted assistant at the department.

Acheson had kept a comparatively open mind about the prospective new bomb longer than anyone else in the higher reaches of government. But on January 26 an event occurred that taxed even his capacity to stand above the fray. A reporter asked him to comment on the case of Alger Hiss, who had been sentenced that day to serve five to ten years in a federal penitentiary following his conviction for perjury. Conscious of "the yelping pack" at his heels and his own vulnerability to "the fall of some fool's question at a press conference," Acheson referred the questioner to a passage from Saint Matthew on the virtue of compassion, and uttered eleven words that were to haunt him for the rest of his life: "I do not intend to turn my back on Alger Hiss."[7]

He drove to the White House that afternoon and offered his resignation. Truman declined it.

Lilienthal went to see Acheson the next day, and found the secretary looking unruffled. The weather was unseasonably warm, Acheson was at work with his window open, and the two men discussed the upcoming decision about the bomb as though neither of them had another thing on his mind.

Lilienthal then changed the subject, and congratulated the secretary of state on his statement about Hiss: "I am looking at a *man*."

"After a while you get tired of the curs yiping," Acheson replied.[8]

The secretary of state sat up late on Sunday and Monday nights replying to the "flood of letters" he had received after his comment on the Hiss case. To the watchful eye of his assistant, Gordon Arneson, "the Dean" looked weary Tuesday morning as he opened the final meeting of the special committee that was to advise the president on the Super. There were eleven men in the room: Acheson, with Arneson and State Department legal counsel Adrian Fisher; Defense Secretary Johnson and three aides; Lilienthal with Commissioner Smyth; and Souers with his deputy, James Lay. Acheson led off by reading a draft recommendation that the president direct the AEC to determine whether a thermonuclear weapon was technically feasible, while deferring a decision to produce the weapon pending reconsideration by State and Defense of overall U.S. plans and objectives. Johnson objected to the proviso that a decision to produce be deferred, and even though they realized that the defense secretary was trying to accelerate building of the bomb, Lilienthal and Acheson yielded. And when Pentagon press secretary Steven Early suggested that the president not make a special announcement but merely issue a press release, Johnson weighed in again. The thing to do was "play it down, make it just one of those things."[9]

Lilienthal wanted to present his objections. The atmosphere resulting from a decision to go ahead, he said, would in all likelihood render a new approach to the atomic arms race impossible. It would confirm us on our present path and conceal from us the weakness of our position—our reliance on the atomic bomb for the defense of Europe. We were assuming that there would be no war with Russia for a few years at least. Instead of building a new bomb, why not spend a few months on "an intensive . . . re-examination of the worsening of our position as a result of our preoccupation with nuclear weapons?"[10]

Acheson agreed with most of what Lilienthal had said. But without an alternative—and in his view Lilienthal had not suggested one—the pressures for a decision had reached such a point that he did not feel he could recommend delay. To Acheson's surprise, Lilienthal agreed to join in and make their recommendation to the president unanimous, provided he be given a chance to express his objections to the president in person.

Truman was seated at his desk in the Oval Office when Johnson, Acheson, and Lilienthal appeared. Slightly surprised to see the three of them when he had expected only the secretary of defense, he greeted them with a "quick, owlish look." Acheson told him that Lilienthal had something he wanted to say. Turning to Lilienthal, Truman said he hoped we would never have to use these new weapons, but in view of the way the Russians were behaving, we had no choice but to go ahead. Lilienthal objected that he did not agree with the course the country was about to take. It would magnify our reliance on nuclear weapons and mislead the nation into thinking there was no other way. The president broke in to say that if Senator Johnson of Colorado hadn't made his televised remarks, calmer deliberation might have been possible. Now, however, so much excitement had built up that he had no alternative.[11]

At 12:45 the visitors left the Oval Office. They had been there all of seven minutes.

As his special committee had suggested, the president refrained from calling a press conference. The White House merely issued a press release: "I have directed the Atomic Energy Commission to continue its work on all forms of atomic weapons, including the so-called hydrogen or super bomb." That afternoon, acting on another Lilienthal caveat, Truman ordered State and Defense to reexamine national objectives "and the effect of these objectives on our strategic plans in light of the probable fission bomb capability and possible thermonuclear bomb capability of the Soviet Union."[12]

That afternoon David Lilienthal learned from McMahon that his committee had been on the point of demanding publicly that the president go ahead, the very act of preemption the president had anticipated.

Lilienthal later wrote that speaking up in the Oval Office had been one of the hardest acts of his life, "saying No to a steamroller." He knew that Acheson was at least as unhappy as he was about the course they were suggesting and that his own insistence on speaking out distressed the secretary, lest his doing so without putting forward an alternative merely confuse the president, who had already made up his mind. If Lilienthal had had anything but "the most unbounded admiration" for Acheson, "the deepest loyalty and fealty for the President," and compassion for the load each man had to carry, he would not have found his dissent so painful.[13]

"Now to be a good sport," he thought as he broke the news to the GAC. The mood was "like a funeral party," and became bleaker still when Lilienthal added that the president had issued a second order forbidding GAC members to speak out. Not only had the president overruled his scientific advisers; he had bound them to secrecy at a moment when they had urged that the public be more fully informed. Conant and Oppenheimer asked whether they ought to resign. Lilienthal asked them to remain.[14]

Later there was an evening gathering, the fifty-fourth birthday party Lewis Strauss gave for himself at the Wardman Park. For the GAC members it was like the second funeral they had been to that day. While Strauss celebrated, a dejected Robert Oppenheimer sat with his back to the other guests, the inevitable cigarette dangling from his fingertips. When Strauss approached to introduce his son and his son's new wife, Oppenheimer did not bother to turn around. As the Strausses remembered it, he merely extended a hand over his shoulder.[15]

Before going to bed that night, Lilienthal wrote in his journal: "This is a night of heartache. . . . We have to leave many things to God; this one He will have to get us out of."[16]

CHAPTER FIVE

Lost Opportunities

THE PRESIDENT HAD NOW committed the country to building a weapon no one knew how to make, or even whether it could be made. Against the advice of nearly all his scientific advisers, he had placed his weaponeers in a position where they *had* to produce—or make his government look catastrophically inept. And he had handed the Russians information that ought to remain secret. If they had not already embarked on a program to build the hydrogen bomb, they would do so now. And if they had begun, they would step up the pace.

We know now, as we did not know then, that the Russians were working on the H-bomb and that their physicists were just as capable as ours. After Truman's announcement of January 31, 1950, Stalin ordered them to move faster, and the Soviet scientists succeeded brilliantly. For the second time, Hiroshima having been the first, the United States had set the pace of the arms race.

Air Force officials wanted the Super because its radius of destruction—ten times that of the atomic bomb—would "compensate for bombing error." It is appalling today to read secret congressional testimony of January 1950, in which officials of the Pentagon explained that instead of ten or twelve A-bombs, a single hydrogen bomb would more efficiently do the job of wiping out a division of troops massed for a river crossing or a beachhead landing. These men understood neither the H-bomb nor the A-bomb. Air Force officials and congressional assistants such as William Borden, who drafted McMahon's emotionally charged letters to the president, had access to all the secrets. But what the H-bomb was—what it would do and what the effects would be—of this they had no understanding. The damage inflicted by the weapon could not be limited to the battlefield. A single bomb could probably "take out" any capital city in the world and, because of the pulse it emitted, wreak havoc on the communications of the country that received it. Industry, agriculture, communications, all would be so severely crippled that the conquering nation would be unable to put civilization together again. Those who understood this were the physicists, mathematicians, and engineers who had built the atomic bomb. The GAC was composed of such men, and they were horrified by the idea of a new weapon a thousand times more destructive than the one they had brought into being. But as far as the politicians were concerned, the new bomb would be bigger, therefore better, than the old, and it would be political suicide not to build it. They brushed aside any thought that it might also be a weapon of genocide.

There were other respects in which scientists and political people were at cross-purposes. The model the GAC had been looking at was the Classical Super, which Teller and others had been working on without success for more than three years. The weapon U.S. scientists ultimately developed was not the model the GAC had before it in 1949 but a new weapon, built on different principles. Thus when Oppenheimer wrote in his covering report that the GAC's recommendations "stem in large part from the technical nature of the Super," he was referring to a fact difficult for nonscientists to understand: while it had been impossible to prove the feasibility of Teller's Super, it might likewise be impossible to prove decisively that it was not feasible. The situation was an open-ended one in which the odds of the bomb's being possible did not look good enough for the nation to commit itself publicly to building it.[1]

Readers of the GAC report in Washington did not understand this. Instead, they looked at its moral language—"weapon of genocide," "necessarily an evil thing in any light"—and were put off by the fact that advisers picked for their scientific expertise had ventured into moral territory. Unaware that David Lilienthal had asked the GAC to advise on "as broad a basis as possible," the few who had seen the report believed that the GAC had bent its technical advice to fit its ethical predilections. The fact that it had dealt with the moral issue obscured its technical advice and tended to discredit its recommendations.

Why didn't the GAC press its case? Manley said later that it "leaned over backwards" not to lobby, adding that the members were not accustomed to fighting for their views, since their advice had almost always been taken. That, I. I. Rabi was to say later, left the lobbying to the other side. And lobby the other side did. While Oppenheimer, Rabi, and the rest felt inhibited from lobbying members of the legislative branch while the issue was being considered by the president, men like Strauss and Johnson were not troubled by such scruples. The same was true of the president's secrecy directives: the scientists observed the prohibition against going public, while the political men, aided by tips from a collusive FBI, felt free to leak to the press. It was not until five years later, when the transcript of the Oppenheimer hearing was published, that Americans learned that of the president's fourteen atomic energy advisers, ten had opposed an accelerated H-bomb program and one had abstained, and it had been the two nonscientists who had been most eager to go ahead.

Robert Oppenheimer had a history of thinking long thoughts about atomic weapons. In the course of six wartime visits to Los Alamos by the great Danish physicist Niels Bohr, he had become imbued with Bohr's belief in international control. Both men were convinced that once the war was over, the "secret" of atomic weapons should be shared with other nations and that the capacity to make atomic weapons should be controlled not by a single nation but by a consortium. Oppenheimer never wavered from his and Bohr's vision of international control.

As soon as the war was over, he chaired a panel to make recommendations on the future of the atomic bomb to a group consisting of Secretary of State Acheson, General Leslie R. Groves, James B. Conant, Vannevar Bush, and John J. McCloy, former assistant secretary of war. After four days' intense deliberation at the historic meeting place of Dumbarton Oaks in Washington, D.C., the group proposed that an Atomic Development Authority be created to control everything about atomic energy, from the mining of thorium and uranium to production. No nation would be allowed to make atomic bombs, and the United States would effectively give up its monopoly. The proposal, called the Acheson-Lilienthal plan, was Oppenheimer's inspiration and was drafted by him and Rabi during Christmas week, 1945, in Rabi's apartment overlooking the Hudson River. The plan, which Acheson described as "brilliant and profound," was introduced at the United Nations in amended form by the American financier Bernard Baruch, and promptly rejected by the Russians. Meanwhile Oppenheimer, as adviser to Baruch's delegation, got a chastening look at Stalin-era intransigence.

When the H-bomb issue arose in 1949, he remembered that experience. He was convinced that development of the H-bomb would make things worse, and likewise convinced that any system of inspection rigorous enough to pass the U.S. Senate would be turned down by the Russians in a way that might close the door to future negotiations. "It seems to me," Oppenheimer wrote to Kennan, "that the time for plans, proposals and systems offered unilaterally by our government is past, if it ever existed; and if we ever again come up with a set of proposals, it should be on the basis of some prior agreement."[2]

He continued to believe in international control, but he did not know how to get there. With the rest of the GAC majority, Oppenheimer considered it neither the obligation nor the prerogative of their committee to say what the president ought to do, but only to advise as to what he ought not to do. Fermi and Rabi, on the other hand, considered it incumbent on them to suggest a positive as well as a negative course of action, and proposed an attempt at a self-enforcing agreement with the Russians not to develop the bomb. Uncertainty as to which was truly the better course evidently stayed Oppenheimer's hand and kept him from fighting for the majority view. On this issue, as on a good many others, he was the possessor of a divided mind and extraordinarily divided emotions.

Why did Harry Truman come to the decision he did? The Truman of 1950 was no longer the accidental president who had, almost jauntily, it seemed, ordered the bombing of Hiroshima in the summer of 1945. Five years later, he was more confident and more humane; he understood a great deal that had been obscure to him before. In the late

1940s he told a group of military and civilian advisers, "I don't think we ought to use this thing [the atomic bomb] unless we absolutely have to. It is a terrible thing to order the use of something that is so terribly destructive. . . . You have got to understand that this isn't a military weapon."[3]

The American people, too, seem to have understood. A Gallup poll in early 1950 showed support, by 73 to 18 percent, for the president's decision, but also showed that half of those who responded wanted to try to reach agreement with the Russians before proceeding to build the hydrogen bomb. With the public, although not with the Super's more vociferous advocates in Congress and the Pentagon, the president had more leeway than he supposed.[4]

Had he been willing to brave the political fallout, Truman could have omitted any public announcement and left the scientists to continue secretly to investigate the bomb's feasibility. Meanwhile he could quietly have felt out Soviet willingness to make a deal. As long as Stalin was still alive, negotiations would not have been successful. Once Stalin was gone, however, and he died in 1953, a legacy of trying to find a solution would have been there—and might have made a difference. Khrushchev and Eisenhower might by the mid- to late 1950s have reached agreement to end the fateful competition.[5]

The outcome was a disaster for everyone. It marked a lost opportunity for the president to level with the American people on a life-or-death decision from which they would be the first to suffer and about which they showed heartening signs of common sense. And it failed to buy security for the United States. Believing that we had a greater supply of atomic weapons than we did, the Russians reversed their earlier demobilization and built their ground forces from a low of three million back up to five million men. To counter the resulting superiority of Soviet troop strength in Europe, the president ordered full steam ahead with the H-bomb. So it was to go with decision after decision for forty years, and with each upward ratchet of the arms race, each side became less secure. The decision to produce the H-bomb enshrined secrecy and made the cold war a way of life for both countries.

PART TWO

1950

CHAPTER SIX

Fuchs's Betrayal

"THE ROOF FELL IN TODAY," David Lilienthal wrote in his journal on February 2. He called what had happened "a world catastrophe, and a sad day for the human race." A German-born member of the Manhattan Project had confessed in London to passing atomic secrets to the Russians. His name was Emil Julius Klaus Fuchs, and he had been a member of the British mission to Los Alamos during the war.[1]

The president was told on February 1, 1950, the day following his H-bomb announcement. To official Washington, as to the rest of the country, the news was as shattering as Joe One, the Russian atomic test, had been less than six months before. Physicists who had worked with Fuchs were appalled. Not only might his betrayal explain why the Russians had tested an atomic device sooner than expected, but it might also explain another fact—known to Oppenheimer and one or two others who had studied the debris from Joe One—that the Soviet device appeared to have similarities to the bomb we had dropped on Nagasaki. What else might Fuchs have passed on? The tiny circle of men who knew about these things quickly learned that Fuchs had attended a conference at Los Alamos on thermonuclear reactions in the spring of 1946 before going home to Britain. Had he passed H-bomb tips to Moscow? American physicists did not think so. We were on the wrong track with the H-bomb, and we had been in 1946: anything Fuchs might have transmitted could only have misled the Russians. Robert Oppenheimer expressed the belief of knowledgeable physicists when he said that if the Russians had made progress on the basis of what Fuchs could have told them, "they were marvelous indeed." Still, what Fuchs knew was important enough: that with the war barely over, the Americans already were at work on the H-bomb.[2]

One American physicist was convinced that Fuchs had given the Russians a head start with the hydrogen bomb. That physicist was Edward Teller. Teller had known Fuchs a long time, as a student in Fuchs's native Germany in 1928, and in Los Alamos during the war, when Fuchs, a bachelor, was sought after by the Tellers and other couples to babysit their children. Not only had Teller and Fuchs both been present at the 1946 Super conference, they had seen each other every year since, at the Tellers' home and elsewhere. Only a few months before, in September 1949, while Oppenheimer and Vannevar Bush in Washington were poring over fallout data from Joe One, Teller and Fuchs had made a train trip together in England. News of Fuchs's treachery must have been a fearful blow to Teller. Already he had been warning that the Russians were probably ahead with the H-bomb. Now he proclaimed it insistently.

Fuchs's betrayal had other shattering consequences, among them the growth of doubt in some quarters about Robert Oppenheimer. As early as October 1949, when the H-bomb debate was getting under way, Lewis Strauss received a tip from the FBI that Fuchs was under suspicion. Immediately, he began making inquiries of General Leslie R. Groves, director of the Manhattan Project, about Robert Oppenheimer, who was known to have had a left-wing past, and his brother Frank, a former member of the Communist Party. Strauss spent an hour with FBI director J. Edgar Hoover, apparently exchanging concerns about the Oppenheimers, and when, during the Halloween meeting in October, Robert Oppenheimer told him that he did not think the Russians would refuse to negotiate about the Super, Strauss's suspicions grew. From then on, he wondered about Oppenheimer's opposition to the H-bomb. Was Oppenheimer simply naive? Or was he, like Fuchs, trying to help the Russians? Informed that Fuchs had confessed to espionage, Strauss, in a response that spoke volumes, told Hoover that the news would strengthen the president's hand on the H-bomb decision and "make a good many men who are in the same profession as Fuchs very careful of what they say publicly."[3]

Hoover shared some of Strauss's reservations, for he informed Strauss of Fuchs's confession on the same day he told the president, thereby enabling Strauss to upstage the chairman, David Lilienthal: at the AEC's meeting on February 2, it was Strauss, not Lilienthal, who broke the news to the commissioners.

If Fuchs's espionage seemed to official Washington and much of the public to strengthen the case for secrecy, in the eyes of many Manhattan Project veterans it did the opposite. It meant, as Glenn Seaborg pointed out after learning about Joe One, that Groves's policy of compartmentalized research had failed. Most scientists believed that there were no atomic "secrets." The basic principles were widely known, and once it appeared that the bomb *could* be made, then the way was clear for others to build it. Some of the country's most distinguished physicists were convinced that had the American people been told the facts about nuclear weapons and the scientists' true opinions, they would not have supported the decision to proceed with the H-bomb. Prohibited from disclosing classified information, these physicists struggled to find a way to keep the public better informed. The way they found was to criticize the secrecy that had surrounded Truman's decision.

A day or two after the announcement of Fuchs's confession, a dozen physicists signed an appeal in the *Wall Street Journal,* describing use of the H-bomb as "a betrayal of all standards of morality and of Christian civilization itself," and calling for a pledge by the U.S. government not to be the first to use it. And a few days after that, three famed theoreticians spoke their minds on Mrs. Franklin Roosevelt's weekly television program. Characterizing the arms race as "inexorable," Albert Einstein called "each step . . . the inevitable consequence of the one before. And, at the end . . . lies general annihilation." Hans Bethe emphasized the H-bomb's genocidal nature. The only reason for developing it, he said, lay in the danger that the Russians might build it first and use it to blackmail the United States. By announcing that we would never be first to use it, we could reduce the odds that they would use it to forestall a strike by us. And Oppenheimer emphasized the "grave danger for us in that these decisions have been taken on the basis of facts held secret." The danger, he said, lay in the fact that "wisdom itself cannot flourish, nor even truth be determined, without the give and take of debate or criticism. The relevant facts could be of little help to an enemy; yet they are indispensable for an understanding of questions of policy."[4]

Oppenheimer spoke from experience: as chairman of the GAC and member of several other governmental advisory groups, he had been frustrated during the H-bomb discussions by being muzzled. Just the day before Truman's H-bomb decision, he had testified to the joint congressional committee—in tightest secrecy, of course—that it had been painful for him and others in the know to stand by "in rigid silence" while uninformed individuals had been free to say whatever they pleased, in some cases misleading the public, and in others violating security. Oppenheimer pointed to public use of the word "tritium"—a key H-bomb component—as a security violation. He added that it would be impossible to "undertake anything as interesting as this [building the bomb] and keep it quiet in this country."[5]

Oppenheimer and Bethe evidently had a conversation after their appearance on the program. Being a consultant at Los Alamos but not a government official, Bethe had greater freedom than Oppenheimer to speak out as long as he did not divulge technical secrets. Two days after their conversation Bethe wrote to his colleague Victor Weisskopf at MIT, "I had a long talk with Oppie, who agreed very much with what we had done and were doing. He emphasized the necessity of keeping the issue alive and I very much agree with him. Can you help?" Bethe's letter marked the beginning of an effort by physicists outside the official framework to keep fundamental facts about the H-bomb before the public while observing the president's security strictures.[6]

In keeping with what he and Oppenheimer had agreed, Bethe and three colleagues that spring of 1950 published a series of articles in the journal *Scientific American* and in the *Bulletin of the Atomic Scientists* in which they deplored the "authoritarian" manner in which the H-bomb decision had been made, and tried to inform the public of the principles underlying the technology. The first article, by Louis Ridenour, dean of the graduate college at the University of Illinois, called Truman's decision a "Pyrrhic reply" to the news of Joe One and noted that we were more vulnerable to the hydrogen bomb than the Russians. He praised the emphasis of Los Alamos since the war on making more efficient fission weapons instead of trying to build a hydrogen bomb, deplored the "bankruptcy" of a secrecy policy that excluded the public from life-and-death decisions, and added that the nation needed better means of delivering bombs more than it needed new, more destructive weapons.[7]

In another of the series former AEC commissioner Robert Bacher complained that the public was being given an exaggerated idea of the H-bomb's effectiveness and being denied facts that would enable it to choose between developing weapons, on one hand, and atomic power for peaceful purposes, on the other; and he warned against the belief that secrecy contributes to security: "We are dangerously close to abandoning those principles of free speech and open discussion that have made our country great," he said. And Ralph Lapp, former head of the nuclear physics branch of the Office of Naval Research, emphasized that development of the H-bomb would require a far-reaching program of civil defense and that the nation had not been informed. Since an H-bomb could level an entire metropolitan area, we would have to build a new type of city, a strip city strung along a straight line hundreds of miles long. Such a restructuring of American society could not be carried out without public assent, yet the issue had not even been raised. In the meantime Congress was making a political football of the atom.[8]

Of all the *Scientific American* articles, however, it was Hans Bethe's contribution on the moral issue that attracted the most attention. After describing the terrifying heat, blast, and radiation effects, Bethe asked, "Can we, who have always insisted on morality and human decency, introduce this weapon of total annihilation into the world?" Use of thermonuclear weapons would usher in a new dark age, with nothing left that we think of as civilization. If the Nazi experience taught anything, said Bethe, it was that physical destruction brings moral destruction, and in the struggle merely to survive, it is every man against the other. How could we, whose quarrel with the Soviet Union was largely about means, take the lead in introducing a type of warfare that was bound to bring mass slaughter? "Shall we convince the Russians of the value of the individual by killing millions of them?" Our failure to eliminate or control atomic weapons was no reason to introduce a weapon a thousand times worse.[9]

Even if the Russians were to develop the hydrogen bomb first and use it on us, Bethe said, our reserve of atomic bombs, distributed among various launching sites, would enable us to even the score. "In fact, because of the greater number available, A-bombs may well be more effective in destroying legitimate military targets. . . . H-bombs, after all, would be useful only against the largest targets, of which there are very few in the USSR." The only reason to develop the bomb would be to deter the Russians from deploying it against us, to prevent its use rather than to use it ourselves. Should we go ahead, therefore, we ought to proclaim our reason to the world and pledge that we would never be the first to use a thermonuclear weapon and would use it only if someone else had already used it in an attack on us or one of our allies.

The straightforward simplicity of Bethe's argument would have attracted attention in any event, but the circumstances in which his article appeared were sensational. On reading an advance copy, which had been delivered to the AEC, Commissioner Smyth spotted technical data which, he thought, should remain secret. The AEC immediately ordered Gerard Piel, publisher of the magazine, to stop publication and informed him that it was prepared to get a court order. Piel obeyed the AEC of his own volition and had the typeset plates, plus about three thousand copies of the magazine, destroyed. Bethe then produced a second version, which with customary prudence he had written in advance and stored in his safe, and the journal appeared, only a few days late, with this version in it. Bethe took the fuss with customary calm: the published version, he felt, was just as good for his purposes as the original. Practical as ever, he was concerned about the cost to *Scientific American,* but consoled himself by thinking that the notoriety had been "good advertising" for Mr. Piel.[10]

Bethe went further than any of the other Manhattan Project physicists to act on his disapproval of the presidential ukase. In mid-February 1950 he wrote Norris Bradbury one of the more remarkable letters in the annals of American dissent.

> You have probably heard about my feelings concerning the hydrogen bomb. . . . The announcement of the President has not changed my feelings. . . . I still believe that it is morally wrong and unwise for our national security to develop this weapon. In most respects I agree with the opinions of the General Advisory Committee although I have not seen their report itself. So much has been said about the reasons on both sides that I do not need to go into them here. The main point is that I cannot in good conscience work on this weapon.
>
> For this reason, if and when I come to Los Alamos in the future I will completely refrain from any discussions related to the super-bomb. I have not completely decided whether this should include work on the booster. This will depend essentially on the question of how many problems the super and the booster have in common. Therefore on my visits I would primarily concern myself with the problems of the implosion, with problems of neutron diffusion and of efficiency, in other words with classical Los Alamos problems. . . .
>
> Because of these very much reduced plans I think it would not be worthwhile to renegotiate my consultant's contract. . . .
>
> In case of war I would obviously reconsider my position.[11]

The letter was remarkable, among other reasons, for the willingness to sacrifice that it implied. Bethe was one of the constellation of scientific geniuses who had sought refuge from Hitler's anti-Semitism during the 1930s, and his work on the fusion of light elements in the sun was the first to point to the possibility of a weapon based on thermonuclear reactions. He was at the time a faculty member at

Cornell, which had become his home in America. Later, as director of one of the Manhattan Project's two Theoretical Divisions, he had come to think of Los Alamos, too, as home, and had returned there as a consultant every summer but one since the war. He loved gazing out at the high mesas, loved hiking in the mountains, and considered his colleagues there not only his cherished friends but his extended family. The prospect of not working with them again was painful to him.

His letter to Bradbury was unique: no one was under as much pressure as Bethe to join the program, and no one was to resist as forthrightly. Others who agreed with him that the weapon was immoral, that possessing it would not contribute to defense, or that their university research was more promising for the country than weapons work, remained silent rather than refusing outright. Bethe alone spelled out his reasons.

Meanwhile his colleague Teller had already started recruiting for the Super program. In the *Bulletin of the Atomic Scientists* that spring he wrote a summons titled "Back to the Laboratories," in which he preached that it is not the scientist's job to decide whether the hydrogen bomb *should* be built. The scientist, Teller said, is not responsible for the laws of nature: it is his job to find out how they work. The scientific community had been "out on a honeymoon with mesons. The holiday is over. Hydrogen bombs will not produce themselves. . . . If we want to live on the technological capital of the last war, we shall come out second best."[12]

Early in March 1950, Teller arranged to have dinner in Washington with Brien McMahon's assistant William Borden. He informed Borden that Oppenheimer had delayed the H-bomb program and had tried to have the Los Alamos laboratory closed after the war. "Give it back to the Indians," he quoted Oppenheimer, apparently unaware that this was the title of a popular song that Oppie must have heard somewhere. Realizing that he could not have the lab disbanded, Oppenheimer, Teller said, had tried to change it from a weapons facility into a center for basic research. While postwar director Norris Bradbury was an improvement over Oppenheimer, he added, Bradbury, too, left a lot to be desired. Under him the lab had, "miraculously," survived, but it was weak and ineffective and composed of mediocrities. It was Bradbury's fault, since he "is loyal to them and . . . refuses to supplant the mediocre with better men." Teller warned that the Fuchs case confirmed our worst fears: thanks to him, the Russians had known our most promising approach to the H-bomb since 1946 and as a result might have developed a hydrogen device concurrently with their atomic bomb. Now, with Bethe, Fermi, and Oppenheimer discouraging the younger men by refusing to join the program, our situation was "desperate." Teller hoped the president would bring his personal pressure to bear on reluctant scientists.[13]

Teller's testimony, given secretly to the congressional committee the next day, was even more alarming than what he had told Borden over dinner, but this time he did not mention Bradbury or Oppenheimer by name or suggest that the president be asked to intervene. He warned that the country was in even greater peril than during the war, since the Germans had not, after all, been working on the atomic bomb. The Russians, on the other hand, might already be ahead of us with the H-bomb. He told the committee that H-bomb work had barely progressed since the war: the best scientists had returned to basic research and many were hesitant to join because they had a bad conscience over Hiroshima. Physicists, he added, are as susceptible to the herd instinct as those of lesser intellect: they would refuse to work on the weapon if their leaders refused. Los Alamos needed to double the size of its theoretical staff and improve it by "much more than a factor of two in talent." Yet a manpower draft or other direct pressure might not be helpful, since a scientist has to put his heart in it if he is to invent something new and original. If the scientists continued to hold back, however, we might have to turn to the British and Canadians and that could be dangerous. Klaus Fuchs had, after all, been part of the British wartime mission. Was there, Teller asked, some form of suasion the committee might be willing to bring to bear? He offered a list of scientists who could be helpful.[14]

Smyth, who had come to the hearing expressly to add nuance to Teller's remarks, intervened, suggesting that an appeal by the White

House to the president of a university might be the best way to secure the services of a scientist reluctant to take time from his academic career to return to the lab. Smyth added that a scientist who did not want to work on the bomb could nevertheless contribute by training younger men to work on it, and pointed out that secrecy damaged recruitment, since it fostered the assumption that there was nothing left to do on the H-bomb but the engineering. If secrecy were eased somewhat, and scientists were told the truth, that there was still a vast amount of work to be done, it would send a signal that we had not gotten very far.[15]

In warning of a scientific boycott, Teller as usual had jumped the gun. Other shortages were more critical at that moment than highly skilled manpower; one of them was the potential shortage of tritium. No one knew how much tritium, an isotope of hydrogen, would be required for a bomb test, but it could be considerable, and the reactor facility in Hanford, Washington, the only one in the country that produced it, already was fully committed to plutonium production. In the tense atmosphere after Fuchs's confession, after an alarming Pentagon report in February that the Russians might already be working on the H-bomb, and after a formal request from the Joint Chiefs of Staff that work on the bomb receive priority status, President Truman issued the directive that put real teeth in his original order. On March 10 he secretly ordered the AEC to prepare production of the materials the weapon would require, especially tritium.[16]

Another bottleneck was the lack of computers to do the millions of computations that would be required. Just after the war a handful of scientists and their wives had performed mathematical calculations on the early IBM punch-card machines. But by 1948 it was clear that further work on either of the H-bomb designs under consideration— both Teller's Super and a simpler, layered device called the Alarm Clock, designed by Teller in 1946—would have to wait until faster machines had become available, a delay to which Teller himself agreed. Since 1948, members of the "T," or Theoretical, Division, had done hand calculations on aspects of the Super problem and had planned the calculations that needed to be done as soon as computers became available. What the lab needed most was not, as Teller thought, a famous theoretician like Oppenheimer, Fermi, Bethe, or Harvard's Julian Schwinger to replace Bradbury, but a way to cope with the staggering mathematical demands imposed by the H-bomb project.[17]

The lab eventually built a computer of its own. Even that effort, however, was slowed by something more mundane—a housing shortage that hampered the growth of personnel. Los Alamos in the spring of 1950, then, was dealing with a number of shortages, each of them related to the others and each, in time, overcome.[18]

During the period of uncertainty after the war, the man who had held the lab together was Norris Bradbury, selected by Groves and Oppenheimer to succeed Oppenheimer only a few weeks after the Japanese surrender. Bradbury was a naval commander and a specialist in ordnance; his first task had been to stanch the hemorrhaging of personnel, which had fallen from about 3,500 in the summer of 1945 to just over 1,200 six months later, and build a stockpile of fifteen or so atomic bombs that could be assembled rapidly. The lab did fission research that had been passed over during the war, especially research into design of the smaller, more efficient fission weapons that were now the country's first line of defense. Sophisticated atomic weapons were important for another reason as well: should the Super ever become a reality, the hydrogen fuel would be triggered by an atomic bomb. It was therefore of great importance to learn more about how fission worked and how fission and fusion interacted during an explosion. Bradbury was not enthusiastic about the Super, but he was convinced that "some day, someone must know the answer" to the question whether it could be built. "The use of nuclear energy," he had told the laboratory on the day he took over in 1945, "may be so catastrophic . . . that we should know every extent of its pathology. . . . One studies cancer—one does not expect or want to contract it—but the whole impact of cancer . . . is such that we must know its unhappy extent. So it is with nuclear energy . . . we must know how terrible it is."[19]

When Truman made his decision to proceed with the hydrogen

bomb, the lab under Bradbury had already held two major series of tests in the Pacific, Operation Crossroads in 1946, which studied the effects of the atomic bomb on naval vessels, and Operation Sandstone in 1948, which tested design principles for the next generation of atomic warheads. And, contrary to Teller's accusations that it was not working on the Super, the lab was preparing a series for the following year, 1951, which would include a critical test of thermonuclear principles. To prepare the series—an enormous theoretical, engineering, and logistical challenge—Bradbury in late 1949 or early 1950 set up what he called the "Family Committee" to evaluate a whole family of thermonuclear ideas—with nicknames like "Daddy," "Sonny," "Uncle," and "Little Edward"—generated by Teller, and decide which should be included in the next year's series. Teller had come up with so many ideas, some good, some not so good, that it had placed a strain on the laboratory. Aiming to harness his formidable energies without allowing them to tear the lab apart, Bradbury passed over Teller and named a tough-minded assistant, Darol Froman, who had managed the Sandstone tests, to be head of the new committee.

Bradbury's choice was preceded by some volatile history. During the war, when Bethe twice asked Teller to undertake critical assignments, Teller accepted responsibility but both times failed to follow through. After the second failure he and his group, at his request, had been relieved of work on the A-bomb, and a British team was brought in to do the work (the team that included Fuchs). It was generally felt that Teller failed to perform because he was bored by the fission bomb, a problem he considered solved, and because he was already far more interested in the H-bomb. Meanwhile the wartime director, Robert Oppenheimer, was under tremendous pressure to get the A-bomb built. To assuage Teller's resentment at not being named head of the Theoretical Division, Oppenheimer set aside an hour in his hectic schedule each week to meet with the Hungarian and listen while he poured out his suggestions. Oppenheimer also permitted Teller to form a special group of a dozen physicists and mathematicians to work on thermonuclear ideas. Years afterward members of the wartime lab still remembered with resentment Teller's having sat out what one of them called "the main event," building the atomic bomb, during the last critical year, when all hands were desperately needed. And right after the war, when Bradbury was struggling to hold the lab together, Teller had presented an ultimatum: Bradbury must promise to conduct a dozen fission tests a year, or mount a vastly stepped-up thermonuclear effort, or he would leave. The laboratory being in no condition to undertake either, Bradbury refused, and Teller returned to teaching and research at the University of Chicago.

But he did not sever his ties to Los Alamos. He had returned every summer to consult on special problems and was back at the lab on a year's leave even before the Soviet test of August 1949. With the Polish mathematician Stanislaw Ulam and the prodigious Russian astrophysicist George Gamow, he was working on the problem of ignition: how to ignite a cylinder of deuterium (an isotope of hydrogen), using a fission bomb near one end of the cylinder as the trigger. It was a daunting problem, since the deuterium would not ignite until it reached a temperature so high that the cylinder would blow apart in the fraction of a millisecond before the explosion could spread through it. With the addition of tritium, a third isotope of hydrogen, to the deuterium fuel, the temperature of ignition could be lowered sufficiently for the deuterium-tritium mixture to burn. But the amount of tritium this would require had to be established with some accuracy, since tritium, produced in the reactors at Hanford, Washington, was scarce and expensive. Producing it would mean a sacrifice of plutonium needed for the A-bomb.[20]

Teller had made several different estimates of the amount of tritium that would be required. At the time of the 1946 conference it was assumed that the Super could be ignited with fewer than four hundred grams of tritium, which was not considered prohibitive, but an estimate by Teller in September 1947 was about twice as large. In December 1949, even before Truman's H-bomb announcement, two parallel sets of calculations were begun in an attempt once again to determine the tritium requirement. One set entailed preparation of a machine calculation to go on a computer called the ENIAC, in Aberdeen, Maryland. Preparing the calculation took six months and was carried out by two husband-and-wife teams, John and Klari von Neumann in Princeton, and Foster and Cerda Evans with John Calkin in Los Alamos. The calculation went on the ENIAC in June 1950 and continued into the summer.[21]

Since the results would not be known for some time, Stanislaw Ulam and a collaborator, Cornelius Everett, undertook a second set by hand. It was expected that their work, a simplified version of the ENIAC calculation, would provide less detailed results than the ENIAC but would do so faster. The two mathematicians worked four to six hours a day, applying slide rules, pencil, and paper to a set of highly simplified calculations and filling page after page with stepwise computations. Everett, a self-effacing workaholic whom Ulam had known before the war at the University of Wisconsin, performed such a large number of calculations that his slide rule wore out, leading him to joke that the least the government could do was buy him a new one. They began their work in early winter and by the end of February 1950 concluded that it would take far more tritium to ignite the Super than any of Teller's estimates, ranging from three hundred to six hundred grams, had foreseen.[22]

Ulam and Everett then began a new calculation, one that assumed that several hundred additional grams of tritium had been added to the model. Françoise Ulam and two other wives were put to work grinding out arithmetical problems on desk calculators. But even assuming the extra tritium, this model, too, would not ignite. Thus the results of the second set of Ulam-Everett calculations, completed by early summer 1950, were even gloomier than the first, indicating that the amount of tritium required would be several times larger than previous estimates. They seemed to indicate that Teller's Super was not feasible.[23]

In April 1950, before the second set of results was known, Ulam flew east to consult the great mathematician John von Neumann, who, like Teller, hoped that the H-bomb in some form would be possible. A day or so after Ulam arrived in Princeton, Enrico Fermi, too, appeared in the busy von Neumann household, and on the after-noon and evening of April 21 the three friends spent hours discussing the implications of the first Ulam-Everett calculations. The next day they were joined by Oppenheimer, who lived near the von Neu-manns in Princeton. When Ulam caught Fermi and von Neumann, the world's most accomplished mathematicians, in a minor arithmeti-cal error, Oppenheimer winked at Ulam in amusement. Comparing Oppie's and von Neumann's attitudes toward the bomb, Ulam no-ticed that Oppie "liked having the difficulties confirmed, whereas von Neumann was still searching for ways to rescue the whole thing." Von Neumann "never lost heart," even after he realized that the amount of tritium required would be so great as to make the Super prohibi-tively expensive.[24]

Immediately after his return to Los Alamos, Ulam wrote to von Neumann that Teller had been "pale with fury" when he learned of their conclusions. Teller also wrote to von Neumann, expressing the dark thought that Ulam had biased his calculations deliberately. To this von Neumann replied that he was "sorry to see that the strain which your work puts upon you is exceedingly great." Françoise Ulam in Los Alamos was a witness to the unhappiness her husband's results caused Teller. She had enjoyed her job up to now, punching out numbers on the desk calculators. She liked working in the T Di-vision, where her husband was, and liked joining in the midmorning coffee hour, where the lab's luminaries and its rank and file ex-changed gossip and planned the next Sunday's hike in the Jemez or Sangre de Cristo Mountains. But now, down the corridor, Françoise heard Teller berating Stan and shouting that his figures were wrong. The angry scenes went on for weeks, until it seemed to Françoise that no one stood up to Teller but Stan. But what Teller denied when it came from Ulam he could accept, at least for while, from his es-teemed friend von Neumann. On June 13, after more than six weeks, Ulam wrote in his diary, "Victorious end of fights with Edward."[25]

Members of the old wartime team had by now arrived for the summer. On hand to consult on fission reactions, Bethe, despite his letter to Bradbury a few months earlier renouncing work on the

Super, looked over the Ulam-Everett hand calculations and concluded that ignition would probably require a kilogram of tritium, almost twice Teller's most recent estimate. Eagle-eyed as always, Ulam noticed that Bethe began to show up more frequently, apparently in hopes of proving once and for all that the Super would not work.[26]

Another visitor was Fermi, with whom Ulam set up a calculation to explore the second, equally crucial, half of the Super problem, the problem of burning. On the dubious assumption that the deuterium could be made to ignite, would the burning "propagate" through the column of deuterium? Programmers from the lab's computing group worked with desk calculators, while Fermi used logarithms and a slide rule and his usual stunning simplifications. By late summer he and Ulam embellished this routine and made their final set of computations a race between them. Assisted by a collaborator named Miriam Plank, Fermi worked on a Marchand calculator. The many hours he spent alone with the fetching Miriam, reviewing her calculations on the Marchand and laying out new ones for her to do, caused smiles of amusement among members of the T Division.

Ulam, on his side of the competition, relied on Monte Carlo, a method of calculation that was largely his invention and that was based on random numbers. Working once again with Everett, he addressed the problem by throwing dice. The race between Fermi and Ulam ended in a draw, with the two sets of calculations producing the same answers at about the same time. Like the three sets of Ulam-Fermi calculations that had preceded them, this one also showed that the explosion would fizzle.[27]

Teller's capitulation was short-lived. Carson Mark heard him roaring in disbelief as one set of calculations came in. But Ulam and Fermi were confident of their results. Ulam's confidence went beyond the issue of accuracy. He was convinced that the work he had done with Fermi was even more important than the earlier calculations with Everett because it turned out to be basic to an understanding of thermonuclear explosions. And it was important in a way that mattered hugely for successful development of the H-bomb. For years the lab had been working on the wrong model, Teller's Super. But before a new approach could be considered seriously, the old one had to be discredited. Ulam and Everett had shown that the Super could not work, but neither of them had Fermi's prestige. His adherence to their conclusions was decisive. Los Alamos was now convinced that the Super conceived by Edward Teller would neither ignite nor burn.[28]

CHAPTER SEVEN

Fission versus Fusion

THE THEORISTS WHO gathered in Los Alamos that summer of 1950 were a stellar group. In addition to Bethe, who had come to work on fission, and Teller and Fermi, who were working on different aspects of the thermonuclear problem, another legendary physicist, John Wheeler, arrived from Paris to answer what he regarded as a patriotic summons to join the H-bomb project.

Wheeler, whose groundbreaking paper on fission with Niels Bohr before the war had identified U-235 as the isotope of uranium that could be made to fission, had been in Europe during the 1949–50 academic year for a Guggenheim-sponsored period of thinking, writing, and renewed collaboration with Bohr. With his wife and three young children, he had settled into a cozy pension on the Left Bank when, one evening in late 1949, he received a transatlantic telephone call. Wheeler took the call on the wall phone in the dining room, where a score of French guests laid down their knives and forks to listen. It was AEC commissioner Henry Smyth. Would Wheeler cut short his fellowship year and come home to work on an all-out project? The Russians, Smyth said obliquely, were almost surely working on the same thing. Wheeler had already heard from Teller and had a notion what Smyth was referring to. Other cryptic telephone calls followed from across the Atlantic.

Still hesitating two months later, Wheeler mentioned his dilemma over breakfast in Copenhagen with Niels Bohr. "Do you for a moment imagine," he heard the Danish physicist say, "that Europe would be free of Soviet control today were it not for the atomic bomb?" Wheeler, an ardent patriot, decided to go home.[1]

He brought two of his most promising Princeton graduate students, Ken Ford and John Toll, to Los Alamos, where the three of them recalculated existing bomb design ideas, altering the parameters to see if they could somehow produce a thermonuclear explosion. They thought of new designs, too, the further out the better, and ran them through the calculators. And they revived an early inspiration of Teller's, the Alarm Clock, to see how large an explosion they could get. Wheeler and his men worked in an office next to the coffee room, and members of the T Division dropped by daily to join in the brainstorming. Besides Teller and his assistant, Frederic de Hoffmann, who had come from France to help out, there were Conrad Longmire, Marshall Rosenbluth, and Emil Konopinski, all of whom were to make significant contributions. And, importantly, the patient and respected division chief, Carson Mark, would come by to ask quiet questions that had a way of ferreting out weak spots. During the morning coffee hour all of them pooled their latest ideas, especially the ones they had tried out on calculators the day before. Teller would drop in, "a dark-haired, bushy-browed prophet," as Wheeler described him, to urge that they chuck it all and try some new approach. Ulam, meanwhile, would float down the corridor from office to office and announce before leaving in midafternoon, "I don't know how you physicists do it. I can't work more than six hours a day." Then he would go home to do pure mathematics late into the night.[2]

Wheeler, too, worked evenings in the log house where he and his family were living. It was the best house on Bathtub Row, Kitty and Robert Oppenheimer's during the war, and it had a small Indian ruin in back. The three small Wheelers loved playing with six-year-old Claire Ulam next door, and observed that, when it came to stacked-up dishes in the sink and round-the-clock hospitality, the housekeeping style of Claire's mother, Françoise, was more relaxed than that of their mother. Janette Wheeler, for her part, found Los Alamos a company town, hard to break into. When, after a year or so, the Wheelers departed for the more civilized life of Princeton, the Los Alamites detected Janette's hand. "She thought we were all savages," one of them said.[3]

While Wheeler had come to explore thermonuclear possibilities, fission exploration, too, had attracted a gifted recruit in twenty-five-year-old Theodore Taylor. A few months earlier, in the fall of 1949, Carson Mark had had a call from Robert Serber, Manhattan Project veteran and professor of physics at Berkeley. He had an outstanding graduate student who had gone to pieces during his preliminary oral exams and flunked not once, but twice. The student was exceptionally creative, and Serber could not bear to see him lost to physics. He asked Mark to try him out. Taylor, who possessed an uncanny ability to visualize the way a collection of metal and wire and high explosives would react together, used graph paper and a hand calculator to eliminate material from the designs tested at Trinity, Bikini, and Sandstone and made them lighter and more efficient. Then he rearranged what was inside the implosion systems so as to get more energy for compression of the U-235 or plutonium core. Soon it was clear that Taylor was a prodigy, capable of designing A-bombs in a whole range of sizes and yields. After his failure at Berkeley, Taylor's confidence had been at rock bottom; his freewheeling status at Los Alamos suited him perfectly. The big men were trying to figure out how to build the Super, no one cared much about fission, and he was left in peace. So little had been done to improve the early fission designs that he felt his job was like skimming cream off the top of a milk bottle. He was getting results—while everyone else at the lab was at a dead end, trying to make deuterium ignite and burn.[4]

Any number of factors, a millionth of a second in timing or the smallest deviation from perfect symmetry, could make such a difference that Taylor decided that multiple small-yield explosions, each testing a different aspect, were needed to perfect the design of his new, more efficient A-bombs. He couldn't go to the Pacific to test merely part of a bomb, and so the AEC built two sites in Nevada, the first in the continental United States, to try out Taylor's ideas. The confidence that the young theorist had lost at Berkeley rebounded. He was given increasing freedom and that precious thing, open access to the computer. Caro Taylor noticed that Hans Bethe would drop by in hiking boots to confer with her husband, that Fermi would seek him out for hikes in the mountains above Los Alamos, and that at the rare dinner party they attended, some famous physicist or mathematician would huddle with him off in a corner.

Taylor's work was partly a hedge in case the thermonuclear bomb proved impossible: indeed, two years later his design, the Super Oralloy Bomb, was tested triumphantly at the Pacific proving grounds on Eniwetok. The successful test of a fission weapon of this magnitude—at half a megaton, it produced a much bigger explosion than earlier atomic bombs and half that of the putative hydrogen bomb—was to raise the question whether the megaton weapon, the thermonuclear bomb, would be needed after all.

The constellation of geniuses at Los Alamos that summer focused on a series of tests scheduled to take place in the Pacific the following spring. The series, code-named "Greenhouse," was to test four devices, two of which would have thermonuclear components. One of these was the Booster, an atomic bomb in which a small amount of deuterium would be added to the fissionable material in order to increase the yield. At their Halloween meeting Oppenheimer and the GAC had endorsed work on this weapon because it appeared to be a promising way to use fusion to produce an enormously enhanced atomic bomb. Carson Mark and the T Division were especially committed to this test because of the information it might provide about the way the fission and fusion elements interacted.

The other test, code-named "George," was the one in which Teller was particularly interested because it was more nearly a true thermonuclear experiment than the Booster test. It was not a bomb test but an experiment to learn how a capsule of thermonuclear fuel, a mixture of deuterium and tritium (D-T), would behave if ignited by a fission explosion outside it. Instead of placing the D-T combination at the center of the explosion, as in the Booster, energy from the explosion would be channeled down a pipe, or tube, to a vial of D-T gas weighing only a fraction of an ounce. After years of trying to think of ways to ignite a D-T mixture and make it burn, Teller wanted to know what would happen once it did burn: how the temperature and density would change, all the "diagnostics" of burning.

This required that the thermonuclear mixture be at a distance from the fission trigger and studied separately. Teller hoped the test would prove that the Super on which he and the lab had lavished years of research was possible, at least in principle. But a portentous fact, to which neither he nor anyone else gave much thought at the time, was that the component of the fission explosion that would move out of the core first and down the tube toward the thermonuclear fuel would be X-radiation.

After a summer of intense theoretical exploration, the lab had continued to make headway with fission weapons. Not only was there no progress on the Super, however, but the ENIAC calculations and the hand calculations by Ulam with Everett and Fermi all had provided evidence that the Super could not be built. In August, Teller and Wheeler produced a paper in which they conceded that it was still too early to say whether a thermonuclear weapon was feasible or economically practical. Instead of blaming possible failure on statistical evidence, however, they blamed it on a shortage of the "right men," or senior theoretical physicists. The number of these, they said, was shrinking when it ought to be growing. Unwilling to give up, they expressed hope that the big new computers scheduled for completion in 1951 and 1952 might disprove the pessimistic calculations so far.

About this time Bradbury wrote a paper agreeing that the chances of success now looked poorer than before. Unlike Teller and Wheeler, however, Bradbury did not blame a shortage of talent. Thermonuclear success, he predicted, "may depend upon entirely new and as yet unforeseen approaches."[5]

At a meeting in Washington in September 1950, the GAC welcomed the laboratory's success in fission research, noting that it was now possible to make a large number of small bombs from a given amount of fissionable material and also to develop atomic weapons with ten times the destructive power of any previous design, improvements that promised effectively to double the size of the U.S. stockpile. The committee contrasted the "uncertainties" of thermonuclear development with the "great promise" of fission weapons and suggested that the laboratory concentrate on fission. The GAC made another comment that was to cause trouble later on for Chairman Oppenheimer. Taking aim at Teller's special project, the GAC expressed "misgivings as to the value and relevance" of the effort expended on the forthcoming George shot. Because of the demands preparation for the test was placing on computer time and on the T Division, the committee concluded that "there is in fact interference between the thermonuclear program and the fission weapon program."[6]

That summer an event occurred that dwarfed even the explorations at Los Alamos. On June 26, 1950, in an attack that Americans believed to have been instigated by Joseph Stalin, the troops of Communist North Korea poured over the border to the south and invaded the Republic of South Korea. With U.S. strategic interests at stake, President Truman asked the United Nations to intervene. The fighting, waged by forces of the United States and the United Nations, lasted three years and was regarded as a kind of surrogate war between the United States and the USSR.[7]

The war in Korea changed everything. With Mao Tse-tung in power in China, the outbreak of hostilities meant that the United States was engaged against Communism in Asia as well as in Europe. It led to a buildup of U.S. armed forces, a change from peace to a semiwar footing, and growing suspicion of everything remotely red at home.

Remote as they were geographically, the men on the mesa in New Mexico were very much affected. There was talk of postponing or canceling the Greenhouse tests scheduled for the spring of 1951 in the Pacific lest they interfere with Navy supply lines to Korea. Hans Bethe reconsidered his renunciation of H-bomb work and agreed to join the project. And at the higher reaches of the U.S. government, consideration was given to using the atomic bomb in Korea. This possibility enhanced the priority of fission research: Korea had no targets large enough for the hydrogen bomb, but plenty of targets for small, or "tactical," atomic weapons should Truman decide to go nuclear.

The Korean War also brought into relief a difference of emphasis in Washington between those who believed the main threat from Stalin lay in Europe and those who worried most about Asia. Those who thought the greatest danger from Communism lay in Asia wanted to give priority to better and cheaper atomic bombs, while those who worried most about Europe tended to favor the bigger bomb. The nightmare of those most concerned with Europe was that with the Americans tied down in Korea, Stalin, who had already overrun Eastern Europe, would unleash his vast land armies on Western Europe. To prevent this, they wanted priority development of a "strategic," or hydrogen, weapon with which to bomb Soviet urban areas should Stalin make a move toward the West. Brien McMahon's energetic assistant, William Borden, belonged to the Europe-first school of thought. Borden wrote a memo that summer pointing out that in addition to its larger cities, the USSR had many smaller, spread-out urban areas with factories and military bases on the outskirts. "One H-bomb would eliminate the entire complex," he wrote, while "A-bombs would be relatively ineffective." Borden also doubted the ability of U.S. bomber crews to deliver A-bombs on heavily defended pinpoint targets, especially at night or in bad weather. "Such targets," he concluded, "might succumb to the H-bomb alone." Such was the strength of Borden's feelings that he opposed use of the A-bomb in Korea not out of pacifist sentiment but because "each weapon used in Korea will leave one less to be used . . . against Russia."[8]

Ted Taylor was exposed to this attitude that fall of 1950 when he and several other New Mexico weaponeers were informed in a Pentagon briefing that Soviet land armies were capable of occupying all of Western Europe in less than six weeks. Taylor, an innocent whose experience up to then had been pretty much limited to what went on in the core of a fissioning bomb, was too startled to question whether what they were being told was true—"we were only kids from Los Alamos."

Taylor spent several weeks in the Pentagon that autumn poring over enormous photographs of Moscow, Baku, and other targets in the Soviet Union, trying to figure out whether he could design an A-bomb big enough to wipe out an entire metropolitan area. "I spent a lot of time drawing circles with ground zero on the Kremlin and the distance corresponding to various calories per square centimeter and pounds per square inch pressure." Pentagon officials were disappointed that none of his circles included the whole of Moscow. If the contents of one big bomb were divided into several smaller bombs, Taylor told them, they could destroy more of the city. "What could you do with a kiloton?" he asked rhetorically later on. "The answer was a great deal, depending on what you could package it in."[9]

Smaller bombs were a specialty of his: thanks to Taylor, a dozen small implosion designs eventually became part of the U.S. stockpile, to say nothing of the design for a tiny atomic bomb ten inches in diameter that one man could lift off the ground. But the Navy and Air Force were not interested in Taylor's boutique bombs. Frightened by the conviction that they were years behind the Russians and uncertain that the Super could be built, they wanted a one-megaton fission bomb, an atomic bomb in the hydrogen-bomb range. They hoped that the twenty-five-year-old prodigy from Los Alamos could give them the miracle they sought.

With war simmering in the Far East and Taylor at work on clever fission designs, Oppenheimer summoned the GAC to Los Alamos in late October for its twenty-third meeting. Here and there the cottonwoods were still yellow in the river valleys, but on the Hill the aspens were bare. The skepticism of the Halloween meeting just one year before had been amply borne out. Oppenheimer reminded those gathered on the mesa that the earlier meeting had been asked to judge a specific Super design and concluded that it showed too little promise to justify an all-out program. Calculations by Fermi and Ulam since then made it appear even less likely than before that the second stage of the explosion, the "propagation," would occur.[10]

The situation was equally grave, indeed it now looked nearly hopeless, with regard to the first, or "ignition," stage. Instead of the one hundred, four hundred, or six hundred grams of tritium that Teller had variously predicted, Ulam and Everett and the ENIAC calculations had shown that "a lower limit" of three to five kilograms would be required. Not only had Teller's estimates been wrong—they had been wrong by an order of magnitude.[11]

Did Teller feel chastened by his egregious miscalculations? Not in the least. He was present at the meeting, along with other members of the lab, and when Carson Mark outlined the ENIAC and Fermi-Ulam results of the summer just past, Teller charged that the assumptions on which they were based had been heavily oversimplified and that their conclusions were wrong. Fermi disagreed, suggesting that more detailed calculations would probably make the picture even bleaker. And when Chicago chemist Willard Libby, a new member of the committee, agreed with Teller that the Fermi-Ulam results had been given too much weight, Oppenheimer, Rabi, and DuBridge responded that any change would be in the direction of making success appear even more unlikely.[12]

Teller returned to the manpower issue, charging that Los Alamos did not have enough qualified personnel to do both the required theoretical work and detailed calculations—"there are just not enough of us." With more than a touch of condescension, he said the lab would be able to cope if the Super's feasibility was disproven, but should the George test the following spring show that the Super looked promising, "then for that we are not strong enough." By "we," he meant the lab and his colleagues there. Bradbury spoke up for the lab and responded that what Los Alamos needed was not larger numbers but "individuals of special abilities and judgment," especially theoreticians. He had opposed pressure to expand more rapidly, he said, lest the place become too cumbersome. Oppenheimer suggested that if the lab were to change emphasis in any way it should be in the direction of obtaining higher yields from smaller amounts of fissionable material.

With the war in Korea making the Pacific proving grounds less secure, the question arose of whether to go ahead with any of the Greenhouse tests and especially whether George, the test of ignition, or first-stage, possibilities would be useful when, in light of the work by Ulam, Everett, and Fermi, there was no apparent solution to the second, or propagation, stage.

Oppenheimer wrote a summary letter to AEC chairman Gordon Dean after the meeting, in which he conceded that the test might yield "relevant" information about burning and radiation flow. "We wish to make it clear, however, that the test, whether successful or not, is neither a proof firing of a possible thermonuclear weapon nor a test of feasibility. . . . The test is not addressed to resolving the paramount uncertainties which are decisive in evaluating the feasibility of the Super." Since George was the test to which Teller attached special importance and on which he had lavished his efforts, he and others later criticized Oppenheimer for his words and accused him of hoping for a failure. To the contrary, Oppenheimer, the GAC, and the lab thought that the test would succeed. But they considered it irrelevant to the question of whether the Super would work and believed that it "made no technical sense."[13]

Summing up the past year as the meeting ended, Bradbury concluded that the thermonuclear program had gotten nowhere. It was of utmost urgency that the lab "do first those things promising the greatest possible gain in minimum time." That meant working on atomic weapons. Bradbury had almost given up on the Super. "Practical success, if it can be attained at all without new and presently unforeseen conceptions, must be regarded as . . . distant."[14]

CHAPTER EIGHT

Teller

SOON AFTER JOINING the lab, Ted Taylor found himself grounded by weather at the Phoenix airport. The only person who looked familiar to him was Edward Teller, and in the course of an eight-hour stopover, the two got to talking. Teller, who had a special liking for young people, asked Taylor what he was working on. Taylor described an idea he had for exploring reactions in the center of the current stockpile bomb by going to low-yield testing. Teller was enthusiastic.

The moment they got back to Los Alamos, Teller called a meeting and asked Taylor to lay out his idea. Carson Mark was there, and Emil Konopinski and even Enrico Fermi. Everyone said yes, that looked like a good thing to do.

That, Taylor said afterward, was Edward Teller at his best. And his best was very, very good. In originality, enthusiasm, quickness to grasp a new concept—in all of these, no one was better. Even colleagues who detested him enjoyed going to Teller's office to chew over a new idea. His math could be unreliable and he was not the person you'd ask to work a problem through patiently, with equations, but he had humor and charm and he could be immensely generous. He could also lean over backward to be fair. In 1948 he was probably the first American scientist to seek out Werner Heisenberg, Carl Friedrich von Weiszacker, and other physicists who had chosen to stay in Germany during the war. He listened to them, sought to understand the ambiguities of their position under the Nazis, and did his best to bring them back into the world scientific community. "It is wrong," he wrote to a close friend, "to act as if the only thing in the world would be politics."[1]

Teller was also astonishingly self-absorbed. Whatever his mood of the moment, that mood simply filled his universe. At such times he would extrapolate outward from his own dark mood and see the whole world in shades of black. By late fall 1950, he had sunk into one of those moods. Gone were the high hopes with which he had arrived from Chicago the year before. He blamed the lab and looked down on his colleagues there. Bradbury and the others who had stayed on after the war were what he called "the second team." His thoughts ran constantly to the first team—Fermi and Bethe and Oppenheimer—who had refused to return and work on *his* bomb as they had worked on Oppie's bomb during the war. If work on the Super was at a dead end, *they* were to blame.

Many an evening that fall and early winter, Teller trudged through the snow to the house of Kay and Carson Mark, three doors away from his own. There he sat in a big chair, chin in hand, staring at the floor, "wrapped in a black cloud you could almost touch," Kay Mark remembered. Her husband was likewise aware of that cloud of despair. Putting it in his usual mild way, Carson Mark saw that Teller was "troubled," that he was "angry and resentful." While Kay was putting the younger children to bed, Carson puffed quietly on his pipe and kept his thoughts to himself. He was reflecting that thanks largely to the man in front of him, "we had spent years working on the wrong thing. The thing Edward had peddled to Truman did not exist."[2]

There were other reasons, too, for Teller's apocalyptic frame of mind. He had received word that his father, Max Teller, had died in Budapest, leaving his mother and sister exposed to the Stalinist cruelties of Hungary's Rakosi regime. And he was tormented by indecision about his future. He had tentatively accepted a job offer from UCLA, only to learn that the regents had fired thirty-two professors who refused to take a loyalty oath. Teller's solidarity with the professors and unwillingness to take the oath himself had led to a bitter scene in Ernest Lawrence's office. Not since Nazi times, he said, had he heard a "little fascist speech" like the scolding Lawrence gave him that day. Teller actually wanted to return to the University of Chicago, but his wife, Mici, hated the place. He was toying with an offer from New York University, not because he meant to take it, but in hopes of persuading Mici that he had done his utmost to save her from the midwestern weather. All this and more Teller confided to Maria Goeppert Mayer, a brilliant former student living in Chicago, on whom he relied for counsel and support.[3]

And there was Korea. "The third world war has started," he wrote Mayer, "and I do not know whether I care to survive it." Not since Pearl Harbor had the nation faced such disaster. After a successful landing at Inchon in September 1950, General Douglas MacArthur had sent his forces up the Korean Peninsula, risking intervention by China. Sure enough, on November 25, a quarter of a million Chinese troops burst from their hiding places just south of the Yalu River and crushed the United Nations forces. President Truman created an uproar by leaving the impression at a press conference that the decision whether to use atomic weapons might be left to General MacArthur.[4]

Teller, as usual, spent much of the winter in travel mode. In December he flew in a tiny airplane from Los Alamos to Norman, Oklahoma, where he delivered a speech at the university and, even though AEC commissioner Sumner Pike was in the audience, criticized both the commission and the U.S. policy of restraint in Korea. He also traveled to Washington, where he informed Louis Ridenour, now chief scientist of the Air Force, that the AEC was dragging its feet on the H-bomb. Teller wanted to leave Los Alamos, where, he said, the research facilities were inadequate. He wanted the Air Force to set up a facility so that he could work on the problem at the University of Chicago instead. And he made a convert of Lieutenant General Elwood R. "Pete" Quesada, a renowned World War II pilot assigned to command the task force that would carry out the Greenhouse tests. Listening to Teller, Quesada realized that his service, the Air Force, stood to gain more than the other services if the H-bomb was built. It followed that he should render all the help he could. Teller warned, however, that the project had powerful opponents, the ring-leader being Robert Oppenheimer. Failure of the tests would enable those opponents to argue that the effort was futile.

Teller's conviction that Oppenheimer was trying to subvert the project received reinforcement when a panel chaired by Oppenheimer made its report in December 1950. The panel, one of many on which Oppenheimer served in addition to the GAC, had been specially created by the Defense Department to advise on the long-range uses of atomic weapons. It met at a moment when hopes for the Super were at their nadir and many in Washington feared that China's intervention in Korea might be the prelude to a Soviet invasion of Europe. Since recent successes at Los Alamos had all been in fission research, the panel—like the GAC at its Halloween meeting of 1949 and its Los Alamos meeting of October 1950—agreed that priority should be given to work on the fission bomb. Only if it was understood and accepted that work on a thermonuclear bomb was long-range in nature, five years or more, could the resources of Los Alamos be freed for concentration on fission weapons. Teller disagreed, and bitterly reproached Luis Alvarez, a member of the panel, for having signed a report that, he told Alvarez, was "being used against our program. It is slowing it down and it could easily kill it."[5]

Oppenheimer had written the report, but all twelve members of the panel, which included three generals and an admiral, were in agreement. The GAC, meeting on January 6, was likewise unanimous (with Walter Whitman, director of the 1948 Lexington Study of aircraft nuclear propulsion, and Oppenheimer, who belonged to both groups, recusing themselves). But as Teller saw it, the culprit was Oppenheimer: he had a golden tongue, and the others must have succumbed to his spell. Teller did not view it as a matter of honest error or difference of opinion. Oppenheimer wanted to kill his, Teller's, program; therefore he must have a hidden motive.[6]

Teller and Bill Borden had been cultivating each other for a year. They wrote flattering letters back and forth, decried what they thought were shortcomings in the H-bomb program, and arranged to see each other over dinner when Teller was in Washington.

In March 1950, only a month after Truman's H-bomb decision, Teller had warned the committee that the country might be in even greater danger than during World War II. By the war's end we had known that the Germans did not, as we had feared, have an A-bomb program. Now, however, with the Russians, we had no such assurance: indeed, thanks to Fuchs, they might well be ahead. Between the war's end and the 1949 Russian test, Teller claimed, work on a U.S. hydrogen bomb had not gone forward "at any appreciable rate." Although he was hesitant to suggest that his colleagues actually be drafted to work on the H-bomb, the number of theoretical physicists on the project must be promptly increased by "more than a factor of two in number and much more than a factor of two in talent."[7]

Teller complained that most of the scientific community was reluctant. Many scientists, he said, were still suffering a bad conscience over the destruction wreaked by the A-bomb and questioning the morality of H-bomb work. "If some of the best among them" showed by their actions that they were doubtful about thermonuclear work, the others would also hesitate.

In his formal testimony before the committee, Teller had not named names. But at dinner with Borden the evening before, he had not hesitated to do so, blaming the scientists' reluctance on Oppenheimer and, to a lesser extent, on Bethe and Fermi also. He had charged that for two years after the war Oppenheimer had tried to have the lab disbanded—"give it back to the Indians"—or make it a center of basic research.[8]

On the strength of what Teller said that night, Borden prevailed on Senator McMahon to call the last-minute session next day in which Teller told the committee that for four years after the war no "appreciable" work had been done on the H-bomb.

Teller was well aware that the man he had chosen to confide in saw things very much as he did. Bill Borden had no training in nuclear physics, but this in no way inhibited his certainties. He shared Teller's belief that the Russians were out to do in the United States and that it was a matter of survival to stay ahead. He expected war in Europe at any moment and believed that the H-bomb could be decisive in subduing the vast territory of the USSR. The usually reticent Fermi implicitly criticized Borden's advice to the senator when he told a member of the JCAE staff that during the critical period in 1949 and 1950 when McMahon had been pushing President Truman to start a crash program, he and the JCAE had been "misinformed" about the real prospects and problems of the Super. Fermi warned that the committee ought to "think twice" before entering scientific controversies in the future, since it lacked the necessary technical competence. Coming from Fermi, who was renowned for his impartiality and cool judgment, this was devastating criticism. The conversation ended with what the staff member in his report described as "admonitory remarks about Dr. Teller. Dr. Fermi says he has the greatest respect for Dr. Teller's scientific ability and also values him as a personal friend," but that, having "very little comprehension of the scientific and engineering problems that lie between the germ of a brilliant idea and the achieving of a perfected weapon," Teller had a tendency to exaggerate the prospects for success.[9]

As for Borden, out of childish bravado and lack of genuine understanding, he made light of what the A-bomb could do. After witnessing his first atomic test, he had written a memo dismissing the impression it had made on him. He and colleagues on the committee staff who felt as he did made a point of calling atomic bombs mere "ordinaries" compared with the hydrogen bomb. He prodded Senator McMahon relentlessly to seek expansion of the program. Borden was an intelligent man who cared about duty and honor. But he was a zealot, and he had the ear of a powerful senator who wanted to be president, and as a result, he wielded an authority that far outweighed his judgment.

So zealous was Borden in pursuing his ends—larger, more powerful nuclear weapons—that he occasionally committed glaring breaches of protocol and even security. For example, after an appearance by Hans Bethe before the committee in May of 1950, Borden outlined Bethe's secret testimony in a letter to Teller that, if not technically a breach of security, was at the very least out of channels, as Borden himself acknowledged: "This information is, of course, just for your personal use. . . . I would appreciate your not circulating it."[10]

Borden's lapses of judgment were compounded by Teller's inclination to question the motives of anyone who stood in his way. Meeting with a committee staff member in Los Alamos during the spring of 1950, Teller had made what was almost—but not quite— his first suggestion to a government official that Oppenheimer might be a security risk. After entering the caveat that he "did not get along" with Oppenheimer, in part because he held him responsible for dropping the H-bomb program at the end of the war, Teller said it was "common knowledge that Oppenheimer was far to the left." Oppenheimer, he said, was "unusually close" to his brother Frank, and Frank Oppenheimer would not have joined the Communist Party if Robert had not approved. Teller believed that Robert Oppenheimer had used his influence to bring his brother to Los Alamos during the war, and he thought that this, too, was grounds for suspicion. (Frank Oppenheimer was, in fact, a first-rate experimentalist whose work checking test results at the Trinity site received high praise from everyone there.) Concluding his report, the JCAE staff member said that Teller had been "careful to explain that he himself did not have any idea that the subject was disloyal or intended to injure the best interests of the country. . . . However . . . Teller did say that were Oppenheimer found, by any chance, to be disloyal 'in the sense of transmitting information,' he could, of course, do much more damage to the program than any other single individual in the country."[11]

Borden lost no time reacting to Teller's remarks. He drafted a memo for Senator McMahon warning that the program was in the hands of highly placed individuals who had "bitterly" opposed the H-bomb decision and whose emotions might be leading them to consider the effort futile. These individuals included AEC general manager Carroll Wilson, all nine members of the GAC including Oppenheimer, and two of the commissioners, Sumner Pike and Henry D. Smyth. Borden urged that special attention be given to filling the position of general manager and vacancies on the GAC and the commission as they arose. Accordingly, when the terms of three

GAC members expired that summer, they were replaced by men who were expected to show more enthusiasm for the H-bomb project than those who were departing. By far the most notable departure was that of Fermi, quite possibly the world's greatest living physicist: his departure was pushed by a new AEC commissioner, Thomas Murray, in hopes of creating a precedent that might lead in time to the departure of Oppenheimer.[12]

The extent to which Borden shared Teller's suspicions—and, indeed, brought his own special twist to them—can be seen from a memorandum he wrote to his boss toward the end of the year:

> I spent most of last week reading several dozen personnel security files. . . .
>
> A number of the "calculated risk" clearances of distinguished scientists having irreplaceable abilities . . . left me with a feeling of apprehension. . . . Usually, too, the subject had intimate access under the Manhattan District—and if he is kept out of the program, our progress very definitely suffers.
>
> It is indeed the unhappy truth that a number of our greatest experts have long lacked—and perhaps occasionally still lack—a sense of moral outrage at the characteristics and ambitions of the Soviet government. This lack, combined with almost fantastic naivete and gullibility, has caused so many of the top scientists to join front groups, associate with Communists, etc., that any real espionage agents among them cannot be identified by reference to such activities.
>
> I conclude that we may well have another Fuchs still in the project today and that all calculations should take into account this strong possibility.[13]

CHAPTER NINE

Ulam

As HE PLAYED on the rug in his parents' house in the Polish city of Lvov, the little boy kept staring at the intricate Oriental pattern. Aware that his father was smiling at him, the boy thought, "He thinks I am childish, but these are curious patterns. I know something my father does not know."[1]

All his life, Stan Ulam was looking for patterns. All his life, too, he had the air of the detached observer. He was not yet forty-two years old when the year 1951 began, an onlooker as Edward Teller and Hans Bethe argued about thermonuclear reactions. "Amusing fights: Hans-Edward," Ulam wrote in his diary on January 18. And a few days later, "big fight fairly amusing." What the fight was about, whether and how it contributed to the pattern taking shape in Ulam's head, is not known. But on January 25 he wrote in the diary, "Discussion with Edward on two bombs."[2]

Ulam had been thinking for some time about a "bomb in a box." And in December 1950 he came upon the idea of using shock waves from an exploding fission bomb inside a "box," or container, to compress the material in a second fission device inside the same "box" to such high density that it would burn. Now it occurred to him that these ideas might be combined in such a way as to solve the problem of making a package of thermonuclear fuel burn. The concept, that of using an exploding fission device inside a container to create so much pressure on the thermonuclear material as to maintain the burn, was called "compression," but in fact it was extreme compression compared with anything that had been contemplated before.[3]

Françoise Ulam later remembered coming home at noon about January 23, 1951, to find her husband staring out the window with a strange expression on his face. Over lunch, he told her he had had an idea that might make the Super possible. If his idea worked, he said, it would change the world. Appalled, since she had hoped the bomb would prove infeasible, Françoise asked what his next step would be. He supposed that he would have to tell Edward. Remembering Teller's fury the previous summer after he learned of Stan's results with Everett and Fermi, she asked whether he ought to try his idea on someone else first, "either Carson or Norris."[4]

Ulam appeared in Carson Mark's office that afternoon and, sketching something on the blackboard, said, "In Nevada we have to be doing something more interesting, like this. If we did it that way, it might produce such and such reactions, which would be interesting to measure." Such was Ulam's style. He seldom spelled out an idea, being so absorbed in it himself that he assumed his interlocutor was following his line of thought. Mark, frantically busy with preparations for the Greenhouse tests and for a series of smaller fission shots in Nevada, did not realize that Ulam's idea pertained to the thermonuclear problem. "It seemed like an unnecessary addition to things that were scarcely manageable as they were," he said long afterward.[5]

Ulam next showed up in Bradbury's office. This time he had no need to explain: Bradbury immediately saw what he was driving at. Both men realized that the next person Ulam had to see was Teller. Bradbury, who was given to minimizing his own role, refused to take credit in later years for so quickly grasping the relevance of Ulam's idea: he took credit only for imparting a hint or two as to how Ulam might present his idea without making Teller as angry as he had been the summer before.[6]

The next morning Teller and Ulam had their discussion "on two bombs." Teller resisted at first, but before long he, too, became enthusiastic. Later in the day he burst into the T Division office, where several of his colleagues were working. "Ulam has had an idea," he announced, "but he hasn't got it quite right." And he set the men—Max Goldstein, Arnold Kramish, and Frederic de Hoffmann—to work on calculations to see whether the new concept might be applied to the George test in the spring. Teller went home to his piano while the others worked through the night.[7]

Ulam met with Teller several times in late January and early February 1951, half an hour or so each time. He drew a sketch, and then Teller added an idea. Ulam's idea was to compress the thermonuclear fuel by mechanical shock from an exploding fission device, while Teller's was to use radiation from the exploding device instead, in order to achieve the extreme compression required. The two men wrote a joint paper in which each described the scheme he had thought of: they had come up with parallel ways of obtaining a thermonuclear burn without using the prohibitive quantities of tritium required by all the other schemes so far. The concept was called "radiation implosion."[8]

The concept seemed simple—but only after someone had discovered it. And the title of LAMS-1225, the paper completed by the two men in late February and dated March 9, 1951—"On Heterocatalytic Detonations: I. Hydrodynamic Lenses and Radiation Mirrors—I"—hints at its extraordinary ingenuity. Hot X-rays from the exploding fission bomb would move in all directions inside the casing that contained the two bombs. Any material inside the casing would then be ionized and exert a strong material pressure that would compress the secondary sufficiently to ignite the thermonuclear fuel. All of this had to occur in a millionth of a second, lest the device explode before the second bomb could ignite. In the half century since it was written, only a handful of people have read the paper, and those who have report that much of it consists of brilliant ideas of Ulam's about "staging," or arranging the components in such a way as to maximize the explosion. Although six other nations—Britain, France, China, the USSR, and probably Pakistan and India—have later developed the hydrogen bomb, the Ulam-Teller paper, which lays out the key concepts of staging (Ulam's), compression (Ulam's), and radiation (Teller's), is classified to this day with no hope of declassification anytime soon, lest some would-be proliferator, whether a terrorist or a nation, learn something from it that would enable him to devise a workable bomb.[9]

Teller assigned his protégé, Frederic de Hoffmann, to do the mathematical work on a second idea he had had that was an ingenious complement to the first: the addition of a second fission element, which came to be called the "spark plug," positioned like a rod inside the thermonuclear fuel, to compress the thermonuclear component by an explosion inside as well as from the outside. The resulting paper, LA-1230, to which, knowing his mentor's emotional identification with the achievement, de Hoffmann signed only Teller's name, and not his own, is dated April 4, 1951, and likewise remains classified.[10]

Teller from the start tried to make Ulam an unperson. Not only did he assign de Hoffmann to write the April 4 paper; he refused to sign a patent application bearing Ulam's signature because it named the two of them as coinventors. Because of Teller's refusal to sign Ulam's application and failure to file an application of his own, the Teller-Ulam, or, as some might call it, the Ulam-Teller, concept, which became the basis of hydrogen bomb design, was never patented. Teller simply took the credit.[11]

Four years later, following a conversation with Fermi on his deathbed, Teller published an article, "The Work of Many People," in which he described the contributions various scientists had made. He mentioned the calculations Ulam had done with Everett showing that the old concept would not work, but omitted Ulam's role in the breakthrough. He did it again in his book *Legacy of Hiroshima,* published in 1962, this time attributing the breakthrough to himself and de Hoffmann. Afterward, in books, articles, and interviews, he did his utmost to excise Ulam from the history books, insisting that since Ulam had not been eager for the bomb to be invented and was skeptical that it would work even after their conversations of January and February 1951, he should not receive any credit. "Ulam invented nothing!" he exclaimed on many occasions.[12]

For a time Teller's claim to sole authorship was virtually uncontested, partly because of government secrecy. Because the ideas he had contributed were considered especially sensitive, Ulam's name was for years censored out of the official literature. In the published transcript of the Oppenheimer hearing of 1954, for example, Ulam's name appears only once, with four asterisks in place of his name the other times it was mentioned in testimony; and when Bradbury, in a press conference later that year, singled out Ulam's contribution, Robert McKinney, publisher of the *Santa Fe New Mexican* and a man well versed in matters atomic, had to ask who Ulam was and how the name was spelled. Ulam declined to press his claim, considering assertiveness of that sort beneath him, and despite Bradbury's effort, the role of the Polish mathematician was for years unknown to the public, while Teller, with his reputation as "Father of the H-bomb," enjoyed tremendous standing with congressmen and Pentagon officials, who did not know the real story.[13]

This distortion of the record, for which both Teller and the system of secrecy were to blame, later became a matter of anger and embarrassment to members of the laboratory who knew how the breakthrough had occurred. Most were critical, even contemptuous, of Teller, not only for claiming credit that was not properly his, but also for the very serious action of using his public reputation to acquire his own lab at Livermore and to promote visionary schemes—the "Clean Bomb" of the 1950s, Projects "Gabriel" and "Ploughshare" in the 1960s, "Palisades of Fire" in the 1970s, and "Star Wars" in the 1980s—which they considered ill-judged and based on false scientific claims.[14] Carson Mark, in particular, felt remorse over having missed what Ulam tried to tell him that fateful afternoon of January 24, 1951. Mark believed that had he caught Ulam's drift and put the T Division to work on the new concept right away, Teller's contribution, the idea of radiation, would have occurred to the lab's theoreticians as a matter of course. In that event the T Division and Stan Ulam would have been known as mother and father, respectively, of the H-bomb. Teller would still have received credit for the single-mindedness he had brought to the quest, but he would not have had the enormous political clout that he acquired and that, in the opinion of Mark and most members of the lab, he misused.[15]

Teller's churlishness had a history, unknown until Françoise Ulam unearthed it in the lab's personnel files during the late 1980s. It was the questionnaire Teller filled out after Ulam had worked for about a year in Teller's subgroup, doing research on the Super.

War Department
Project Y

EMPLOYEE RATING OF SCIENTIFIC ACHIEVEMENT

Name of employee	Stanislaw Ulam
Success in recent work	Unsatisfactory
Theoretical ability	Outstanding
As potential member of lab research	Outstanding
Personality	Unsatisfactory

Comments: Mr. Ulam is a brilliant mathematician but does not have the proper background for the work we are doing and does not seem able to adjust himself to our work. Occasionally he has helped in our research and on the whole the group has profited by his presence.

He is an independent thinker and might conceivably turn up most important results. I think if he could work on pure research in mathematics he would be much more happily placed than in our project.

E. Teller   February 13, 1945[16]

Teller recognized Ulam's independence—and wanted no more to do with him.[17]

Something similar also happened in early 1950 when Ulam, Teller, and Gamow were looking into theoretical problems of the Super. Finding the other two uncomfortably irreverent and independent-minded, Teller seized a moment when they were both out of town to disband their three-man group.

Having shown by his calculations with Everett and Fermi during the spring and summer of 1950 that Teller's design would not work, Ulam in 1951 came up with the solution. Poker player that he was, he was pleased to have trumped Teller, to have trumped him twice, in fact, first by showing that Teller's design would not work, and then by coming up with a workable concept himself. And he had done it, as he did everything, with a beguiling air of nonchalance and not a trace of Teller's obsessiveness, which to him was unseemly and perhaps a little obscene. Ulam was annoyed by Teller's insistence on placing his stamp on the invention: as far as he was concerned, his scheme, that of achieving compression by means of mechanical shock, was enough by itself to do the job. As Ulam put it later, Teller had added a "complication." Belittling it, he said in his book that Teller "had found a parallel version, an alternative to what I had said, perhaps more convenient and generalized."[18]

But Teller's idea was crucial. Why did the idea of radiation occur first to him and not to Ulam? Carson Mark believed that Teller's concentration on George was the explanation. "Edward had just finished a year of work on the George shot," of which radiation was a feature. George was Teller's test: not only had he worked on it, he had promoted it to the point of trying to have "Item," another shot in the series, canceled. Ulam, Mark added, "did not have that immediate, close-in exposure to the radiation picture." Mark did not consider it surprising that Teller came up with the idea, since "once you try to achieve fantastic compression by means of an atomic bomb, you'd have to face the fact that radiation was there. You'd have *had* to think of it. Edward was in a better position to be aware that radiation could be decisive. He was thinking about radiation in a way that Ulam was not." Mark believed that anyone in T Division who had worked on George would have called attention, as Teller did, to radiation as a way of producing extreme compression.[19]

Another physicist, who attended the 1946 Super conference but was no longer working on weapons in 1951, agreed. "Once you think of implosion," he said, "you think of radiation. After the idea of compression occurred, a day's discussion would have produced the idea of achieving compression by means of radiation." This scientist, Philip Morrison, did not find Teller's idea surprising. Rather, what surprised him was the importance given by the new concept to "radiation mirrors."[20]

Legends surround Ulam, among them the legend that he was lazy. No one ever saw Ulam working; nor did anyone ever see him when he was not, almost visibly, engaged in thinking. Some mornings he did his thinking at home, and Bradbury would drop by at eleven or so to ask when he was coming to "work" at the two-story wooden Tech Building. There was joking at the lab that "Everett did Ulam's best work," and in later years one or two of the division chiefs were "ferociously critical" of Ulam for failing to complete his projects. But Mark, with Bradbury's support, insisted on keeping him because his presence was so stimulating to the younger scientists. Mark conceded that Ulam did not exactly "work" on things. Instead, he sowed ideas as if he were "a landed seigneur back in Poland strolling around his estates, waving a hand and ordering his minions to plant a walnut seed here, a sapling there, and leaving others to tend the young trees."[21]

Ulam was to the manor born. Stan's father, Jozef, was a lawyer; his uncle, Szymon, was a banker; and his mother, Anna Auerbach, was from a wealthy industrial family. Genius ran in the family, some of the finest buildings in Lvov being the work of an earlier Ulam, an architect. For a few years, beginning when Stanislaw was five, the family took refuge in Vienna, since Russian troops had occupied Lvov, then part of the Austro-Hungarian Empire. While still in his teens, Ulam was accepted by the coterie of mathematicians who made up the well-known Lvov school, who quickly noticed his altogether exceptional originality. Huddled in the coffeehouses and tiny inns of Lvov, these mathematicians spent hours drinking coffee and scribbling formulas on white marble tabletops. Recalling one seventeen-hour session at the Scottish Café in which the silence was broken only by occasional bouts of laughter or a pause for drinks and a bite to eat, Ulam later said that long hours of silent concentration were a requirement of creative mathematical work. But thinking very hard about the same problem for hours on end could produce severe fatigue, even breakdown. Ulam, who was as fascinated by the workings of the brain as by mathematics, wrote that he never experienced a real breakdown, but on two or three occasions he had felt "strange inside" and had to stop.

In 1932, at the age of twenty-three, he was invited to work in the Soviet Union, but because of his capitalist origins considered it the better part of wisdom to decline. Two years later, von Neumann invited him to the Institute for Advanced Study at Princeton, and in the fall of 1936 he began a three-year appointment as a junior fellow at Harvard, returning each summer to Poland. Finally, in the summer of 1939, with war impending in Europe and at his uncle's insistence, he left Poland for the United States, accompanied by his seventeen-year-old brother, Adam.

Neither Adam nor Stan ever recovered from the loss of the life they had known in Europe. Although both were to make distinguished careers in the United States (Adam as a historian), neither felt at home in what they experienced as a puritanical Anglo-Saxon culture. Nor did they know the full dimensions of their loss until after the war. Only then did they learn that the Nazis had shot their sister, Stefania, and her infant daughter; that her husband, too, had disappeared; and that the uncles and aunts who had stayed in Lvov were sent to concentration camps and died there. The Russians permitted their father, Jozef, to remain in his apartment, where he offered shelter to a seventeen-year-old student who was wanted by the authorities. During the fall and winter of 1939–1940 the two of them burned Jozef's law books for warmth and had conversations in which the older man spoke with pride about the two sons he had sent to America. Before the war ended, no one knows exactly when, Jozef died of heartbreak and ill health. The Russians, meanwhile, confiscated the family properties.[22]

Immediately after the war Stan, who was teaching at the University of Southern California, was stricken by mysterious headaches. Upon operating, the doctors found inflammation of the brain and not, as they had feared, a tumor. Their intervention relieved the intracranial pressure, and the patient recovered. But for Stan the observer of mental processes, the threat of losing his memory and capacity for logical thought had been terrifying, and he never completely recovered from the fear. After he died in 1984, his friend Gian-Carlo Rota wrote that Ulam's mental capacity had been affected by the illness, but Françoise and Adam Ulam, and two mathematicians who worked with Stan before and afterward, Mark Kac and David Hawkins, insisted that they had seen no change. When they discussed the cause of Stan's illness, colleagues speculated that he might have been trying unconsciously *not* to solve the problem of the H-bomb. But Françoise, whose mother also had died in the Holocaust, disagreed with the speculation. If Stan's illness had a psychological component, and she was by no means persuaded that it did, she thought it was caused by the realization that all of his family were gone, the old life in Europe gone forever.[23]

When Stan was invited to return to Los Alamos after his illness, he gladly accepted, and the unlikeliest part of his unlikely odyssey began. There on the dusty mesa, he managed to re-create some of the warmth and conviviality of his beloved Scottish Café: he and a colleague even opened a coffeehouse. What he missed in America was a culture in which mathematics was done orally and at leisure, in conversation upon conversation, as it had been in Warsaw and Lvov. Paradoxically, he found this culture at the lab. Being at the very frontier of science with some of the most brilliant minds in the world excited his imagination. It reminded him of Lvov. And Los Alamos, a kind of factory for most of the people who worked there, allowed him to work as he pleased.[24]

One friend said that Ulam had "not an ounce of modesty in him." Indeed, he was heard to boast, "I am the most imaginative man in the world." Aware that his greatest gift was his originality, he was at pains to conserve it. When he read a book, his eye would race down the page, plucking out the nuggets, and then he would toss the thing away, "in order not to be influenced." In conversation it was the same, with friends occasionally complaining that he gave short shrift to their ideas. When I. I. Rabi, for whom he had great respect, twice came to see him—in 1949, during the H-bomb debate, and 1954, at the time of the Oppenheimer hearings—to ask him to join the behind-the-scenes political scrimmaging, Ulam, to Rabi's annoyance, remained aloof. Similarly, although he disdained Teller's lust for the H-bomb, he refused to waste himself on anger. Indeed, some of Ulam's personal style, the air of amateurish ease, the laziness, appears to have been a cover to protect the "ability to see around corners," which, along with uncanny luck, was the Ulam signature in mathematics.[25]

Surprisingly for one so original, he required the stimulation of other minds. He was never alone if he could help it, entertained people by the hour with jokes and stories, and did nearly all his work in collaboration with others, even though, as his colleague Mark Kac put it, he was the giver 99.99 percent of the time. Ulam's work with Cornelius Everett appears to have been the exception. The two of them had written a major paper and three or four lesser ones together before they sat down to calculate tritium requirements for the Super. Everett, who combined extraordinary technical prowess with an unusual willingness to work on someone else's ideas, would listen as Ulam tossed out ideas, then check them with brilliant computations of his own. But somewhere along the way Everett, who was as reclusive and self-effacing as Ulam was outgoing, came to feel shortchanged; after his death his widow, Dolly, said that he was "disillusioned and brokenhearted" over his collaboration with Ulam. According to her and other members of her family, Everett felt that Ulam had shoved him aside and usurped the credit, as Teller was to do with Ulam.[26]

The collaboration with von Neumann was another matter. The two never wrote a paper together, yet they were so close that to understand the work of either, Françoise thought, one had to understand their relationship. The friendship went back to prewar Europe: in 1937, at Ulam's invitation, von Neumann went to Lvov, where he met Ulam's parents and visited the Scottish Café. Ulam, in turn, visited von Neumann in Budapest the following summer, met his family, and accompanied him to a mountain resort where he met two of his friend's elderly professors. And there was the matter of background. Von Neumann did not feel at ease with people whose social origins differed much from his own: he and Ulam were both well-to-do central European Jews of the third or fourth generation. Both were cultivated, with backgrounds in the Latin and Greek classics, and a wry humor was seemingly native to them both. Although something in the air stimulated them to do great work in America,

both suffered from culture shock here, and from absence of the con-
versational art. And they had a common sensibility. Although he was
six years younger and nowhere nearly as accomplished a craftsman,
Ulam sensed von Neumann's deep-seated doubt about his own ability
and knew how to tease him out of it. Especially in the early days, it
was the older man who sought out the younger one, and by some accounts Ulam was the only close friend von Neumann ever had.[27]

On the basis of Ulam's work on random processes, the two
friends, with input from Nicholas Metropolis, Stanley Frankel, Enrico
Fermi, and others, invented Monte Carlo, a method of extending the
use of computers to statistical sampling. Monte Carlo, so named because an uncle of Ulam's had borrowed money from others in the
family to fuel his frequent visits to the gaming tables, became invaluable in estimating neutron multiplication rates and predicting the explosive behavior of fission weapons. An indispensable tool in computer
science to this day, Monte Carlo exemplifies the ways in which computer development and invention of the hydrogen bomb were inextri-
cably linked.[28]

Thinking of how Ulam broke the logjam in 1951, one has to ask
whether Truman's H-bomb order made a difference. Did it speed up
the pace of Ulam's thinking? Ulam himself was dismissive. He said
that "the number of people working on something does not increase
in proportion the yield" and hinted that the visiting dignitaries and influx of talent brought by Wheeler had merely been a distraction. But
Françoise Ulam at first believed that without the forcing-house atmosphere produced by the president's decision, Stan might in 1950–1951
have devoted his best thinking to some other problem. Carson Mark
had a different view, with which Françoise later came to agree. He
concluded that Ulam "resonated" neither with Truman's order nor
with Teller's enthusiasm, but with von Neumann's desire—on political as well as scientific grounds—to find a solution. Ulam did not
share von Neumann's right-wing political ideas, but he did share his
intense interest in fusion reactions. It was to von Neumann, and to the
intellectual challenge of the thermonuclear problem, that Ulam responded. Ironically, when the younger man came up with a solution,

von Neumann, the greatest mathematician of the century, felt a pang of regret that he had, once again, been trumped in originality.[29]

Ulam's enormous contribution did not at first bring him much recognition. Members of the lab were too busy with the tests of spring 1951, and then with preparing the first test of the Ulam-Teller, or Teller-Ulam, concept, to worry about questions of credit. Besides, everything Los Alamos did was a group effort: no one felt any need to sort out the question of who contributed what idea, or in what sequence, until later, when Teller's claims made it an issue. Ulam, meanwhile, disappointed by what he took to be the lab's indifference, departed for Harvard, where he spent the 1951–1952 academic year. He took no part in preparations for the "Mike" shot of autumn 1952, the first test of his ideas.

A gentle man, he was wounded more than he ever admitted by Teller's brutal rejection. While privately he despised Teller, he refrained from joining the Teller-bashing at dinner parties in Los Alamos and Santa Fe. They had needed each other once: "If either of those guys had had to work alone," Bradbury said, "each would have accomplished about one quarter of what he did." But after that brief moment in 1951 they never spoke to each other or communicated in a meaningful way again.[30]

PART THREE

1951-1952

CHAPTER TEN

Teller's Choice

LEWIS STRAUSS AND EDWARD TELLER first met in a synagogue in New York City. The year was 1948; the occasion, a speech by Teller advocating world government. After the speech an elderly woman came up to him and introduced her son. The serious-looking, bespectacled man at her elbow turned out to be AEC commissioner Lewis Lichtenstein Strauss. Despite the differences in their religious practices—Strauss, an Orthodox Jew who prayed twice a day, was distressed by the fact that Teller was nonpracticing—the two became friends, and the friendship was cemented a year later during the debate over the hydrogen bomb. From then until Strauss's death many years later, Teller and Strauss were allies who frequently acted in concert.

In February 1951, only days after Teller and Ulam had their talks in Los Alamos hammering out the concept of radiation implosion, Teller appeared on the East Coast for one of his démarches with Strauss. Strauss was no longer a commissioner, he was working in New York for the Rockefellers, and he knew nothing about the Ulam-Teller breakthrough. But he held a couple of part-time appointments that gave him leverage in Washington. As he saw it, the president had issued his order more than a year earlier and there was still no hydrogen bomb. Someone must be to blame. That someone, he decided, was Robert Oppenheimer. There were rumors that Oppenheimer had been a Communist, and two former Party members had lately surfaced and testified that they had attended a Party meeting eight years before at Oppie's house in California. Whatever his intentions, Oppenheimer was helping the Soviet Union.[1]

And so on February 9, 1951, Strauss went to see Gordon Dean, David Lilienthal's successor as chairman of the AEC. Clutching several pages of notes, he treated Dean to a scathing critique of Los Alamos: the lab was dragging its heels and Oppenheimer was "sabotaging" the project. When he described Oppenheimer as "a general who did not want to fight," Dean disagreed that the program was in the hands of people who did not believe in it. Suggesting remedies nonetheless, he noticed one in particular that Strauss did not object to—creation of an entirely new laboratory. Before the visitor left, Dean asked to keep his talking points. To his surprise, Strauss strode to the fireplace and tossed them, with a dramatic gesture, into the fire. Dean thought this a little bizarre, and was mystified further when he was told later that the notes had been intended for Truman. Dean was miffed both by Strauss's intention of going over his head to the president and by his failure to mention it. A straight shooter himself, Dean viewed it as his job to protect a president besieged by a thousand headaches. Had he read the notes, which bore the Tellerian title "The Russians May Be Ahead of Us," he would have seen what he probably suspected anyway, that Strauss's informants had been Teller and his acolyte Freddie de Hoffmann.[2]

The other member of the two-man team was also in the AEC building that day. Teller had come at Strauss's suggestion to see AEC commissioner Thomas Murray, who was also dissatisfied with thermonuclear progress. Meeting Murray for the first time, Teller attacked the panel report on long-range objectives that Strauss had criticized to Dean. Singling out the author, Oppenheimer, Teller charged that the report was "designed to discourage" enthusiasm and had effectively put the project "on ice." He added that Los Alamos had lost competent men and seemed unable to attract new ones. Time and again, Teller said, Bradbury had yanked him and others off the H-bomb project and assigned them to other work. If the program remained at Los Alamos, Bradbury should be fired and a new division created to focus on thermonuclear problems. But there was a better way: take the project away from Los Alamos and set up an entirely new laboratory.[3]

While he was in the AEC building, Teller also stopped by to see General Manager Marion Boyer and told him, too, that the program should be moved away from Los Alamos. Then he took a taxi to the Capitol, where he insinuated to William Borden that the tritium estimates by Ulam, Everett, and Fermi were wrong. He warned that the design for the upcoming George shot, the first test of thermonuclear principles, had been deliberately made highly experimental and might not succeed. Borden realized that Teller was embarrassed by his erroneous tritium estimates. Fearful that George, too, might be a failure, Teller was accusing Oppenheimer and the GAC of pushing for a premature test in hopes of a failure that would kill the whole program.[4]

Gordon Dean had been AEC chairman for about a year. At the time of his appointment, he was known in atomic energy circles mainly as Senator McMahon's onetime law partner, and his selection had been viewed as a presidential sop to the nuclear enthusiasts in Congress. Dean's appointment prompted such foreboding in Carroll Wilson, David Lilienthal's loyal deputy and the man entrusted with day-to-day management of the commission, that he had taken the unusual step of resigning publicly in protest. Wilson need not have worried, for Dean proved to be an experienced administrator and a first-rate judge of character. A Californian by birth, he had joined the Duke University law faculty at twenty-five, argued his first case before the Supreme Court at twenty-eight, served in the Justice Department's antitrust division under the legendary Thurman Arnold, and been special assistant to two of FDR's attorneys general, Homer Cummings and Robert H. Jackson. When Jackson was appointed chief U.S. prosecutor at Nuremberg, he took Dean along as an adviser.[5]

The joint descent by Teller and Strauss on the AEC, plus Teller's call on Borden and his visits to the Pentagon, planted the thought in high places that the program was lagging and a new lab might be the answer. Meanwhile, the men at Los Alamos were enjoying a breather after completing work on the Greenhouse series, and Norris Bradbury circulated a plan to reorganize the place. Bradbury was responding to a demand by Teller for a special division at Los Alamos, with himself as leader, to work solely on the thermonuclear bomb. Teller was convinced that success could come only from men who were giving it their undivided attention, a premise that made no sense to the rest of the lab. Since a small and efficient fission "primary" was the key to making the fusion "secondary" burn, and success of the weapon depended on the interaction between the two, most people were working on both.[6] Placing Teller in charge made no sense to most of them either, since Teller's idea for organizing things was to insist each day that the laboratory drop what it had been doing the day before and turn to his newest brainstorm. So while Teller—without leveling with Bradbury—was politicking in Washington for a laboratory of his own, Bradbury in Los Alamos was ceding as much as he could, short of creating a separate thermonuclear division run by Teller.[7]

In Washington again, Teller this time presented his case directly to the chairman of the AEC. It was a dark moment for Gordon Dean, who had been wrestling with a dilemma: how much of the evidence in its possession could the government use in its prosecution of Julius and Ethel Rosenberg without risking the loss of atomic secrets.[8] Dean had no sooner dealt with that issue than he learned that the Russians might be on the point of entering the war in Korea, an action that could trigger World War III. The news, a false alarm received by Pentagon Intelligence, marked the moment when the United States came closer than at any other juncture to using nuclear weapons in Korea. The Joint Chiefs asked the AEC to transfer part of its stockpile to the Air Force for possible use in the Far East, and this in turn raised the delicate issue of civilian control. And another delicate question loomed over the White House: how to handle General Douglas MacArthur, who had recently—without authorization—proposed a series of actions in the Pacific likely to expand the war. A few days after the Dean-Teller meeting, the president, at fearful political cost, fired his most famous general for insubordination.[9]

At the meeting on April 4, Teller noticed that Dean's attention seemed to wander. But the chairman's air of distraction did not restrain the scientist from giving a long and one-sided recitation on thermonuclear ideas, criticizing Bradbury's proposal for a separate thermonuclear division and discussing how and why he would hand in his resignation. Teller asked for a new laboratory devoted entirely to the thermonuclear effort and staffed by fifty senior scientists, eighty-two junior scientists, and 228 assistants. Aware of Teller's awesome political support, Dean prevailed on him to postpone any decision to quit Los Alamos.[10]

After leaving the chairman's office, Teller discovered that his zipper was broken. He thereupon attributed Dean's apparent inattention to his open fly rather than, as was in fact the case, to Dean's worry that atomic war was about to break out.[11]

Soon afterward Dean received a long memo from Teller, again asking for a new laboratory and hinting that without it he might leave the project. This was not to be the last time Teller would threaten to quit.[12]

A few weeks later Teller and Dean met again, this time on remote Eniwetok Atoll. What brought the AEC chairman all the way to the Pacific was the long-awaited George shot, on which Los Alamos had been working for two years. Detonated on May 9, local time, George produced by far the largest nuclear explosion ever: it vaporized the two-hundred-foot test tower and 283 tons of diagnostic equipment. Dean heard Teller boast that Eniwetok would not be large enough for the next test.[13]

But size was not the main thing.[14] George, in which radiation from exploding a large atomic bomb was channeled to a container of thermonuclear fuel outside it, demonstrated that with sufficient heat and pressure, tritium and deuterium could be fused.[15] The result had been expected, so beyond that was the question of the test's usefulness, since Ulam and Fermi had already shown the second part of the Super—the propagation—to be infeasible. Not only that, but during preparations for the George shot, and partly as a result of them, the Ulam-Teller idea had come along and rendered moot the problems to be addressed by the test. Theoreticians at Los Alamos were delighted all the same by the outcome, which, Carson Mark said afterward, confirmed "that the methods we were using to calculate the elements of the process were . . . accurate" and "could be relied on wherever similar processes might be involved." Mark realized that calculations for the next big test, that of the Ulam-Teller idea, would be more elaborate than any the men of the T Division had done so far. He was encouraged to know that they had been going about it the right way.[16]

Almost no one at Eniwetok had heard about the Ulam-Teller concept, but a Lawrence protégé from California named Herbert York learned of it on a warm tropical evening spent alone with Teller. The two men were in a corroded old aluminum building, and York later remembered that, using a blackboard as his prop, Teller sketched the new idea. "I instantly recognized that this was it."[17]

York was one of only a handful who had heard about the Ulam-Teller idea, and Gordon Dean decided in the spring of 1951 that it was time to inform those closest to the project of the recent developments. The new concept, known as "radiation implosion," required theoretical investigation, as did results of George and the other Greenhouse tests. In addition, Teller's 1946 Super—the concept so difficult to disprove—was still on the table. With an enormous workload ahead, Dean wanted to establish priorities. He called a meeting for mid-June at the Institute for Advanced Study, with Robert Oppenheimer as host.

All of the commissioners came, and five GAC members and, from Los Alamos, Norris Bradbury, Associate Director Darol Froman, and Carson Mark. Several consultants—Bethe, Teller, Wheeler, von Neumann, and the theoretical physicist Lothar Nordheim—were invited because of their close familiarity with the project. The gathering turned out to be the turning point in the development of the hydrogen bomb.[18]

At the meeting, which assumed the importance of the new Ulam-Teller concept, Carson Mark led off with an analysis of the Pacific test results, and Wheeler reported on ways in which findings from those tests, particularly Item and George, might be applied in a test of the radiation-implosion idea. Norris Bradbury discussed the allocation of lab time between fission and fusion; Bethe, who had been in Los Alamos checking calculations, described the new concept as hopeful; and Oppenheimer pronounced it "technically sweet." Oppenheimer's words expressed the sense of the gathering, which welcomed the breakthrough as the right course to follow.[19]

Teller apparently did not understand. Bradbury had intentionally left him and the other consultants off the Los Alamos delegation so that they could express themselves independently of the laboratory. Foreseeing trouble, Bradbury had sent a memo to Oppenheimer in which he warned that emotions were a bigger roadblock than either the physics or the engineering, and he even arranged to accompany Oppie on the train ride to Princeton to discuss how to deal with both the science and the personalities.[20]

But his omission of Teller from the lab's delegation provoked the very outburst he had been hoping to avoid: from the outset, the Hungarian treated the gathering as a "battle" for acceptance of his ideas. He listened to the speakers with growing impatience. "Finally, I could contain myself no longer. I insisted on being heard. . . . It was decided that I should be allowed to speak."[21] Outside the meeting, Bethe and Teller were overheard in some sharp exchanges, and when Gordon Dean privately asked Bethe whether there was any way to alleviate the ill feeling between Teller and the rest of the lab, Bethe sadly shook his head.[22]

During the half century since, Oppenheimer has been accused of inconsistency, at the very least, in welcoming the new ideas as "technically sweet," and many people felt that he had betrayed the principles enunciated by him and the GAC majority in 1949 when they opposed the crash program partly on moral grounds. No sooner did the bomb look feasible, critics say, than Oppenheimer tossed morality out the window. If so, Oppenheimer was not alone. Fermi was at Princeton, too, and although in 1949 he, with Rabi, had called the H-bomb "necessarily an evil thing in any light," neither Fermi nor Rabi expressed doubts now. The difference was that with the Ulam-Teller inspiration, the weapon was now within reach. In 1949, when it looked impossible, Fermi and Rabi hoped, while there was time, to agree with the Russians not to go ahead. But by 1951 it was too late. As soon as they learned of the new concept, Bethe, Fermi, and Oppenheimer, along with everyone else, realized that the bomb was possible. And if it was possible for the United States, it was possible for the Russians, too. Oppenheimer's remark announced that the landscape was irrevocably altered.

After the Princeton meeting, Bradbury asked Teller to take charge of all theoretical work on the H-bomb. Aware that many of the men he relied on would quit if he were to put Teller in overall charge, he did not offer the one thing Teller really wanted: directorship of the entire program. Bradbury did his best to "soften the blow," but each of them found the conversation so painful that neither ever again mentioned it in the other's presence. Teller for the time being stayed on, but not without a new warning to Gordon Dean, via Freddie de Hoffmann, that he might quit—and not just the lab, but the entire H-bomb program.[23]

Meanwhile the work went on, with Carson Mark and his Theoretical Division analyzing results from the Pacific tests. Twice in the summer of 1951 the unhappy Teller flew to Washington to complain to higher-ups: once over dinner with William Borden at his club, then at a meeting with Gordon Dean. Both men begged him to remain.

A few weeks later, twenty-three-year-old Richard Garwin, a protégé of Fermi's from Chicago, happened to attend a Los Alamos meeting where the schedule for Mike, the first and crucial test of the Ulam-Teller concept, was being discussed. Teller wanted the shot scheduled for July 1, 1952, while Bradbury and Marshall Holloway, leader of the Theoretical Megaton Group, said that it could not practicably be held before fall. Teller was furious. "You guys don't have your heart in it," he scolded, and he threatened to leave the lab. Garwin, who was friendly with Teller and had, at his request, done the essential early blueprint for Mike, was flabbergasted. He thought these "guys" had their hearts wholly in it, and he found their dedication impressive.[24]

About this time, late September of 1951, Bradbury made a crucial decision: he put Holloway in charge of preparations for Mike. This,

Teller's friend de Hoffmann pointed out, was "like waving a red flag before a bull." Around the lab it was said that more than anyone else, "Holloway really had Teller's number." The two men had had so many passages at arms during the preparations for the George test that Holloway, hard-shelled, even impervious, though he was, refused any longer to deal with Teller directly. Holloway would describe the calculations he needed to Carson Mark, who would go to de Hoffmann, who would then put the matter, with utmost delicacy, to Teller.[25]

Informing the AEC of his decision to elevate Holloway, Bradbury told Dean that the lab could live with Teller if he "is willing to settle down and work with the rest of us," but "after the experience of the past year I am not persuaded that this is likely." Bradbury concluded that "equally rapid and certainly more stable and unemotional progress" would be made if Teller contributed from outside, "rather than as a continually dissatisfied and rebellious member of the laboratory."[26]

For his part Teller considered Holloway cantankerous and unreasonable and altogether an insulting choice. Besides, Teller had all along wanted someone "big" to head the program—Bethe, Fermi, or Oppenheimer. Fermi and Bethe had turned it down. Now Oppenheimer, sensing that Teller was emotionally off balance, told Dean that much as he doubted he could "make the omelet rise twice," he had not closed the door on returning to Los Alamos. He telephoned Bradbury and felt him out, but sensed no eagerness on the director's part to have him back. "Oppie couldn't come here and act in a limited way," Carson Mark explained years afterward.[27]

The question of Teller's future inevitably came to a head as the AEC commissioners finally faced the decision of whether to build a second Los Alamos. Teller had been pushing this behind the scenes, telling anyone who would listen that the lab had grown stodgy, unimaginative, and unequal to the task of producing an H-bomb anytime soon. He had a supporter in former commissioner Strauss and another in Commissioner Murray. And in a speech before the U.S. Senate, Brien McMahon, chairman of the joint congressional committee, piled on the pressure by urging that all three services be equipped with nuclear weapons—"an atomic army, an atomic navy and an atomic air force."[28]

Teller's next step was to announce one more time that he was leaving Los Alamos, with the caveat that he would keep track of developments from his post at the University of Chicago and perhaps visit the lab briefly from time to time. Over lunch with Borden and another staff member from the joint committee, he made it very clear that "his primary interest . . . was the second laboratory." His departure, he pointed out, would undercut one of the chief arguments against it, since "he had already left and to that extent the new laboratory would not be cutting into the manpower" available to the old one.[29]

Gordon Dean had been staving off the pressure. First, there was the problem of personnel: a new lab would divide the small cadre of available physicists. Second was the morale factor. A new lab would constitute a staggering no-confidence vote in the men who were doing the work and showing every sign of success. Dean was impressed by Teller's cleverness and political clout, but knew that the last thing he was, was an administrator. Nor could Dean overlook the monumental self-absorption of the man who had come to him in April 1951, at a moment when Dean had thought the world was on the brink of World War III, to hand in his resignation, and had been threatening to quit ever since.

Dean and the three other commissioners who were trying to hold the line received an assist from the GAC in October when it opposed a new lab on grounds that virtually everyone qualified was at Los Alamos already, except for Teller, and that "a solution to the major thermonuclear problem" appeared likely within a year. But Oppenheimer had misgivings of his own. He considered the lab's leaders—Bradbury, Froman, Holloway, and Mark—capable but cautious and risk averse. For this or some other reason, following a visit from Teller, who again expressed doubt about the laboratory's competence, Oppenheimer invited the Hungarian to appear before the GAC. There, in December, Teller blasted the lab's senior staff for lacking imagination and failing to attract the best scientists. He did this just as the Russians announced their second and third atomic tests: these signs of progress fed anxiety in Washington that, thanks to Klaus Fuchs, they might already be ahead. Pointing to these new indicators of Soviet progress, Teller charged that even the laboratory's success at Greenhouse was proof of earlier failure to develop its potential.[30]

Despite Teller's imprecations, the GAC for the second time formally opposed a new lab, fearing it would damage Los Alamos and "create general havoc." Hoping, however, to reengage Teller and deal with its own sense that the lab had become too conservative, the committee suggested creating an advanced division to work on long-range, even far-out, ideas, with a leader who would be persona grata to both Bradbury and Teller. Bethe's name was floated, since he got along well with both men. Oppenheimer urged that the suggestion be carried out quickly, since, as he put it, "the present ambiguous situation cannot be held ambiguous very long."[31]

Bradbury was under fearful pressure. Again and again he flew east to appear before the Washington brass. Aware, as he put it, of "rather thinly veiled criticism," he nonetheless reminded skeptics that every weapon development currently under way had "arisen out of the suggestion and, in many cases, the urging, of this laboratory," and warned that siphoning off manpower and resources would only slow things down.[32]

Under tremendous pressure themselves, the lab's theoreticians, explosives experts, cryogenists, and metallurgists were working all-out to prepare two series of tests: one, a preliminary fission series in Nevada in the spring; the other, a first test of the radiation-implosion concept in the Pacific the following fall. While lab members noticed occasionally that the director was out of town, Bradbury took pains to keep them from any inkling of the ordeal he was undergoing back east. Mark, who worked with him as closely as anyone, had no idea of this pressure on Bradbury until he read a partially declassified version of Gordon Dean's diary when it was published thirty-six years later. "He never let himself sag in my presence. He kept it to himself and shielded me and the rest of us from the miserable time he was having."[33]

Why, in the midst of the enormous outlay of effort on the project, did Bradbury and the rest of the laboratory try so hard to hold on to the fractious Teller? Much of the reason lay in the man's tantalizing originality. His insight and curiosity were relentless, and he promoted his ideas with evangelical fervor. Moreover, he had been right just often enough so that each time he had an inspiration, the others strove to divine whether this might be the long-awaited stroke of genius. "It would be impossible to run a laboratory if you had no Dr. Tellers," said Max Roy, head of the Physics Division, "and equally impossible if you had all Dr. Tellers." Carson Mark put it generously: "He discussed nearly every physical detail of almost every problem. . . . He called attention to possibilities. He resolved difficulties, elucidated complicated phenomena. His speculations induced speculations in others." But Jacob Wechsler, an engineer who had to coax designs into reality, thought otherwise. "You can't take a massive program and keep changing it," he said. "Such a brilliant, destructive man! It got so that each time he came back to visit, we were terrorized. We almost hated to see him show up."[34]

No one had any idea about the true extent of Teller's disloyalty. Marshall Rosenbluth, a talented young physicist whose contributions were critical, had heard that there was tension, but commented that "it didn't make much difference" at the working level. Some lab members were amused by the Hungarian; others thought his ideas gained disproportionate attention just because he was "obnoxious." None knew how egregiously he had maligned them, and the lab, behind their backs. Teller's faith and enthusiasm were compelling—so they mostly put up with him.[35]

It was Bradbury's ironic lot, in order to save the program and build the H-bomb at the earliest possible moment, that he had to deny Edward Teller.

CHAPTER ELEVEN

The Second Lab

THOMAS MURRAY of New York was a well-known inventor and entrepreneur. A Democrat and a devout Roman Catholic layman, he had been appointed by President Truman to the Atomic Energy Commission after David Lilienthal's resignation in 1950. Murray held two hundred patents, had founded his own company, acted as receiver of the IRT subway system in New York during World War II, and had successfully arbitrated major labor disputes. But he was new to the atomic energy program.

From the moment Edward Teller appeared in his office in February 1951, Murray had been a convert to the idea of a second laboratory. Each time the matter came up at commission meetings, he had spoken strongly in favor. And each time the commissioners voted against the idea, he had written a withering dissent. Murray used Teller's criterion, the number of topflight scientists at Los Alamos engaged solely in thermonuclear work. Persuaded by Teller that a new facility was needed, Murray strove energetically to bring it about. Being a solo operator, accustomed to ignoring channels, he felt no compunction about going straight to the White House. Twice in October 1951 he expressed dissatisfaction with the thermonuclear effort directly to President Truman, then pressed the case for a new lab with Truman's national security adviser, Sidney Souers, as well.[1]

In December 1951, a few days after the GAC rejected the proposal for a new laboratory for the second time, Murray placed a call to Ernest Lawrence, Nobel laureate and inventor of the cyclotron, in Berkeley. He outlined the thermonuclear situation as he saw it and said that all of his fellow commissioners and Oppenheimer's GAC were claiming that there were too few qualified physicists to staff a second facility. Lawrence scoffed and suggested that he and Teller become the core of a new enterprise. Murray urged Lawrence to become director, saying that Lawrence's prestige would be needed if the opposition from Oppenheimer and those who thought as he did was to be overcome.[2]

At a party in Berkeley on New Year's Day, 1952, Lawrence asked a promising postdoctoral student, Herbert York, to stop by his office. York was one of a handful of men at Berkeley who had worked on the thermonuclear program, having performed diagnostic tests on the George shot the year before, and Lawrence wondered whether he had an opinion about the need for a second lab. The thirty-year-old York, whose experience until then had been mostly confined to experimental physics, told Lawrence that he had not given it much thought. And so, with the boss's blessing, he set off on a fact-finding tour. After listening to the views of Teller in Chicago, Wheeler in Princeton, and officials of the Air Force in Washington, he reported back that a new laboratory would be a good idea, the very conclusion Lawrence had hoped he would come to.

Lawrence instructed York to draw up preliminary plans. This York did, flying back and forth between Berkeley and Chicago all winter in an effort to reconcile the vastly different visions of Lawrence and Teller. Each time, he found himself editing his account so that neither man would be totally alienated by the other's concept. Teller wanted a lab focused on a single objective and staffed by world-famous scientists, like Los Alamos during the war, while Lawrence wanted something smaller, less ambitious, and in fact more open-ended. A product of the plains of South Dakota, Lawrence was the kind of leader who had little use for rank or organizational charts. He believed in selecting talented young men and giving them their head. Since York shared his predilections, the emerging plans bore the Lawrence stamp.[3]

During the winter of 1952, Teller paid a visit to Berkeley. Lawrence escorted him to the nearby townlet of Livermore amid orchards and vineyards to show him the Materials Testing Accelerator, a pet project of his. Suggesting this as a possible site for the new laboratory, Lawrence inquired whether Teller might be willing to join. Yes, Teller replied, but only if the lab worked solely on thermonuclear weapons.[4]

Back east, however, with the AEC and the GAC firm in their opposition, the drive for a new facility had stalled. In February 1952, the GAC again declared itself opposed, again praised Los Alamos, and pointed out that fission and fusion processes within the H-bomb were so closely intertwined that separation between them was impossible. The committee concluded for the third time that creating a new facility would hurt Los Alamos, while producing "no compensating advantages for many years."[5]

Over at the joint congressional committee, even Borden and committee counsel John Walker appeared resigned to the thought that it would take an impressive new advance by the Russians to rekindle enthusiasm here. One of them, however, offered a suggestion not too far removed from what eventually happened. Why shouldn't an eminent scientist, someone in private life, organize a small group of theoretical physicists to work on the H-bomb, then approach the AEC to seek funds for a new facility?

Teller, meanwhile, was his usual mercurial self. After his February visit to Lawrence he had a conversation with Murray, who advised him to lie low. Afterward Teller thanked him "for your good advice. . . . I have now a much clearer picture of the situation and consequently a much better feeling about the way I must continue to act. I shall be, as you advise me, very patient and I believe, like you do, that things will work out as we hope and as they must." Teller's optimism, as usual, was short-lived: a few days later he confided to Borden that he had given up hope.[6]

Yet events continued to unfold. In March, Murray flew to California, where he and Lawrence agreed on the need for a change of leadership. Lawrence told Teller he hoped that Oppenheimer would not be reappointed to the GAC when his term expired the next summer, that Arthur Compton of the University of Chicago would take his place as chairman, and that Luis Alvarez, leader of the Materials Testing Accelerator, would be appointed a member. Murray was a friend of fellow industrialist Henry Ford: it occurred to him and Lawrence that either the Ford Foundation or the RAND Corporation, a recently created Air Force think tank, might be persuaded to offer subsidies so that the top advisory jobs would be more appealing to those who agreed with them.[7]

Finally, to finesse a prediction attributed to Gordon Dean—that Bradbury would quit in protest if a new lab were to be set up—Murray flew home by way of New Mexico, where he was assured by Bradbury himself that he would never resign over such an issue.[8]

Meanwhile Senator McMahon, his enthusiasm for a second lab undiminished, requested a formal report from the Defense Department, an action that proved to be the turning point. Defense Secretary Robert Lovett's first response was to praise Los Alamos and declare that it would be a mistake to move the thermonuclear program. But two weeks later Lovett did an abrupt about-face, urging immediate consideration of a new laboratory and a vastly expanded thermonuclear effort.

Why did Robert Lovett, one of the most self-assured men ever to serve in Washington, suddenly have second thoughts? David Tressel Griggs, chief scientist of the Air Force, was the key. He had known Lovett very well during World War II, when Lovett was assistant secretary of war for air. Teller told a member of the joint congressional committee staff that a briefing he had given for Lovett and the three service secretaries on March 19—a briefing arranged by Griggs—had been for the express purpose of turning Lovett around, and apparently it did. Possessor of one of the early U.S. pilot's licenses, Lovett had flown countless bombing missions with the British over Germany during World War I and was a devotee of airpower and Air Force prerogatives alike. His reversal on the second laboratory came about not because of any change in his beliefs about air warfare but because of the intense campaign waged by Teller, Lawrence, and Murray to win him over. Griggs had also introduced Teller to General James H. "Jimmy" Doolittle, the Air Force hero who had led the famous incendiary raids over Tokyo during World War II. Quickly won over by Teller, Doolittle spoke to Air Force Secretary Thomas Finletter, who was hearing similar advice from his assistant, William A. M. Burden, another convert to Teller's views.[9]

Out of the blue, Teller in Chicago now received a summons from Finletter. As Teller later described it, the secretary, an austere, self-contained lawyer from New York, listened "in icy silence" as Teller described the shortcomings of Los Alamos and the likelihood that Fuchs had speeded up the Soviet program, and sketched a future with a variety of thermonuclear weapons, not just a single big bomb. A few days later, Finletter flew to Los Alamos. There he found—or thought he found—the same halfhearted attitude Teller had told him to expect. Finletter was no sooner back in Washington than Teller received another summons, this time from Lovett.[10]

As Teller waited in the outer office of the unflappable secretary of defense, his mood was shaken when Robert LeBaron, chairman of the Pentagon's Military Liaison Committee, said to him, "Edward, I've done everything I can, but it's a lost cause." In Lovett's inner sanctum, however, Teller's powers of persuasion did not fail him: "before I left the Secretary's office I knew that I had won."[11]

Finletter played the decisive role: he sanctioned the clandestine, out-of-channels meetings between David Griggs and staff members of the joint congressional committee, and he encouraged Griggs to set up half a dozen briefings by Teller and his RAND associates which added immeasurably to the pressure, especially from the Air Force. At these sessions for officials of State, Defense, and the Joint Chiefs, the RAND scientists displayed charts illustrating thermal, gamma, and shock effects from thermonuclear bombs at various megatonnages, dropped from various altitudes. Teller followed up by emphasizing the Russians' competence, the risk that Fuchs had put them ahead, and the appalling danger should the Soviet Union build the thermonuclear first. Finally, he pleaded for new talent and a new laboratory to supplement the current desultory effort. To these briefings was added the threat that if the AEC refused to establish a new laboratory, the Air Force might do so on its own.[12]

Gordon Dean was ordinarily a virtuoso at rising above pique. But he was infuriated by Teller's latest end run. Privately, he fumed that

Lovett "knows virtually nothing about the atomic program." And, in as restrained a manner as he could summon, he complained to Secretary of State Dean Acheson and to Lovett's deputy, William Foster, both colleagues on the atomic energy subcommittee of the NSC, that he had endured Teller's complaints for two years now and that "while representing the finest in scientific brains, Teller did not always have a good feel for . . . administrative headaches." To the president's incoming national security adviser, James Lay, Dean attributed Lovett's change of heart to "one man's [Teller's] kicking up a fuss with people . . . who don't know the background." It would be "the worst thing in the world . . . to disrupt the morale of the lab when they are breaking their necks" to prepare the first test of a true thermonuclear device.[13]

But Dean recognized handwriting on the wall when he saw it and reluctantly agreed to meet with Ernest Lawrence. First, however, the GAC in late April praised the existing program as "sound, constructive, and very likely indeed to lead to success," and made one last effort to deflect the pressure. Noting that scientists from Berkeley had worked on instrumentation at Greenhouse, and that York was interested in testing componentry, the committee suggested by way of compromise that the Berkeley group be invited to help with the testing program and even with broader problems—so long as it did not drain manpower from Los Alamos. Characterizing the situation as "an unhappy one in which a fairly technical decision is being forced by high-pressure methods," Oppenheimer observed that the new enterprise would "have to go fast, or it will not go at all," his way of saying that Los Alamos was on the verge of a breakthrough that would prove a new lab unnecessary.[14]

Soon afterward, the AEC echoed the GAC's praise for Los Alamos and repeated its opposition to a new laboratory. The commissioners agreed with the GAC's recommendation and invited the Berkeley scientists to join in "securing diagnostic information on the behavior of thermonuclear devices." Once established in this work, they added, the California group would be "encouraged to submit . . . proposals of areas of further thermonuclear research."[15]

Ernest Lawrence was content. Experienced entrepreneur that he was, he knew that the goals of the new operation needed no spelling out. In Washington, second lab supporters were likewise satisfied. What mattered to them was not the AEC's rhetorical opposition but the reality that it was pulling Berkeley into the program. With Lawrence in the picture, the rest would follow. But Teller disagreed, demanding a clear mandate. He distrusted the AEC and doubted that it would ever sanction a new lab devoted wholly to thermonuclear weapons, he was suspicious of Lawrence's priorities, and he considered Herbert York too inexperienced to run the place. Besides, Teller wanted to stay in Chicago, where the Air Force had, he believed, promised him a laboratory of his own. By early summer 1952, his allies—Murray, David Griggs, and Robert LeBaron of the Defense Department, and Walker and Borden of the joint congressional committee—were all trying to persuade him to go to Berkeley, while he was inclined to refuse.[16]

Teller was on hand, however, at Berkeley's Claremont Hotel in mid-July for a celebration of the new laboratory. Unexpectedly, after a considerable amount of alcohol had been imbibed by all, Teller announced that he would not be joining after all. Lawrence was unfazed, having already intimated to York that they might be better off without him. But Captain John T. Hayward of the AEC's Division of Military Applications intervened: some of those at the celebration spotted Gordon Dean racing downstairs to dictate a "warm and cordial" letter committing the AEC to the new facility's going ahead on a broad front. Teller, whose wife and children had already arrived in California, agreed to remain.[17]

The new laboratory, set in Livermore, opened officially on September 2, 1952, and was at first called Project Whitney, after the highest mountain on the West Coast. Although Lawrence continued to insist that it was not, and never would be, *the* second laboratory, within a few years it became just that, moving from diagnostics to full-scale design and development. In the beginning, Lawrence was the nominal director, with York the acting director and Teller the presiding genius. The lab grew quickly, and it did, as proponents had prophesied, draw new talent into the program. To Teller's initial chagrin, those who came were not the world-class physicists he had dreamed of but young, newly minted Ph.D.'s. Nearly all had been students of Lawrence's. Charles Critchfield, a former student of Teller's, refused to join. Like many others, he was fond of the man but did not want to work for him—"If he's not in charge, he's not happy." Another refusenik was Francis Low, a thirty-year-old postdoc at the Institute for Advanced Study. Oppenheimer summoned Low and young Murray Gell-Mann to his office in Princeton. He sat by without comment while Teller made his pitch, asking the younger men to work with him. Low drove Teller to the railway station afterward, but he did not join the project.[18]

Besides increasing the number of physicists in the program, especially experimentalists, the new laboratory greatly expanded the number and variety of new weapons in the U.S. arsenal. That is, after early failures—its first two tests, of uranium devices designed by Teller, were embarrassing fizzles. But by 1956, the Livermore lab was finally on its way. Ironically, the Air Force, which had done so much to bring the new lab into being, continued to order its weapons from Los Alamos, while the Army and Navy, which had not pushed for the lab, patronized Livermore. Livermore made a specialty of building miniaturized warheads and is perhaps best known for designing the warhead for the Navy's Polaris missile.

The Air Force's continuing patronage of Los Alamos illustrates what had happened. Top brass at the Air Force, including Secretary Finletter, believed what Griggs and Teller told them, while officers at the working level, who dealt day to day with Los Alamos, trusted Bradbury. Bradbury did not overpromise, he did not stimulate military requirements for weapons he was not ready to produce, and he stayed well within his cost estimates. But the higher-ups mistook his workaday manner and his too-evident lack of enthusiasm when they arrived on time-consuming inspection trips for absence of charisma and lack of commitment to the program.

Herbert York in later years said that Teller's politicking failed—"It was Lawrence who rescued the enterprise." To have him, even nominally, at the helm was a gold-plated guarantee. And Lawrence wanted the lab that came into being at Livermore. The Materials Testing Accelerator, the huge device he had been building there and in which he had invested his prestige, had become an embarrassment, and he was anxious to save face. The new lab solved his problem. It likewise provided a graceful way out for the AEC, with Gordon Dean and his supporters now able to claim that it was not a new facility being created but an existing one converted to new uses.

The country now had two enormously costly laboratories competing with each other to produce ever more streamlined designs. Together, Livermore and Los Alamos created the vast arsenal of superfluous nuclear weaponry that curses us today.[19]

CHAPTER TWELVE

A New Era

THE MEN AND WOMEN of Los Alamos took creation of the new lab hard. It was an ill-deserved slap in the face, and at a moment when they were working all-out to prepare the first trial of the Ulam-Teller concept. The test, christened Mike in honor of the expected megaton yield, was scheduled to take place in the fall of 1952 on Elugelab, an island at the northern end of the Pacific atoll of Eniwetok.

The work to be done was awe-inspiring, in scale and complexity something like the logistics for one of the great Pacific landings in World War II. Sections of the test device, plus experimental and support material, were being fabricated in shops all over the United States; for reasons of secrecy, no subcontractor was told the complete story about how the parts he made were to be used. A major sea- and airborne task force would be required, with the components— hundreds of tons of them—hauled to Oakland, California, for shipment, and other parts flown directly to Eniwetok in airplanes far less capable than those used today. Making sure that the parts arrived in the right place at exactly the right moment entailed almost unimaginably close coordination.

To make the test, and analysis of the results, as simple as possible, liquid deuterium had been selected as the hydrogen fuel. This decision caused cryogenic problems never dealt with before: for these, the engineer Jacob Wechsler was in charge. Every month, sometimes more frequently, Wechsler traveled by train from New Mexico to Boulder, Colorado, where the National Bureau of Standards had built a hydrogen liquefaction plant; to Buffalo, New York, where American Car and Foundry was casting and welding the heavy steel casing and the cab under which the device would be assembled; and then to the Boston area, where the A. D. Little Cambridge Corporation was producing enormous dewars in which liquid deuterium and other liquefied gases would be stored at Eniwetok. Transporting the dewars from the East Coast to Oakland, and from there to the Pacific, was itself a vast undertaking, and one that, again, required the most precise coordination. Ultimately, to achieve, by the explosion itself, the highest temperatures ever attained on earth, the hydrogen fuel had to be cooled to minus 423 degrees Fahrenheit, one of the lowest temperatures ever generated, and maintained there in the scorching heat of the Pacific.[1]

Calculations for Mike had begun in June of 1951 and entailed millions of computations, so many that at one point, in 1952, they required the full-time use of four large calculators, the Princeton and Los Alamos MANIACs designed by John von Neumann, and two others: the UNIVAC in Philadelphia and the SEAC in Washington, D.C. The questions that were fed into these calculators originated mostly at Los Alamos, where design and engineering were directed by the Theoretical Megaton Group (also called the Panda Committee) under Carson Mark and Marshall Holloway.[2]

Years afterward, as Wechsler recalled the preparations for Mike, he gave credit first to Holloway, for managing the extraordinarily complicated logistical details, and second to Mark, for his willingness to compromise on design problems to help minimize the chances of failure. Wechsler described sitting in Mark's office trying to think of ways to channel radiation from the fission primary down the cylindrical container so that it would bombard the back of the fusion secondary. And he remembered Mark's saying, "Look, if we firm up the plan and do this, can we then hold this other thing open?" Mark considered Holloway a steady manager and someone he could rely on. For example, if the theoreticians lagged a little in delivering computations, he knew Holloway would find a margin of a week or two. "I was always sure he had a little something up his sleeve."[3]

Teller at one stage predicted that Mike would fail: because of a physical law called Taylor instability, radiation from the primary would be absorbed in the casing. But Hans Bethe, a genius at understanding the physical interaction between radiation and shell, asserted, confidently, that there would be no Taylor instability.[4]

The lab could not afford failure, or even delay. Each time a potential glitch threatened, the question was not Can the device be made perfect? but Can it be made to work at all? The result was what weaponeers call overdesign. One example was the outer casing, manufactured in Buffalo and shipped from Oakland aboard the USS *Curtiss,* disassembled, for reasons of secrecy, in heavy steel rings. To keep the device from blowing apart prematurely, the casing had welded steel walls a foot thick, which accounted for much of Mike's eighty-two-ton weight. Later, with the experience of Mike behind them, the engineers were able to design walls that were much thinner, a key to making bombs that could be carried by aircraft. But for Mike, most choices were on the conservative side. The result was a device that was not—and not meant to be—a deliverable weapon. Nicknamed "the Sausage" because of its shape, Mike has been described as "essentially a large thermos bottle," standing just over twenty feet high and not quite seven feet in diameter, with diagnostic tubes protruding at either end. Design changes were made until the moment of final assembly, with Carson Mark on hand to interpret theoretical questions into language the experimentalists could understand.[5]

Even the primary, one of the least problematic parts of the design owing to the lab's work on fission, required last-minute changes: to reduce the risk of predetonation, a new core, with altered quantities of plutonium and enriched uranium, was flown to Eniwetok and installed only a day or two before the test.[6]

While the lab was going at it full steam, four well-known scientists questioned whether the test should take place at all. In the billiard room of Washington's august Cosmos Club in the spring of 1952, Robert Oppenheimer, I. I. Rabi, and Charles Lauritsen, the president of Caltech, found themselves comparing notes about the danger that Mike would end—for all time—any hope of agreement with the Russians not to develop hydrogen weapons. Once we held a test, the USSR was sure to follow. And since any hydrogen explosion would throw up debris, secrecy was out of the question: either nation would know when the other set off a thermonuclear device. Once again, the men discussed an alternative: prepare a test, and then tell the Russians that we would not go ahead unless they did so, an idea similar to the Fermi-Rabi proposal of 1949. They telephoned their wartime colleague, Vannevar Bush, the crusty, independent-minded president of the Carnegie Institution of Washington, and asked him to join them. On Bush's arrival, they found that he was thinking along the same lines.

The Mike test was scheduled for November 1, three days before the election of a new president, and the four scientists considered it unconscionable for either candidate, Republican Dwight Eisenhower or Democrat Adlai Stevenson, to be confronted upon his election by a fait accompli of such fateful import, and with consequences for which he would be responsible. With engineers and other specialists building test components all over the country and servicemen helping in the Pacific, word could easily leak out and become an issue in the closing days of the campaign. Moreover, they were certain that a test would be invaluable to the Russians as they studied our fallout, and would help them on their way to an H-bomb of their own.[7]

Vannevar Bush, wartime director of the Office of Scientific Research and Development and a member of the Acheson-Lilienthal working group in 1945, was so concerned that Mike would end any hope of ever reaching an agreement with the Russians that after meeting with his colleagues at the Cosmos Club he immediately went to Secretary of State Acheson to urge that the test be postponed. Acheson turned a deaf ear.[8]

Hans Bethe, too, was drawn into discussions of postponement. In the early summer of 1952, he was in Los Alamos when Oppenheimer asked him to seek Bradbury's views about the consequences of a delay. Bradbury answered that a delay of ten days or so would do no harm. After that, however, bad weather might force postponement until spring. Bradbury suggested that the candidates be told of the pending test ahead of time so that the new president would be prepared for what faced him on taking office.[9]

Bethe was in a painful position. Here was someone who had, in his words, been "terribly shocked" by Truman's decision to proceed with the H-bomb, who had at first refused to work on thermonuclear weapons, who had joined the effort with great reluctance and had been cheered by every indication that the bomb might not work. Yet here he was at Los Alamos in mid-1952, doing the final calculations for Mike. About this time Gordon Dean, beset by Air Force warnings that the Russians were probably ahead, asked Bethe to compare H-bomb progress by the two countries in light of Fuchs's spying. Bethe responded in a long and thoughtful memo expressing doubt that Fuchs had been of much help to the Russians, since the ideas he was in a position to give had turned out to be invalid. He said that thermonuclear development in this country had been "about as rapid as was technically feasible" once the Ulam-Teller ideas appeared, and he pleaded for the utmost secrecy. "If we now publicly intensify our efforts, we shall force the Russians even more into developing this weapon which we have every reason to dread."[10]

Then, late that summer, Bethe wrote a second letter to Dean, pointing out that a successful test three days before the election could become a last-minute campaign issue. He urged that Mike be postponed until the day after the election or, better yet, until mid-November, when the "smoke of [campaign] battle" would have cleared. As Bradbury had done earlier, Bethe urged that Eisenhower and Stevenson be briefed. He suggested that if Dean did not wish to do the briefing, someone like Oppenheimer could do it.[11]

Oppenheimer, too, entered the discussion of test postponement once again. He had been appointed chair of a panel tasked by the secretary of state to survey relations with the Soviet Union one last time for the outgoing Truman administration and consider whether there was any way to break the impasse over arms control. The new group, called the Disarmament Panel, wanted to try for an agreement with the Russians not to engage in thermonuclear testing, and in early September, some of its members paid a call on Acheson. They, like Bethe and Bush before them, suggested that the test be postponed so that the new president would have a chance to think about thermonuclear weapons in a much larger context, that of the U.S.-Soviet relationship overall. Once a hydrogen device had been tested, a threshold would have been crossed, and it would be too late.[12]

Bethe, members of the Disarmament Panel, and Rabi, who had known Eisenhower well when he was president of Columbia University, probably hoped that a postponement until mid-November would lead to a longer delay so that the new president would have time to test Soviet willingness to negotiate.

Displeased at seeing Oppenheimer as part of the discussion, Gordon Dean told a colleague that he was "a little concerned at Oppenheimer's recently undue interest in postponement. I can see the plays from where I am sitting and I am not happy." Dean's position and that of the president on the timing of the test were delicate enough without meddling by a scientist whose left-wing past, amid the increasingly clamorous musings of Senator McCarthy, made him a point of vulnerability for the atomic energy program. Truman and Dean were Democratic loyalists who hoped for a victory by Stevenson. Years afterward, Deborah Gore Dean said that her father had wanted the Mike test held on schedule in hopes that a successful shot might swing the election to the Democrats, and the president probably felt the same way. In addition, he surely wanted to leave a successful test as his administration's legacy. But if he was tempted to go ahead prior to the election on political grounds, he gave no hint, putting out word instead that he would have no objection if operational difficulties should cause postponement. By mid-October it was clear, however, that no such difficulties existed, and Dean instructed AEC commissioner Eugene Zuckert, who was on his way to the Pacific, to find out whether a brief postponement would cause problems. Zuckert's answer was yes: commanders on the ground feared a hydrogen leak if the test was delayed.[13]

And so Mike went off as scheduled at 7:15 a.m. on November 1 (October 31 in the United States). Almost immediately an enormous white fireball appeared in the sky like a half-risen sun, and as it rose higher, the ocean around it turned red. Elugelab, the island on which the shot was set off, likewise turned a brilliant red, and after burning six hours, it disappeared. A mushroom cloud one hundred miles across rose to fill the horizon, spreading eighty million tons of radioactive earth, gases, and water into the air and atmosphere. At 10.4 megatons, it was the largest man-made explosion ever, forty-six times the size of the George shot eighteen months earlier, and a thousand times the size of the bomb that had destroyed Hiroshima. A sailor who witnessed the shot remarked: "You would swear that the whole world was on fire."[14]

With the success of Mike, the world moved into a new era just as surely as it had on that fateful day in August 1945. Proportionally, a weapon producing an explosive force of a single megaton represented as large an increase in destructive power as the atomic bomb had over a conventional high-explosive weapon. Moreover, with much of Mike's yield, more than three-quarters, coming from the layer of U-238 that surrounded the fusionable fuel, it was clear that depending on the amount of uranium used, a thermonuclear device could be built to have unlimited destructive power. As Herbert York said afterward, "fission bombs, destructive as they might be, were thought of as being limited in power. Now, it seemed, we had learned how to brush even these limits aside and to build bombs whose power was boundless."[15]

Edward Teller, who had for so long sought a weapon of unlimited destructive power, did not witness the test. Having predicted that Mike would fail, he chose to sit out the event close by a seismograph in Berkeley; when the lines on the graph registered a large explosion, he sent a triumphal telegram to Los Alamos: "It's a boy." Later he told a friend there, Fred Hoyt, that had he known Los Alamos was capable of pulling it off, he would not have insisted on a second laboratory.

Vannevar Bush viewed Mike as a lost opportunity. Gone was the possibility of an agreement with Russia never to cross that threshold. "I still think we made a grave error in conducting that test at that time and not attempting to make that simple agreement with Russia. I think history will show that was a turning point . . . that those who pushed that thing through . . . without making that attempt have a great deal to answer for."[16]

PART FOUR

1952-1954

CHAPTER THIRTEEN

Sailing Close to the Wind

THROUGHOUT THAT SUMMER and fall, the ad hoc panel appointed by Acheson and chaired by Robert Oppenheimer had been meeting to consider the largest questions of atomic policy. Besides Oppenheimer, the panel was composed of four other distinguished Americans: Vannevar Bush; John Dickey, president of Dartmouth College; Joseph Johnson, president of the Carnegie Endowment for International Peace; and Allen Dulles, deputy director of the CIA. It was a sign of the increasingly security-conscious times that the panel had to begin its work late because a question had arisen about clearing one of the distinguished members. As for Robert Oppenheimer, who had chaired innumerable government groups and was the natural leader of this one, he was sailing close to the wind—closer, perhaps, than he knew.

His enemies found an opening in the fact that his term on the GAC, along with the terms of two other members who had opposed the crash program, would expire in the summer. Commissioner Murray, an archconservative who maintained a channel of his own to J. Edgar Hoover, started the ball rolling in early 1952 by complaining to Hoover that Oppenheimer had delayed the weapons program. Soon afterward, in California, Murray discussed with Ernest Lawrence the names of possible replacements for Oppie as chairman of the GAC. Next, the California scientist Kenneth Pitzer brought matters into the open by delivering a speech in which he charged that there had been "serious and unnecessary delays" in the H-bomb program and urged that the influence of "scientific kibbitzers" be reduced. Pitzer's were not the accusations of an obscure West Coast chemistry professor: as

AEC research director, he had spent two years watching the Washington goings-on at close range. After his speech in California, when the FBI came to him, Pitzer said that in contrast to an earlier time he now had doubts, not just about Oppenheimer's judgment, but about his loyalty as well. He suggested that Teller might have something to add.[1]

Teller now made charges that carried special weight. Contacted by the FBI in New Mexico, where he was working on Mike, Teller for the nth time accused Oppenheimer of discouraging others from working on the H-bomb. Oppenheimer, he said, was motivated not by subversive tendencies but by "personal vanity": he did not want his bomb, the A-bomb, trumped by another, more powerful, weapon. According to the FBI report, Teller added that he would do "most anything to see subject separated from General Advisory Committee because of his poor advice." A couple of weeks later Teller—taking the initiative this time—sought a second FBI interview in hopes of making sure that the earlier one remained secret. To his previous comments, Teller added that as a young man, Oppenheimer had suffered "physical and mental attacks which may have permanently affected him." He warned that he "had never had the slightest reason to believe that Oppenheimer is in any way disloyal," but that he did not want it known that he had raised the loyalty question lest he be asked about Frank Oppenheimer and his Party membership. Having raised questions about both Robert Oppenheimer's loyalty and his emotional stability, Teller concluded with what was by now a trademark threat: if fellow scientists were to learn what he had said, the embarrassment would be such that he would have to "sever his connections" with the program. Keep my comments secret, he warned the FBI, or I'll quit working on the H-bomb.[2]

Teller's complaints were not new. He had made them before, to officials at various levels; but the circumstances this time were different. Senator McCarthy was now a power, and Teller was talking, not to a lowly congressional staff assistant as he had in 1950, but to agents of the FBI.[3]

Not surprisingly, with members of the scientific community being questioned by the FBI, rumors about Oppie floated to the surface that spring during the American Physical Society's annual meeting in Washington. At a Cosmos Club gathering in May 1952, James Fisk, the AEC's former director of research, picked up "almost vitriolic talk against Dr. Oppenheimer—implying that he was unpatriotic." Gordon Dean told Fisk that he, too, had "seen signs of this," and termed Pitzer's actions, in particular, "despicable."[4]

But Pitzer did not quit. He wrote a personal letter to the president asking that Oppenheimer be "eased out." (In an interview with the author years later, Pitzer denied that he had written to the president.)[5] Others, too, weighed in. Wendell Latimer, another Berkeley chemist, and Harold Urey, a nuclear chemist and Nobel Prize winner at the University of Chicago, also wrote to Truman. Berkeley physicist Luis Alvarez made a special trip east to lobby Air Force Secretary Finletter against reappointing Oppenheimer, and former commissioner Lewis Strauss, now a financial consultant in New York, raised the issue with Souers and the president in person.[6]

In addition to Strauss, Alvarez, and the chemists—none of whom had participated in the H-bomb program or knew it at first hand—others got into the act. Murray tried to enlist his fellow commissioners, and Finletter arranged to have the matter voted on by the special subcommittee of the National Security Council. Gordon Dean of this group voted to reappoint Oppenheimer, along with Conant and DuBridge, the other GAC members whose terms were expiring, while Lovett and the State Department representative who stood in for Acheson voted against.[7]

Just then, in the early summer of 1952, Gordon Dean learned something that could at any moment erupt into disaster for the atomic energy program: the Justice Department was about to indict a physicist named Joseph Weinberg for perjury. The potential for disaster lay in the fact that Weinberg, a onetime Communist Party member, had been a student and a friend of Oppenheimer's. The FBI had been tailing him for years and, in 1943, had recorded a conversation between him and the Party organizer of Alameda County, California, which seemed to implicate Weinberg in espionage. The Justice

Department now charged Weinberg with lying when he had denied to the government under oath that he had attended a Party meeting at Oppie's house in Berkeley in July 1941, at which the scientist had allegedly been present. The government had only one witness, a man named Paul Crouch, a former Communist Party organizer in California who was now a paid informer for the FBI. The charges had been simmering for a while, Oppenheimer having told a California investigating committee in 1950 that he had been in New Mexico in July of 1941 and had never attended such a meeting, much less hosted it at his house. For Gordon Dean, the disastrous potential lay in the fact that neither he nor Jay McInerny, the assistant attorney general charged with bringing the case, was convinced that Oppie had told the truth. They feared that should he be called to testify, he would lie under oath and subsequently be indicted for perjury. Dean was worried about the likelihood that such a sequence of events would make the AEC a sitting duck for McCarthy or some other red-hunting committee chairman in Congress. Dean was therefore anxious to get the count naming Oppenheimer dropped from the Weinberg indictment—and maneuver Oppie off the GAC before the press got wind of the case. Oppenheimer's attorney, Joseph Volpe, made it "crystal clear" (Volpe's words) to Oppie that Dean wanted him off the GAC. Meanwhile, ill with the brain tumor that would soon kill him, JCAE chairman Brien McMahon met with McInerny's and Oppenheimer's lawyers and brokered a deal. Oppenheimer decided not to make a fight of it, and Gordon Dean wrote him a letter of thanks—"I fully appreciate the reasons behind your unwillingness"—that hinted at the behind-the-scenes negotiations.[8]

Had Oppie chosen to fight for his place on the GAC he would not have succeeded, since National Security Adviser Sidney Souers advised the president against reappointing him. Souers said afterward that in making his decision he had discounted the "loyalty talk" against Oppenheimer but considered it time for "new blood" who "believed in the policy of the President." Despite Souers's denial, the FBI interviews with Teller, Pitzer, and Libby and the letters to the White House from Pitzer, Urey, and Latimer accomplished their goal: they persuaded Souers that Oppenheimer had been opposing the program and should be replaced.[9]

Oppenheimer enjoyed being chairman of the GAC. Volpe, Oppie's friend as well as his attorney, called him "Mr. Atom, the giant of the business. He loved being sought out for his advice and to some extent it went to his head." Now, facing the possibility that he might have to testify in a felony trial, Oppie was distressed by the likelihood that he would forfeit his enormous stature with the public, the government, and the scientific community. Kitty Oppenheimer, Volpe remembered, "took it more calmly than he did, and was extremely supportive." Gordon Dean, too, treated Oppenheimer with kid gloves. "Mr. Atom" had on occasion been a headache for Dean, personifying, as he did, traits that made the scientists difficult for a government official to deal with: they had been thrown into the public spotlight unprepared, they did not know the political game, and they enjoyed their newly acquired renown all too much. Dean felt a measure of personal attachment for Oppenheimer, however, and a respect that had risen during the second-lab affair, and did his utmost to balance fairness to the man with the best interests of the atomic energy program.[10]

The Weinberg case was like a high explosive that could blow up at any moment. Dean now made a highly unusual request: he asked the president to intervene with the Justice Department to keep Oppenheimer's name out of it. Should the prosecution call Oppie as a witness, Dean warned, "it will mean that Dr. Oppenheimer must take the stand and contradict the testimony of Crouch, the only government witness. It will be Oppenheimer's word against Crouch's. . . . Such a conflict in the atmosphere of a criminal court, involving two such colorful figures, will attract great attention. . . . Dr. Oppenheimer's good name will be greatly impaired and much of his value to the country destroyed." Such was the risk that the president overcame his reluctance to intercede and wrote to Dean, with a copy to Attorney General Tom Clark, "I am very much interested in the Weinberg-Oppenheimer connection. I feel as you do that Dr. Oppenheimer is an honest man. In this day of character assassination and unjustified smear tactics, it seems that good men are made to suffer unnecessarily." The president's words were brave, but the White House in reality was wary of embarrassment, so much so that Truman did not send his ritual letter of thanks to the outgoing members of the GAC until the eve of his departure from office.[11]

Fortunately for Dean and the AEC, the outcome was anticlimactic: the trial did not take place until March 1953, safely past the new president's inauguration; the incident involving Oppenheimer was somehow, miraculously, never mentioned; and the jury—to everyone's astonishment—found Weinberg innocent.[12]

The Weinberg affair, nonetheless, showed the difficulty of conducting rational policy with political dynamite in the air. At a meeting of the special subcommittee of the National Security Council in October, for example, Acheson suggested that the United States might use the upcoming Mike test as an opportunity to try a new arms control approach to the USSR, and Paul Nitze, chief of the State Department's Policy Planning Staff, raised the possibility of a test moratorium. At this, Secretary of Defense Robert Lovett nearly leaped out of his chair. Such ideas, he said, must be put out of mind and any documents that so much as mentioned them destroyed. The reason? Proposals such as these might be traced to "fellows like Dr. Oppenheimer, whose motivations in these matters were suspect." It turned out that Lovett had been talking with Gordon Dean about Oppenheimer and was fearful of "adverse developments," by which he meant the still ticking Weinberg case.[13]

At this very time, Oppenheimer and his colleagues on the Disarmament Panel were putting the final touches on their thoughtful and farsighted report, in which they said that nuclear weapons were not merely a military problem but were "intimately connected with the largest questions of national policy." The United States, they said, had allowed itself to become frozen in a posture of "rigidity and totality of commitment which seem to us very dangerous," and they warned of catastrophe unless our policies became more flexible. The panel singled out for special criticism the excessive secrecy whereby the public had not been told even minimal facts about the size of the nation's stockpile, about the phenomenal pace at which both sides

Robert Oppenheimer at a party in Fuller Lodge, Los Alamos, probably August 1945.

David Lilienthal a few years after his retirement as chairman of the AEC.

Lilienthal testifying at Senator Bourke Hickenlooper's "terrible mismanagement" hearings in 1949. AEC general manager Carroll Wilson sits next to Lilienthal at left, and Commissioners Gordon Dean, Henry DeWolf Smyth, and Lewis Strauss are behind him, slightly to the right.

Niels Bohr visited Los Alamos six times during the war. His views shaped Oppenheimer's approach to postwar use of atomic knowledge.

Hans Bethe *(center)* at Wheeler Peak, a favorite hiking spot near Los Alamos.

Carson Mark *(left)* and Bethe in Ithaca, New York, during the early 1960s. They worked together on the hydrogen bomb and remained close friends and collaborators afterward.

Enrico Fermi's colleagues called him "the pope" because of his total knowledge of both theoretical and experimental physics.

Edward Teller *(left)* consulted Fermi while they were colleagues at the University of Chicago after the war. Photograph taken 1951.

John Manley *(left)* helped Oppenheimer organize the lab. He became secretary of the General Advisory Committee. Photograph probably taken August 1945.

Maria Goeppert Mayer with her teacher Edward Teller *(left);* her husband, Joseph Mayer; and James Franck, conscience of the physics community, 1930s.

Charles J. V. Murphy at Cap d'Antibes in 1949, at work on *A King's Story*, the memoir of the Duke of Windsor.

Lewis Strauss points to the area where the Bravo test took place. At this press conference, on March 30, 1954, he said that the hydrogen bomb could be made big enough to "take out" a city as big as New York.

Vannevar Bush, head of the Office of Scientific Research and Development during the war, warned the commissioners in June 1954, while they were still deliberating, that the Oppenheimer hearing might forever impair trust between scientists and the government.

A brilliant student of Oppenheimer's at Berkeley, Robert Serber *(right)* wrote what became the *Los Alamos Primer,* which was required reading for every newcomer to Los Alamos during the war. He remained close to the Oppenheimer family afterward.

Cornelius Everett at the University of Wisconsin, where he met Stanislaw Ulam in the early 1940s.

Stanislaw Ulam and Françoise Aron, then an exchange student at Mount Holyoke College, during their courtship, 1939 or 1940.

Stanislaw Ulam *(center)* with his wife, Françoise, and a Polish colleague at the second postwar International Congress of Mathematicians in Edinburgh, 1951.

Army general James M. Gavin, an Oppenheimer ally and a strong
supporter of tactical, or "battlefield," nuclear weapons, speaks with an
adversary, Edward Teller.

The AEC's director of research from 1948 to 1951, Kenneth Pitzer wrote to President Truman in 1952, opposing reappointment of Oppenheimer to the General Advisory Committee.

Henry Smyth considered his work at the International Atomic Energy Agency the most important achievement of his life, but it was his dissent in the Oppenheimer case that earned him a place in history.

I. I. Rabi *(left)* with Enrico Fermi at Westhampton Beach, New York, in 1953. Rabi was Oppenheimer's closest friend and counselor and an eloquent defender who tried to stop the hearing.

After Truman's order to develop the hydrogen bomb, Victor Weisskopf used the stature he had acquired at Los Alamos to insist that questions of weapons development be kept before the public.

OVERLEAF: After learning that he was to receive the Fermi Prize, on April 5, 1963, Oppenheimer called his friend and neighbor Ulli Steltzer and invited her to take his photograph.

were accumulating "unprecedented destructive power," or about the fact that beyond a certain number of weapons it was futile to try to meet the Soviet threat simply by "keeping ahead of the Russians." Finally, the panel urged the nation's leaders to deal more openly with the American people and reach a collective understanding with the "other major free nations" whereby the responsibility for nuclear weapons would be shared. Despite its pessimism—the panel could see no path to arms control as long as Joseph Stalin was alive—the report closed on a note of prophecy. It exhorted the U.S. government to keep channels open and listen carefully for the slightest change in attitude once the Soviet dictator passed from the scene. Two months later, the seemingly immortal Stalin lay dead.[14]

It was a measure of Robert Oppenheimer's fatalism, arrogance, and, possibly, despair that he and the panel of which he was chairman had ventured far beyond their mandate, into the deepest waters of foreign and domestic policy.

He could not have been oblivious of the storm clouds gathering in the summer of 1952. He had been maneuvered off the GAC, and the GAC itself had suffered major defeats with rejection of its H-bomb and second-lab positions. At lunch at the Cosmos Club in May 1952, he, Conant, and Lee DuBridge had discussed the "dark words" in circulation about him, as well as reports that the three of them had sabotaged the H-bomb program. He had heard about a rancorous luncheon in Georgetown that spring at which David Griggs, chief Air Force scientist, had argued about the H-bomb with two of Oppie's closest colleagues. In response to Griggs's charge that the GAC had obstructed the effort, one of them, Rabi, arranged for Griggs to meet with Oppenheimer in Princeton so that he could read minutes of the various GAC meetings at which the H-bomb project had been discussed. Griggs was disappointed, however, when Oppie showed him, not the minutes he had hoped to see, but the Halloween meeting annexes in which the GAC members spelled out their reasons for opposing a crash program. This effort at rapprochement led to disaster when Oppie's failure to make "minutes" available only deepened

Griggs's suspicions. It is not clear from existing accounts, however, which minutes Griggs had expected to see, those of the Halloween meeting—because of their sensitivity, Manley's minutes had been destroyed—or those of subsequent meetings, which, in Rabi's view, would have proven to him that the GAC had spared no effort to comply with the president's order.[15]

The meeting at Princeton veered toward acrimony, moreover, when Griggs asked whether Oppenheimer was spreading a story that Thomas Finletter had said that if only the United States had a couple of hundred hydrogen bombs, "it could rule the world." Oppenheimer bluntly replied that he believed the story and did not deny relaying it to others. Then Oppenheimer asked whether Griggs considered him pro-Soviet, or merely confused. Griggs said he wished he knew. Next, Oppenheimer asked whether Griggs had raised questions about his loyalty with Finletter and General Hoyt Vandenberg. Griggs admitted that he had. Their meeting ended with Oppenheimer's telling Griggs he was paranoid.[16]

What Oppie did not know was that a full year before, in May 1951, Finletter had canceled his Air Force clearance in the wake of a conversation with California physicist Luis Alvarez and after reading portions of Oppenheimer's FBI file. Not only were Air Force Secretary Thomas Finletter and Air Force Chief of Staff Hoyt Vandenberg convinced that Oppenheimer was a security risk, but he had infuriated the Air Force by participating in a study with Caltech scientists about ways to adapt atomic weapons to ground warfare. The study, Project Vista, had been commissioned by the Army and the Air Force as a result of their experience in Korea, where the A-bomb would have been useless against troops on the ground. The study was addressed to fears that the Russians, with their vast superiority in manpower, could roll over Western Europe and annex its industrial power. Should the Russians make such a move, the Western allies would have no way to counter them except by bombing Soviet cities and civilians. Was there a way to adapt nuclear weapons, by making them small and precisely targeted, so as to deter the Russian land armies and ward off an invasion of Western Europe?[17]

After working on the study during the spring and early summer of 1951, the chairman—Lee DuBridge—and the rest of the Vista group had invited Oppenheimer to Pasadena. With his genius at synthesizing the ideas of others, Oppenheimer redrafted the committee's work and helped write what was to become the controversial chapter 5 of the report, dealing with the question of tactical weapons. Although Oppenheimer was a latecomer to the project and his views were shared by all the other scientists who were working on it, he inevitably became the lightning rod. To the Air Force, Vista's recommendation that the Strategic Air Command relinquish its monopoly of fissionable material and share with the other services could only mean abolition of its strategic air arm. Similarly, the Air Force objected to the proposal that instead of the SAC's being assigned to carry out major bombing strikes inside the Soviet heartland, a new tactical air force be created that could drop small nuclear bombs on enemy airfields and supply lines in Europe. To the "big bomb" advocates in the Air Force, these proposals spelled heresy. And to powerful individuals already suspicious of Oppenheimer, chapter 5 of Vista smacked of treason.[18]

Oppenheimer did not help his cause when Finletter, at the suggestion of two assistants, invited him to lunch in his private dining room at the Pentagon. He arrived late, rebuffed the secretary's efforts to be gracious, and became, in the words of one of those present, "rude beyond belief." He questioned the morality of the big-bomb strategy. Finletter replied that it would be more immoral to forgo our most effective weapon before conditions were ripe for disarmament. Their meeting ended in disaster. Oppenheimer was said to have exuded contempt for everyone in the room and, the moment the meal ended, rose, turned on his heels, and walked out.[19]

The Pentagon luncheon did nothing to quell the secretary's suspicions, and, learning that a group of Vista scientists, including Oppenheimer, were on their way to Europe to present their ideas to NATO commander Dwight D. Eisenhower, Finletter tried but failed to scuttle the visit. Next, he summoned General Lauris Norstad, the ranking Air Force officer at NATO near Paris, back to Washington for a briefing. The scientists—DuBridge, Oppenheimer, Charles Lauritsen, and Walt Whitman, now chairman of the Pentagon's Research and Development Board—first called on Eisenhower, who, according to Lauritsen, was "fascinated" by the idea of using tactical airpower to defend Europe, favored publication of chapter 5, and said he wished he had written it himself. Next they met with Norstad. Fresh from his briefing at the Pentagon, Norstad at first gave an impassioned defense of the strategic concept. When the scientists saw him a second time, however, they found him calmer, and after Oppenheimer had hastily redrafted one or two provisions, Norstad pronounced himself satisfied.[20]

The Air Force in Washington was another story. Having first tried to water down the report, Finletter now moved to suppress it entirely. All copies were recalled and chapter 5 disappeared from view until its partial declassification in 1980, nearly thirty years later. Even today, it is not available in its entirety. While chapter 5 was never allowed to become part of the dialogue, the suggestions put forward there soon became policy. In early 1952, even before the complete Vista report was issued, the Joint Chiefs of Staff authorized General Eisenhower to start planning for the use of tactical nuclear weapons in Europe, and two years later NATO made a formal commitment to use them for defense. Progress in the aim and design of nuclear weapons, along with the imperatives of strategy, vindicated chapter 5 long before the Air Force could bring itself to accept it.[21]

Meanwhile, on a personal level, chapter 5 seemed once again to bear out Finletter's suspicions. If in the spring of 1951 he had judged Oppenheimer a security risk, by autumn, with the Vista affair at its height, he had concluded that the scientist might be something more sinister. One of Finletter's subordinates, Garrison Norton, came to share these suspicions, confiding to a congressional staff member that he "was awake nights worrying" about the physicist.[22]

Air Force officials were not alone. Bill Borden, executive director of the joint congressional committee and Brien McMahon's trusted right hand, had first doubted Oppenheimer's loyalty back in early 1950, following the GAC's verdict against the crash program and Fuchs's arrest for espionage. Since then Teller had fueled Borden's doubts by telling him repeatedly that the thermonuclear program was lagging, and Oppenheimer was to blame. All this time Borden had been engaged in a dialogue with himself over whether Oppenheimer took the positions he did because he was (a) an agent of the Soviet Union or (b) simply wrongheaded. In the space of just a few days in the spring of 1952 Borden took several contradictory actions. He drafted a letter for McMahon to send to the president warning that the scientist might have been in touch with the Soviet spy network even before the opening of Los Alamos, and an alternative suggesting that "sincere and patriotic" as Oppie's motives might be, his influence was nonetheless harmful. And he wrote a memo to himself summarizing the FBI's most up-to-date file. "The whole trend and connotation of this summary is to the effect that Dr. Oppenheimer is not that which might be most feared."[23]

With Borden engaged in debate with himself, he and McMahon decided to hire Frank Cotter, a former FBI agent with a year's experience at Los Alamos. On the morning Cotter reported for work in June 1952, Borden handed him the transcript of the FBI's interview with Fuchs in England, told him it hinted that there had been a second spy in the Manhattan Project, and instructed him to find out whether it was Oppenheimer.

The thirty-year-old Cotter, whose fair hair, blue eyes, and open countenance belied his extensive experience as a street agent, had grown up in the Bronx and attended New York University, where— he later pointed out—every tenth professor had been a Marxist. The idea that someone might be a real, live Communist didn't faze him. But as he read the AEC files on Oppenheimer, Cotter was appalled by the fact that Oppenheimer had kept on making monthly payments to the Party even after the Hitler-Stalin pact of 1939. Cotter knew that many Communists, especially Jewish members, had abandoned the Party after that, and he thought it remarkable that Oppenheimer should have kept up his payments. Then he noticed that nearly everyone close to the scientist—his brother, wife, sister-in-law, former students, friends—had been Party members. And he noticed that San Francisco police records of the death, thought to be suicide, of Oppie's onetime fiancée, Jean Tatlock, were missing from the file. She, too, had belonged to the Party. Was there cause for suspicion in this apparent disappearance of records?[24]

On sweltering evenings that summer of 1952, Cotter sat in the joint congressional committee offices on the Hill and talked over his findings with Bill Borden, who, to his surprise, now seemed to take Oppie's side. "No, no," Borden would say at Cotter's newest discovery. "That doesn't make him a spy." Cotter looked up an acquaintance, Maurice "Gook" Taylor, a field agent whose judgment he respected, and every week or two they met for a beer after work. Taylor, who dealt with coded messages coming in to the FBI via Soviet cable traffic, was unequivocal. There was, he said, "no way" someone as big as Oppenheimer could be engaged in espionage without its coming through the signals system. And after four months working on the case and finding nothing, Cotter was persuaded. Not only Taylor, but Don Walters and Charlie Lyons, agents whose job it was to tail Oppenheimer when he was in town, assured Cotter that the scientist was beyond suspicion.[25]

Cotter reported these assurances to Borden and other congressional staffers who had taken part in their discussions. He was therefore very much surprised in the fall of 1952, after what must have been fifty or sixty hours of conversation, to find that he and Borden had switched sides. Cotter's suspicions had been allayed. Borden's had flared up again.

Although McMahon chose not to send either of Borden's draft letters in May warning the president about Oppenheimer, he had sent Truman a third missive, also drafted by Borden and apocalyptic in tone, which demanded production of H-bombs by the hundreds, and had attached a forty-page history of the nuclear weapons program compiled by the joint committee staff. Realizing that a new administration would soon take office and that he might no longer enjoy his accustomed influence, Borden now churned out more of these papers, or "Chronologies," critical of Oppenheimer and the AEC. By the fall of 1952, John Walker, committee counsel and a Yale Law School friend of Borden's, was putting final touches on an H-bomb chronology that Borden hoped to have on the new president's desk as soon as he was inaugurated. Lewis Strauss, like Borden a fervent believer that the bomb had been dangerously delayed, contributed material from his copious files, and Teller invited committee staffers to spend two weeks with him in California so that he, too, might contribute.[26] Since the document was filled with theoretical material, Walker and Borden sought a consultant. In view of the report's criticisms of the GAC, Oppenheimer, and the AEC for allegedly obstructing the H-bomb program, they dared not turn to a scientist from Los Alamos or the AEC. Instead they chose John Wheeler, who had sided with them in the H-bomb and second-lab controversies and was currently director of a project in Princeton that was doing sensitive computations on the H-bomb. One of the world's great physicists and philosophers, Wheeler was notoriously absentminded, and somewhere on the train ride between Princeton and Washington on January 6, 1953, he managed to misplace the six highly classified pages that Borden had sent to him by registered mail. Those pages have never been recovered.

No document could have been of greater help to a would-be enemy: it revealed the basic concepts of staging, compression, and radiation implosion; the existence of the spark plug; and the length of time it had taken the United States to progress from discovery of radiation implosion to its first test of the concept. The pages also mentioned names for secret devices and codes and summarized a highly classified debate between Bethe and Teller about the American H-bomb program. A panel comprising Bethe, Bradbury, Teller, and von Neumann quickly concluded that, together with information gleaned from the Mike test of November 1, the document lost on that train ride could be the basis for a full-scale Soviet thermonuclear program.[27]

By the time news of Wheeler's gaffe had filtered through the bureaucracy, Dwight Eisenhower was in the Oval Office. Appalled by the episode, and convinced that it had been an "inside job" perpetrated by Soviet intelligence, Ike treated the five AEC commissioners to a display of temper the likes of which they had never before experienced. Painstakingly, Gordon Dean laid the facts before the president. The

AEC was in no way responsible for what had happened. It had not originated the document and had, indeed, never seen it. Wheeler, Dean explained, was far from being an agent of the worldwide Communist conspiracy. He was a distinguished theoretician and much too valuable for the program to lose.

Borden, too, was called to account, and by the committee that employed him. In breathtaking defiance of logic and common sense, he tried to place responsibility on the AEC, against whom his démarche had in fact been directed. He even blamed the commission for his and Walker's decision to send the document, classified top secret, by registered mail rather than by armed courier. Borden's presumptuousness, his conviction of his own rightness, his certainty that he was duty-bound to act as he thought best without even consulting the senators he worked for—all of these foreshadowed the still larger event in which his failed judgment was to lead not to a stand-alone breach of security, serious as it was, but to a national calamity.[28]

CHAPTER FOURTEEN

Strauss Returns

DWIGHT EISENHOWER RAN for president in 1952 to keep the Republican Party from being captured by its isolationists, led by Senator Robert A. Taft of Ohio. Eisenhower had done as much as anyone to save Europe from Hitler, he felt committed to the nations he had helped liberate, and he did not want the United States to retreat from its new responsibilities abroad. Even though he had been commander of NATO, however, he was not up-to-date on nuclear weapons. He was astonished when—nearly three weeks after the fact—Gordon Dean told him about Mike, the test in the Pacific held days before his election. Ike was subdued when he learned about Mike's enormous explosive power and the fact that the island on which it was detonated had disappeared, giving way to a vast underwater crater. Hearing about the world's first thermonuclear test, he worried that mankind would prove unequal to the challenge of managing such awesome power and would stumble into the destruction of all life on earth. And he expressed hope that news of the breakthrough could be kept secret.

Against this inclination toward secrecy, the new president had a countervailing inclination toward openness. Shortly after his inauguration in January 1953, he met with Oppenheimer and other members of the Disarmament Panel and was impressed by what they told him, and especially by their recommendation that his new government share more information with the American people about how nuclear weapons were growing exponentially in power. Indeed, he was so impressed that he devoted one of the first meetings of his National Security Council to the panel's suggestions, especially its plea for greater openness. Almost immediately thereafter, however, Ike made an appointment that was to doom the panel's proposals; he named Lewis Strauss to a new post, that of White House adviser on atomic energy. The president knew that Strauss was a successful banker and an early Taft supporter who had made amends by helping the Eisenhower campaign in New York. What he did not know was that Strauss was entering his new job with an agenda of his own.[1]

That agenda was, in part, to reduce the public stature of Robert Oppenheimer. Within days of acceding to his new office, Strauss made his first move. He had lunch with a man whose role in the events that lay ahead was to be truly extraordinary. Charles J. V. Murphy was a writer for *Fortune* and *Life* magazines and had for years been a close friend of the publisher, Henry R. Luce. But in addition to writing on defense and intelligence issues for Luce's influential publications, Murphy wore another hat, that of lieutenant colonel in the Air Force Reserve. Somehow enjoying special status, he had the run of the Pentagon and served as speechwriter and part-time adviser to outgoing secretary Finletter and his undersecretary, Roswell Gilpatric, Air Force Chief of Staff Hoyt Vandenberg, General Jimmy Doolittle, and others. Even before his luncheon with Strauss on March 12, Murphy had been thinking about a story for *Fortune* on the hydrogen bomb program, in which, he agreed with the Air Force chieftains, there had been "literally criminal negligence."[2] Pursuing his story, he had flown to Independence, Missouri, to call on the newly retired president. To Murphy's amazement, Harry Truman refused to speak to him about his decision to accelerate development of the H-bomb. Undeterred, Murphy flew on to Pasadena to interview Vista scientists Lee DuBridge, Willy Fowler, and Charles Lauritsen. Then he flew to Boston to see MIT physicist Al Hill. All the while he kept working his Air Force sources.[3]

A spellbinding Irishman from Massachusetts, Murphy had accompanied Admiral Richard E. Byrd to the Antarctic and spent two years there, and had ghostwritten Byrd's bestselling books on his Antarctic expeditions. During Murphy's years as a Luce reporter he had acquired champagne tastes—first-class restaurants, the finest private schools for his four children, and a house in Georgetown, in the nation's capital. To sustain these tastes, he juggled ghostwriting tasks along with his magazine assignments, and on a given day that spring of 1953, the afternoon might find him in New York City discussing a writing project over tea at the Waldorf with the Duke of Windsor, while in the evening he might be in Georgetown discussing air strategy with influential columnist Joseph Alsop or downing martinis with some hero of covert action at the CIA. Editors at *Time* could count on a Murphy story to be sweeping and portentous, yet the author of those stories had an odd way of taking a backseat. Though always strapped for cash, Murphy might quixotically refuse payment for a ghostwriting stint, and invariably he made the heroes of his articles larger, nobler characters than they were in real life. Such were his enthusiasms that one didn't lightly enlist him in a cause lest one find oneself mounted on a charger that might slip its harness. Only one man could keep Charlie Murphy in harness, and that was Henry R. Luce.[4] Still, Lewis Strauss tried, and his meeting with Murphy over lunch marked the confluence of two conspiracies to end Oppenheimer's influence, one masterminded by Strauss, the other by officials in the Air Force.

The highest of these officials, Thomas Finletter and Roswell Gilpatric, spent hours with Murphy that spring as they said their good-byes in Washington and moved back to their old law firms in New York. Finletter, whose conversations with Murphy covered the entire range of strategic issues confronting the Air Force, was tight-lipped and contained, not given to expressing what were said to be powerful currents of emotion underneath.[5] Thus it fell to Gilpatric, over drinks, dinners, and late-night conversations at his apartment, to provide the details. Questioned years afterward as to why he had given so much of his time to the project, Gilpatric explained that before his stint in the Air Force, as an attorney for Henry R. Luce, he had vetted Murphy's articles for *Life,* and that he had known the writer socially for years. The interviews dealt with dissension inside the Air Force over what type of aircraft should carry the H-bomb, why Finletter had supported the second lab, and Finletter's suspicion that the so-called delay in building the H-bomb was somehow tied to Oppenheimer's support of Vista. "As this conviction took hold," Gilpatric explained, the secretary "fought for giving Teller a free hand."[6]

Three years before his death in 1996, Gilpatric expanded on the personal aspect. He explained that while Finletter had relied on his assistants, William Burden and Garrison Norton, to handle the scientists, there was one scientist whom he made a point of seeing personally. That was Edward Teller. Gilpatric's office was next to the Air Force secretary's, he was aware that Teller was "in the building all the time," and he knew that Finletter frequently had Teller to lunch. Describing the secretary as "completely sold" on Teller, Gilpatric added that, "carried along by the force of his personality," Finletter had championed Teller with the other services. To Gilpatric it had seemed that his boss was "under a spell," and he did not understand how Finletter, who appeared "unemotional and moved solely by cold logic," could make an exception for this one man. He also noticed that much as Finletter resented Oppenheimer's meddling in Air Force policy, he made no objection when Teller did the same thing.[7]

This complaint, that Oppie was meddling where he did not belong, became the theme of Murphy's article, "The Hidden Struggle for the H-Bomb: The Story of Dr. Oppenheimer's Persistent Campaign to Reverse U.S. Military Strategy," which was published anonymously in the May 1953 issue of *Fortune* magazine. A hysterical, overwritten account of an alleged life-and-death struggle over Air Force policy, "it contained so many errors," one scientist said, "that it wasn't even wrong." It scolded Oppenheimer and the GAC for allegedly obstructing the H-bomb program, blocking Teller at every turn, and campaigning to give up the Air Force advantage in big bombs in favor of smaller, defensive weapons. It accused the GAC scientists of hubris in "trying to settle such grave national issues alone, inasmuch as they do not bear responsibility for the successful execution of war plans." The article's admonitory tone, and the fact that it was unsigned, lent it an ominous, somehow official, air, and made it the shot across the bow of Oppenheimer and the other "liberal" scientists that much of the scientific community had been expecting.

Teller, whom Murphy had not interviewed for the story, was one of its heroes, and another was Strauss, who can be seen from the notes of Murphy's interviews to have been the source of many of its fallacies. In explaining the GAC scientists' alleged opposition to the H-bomb, for example, Strauss told Murphy that they had mistakenly assumed that the Russians would be unable to produce an atomic bomb for decades, if ever (most scientists actually expected that it would be about five years after Hiroshima); that it was he who insisted on convening the GAC after the AEC met in the fall of 1949 (it was Lilienthal, the chairman, who convened the GAC before the AEC met); that Strauss was the only AEC commissioner who favored a crash program (Gordon Dean favored it also); and that, among GAC members, "only Fermi forthrightly supported Strauss" (Fermi, with Rabi, forthrightly dissented).[8]

These and other falsehoods added up to what Joseph Alsop, a sometime friend and sometime foe of Murphy's, called a "rich compost of hints, inaccuracies and special pleadings."[9] But even these paled before the article's most astonishing invention, a cabal called ZORC, supposedly made up of scientists who were accused of promoting a futuristic system to defend North America at the expense of the Strategic Air Command. ZORC, Murphy claimed, got its initials from its members, Jerrold Zacharias, Robert Oppenheimer, I. I. Rabi, and Charles Lauritsen, who were said to be guilty of believing that defense was more moral than offense. Outside the Air Force, where the imaginary ZORC had been the subject of rumors for some time, no one, and certainly not the scientists for whom it was supposed to be named, had ever heard of it. Murphy's source was a shadowy retired lieutenant colonel by the name of Thaddeus F. "Teddy" Walkowicz.[10]

ZORC—later to assume crucial importance in the Oppenheimer security trial—was not Walkowicz's only fabrication. He told Murphy that the Greenhouse George shot in May 1951 had been "an experiment to determine whether you could use a fusion bomb as a match to light a fission weapon," when the opposite was true.[11] Walkowicz, whose misinterpretation of secret intelligence data had led to a false alarm in 1951 that the Russians had beaten the United

States to a working thermonuclear device, was the source with whom Murphy, sometimes accompanied by Jimmy Doolittle, had met more frequently than anyone else while preparing his story.[12]

Who was this character who emerged from the Pentagon from time to time to spread dire and misleading reports? Tall, handsome, and in his forties, Walkowicz, like Murphy, was a mesmerizing story-teller whose presence could electrify a room. But he was a much darker character than Murphy, a heavy drinker and a "black Catholic" whose father had arrived in 1908 on a cattle boat from Poland. A member of the Murphy family described the friendship between the two men as "a dark chapter," while Walkowicz left so much human wreckage behind that it is difficult to find an acquain-tance or family member who will speak of him at all. Brilliant in technical matters, Walkowicz had degrees in aeronautical engineering from Caltech and MIT, had been executive officer of the Scientific Advisory Board of the Air Force, and in the spring of 1953 was a fi-nancial adviser to the Rockefeller brothers. Someone who knew him well described him as "hateful," and for all his success—by the 1980s he was a board member of NASA, Eastern Airlines, and the Civil Aeronautics Board—he remained angry and sometimes violent to-ward those who were close to him. Rabidly anti-Communist, he was so convinced that war between the United States and the Soviet Union was about to break out that throughout his years at 30 Rocke-feller Plaza, he kept a fallout detector on his desk.

After cutting his first draft from 6,600 to 3,400 words, Murphy cleared the article with Strauss, who pronounced it "accurate" as far as his role was concerned. Murphy sent the final draft to Finletter and Gilpatric, went over "last points" with Walkowicz, and twice visited Finletter at his apartment to check last-minute changes. "He had few more corrections to make and was enthusiastic," Murphy com-mented, adding that a final check with Gilpatric produced the same result.[13]

The article created a sensation, especially the ZORC accusation with its dark suggestion that four of the government's top advisers had formed a conspiracy to weaken the United States. And, as it happened, at the very moment of its appearance in May 1953, two longtime friends of Oppenheimer's were summoned before the Senate Internal Security Subcommittee and its chairman, Senator William Jenner of Indiana. One was Philip Morrison, professor of physics at Cornell who had been Oppenheimer's student, and the other was David Hawkins, a philosopher of science who had been Oppenheimer's administrative assistant at Los Alamos. Back in the 1930s, in Berkeley, the two men had been Communist Party activists and devoted supporters of Loyalist Spain. Appearing before a session of the Jenner committee in Boston, each took the "diminished Fifth," meaning that he agreed to answer questions about himself, but not about anyone else.[14] In closed session on the morning of May 7, Morrison was asked—and refused to answer—a series of questions about Oppenheimer. During the lunch break Morrison explained to his attorney that he was not the committee's real target. It was Oppenheimer. The attorney, Arthur Sutherland of the Harvard Law School, did not believe it. "But he's an overseer of Harvard," Sutherland objected, by which he meant that someone so respected could not possibly be under suspicion. But when, in open session that afternoon, lawyers for the committee omitted the questions about Oppie that they had asked in secret session earlier in the day, Sutherland, in Morrison's words, "nearly fainted," and accepted what Morrison, Hawkins, Rabi, and other friends of Oppenheimer's had known for years: that eminent as Oppie was, he was not too eminent to be the object of a political vendetta. Someone in Washington, however, judging the moment not yet ripe, apparently telephoned the committee's lawyers during the lunch break and ordered them to drop the questions about Oppenheimer. The famed scientist was still above public attack.[15]

And what of Oppenheimer? How did he react to the article in *Fortune* and to news that two of his old and close friends, both former members of the Communist Party, had been called before a congressional committee and asked questions designed to incriminate *him*? Oppenheimer had had plenty of warnings. He had lost his place on the GAC and, over cocktails at his house in Princeton in late 1952, had heard from colleagues the rumors that he was about to come under attack by the Air Force.[16] Oppenheimer had long known that his left-wing past made him vulnerable, and with Senator McCarthy ascendant, the danger now was even greater than before. Over the years, Joe Volpe had seen the scientist trying to ingratiate himself with such powerful senators as Hickenlooper and McMahon, seen him flatter them and treat them like high priests of atomic energy, only to make fun of them later behind their backs. "He was a genius in some respects and a child in others," Volpe commented. There were individuals, especially those he regarded as stupid, with whom Oppenheimer could not hold himself back. With them he was capable of unleashing a fusillade of feline, almost involuntary, cruelty which witnesses never forgot and the victims—some of them, anyway—never forgave. Volpe saw Oppie make mincemeat of Pitzer at a meeting of the GAC, watched him ridicule Strauss at the Halloween meeting of 1949, and even saw him make withering remarks to Commissioner Henry D. Smyth, with whom Oppenheimer was mostly in agreement but whom he did not regard as a first-rate physicist.

Was he aware of the effect his sharp tongue had on others? "Yes and no," Volpe thought. "Oppie was his own worst enemy. If he did not like someone, he was not content just to win the argument. His propensity for destroying an adversary led to his downfall." Volpe, a vigorous, direct, and wise counselor, called him on it repeatedly and told him to cool it. Oppenheimer would thank him, but somehow that didn't stop him next time.[17]

The decisive occasion with Lewis Strauss was a congressional committee hearing in May 1949 which had been called to discuss the shipment of iron isotopes abroad, a step Strauss bitterly opposed because he feared that the isotopes might be put to military use. Strauss was seated in the hearing room with his fellow AEC commissioners, Oppenheimer with Volpe at the witness table. "No one," Oppie started out, "can force me to say that you cannot use these isotopes for atomic energy. You can use a shovel for atomic energy. In fact, you do. You can use a bottle of beer for atomic energy. In fact, you do. . . . My own rating of the importance of isotopes in this broad sense is that they are far less important than electronic devices but far more important than, let us say, vitamins, somewhere in between." As laughter punctuated these remarks, Volpe stole a look at Strauss. His eyes had become narrow slits; the muscles in his jaws were working; his face had reddened and taken on a menacing look.

Afterward Oppenheimer turned to Volpe like a triumphant schoolboy. "Well, Joe, how did I do?"

"Too well, Robert, much too well."

"Somewhere along the way," Volpe said later, "he had learned to go for the jugular."[18]

What made this particular put-down different from the others was the fact that it happened in public. Strauss did not enjoy being mocked in closed meetings before Fermi and Rabi and Conant, of whose intellectual stature he was in awe, but he truly hated having the same thing happen within camera range, hated reading about it the next day in the *Washington Post*.[19]

The one response Oppenheimer did not evoke was indifference. According to Volpe, there were those who disliked him, those who disliked him a lot, and those who disliked him to the point of enmity. But those who liked him, loved him. Louis and Eleanor Hempelmann were among those who loved him without reservation. Dr. Hempelmann was a broad-shouldered, handsome man with deep-set eyes who had been trained in the unusual—for the times—subject of radiology at Washington University in St. Louis and the Brigham Hospital in Boston. He and Oppenheimer first met during the 1930s in Berkeley, where he was working with John Lawrence, brother of Ernest, on radiation treatment for cancer. They saw each other again in Chicago in 1942, when Oppenheimer asked Hempelmann to come to Los Alamos. The two couples became close friends, and Eleanor Hempelmann, a member of the Pulitzer family of Maine and St. Louis, became close to Kitty. The Hempelmanns were still at Los Alamos when Kitty and Robert returned to New Mexico for a visit in 1946. Dining with the Oppenheimers at the La Fonda Hotel in Santa Fe, the Hempelmanns noticed that Robert turned to the walls from time to time and made announcements for the benefit of the microphones he assumed were implanted there. Here, they reflected, was Robert Oppenheimer, hero to the entire nation, still under surveillance, as he had been throughout the war. Another time they were visiting the Oppenheimers at their ranch in the Pecos Mountains and the two couples spent hours on hands and knees, scouring the earth for four-leaf clovers. But when Louis Hempelmann came upon a rare five-leaf clover, Kitty was upset: the five-leaf clover was thought to bring bad luck, rather than the good luck she and Robert knew they would be needing.[20]

CHAPTER FIFTEEN

Two Wild Horses

THE DISARMAMENT PANEL, led by Oppenheimer, had summed up the Truman administration's accomplishments in arms control and made further suggestions for the incoming Republican administration. Paradoxically, although the panel had recommended far greater openness in nuclear matters, the report itself was held in tightest secrecy. In hopes of getting its suggestions before movers and shakers of the Eastern Establishment, Oppenheimer in February 1953 presented an unclassified version in a speech before the Council on Foreign Relations in New York. He had been encouraged by the new president's favorable response to the panel's suggestion of greater candor. In Paris a year or so before, Oppenheimer had heard Eisenhower—then NATO commander in Europe—complain about excessive secrecy. Therefore he was not surprised that of all the panel's suggestions, it was the candor proposal that the new president responded to first. If the government were to share more weapons information with the public, Oppenheimer believed, other priorities—the need for better defensive measures at home, more exchange of information with our allies, reconsideration of the mindless buildup of redundant weapons—would sooner or later fall into place. As he told an interviewer, "the only way to bring this candor into being is through the President. He is the only person who has the right to do it, the only person who has the authority to transcend the racket of noise, mostly consisting of lies, that has been built up around this subject. Only the President can make this known. All I can do is make it easier for the President to do it."[1]

On May 28, 1953, Oppenheimer visited the Oval Office and

handed the president a draft of an article he had written for *Foreign Affairs*, the influential journal of the Council on Foreign Relations, based on his speech the winter before. Eisenhower gave the article to his national security adviser, Robert Cutler, and it was published with Cutler's approval in July. Oppenheimer had written that because of secrecy, he had to tell about the arms race "without communicating anything. I must reveal its nature without revealing anything." He pointed out that merely staying ahead of the Russians did nothing for our security because "our twenty-thousandth bomb will not in any deep strategic sense offset their two thousandth." To be ready if an opportunity to negotiate with the Russians should present itself, the leaders of the two sides needed to get past the rigidity imposed by the "terrifyingly rapid accumulation of nuclear weapons." He compared the situation of Russia and the United States to that of "two scorpions in a bottle, each capable of killing the other, but only at the risk of his own life."[2]

Lewis Strauss, apostle of secrecy, did not stand idly by while Oppie was scoring points with the president. Before the scientist's visit to the Oval Office at the end of May, Strauss warned the president that he had misgivings about Oppenheimer's security record. And when the president invited Strauss to add the AEC chairmanship to his portfolio as White House adviser, Strauss is said to have told the president, before accepting, that he "could not do the job" if Oppenheimer had anything to do with the nuclear weapons program. Meanwhile, intent on keeping the threads in his own hands, Strauss helped head off a threatened investigation of Oppenheimer by Senator McCarthy, warning Senate majority leader Robert Taft that "some of the so-called evidence will not stand up. The McCarthy committee is not the place for such an investigation and the present is not the time."[3]

On June 30 Gordon Dean completed his three-year term as AEC chairman. For months after Strauss's appointment as White House atomic energy adviser, the two men had been working in tandem. Dean disliked and distrusted Strauss but had chosen to finish out his term partly because the new president asked him to, and partly

because he had been appalled by the incoming administration's ignorance about nuclear weapons. Oppenheimer, who no longer held an
advisory position and—as the unsigned *Fortune* article had made
clear—was facing brisk headwinds from the Air Force, now asked
Dean to extend his AEC consultancy. From that perch, he would still
have access to classified information and still be able to influence policy. Dean agreed. Oppenheimer's Q clearance was good for another
year, until June 30, 1954.[4]

Now that he would be wearing both hats, that of White House
atomic energy adviser and chairman of the AEC, Strauss was again in
touch with Charlie Murphy, this time about a second article for *Fortune.* The new article reported that Oppie's advocacy of greater openness had placed him "once more squarely in conflict" with Strauss, "a
man of rare sagacity, enlightenment and courage." Before the draft
went to press, however, Strauss asked Murphy to "omit the references
to me, even though they are very flattering. . . . For the next month
or two, until I am firmly in the saddle, I would like to remain very
much in the background." Accordingly, the piece appeared without
the praise of Strauss, but with a small photograph of him and a caption saying that he wanted to "keep a tight lid" on atomic secrets. The
article was mainly an attack on Oppenheimer, accusing him of a cardinal sin, that of advocating publication of—holy of holies—the
number of weapons in our atomic stockpile. It also criticized the
president—because he favored relaxation of nuclear secrecy. Murphy
met with Strauss four times while he was preparing the article, which
appeared, not anonymously like the one in May, but under Murphy's
byline, in the August issue of *Fortune.*[5]

Murphy rarely pulled his punches. If a man is a traitor, then, to
his way of thinking, get rid of him! Strauss's desire to stay in the
background disappointed Murphy, who decided that the new chairman was a trimmer. But Murphy knew only part of the story. Strauss
had another steed in his stable, and that was the obsessive Bill Borden. At the end of April 1953, badly compromised by his handling of
the Wheeler affair and a Democrat who stood to lose his job with the
new Republican Congress, Borden carried a mysterious "paper" to

Strauss and spoke with him briefly. The content of his "paper" is not known but was probably a compilation of Borden's suspicions about Oppenheimer. The May issue of *Fortune,* containing Murphy's anonymous attack on the scientist, was about to appear on the newsstands. Strauss telephoned several opponents of Oppenheimer at this time, probably to warn them that a public attack was imminent, and he may have used Borden's paper as backup.[6]

Borden spent May struggling with the question that had nagged at him for so long. He asked to see Oppenheimer's AEC security file one more time, and a day or so before he left Washington, he handed his successor at the joint committee a fifteen-page document. The document's 189 questions about Oppenheimer's record were mainly a brief against the FBI for sloppy investigatory procedures. But Borden also appended a separate, handwritten document in which he painstakingly weighed the scientist's actions: had Oppenheimer been acting "under a directive from his own conscience or a directive from the Soviet Union?" Borden considered either explanation consistent with the evidence, but concluded that "Dr. Oppenheimer's influence upon atomic policy has been more harmful to the United States than even would have been the betrayal of all the military-atomic information in his possession from 1940 to the present."[7]

Borden then repaired for the summer to his family's place in Chaumont, New York, near Lake Ontario, where he spent six weeks alone, without his wife and sons, ruminating over the unfinished business he had left behind. He spoke to Lewis Strauss by telephone during the summer, and in the fall he moved his family to Pittsburgh. But before starting on his new job, at the Westinghouse Electric Corporation, Borden felt that he would not have done his duty until he had reached a verdict on Oppenheimer. This he did, and in November he sent his verdict to the FBI.

The verdict was that "more probably than not," Oppenheimer had for years been acting as an espionage agent of the Soviet Union. Borden sent the letter to J. Edgar Hoover, rather than the head of the AEC or some other government agency, because he thought that the

FBI had grown lax and he hoped it would reopen its investigation of Oppenheimer.[8]

What sort of man was William Borden and what led him to his conclusion? Did Strauss know about his letter in advance? Had Strauss put him up to it? One August afternoon two years earlier, Borden and Strauss had had a lengthy conversation about Oppenheimer. Since then, they had remained in contact. It seems likely that during the early fall of 1951, the two men had agreed on some kind of joint action with regard to Oppenheimer, but, faced by a long absence from Washington and an apparent cooling in Strauss's regard, Borden had gone off on his own and taken a step the older man did not anticipate. But Borden's colleagues in the schoolboyish, rather Yale atmosphere at the joint congressional committee disagreed with this reading of Borden's actions. They did not think that Strauss was implicated in what Borden had done. It was not Borden's nature to conspire, they insisted, "and besides, he didn't like Strauss." He had even nicknamed Strauss "Luigi" because he considered him Machiavellian. And he still blamed Strauss for inspiring the 1949 Hickenlooper hearings, for which Borden had had to write the final, embarrassing report saying that there was nothing to the charges of "terrible mismanagement" by Lilienthal.[9]

Borden was a child of Washington. He was born there in 1920 and attended the select St. Albans School and then Yale. On his graduation in 1942 he enlisted in the Army and became a bomber pilot over Europe. One night near the end of the war, flying his B-24 home after a mission to Holland, he saw a German V-2 rocket whizzing past him on its way to London. From then on Borden was haunted by the horror that could be wrought by marrying rocket technology to that of the atomic bomb. At twenty-six, he wrote a book called *There Will Be No Time,* arguing for world federation. After graduating from Yale Law School, he was singled out by Brien McMahon, father of the Atomic Energy Act and a neighbor of his parents, to work for the JCAE.

Borden was from a protected, orderly world. The mother who left her imprint on him was known for her upright character; his father was a Washington surgeon famous for having barred from his operating room an intern who had arrived only five seconds late to assist him. There was military tradition in the family, and an uncle Liscum (Borden's middle name) who had won the Congressional Medal of Honor. Lacking much experience of everyday life, young Liscum, or "Lic," as he was known to his friends, believed things happen in a tidy, logical way. Upon becoming staff director of the joint congressional committee, he had been shaken to discover how few atomic weapons the U.S. stockpile contained—he was not told the precise numbers but was able to make a rough guess—and right away set to work to expand it. His writing had a kind of hysteria to it: he wrote lines for Senator McMahon like "total power in the hands of total evil equals total destruction" that illustrate the absolute cast of his thought. If x or y was obvious to him, he wondered, why wasn't it obvious to a genius like Oppenheimer? From there it wasn't far to the question, How can someone as clever as Robert Oppenheimer take the positions he does if he is not an agent? Extrapolating from his own character, Borden knew that *he* could not have taken those stands unless he had been an agent.[10]

Borden was a liberal Democrat. He had a strain of idealism and was an active board member of the Experiment in International Living, which sought to improve international understanding by sponsoring exchanges between European and American students. He loathed Joe McCarthy and agreed with Oppenheimer's proposal for greater candor. Far from being obsessed by security, he had been known to look the other way when something was not as it ought to have been in the dossier of a loyal congressional committee staff member. He was decent and courteous and might enjoy three or four scotches during an evening's conversation, but he would not countenance an obscenity or a dirty joke. Everyone who knew him uses the word "integrity," as in "he had more integrity than anyone I ever met." He was an exceptionally conscientious man, driven by what he saw as his duty. But he was an intense workaholic, and one colleague said, "I think that destroys judgment." Those who worked with Borden liked and respected him. Said one, "The most negative thing I thought was that he might have flown a few too many missions during the war."[11]

Why did this man who ordinarily showed little interest in people, and no interest whatever in sizing them up, focus on Oppenheimer—and reach the conclusion he did? Frank Cotter thought it was Teller, who saw Borden every time he came to Washington. They were not close personally—Borden was not close to anyone—but their views on policy were very close indeed. "An impressionable man like Bill, hearing someone of Teller's stature tell him that Oppenheimer was sabotaging the program, and always with the innuendo that he was a Communist, that would have done it."[12]

When Borden's colleagues at the joint committee read his letter to the FBI that fall, they were horrified. John Walker, J. K. "Ken" Mansfield, Frank Cotter, Corbin Allardice—none of them agreed with him about Oppenheimer. They thought his isolation that summer had contributed to his taking such a drastic step and that talking things over with them every day, as he had done at the committee, would have tempered his judgment. They noticed that he missed Senator McMahon, missed the give-and-take, missed writing overheated letters for the boss that the boss sometimes did not send. McMahon's death in the summer of 1952, they believed, left him feeling that it was up to him to carry the burden of national security alone and removed a restraint from his actions. They thought it was tragic, that it was bound to destroy both Oppie and Borden, and that Borden would carry the weight of it with him to his grave. And they were certain that he and Strauss had not been in collusion.

But it was not so simple. Although not nearly as devious as Strauss, Borden, too, could be manipulative, his handling of the JCAE's thermonuclear history of January 1, 1953, the so-called Walker-Borden report, being a case in point. Borden had told Carl Durham, the inexperienced interim chairman of the joint congressional committee, that the report was a "compilation," not the one-sided attack on Oppenheimer and the AEC that it actually was. He had tried to withhold it from the AEC, he had delayed several hours before informing the FBI that Wheeler had lost an extract, and he had given misleading answers to members of the JCAE at their hearing on the episode. He had even used threats against Gordon Dean in an effort to force the AEC to assume responsibility. Similarly, Borden's correspondence shows him trying to manipulate Teller, and his exchanges with Strauss are so conspiratorial in tone as to suggest shared purposes that they did not care to put in writing.[13]

Borden had all along funneled information to Strauss, who in turn assumed that he could count on the younger man when the time was right. But what Strauss seems to have had in mind was some action that would tarnish Oppenheimer's public image and reduce his influence, not a dramatic move that might force the president to act.[14]

Lewis Strauss had two wild horses in his stable, and one of them threw off his harness. Only, it wasn't the spirited Charlie Murphy who got out of hand, but quiet, intense Bill Borden.

CHAPTER SIXTEEN

The Blank Wall

ON SATURDAY EVENING, November 7, 1953, Bill Borden, anxious to rid himself of the burden that was weighing on him, drove to the main post office in downtown Pittsburgh and mailed a copy of his three-and-a-half-page letter to Lou Nichols, an FBI acquaintance, to be passed along to J. Edgar Hoover. He sent the letter, which contained highly sensitive material, by ordinary mail and with a covering note in cramped handwriting, and with errors that might suggest that the author had had two or three drinks, or was under severe stress.[1]

Borden's letter stated that Oppenheimer, as member or chairman of more than thirty-five advisory groups, had shaped more government policies and been in a position to compromise more secrets than any other individual in the country. It gave twenty-one reasons why it was Borden's "exhaustively considered opinion, based on years of study, that more probably than not J. Robert Oppenheimer is an agent of the Soviet Union."

When Hoover received Borden's letter, he treated it like a grenade that might go off at any moment. He had been living with the Oppenheimer problem for years, saw nothing new in the letter, and was only too aware of Oppenheimer's formidable standing in the scientific community. Six months earlier, Hoover had headed off Joe McCarthy when the rambunctious senator—primed by Murphy's anonymous blast in *Fortune*—had come to see him about investigating Oppenheimer. Hoover also agreed with Strauss that there should be no public move against Oppie without the most careful preparation. The thing Hoover cared most about was not the arrogant physicist but protecting the FBI's sources. His FBI had kept Oppenheimer

under surveillance for years. Ever since 1946 the bureau had, inter-
mittently, opened Oppenheimer's mail, tapped his telephones, and
followed his movements, and it was of utmost importance to Hoover
that these methods—most of which were illegal—not be compromised. Mindful of the adage that if you strike at a king, you must kill
him, he was convinced that the destruction of this particular king
could not be accomplished without the use of every bit of ammuni-
tion in the FBI's arsenal. The best way to handle Borden's charges,
Hoover believed, was for the Defense Department—to which, along
with the White House and the Justice Department, he had sent Borden's letter—to abolish the only official board on which Oppenheimer was currently serving and thereby, in effect, cancel his
clearance without the hazards of a public hearing. And there were
other considerations. For one, Hoover seems to have been wary of
Strauss, lest the AEC chairman in his zeal give away FBI methods,
particularly its use of wiretaps. And there was the uncomfortable fact,
which Hoover had until now forgotten, that back in 1947, with a single caveat, he had signed off on Oppenheimer's Q clearance.[2]

Responding to a hurry-up call from the White House on the after-
noon of December 2, Lewis Strauss found the president, his adviser
Robert Cutler, and one or two others in an anxious huddle in the Oval
Office. Borden's bombshell had landed in a highly charged situation:
Attorney General Herbert Brownell had accused former president
Truman just a few weeks earlier of having knowingly protected a
Communist spy in the Treasury, and McCarthy had followed up with
an attack on Truman that was seen in the White House as an attack
on the new president as well. Resisting the pleas of some in his entourage that he take on McCarthy openly, Eisenhower had that very
morning told an aide that he would "not get in the gutter" with the
Wisconsin senator. But he could not afford to open himself to the
charge that he, like Truman, had knowingly protected a security risk.
Strauss helped Ike reach his decision that afternoon, and the next
morning Eisenhower told his national security advisers that he had decided to lower a "blank wall" between Oppenheimer and the nation's
secrets. How it was to be done was left to them to decide.[3]

Robert Oppenheimer was in Europe, delivering the BBC's prestigious Reith Lectures, and was scheduled to return in mid-December. It was decided that he must be kept in the dark lest—nightmare of Hoover and Strauss—he slip off to Russia as the suspected Soviet spies Guy Burgess and Donald Maclean had done three years before. But defense installations and AEC laboratories were notified right away that Oppie's clearance had been suspended. At the Pentagon, Rear Admiral William S. "Deak" Parsons, head of ordnance at Los Alamos during the war and the closest of friends with Robert and Kitty Oppenheimer, heard about the "blank wall" order on December 4 and made up his mind to protest to the secretary of the Navy. But he was stricken with chest pains in the night and died at Bethesda Naval Hospital the next day. In the minds of Martha Parsons and their daughters there was never any doubt that Deak's heart attack had been precipitated by the news about their friend.[4]

For the next couple of weeks Hoover, Strauss, AEC general manager Ken Nichols, Commissioners Murray and Smyth, Assistant Secretary of Defense Donald Quarles, Attorney General Brownell, and National Security Adviser Robert Cutler all tried to devise a way to rescind Oppie's clearance without provoking a public outcry. Murray wanted to cancel Oppenheimer's AEC consultancy, while Smyth favored a secret hearing that he hoped would clear the scientist. Nichols wanted to hand the whole thing over to McCarthy, and Quarles was so concerned about feeling in the scientific community that he wanted to do nothing about the charges and let the government go on living with the risk. Cutler, a Harvard overseer along with Oppenheimer, preferred to inform the scientist in secret that his clearance was being revoked and ask him, for the nation's sake, not to make a fight of it. Everyone understood that if challenged in public, Oppenheimer would have to defend himself. Finally it was decided that on Oppie's return from Europe, Strauss would present him with a letter of charges and leave it to him whether to give up his clearance quietly or insist on a hearing.[5]

Lewis Strauss later falsified the events of those days in an effort to minimize his own role—and for many years he got away with it.[6] In his book *Men and Decisions,* published in 1963, Strauss claimed that the president summoned him "in the chill of late afternoon" on Thursday, December 3, to help him decide what to do. After meeting with his national security advisers, Strauss said, the president informed them that he was lowering a "blank wall" between Oppenheimer and all classified information. But from Strauss's own daybooks and from notes by his assistant Bryan LaPlante, it is clear that Strauss first saw the president "in the chill of late afternoon" on December 2, a day earlier than he wrote in his book, and for the second time at a National Security Council meeting the next morning, at the close of which Eisenhower announced his "blank wall" directive. Why, nine years after the event, did Strauss choose to make it appear that he had seen the president only once, and only after Eisenhower had already decided to lower the "blank wall"? Because it was he who suggested the "blank wall," and he did so on December 2.[7]

There is more. On December 1, Strauss spent an hour and a half with Edward Teller. Two days later, returning from his second visit to the White House, Strauss found Teller awaiting him again, this time for a luncheon appointment. Teller returned to California later in the day. That evening Strauss sent him a telegram: "Take no action on personal matter we discussed. Nichols will call you." And the next day Ken Nichols telephoned to inform Teller of changes in his "previous instructions by Mr. Strauss on Thursday, December 3, 1953." In an interview many years later, Teller could not recall what the "personal matter" was.[8]

In later years Teller described the AEC chairman as extremely upset on his return from the White House that day. "I just had a terrible piece of news," he quoted Strauss as saying. "The President insists that we open the case" of Oppenheimer's clearance. Strauss, Teller added, did not want this known, because he hoped to settle it without a public hearing. He cited Strauss's secretary, Virginia Walker, as saying that Strauss was "horrified and deeply disturbed" by the president's order. Was Strauss actually "appalled," as John MacKenzie, his personal assistant, described him, or was he secretly gratified to be going head-to-head with his nemesis at last? Someone who knew him very well, and from a position of equality, was William Golden, the self-made financier who had from time to time helped Strauss at the AEC as an unpaid, highly respected adviser. Golden thought that Strauss and Oppenheimer were in some ways alike. Each of them was courtly in manner, each had the capacity to mask his feelings, and each was, above everything, "inscrutable." Golden believed that Strauss, out of deep partisanship as a Republican and deep animosity toward Oppenheimer, had been capable of urging the "blank wall" on Eisenhower, and then coming back to his office and feigning dismay. Victor Mitchell, who worked for Strauss for three years, and his wife, Donna, who also knew the chairman well, agreed.[9]

So inscrutable was Strauss that it is still impossible to say whether he was horrified when he read Borden's letter or whether Frank Cotter was closer to the truth when he said that "Borden accidentally and without design gave Lewis Strauss the thing he wanted most in life."[10]

CHAPTER SEVENTEEN

Hoover

HAROLD GREEN, a thirty-two-year-old lawyer in the AEC's Security Division, was not surprised that someone had pulled the trigger. He had expected something like this ever since he had learned from Bryan LaPlante, one of Strauss's closest aides, that Strauss had made an unsolicited promise to Hoover that he would purge four officials at the AEC, including Oppenheimer, whom he knew to be anathema to the FBI chief. Neither Green nor others in his division considered Oppenheimer a security risk despite his appalling dossier. They simply hoped to muddle through until expiration of his clearance without another close call such as they, and Gordon Dean, had experienced with the Weinberg case.[1]

A Chicago native and graduate of the University of Chicago Law School, Green had had extensive experience evaluating security files during his three years at the AEC. He was nonetheless surprised when William Mitchell, general counsel of the AEC, called him in on the afternoon of Friday, December 11, and showed him a copy of Borden's letter. Mitchell pointed to an enormous stack of papers—the AEC's investigative files on Oppenheimer—and told Green to draft a statement of charges for the commissioners to consider on Monday morning. He instructed Green not to include Oppenheimer's opposition to the H-bomb: the commissioners did not want the scientist placed on trial for his opinions.[2]

If Green had been surprised by Mitchell's telling him to draft the charges, he was still more surprised by the behavior of Ken Nichols that weekend at AEC headquarters. Nichols, who was to be the signatory to the charges, called Green again and again that weekend and summoned him twice to his office. He told Green how difficult Oppenheimer had been to work with during the war, when he was General Groves's deputy. He described Oppenheimer's arrogance and indifference to security, and recounted the bad advice he had given the government. His attitude toward Oppie was anything but dispassionate. "Be sure you get *that* in," he would say. "I've got the son of a bitch now. I don't want him wriggling off the hook." Green thought it peculiar that a man who would probably be a judge in the case should be doing double duty behind the scenes as prosecutor.[3]

Green finished early on Sunday and decided to try his hand at adding charges about the H-bomb, doing it in such a way as to test Oppenheimer's truthfulness, rather than the validity of his advice. To the counts he had already written, Green added seven more, based on Teller's interviews with the FBI in May 1952. When Mitchell came in later on Sunday, he approved. "Let's try it on Nichols tomorrow."[4]

On Monday, Green got another surprise: a call from one of Hoover's closest assistants inviting him to call on the FBI if he needed help. Green was astonished, since in the hundreds of security cases he had handled, the FBI had until then met his requests for assistance with hostility and had helped out grudgingly if at all.[5]

Strauss, meanwhile, had outraged three of his fellow commissioners. In a hurry to accompany the president to a conference in Bermuda on December 4, he had told the two who happened to be in town about Borden's letter—but had said nothing about the president's "blank wall" directive. Nor had he told his supposedly coequal colleagues that he had for months been meeting with C. D. Jackson, the president's assistant for psychological warfare, to draw up a plan for international atomic cooperation. Under the plan, which Strauss had embraced in hopes of subverting Oppenheimer's call for candor, the United States and the USSR would contribute a pool of fissionable material to the United Nations to be devoted to peaceful purposes. The first Strauss's colleagues knew of the proposal, which had been christened "Atoms for Peace," was on December 8, when the president, on his way home from Bermuda, unveiled it at the UN General Assembly to enthusiastic applause. At dinner that night Gerard

Smith, assistant to Commissioner Murray, heard Harry Smyth describe the plan as "a thoroughly dishonest proposal" and express anxiety over the danger that it would spread nuclear know-how to
nations that did not have it. It was to avert such contingencies that
the commission had traditionally had a scientist member. While
Smyth, the current scientific member, worried that Atoms for Peace
would put tightly guarded secrets at risk, the security-obsessed
Strauss, whether ignorant of reactor physics or simply elated at having his plan adopted and Oppenheimer's proposal foiled, appeared
serenely unconcerned with the danger.[6]

Smyth and Zuckert were so unhappy with the chairman's decisions
and his abuse of commission prerogatives that by the time Strauss
called his colleagues together on December 10, they were thinking seriously about resigning. Once again Strauss failed to level with them,
neglecting to inform them that he had spoken with the president
about the Oppenheimer matter and had himself had a role in the
"blank wall" order. Now it was too late: Hoover had already sent Borden's letter and a sixty-nine-page summary of Oppenheimer's FBI file
to several government agencies, the president's "blank wall" directive
had been circulated, and the Defense Department had notified its installations at home and abroad that Oppenheimer's clearance had been
suspended. The only thing left for the commissioners to decide was
how—not whether—to implement the president's order.[7]

Commissioners Murray, Smyth, and Zuckert remained unhappy,
and with good reason. The H-bomb charges drafted by Green were
neither discussed at a meeting of the commissioners nor formally
approved by them. Twice, Harry Smyth objected to inclusion of the
H-bomb count in the letter that General Manager Nichols was to present to Oppenheimer, and he gave up only after being told—falsely—
that his colleagues were going along. Informed of AEC decisions only
after they had been taken, misinformed and even lied to, the restive
commissioners found at every step that their options—above all, the
option of keeping the matter quiet—had been foreclosed.[8]

In the middle of December the president summoned Hoover,
Brownell, Strauss, and two other high officials. They decided that

Strauss would tell Oppenheimer that his security status had been challenged and that the president had suggested that the AEC investigate the charges. The scientist would be given a choice between resigning and asking for a hearing. If he chose the latter, his case would be heard by an ad hoc AEC committee with provision for review.[9]

That meeting was a turning point for Hoover. Returning to the bureau that day, he informed his underlings that "this is a most important and urgent project" on which they were to give the AEC "the fullest cooperation," provided only that the bureau's confidential techniques—especially its bugging and wiretapping practices—be protected. For years, Hoover had been watching, gathering evidence, and waiting for his opening. Now at last he committed the FBI to an all-out effort to banish Oppenheimer from the councils of government. His decision was, in part, the culmination of a protracted courtship between him and Strauss. For years, in and out of public office, Strauss had volunteered information to the FBI; the bureau, on the other hand, had, at his request, checked the security status of faculty appointees to the Institute for Advanced Study at Princeton and the Brookings Institution in Washington, of which he was a trustee. FBI agents had greeted him at Orly Airport when he went to France and met his mother-in-law at Idlewild (now John F. Kennedy International) Airport when she returned from abroad. He had promised the FBI chief that he would get rid of Oppenheimer, and Hoover at last was persuaded that the effort was likely to succeed.[10]

Ex–FBI man Frank Cotter explained the director's change of heart. From Gook Taylor, Cotter's friend who monitored the Soviet intelligence cables, and from others, Hoover knew perfectly well that Oppenheimer was not an espionage agent. His reason for hating him could even have been mere conviction that Oppenheimer was an adulterer. But "Hoover was a master politician. Eisenhower was going a certain way, so he did, too."[11]

Kitty and Robert Oppenheimer spent their final evening in Europe with Haakon and Carol Chevalier at the Chevaliers' apartment in the Montmartre section of Paris. Haakon, a professor of Romance

languages, and Robert had been the closest of friends in Berkeley before the war, sharing a love of French poetry and French culture generally. Chevalier, a Communist Party member, and Oppenheimer,
who during the late 1930s had probably occupied a niche just outside
the Party, had also shared a great deal politically in their sympathy for
Republican Spain and for the Soviet experiment in Russia. As the evening of December 7, 1953, drew to a close, it struck Chevalier that his
old friend seemed apprehensive, as if he felt that trouble might await
him in America.[12]

A couple of weeks later, Oppenheimer was facing Lewis Strauss in
Strauss's office, the one man stocky, balding, with heavy spectacles
shielding a partially blind right eye, the other man angular, rumpled,
with large, almost transparent blue eyes. Strauss had gotten where he
was on his own, from itinerant shoe salesman in Virginia, to protégé
of Herbert Hoover in European war relief in 1919, to fabulously successful investment banker who married the boss's daughter. Strauss
was controlling and conniving: a man who would walk into a social
gathering, pick his moment, and dominate the room by telling stories. What one man had by effort, the other had by birthright, as son
of a German Jewish immigrant who had made a fortune selling suit
linings and real estate and left his sons an inheritance of Cézannes
and Van Goghs. A natural of such magnetism that he could hold a
roomful in his hand just by being there. Agnostic bohemian versus
dutiful elder of an Orthodox Jewish congregation. One might almost
have taken it for an even match.[13]

The two men sat there, and one of them told the other that he was
in trouble. A former government official had raised questions about
Oppenheimer's right to a security clearance, Strauss explained, and
the president had ordered an inquiry. Oppenheimer looked over the
letter of charges and asked whether anyone with such a record had
ever been cleared in a formal hearing. The two discussed the possibility of Oppenheimer's resigning his contract, thereby obviating the
need for a hearing. Strauss tried not to make a recommendation, but
it was clear to the other man that this was the course Strauss wanted
him to take. Oppenheimer asked for a few days to think it over:

Strauss pressed for an answer right away. He would be at home after eight that evening, and Oppenheimer could reach him there. The scientist was not even allowed to take the letter of charges with him. He could have a copy only if and when he decided to go through with a hearing.[14]

As he was leaving, Oppenheimer said that he was going to see his friend and attorney, Herbert Marks, and Strauss loaned him his official Cadillac. But the scientist changed his mind and at the last minute went instead to the office of Joe Volpe, where they were joined by Marks. Unknown to the three of them, the FBI had anticipated Oppenheimer's moves and placed a tap in the offices of both Volpe and Marks, with the result that Oppie's very first conversation with his attorneys was recorded. The three men later proceeded to Marks's house in Georgetown, where Anne Marks cooked steaks and the four of them reviewed Robert's options.[15]

The next day Oppenheimer sent Strauss his answer.

> Yesterday, when you asked to see me, you told me for the first time that my clearance by the Atomic Energy Commission was about to be suspended. You put to me as a possibly desirable alternative that I request termination of my contract as a consultant. . . . I have thought most earnestly of the alternative suggested. Under the circumstances this course of action would mean that I accept and concur in the view that I am not fit to serve this government that I have now served for some twelve years. This I cannot do. If I were thus unworthy I could hardly have served our country as I have tried, or been the Director of our Institute in Princeton, or have spoken, as on more than one occasion I have found myself speaking, in the name of our science and our country.

About this time Hoover, at Strauss's request, asked the attorney general for permission to "install a technical surveillance" on Oppenheimer's telephone at home or at "any address to which he may later move." Authorization arrived the next day. Although Attorney General

Brownell told the author many years later that he had not been "directly involved" in the Oppenheimer affair, this decision was one of many he signed off on.[16]

Oppenheimer saw Strauss a second time to accept the letter of charges. It was Strauss's impression that the scientist preferred to "terminate his contract quietly," but that his attorneys, seeing "a big fee in it for themselves," had advised otherwise. (In fact, they represented him free of charge.)[17]

Among the humiliations visited upon the Oppenheimers was a visit to their house on Christmas Eve. Their caller was Roy Snapp of the AEC, who presented them with a letter ordering Robert to hand over any official documents remaining in his possession. Oppenheimer and Snapp had had many dealings when Oppie was riding high, and the occasion can only have been excruciating for them both. Eleanor Hempelmann, on hand with her husband for the holiday, later described Oppenheimer's "consummately polite, even courtly" behavior toward the visitor. "He put on a wonderful performance."[18]

Oppenheimer suffered a disappointment after he visited the leading law firm in Washington to ask the highly regarded attorney John Lord O'Brian to represent him. O'Brian was anxious to do so but, after consulting his colleagues, felt obliged to decline. The firm's founding partner, Edward Burling, had an affectionate relationship with a younger member, Donald Hiss, who, like his brother, Alger, was the subject of espionage rumors. Because of its refusal to fire Donald Hiss, the firm had lost four or five major clients, and in the atmosphere of the day, the partners did not want O'Brian to take the case. O'Brian's stature, talent, and devotion were such that his inability to handle the case came as a severe blow to Oppenheimer.[19]

About this time FBI special agent Kenneth Commons in Newark telephoned Washington headquarters to report that the "technical surveillance" reflected the scientist's search for an attorney. Because of the danger that the wiretaps might disclose an attorney-client relationship, the agent wondered whether to continue. He was told to do so.[20]

From now on, the FBI's wiretap reports were the AEC's main source of information about Oppenheimer's search for an attorney, his attorneys' conversations with him and one another, and other defense preparations. To obscure the fact that the information had been obtained illegally, most of the reports were written in the form of letters from Hoover to Strauss that started out "according to a reliable confidential informant," code for wiretapped information. In addition to reports obtained from telephone taps, others were derived from physical surveillance. On receipt of one report, Strauss wrote to Hoover: "This is to acknowledge and thank you for your letter of February 1, 1954, concerned with the reported discussion between Dr. Oppenheimer, his counsel, and other individuals." But Strauss tired of penning acknowledgments, and a few days later wrote a letter with the notation "Strauss asked if it were necessary for him to acknowledge each letter from bureau. He was advised not necessary since letters were delivered personally to him." The person who carried the FBI reports to Strauss was Hoover's liaison to the AEC, Charles W. Bates.[21]

Hoover had chosen his go-between with care. At the age of thirty-four, Bates, a good-looking, gregarious man with slicked-back dark hair, dark skin, and, sometimes, dark glasses, had become part of Strauss's inner circle. "An able but shadowy figure," as Harold Green described him, Bates did not so much enter a room as burst in, as if he were leading an FBI raid. He spent nearly all his time at the AEC and had entrée to everyone in the building. Not only did he deliver the FBI's wiretap reports, but he carried verbal messages between Hoover and Strauss. Bates had been around politics for a long time. Raised in a tiny town in north Texas where his mother worked at the polls and his aunt was secretary to Collin County congressman Sam Rayburn, Charlie Bates and his twin brother remembered visiting Rayburn's house as children and being given lemonade and watermelon. They looked to Rayburn as a father and even carved the wooden gavel with which he called the U.S. House of Representatives to order when he was first elected Speaker in 1940.[22]

Impressed by Bates and the Rayburn connection, J. Edgar Hoover elevated the young man to the rank of supervisor when he was only twenty-seven. Bates now looked on Hoover, too, as a second father, and came up with pretexts to drop in at his office now and then. It got so that Hoover would address Bates by name when they saw each other in the elevator and sound off about whatever was on his mind: "Hoover," Bates said, "always had something he wanted to talk to you about." Bates got along with Strauss, too, but not to the point where he viewed him as another father. Strauss called the younger man "Charlie," while Bates called him "Admiral" and sometimes "Lewis." Eventually Strauss relied on Bates and sometimes turned to him for advice. Hoover relied on Bates too—to help him gauge Strauss's frame of mind. For, as the weeks went by, the Admiral was less and less a cool customer who wanted to rid himself of his quarry gracefully, more and more an implacable foe who wanted to destroy him as ruthlessly as possible. Hoover wanted to make sure that matters did not slip out of hand.[23]

Oppenheimer spent the first three weeks of 1954 seeking an attorney. His friend Herb Marks thought he should be represented by someone whose stature was comparable to his own, yet it was asking a good deal to expect a prominent attorney to accept any case, let alone this one, on such short notice. O'Brian had advised Oppenheimer to settle for no one but Simon Rifkind, senior partner in the New York firm of Paul, Weiss, Rifkind, Wharton and Garrison, but for reasons of health and at his wife's insistence, Rifkind turned him down. At that point Rifkind's partner, Lloyd Garrison, volunteered, and Oppenheimer accepted with relief. He and Garrison were on friendly, respectful terms already, since Garrison was a trustee of the Institute for Advanced Study. A great-grandson of famed abolitionist William Lloyd Garrison, Lloyd K. Garrison was intensely public-spirited, a national leader in civil rights, civil liberties, and labor arbitration. He cleared his calendar and took the case on a pro bono basis, his only payment the firm's out-of-pocket expenses. Assisting him would be Marks; Samuel Silverman, a litigator in Garrison's firm; and Allan Ecker, an associate in the firm who had written a 1948 cover story on Oppenheimer for *Time.* Eighty-year-old John W. Davis, Democratic candidate for president three decades earlier, was to serve as senior counselor.

The AEC, too, was seeking a lawyer. Strauss had no one in his general counsel's office whom he trusted—all of them being holdovers from Democratic days—so he asked the Justice Department to lend him an attorney. When Brownell refused, Strauss asked the FBI to suggest a former agent. Hoover likewise refused. Finally, on the recommendation of Deputy Attorney General William P. Rogers, Strauss hired Roger Robb, a Washington attorney who represented McCarthyite radio commentator Fulton Lewis Jr. and who, as a district prosecutor, had acquired a reputation as a fierce cross-examiner. Hoover approved, commenting that Robb had been "cooperative and honorable" with the bureau and agreeing to expedite his security clearance.[24]

That Strauss, certain to be a judge in the event of an appeal to the commissioners, should select the prosecuting attorney was remarkable enough. Equally remarkable, he also chose the chairman of the Personnel Security Board, in effect, foreman of the jury that would hear the case. His choice, seconded by President Eisenhower, was Gordon Gray, a Democrat, former secretary of the Army, and president of the University of North Carolina. (As it happened, Gray, Brownell, and Robb had all attended Yale Law School at the same time.) It was felt that the board should also include a captain of industry, and it fell to AEC general counsel William Mitchell to make the choice: Thomas Morgan, a North Carolina native who had risen from a hands-on job repairing gyrocompasses to the presidency of the Sperry Gyroscope Corporation.

The third member was to be a scientist. Lee Hancock, a onetime FBI man employed by the AEC, happened to be on hand when C. Arthur Rolander, an AEC employee who was assisting General Manager Nichols with the prosecution, appeared at the AEC Security Division for help in finding someone to fill the third slot. Rolander was seeking a scientist who had served on other Personnel Security Boards and had "the right attitude toward security." Members of the division checked the transcripts of board hearings all over the country, looking for individuals who had taken a tough line, and they chose a retired chemistry professor at Loyola University with a record of exceptional severity. His name was Ward Evans. Hancock considered the process a "cold, calculating exhibition of trying to stack the deck."[25]

During the weeks and months that followed, Hancock received an education in what a politically motivated prosecution could be. Carpooling from Virginia to work each day, Hancock found himself coaching the neophyte Rolander on AEC rules and procedures. During the commute, and at lunches with Strauss's assistant Bryan La-Plante, Bates, and others, Hancock became aware of the pervasive "get Oppie" atmosphere on the AEC team. He constantly heard remarks like "Strauss wants to win" and "if we deliver, our futures will be taken care of." And on days when Robb joined them for lunch, it was "the Republican Party needs this." Bates described the pressure in a report to Hoover: "Strauss felt the importance of the Oppenheimer case could not be stressed too much. He felt that if the case is lost the atomic energy program . . . will fall into the hands of left-wingers. If this occurs, it will mean another Pearl Harbor as far as atomic energy is concerned. Strauss feels that the scientists will then take over the entire program. Strauss stated that if Oppenheimer is cleared, then anyone can be cleared regardless of the information against them."[26]

The charges fell into two categories. The first twenty-three had to do with Oppenheimer's alleged Communist and left-wing associations in California between 1938 and 1946: organizations he had sponsored; publications he had subscribed to; the Communist Party memberships of his brother, wife, sister-in-law, and former fiancée; funds he had donated to the Party for Spanish war relief; fund-raisers he had attended; claims by Party organizers that he was a covert member; and, by far the most important, the Chevalier affair. In that contretemps, Oppenheimer's close friend Haakon Chevalier in late 1942 or early 1943 passed on a feeler as to whether Oppenheimer would provide information to the Russians through a Soviet consular official in San Francisco. Oppenheimer immediately refused, but he delayed several months before reporting the feeler to Army intelligence and then lied about the circumstances in the hope of protecting Chevalier. The AEC's charges also included Kitty and Robert's continuing friendship with the Chevaliers after the war, until 1947.

Appalling as these charges appeared to anyone reading them for the first time, General Leslie R. Groves and his top security man, John Lansdale, had known about nearly all of them when they cleared Oppenheimer for the Manhattan Project in 1943, and the AEC had reviewed the charges, updated to include the Chevalier affair, in 1947 and cleared Oppenheimer without a dissenting vote. Among those who had agreed to the clearance were Strauss and J. Edgar Hoover, with Hoover stipulating that he had no reservations about Oppenheimer's loyalty but only about the Chevalier matter, which he considered a matter of bad judgment, and not disloyalty.

The final charges had to do with the hydrogen bomb. Oppenheimer was accused of having altered his estimates over the years as to the bomb's feasibility, of having opposed its development for moral and political reasons, and of having continued to oppose the bomb and declining to cooperate fully even after Truman's order to go ahead. He was also accused of having tried to turn the top scientists at Los Alamos against the project by instructing John Manley to disseminate the GAC reports there in November 1949, and of having persuaded colleagues not to work on the bomb; and he was told that the opposition, "of which you are the most experienced, most powerful and most effective member, has definitely slowed down its development."[27]

Ironically, while Oppenheimer was preparing to defend himself against charges that he had delayed the hydrogen bomb, Strauss was on Bikini Atoll, witnessing the largest test the United States had ever detonated. It was called Bravo, and it exploded with a force of fifteen megatons, three times as large as expected and more than seven hundred times as powerful as the Hiroshima bomb. Bravo's size prompted rumors that it had gotten out of control, and even the president said publicly that "something must have happened that we have never experienced before." And it was not just a matter of size. Eighty-two nautical miles to the east of Bikini, twenty-three Japanese sailors on a ship called the *Lucky Dragon* sickened from fallout, and one of them died. Once again, America had inflicted nuclear damage on Japan. Seeking to distract the U.S. public from its fear of fallout,

Strauss told a press conference on his return from the Pacific that the H-bomb "can be made as large as you wish . . . large enough to take out a city." A city as big as New York? someone asked. "The metropolitan area, yes," Strauss replied, adding measurably to the panic. A photograph taken as they left the press conference showed Eisenhower scowling. "I wouldn't have answered that one that way, Lewis," the president chided. "Other than that, I thought you handled it well."[28]

Bravo was the first in a series of tests in the spring of 1954, the Castle series, that ushered in a new, more advanced phase of thermonuclear development. But U.S. officials continued to worry: six months earlier, the USSR had tested "Joe Four" (after Stalin), the first Soviet device that involved thermonuclear reactions. In Los Alamos, poring over debris that had been gathered by aircraft, Hans Bethe, Enrico Fermi, and Carson Mark concluded that while the Soviet Union was on the track, it had not yet discovered radiation implosion. Joe Four consisted of alternating layers of uranium and lithium deuteride, like our Alarm Clock. It was a single-stage and not a multistage device, like ours, and it used high explosives, not radiation, to achieve compression. Without radiation compression, the Russians would be unable to explode a megaton weapon.[29]

Ever since Joe One five years before, the United States had known that it had underestimated the talent of Soviet physicists and the capacity of the Soviet industrial machine. Americans had lost their complacency and tried incessantly to assess their lead—if indeed they still had one—over the USSR. Yet it seemed strange, at the very moment of reassurance, when the United States had just set off a device so enormous as to engender first and foremost the fear that it might get out of control, to be trying a man for having delayed development of the hydrogen bomb. The hydrogen bomb, or at least a thermonuclear device that could be weaponized with comparative ease, was already a fact. And we knew that the Russians did not yet have it.

CHAPTER EIGHTEEN

The Hearing Begins

ONE MORNING IN JANUARY, a Scottish-born reporter for a famous newspaper was looking for a seat on an airplane out of Washington. He found one next to a rumpled-looking blue-eyed man who did not seem happy to see him. Well aware of the man's identity, the reporter engaged Robert Oppenheimer in chitchat about Eisenhower's first year in office. Although he steered away from topics he thought might be troublesome, the man noticed that his companion nonetheless seemed nervous and under strain.[1]

That was all James Reston needed. On his return to the capital, he started asking around. What he found was dynamite, and before long Lloyd Garrison confirmed Reston's scoop: the government had confronted the scientist with charges, suspended his clearance, and scheduled a hearing. Garrison asked Reston, Washington bureau chief of the *New York Times,* not to publish until Oppenheimer had had time to complete his response, so that charges and rebuttal could appear simultaneously. The *Times*'s publisher, Arthur Hays Sulzberger, agreed, and for six weeks the paper held the story amid worries that Senator Joseph McCarthy or a *Times* competitor might break the news at any moment. Finally, only days before the Oppenheimer hearing was to begin, McCarthy charged on nationwide TV that Communist sympathizers in the government had caused a "deliberate eighteen-month delay" in the hydrogen bomb, a figure he had apparently lifted from Charles Murphy's anonymous article in *Fortune* the year before. Eisenhower replied that he knew of no such delay.

Anxious to trump McCarthy, Lewis Strauss and presidential press secretary James Hagerty concocted a strategy to trigger publication, and on April 13, the second day of the hearing, Reston's story appeared on page 1 of the *New York Times*. Gordon Gray, chairman of the hearing board, was outraged. Garrison had promised that he would try to restrain publication, and Gray thought Garrison had double-crossed him. Since no one at the AEC or the White House informed him that it was they who had double-crossed him, Gray scolded Garrison as the hearing opened and in the weeks that followed reprimanded him repeatedly for having—so Gray thought—broken his promise. The duplicity of this maneuver, whereby high officials of the AEC and the White House deceived their own hand-picked chairman, was typical of what was to happen in the weeks ahead.[2]

Oppenheimer's friend Joseph Volpe later said the proceeding was "like a hearing on your wife after you've been married twenty years." In his dozen years of government service Oppenheimer had been through four high-level reviews, among them the 1947 review in which Hoover and Strauss had agreed to clearance.[3] This new proceeding was unlike any of the others in that it resembled a criminal trial, with the burden of proof on one side only: the defense. It was held in a dilapidated government building with only lawyers, witnesses, and a handful of officials present. The location was not announced, reporters were not permitted—indeed, they were not formally told that it was happening—and each witness was informed as he took the stand that the proceeding was "confidential," meaning that he was not supposed to speak about it with anyone outside the hearing room and that government representatives would not do so either. On completion of the proceeding, the Gray board was to vote on whether Oppenheimer's clearance should be restored, and it was understood that, either way, the verdict would be appealed. The defense decided at the outset that, should it lose, it would not appeal within the federal court system. Instead, the five commissioners would act as the court of final appeal. In an improvised, and egregious, intermediate step, once the Gray board rendered its decision, AEC general manager Kenneth Nichols, who had signed the original letter of charges, sent the commissioners his recommendations. The

government made up rules as it went along, and the defense was not
consulted about what the rules should be. Lloyd Garrison objected
again and again that he did not know what type of proceeding it
was—was it a trial, with the normal protections of the courtroom?—
but in the fear-laden climate of the day, his objections were overruled, and Chairman Gray even reprimanded him for making them.

The whole affair was after the fact: Oppenheimer's contract as an
AEC consultant was to expire on June 30, and Strauss was free at any
time before that to cancel the contract, which would automatically
have precipitated revocation of his Q clearance. Instead, paradoxically, members of the Gray board and the AEC commissioners had to
rush the writing of their opinions in order to get a verdict in before
the contract was to lapse. With common sense turned on its head, it
is impossible to escape the conclusion that Strauss's determination to
win at any cost was colored by an implacable desire for revenge.

The week before the hearing began, Gray, Morgan, and Evans
were closeted with three thousand pages of documents—Borden's
letter, the denunciations by Pitzer, Teller, and Latimer, other items
from Oppenheimer's FBI file—compiled by the prosecution. Roger
Robb, the outside prosecutor hired for the case, and his chief assistant, C. Arthur Rolander, were on hand to interpret, and with the
board members taking meals together every day, Robb very often ate
with them. Not only was the defense prevented from seeing the documents the board members were reading: it was not told what the
documents were or what they contained. Silverman called the board's
prehearing immersion in files that the defense was not allowed to see
"unheard of," while Green later said that the board members emerged
"brainwashed," coming to the presentation of testimony steeped in
the prosecution's case and on friendly terms with the prosecutor himself. But when Garrison asked to meet with the board, he was
brusquely refused. There was no discovery process and no rules of evidence. The defense, mistakenly assuming that the proceeding might
bear some resemblance to a normal trial, furnished the prosecution
with the names of its witnesses ahead of time, but when Garrison
asked for a list of prosecution witnesses, Robb refused and was upheld

by Gordon Gray. Meanwhile, knowing in advance who the defense witnesses were to be, Robb repeatedly embarrassed them with disclosures from their FBI files.

The biggest handicap of all for the defense was its lack of security clearance. Many of the documents entered in testimony had been confiscated from Oppenheimer's files and some had even been written by Oppenheimer himself, but now they were classified and no one on the defense team was permitted to see them. Prior to the hearing, the AEC had offered to expedite a clearance for Garrison but refused to extend the offer to Silverman and Marks, and Garrison withdrew his request. (The truth, which the prosecution did not want to tell Garrison, was that they anticipated difficulty clearing Marks, a liberal who had been a close adviser to Acheson in the State Department.) As opening day approached, however, Garrison, anxious that Oppenheimer not be left unrepresented in the hearing room, renewed his request for clearance. Strauss refused outright, instructing Nichols to "make it perfectly clear to Garrison that we offered to do this last January and . . . we won't give any special consideration to this and should not give him emergency clearance." (Robb, of course, had been cleared in just a few days.) Several times Robb declassified a document on the spot, while questioning a witness, but refused to let the defense attorneys see it on grounds that they were not cleared. Barred by classification rules even from seeing Oppenheimer's FBI file, the defense lawyers were unaware both of derogatory items they should try to answer and positive items that might help their client. It was like trying to defend someone while blindfolded and with one arm tied behind one's back.[4]

Most ironic of all, the hearing was a massive breach of security. Roger Robb would ask bluntly about the core of the hydrogen device, while the witness—Oppenheimer, Bethe, or Rabi—would do his best to answer without giving anything classified away. All of the defense witnesses were more careful about secrecy than the government prosecutor, and Rabi was especially outspoken. He insisted that James Beckerley, the government's classification officer, be present at every moment while he was on the stand. He was afraid, he said, that the hearing would make it easier for the Russians to get the H-bomb by enabling them to put "bits and pieces together" and by "the attrition of the security of technical information." Beckerley remarked afterward, "If Oppenheimer or his witnesses had given anything away, they'd have been had up for it, but they knew better than the prosecution what ought not to be said." Their efforts did not wholly succeed. Scientists all over the world pored over the transcript after it was published, and the official British historian Lorna Arnold wrote that the transcript of the Oppenheimer hearing helped British weaponeers invent an H-bomb of their own.[5]

Since the defense attorneys were denied access to material they needed, Oppenheimer and Marks served instead as their historical memory, and Silverman, chief litigator for the defense, was astonished at how much they remembered. Oppenheimer also served as Silverman's tutor in physics. Silverman called these sessions "fantastic," but added that because of security Oppie censored what he told him even when a fuller explanation might have made his case more persuasive. "Oppenheimer was very careful even with us, his counsel. If a thing was classified, he didn't tell us." It was one of innumerable respects in which the government assumed Oppenheimer's loyalty and discretion even as it challenged them.[6]

A final crippling circumstance, which Garrison and Oppenheimer suspected but may have underrated, was that every detail of their strategy was known to the prosecution in advance because of the wiretapping, euphemistically called "electronic surveillance," of the Oppenheimers' conversations with their attorneys and the attorneys' conversations with one another. Robb had detailed information about Oppenheimer's state of mind, his search for an attorney, the presence of former secretary of state Acheson at dinner at the Oppenheimers' in Princeton just prior to the hearing, Kitty Oppenheimer's approach to General Groves at a New York cocktail party in an effort to find out what he was going to say on the witness stand, and Robert's conversations with potential witnesses, to say nothing of evidence the defense attorneys planned to introduce.

Charles Bates, Hoover's liaison to the AEC, carried the wiretapped reports, plus letters and memoranda from the FBI files—sometimes as much as a briefcaseful—from the FBI to Strauss, and from Strauss to Robb or his assistant Art Rolander. Bates, who strongly favored the prosecution, read all the messages stamped "via Liaison," since it was his job to advise Strauss or the FBI recipient about the matter at hand and deliver an oral reply. He would run errands and schmooze at the AEC, then return to the FBI in late afternoon. During the first six months of 1954, before, during, and after the hearing, he carried at least 273 wiretapped reports to Strauss or Robb, as well as oral messages back and forth between the two men, including Strauss's suggestions as to the questions Robb should ask witnesses.[7]

Over twenty years later, on December 1, 1976, Judge Roger Robb of the United States Court of Appeals for the District of Columbia wrote a letter to Samuel B. Ballen, a businessman in Santa Fe, New Mexico, about his role in the Oppenheimer case. "I had no knowledge of any bugging. Neither did I have any information about any conversation between Oppenheimer and his lawyer, and the suggestion that I used such information in 'strategy planning' is preposterous. I trust you will not persist in circulating false and libelous statements about my professional conduct." Robb sent a copy of his letter to Gordon Gray, and published a similar letter in *Life* magazine. As an attorney, Robb had represented clients as diverse as Earl Browder, chairman of the U.S. Communist Party, and Barry Goldwater, Republican candidate for president in 1964, and there was no way he did not know the source of the FBI documents he used in prosecuting Oppenheimer. Asked in the mid-1970s whether he would be interested in an appointment to the U.S. Supreme Court, Robb indicated that he would not, perhaps in part because he feared that his use of illegally obtained evidence in the Oppenheimer case would come to light.[8]

The hearing opened on Monday morning, April 12, in T-3, a rundown temporary building off Constitution Avenue within sight of the White House. Room 2022, where the hearing took place, was a long, rectangular office that had been converted into a makeshift courtroom. When he was not on the stand, Oppenheimer sat on an old leather couch just behind it. Roger Robb's desire to throw the defendant off balance was manifest even in the old courtroom trick of placing the couch at such an angle that Oppenheimer had to squint into the sun throughout the proceedings.[9]

Oppenheimer started off with panache. Under Lloyd Garrison's gentle probing he described his years of service to the government, beginning with Los Alamos, his efforts after the war to get an atomic energy bill passed by Congress, and his work on the Acheson-Lilienthal plan. He described the reasoning behind the GAC's advice against a crash program to build the H-bomb and denied that he had ever attempted to dissuade anyone from working on it.

But the wind went out of his sails under cross-examination when Robb grilled him about the Chevalier affair. The facts were that one evening in late 1942 or early 1943, when Oppenheimer was already involved in the secret project, his close friend Haakon Chevalier, on a visit to the Oppenheimers, passed along a feeler from George Eltenton, a Communist Party member with whom they were both acquainted. Eltenton, a British-born engineer who had lived in the USSR, had asked Chevalier to inform Oppenheimer that he knew of a way to transmit information to our then ally, the USSR, through the Soviet consulate in San Francisco. Oppenheimer, shaking a pitcher of martinis in the kitchen, immediately responded, "But that would be treason," or words very like those. The two men dropped the subject, and Oppenheimer tried to forget the conversation. Six or seven months later, on a visit to Berkeley from Los Alamos, hearing that Army security was worried about espionage at the Berkeley laboratory, he dropped by the Army security office on campus and told Lieutenant Lyall Johnson, the officer on duty, that George Eltenton, an employee of the Shell Development Company in the Bay Area, might bear watching.

Johnson's superior, Boris Pash, head of Army counterintelligence on the West Coast, was stunned. He ordered Johnson to place a wire in the office and, when Oppenheimer appeared the next day, pressed him for the name of the intermediary who had passed on Eltenton's approach. Anxious to protect Chevalier, Oppenheimer equivocated.

All he had meant to convey, he said, was that it would be a good idea to keep an eye on Eltenton.

Oppenheimer returned to New Mexico, and Army security went into overdrive. General Groves and his deputy for security, John Lansdale, tried without result to pry more out of Oppenheimer. Finally, about a year after the initial approach, Oppenheimer yielded and gave Groves the name of Haakon Chevalier.

Oppenheimer testified about these events on the third day of the hearing. Under questioning by Robb, he admitted that in Pash's office in 1943 he had, in his words, "invented a cock and bull story":

Q: Did you tell Pash that X had approached three persons on the project?
A: I am not clear whether I said there were 3 X's or whether X approached three people.
Q: Didn't you say that X had approached three people?
A: Probably.
Q: Why did you do that, Doctor?
A: Because I was an idiot.
Q: Is that your only explanation, Doctor?
A: I was reluctant to mention Chevalier.
Q: Yes.
A: No doubt somewhat reluctant to mention myself.[10]

Robb next read from the transcript of the 1943 interview to show that Oppenheimer had said more than he had reported in earlier testimony. Much of what he had said in 1943 had been false, and Oppenheimer, unnerved at hearing his own words read back to him, commented: "This whole thing was a pure fabrication except for the one name Eltenton."[11]

Robb concluded, "Isn't it a fair statement . . . that you told not one lie to Col. Pash, but a whole fabrication and tissue of lies?" Oppenheimer lamely answered, "Right."[12]

When he went home that night, Robb said to his wife, "I've just seen a man destroy himself."[13]

But if Oppenheimer destroyed himself, Robb had supplied the script. He had prepared with the utmost care, then handed a piece of rope to the man on the gallows.

The defense attorneys were dismayed. Robb's bullying, his innuendos, his heavy-handed insistence on yes-or-no answers, all these, along with Gray's supine failure to rein him in, soon made them realize that they were in an uphill battle. "There was a general feeling of depression," Silverman said later.[14]

On Easter Sunday, April 18, Joe Volpe was asked to the house of Randolph Paul, Garrison's law partner, in Georgetown. The Oppenheimers were staying there, and Robert, miserable over the way things were going, wanted Volpe's advice. After Garrison and Marks described what had gone on in the hearing room so far, Volpe told them that if things continued this way, they should pack their bags and walk out. Randolph Paul agreed.[15]

Volpe had been counsel to the AEC in the early days and helped draw up its security regulations. He and Herb Marks had designed the AEC security board hearings to be nonadversarial, to bring out the favorable as well as unfavorable sides of an individual's record and weigh the "whole man," in part because the AEC could not otherwise attract the highly qualified personnel it was looking for. It was clear to Volpe that the proceedings in room 2022 were a long way from long-standing AEC procedures, which were known to be the fairest and most effective in government.

Events a day or so later proved the point. On Monday the nineteenth, preparing to testify, David Lilienthal visited the AEC building to review documents about Oppenheimer's 1947 clearance and the GAC's Halloween meeting. He was assigned a desk and files that purportedly contained the documents he was seeking. Once he was on the stand, however, it became apparent that the documents he was being questioned about had been purposely lifted from the files to make it appear that he had forgotten critical facts and that his testimony should be discounted. Garrison protested that Robb's trick made "a lapse of memory seem like a deliberate falsification," adding that the hearing as a whole was more like a criminal prosecution than an inquiry to find the truth. Robb accused Garrison of challenging his professional integrity and went on questioning Lilienthal unabashed. All without a peep from Gordon Gray.

Lilienthal's entrapment was just the sort of outrage Volpe had had in mind when he had advised the defense lawyers to walk out. But Silverman explained years afterward that they had not taken the idea seriously. "In those days you didn't protest. We just accepted that this was the way things were. And who would we have appealed to?"[16]

Had he known what was happening behind the scenes, the pessimism of the forty-six-year-old Silverman might have turned to anger. The tiny basement office in building T-3 that had been assigned to the defense to work in at night was wired. Oppenheimer and Garrison correctly assumed that they could talk privately in the evenings only at the Pauls' house, but the more innocent Silverman thought they were "paranoid" and remained unaware of the tapping until passage of the Freedom of Information Act more than twenty years later gave it away.

In his testimony, Oppenheimer conceded almost every charge having to do with his life in Berkeley prior to World War II. A product of the Cambridge-Göttingen-Berkeley Ivory Tower, he had known almost nothing about events in the world outside physics, learning of the 1929 stock market crash, for example, only some time after it occurred. But after falling in love in 1936 with Jean Tatlock, a Communist Party member, he, too, became close to the Party and was eventually, in his own words, a "fellow traveler." He sympathized with the effort to create an egalitarian society in Soviet Russia, but what he cared most about was the rise of fascism in Europe and the cause of Republican Spain. Like other leftists of that era, he hoped for a defeat of fascism in Spain that would deter Hitler from unleashing war on the rest of Europe. People joked that the easiest way to find Oppenheimer was to attend a fund-raiser for victims of the Spanish civil war. What the ultrarespectable Gordon Gray and his colleagues made of Oppenheimer's life on the bohemian left in Berkeley during the 1930s has to be guessed at, since it did not remotely resemble their own experience, and like most Americans, they were not touched personally by the Spanish war. The Chevalier affair was the most damning, not because it was about espionage or treason—it was not—but because it was about lying. Oppenheimer in 1943 had lied to protect a friend. Throughout the hearing, the question that hung over room 2022 was, would he do it again? Would he put loyalty to a friend ahead of loyalty to his country? The question was the more pointed because Oppenheimer admitted that he had seen Chevalier from time to time after the war, and revealed—a startling fact that became known to the prosecution only when Oppenheimer mentioned it in his testimony—that he had seen Chevalier on two separate occasions in Paris in December 1953, only four months before the hearing.

One after the other, witnesses for the defense argued not only that Oppenheimer would place loyalty to the country above loyalty to a friend but that he had already done so. They emphasized that he, like the rest of them, had changed and grown when it came to accepting the need for security. John von Neumann, the world's greatest mathematician, who occupied the office next to Oppenheimer's in Princeton, emphasized the strange new world of espionage and counterespionage into which they had all been thrust. "We were little children," he said. "We suddenly were dealing with something with which one could blow up the world. . . . We had to make . . . our code of conduct as we went along." Even if Oppenheimer's 1943 version of the Chevalier approach had been true, von Neumann said, "it would just give me a piece of information on how long it took Dr. Oppenheimer to get adjusted to this Buck Rogers universe, but no more." Later he "learned how to handle it, and handled it very well." Robb asked a final question. "Doctor," he said to von Neumann, "you have never had any training as a psychiatrist, have you?" Von Neumann was only one of several distinguished witnesses who attested to Oppenheimer's loyalty, only to be faced by insulting innuendo.[17]

Emphasizing that events of the early 1940s, such as the Chevalier affair, had to be weighed in terms of the period in which they occurred, Gordon Dean conceded that had he first met Oppenheimer in Berkeley in 1939 or 1940, he might not have cleared him. But, "I feel quite differently having watched him closely and . . . evaluated quite carefully his service to his country." Here, said Dean, was "one of the few men who can demonstrate his loyalty to his country by his performance." Lee DuBridge, who had spent five years with Oppenheimer on the GAC, agreed: "There is no one who has exhibited his loyalty to this country more spectacularly."[18]

George Kennan, the expert on Russia whose last official post had been that of ambassador to the USSR, defended Oppenheimer against any implication that he had bent his policy advice in the Soviet Union's favor. Pointing out that the gifted individual is less likely than others to have led a wholly conventional life, Kennan said that Oppenheimer had one of the great minds of his generation. "A mind like that is not without its implications," he added. "You might just as well have asked Leonardo da Vinci to distort an anatomical drawing as . . . ask Robert Oppenheimer to speak responsibly to the sort of questions we were talking about and speak dishonestly."[19]

While all twenty-eight defense witnesses—most of them far more distinguished in American life than any prosecution witness—praised Oppenheimer's contributions, Vannevar Bush, director of the wartime Office of Scientific Research and Development and the most venerable of them all, treated the board with defiance. It ought to have rejected Nichols's letter of charges and sent it back for redrafting, he said, to eliminate any suggestion that Oppenheimer was being tried for advice he had given the government. The board's failure to do so, scolded the austere New Englander, had resulted in "a very bad mess" in the government's relations with the scientists. The National Academy of Sciences and the American Physical Society would be holding their annual meetings in Washington the following week, and he hoped "they would do nothing foolish," such as decide to boycott government programs. The scientific community was alarmed that a colleague who had "rendered great service to his country, service beyond almost any other man, is now being pilloried and put through an ordeal because he had the temerity to express his honest opinions. . . . When a man is pilloried for doing that, this country is in a severe state."[20]

But the witness who may have gone furthest of all was Rabi, a close friend of Oppenheimer's since 1929 and his successor as chairman of the GAC. Rabi conceded that Oppenheimer's failure to report the Chevalier feeler accurately "was a great mistake in judgment" but, as von Neumann had, pointed out that Oppie need not have reported it at all. "I read no sinister implication in it." Asked about his attempts to persuade Strauss to call off the hearing, Rabi replied that he had told Strauss from the outset that the suspension of Oppenheimer's clearance was "a very unfortunate thing and should not have been done. In other words, there he was; he is a consultant, and if you don't want to consult the guy, you don't consult him, period. . . . It didn't seem to me the sort of thing that called for this kind of proceeding at all against a man who had accomplished what Dr. Oppenheimer has accomplished. There is a real positive record . . . we have an A-bomb and a whole series of it, and what more do you want—mermaids? This is just a tremendous achievement. If the end of that road is this kind of hearing, which can't help but be humiliating, I thought it was a pretty bad show. I still think so."[21]

Behind the scenes, Rabi had made six attempts to have the hearing called off, only to be foiled each time by Strauss. Once, before the proceeding began, he telephoned the White House to request an appointment with the president. Spotting Strauss in the outer office, the president's secretary asked who Rabi was. Strauss intercepted the call and then obtained a commitment from the president to refer any call from Rabi—who had seen a good deal of Eisenhower during his brief time as president of Columbia University—back to Strauss. Another time, a few days after the start of the hearing, Rabi asked the AEC chairman to request a formal presidential directive to call it off. This time, worried about criticism that was beginning to appear in the press and wary of a scientific boycott, Strauss asked Robb to curtail his questioning of prosecution witnesses.[22]

Rabi let Strauss know later on that he would be appearing as a defense witness and would testify that Oppie was not a security risk. Strauss tried to warn him off and cautioned that Rabi might find himself trapped on the stand if he had not seen Oppenheimer's FBI file. Strauss got an okay from J. Edgar Hoover to let Rabi see the file, but found himself outmaneuvered when Rabi mentioned offhandedly on the witness stand that Strauss had already shown it to him. Thrown into disarray by the revelation that Strauss had shown the witness the highly classified dossier, Robb asked for an immediate recess.[23]

Finally Rabi informed Strauss that the GAC had passed a resolution declaring it the intention of all nine members to appear as witnesses for the defense, and Strauss answered that he refused to be blackmailed.[24]

Neither man wanted to alienate the other, since both were keenly interested in the Atoms for Peace conference, which was to take place in Geneva the following year. Strauss needed Rabi, a Nobel Prize winner known all over Europe, for the conference, while Rabi wanted the world to get something besides weapons out of the atom. Rabi later explained, "My way of keeping straight with Strauss was to tell him at every point what I was doing and what I thought. I never hid what I thought. Had I taken part in the defense—gone over to Oppenheimer or his damn-fool lawyers—the outcome might have been different, but I wouldn't have had my Geneva conference." Rabi was angry at Oppie and thought he had brought the whole thing on himself. Had he been part of the defense team, he said, he would have urged him to tell his accusers, " 'who the Hell are you to try *me*, who saved your country for you?' " Disgusted by Oppie's caving in under Robb's savage cross-examination, Rabi said of his friend, "He was such a great actor, so he played the role of victim. That is what they wanted of him, and he did it."[25]

Still, Rabi regretted all his life that he hadn't done more. As a member of the GAC, he held a presidential appointment and was entitled to approach the president directly, and afterward—perhaps not remembering that he had been intercepted on precisely such a mission by Strauss—he blamed himself for failing to tell Eisenhower in person that he should call the whole thing off. He did go up to the president at a White House reception one night intending to speak to him, but before he could open his mouth, Otis Chandler, publisher of the *Los Angeles Times* and backer of the Republican Party, broke in with some comment to Ike about Oppie's romance with Jean Tatlock. Rabi could not summon the heart to talk to the president that night.

It was as though Rabi, as steady as anyone could be, was standing like a rock beside Oppie and trying to impart to him the staunchness he needed. He loved Oppenheimer for the power of his mind and his superb education, so much better, he felt, than his own. He relished being with him, discussing history, philosophy, literature, and psychology with him—and knew precisely what he lacked. Oppenheimer's brain, Rabi thought, was too much for his frail body and his emotional capacity. He could be "sublime" when things were going his way, but he was not a street fighter. "Kitty was better in that way. She supplied the backbone."[26]

Groves at Los Alamos, Rabi thought, had understood what Robert lacked and supplied the "backbone" himself. And if he was too busy or was off somewhere, Groves brought in others to supply it. During the early days, in 1943, some of the Europeans thought that they were greater scientists than Oppie and that one of them should be leading the project. At moments when Oppie seemed to doubt himself, Groves would encourage Rabi or Bacher to fly in from the Radiation Lab at MIT to buck him up. Now, in the spring of 1954, Kitty Oppenheimer, herself the possessor of a keen fighting spirit, was doing her best to shore Robert up. And Rabi, as loyal in his way as Kitty was in hers, tried, quite simply, to make a gift to Robert of the staunchness, the stiffness of spine, that he himself had and that his brilliant, mysterious friend lacked.

The cost to Kitty was beyond reckoning. On weekends during the hearing, the two of them went back to Princeton. Robert caught up with institute affairs, and they spent time with their children, Toni, aged ten, and Peter, fourteen, who especially needed comforting. One spring evening Harold Cherniss, an art historian at the institute, and his wife, Ruth, a childhood schoolmate of Robert's, were with the Oppenheimers. After dinner, Robert walked them to their car. As the three of them were saying good-bye, they heard a prolonged wail coming from the house, like the baying of a wounded animal.[27]

CHAPTER NINETEEN

Smyth

THE OPPENHEIMERS would have been surprised had they known what was going on in the household of another couple—whom they knew, but were not close to—who were just as upset as they were, and on their account. AEC commissioner Henry Smyth was Oppie's senior by six years and had received his Ph.D. from Princeton in 1921, before quantum mechanics arrived in the United States. Oppenheimer respected Smyth but did not consider him a first-class physicist and had, on more than one occasion, let him know it. But Smyth, who had a lively sense of justice and an overriding desire for the well-being of the atomic energy program, was not one to hold Oppie's attitude against him. So acute was his feeling, and that of his wife, that what was happening to Oppie was unjust, outrageous, and bad for the country, that the redoubtable Mary deConingh Smyth kept a detailed record of their actions throughout this period and left it behind for history.

A little over six feet tall, with an angular face and wavy gray hair parted on one side, clad always in subdued grays and browns, Henry DeWolf Smyth was the picture of austere rectitude. A commissioner for five years, he had been disappointed when Eisenhower passed him over for AEC chairman in the spring of 1953 and selected Strauss instead. By the autumn of that year he was thinking seriously of returning to his professorship at Princeton, not because he had been passed over but because he deeply distrusted the new chairman. Once he realized that the hearing was to take place, however, he put his personal plans on hold. He knew Strauss too well not to fear a collision between scientists and the administration that could endanger the weapons program.[1]

After New Year's, 1954, he and Mary stayed up nights discussing the resignation and worrying what would happen to Oppie if no one was left at the AEC to stand up to Strauss. Mary wrote in her diary on January 11, "We decide what is right for H to do about RO." And an evening or two later, "H so tired from worry over RO. We talk late." They shared hard truths about themselves, too: walking in Rock Creek Park one Sunday, husband and wife discussed their "real incompatibility," and Mary wrote later that she was "sunk." They had their lighter moments, too. Klari and Johnny von Neumann stayed with them the week Johnny testified—he had not wanted to appear, and rumor had it that Klari threatened him with divorce if he did not testify in Oppie's favor—and another time Rabi came for dinner and stayed overnight: "Rabi here for dinner. Wonderful ping-pong."[2]

The week of April 26, the last full week of the hearing, scientists converged on Washington from all over the country for their annual meetings. Despite the warning to each witness that the hearing was to be treated as "confidential," news had spread throughout the physics community as to what kind of proceeding it was. Hans Bethe, president of the American Physical Society, invited Oppenheimer to sit on the dais during dinner at one of the big Washington hotels. When Bethe introduced the worn and tired-looking physicist he received a standing ovation.

All of the government witnesses testified that final week: the prosecution had arranged it that way so that hostile testimony would be fresh in the minds of the board members when they made their decision. During that frantic week, Strauss managed to squeeze time for four prosecution witnesses into his schedule. On Monday he saw Wendell Latimer and Kenneth Pitzer, the professors of chemistry at Berkeley who had informed against Oppie to the FBI two years earlier and were to testify against him that week. And late Tuesday he had a visit from Edward Teller, who was scheduled to testify on Wednesday.[3]

After seeing Strauss, Teller stopped by the office of Roger Robb, who had interviewed him six weeks earlier in California. On that occasion Teller had told Robb about an episode in 1942 or so when Oppenheimer had sought his advice as to whether he should accept leadership of the Manhattan Project in view of left-wing friendships he had had during the 1930s, and Teller had urged him to go ahead. Robb now told Teller that since their meeting in California, Oppenheimer had testified to an involvement with the Communist Party far more extensive than the one he had described to Teller. Robb showed Teller the passage in Oppenheimer's testimony in which the scientist admitted that he had given Pash in 1943 a false story about Chevalier, and Teller professed to be shocked. "Oppenheimer lied to me," he said, adding that his father had taught him as a boy that a half-truth was as bad as a lie.

When Teller returned to his hotel that evening, three of his oldest friends begged him not to testify for the prosecution. Thirty-two years later John Wheeler still remembered Teller's pacing back and forth in his room at the Wardman Park Hotel, worrying about the flaws in Oppie's character, while Hans and Rose Bethe also sorrowfully recalled pleading with Teller that night. Teller and Bethe had met in 1928, as students of Arnold Sommerfeld in Munich. When Bethe arrived in the United States in 1935 as a refugee from Hitler, he had gone straight to the Tellers' home in Washington, D.C., and a year or so later the Tellers had chaperoned Bethe and Rose Ewald, then in their courtship, on an automobile trip across the United States. Bethe had already implored Teller to testify *for* Oppenheimer, and Rose, too, now begged him not to turn against their old friend. This time Teller did not mention the "issue of character" of which he had spoken to Wheeler, nor did he question Oppie's loyalty. Instead he deplored his opposition to the H-bomb and complained that he had slowed down another program, the nuclear reactor effort, as well. As the old friends said good night, the Bethes knew they had failed.[4]

Teller did not mention his session with the prosecutor that day to either Wheeler or the Bethes. But in later years he insisted that his afternoon meeting with Robb—which he remembered, inaccurately, as having taken place early Wednesday morning, April 28, when he was on his way into the hearing room—changed his mind. Until that moment, he claimed, he had intended to limit his testimony to his belief that Oppie had slowed the H-bomb program and given bad advice.

But on reading Oppie's admission that he had lied, he had decided to say more.

Robb proceeded with surgical delicacy the next day. Asked whether he thought that Oppenheimer was disloyal, Teller answered that he had always considered him a loyal citizen. Describing his old colleague as "intellectually most alert" and "very complicated," Teller volunteered that "it would be presumptuous and wrong on my part if I would try in any way to analyze his motives." Robb moved in for the kill: "Do you or do you not believe that Dr. Oppenheimer is a security risk?"

"In a great number of cases," Teller answered, "I have seen Dr. Oppenheimer act in a way which for me was exceedingly hard to understand. I thoroughly disagreed with him in numerous issues and his actions frankly appeared to me confused and complicated. To this extent I feel that I would like to see the vital interests of the country in hands which I understand better and therefore trust more. In this very limited sense I would like to express a feeling that I would feel *personally more secure* if public matters would rest in other hands" (italics added).[5]

With these words, the deed was done. In California only a few days before, Teller had told an AEC official that he was sorry the case was being "brought on security grounds because such charges were not tenable." But in their session Tuesday night, Robb evidently persuaded Teller to utter the word "secure." And the moment he did so, Robb switched abruptly to a different line of questioning. He aimed at all costs to avoid giving Teller a chance to take back the words he had spoken.[6]

Teller then said under oath that Oppenheimer was "just a most wonderful and excellent director" of Los Alamos during the war. But if scientists had gone to work on the H-bomb immediately after World War II—a course he said Oppenheimer had discouraged—the United States could have had the weapon four years earlier than it had, indeed possibly as early as 1947. And he added that Oppenheimer's influence and that of the GAC had been "a brake rather than encouragement" to the thermonuclear program, "more frequently a hindrance than a help."

Toward the end of Teller's testimony Gordon Gray asked whether he thought the common security would be endangered if Oppenheimer were allowed to keep his clearance. If it was a question of intent, the answer would be no, Teller replied. Oppenheimer would not "knowingly and willingly" do anything to endanger the nation. But "if it is a question of wisdom and judgment, as demonstrated by actions since 1945, then I would say that it would be wiser not to grant clearance."[7]

As he left the stand, Teller turned to Oppenheimer, who was seated behind him on the sofa, and put out his hand. Stunned, Oppenheimer took it. "I'm sorry," Teller said. "After what you've just said, I don't know what you mean," Oppenheimer replied. Teller turned and limped from the room.[8]

Strauss and Robb were disappointed by the failure of another witness to make it to Washington that week. That witness was Ernest Lawrence, the only leader whose stature in the scientific community came close to that of Oppenheimer. A few weeks earlier, talking with Robb, Lawrence had bitterly criticized Oppenheimer: his hypnotic influence, his opposition to the H-bomb and the second lab, and his participation in Project Vista. Strauss, who for nearly twenty years had helped Lawrence acquire expensive equipment for his laboratory, had told Lawrence that it was his duty to testify, and Lawrence had reluctantly consented. Reluctantly because Lawrence and Oppenheimer went back even further than Lawrence and Strauss, and had been the closest of friends and collaborators during the 1930s. So close were they that Lawrence had named his younger son Robert after him. Lawrence, as leader, had very much at heart the "unity" part of the words "scientific community." He was a man of unusually deep loyalties, and the idea of reading Oppie out of that community pained him. But he felt betrayed. It wasn't just Oppie's left-wing opinions—Lawrence thought he had outgrown them—but the fact that prior to his recommending Oppenheimer's younger brother Frank for a teaching job at the University of Minnesota, Robert had assured him that Frank had never belonged to the Communist Party, knowing full well that he had.

Because of his bitterness, because he believed that Oppenheimer's advice had been mistaken and maybe dangerous, and also perhaps out of irritation that Oppenheimer seemed to enjoy his fame all too much, Lawrence had given Strauss his word that, on the way home from a meeting on reactors in Tennessee, he would stop in Washington to testify. Lawrence had allowed himself to be persuaded that the proceeding was Oppenheimer's fault: Strauss had given him a chance to renounce his clearance quietly; it was Oppie who had insisted on a hearing.

The woods outside Topoca Lodge in the Great Smoky Mountains were breathtakingly beautiful that last weekend of April 1954 as the country's best-known specialists on nuclear reactors met under the auspices of the AEC. They had gathered to discuss technical problems, but the immolation of Oppenheimer dominated their meeting. Lawrence was surprised by the unanimous sympathy for his old friend. When he said that Oppenheimer himself was to blame, they told him that, to the contrary, Oppie had had no choice but to ask for the hearing once he was charged as a security risk. When Lawrence argued that fame had gone to Oppie's head and he had strayed from science into moral preachment, they asked whether being a scientific adviser to the government meant that a man must renounce his beliefs. Was it his duty to approve a course of action that offended his moral code? And was it a crime to be wrong, assuming that Oppenheimer had been wrong in opposing the hydrogen bomb? Lawrence heard the words "martyrdom" and "persecution" applied to the goings-on in Washington, and approval of Oppie's stance on the H-bomb. And when one of the conferees pointed out that the hostile testimony so far had all come from Berkeley, Lawrence found himself defending his lab from the charge that it was waging a vendetta. But the arguments that weighed most with him had to do with the scientific community—the damage a split would cause, not just to science, but to the weapons program and the country.[9]

The discussions exacted a toll, and Lawrence suffered an attack of the ulcerative colitis that was eventually to kill him. Before he flew home—to California and not Washington—he summoned three other conferees to his bathroom and showed them the blood he had lost, so they would not think that he had lost his nerve.[10]

Luis Alvarez in Berkeley was surprised to receive a call from Lawrence, before he left Tennessee, telling him not to testify. Lawrence added that the four of them, Lawrence, Alvarez, Ken Pitzer, and Wendell Latimer, were viewed as a Berkeley cabal bent on destroying Oppenheimer, and that he was afraid the lab would suffer reprisals if he and Alvarez took the stand. Alvarez canceled his flight to Washington.

That evening he had another call, this one from Lewis Strauss. Maybe Lawrence had caved in because of illness, Strauss scolded, but what was Alvarez's excuse? Lawrence had ordered him not to go, Alvarez objected, and it was Lawrence he worked for. Strauss told Alvarez that it was his duty to appear; Alvarez responded that he had already done his duty to the country—during the war, at Los Alamos. Strauss became more and more exercised, and finally warned that if Alvarez failed to show up the next day, he would be unable to look at himself in the mirror for the rest of his life.

Alvarez reconsidered. He poured himself a drink and booked a seat on a midnight flight to Washington. On the drive to the airport, he reflected that it was the first time he had ever disobeyed Ernest Lawrence.[11]

CHAPTER TWENTY

Borden

ON WEDNESDAY EVENING Allan Ecker, a junior member of the defense team, was in the AEC building reading declassified transcripts of the day's testimony when he heard the crackling sounds of an ancient recording machine through the thin wall between him and the office next door. As he left the building that night, Ecker saw Roger Robb leaving with two men Ecker later recognized on the witness stand: Luis Alvarez, just in from California, and Boris Pash.[1]

When his turn came the next day Alvarez, like his Berkeley colleagues Latimer and Pitzer, testified that Oppenheimer had persuaded others, especially younger men, not to work on the H-bomb. But all three of them hedged a little. Pitzer said, "I am not myself a physicist," and Latimer, "my impressions would be based very largely on what Dr. Teller has told me." Alvarez put it this way: "This I have been told by Edward Teller. That is my only source of information on this point." Along with Teller, all of them emphasized Oppenheimer's persuasiveness—"one of the most persuasive men that has ever lived," Alvarez said—to back up the prosecution's claim that Oppenheimer had discouraged fellow scientists from working on the project. And when Robb asked whether Oppenheimer was still essential to the weapons program, Pitzer, Teller, and Latimer answered emphatically that he was not. Interestingly, Strauss had seen the three other men, and probably coached them on this very point, before they gave their testimony, but saw Alvarez, who was not asked that question, only for a brief moment Friday morning, after he had testified. Strauss apparently did not coach Alvarez but presumably thanked him for coming all the way from California: Lawrence's change of heart had, in a sense, left Teller out to dry, left him the only Berkeley physicist to take on Oppenheimer, Latimer and Pitzer being chemists. And, having seen Teller twice that week, on Tuesday, before he testified, and on Thursday, afterward, Strauss knew how shaky his star witness felt. Alvarez had no more firsthand knowledge of the thermonuclear program than Pitzer or Latimer, but at least he was a physicist and could be counted on because of his long-standing, and well-known, animosity toward Oppenheimer.[2]

Unlike the other four, a fifth prosecution witness, Major General Roscoe Charles Wilson, had no personal animus against the defendant and appeared only reluctantly, on orders of the Air Force chief of staff. Wilson had known Oppenheimer since 1944, when as Air Force liaison officer to General Groves he had helped pick Alamogordo as the site of the first atomic bomb test. He testified that despite his admiration for Oppenheimer, he had warned the director of Air Force intelligence in early 1951 about a "pattern of activity" on the scientist's part that he thought could "jeopardize the national defense." The "pattern" included Oppenheimer's advocacy of internationalizing atomic energy (the Acheson-Lilienthal plan) at a time when this country still had a monopoly, his opposition to two of three devices favored by the Air Force for detecting a possible test by the Soviet Union, and his opposition, on technical grounds, to development of a nuclear-powered airplane. In the fall of 1949, immediately after Joe One, Wilson had been briefed by Teller, who sent him to top Air Force officials to alert them to the fact that something called the hydrogen bomb might be the answer to the Soviet A-bomb. The intervention by Teller and Wilson led Air Force chief of staff Hoyt Vandenberg to testify in favor of the H-bomb in Congress, on October 14, 1949, only the day after he had learned that the bomb might someday be a possibility.[3]

Calling himself "a big bomb man," Wilson described his testimony as "one of the great sorrows of my life." Years afterward he explained that Oppenheimer had been "remarkably kind to me, and really a great mind, an incredible mind. . . . I liked Oppenheimer," he said, "we were friends. I have been to his house many times. . . . As I sat there I could see tears running down the guy's face. . . . This really has been on my conscience."[4] (Joe Volpe later denied that Oppenheimer wept at any time during the hearing.)

If Lawrence's defection left Teller out on a limb, Thomas Finletter's decision not to testify left the Air Force's other witness, David Tressel Griggs, very much on the spot as well. Ivan Getting, a former Air Force scientist and close friend of Griggs's, stopped by Griggs's house in Los Angeles one day in 1954 and found his friend talking on the telephone to someone back east. That someone was their old boss, the former secretary of the Air Force, breaking the news to Griggs that he was not going to appear. Getting noticed that Griggs looked "ashen" and "let down."[5]

Griggs nonetheless appeared during the final week to support the prosecution's case that Oppenheimer had engaged not in a single act but a pattern of actions designed to weaken the Air Force and its offensive arm, the Strategic Air Command. Griggs described the 1951 Vista meetings at Caltech and a meeting outside Boston in September 1952 on air defense of the United States. During the Boston meeting, Griggs testified, he had seen Professor Jerrold Zacharias of MIT go to the blackboard and write the letter Z at the top, followed by the letters O, R, and C, in capitals eighteen inches high, diagonally to the bottom of the board. The initials were those of Zacharias himself, and of Oppenheimer, Rabi, and Charles Lauritsen, who, Griggs alleged, had conspired to weaken SAC, if not abolish it altogether. The charge that there was a cabal called ZORC had created a sensation when, as mentioned earlier, it appeared in Charles Murphy's *Fortune* article of May 1953, and was raised again at the hearing to suggest a conspiracy. Although Zacharias denied writing the fateful letters on the blackboard and MIT physicist Al Hill, who was also present at the Boston meeting, testified that the episode never took place, the ZORC story had staying power: Ivan Getting believed it and in 1989 sent the author a letter from a scientist who had allegedly been present, offering to swear under oath that he had seen Zacharias write the initials on the blackboard. However, after the hearing two prominent scientists who had attended the Boston meeting, Emmanuel Piore and Carl Overhage, told the FBI that they had never witnessed such a scene nor heard of ZORC prior to Murphy's story in *Fortune*. Griggs himself was unsure: three weeks after testifying at the hearing he told the FBI, according to bureau records, that "doubts have arisen in his mind as to whether his recollection was true. . . . He said that he is somewhat confused concerning this matter and stated also that he has a poor memory."[6]

Guyford Stever, an aeronautics specialist who became science adviser to President Gerald Ford, in later years recalled seeing Zacharias at the blackboard, writing down names of those who had taken responsibility for drafting parts of a paper or report. "It was a simple technique, and not a consequential thing," Stever said, adding that after Zacharias had written down the four names, or initials, he exclaimed, "Look at that, ZORCH."[7]

From FBI interviews of May and June 1954, it appears that the ZORC story sprang from the brain, and almost certainly the imagination, of Air Force Colonel Teddy Walkowicz, the author of much other misinformation. This, for example, from an FBI report in June: "On June 12, Mr. Charles J. V. Murphy was interviewed. . . . He stated that he had no direct or first-hand knowledge relative to the origin of . . . the term ZORC. It is Murphy's recollection that Teddy Walcowicz [*sic*], former Air Force officer, was Murphy's main and possibly only source of information."

Griggs's story, with its accusation that Oppenheimer had been leader of a conspiracy, was unsupported by any other witness at the hearing. But it was allowed to stand. Unlike so much else that had found its way into the FBI files, Griggs's refutation in May was not leaked to the press, nor was Murphy's of June 12. The bureau had both when the commissioners sat down to consider their verdict in late June. There is no evidence that they were informed.[8]

On Friday, April 30, Boris Pash, whom Allan Ecker had seen emerging from Robb's office on Wednesday evening, testified about the meeting in Lyall Johnson's office in the summer of 1943, when Oppenheimer described the feeler from Soviet intelligence that had been relayed to him by Haakon Chevalier. The recording made by Pash, the Army's counterintelligence chief at the Presidio of San Francisco at the time, had already been played to the Gray board, and Pash now testified to his belief that Oppenheimer was a security risk, that he was merely pretending to have changed his allegiances, and that he had been in 1943 and probably remained a member of the Communist Party. (Pash was the sole prosecution witness whose testimony was not based in part on information supplied by Teller.)

Dramatic as the statements of Griggs and Pash had been, the appearance of the week's final witness was the most stunning event of all. On Friday afternoon the blond, slight, thirty-four-year-old William Borden entered the hearing room and raised his right hand while his November 7 letter to Hoover was handed to lawyers for the defense. Until this moment, they had not known about the letter. Now, seeing it for the first time, they were appalled, both because the board members had had it in front of them the entire time, and because of its conclusion: Borden's "exhaustively considered opinion . . . that more probably than not J. Robert Oppenheimer is an agent of the Soviet Union." The letter even said that Oppenheimer could have been acting on Soviet orders as far back as the time when he chose atomic weapons as his specialty in the early 1940s, and that in addition to performing espionage, he had probably also "acted under a Soviet directive in influencing United States military, atomic energy, Intelligence and diplomatic policy." Lloyd Garrison was quick to point out that in introducing accusations that were not part of the AEC's original letter of charges and that had not arisen at the hearing, "we now have a new case," and even Gray dissociated himself and his fellow board members from Borden's claim that Oppenheimer might have volunteered information to the Russians. The board had no evidence before it to show that Oppenheimer was an espionage agent, Gray said, to Borden's chagrin and the outrage of his friends, one of whom later protested that "Gray kicked Borden in the teeth."[9]

By the time Borden had read his letter aloud, it was 4:30 p.m., early enough in the afternoon for the defense to start cross-examination before adjournment for the weekend. But defense attorneys were at odds among themselves as to whether they even wanted to cross-examine, and a recess was called. Silverman did not want to give Borden a chance to make Robb's case for him or to spread innuendo on the record. Herb Marks, on the other hand, wanted to question Borden on every single assertion. By Sunday night, however, Marks had come around to Silverman's view, and the defense decided not to cross-examine. Even after Borden's surprise appearance, Silverman later admitted, it was several days before he began to suspect that this was the letter that had triggered the hearing.[10]

On Thursday, May 6, the hearing ended with a three-hour extemporaneous summation by Garrison, who stated that the hearing should not have been brought at all in view of Oppenheimer's overall record and the fact that there had been no new security information against him since his clearance in 1947. The charges, Garrison said, fell in two categories: Oppenheimer's opposition to the H-bomb, in which he had been joined by nearly all the top scientists, and the Chevalier affair. The latter, he concluded, "must be judged in perspective. It happened in a wholly different atmosphere from that of today. Russia was our so-called gallant ally. The whole atmosphere toward Russia, toward persons who were sympathetic with Russia, everything was different from what obtains today. I think you must beware of judging by today's standards things that happened in a different time and era." With that, after three and a half weeks, and nineteen days of testimony, the board adjourned. The members departed for their homes, Morgan and Gray for North Carolina, Evans for Chicago.[11]

When they reconvened on May 17, Gray and Morgan found, to their surprise, that Evans, whom they had believed to be firmly in the prosecution's camp, had changed his mind. Aware of Gray's concern that, in light of the 1947 clearance, the hearing might violate rules against double jeopardy, and that he might vote in Oppenheimer's favor, Strauss and Robb decided to act. Shortly after noon on May 20, they had Charles Bates telephone the FBI with a request that Hoover meet with the board members. They "feel that the board may be trying to find a way out to clear Oppenheimer," and wanted to "come over and talk to the director before the board does." A series of follow-up calls ensued. At 12:20 p.m., Robb called the FBI, said that it would be "a tragedy if the decision of the board goes the wrong way," and declared it "a matter of extreme urgency" that Hoover meet with the board. Ten minutes later Strauss placed a telephone call to Alan Belmont, Hoover's top counterintelligence official, and said he had just come from the White House, implying that he had spoken to the president. Things were "touch and go," Strauss said, and "a slight tip of the balance could cause the board to commit a serious error." Therefore Robb and the board members would gladly go to Hoover's out-of-town location, wherever he might be, in order to meet with him. Hoover, of course, refused. "I think it would be highly improper for me to discuss Oppenheimer case now with anyone connected with AEC or the board—JEH."[12]

Fully as remarkable as the request itself were the reactions years afterward of two participants in the approach to Hoover. In 1978, when BBC producer Peter Goodchild showed Robb, by then a federal district judge in Washington, D.C., a recently declassified FBI memo outlining the events of May 20, 1954, Robb responded, "Damned if I remember this." He subsequently dictated a statement: "I specifically and categorically deny that I ever encouraged a meeting between the board and the director for the purpose of having the director influence the board [and] have no knowledge whatsoever of any conversation between Admiral Strauss and Mr. Belmont. I never heard of any such conversation, had nothing to do with it if it occurred, and any implication to the contrary is unwarranted."[13]

Yet Robb failed to sue to prevent Goodchild's TV program from being shown in the United States. Appointed by the chief justice of the United States about this time to a panel on ethics, he subsequently named special prosecutors to investigate alleged wrongdoing by President Carter's chief of staff Hamilton Jordan, and two Reagan cabinet officers, including Attorney General Edwin Meese.

Before making his 1978 statement to Goodchild, Robb telephoned Gordon Gray; Art Rolander, his assistant at the hearing; and Charles Bates, who had carried the May 20 messages between Robb and Strauss on one hand, and high officials of the FBI on the other. Five years afterward, in an interview with the author, Bates strenuously defended Robb against any suggestion that he had wanted to influence the hearing board. "Roger is too honorable a man. It would have been suicide," he said. In an interview two weeks later, however, confronted again by Robb's statement to Goodchild and the May 20 FBI memo, Bates defended the memo's accuracy and grew angry at Robb. He had not had the memo in front of him when Robb called him in 1978, and had not known that it was declassified. "If he had shown me *that* memo, I'd have stood by it, *absolutely*" (the emphasis is Bates's). Pointing to a remark Robb had made to Goodchild, he added, "Here, he admits he took the first step. If I had him up on the witness stand, he'd be in a lot of trouble." Bates concluded by saying that he resented the Freedom of Information Act's placing him in the situation he had just been in. He had handled many high-profile cases for the FBI—Patty Hearst, the Chicago Seven, the Black Panthers—and had managed to request a transfer out of Washington just in time to avoid Watergate, but he had been sued repeatedly because of FOIA, he said, and did not like having to defend actions he had taken thirty years earlier in a different context and atmosphere.[14]

Caesar's Wife

GORDON GRAY was born at the top and had never had a failure in his life. In North Carolina as he was growing up his father was president of the R. J. Reynolds Tobacco Company. After graduating from the Yale Law School, Gray had spent two years practicing corporate law in New York City. He enlisted in the Army during World War II, rose to the rank of captain, and in 1949 was appointed secretary of the Army by President Truman. When Eisenhower asked him to serve on the board that was to hear the Oppenheimer case, he was president of the University of North Carolina and might have seen the security board as a step on the way back to public life in Washington.

Besides being virtually above criticism, Gray, a forty-four-year-old widower and father of four young boys, had a reputation for fair-mindedness. Despite this, and despite his own feeling that he had leaned over backward to protect Oppenheimer, Gray's rulings were tilted harshly against the defense, so harshly that a reader of the transcript might get the impression that he had had no training in the law and very little notion what due process was. With Oppenheimer's clearance due to expire on June 30, Gray's effort to speed up the proceeding led him at least twice to turn down requests from an exhausted Lloyd Garrison for a half hour's delay in the start of testimony the next day. But the notes he made in North Carolina during the board's ten-day recess in May show that Gray made an effort to be fair as he weighed the imperatives of security against Oppenheimer's contributions. He was impressed by the prominence of the defense witnesses and the solidarity of the scientific community in defense of Oppenheimer, and he attached special weight to the suggestion of George Kennan in his testimony that men of unusual brilliance should be held to a different standard than those of more modest capacities.[1]

On their return to Washington he and the board devoted ten days to their deliberations. Finally, by a vote of two, Gray and Morgan, against one, Evans, they decided that Oppenheimer's clearance ought not to be reinstated. The majority opinion, written by Gray and released on May 27, found nearly all of the charges having to do with the scientist's left-wing associations in Berkeley before the war to be "substantially true." Despite "poor judgment" in continuing some of those associations to the present day, however, the board found "no evidence of disloyalty. Indeed, we have before us much responsible and positive evidence of the loyalty and love of country of the individual concerned." Its decision against clearance was based on the twenty-fourth, or H-bomb, count. It found Oppenheimer inconsistent in changing his views between 1945 and 1949 as to whether the H-bomb was feasible, and inconsistent—or, worse, untruthful—in testifying that what he opposed in 1949 was only the "crash program," when he had in fact signed the GAC recommendation that the "super bomb should never be produced." While it found that Oppenheimer had done nothing actively to obstruct the H-bomb project, the board declared that his failure to make his support known among the scientists had had a negative effect on recruitment, since his "enthusiastic support" would have led others to join the program. The board believed that the opposition of many scientists, of whom Oppenheimer was the "most experienced, most powerful and most effective," had slowed development of the H-bomb. Although it considered Oppenheimer "a loyal citizen" with "a high degree of discretion reflecting an unusual ability to keep to himself vital secrets," it nonetheless ruled that clearance would not be "clearly consistent with the security interests of the United States." He was "susceptible to influence," his conduct and associations showed "serious disregard for the requirements of the security system," his conduct over the H-bomb had been "disturbing," and he had been "less than candid in several instances in his testimony."

While tortured reasoning and a tone of regret pervaded the opinion, one caveat stood out. Astonishingly, the board said that it might have reached a different conclusion had it been "allowed to exercise mature practical judgment without the rigid circumscription of regulations and criteria established for us." The regulations to which it was referring were provisions of Executive Order 10450 of the Eisenhower administration stipulating that clearance should be withheld from anyone against whom there was reliable derogatory information. This was called the "Caesar's wife" principle, it being a truism in Roman days that Caesar's wife must be above reproach. Against this was the "whole man" standard, prevalent at AEC security hearings during the Truman years, which required that favorable information should be balanced against unfavorable information.

It might have been supposed that the Eisenhower, or Caesar's wife, rule, being the more recent, should prevail, except for a June 8, 1953, ruling by the Justice Department that the AEC's existing security program exceeded requirements of the new order and that the Eisenhower rule was inapplicable. The hearing had, then, been conducted under an ad hoc combination of both regulations—with the harsher ruling prevailing in every instance. Harold Green, who had crafted the letter of charges, felt strongly at the time and afterward that among its many failings, the entire proceeding had been conducted under the wrong rules.[2]

The only member to dissent from the majority opinion was Ward Evans, the chemistry professor from Chicago who had been specially selected to be "a hanging judge." Of Oppenheimer, Evans wrote in his opinion that "to damn him now and ruin his career and his service, I cannot do it." He concluded, "I personally think that our failure to clear Dr. Oppenheimer will be a black mark on the escutcheon of our country."

And how did Gordon Gray feel about his role in a case that in his closely knit circle divided family members from one another and tempted even close friends of his to shun him? Harold Green said later that Gray never understood the nature of the proceeding he had been party to. But the columnist Roscoe Drummond wrote at the time that Gray was profoundly upset, and the widow of his closest friend, Frank Wisner, agreed, saying that she thought the case "bothered him the rest of his life." Some members of the Gray family disagree. Gray's second wife, Nancy, said Gray had "moved on" by the time she met him six months after the hearing, and his son Boyden, with whom he had many conversations over the years, said that his father told him he "never lost any sleep" over the case. But the oldest son, Gordon junior, who spent hours with his father at Walter Reed Hospital in the two weeks before he died, believed that Gray went to his grave "with very serious doubts." Again and again the father told his son how much he had admired Oppenheimer, how sorry for him he had been during the hearing, how he had worried that Oppie might break down, and how he had tried to get the hearing called off. "My father had very few failures," said the younger Gray. "He had an unblemished record, and this was the one blot on it."[3]

After publication of the opinion at the end of May, newspaper editorials in many parts of the country approved. But opinion in the *New York Times,* the *New York Herald Tribune,* and other influential dailies ran strongly against the Gray board, and Strauss quickly regretted Gray's pledge to the witnesses that their testimony would remain secret. If people could read in Oppenheimer's own words his admission that he had lied about the Chevalier affair and had spent a night in 1943 with a woman who might be a Communist Party member, Strauss thought, then opinion among the East Coast elite would turn against him.

And so it happened one evening in the first half of June that Lee Hancock of the AEC Security Division was again kept waiting while Art Rolander made a flurry of phone calls. As they drove home along the Shirley Highway, Rolander explained what had kept him. He had been telephoning the witnesses to let them know that their testimony was being released to the newspapers. Hancock was stunned. "How could you?" he asked, thinking of Gray's promise to the forty witnesses that their testimony would be treated as confidential and that the AEC would not initiate any public release. Rolander told Hancock that Robb had learned from a telephone tap that Oppie's lawyers thought his testimony showed their client in a negative light. Hancock was stunned once again. He knew, of course, that for years Oppenheimer's mail had been opened and his telephones tapped and that he was often under physical surveillance. But Hancock never got over the shock of learning that the telephones of the defense attorneys had been wiretapped throughout the hearing.[4]

As for the witnesses, some were asked for permission to have their testimony released and agreed. I. I. Rabi later said that he was not asked but was simply told that his testimony was about to appear; Norman Ramsey asked to have his remarks about the wife of a colleague excised and was embarrassed to have his request ignored and his words published as he had spoken them; those who saw George Kennan that day believe that he was not contacted, since he was giving the commencement address at his daughter's college; and Jerrold Zacharias flatly refused permission.

Strauss briefly had a pretext for releasing the testimony when Commissioner Eugene Zuckert left a notebook containing a hundred-page analysis of the evidence in a railway car near New Haven. The notebook was soon recovered, but Strauss was able to use the loss to wangle a 4–1 vote in favor of releasing the transcript, with only Harry Smyth dissenting. Gray, whose promise to the witnesses was being broken, not only went along but urged that the transcript be published. This he was persuaded to do after Strauss and Charles Murphy, another friend, warned him—untruthfully—that Lloyd Garrison was negotiating with a public relations firm in hopes of manipulating public opinion in Oppenheimer's favor. "There appears to be no respect for truth in either client or counsel," Strauss said to Gray.[5]

As relieved as they were by the Gray board's decision, Murphy and Frank Wisner, members of an influential coterie of journalists and highly placed officials who lived in Georgetown, regarded Gordon Gray's opinion as a disaster. First, it pronounced Oppenheimer "loyal" and "discreet," which they believed to be untrue. And second, by blaming him for his failure to show enthusiasm for the H-bomb, it implied that Oppie was being punished for advice he had given the government. One evening Gray's friend Wisner, head of covert action at the CIA, invited Murphy to his house after dinner to discuss the unfortunate opinion. A day or so later Murphy discussed it again with Wisner and Strauss. "The Oppenheimer ruling haunts every conversation," Murphy wrote, adding that Gray was "hurt and disturbed" by newspaper "distortion" of his opinion. But following release of the transcript in mid-June, a strategy was worked out during a dinner at the Carlton Hotel given by James Shepley of *Time* magazine, where the guests were Gray, Strauss, Murphy, Wisner, and General Wilton D. "Jerry" Persons, political adviser to the president. In accordance with the new strategy Gray flew the next day to New York, where Murphy introduced him to Henry R. Luce and Ogden Reid Jr. The *New York Herald Tribune,* the newspaper belonging to Reid's family, published the influential Walter Lippmann, whose columns were extremely critical of the way the case had been handled, and Joseph and Stewart Alsop, the most outspokenly pro-Oppenheimer and anti-Strauss reporters in the country. "The purpose of the meeting," Murphy wrote in his diary, "was to impress upon Reid that his newspaper had not reported the Oppenheimer findings objectively."[6]

With Wisner and Murphy at work on public relations, the AEC's Ken Nichols was engaged in damage control of his own. Charged with evaluating the Gray board's findings and forwarding his recommendations to the commissioners for a final decision, he faced the difficulty that six of the eight prosecution witnesses and three-quarters of the testimony had dealt with Oppenheimer's opinions on policy. With drafting help from Roger Robb, he now shifted the ground away from Oppenheimer's views and based his recommendation—that he be judged a security risk—solely on Oppenheimer's early Communist associations, his falsehoods in the Chevalier affair, and the fact that he was no longer indispensable to the atomic energy program. This shift in the prosecution's charges, together with the fact that the defense was not allowed an appeal from them, has been called the "gravest procedural defect" in the entire case.[7]

As Harry Smyth had foreseen, publication of the transcript and the Gray board's verdict did nothing to lighten the pressures under which the commission was working. Inside the AEC, the appetite for vindication was so strong that one employee compared the atmosphere to that of "a lynching." With the burden now on Strauss to come up with a persuasive and, if possible, unanimous verdict by the commissioners, the chairman was gratified to receive a telephone call on June 21 from a friend in New York. The friend was William E. Robinson, vice president of the *New York Herald Tribune,* sometime public relations man, and later president of Coca-Cola. Robinson, a "large, beefy Irishman who was probably Eisenhower's closest friend," urged Strauss to seek help in drafting his verdict and suggested Charles J. V. Murphy, author of the anonymous attack on Oppenheimer in *Fortune* the year before.[8]

Two days later Murphy and Strauss dined together, and the next day Murphy reread the Gray report with a view to correcting the impression that Oppenheimer was being punished for his opinions. When Strauss sent a rough draft of his proposed opinion to Murphy at the Time Inc. office on Connecticut Avenue, Murphy immediately found it "too short and inconclusive." To avoid the Gray board's errors, he advised that the AEC opinion should steer clear of Oppenheimer's views on policy and concentrate on "his falsehoods and his continued association with Communists," an allusion to the Oppenheimers' luncheon and dinner with Chevalier in Paris only six months before. In the course of a two-hour drafting session at Strauss's office on Friday, June 25, Murphy had the impression that Strauss was "wavering between optimism and apprehension" over the outcome of the vote. The two men spent all day Saturday working together, and before Strauss departed for a black-tie dinner honoring Winston Churchill at the White House, Murphy suggested that he bring Roger Robb along the next morning. Robb, Strauss, and Murphy had a four-hour breakfast on Sunday in Strauss's suite at the Shoreham Hotel and thoroughly revised the draft of the day before. "It was the first time Strauss seemed sure of his position," Murphy observed. That night Murphy made further changes, which he showed to Strauss over breakfast Monday morning. Strauss left for the AEC in what Murphy judged to be "a confident frame of mind."[9]

Meanwhile, at Harry Smyth's house on Woodland Drive, on a steep hill just behind the Shoreham, work was going forward on the dissent. Smyth knew that he would be in a minority, but he hoped to be joined by Zuckert or Murray in a 3–2 vote. But when he arrived home on Tuesday evening, June 22, Mary Smyth saw that he was in low spirits. He had learned that the vote would be 4 to 1, with his the only dissent. The other commissioners had given him some notion of the arguments they would be making, however, and he decided to address those with an opinion that was "shorter, stronger, and less philosophic" than the one he had originally had in mind. For the rest of the week he and Mary, together with Philip Farley and Clark Vogel, AEC employees whose help he had requested, stayed up into the wee hours each night working on successive drafts. On Saturday, Smyth wrote what his wife called a "good, short opinion," adding at the top of her diary, "H looks close to exhaustion."[10]

The other members of the drafting team were exhausted, too, and when AEC chief counsel William Mitchell delivered a first version of the majority opinion to the house at noon on Sunday, June 27, they did not read it right away. But late that afternoon, Smyth looked at it and saw that it was not what the other commissioners had told him to expect. With Oppie's clearance due to expire on Wednesday, he did not have much time in which to produce a wholly new opinion.

The same thing was repeated on Monday, when Roy Snapp of the AEC appeared at 3000 Woodland Drive about 7:00 p.m. with the majority opinion. Having no inkling about the sessions at the Shoreham and no idea that Murphy and Robb had worked on the decision too, Smyth was greatly surprised by the final version. The wording, the emphasis, and, above all, the tone of the new opinion differed so much from the draft he had seen on Sunday night—the Strauss-Murphy version of Friday and Saturday—that he knew he would have to start all over again. As they began work that night he worried whether his loyal secretaries, Mary Sweeney and Evelyn McQuown, would lose their AEC jobs and pensions, and he was concerned about Farley, who had been matter-of-factly informed by Nichols that helping Smyth with his opinion would do his AEC career no good. And he was aware of a car parked in the cul-de-sac down the street. He assumed it was the FBI, keeping track of their comings and goings.[11]

The decision had been hammered out by the majority commissioners during an all-day session on Monday and was signed by Strauss, Commissioner Joseph Campbell, and Zuckert. Strauss had agreed to a slight weakening of the version he had approved that morning with Murphy, probably to placate Eugene Zuckert, but it was still a stunning personal attack on Oppenheimer. Specifying at the outset that Oppenheimer's position on the H-bomb had nothing to do with its decision, the board stated that Oppenheimer was no longer entitled to the government's trust because of "fundamental defects in his character." The proof was that "his associations with persons known to him to be Communists have extended far beyond the tolerable limits of prudence and self-restraint" to be expected from one holding high positions of trust. "These associations have lasted too long to be justified as merely the intermittent and accidental revival of earlier friendships." The opinion listed six associations about which he had allegedly lied, with emphasis on the Chevalier affair, concerning which he had either lied to Boris Pash in 1943 or to the Gray board in 1954. It added that the associations themselves, and not just his lying about them, were "part of the pattern of his disregard for the obligations of security."[12]

In addition to signing the majority statement, Zuckert and Campbell each wrote a separate concurring opinion that pointedly excluded Oppenheimer's advice to the government as a factor. Thomas Murray, meanwhile, also voted to revoke Oppenheimer's clearance, but such was his resentment of the way Strauss had handled the case that he refused to sign the majority statement. Instead he produced a separate decision pronouncing Oppenheimer disloyal because he lacked loyalty to the security system as such. "It will not do to plead that Dr. Oppenheimer revealed no secrets to Communists and fellow travelers," Murray said. It was the associations themselves that offended. That Oppie should have maintained them at all was an act of disloyalty. To allow him to place himself above the security regulations was "to invite the destruction of the whole security system."[13]

Strauss had violated a promise to Smyth that he would have a full twenty-four hours in which to write his dissent, and the six of them on Woodland Drive once again worked all night, revising a passage here, putting in a stronger word there, and trying to make the dissent responsive, point by point, to the majority opinion. Smyth at one point looked up and said, "You know, I'm doing all this for a fellow I've never liked very much. Of course," he added, "I'm not doing it for *him*." He and his helpers felt that what they were doing, they were doing for history, a mission larger than the cause of justice to any one individual. And they hoped their dissent might serve as a basis for reopening the case someday.[14]

Smyth brought up the fact, about which the majority statement maintained a stunning silence, that Oppenheimer had not been charged with, or found guilty of, ever having divulged a single secret. In this, Smyth wrote, lay proof of his future trustworthiness. "The past fifteen years of his life have been investigated and reinvestigated. For much of the last eleven years he has been under actual surveillance. This professional review . . . has been supplemented by enthusiastic amateur help from powerful personal enemies. Few men could survive such a period of investigation and interrogation without having many of their actions misinterpreted." Smyth refuted the charges having to do with Oppenheimer's personal associations and called the Chevalier affair the only "inexcusable" episode in the story (a word he later wished he had weakened). He denied that Oppenheimer had impeded the H-bomb, adding, "The history of his contributions stands untarnished." Finally, he dismissed the alleged "fundamental defects in his character," describing Oppenheimer instead as "an able, imaginative human being with normal weaknesses and failings." He said that the board should have exercised "overall commonsense judgment." It was the conclusions of the majority, he said, that were "so extreme as to endanger the security system."[15]

About four o'clock in the morning Smyth took the unfinished draft to his study and worked alone. Two hours later he emerged with the final opinion. The weary secretaries typed it up, Mary Smyth made breakfast, and Farley took the dissent to the commission, where he stood watch over the mimeograph machine to be sure that no one changed it. On the following day, June 30, Mary Smyth wrote in her diary: "We buy newspapers and wonder what we have done."[16]

As for the other commissioners, Murray was a devout Roman Catholic whose faith frequently impelled him in directions where other men did not go. For years he had maintained a special channel to his fellow Catholic J. Edgar Hoover, and in accordance with what the FBI chieftain had said to him, Murray did not think Oppenheimer was a Communist. But he felt that the issue of Oppie's observance of security regulations "outweighed any question of equity to an individual." Murray's fellow commissioners viewed him as a wild card. They had no idea how he was going to vote, but since he was not much of a writer, they assumed that someone else had written his opinion for him. They thought the author was either his son, Daniel Bradley Murray, who was then in training for the priesthood, or the worldly and highly regarded Jesuit theologian John Courtney Murray, spiritual counselor not only of Tom Murray but of Clare and Henry Luce (he was known as the "Luces' Richelieu"). Queried about his father's opinion years afterward at the boys' school outside Baltimore where he was teaching, Father Daniel Bradley Murray said that he did not know how his father had voted in the Oppenheimer case but added, however, that he had consulted John Courtney Murray about "everything." His father would "put together all the problems he had at a particular time and consult him about them all at once." While a search of John Courtney Murray's papers has turned up no early drafts or other evidence that he was the true author of Thomas Murray's opinion, it remains a good guess that he was.[17]

Strauss did not leave the votes of the other two commissioners to chance. One, Joseph Campbell, was his creature. Campbell had been chief financial officer of Columbia University when, in the early 1950s, Strauss, in behalf of the Rockefeller family, negotiated a new lease of the land under Radio City with the university. Strauss, whose acquaintance with Eisenhower dated from this period, had had Campbell appointed to the commission and, after the hearing, had him shunted to the post of comptroller general of the United States so that he could make a new appointment to the AEC.[18]

Eugene Zuckert's vote was a different matter. Like Gordon Gray, Zuckert was a Democrat and a Yale Law graduate, and his friends were mostly New Dealers. He had been assistant secretary of the Air Force and was later to be secretary, but at this moment his term as commissioner was expiring and he had no new job in sight. He remembered years later that in December 1953, when the case was getting under way, Strauss had sent his car for him, had him brought to the commission, and offered him a job as head of a foundation Strauss had created in his mother's memory. It was such a "barefaced" attempt to bribe Zuckert into leaving that "I was completely shocked." What governed his opinion, Zuckert said, was concern about Oppenheimer's judgment. "I've lain awake at night. This man had national security responsibilities of the absolutely highest order. It was a question of what his judgment would be in the ultimate case and you had no way of predicting when that case might be presented to him. I just didn't go along with his judgment, particularly on security matters. The scientists tend to have contempt for security anyhow. He had a very condescending attitude toward security." Gray wondered whether Oppie was unstable, while Zuckert wondered about his judgment. It seemed to Zuckert afterward that, intellectually, he and Gray were "on the same plane."[19]

But Zuckert's written opinion seems forced, as if every word had to be wrung out of him. After the hearing, and after his departure as a commissioner, Strauss kept him on as a consultant and did other minor favors for him but apparently did not offer Zuckert the one thing that might have tempted him, a new term as commissioner. Harold Green, who admired Zuckert as "a man of massive integrity," found him, two or three days before the vote, intending to vote in Oppenheimer's favor. Something made him reconsider, presumably something more compelling than the last-minute changes in the majority statement that he managed to obtain from Strauss. Phil Farley, an outstandingly objective AEC employee, considered Zuckert an ambitious man of limited ability who was worried that he did not have a job awaiting him after his term expired. "He didn't think Oppie was a security risk, he was afraid his own career would be at risk" if he voted the wrong way. Avoiding the enmity of Lewis Strauss, Farley thought, was probably sufficient.[20]

Zuckert's later years reeked of regret, and he told friends many times that it had wounded him to reach the conclusion he did. "Here was this brilliant, accomplished man. It hurt to be objective." And he would quote Supreme Court justice Abe Fortas, whom he had known since Yale Law School days. Fortas had told him that "there are times when you have to rise above principle," meaning that he should have voted to clear Oppenheimer because Oppie was exceptional. Joe Volpe, who was close to Zuckert, was convinced that he regretted his vote as long as he lived. Asked about it a decade before he died, Zuckert nodded. "It was the saddest thing I ever took part in. It cost me a lot of friendships and I had to be on the same side as people I did not respect."[21]

CHAPTER TWENTY-TWO

Do We Really Need Scientists?

ON THE AFTERNOON of June 29, the day the AEC announced the
verdict in Washington, Strauss telephoned James Hagerty at the
White House with news of the 4–1 vote. The president, who had just
concluded a four-day visit with British prime minister Winston
Churchill, called back to congratulate him on the "fine job" he had
done and said he hoped Strauss's handling of the case "would be such
a contrast to McCarthy's tactics that the American people would immediately see the difference."[1]

Throughout the Oppenheimer affair Strauss had consulted regu-
larly with presidential press secretary James Hagerty, and on critical
days he had met with Hagerty or the president first thing in the morning. He met at least a dozen other times with the president alone or his
assistants Sherman Adams or Robert Cutler, and on some if not all of
those occasions the hearing was a subject of discussion. In addition,
the president's personal assistant, the normally acidulous Ann Whitman, made an exception for Strauss, whom she called "the sweetest
man I ever did see," and gave him access to the Oval Office whenever
he wanted a word with the president. Strauss had told Eisenhower, untruthfully, that the Oppenheimers had stayed with the Chevaliers for
several days the previous winter, instead of having had two meals together, and this misinformation is said to have weighed heavily with
Eisenhower. Strauss had told the president about the trouble he was
having with the Democratic members of the commission, all three of
whom, Murray, Zuckert, and Smyth, had, during the hearing, testified in Congress against his effort to codify his de facto role as ruler of
the commission. The president was "concerned" by what Strauss told

him about growing Democratic resistance to him inside the AEC and was "more determined than ever" to appoint someone who could work with Strauss when Zuckert's appointment expired at the end of June.[2]

In addition to Hagerty and the president himself, Attorney General Herbert Brownell had had a role in the case. Three years before his death he wrote the author, "I wasn't directly involved in the Oppenheimer affair, but I do recall that President Eisenhower took an active interest in the progress of the Gray board hearings and asked me to review their findings from the standpoint of procedural due process." The record shows, however, that Brownell had taken part in all the major decisions: the president consulted him before deciding to lower the "blank wall"; he gave the FBI permission to wiretap Oppenheimer's attorneys; and the day before the hearing began he spent three hours at Strauss's farm discussing, among other things, whether Oppenheimer might be subject to criminal charges.[3]

On the afternoon of June 29, when the commissioners' decision was announced, Strauss paused to honor and to thank. He called on J. Edgar Hoover at the FBI, and had dinner with the other Hoover, the former president who had made his career and on whom he still looked as a father. A day or two later he paid an afternoon visit to the president and celebrated over dinner with Charles Murphy and Frank Wisner. In many respects it was Murphy whose contribution was the most spectacular of all. Not only had he written the 1953 *Fortune* articles opening the attack on Oppenheimer, but he had been the first to realize that the Gray opinion was a disaster for the government, since it gave the impression that Oppenheimer was being punished for his opinions. He had taken charge immediately and masterminded the campaign to turn public opinion around. And he was principal author of the savage majority opinion. Which of them it was, Strauss, Robb, or Murphy, who coined the phrase "substantial defects in his character" is anybody's guess. One individual who knew Murphy well considered him the likeliest candidate, although any of the three could have done it.[4]

Recompense was in Strauss's mind, but Murphy refused payment, viewing what he had done as a public service. So Strauss did the next best thing—he shared his incomparable contacts. After the *Fortune* articles the year before he had, unsolicited, given Murphy an introduction to young King Baudouin of Belgium, who had come to his throne in difficult circumstances and was said to be looking for public relations help. Now that the Oppenheimer case was over, Strauss sent a car for Murphy in Georgetown one evening in August 1954 and had him delivered to his country home in Culpeper, Virginia. There, he told Murphy over a magnificent dinner that his friend Helen Rogers Reid was looking for someone to buy her newspaper, the *New York Herald Tribune*. Would Murphy like to be the editor?[5]

Of the two wild men Strauss had enlisted to help diminish Oppenheimer, one, Charlie Murphy, had stayed in harness and come through with flying colors. But what of the AEC chairman's other charger, Bill Borden? Borden was now working for Westinghouse in Pittsburgh, but he had not forgotten his glory days at the congressional committee. For him it was not enough that his letter to Hoover had prompted the president to take action against Oppenheimer: the scientist's destruction was merely act 1 of a two-part scenario which he and Strauss probably concocted together in the late summer or early fall of 1951. Act 2 was to make Teller the new Oppenheimer. And so in January 1954, Clay Blair, the twenty-nine-year-old Pentagon correspondent of *Time* magazine, received a letter postmarked Pittsburgh. The author of the letter congratulated Blair on his newly published book about Hyman Rickover, father of the nuclear-powered submarine. He added that the story of Edward Teller and the hydrogen bomb was equally impressive and expressed surprise that *Time* had not yet found room for Teller on its cover. The author's name was not familiar: William L. Borden.[6]

A week or so later Blair found himself in a mansion overlooking Rock Creek Park in Washington. Down from Pittsburgh for the weekend, Borden had invited Blair to his mother's house to tell him about Teller's battle to build the hydrogen bomb over the opposition of Robert Oppenheimer. And he had a story to tell! Blair's usual beat was the Navy and he did not know much about Teller and Oppenheimer, but what he was hearing reminded him of the story he had just written: Teller fought Oppie and the GAC to build the hydrogen bomb, Rickover was said to have fought the same opponents to build his nuclear sub, and Blair wondered what Oppenheimer had been up to, opposing these projects to strengthen the United States. Borden hinted at an answer: was Oppie, with his left-wing past, trying to help the Soviet Union? Borden did not mention Oppenheimer's being in trouble with the government or say anything about a prospective hearing. He struck Blair as disinterested, idealistic, anything but a huckster with something to sell.

Blair raced back to his office at *Time* on Connecticut Avenue and informed his bureau chief, James Shepley, that this guy Teller was a hell of a story. Shepley wanted to meet Borden, and Blair introduced them over lunch. He did not see Borden again.[7]

A week or two later, Shepley and Blair found themselves at the Tellers' house in California. Mici Teller cooked a "fabulous" dinner, Edward played Beethoven on the piano, and they had a "wild" evening lasting six or seven hours. Early in the evening, as Teller and Shepley discussed philosophers, Blair realized that Teller, like Rickover, had an "awesome" mind. One bibulous evening led to another as Teller dispatched them to San Diego to see Freddie de Hoffmann, Los Alamos to see Ulam, and Livermore to see Lawrence and York. Everyone they talked to seemed enthusiastic about Teller and the H-bomb.[8]

The fifteen-thousand-word "take," or raw file, that Blair wrote after his return created a sensation at *Time*. Although it was not yet in print (being raw material for the planned cover story), everyone in the New York office was reading it. Even Turner Catledge, top editor at the *New York Times,* got a glimpse of it and said that this young fellow Blair ought to get the Pulitzer. Given Blair's story and the flap it caused, it was natural for an outgoing, fabulously well connected *Fortune* writer with a desk in *Time*'s Washington bureau to take Blair under his wing. Charles J. V. Murphy was, as usual, commuting between Washington and New York, working on a dozen projects at once, but he had lost none of his enthusiasm for the Air Force. He introduced

Blair to what Blair later called the Air Force "cabal." The most flamboyant member of the cabal was Teddy Walkowicz, like Murphy a commuter to New York, where he advised Laurence Rockefeller on aviation investments. Walkowicz's franchise at the Pentagon appeared to be the care and feeding of the in-house Hungarians: Theodore von Karmann of the rocket program, Edward Teller, and Johnny von Neumann. Blair later remembered nonstop discussions of weapons systems in a tiny room in the science area of the Pentagon. At the blackboard a bald, emaciated professor would be jotting down statistics about the number of Russians who could be wiped out by a single atomic bomb, all the while sipping from a glass of milk for his ulcers. He was W. Barton Leach, wise man of the cabal and professor of property law on leave from the Harvard Law School. Another member was Colonel Bob Orr, a frequent source of Murphy's stories on science and strategy. The cabal was anti-Army, anti-Navy, anti-Russian, and out to "kill Oppenheimer" if they could. Blair later remembered the cabalists as "fanatics," very, very different from the low-key, intellectual-appearing Borden.[9]

That spring, *Time*'s Teller cover was shelved at Teller's request. He had learned that his mother and sister were alive and still in Hungary. He was worried about them, and the U.S. government was worried about him and the pressure he would be under from both the Russians and the Hungarians should their attention be drawn to his role in building the H-bomb. Blair started to interview Strauss with the idea of converting his Teller take into a book. And, always the prodigal friend, Charlie Murphy took Blair and Shepley to lunch with his book publisher, Ken Rawson (publisher also of the Duke and Duchess of Windsor) in New York, and a contract was signed for *The Hydrogen Bomb.*

By the time Blair learned about the Oppenheimer hearing, he said later, his book was three-quarters written. Fortunately his coauthor, James Shepley, a great reporter but one who lacked fluency and did little if any writing on the book, knew Gordon Gray. One day in June, Shepley called him into his office and, pointing to a stack of papers, explained that these were galleys of the Oppenheimer hearing. Blair's surprise turned to incredulity when Shepley told him that the transcript had been leaked to him by Gordon Gray.*

By now it was almost mid-June, and the book was due at the publisher's. For three or four days Shepley and Blair stayed up around the clock, feverishly extracting anecdotes from the testimony and back-feeding them into their manuscript. No sooner had they finished than Shepley had a summons from Lewis Strauss. The two reporters arrived at the AEC in early evening and, Blair recalled, found a fire going in Strauss's office. Strauss had been up all night reading their manuscript and greeted them with an astonishing offer: if they would agree to withhold publication, he would place twenty-five thousand dollars of his own funds in a safe-deposit box and it would be theirs upon his death. If the book was published now, he explained, the scientific community, which was already overwhelmingly in favor of Oppenheimer, would turn irrevocably against Teller. And that would undermine what he was trying to do: turn Teller into the new Oppenheimer.[10]

Blair and Shepley explained to Strauss that with everyone leaking to everyone else and most of the leakers convinced that Oppenheimer was a spy, there was no way to put twenty-five thousand dollars in a safe and make the story go away.

The authors met their deadline, and throughout the summer their book was at the publisher's in New York, ticking like a time bomb.

Most of the public was shocked by the verdict. As for the physicists, nearly all of whom had agreed with Oppie about the H-bomb, they began to wonder when *they* might be hauled before some tribunal and have their reputations ruined for opinions they had expressed years before, under wholly different circumstances. Vannevar Bush spoke for virtually the entire community when he wrote in the *New York Times* in June that the partnership between government and the scientists that had grown up during the war was being destroyed by a security

---

*The author doubts that Gray leaked the transcript and believes the leak was the work of one of Strauss's minions.

system gone wild. Bush pointed out that service to the government was not a privilege, as Lewis Strauss liked to say, but a duty, sometimes a disagreeable duty, which scientists would perform wholeheartedly only if they had confidence in the government. They had shown solidarity in defense of Oppenheimer because they believed he was being persecuted for expressing opinions that were not official policy of the moment. Scientists would not boycott government projects, Bush said, but they would work with a heavy heart—and at a moment when the country needed the utmost they could offer. He urged scientists to remain united and said that ordinary citizens, too, should ask whether they were being led into the "fallacies of totalitarianism."[11]

It was August before most of the scientists at the weapons labs had time to wade through the 992-page transcript. At Los Alamos, 493 scientists signed a statement of protest, and at the Argonne National Lab in Illinois, another 214. In a letter to the *Bulletin of the Atomic Scientists* Carson Mark, self-described "midwife" of the hydrogen bomb, compared the Oppenheimer hearing to the "Salem witchcraft delusion," and Vannevar Bush declared that nuclear research was nearly at a standstill because of Strauss's "gumshoeing" against the scientists. In an effort to stanch the damage, Strauss flew to Los Alamos to award the lab a presidential citation. But "Operation Butter-up," as the Los Alamites called it, fooled no one, and the scientists angrily told Strauss that the hearing had created a "very grave morale problem." To this day it is said that after Strauss snapped some photographs, Ralph Carlisle Smith, the lab's patent officer, confiscated the film on grounds that the picture taking had been a breach of security. A month or so later Harry Smyth was sent to New Mexico to pour oil on the troubled waters.[12]

Edward Teller visited Los Alamos that summer and had an experience he did not forget. After giving an interview to Robert Coughlan of *Life* magazine, Teller joined a picnic on the terrace outside Fuller Lodge. He went up to Bob Christy, an old friend who had shared his house in Chicago, and offered his hand. Christy looked at him coldly, refused his hand, and turned away. "I realized that my life as I had known it was over," Teller wrote later.[13]

Those who had been at the lab during the war could not help re-membering Teller's wartime record: he had sat out "the main event," as Carson Mark called the effort to build the A-bomb, and chosen in-stead to work on the hypothetical hydrogen bomb just when all hands were needed to work on a bomb that would end the war. And those who had been present later, during work on the thermonuclear bomb, remembered him as a contentious colleague whose lobbying led to the establishment of a new laboratory at the very moment when Los Alamos was going all-out to test Mike. Now, as they read his testimony, they were appalled. He was Brutus. He had sunk his knife into Oppenheimer and betrayed every one of them.

Imagine their feelings when a book called *The Hydrogen Bomb: The Men, the Menace, the Mechanism* appeared that fall, accusing Op-penheimer, Bradbury, and the lab of what amounted to treason. The authors, James Shepley and Clay Blair, had written that Los Alamos during World War II had been "loaded with Communists and former Communists" hired by Oppenheimer. After Joe One, the lab, still "soft on Communism," had opposed the hydrogen bomb, and Op-penheimer's stooge, Bradbury, had dragged his feet. Even after Tru-man's decision, the authors claimed, Bradbury had refused to put his best men at Teller's disposal, and the lab had remained "indifferent, more often hostile," to the H-bomb. Most of the key wartime scien-tists had not only refused to participate in the program but had lob-bied against it while, following their elders' lead, younger scientists had "stayed away in droves." Shepley and Blair charged that most of the lab members who attended the Greenhouse test in 1951 had been hoping for a failure. And they dealt with the Ulam-Teller break-through merely by saying that something Ulam suggested had "turned on a small light in Teller's storehouse of ideas" and that the laboratory continued to resist Teller's new approach. Oppenheimer, they said, opposed the new concept but at the June 1951 conference at Princeton had had no choice but to give in. Finally Teller realized that he was outflanked and that the nation would be in danger if he did not leave Los Alamos. Not until Livermore opened its doors was Los Alamos finally goaded into building the H-bomb.

The truth was that in 1954, when the book was written, Livermore had been in existence for two years and had so far had nothing but failures. It had held two tests, both designed by Teller, and they had been inglorious fizzles. Because of secrecy, Bradbury was not allowed to correct the record. All he could say was that Los Alamos had "developed every successful thermonuclear weapon that exists today in the free world."[14]

Gordon Dean, chairman of the AEC during the period in question, wrote that the book was "vicious" and that Shepley and Blair were like a pair of "plumbers going to work on a delicate Swiss watch." Along with everyone else in a responsible position, he worried about the harm their hatchet job might do to the weapons program. But he and Bradbury could respond only up to a point: the H-bomb, as Dean had said, was like a delicate Swiss watch whose workings could not be described because the name of each component was secret, as was the interaction between them. Only two people were in a position to discredit the Shepley-Blair book. The president wasn't going to do it because he had been deceived by Strauss and did not know the truth. And Strauss declined pleas from two of the parties who had been libeled, Bradbury and Dean, that he repudiate the volume. Likewise, he turned down an appeal from the ten Los Alamos division leaders on the specious ground that if he spoke out, it would boost sales. Strauss's refusal to repudiate the book was an act of unbelievable disloyalty, since he was head of the AEC, Los Alamos was his lab, and the scientists were his scientists. And it was painfully clear that many of the book's so-called facts could have come only from him.[15]

Bradbury was so outraged that on September 24 he gave an extraordinary press conference at Los Alamos, only the second such appearance he had ever made. Despite the stifling secrecy regulations, he managed to answer the book's most egregious calumnies. And, in his desire to set the record straight, he did something no one would be allowed to do even today: he held aloft what he called the "Ulam-Teller" paper of March 9, 1951, to let reporters know that Teller had not invented the H-bomb alone. There had been another author, and his contribution was such that perhaps the usual alphabetical order should be reversed to "Ulam-Teller." No one in the room had heard of Stanislaw Ulam, not even the best-informed among them, Robert McKinney, publisher of the *Santa Fe New Mexican,* and Bradbury had to spell out the name Ulam.

That fall Joseph and Stewart Alsop published a column asking, "Do we really need scientists, or can we just make do with Lewis Strauss?" The Alsops said that, coming on the heels of the hearing, the Shepley-Blair volume had "turned what was formerly a brush fire into a perfect conflagration of fury." That the book was the second part of a two-part plan to destroy Oppenheimer and make Teller the leader of the scientific community, and that both parts of the plan had been set in motion by William Borden, was known to no one except, perhaps, Lewis Strauss. One observer got the drift, however. Writing in the *Reporter* magazine, Elie Abel said that the book "set out to topple a particular god from his pedestal and to raise a new one in his place. The protagonists remain larger-than-life figures, casting portentous shadows on a darkened stage."[16]

Did Teller know that he was to be the beneficiary of Oppenheimer's downfall? Probably. But he would have given his testimony without that. For years he had been saying that Oppenheimer did not have good judgment. He had made secret statements against Oppie to the FBI since 1949 and to Borden and the JCAE since 1950, and had criticized him in devastating terms to the FBI on two occasions in 1952. Teller had not expected his testimony to be made public, and fear of becoming a pariah among scientists led him, within days of the commission's decision, to draft a press statement seeking to correct the impression that he might consider someone a security risk because of his opinions. He sent his proposed statement to Strauss, who in turn sent it to Roger Robb. Robb got back to Teller with an edited text but advised that silence was best. Teller followed Robb's advice and dropped the idea.[17]

Teller wrote Strauss a letter of thanks. "It is not possible for me to tell you in any short or simple way how grateful I am to you for many things you have done. The list would be too long and *the most*

important item I cannot mention" (italics added). The unmentionable
item had to do with Teller's relatives. Strauss had already spoken to
Allen Dulles, director of the Central Intelligence Agency, about getting Teller's mother, sister, and nephew out of Hungary. Now, after
receiving Teller's thanks, he sent Dulles a reminder.[18]

But Teller still wanted to retract. About the time the Shepley-Blair
volume appeared, an article lionizing him appeared in *Life* magazine
by another writer for the Luce publications, Robert Coughlan. It was
clear that Coughlan had not only drawn on Shepley and Blair's material in the *Time* files but had had help from Teller himself. All this
deepened the animosity of the other scientists and made Teller afraid
that he would be unable to set foot in Los Alamos again. He therefore
drafted an article outlining a history of the hydrogen bomb in which
he shared the credit.

Once again he consulted Strauss, who advised against publishing.
Meanwhile he had a letter from Laura Fermi telling him that her husband, Enrico, was dying of stomach cancer. Teller flew to Chicago to
see Fermi, bringing along a copy of his draft. Anxious to mend the split
among the scientists, Fermi asked to see it. He read for half an hour or
so, then looked up and inquired, "What reason would you have *not* to
publish this?" Teller explained that after all the criticism, he no longer
knew what to do. "Enrico advised me strongly and insistently to publish it."[19]

The article, "The Work of Many People," appeared in *Science*
magazine in February 1955. After recounting the early theoretical
discoveries of George Gamow, Bethe, and Fermi, Teller described
H-bomb work at Los Alamos, naming many of those who had contributed and singling out his protégé, Freddie de Hoffmann, for special praise. He credited Ulam and Everett with showing that early
calculations on the H-bomb had been in error and eliminating the
flawed model the lab had been working on, but added only that the
impasse had been broken by two hopeful indicators, "one an imaginative suggestion by Ulam, the other a fine calculation by de Hoffmann." He was modest about his own contribution, giving himself
credit mostly for his steadfast belief that the bomb could and should

be made. "I find myself in a position of being given certainly too much credit and perhaps too much blame for what has happened." He concluded that the H-bomb ought to unite, not divide, those who had contributed to it and warned, "Disunity of the scientists is one of the greatest dangers for our country."[20]

This was the most credit Teller would ever extend to Ulam. He gave many versions of the H-bomb story in the years ahead, and Ulam's role shrank with each version. One reason for this, he said, was that Ulam had not really believed the bomb would work, since he had cast doubt on it in a letter to von Neumann in 1951 ("Edward is enthusiastic, possibly a sign that it will not work"), and that if he did not believe in his own invention, then he did not deserve credit.

But Teller's outcast status bothered him and he wanted to make amends. In 1961, when he was writing a book called *The Legacy of Hiroshima,* Teller asked Lewis Strauss for advice about his chapter on the Oppenheimer case. Strauss warned that he would be seen as a "repentant witness" and advised him not to publish the chapter. Strauss also passed it along to Charles Murphy, who met with Teller three times in an effort to dissuade him and even brought Gordon Gray along. Murphy advised: "Believe me, Edward, I know how hard all this is for you. The world is also hard. It is replete with ambushes. I suggest that you walk warily and keep a sharp look in all directions."[21]

The Legacy of Hiroshima appeared the following year without a chapter on the Oppenheimer affair.

In the decade between 1944 and 1954, Teller had settled old scores. With the AEC hearing, he avenged himself on Oppenheimer for refusing to make him head of the Theoretical Physics Division of the Manhattan Project in 1944 and, very likely, for a number of perceived slights since then. With Livermore, he took revenge on Bradbury for refusing the conditions he had put on staying at Los Alamos in 1946 and refusing to place him in overall charge of the H-bomb program in 1951: if he couldn't be master of the first laboratory, he would have a laboratory of his own. The third case, that of Ulam, was the most complicated: Ulam had trumped Teller twice, once when he proved that the Super conceived by Teller was unworkable, and again when he himself conceived two of the three ideas that made the radiation-implosion bomb possible. To get even with Ulam for undermining his proudest claim, that of being father of the H-bomb, Teller avenged himself by trying to erase his rival from the history books and make him a nonperson.

Looking at all this, the Freudian observer might say that during the decade between 1944 and 1954 Teller symbolically destroyed each of the three men who had dealt him a severe narcissistic blow. The layperson might conclude, more simply, that he sought to destroy the three men who had stood in his way.

Oppenheimer

KITTY AND ROBERT returned to Princeton, where he continued to run the Institute for Advanced Study and she gardened in the greenhouse they had built at Olden Manor. Ten-year-old Toni and fourteen-year-old Peter came home from the Hempelmanns' in Rochester, New York, where they had stayed in May, and that summer the four of them went sailing off St. John's, in the Virgin Islands. Meanwhile, Lewis Strauss tried to build a majority on the institute's board of trustees for firing Robert.

Robert did not tell his closest friends in the physics community, Rabi, Bethe, Victor Weisskopf, and Abraham Pais, about this new humiliation, and when the trustees voted on October 1 to retain him, it was with McGeorge Bundy, who had helped draft the Oppenheimer panel report two years before, Mary Bundy, and newspaper columnist Joe Alsop that Kitty and Robert celebrated at the Alsops' family home in Avon, Connecticut. Physicist friends of Robert's who still had Q clearances and had stayed on as advisers to the government found themselves in an excruciating position. Virtually everything they had discussed with him during the past dozen years, all the questions about weapons policy, were off limits now. Old friends from Pasadena like Bacher and Lauritsen made a point of visiting when they were in the East, and Bethe and Weisskopf when they were anywhere near Princeton, but as Rabi's daughter Nancy Lichtenstein said later, it was as though they had been cut off in midconversation with Robert.

The autumn after the hearing Schatzi Davis, wife of lab member Bob Davis and neighbor of the Oppenheimers' at Los Alamos, went to see them and found everything changed. Instead of dust in the air and Navajo rugs on the floor and the smell of one of Kitty's pot roasts on the stove, instead of Robert's coming home from work filled with life and eager to see his family, she found the two of them spent and rather formal and sad. Even the food and the serving of it were different—a coddled egg, a butler, a canned half peach without liqueur—and, seeing how it all had changed, Schatzi could not hold back tears. Desperate to change the mood, Robert took her to inspect their new refrigerator, then went off alone to his study.

Robert was more of a presence at the institute than he had been when he was commuting to Washington, and his friends Harold Cherniss and Freeman Dyson thought he was a better director. As he had done before at Berkeley and Los Alamos, he had built the institute into one of the world's great centers of physics, and while he no longer did much original work in physics himself, he stayed abreast through institute luminaries such as T. D. Lee and Dyson and Abraham Pais, and went right on making his famously downputting remarks at seminars. At home and abroad, he lectured on larger questions of science and human values and took up with a group of cold war intellectuals clustered around the Congress for Cultural Freedom of Paris and New York, a group later found to have been secretly funded by the CIA. One of his most valued friends in the congress and at the institute was George Kennan, whose appointment as a permanent faculty member Oppenheimer secured in 1955 over the fierce opposition of the institute's fractious mathematicians.

Dyson, who frequently came upon Kitty up to the elbows in earth in her greenhouse, and Cherniss, a great listener who saw a good deal of Robert, thought the Oppenheimers recovered surprisingly well. But nearly everyone else thought they were devastated. This was especially obvious with Kitty, who had been Robert's chief support and on occasion could still put up a valiant front. But even during Los Alamos days, Kitty used to drink more than was good for her, and now her drinking grew worse. Alcohol, together with medicine she took for her pancreatitis, made her already sharp tongue even sharper. The atmosphere around her could be withering, and the children suffered. Peter, to whom by all accounts she was not a loving parent, said years later, "My father's tragedy was not that he lost his clearance, but my mother's slow descent into the hell of alcoholism." Then he added, "Cut that word 'slow.' "[1]

Early in their marriage Kitty had made Robert break with old acquaintances, and now her biases about people and her not infrequent cruelty drove even loyal friends away. If a woman who at some time or other had meant something to Robert came to see them, Kitty would withdraw to her bedroom and make her displeasure unmistakably plain. Ruth Tolman, widow of Oppie's mentor Richard Tolman, was one of these; Anne Marks, wife and then widow of Herb Marks, was another; and so was Robert's favorite cousin, Babette, who after Hiroshima had sent him a postcard of congratulations: "We always knew you'd set the world on fire."

Peter Oppenheimer, now in his sixties, says that his father coped well. But George Kennan observed that Kitty was a grave liability in Robert's relationships with others. "He was accused of being arrogant, but she made him more arrogant than he was and would egg him on to be intolerant of this or that person. If he hadn't been a pretty strong person and had a touching devotion and a willingness to put up with almost anything, he'd have been destroyed by her as the children were. I think she was a great burden to him." Even those who agreed with Kennan—and nearly everybody did—conceded that the Oppenheimers were, in the words of one witness, "welded" to each other, that they were deeply and mutually loyal, and that, along with the destructiveness, they gave each other unqualified support.[2]

Verna Hobson, Oppenheimer's secretary, a person of great distinction, saw Robert up close. She had worked for him for nearly a year when, around Christmas of 1953, she saw that he was in trouble. After she had made what she calls, without specifying, "a gesture of trust," he invited her into his office, told her about his earlier life as a fellow traveler, and asked her to be his principal secretary. When, soon afterward, seeing the toll the hearing was taking on him, she urged him to fight tooth and nail, his response made her realize that, as he saw it, the hearing was the unavoidable outcome, not of any single misstep, such as his humiliation of Strauss at the isotopes hearing, but of his entire life and the way he had lived it. It was this sense that the government had pronounced judgment on him, not for what he had done, but for what he was, that kept him from walking out as Volpe suggested. He had to fight *his* way, and Mrs. Hobson believed it was this that led him to choose the gentlemanly Lloyd Garrison as his attorney. She had no sense that he ever felt, as Kitty and many of his friends did, that Garrison failed him.[3]

But from feeling that the hearing was inevitable, how far was it to feeling that his prosecutors were right and that he was guilty of *something*, even if not of the specific offenses with which he was charged? For a man who, for all the vaunted "arrogance," had lived most of his life in a state of existential uncertainty, what was it like to be pronounced unworthy because of "substantial defects in his character"? Was it not crushing confirmation of what, beneath the mystique, he had believed all along?

Verna Hobson later said that Oppenheimer's growth during his last ten years or so was the most exciting thing she had ever witnessed. By this she meant primarily that he grew in his capacity for relationships and in his understanding of others. His time as a Harvard undergraduate had been "perfect," he told her, except that he had had no talent for friendship then. Mrs. Hobson, like Joe Volpe, pointed to something else. After the hearing, Oppenheimer never said a word in public to disparage the AEC—much though there was to disparage. Nor was he critical of the government. Once again, just as at his trial, the government counted on his loyalty even as it tried to destroy him.

In smaller ways, Oppenheimer still fell short of the perfection he required of himself. He was a "totally demanding" boss, expecting Mrs. Hobson, when she first worked for him, to take dictation in English, French, and German and in mathematical formulas. He preempted the private lives of those who worked for him. And when the White House announced in April 1963 that President Kennedy would present him with the Fermi Prize that fall, Robert "could hardly bear it" and wanted to decline. "But of course you have to accept," she told him. "I know," he said. But he hated the whole thing—because Teller had won the year before, and because the award to him was so clearly a political gesture.

When the time came, within days of the Kennedy assassination, for President Johnson to present the award in a White House ceremony, Oppenheimer performed graciously and did not blanch even when Teller maneuvered himself within camera range in order to be photographed shaking his hand. It was a "bittersweet" occasion, Anne Marks said, and Kitty Oppenheimer saluted it in her own way. She went to New York and, for ten thousand dollars, bought a mink coat, a slender, saronglike wrap in which she was resplendent. When someone asked Robert what he was going to do with the prize money, he said, "I've already spent it."[4]

We Made It—and We Gave It Away

THE BRITISH TESTED their first hydrogen weapon in 1957, and the three thermonuclear powers, the United States, Britain, and the USSR, conducted larger and larger tests in the Pacific. The public began to worry about radioactive fallout, and when the Democratic candidate, Adlai Stevenson, proposed a self-enforcing ban on large-scale nuclear tests during the presidential election campaign of that year, he did so, ironically, on the advice of Thomas Finletter and Thomas Murray, two of the most avid proponents of the H-bomb—and opponents of Robert Oppenheimer—only a short while before. In 1957 *On the Beach,* a novel about nuclear war by Australian writer Neville Shute, was an overnight bestseller, and popular response to appeals by Bertrand Russell and Prime Minister Jawaharlal Nehru of India for a test ban showed that men and women the world over were alarmed by the dangers of nuclear testing in the atmosphere. In 1958 Nikita Khrushchev, now more or less firmly in the saddle as leader of the Soviet Union, and the safely reelected Dwight Eisenhower embarked on test-ban talks in Geneva and began a test moratorium that lasted three years.

Lewis Strauss tried to apply the brakes. In 1957 he brought three test ban opponents from Livermore, Edward Teller, Ernest Lawrence, and Mark Mills, into the Oval Office, where they promised Eisenhower that a "clean," or fallout-free, bomb could be developed with a mere seven more years of atmospheric testing. Doubts next arose about whether small tests underground could be distinguished from seismic events, such as earthquakes, and these doubts—doubts about Soviet cheating—were fanned by Teller and others for decades.

When Kennedy and Khrushchev agreed in 1963, after the Cuban missile crisis, to ban nuclear testing in the atmosphere, and a limited test ban treaty was initialed in Moscow, Teller testified against it in the U.S. Senate. To him belongs a large share of responsibility for the fact that a comprehensive test ban treaty, banning tests underground as well as in the atmosphere, was never ratified. With his heavy eyebrows, his Hungarian accent, and his only partly deserved reputation as father of the H-bomb, Teller was a mesmerizing advocate of his pie-in-the-sky schemes. Just as he persuaded President Eisenhower for a brief time in 1957 that a "clean" bomb was possible, so, twenty-five years later, he persuaded President Reagan that the perfect defensive shield known casually as "Star Wars" could be achieved.

Strauss's influence persisted, too. At first he adopted Eisenhower's Atoms for Peace idea as a way to preempt Oppenheimer's Operation Candor, but he and the president sincerely hoped by way of the Geneva conferences of 1955 and 1958 to promote the use of atomic energy for peaceful purposes. What neither Strauss nor Eisenhower understood was that the facilities required to produce electricity by way of nuclear fission could also be used to make nuclear weapons. The Russians, of course, did understand, and Soviet foreign minister Vyacheslav Molotov wasted no time asking Secretary of State John Foster Dulles what on earth the Americans thought they were doing, proposing to spread weapons-grade nuclear material all over the world. It is the ironic legacy of the secrecy-obsessed Strauss that he was promoter of a program that has contributed to the spread of nuclear knowledge—and nuclear weapons—throughout the world.[1]

Percival King, an experimental physicist who specialized in reactors, observed the consequences of Strauss's ignorance at close range. Before the Geneva conference of 1958, Strauss, as AEC chairman, offered generous funding to three laboratories for peaceful fusion research. No one, not even Teller, thought that peaceful hydrogen power lay around the corner, and one of the scientists to whom funds were offered declined it for himself and his lab. But Strauss refused to be coached in physics. He counted on a breakthrough and believed that peaceful thermonuclear power would develop rapidly enough so that by 1956 or

1957 he would be the big man. King thought there was an element of competition here. Teller was father of the H-bomb; Strauss would be the father of peaceful hydrogen power. He was certain that if he threw enough money at the problem, scientists would solve it. They, on the other hand, felt that they ought to be in on decisions such as this one— political decisions—so as to help the government avoid wasting valuable resources on projects that defied the laws of nature.

The scientists came into their own again, and Strauss's influence receded, after the Russians launched *Sputnik,* the world's first artificial satellite, in October 1957. The president took it calmly, but from his intelligence he knew that the Russians had already launched an intercontinental missile—the first in the world—and that they were developing increasingly powerful thermonuclear warheads. The fact that the boosters that had lofted *Sputnik* into space would soon be able to deliver the hydrogen bomb meant that a new era was at hand—and the president knew it. Later that autumn he convened a large group of scientists. At the meeting, I. I. Rabi asked for the floor and suggested that the president bring scientists directly into the White House to advise him on the technological problems raised by the Soviet success. Rabi was known for his genius at coming up with the right solution at the right moment, and he had the backing of the scientific community. The president accepted his proposal, and an advisory panel that had previously been attached to the State Department was upgraded, brought into the White House, and christened the President's Scientific Advisory Committee (PSAC). James Killian, president of MIT, became its chairman. From then on, President Eisenhower began to get the kind of informed scientific judgment he should have been receiving all along, and would have but for his misplaced faith in Lewis Strauss. It was ironic that scientists should have regained some of their old clout under the very president who had overseen the demolition of Oppenheimer, and typical of the scientists of that era that they served him in spite of what had happened.

And there were other ironies. During the debate over whether to build the H-bomb, there had been almost no discussion of how the bomb was to be delivered. The Air Force drove the debate, and the

Strategic Air Command begged the question by demanding more and bigger airplanes for itself. The Russians were wiser. They saw that aircraft wouldn't do, and that an H-bomb without an intercontinental missile to deliver it made little sense. So they started intensive work on rocketry well ahead of the United States. In means of delivery, if not in small, sophisticated warheads, they had outstripped us. With all its lobbying for bigger bombs and bigger bombers, and its labeling as "traitors" those, like Oppenheimer, who stood in its way, the Air Force had not helped our military posture but had held us back. The generals had failed to see that the future lay not with bombers but with missiles. Scientists on the PSAC and on a pair of other high-powered committees went to work and in time made up for what one called "seven lost years" in developing long-range missiles.[2]

Strauss, who for four years had controlled the access of scientists to the president, was furious, and sabotaged the PSAC whenever he could. Killian, not one to magnify personal differences, nonetheless noticed that Strauss could be a charming host, welcoming him and Mrs. Killian to his apartment at the Shoreham and his farm in Virginia, but that at work he battled the head of the PSAC at every turn and did his utmost to block Killian's access to the president.

Eisenhower was delighted with his new scientific advisers. People in Washington, he complained, had axes to grind, but scientists were trained to be objective. He soon began to call on the PSAC for advice in matters outside science. But he never realized how badly Lewis Strauss had served him. When Strauss left the AEC in 1959, the president nominated him to be secretary of commerce, a job Strauss coveted because it had been held by his mentor, Herbert Hoover. After long and contentious hearings, however, the nomination was rejected by the Senate, only the eighth time in American history that a cabinet nominee had been turned down. One of the reasons the senators gave was "defects of character," the very words the AEC had used when it took away Oppenheimer's clearance. The president, having no understanding of the resentments stirred by the Oppenheimer case, was enraged. And in another ironic twist, Strauss, who could be so callous in inflicting harm on others, almost literally wept on the president's shoulder. In later years Lewis and Alice Strauss visited the Eisenhowers at Gettysburg, and for the rest of their lives the two men corresponded about their hobby of cattle breeding.

At least in the short run, the two sets of hearings during the spring of 1954 served the president's purposes. The Army-McCarthy hearings led to the Senate resolution in December of that year censuring the demagogue from Wisconsin and ended by breaking McCarthy's power. And, dominating the headlines as they did, they drowned out the Oppenheimer hearing and helped stifle debate over the momentous issues that had led to it. As Eisenhower's biographer Stephen Ambrose pointed out, the uproar over McCarthy enabled the president and Strauss to get rid of Oppenheimer with no public discussion of whether it had been a breach of policy or morality to build the H-bomb. Similarly, the McCarthy hearings diverted public attention from the fears aroused by the Bravo test and obscured the fact that thanks to both Truman and Eisenhower, the United States was now engaged in an all-out hydrogen bomb race with the Russians.

Mike, the November 1952 test of the Ulam-Teller principles that Bush, Bethe, and Oppenheimer had hoped at the very least to postpone, was the watershed marking the world's entry into the thermonuclear age. By the time of the next American test, Bravo in March 1954, the Russians had developed instruments that showed that the Americans had indeed made a breakthrough. Under tremendous pressure to keep up, Andrey Sakharov and Yakov Zeldovich in Moscow also made a breakthrough and, about the time of the Oppenheimer hearing, came up with their own version of the Ulam-Teller concept. A year and a half later, in Central Asia, the Russians tested their first radiation-implosion bomb.

Once again—Hiroshima in 1945 being the first time, Truman's H-bomb announcement of 1950 the second, and Mike in 1952 the third—the United States had led the way in the competition to build weapons of mass destruction.

At the end of World War II, scientists were heroes. It was scientists who had made possible an end to the fighting in time to save the hundreds of thousands of American lives that, but for the atomic bomb, would have ebbed away on the shores of Japan. It did not occur to anyone that these same scientists would now turn their talents to the political arena.

It did occur to those who had worked on the bomb, the young Los Alamos physicist Charles Critchfield for one. On August 16, 1945, days after the Japanese surrender, Critchfield wrote a memo saying that, with the coming of peace, the responsibility for the effects of science on human beings would shift from politicians to the scientists themselves. It had to happen, he said, because scientists would be the first to understand the effects of their discoveries on humanity.

Only a few weeks later physicists, chemists, and metallurgists poured out of the laboratories that had produced the bomb— Chicago's Met Lab, Oak Ridge in Tennessee, Los Alamos in New Mexico—to protest the May-Johnson bill, legislation drawn up by the War Department that would have kept atomic energy under military control. Scientific statesmen who, under pressure of war, had found a way to cooperate with the Army—Oppenheimer, Arthur Compton, James Conant, and Vannevar Bush—favored May-Johnson and believed that the military men they had dealt with, men like General George C. Marshall and former secretary of war Henry L. Stimson, could be trusted with management of the atom. But other, mostly junior, scientists who had worked on the bomb wanted no part of the military, with its secrecy and the obedience to orders from above that were stifling to the spirit of invention. On the basis of their experience with General Groves, they wanted to keep work on atomic weapons free of the Army's system of command and open to the adventurous, questioning spirit that had made their great achievement possible.

The passion with which these men pleaded their case and the awe in which atomic scientists now were held by Congress and the public proved surprisingly persuasive, and May-Johnson was quietly shelved. In its place Congress passed the McMahon Act, which physicists and mathematicians had helped to draft and which provided for civilian control. There was no reason why the scientists' cleverness should have extended to writing laws and lobbying Congress. But those who had contributed to the stunning white flash over the desert at Alamo-gordo in July 1945 were aware that they had handed man a strange new power, the power to alter nature, and, as Critchfield wrote, they felt that it was up to them to exercise responsibility.

They created their own organization, the Federation of Atomic Scientists (now the Federation of American Scientists), and a journal of their own, and they taught academic courses, gave public lectures, and wrote articles in the press. But the vehicle through which they exercised their responsibility most effectively during the early years after the war was the General Advisory Committee of the Atomic Energy Commission, the civilian agency created by the McMahon Act. The nine members of the GAC, as it was called, were nearly all senior scientists who had played leading roles in the Manhattan Project. They were brilliant men with no ax to grind except passion to save the world from atomic war, and, surprisingly, they were very nearly the only people in government with any real understanding of atomic weapons. Because of the members' disinterestedness and ability, the GAC from 1947 to 1952, the Oppenheimer years, acquired remarkable authority inside the government. And much of that authority it owed to Oppenheimer himself, with his mastery of atomic physics, his brilliance at synthesizing the opinions of others, and his breathtaking command of language.

The Oppenheimer GAC suffered two major defeats: President Truman's decision in 1950 to go full steam ahead with the H-bomb, and the Defense Department's decision two years later to build a second nuclear weapons laboratory. But it was the Oppenheimer hearing that put an end to the unique partnership between scientists and the government. By taking away the clearance of the man who had replaced Albert Einstein as the public face of scientific genius, the government told the scientists: We want your work, but we don't want you. We want the fruit of your research, but we have no use for the deeper wisdom you acquired as you were exploring the laws of nature. The hearing marked the end of the scientists' putting themselves and their imaginations on the line to help government with the long-range problems they had created.

Nearly three decades later, in a speech at Los Alamos in 1983, Rabi took the scientific community to task for allowing its political power to slip away. In a speech entitled "How Well We Meant," Rabi said that he and others had known when they saw the fireball at Alamogordo that they were witnessing the end of one world and the beginning of another. "We now had a power that put humanity on a new plane. And, having given this great power to our country, we were in a position to start on a new road." At first, he said, the generals seemed to agree with the scientists, but then they returned to their old ways. The men who created the bomb, on the other hand, had no way of escaping *their* responsibility. "It's gotten out of our hands and how to recover that?" Rabi asked. "We meant well and we sort of abdicated. We gave it away. We gave away the power to people who didn't understand it." In conclusion he lamented what happens when scientists "hand over the products of their knowledge to people who don't have it, to people who don't have the fundamental feeling and appreciation, who don't have a feeling for the glory of the human spirit, who don't respect science as such."

The question at issue was secrecy. Without the suffocating effects of secrecy, none of the events of the 1945–1955 decade would have happened in the way they did and some would not have happened at all. During the Manhattan Project, Oppenheimer had navigated superbly the impasse between the scientists' desire to share their research and the Army's insistence on secrecy. But after the war, because he advocated the Acheson-Lilienthal plan and opposed the H-bomb, Oppenheimer was accused by some of wanting to "give away the secret," as if there were some single, magic secret to the atomic bomb. Lewis Strauss warned before the hearing began that if the case were lost, the atomic energy program would "fall into the hands of left-wingers." The government, he added, would have "another Pearl Harbor" on its hands and scientists would take over the program. Three decades later Charles Bates, the FBI's point man during the hearing, complained to the author that "scientists observe no restrictions. They exchange information about everything. They said that any information a scientist develops, he should be free to pass on to anyone anywhere. I got so sick of hearing that, because scientists are no different from the rest of us."[3]

"That was Oppenheimer's idea," Bates added, "but it was not his government's idea, and it was the government that was paying the bills. Without the government's resources, the bomb could not have been developed. Without the government's money, labs, and support of all kinds, the scientists could not have made these discoveries, yet they had little patience for government restrictions and felt that scientific information ought to be exchanged in complete freedom." Bates overstated the views of Oppenheimer and the other scientists, and the dilemma of which he spoke is now more complex than it was in Oppenheimer's time. A scientific discovery in our time is likely to be not the work of a solitary researcher or a small team working with improvised equipment, but the product of a big team in an expensive lab operating with government funds. In such conditions the scientist is less and less likely to speak out against government policies. Today, for example, there is scarcely a physicist who thinks the Strategic Defense Initiative or its successor, National Missile Defense, can be made to work in anything like the way the Defense Department claims. Some disbelievers, however, accept government funds for the project in hopes of making an ancillary contribution to science, and cover their doubts with silence. The public has been lied to as a result, and billions of dollars have been wasted on an illusion.

The Oppenheimer hearing claims our attention not only because it was unjust but because it undermined respect for independent scientific thinking at a time when such thinking was desperately needed. Had there been no Oppenheimer affair, the government would almost surely have tried to find some other way to chasten scientists and let them know who was boss. "The more we grew," Rabi said, "the more we, the committee [the GAC], the scientists, grew in influence, the greater the worry that they were losing power." He concluded, "Science can be misused. And it's natural to misuse it, natural for politicians, people in power. It gives them a great deal of power, personal power and national power. You give politicians and people in government more power than they have the imagination and spiritual equipment to have."[4]

Among the scientists who created the bomb there were heroes, men who understood what they had done and tried desperately, each in his way, to control the outcome. Hans Bethe was one; Philip Morrison was another; Norris Bradbury, Jerrold Zacharias, Carson Mark, Victor Weisskopf, and Andrey Sakharov tried, and there were others. Of them all, Robert Oppenheimer was the American who could see the furthest, was the most articulate, had the tragic sense. If anyone could have moderated man's rush to extermination, or at least articulated the danger with such eloquence that we would all have been forced to consider, it was Robert Oppenheimer.

Postlude

WHEN I WROTE to him in the fall of 1985, Henry DeWolf Smyth did not want to see me. "Why exhume the case now?" he wrote. "It will only reopen old wounds." He was still reluctant when I arrived at the big old wooden house in Princeton. "Oppenheimer is dead," he said to me at the door. "His wife and daughter are dead. Strauss is dead. All the others are dead."[1]

But as we entered the airy paneled library, he reproached me for another reason. "Why didn't you come to me first? After all, I wrote the only dissent." Apart from his fair skin, everything about Harry Smyth was gray. His suit was dark gray, his hair was gray, the air around him seemed gray—and charged with loneliness. There were books all over the floor, so many of them that I had trouble picking my way to a chair. Dr. Smyth explained that he was giving them away in order to make room for more. This gentleman is not going to acquire more books, I said to myself. He is getting rid of them for another reason. I thought this because each time a new name entered the conversation he would ask, "Have you been to see him—or is he dead, too?"

Dr. Smyth was eighty-seven years old when I saw him in December 1985. He had been an obscure professor of physics at Princeton forty years earlier when, after the dropping of the atomic bomb, the U.S. government published *Atomic Energy for Military Purposes,* the official story of the building of the bomb. The book was christened the *Smyth Report,* and the author became famous overnight as governments and scientists the world over vied with one another to obtain copies. With the report, Smyth's notable public career began. He served for five years (1949–1954) as a member of the Atomic Energy Commission in Washington, and in 1961 President Kennedy named him U.S. ambassador to the International Atomic Energy Agency in Vienna, a job he performed with distinction for nearly a decade.

While he felt that the job in Vienna mattered more than anything else he had done, Dr. Smyth seemed aware, with some regret, that history would remember him best for his dissent in the Oppenheimer case. Talking about the case upset him, and as he was describing the tense night of June 28, 1954, when he wrote his opinion, he called in his secretary, Grace Anderson, and instructed her to take down his words. He pointed to a leather-bound copy of the hearing transcript and told me to open it to page 1063. He had marked the page with the letter I had written asking to meet with him. Near the top of the page, there was a word he wanted to change. In an early version of his opinion, he explained, he had called Oppenheimer's conduct in the Chevalier affair "unforgivable," but Lewis Strauss had remonstrated with him: "You said it was unforgivable, but then you forgave it." So in the final version, Smyth used the weaker "inexcusable." Now, three decades later, he wanted to soften his appraisal a little more. He wished the sentence to read "The Chevalier incident involved temporary concealment of an espionage attempt and admitted lying, and is *unfortunate*" (italics added).

Did you realize how strongly Strauss felt about getting rid of Oppenheimer? I asked. "Yes," Smyth replied, and then he told me an astonishing story. When he informed Strauss, the winter before the hearing, that he planned to resign in the fall, Strauss, without a moment's pause, started offering him inducements to leave right away, so that he would be unable to vote on Oppenheimer's clearance. "Twice between January and June he offered me bribes." First he offered Smyth "a fancy job somewhere" that, Smyth found out later, had not been his to offer. Then he made an offer that was almost past belief—Oppie's job. "He said he assumed that Oppenheimer would not want to continue as director of the Institute for Advanced Study after the ordeal he was going through and therefore he, as chairman of the institute's board of trustees, was searching for a new director.

He described the qualifications he was looking for, and they were nearly identical to qualities I would like to think I possessed. He didn't go quite so far as to say that he wanted someone with degrees from both Princeton and Cambridge University, but he came close. They were qualifications no one else could have possessed." Smyth, who had engaged in a running battle with Strauss over procedures in the Oppenheimer case and other crucial issues, told me how he felt in Strauss's presence. "When I went to see him in his office, I was glad to get out. I didn't want my back to him. I'd have made a perfect target."

When I asked whether Strauss had retaliated against him for his dissent, Smyth said no; he had seen no sign, for example, of Strauss's trying to have him removed from his tenured job at Princeton. "Mrs. Smyth had money," he told me, "so there was nothing he could do." But he had been in no doubt that Strauss would have taken revenge if he could have. "After the case was over, Lewis suggested that I resign, but I refused. I said it would be bad for the country and bad for the scientific community to show that the commissioners were so badly split. I told him I would resign at the end of summer, and I did."

During the hearing Smyth carried out all his day-to-day duties at the commission. He had even flown to the Pacific for the Bravo test. Throughout that time—the hearing, the Gray board's deliberations, the month of June just before the final decision—Strauss had insisted on his right, as chairman, to act as the commission's sole spokesman. He himself saw two or three newspapermen a day but treated any other commissioner who talked to the press like a pariah. Along with two other commissioners, Smyth openly disagreed with this policy. Then he and his spirited wife, Mary, devised a way of seeing to it that the chairman's was not the only view to come before the public. On Friday, May 14, 1954, Mary Smyth wrote in her diary, "JR here for talk with M," JR being James Reston of the *New York Times,* and the next day she wrote, "Al Friendly here to talk with M." Al Friendly was a reporter for the *Washington Post.* She was pleased with the result and on Sunday wrote, "Reston article just what I wanted." The next week she wrote, "M. to see Alsop suddenly," and a couple of evenings later, "Stewart Alsop asks to talk here with us two hours." In this fashion husband and wife saw to it that the public got a fuller picture than it would have otherwise.[2]

Smyth's independence and his belief, as he wrote in his opinion, that the security "system itself is nothing to worship," were exemplified by his handling of Mary's papers after she died. Mary Smyth's diary included a day-by-day account of the Oppenheimer case and Strauss's efforts to doctor the record. After she died in 1980, Harry Smyth, correct and proper though he was in every way, shipped her diary and other papers not to the AEC's successor agency, the Department of Energy, where they might be moldering to this day under a "classified" stamp, but to the American Philosophical Society in Philadelphia. There, in her bold, penciled handwriting, any visitor can read "Items of Possible Interest in Oppenheimer File," "M's Summary on Strauss Data," and dozens of other legal-sized pages documenting Strauss's deceptions from the moment he became chairman of the AEC.

Smyth told me why he had not especially warmed to Oppenheimer. "He was arrogant, and I think that is a dangerous trait when it comes to security. But what an incredible, magnificent job he did at Los Alamos! He was just about the last person I'd have picked for it." Wondering why Oppenheimer did not walk out of the hearing, as Volpe urged him to do, Smyth had concluded that Oppie was disarmed by the sheer brutality of the attack. He had expected something, but nothing this savage. Had the hearing changed him? "Oh, yes," came the reply. "It killed him."

Smyth did not remember that Oppenheimer had expressed much gratitude to him afterward. "He may have said, 'Thank you.'" But the record is a generous one on both sides. Days after the verdict, on July 5, 1954, Oppenheimer wrote:

Dear Harry:

For the past weeks you and Mary have been in my thoughts more than anyone else; and, since the 29th, I have thought often of the skill, fortitude and high courage of your action. . . . It has needed no telling for me to know how great a toll this effort will have taken of you. I wish for you both some quiet and some restoration, and that peace in an act of courage and honor that you have won for all of us and for all time.

With admiration and affection,

Robert[3]

When Oppenheimer died in February 1967, just short of his sixty-third birthday, Smyth, who had just flown across the Atlantic to bury his mother, made a second flight back from Vienna within a day or two to deliver a eulogy at Oppenheimer's memorial service in Princeton.

Kitty died of a mysterious infection in Panama in 1972 while sailing to Japan with her friend and Robert's, Bob Serber. Toni committed suicide in 1977 after the failure of her second marriage. Peter Oppenheimer lives today in a place he loves, Santa Fe, forty miles from Los Alamos, and knows everything there is to know about the Manhattan Project. Like his father and his own three children, Peter has spent much of his life worrying about the legacy of atomic weapons that Robert Oppenheimer left behind.

ACKNOWLEDGMENTS

THIS BOOK is the work of many hands and minds besides my own, first and foremost, Samuel B. Ballen and the J. Robert Oppenheimer Memorial Committee of Los Alamos and Santa Fe. Thanks to them I met, early on, pioneers of the atomic and hydrogen bomb projects whose views have informed my own: George Bell, Hans and Rose Bethe, Norris Bradbury, Charles Critchfield, Robert Raymond Davis, Percival L. D. P. King, Jim and Betty Lilienthal, M. Stanley Livingston, John and Kay Manley, Carson and Kay Mark, Louis Rosen, Max Roy, Raemer Schreiber, Richard Slansky, Robert Thorn, Robert Walker, and Jacob Wechsler.

Through them I also met Harold P. Green; Lee Hancock; Frank, Judith, and Peter Oppenheimer; Cyril and Alice Smith; Victor Weisskopf; Jane and Robert Wilson; and Jerrold Zacharias.

I owe a particular debt to an old and dear friend, Nancy Lichtenstein, to her husband, Immanuel, and to her parents, Helen and I. I. Rabi.

Others who knew the Oppenheimers well and whom I wish to thank especially include Ruth and Harold Cherniss, Priscilla Greene Duffield, "Shotsy" Durgin, Eleanor and Louis Hempelmann, George Kennan, Anne Marks, Honora Fergusson Neumann, Abraham Pais, Joseph Volpe, and Stephen White.

Sad to say, many of these individuals, some of them dear to me, are gone now, but I thank them from the bottom of my heart.

The challenge to anyone writing about the events in this book is that for decades key materials were classified, and many remain classified still. The veil lifted a little in the late 1970s, after passage of the Freedom of Information Act, when portions of Robert Oppenheimer's FBI file were released. As far as I know, the first person to use these documents in the FBI reading room was Caroline Davidson, in the course of her research for BBC producer Peter Goodchild, and I wish to thank her for sharing her notes with me after her work was done. Next to be reviewed for declassification were papers of the Joint Congressional Committee on Atomic Energy, which were bottled up entirely until 1987 and have now been released in part. Finally, beginning in 1993, Energy Secretary Hazel O'Leary took a fresh look at her department's secrecy policies, and some of the AEC's documents on the H-bomb program, the Second Lab affair, and the Oppenheimer hearing were declassified. As these materials became available, the work of historians of nuclear weapons became intensely collegial and many of us shared our discoveries with one another. I owe a particular debt to Gregg Herken for his generosity, as well as to R. Standish Norris, Richard Rhodes, and Silvan Schweber, and to the late Stanley Goldberg and Chuck Hansen. I am indebted also to Steven Aftergood, Brian Balogh, Barton Bernstein, William Burr, James David, James Hershberg, Robert Seidel, Richard Sylves, Samuel J. Walker, and Jonathan M. Weisgall. And I owe special thanks to several individuals who shared their deep knowledge of Russian and Soviet physics with me: Gennady Gorelik, Loren Graham, David Holloway, Ed Kline, and Mark Kuchment.

I gained special appreciation for the devoted work of archivists and librarians, and I wish to thank Hedy Dunn of the Los Alamos Historical Society; Marjorie Ciarlante, William Davis, and Rodney Ross of the National Archives; Arthur Freed, Roger Meade, Mollie Rodriguez, and Linda Sandoval of the Los Alamos National Laboratory; Ronald Grele and John Verso of the Columbia Oral History Research Office; Lori Hefner of the Lawrence Berkeley Laboratory; Joseph Anderson, Jean Hrichus, and Spencer Weart of the American Institute of Physics; David Haight of the Dwight D. Eisenhower Presidential Library; Dale Mayer of the Herbert Hoover Presidential Library; Dennis Bilger of the Harry S. Truman Presidential Library; Charles Greifenstein of the American Philosophical Society;

and Susan Gardos Bleich of the Davis Center Library at Harvard University.

I thank the Davis Center and, above all, Marshall Goldman for unfailing encouragement and support, and the John D. and Catherine T. MacArthur Foundation for its research and writing grant in 1988–1989. I also wish to thank Ruth Adams, Kurt Campbell, and James Cracraft.

For enhancing the audiotape of the 1982 interview of Lee Hancock at Albuquerque Airport by Jack Holl of the Department of Energy, I thank Robert Berkovitz and Haila Darcy of Bolt, Beranek, and Newman.

For advice about wiretapping law during the 1950s, I thank John Pound, Susan Rosenfeld, Herman Schwartz, and Katherine Triantafillou, and for help in interpreting key FBI documents, I thank Paul Farrell and Guy Goodwin.

For making themselves available so that I could better understand Edward Teller's contributions, I wish to thank Greg Canavan, George Chapline, and Harris Mayer, as well as Bill Beyer for arranging our meeting.

For state-of-the-art dissertations that have, alas, not been published, I thank Anne Fitzpatrick and Sybil Francis.

For making invaluable material available, I wish to thank Captain Jack Crawford and Edythe Murphy Holbrook. For additional material, I thank Theodore Conant, Dolores Everett, Ivan Getting, Gwen Groves, Elaine Kistiakowsky, J. K. Mansfield, Phillip S. Meilinger, and Ed Regis. For their understanding of key individuals, I am indebted to William Golden, Gordon Gray Jr., Joan Harrington, and Donna Mitchell.

For their comments on all or part of my manuscript, I thank Hugh De Witt, Max Holland, William Lanouette, David E. Lilienthal Jr., and Herbert York. And for the title of this book, I thank Andrew Szanton.

For support and assistance of all kinds, I thank Daniel P. Asnes, Drew Colfax, Michael Day, Allan Ecker, Joseph Finder, Lester Grinspoon, Richard and Priscilla Hunt, Coit Johnson, Steve Kaiser, Roman Laba, Cecily McMillan, Thomas McMillan, Thomas Mallon, David Metcalf, Thomas Powers, Jay Topkis, Charles Weiner, and Eunice Winslow. For their talent, experience, and sheer staying power, I thank my editors, Wendy Wolf and M. S. Wyeth Jr. And for friendship and assistance beyond price, I thank the late David Hawkins, the late Carson and Kay Mark, Emily Morrison, Philip Morrison, and Françoise Ulam.

NOTES

Abbreviations

AEC—Atomic Energy Commission

AIP—American Institute of Physics

APS—American Philosophical Society

AS—*Atomic Shield: A History of the United States Atomic Energy Commission,* vol. 2, *1947–1952,* by Richard G. Hewlett and Francis Duncan

BAS—*Bulletin of the Atomic Scientists*

CIC—Coordination and Information Center, U.S. Department of Energy, Las Vegas, Nevada

CJVM—Charles J. V. Murphy papers, property of Edythe M. Holbrook

COHP—Columbia University Oral History Project

DDEPL—Dwight David Eisenhower Presidential Library

DEL—*The Journals of David E. Lilienthal: The Atomic Energy Years, 1945–1950*

DOE—Department of Energy, successor to the Atomic Energy Commission, College Park, Maryland

FRUS—*Foreign Relations of the United States,* publication of the U.S. Department of State

GAC—General Advisory Committee, Atomic Energy Commission

HHPL—Herbert Hoover Presidential Library

HSTPL—Harry S. Truman Presidential Library

IMJRO—United States Atomic Energy Commission, *In the Matter of J. Robert Oppenheimer: Transcript of Hearing Before Personnel Security Board and Texts of Principal Documents and Letters* (published by MIT Press, 1971)

JCAE—Joint Congressional Committee on Atomic Energy

JFKPL—John F. Kennedy Presidential Library

JRO—J. Robert Oppenheimer

JRO/FBI—J. Robert Oppenheimer file no. 100–17828, FBI Reading Room, Washington, DC

LANL—Los Alamos National Laboratory

LASL—Los Alamos Scientific Laboratory
LBL—Lawrence Berkeley Laboratory
LC—Library of Congress
LLS—Lewis Strauss papers, Herbert Hoover Presidential Library
NARA—National Archives and Records Administration
NYHT—New York Herald-Tribune
NYT—New York Times
OP—Oppenheimer Papers at the Library of Congress
RG 128—Record Group 128, papers of the Joint Congressional Committee on Atomic Energy, located at the National Archives and Records Administration, Washington, DC
RG 326—Record Group 326, papers of the United States Atomic Energy Commission, located at the National Archives and Records Administration, College Park, Maryland
TEM—Thomas E. Murray papers, in the possession of the Murray family
UC—University of California
UCSD—University of California, San Diego

Introduction

1. Emily Morrison, interviews with author, February 2 and February 15, 1985; *IMJRO,* p. 8.

2. Hilde Stern Hein, interview with author, March 7, 1987.

3. www.BrotherhoodoftheBomb.com, Web site of Gregg Herken's *Brotherhood of the Bomb:* Herken's notes of Barbara Chevalier's diary; Chevalier to unknown researcher, April 25, 1973.

4. Steve Nelson, interview with author, August 28, 1985.

5. Steve Nelson, interview with author, August 28, 1985.

6. Philip Farley, interview with author, February 2, 1987.

7. David Hawkins, interviews with author, January 30, 1985, and January 1, 1997.

CHAPTER ONE: David Lilienthal's Vacation

1. *DEL,* pp. 566–573.

2. When Lilienthal informed Truman on April 3, 1947, that the United States had components for only seven complete atomic bombs, the president was visibly upset. By the end of 1949, the United States had 235 stockpiled warheads (Natural Resources Defense Council Table of U.S. Nuclear Warheads 1945–75, www.nrdc.org/nuclear/nudb/datab9.asp). Lilienthal earned

$8,000 to $10,000 per year as director of TVA and $17,500 as chairman of the AEC.

3. A CIA memorandum of September 20, 1949, predicted, "The earliest possible date by which the USSR might be expected to produce an atomic bomb is mid-1950 and the most probable date is mid-1953." Intelligence Memorandum 225, "Estimate of Status of Atomic Warfare in the USSR" (National Intelligence estimate from CIA records, Record Group 263, NARA, College Park, MD).

4. Robert Oppenheimer, interview with Warner Schilling, 1957, OP, box 65, and *AS,* p. 366. Oppenheimer told Schilling that the British had opposed announcement of the test, while Truman felt that the U.S. public should be told.

5. For the president's announcement, see Harry Truman's *Memoirs,* vol. 2, pp. 307–308.

6. The GAC has been criticized for going beyond the offer of technical advice at its October 29–30 meeting, but in a letter of October 22, 1949, the GAC was asked a second time, this time by Acting Chairman Sumner Pike, to provide policy advice. AEC's 1954 "Thermonuclear Weapons Program Chronology," compiled at the request of H. D. Smyth in 1954 for use by the commissioners in the Oppenheimer case, and declassified in 1982, pp. 22(c) and 22(d), RG 326, NARA.

CHAPTER TWO: **The Maneuvering Begins**

1. AEC "Thermonuclear Weapons Program Chronology," p. 21, RG 326, NARA.

2. Interview with Alice Strauss, November 28, 1990.

3. AEC "Thermonuclear Weapons Program Chronology," 1954, p. 22, RG 326, NARA.

4. Strauss to Souers, May 13, 1947, and September 2, 1947; Souers to Strauss, September 25, 1947 (LLS); Souers oral history interview, December 16, 1954, part 1, HSTPL.

5. Timing of this conversation is important: if all of it took place on October 5, 1949, as the Souers oral history interview of December 16, 1954, suggests, then Strauss was misrepresenting the facts, since Lilienthal, the AEC, and the GAC had not yet taken formal positions. The dialogue recounted in the oral history could, however, be a composite of several conversations between Souers and Strauss that fall.

6. *IMJRO,* p. 714.

7. From "Take One" of an unpublished March 7, 1954, dispatch from

Clay Blair and James Shepley to Larry Laybourne of *Time* magazine for a planned cover issue on Teller, Blair Papers, Archive of Contemporary History, University of Wyoming, Laramie; Alvarez Diary, October 5–7, 1949, RG 326, NARA; *AS,* pp. 376–377.

8. The Russian physicist Pyotr Kapitsa was under house arrest from 1946 to 1954 and did not work on the hydrogen bomb. It is illustrative of the state of Western knowledge of the Soviet bomb program that during the war the United States and Britain assumed that Kapitsa was head of the project, if there was one; the actual scientific director was Igor Kurchatov; Borden memorandum to files, October 10, 1949, RG 128, doc. no. LXVI, and Walker-Borden Chronology, p. 27, RG 128, NARA. "Take Two" of the unpublished Shepley-Blair *Time* cover file of March 7, 1954, reports on the luncheon: "Slowly a fire was ignited inside McMahon. By lunch's end, he was an enthusiastic convert. . . . Lawrence went back to California to whip up enthusiasm in the university laboratories. Meantime Teller and De Hoffmann, getting word of Lawrence's partial success in Washington, began to try to whip up support at Los Alamos."

9. Alvarez Diary, p. 29, RG 326, NARA; *DEL,* p. 577.

10. According to Phillip S. Meilinger, *Hoyt S. Vandenberg: The Life of a General,* Vandenberg's testimony was occasioned by Teller's visit to Major General Roscoe Wilson. See also Walker-Borden Chronology, p. 29, RG 128, NARA.

11. *IMJRO,* p. 328; author interview with Hans and Rose Bethe, December 3, 1986.

12. Hans Bethe, interview with Charles Weiner, part 3, May 1972, p. 24, AIP.

13. *IMJRO,* p. 328.

14. Hans Bethe, interview with Charles Weiner, part 3, May 1972, p. 25, AIP; *IMJRO,* p. 329; Victor Weisskopf, interview with author, February 25, 1985.

15. According to James Hershberg in *James B. Conant: Harvard to Hiroshima and the Making of the Nuclear Age,* p. 471, Oppenheimer was in Cambridge on October 9–10. On Wednesday, October 12, he spent a full day discussing the H-bomb dilemma with his close friend I. I. Rabi (Rabi to Bacher, October 18, 1949, Rabi Papers, LC), and on Saturday, October 15, he discussed it with another close friend, Admiral William S. Parsons. From Oppenheimer appointment books for September and October 1949; Warner Schilling interview notes, p. 19, OP, box 65.

16. *IMJRO,* p. 231; Warner Schilling's notes of June 12, 1957, pp. 6–7 (OP, box 65), quote Oppenheimer as saying that he changed his mind during the GAC meeting as a "result of Conant's intervention" and that it had been a "mistake to go along." Oppenheimer added that his confidential secretary was

surprised when she saw the GAC report, and pointed out that it was not the position he had taken earlier. "She also correctly predicted that it would get me in a lot of trouble."

CHAPTER THREE: **The Halloween Meeting**

1. Oppenheimer interview with Warner Schilling, June 12, 1957, OP, box 65, and letter of Cyril S. Smith to Richard Hewlett, April 27, 1967. In later years Manley, Oppenheimer, and Smith said they had been strongly influenced by Kennan's remarks; Manley and Smith added that they were also impressed by Bethe's description of the technical difficulties.

2. Manley's handwritten notes on seventeenth GAC meeting, LANL; Oppenheimer interview with Schilling, p. 10; *DEL,* p. 581.

3. *IMJRO,* p. 247; Alvarez, *The Adventures of a Physicist,* p. 172.

4. According to Theodore Conant, when Truman asked his father in 1946 to become the first chairman of the AEC, Conant declined because members of the Harvard board of overseers had warned him against serving with Lewis Strauss. Strauss, they said, was deceitful and overly ambitious, and with him as a commissioner, Conant would constantly have to be watching his back. (Conversation with the author, February 6, 1994.) Since Truman had already promised McMahon that he would appoint Strauss, the offer to Conant was moot. Truman left it to the GAC to name its chairman, and according to an FBI wiretap of a conversation between Robert and Kitty Oppenheimer, Oppenheimer assumed that either he or Conant would be elected. Meanwhile I. I. Rabi wrote to Lee DuBridge that Oppenheimer ought to be chairman because he "knows the entire field" and "is not burdened with any other important outside activity and would be able to give it the care and attention which it requires. The delicate question is whether Conant wants it for himself." DuBridge obligingly wrote to Conant that if he did not want the job, then "Robert might fit the bill," and at the GAC's first meeting, on January 3, 1947, Conant nominated Oppenheimer, who was elected without dissent. (See also James Hershberg's *James B. Conant: Harvard to Hiroshima,* pp. 307–309 and 837.)

5. *DEL,* p. 581; Oppenheimer interview with Schilling; Richard T. Sylves, *The Nuclear Oracles,* pp. 145–146.

6. Oppenheimer to Lilienthal with attachments, October 30, 1949, RG 326, NARA.

7. Oppenheimer interview with Schilling.

8. *DEL,* p. 582, and AEC 222/6, minutes of 310th AEC meeting, October 5, 1949, RG 326, NARA.

9. The Gray board concluded in 1954 that Oppenheimer had slowed the H-bomb program, and cited Manley's carrying the GAC recommendations to Los Alamos in November 1949 as evidence, despite an affidavit from Manley to the board that fully explained the circumstances.

10. Manley's diary entries for October 30–November 15, 1949, LANL.

11. Unpublished MS by John Manley, shown to the author by Manley in August 1986.

12. Teller to von Neumann, November 9, 1949, NARA.

13. Ulam to von Neumann, November 15, 1949, NARA; Françoise Ulam, interview with author, November 1991.

14. Bradbury to Chet Holifield, October 15, 1969; Carson Mark, interviews with author, April 2, 1986, and October 18, 1987.

CHAPTER FOUR: **The Secret Debate**

1. Glenn Seaborg, who had missed the Halloween meeting, was present at the December meeting but chose not to take a position. Nonetheless, in his autobiography, *Adventures in the Atomic Age: From Watts to Washington* (New York: Farrar, Straus & Giroux, 2000), he blamed Oppenheimer for allegedly suppressing the letter he had written to Oppenheimer, taking an equivocal, but mildly positive, position on the H-bomb, prior to the Halloween meeting.

2. *DEL*, p. 594.

3. JCAE meeting of January 9, 1950, appendix IV, doc. no. CXXV, RG 128, NARA.

4. *DEL*, pp. 583–584.

5. Arneson, "The H-Bomb Decision."

6. *DEL*, p. 622.

7. Acheson, *Present at the Creation*, p. 360; James Chace, "Sharing the Bomb," *Foreign Affairs*, pp. 226–228.

8. *DEL*, p. 620.

9. Lilienthal's "Memo to File," January 31, 1950, in AEC's "Thermonuclear Weapons Program Chronology," p. 110, RG 326, NARA.

10. AEC's "Thermonuclear Weapons Program Chronology," pp. 111–116.

11. Arneson, "The H-Bomb Decision"; Acheson, *Present at the Creation*, pp. 348–349; *DEL*, pp. 632–633.

12. Acheson, *Present at the Creation*, p. 349. The study ordered by Truman became NSC-68.

13. *DEL*, p. 633.

14. Ibid. At his security hearing in 1954, Oppenheimer testified that Acheson sent word to him and Conant "for heck's sake not to resign or make any

public statements to upset the applecart but accept this decision . . . and not make any kind of conflict about it" (*IMJRO*, p. 86).

15. Pfau, *No Sacrifice Too Great*, p. 123.

16. *DEL*, pp. 633–634.

CHAPTER FIVE: Lost Opportunities

1. In his October 21, 1949, letter to Conant, Oppenheimer called Teller's Super "singularly proof against any form of experiment."

2. JRO to George Kennan, November 17, 1949, *FRUS*, 1949, vol. 1, pp. 222–223.

3. Ferrell, *Harry S. Truman: A Life*, p. 344.

4. Bernstein and Galison, "In Any Light," p. 306.

5. York, *The Advisors*, pp. 94–106.

CHAPTER SIX: Fuchs's Betrayal

1. *DEL*, p. 634.

2. *FRUS*, 1950, vol. 1, p. 173.

3. Hoover to Tolson, Ladd, and Nichols, February 2, 1950, JRO/FBI; Pfau, *No Sacrifice Too Great*, pp. 113–119.

4. *BAS*, March 1950, p. 75.

5. JCAE transcript, January 30, 1950, "Development of Atomic Super Weapons," app. IV, box 4, doc. no. 1447, RG 128, NARA.

6. Bethe to Weisskopf, February 14, 1950, Bethe Papers.

7. *Scientific American* 182, no. 3 (March 1950), pp. 11–15.

8. Ibid., no. 5 (May 1950), pp. 11–15.

9. Ibid., no. 4 (April 1950), pp. 18–23. Bethe's biographer, Silvan Schweber, points out that Bethe was free to publish his article only because he had allowed his Los Alamos consultancy to lapse.

10. Hans and Rose Bethe, interview with author, December 3, 1986; Bethe with Charles Weiner, session 3, May 8–9, 1972, pp. 28–29, AIP; Hansen, *Swords of Armageddon*, vol. 3, p. 113, says there were only four deletions of which one contained disinformation and the other three, information that had appeared earlier in *Scientific American*.

11. Bethe to Bradbury, February 14, 1950, RG 326, NARA.

12. *BAS*, March 1950, pp. 71–72.

13. Borden memo, "Teller Says," March 2, 1950, RG 128, NARA.

14. JCAE meeting of March 3, 1950, on "H-bomb Personnel," RG 128, NARA.

15. *AS,* p. 416.

16. Truman followed up with his June 8 approval of construction of two new heavy-water reactors at Savannah River to produce tritium, and on July 7 asked Congress for $260 million to build them. I. I. Rabi commented, "I regard Savannah River as the way he answered the Russian success." Quoted in Ulam, *Adventures of a Mathematician,* pp. 192–193, and J. Carson Mark, "A Short Account of Los Alamos Theoretical Work on Thermonuclear Weapons, 1946–1950."

17. *AS,* p. 439.

18. Anne Fitzpatrick, "Igniting the Light Elements" (unpublished doctoral dissertation), p. 132.

19. Bradbury to Coordinating Council, October 1, 1945, LANL.

20. Fitzpatrick, "Igniting the Light Elements," pp. 111–112, says that theoretical work on the Super had begun to interfere with work on the fission bomb by spring 1944 "because Teller increasingly devoted more time to this than to the implosion problems he and his group were supposed to work on. . . . Teller . . . declined to take charge of the group that would perform very detailed calculations of an implosion weapon to devote more time to the fusion weapon." In an interview with Silvan Schweber on July 21, 1990, Teller said that the strain between him and Bethe during the war arose, not from Bethe's being placed above him as Theoretical Division leader, but from "Hans' not asking, but telling, me what to do." He added that Bethe considered his reaction "a violation of discipline."

21. To produce one gram of tritium, "one would have to forgo production of 80 grams of plutonium" (Carson Mark to Garrett Birkhoff, February 13, 1990). Fermi in 1948 estimated that in terms of plutonium sacrificed, the United States could afford to produce ten grams a year. Fitzpatrick, "Igniting the Light Elements," p. 192.

22. Carson Mark to Garrett Birkhoff, February 13, 1990; Fitzpatrick, "Igniting the Light Elements," pp. 147–148. The Ulam-Everett paper, LA-1076, "Ignition of a Large Mass of Deuterium by a Burning D-T Mixture: Problem I," March 7, 1950, remains Secret-RD at LANL. Mark remembered Ulam as "smacking his lips" when he brought Mark the negative calculations. Carson Mark, interview with author, June 12, 1990.

23. Ulam, *Adventures of a Mathematician,* p. 215; Carson Mark to Garrett Birkhoff, February 13, 1990; Fitzpatrick, "Igniting the Light Elements," pp. 147–148, citing the second Ulam-Everett report, LAMS-1124, June 16, 1950, which is still secret. Testifying in a patent case years later, Ulam declined to say that the ENIAC results had been wrong. Rather, he said, his hand calcula-

tions with Everett showed the earlier calculations to have been "incomplete" (U.S. District Court of Minnesota, Fourth Division, Honeywell, Inc., v. Sperry Rand and Illinois Scientific Developments, Inc., transcript of proceedings, vol. 47, pp. 7367–7368).

24. *AS,* p. 440; Ulam, *Adventures of a Mathematician,* p. 217.

25. Ulam to von Neumann, April 27, 1950, NARA; Teller to von Neumann, May 10, 1950, NARA; von Neumann to Teller, May 18, 1950, NARA; Françoise Ulam, memorandum of September 25, 1988, "Edward and Mici," AIP; Françoise Ulam memoir, *From Paris to Santa Fe,* AIP; Peter Galison, *Image and Logic,* p. 724.

26. Ulam, *Adventures of a Mathematician,* p. 216.

27. Fitzpatrick, "Igniting the Light Elements," p. 149, citing the Fermi-Ulam paper, LA-1158, "Considerations on Thermonuclear Reactions in Cylinders," September 26, 1950, Secret-RD; Carson Mark to author, October 17, 1991; Wheeler with Ford, *Geons, Black Holes, and Quantum Foam,* p. 209.

28. Ulam, *Adventures of a Mathematician,* pp. 218–219; S. M. Ulam, "Thermonuclear Devices"; George Bell, interview with author, March 8, 2000.

CHAPTER SEVEN: **Fission versus Fusion**

1. Wheeler with Ford, *Geons, Black Holes, and Quantum Foam,* p. 189.

2. Ibid., pp. 20, 206–207.

3. Carson Mark, interview with author, October 9, 1991.

4. John McPhee, *The Curve of Binding Energy,* pp. 58–60; Wheeler with Ford, *Geons, Black Holes, and Quantum Foam,* p. 205; Nuclear History Program oral history interview with Theodore Taylor, April 12, 1989, University of Maryland.

5. Bradbury to McCormack, August 29, 1950, cited in Hansen, *Swords of Armageddon,* vol. 3, pp. 141–142.

6. Oppenheimer to Dean, September 13, 1950, AEC Secretariat Files, RG 326, NARA.

7. With the opening of archives in the former Soviet bloc, Western historians have concluded that the impetus came from North Korean dictator Kim Il Sung, who, after several attempts, persuaded a reluctant Joseph Stalin to permit the invasion.

8. Borden to Sterling Cole, July 24, 1950, app. III, box 62, doc. no. CLXXXVIII, RG 128, NARA; Borden to McMahon, November 28, 1950, app. III, box 62, doc. no. 1785, RG 128, NARA. In 1949 Borden had been denied a top secret Defense Department document because it contained stockpile data.

When he suggested that every bomb be saved for use on Russia, he may have believed the stockpile to be smaller than it was. According to the Natural Resources Defense Council Table of U.S. Nuclear Warheads 1945–75, by late 1950 it contained 369 strategic warheads (www.nrdc.org/nuclear/nudb/datab9.asp).

9. Taylor oral history interview; Taylor, "Circles of Destruction," *BAS* (January–February 1996).

10. Hans Bethe wrote, "The technical skepticism of the GAC . . . had turned out to be far more justified than the GAC itself had dreamed" ("Comments on the History of the H-Bomb," written in 1954 as a reply to Shepley and Blair and classified until its publication in *Los Alamos Science* [fall 1982]); JRO to Dean, November 1, 1950, AEC Secretariat Files, RG 326, NARA. In November 1950, Oppenheimer asked Ulam whether the calculations he had done with Everett showed conclusively that the Super was impossible. In accordance with the principle of indeterminacy, Ulam replied that the calculations were not final.

11. The Teller-Wheeler report of August 1, 1959, said the amount of uncompressed T required to ignite uncompressed D was "of the order of a kilogram or more but not of the order of tens of kilograms" (Fitzpatrick, "Igniting the Light Elements," pp. 222–223, citing the report itself, LAMD-443, secret-RD). The seriousness of the mistake, and of the finding that ignition would require three to five kilograms of tritium, and not a hundred or a few hundred grams as Teller claimed, may be seen from the fact that two years later, in the summer of 1952, the U.S. tritium supply still was measured in grams, not kilograms. On the far-off day when the nation's laboratories might be able to produce a kilogram a year, it would take three to five years to produce enough tritium for a single Super bomb (Hansen, *Swords of Armageddon,* vol. 3, p. 149). As Gordon Dean told a secret session of the JCAE in November, production of one Super would mean sacrificing enough plutonium for between 100 and 150 atomic bombs. Walker-Borden Chronology, entry for November 30, 1950, RG 128, NARA.

12. GAC 23, October 30–November 1, 1950, AEC Secretariat Files, RG 326, NARA, p. 17.

13. Oppenheimer to Dean, November 1, 1950, AEC Secretariat Files, RG 326, NARA.

14. Fitzpatrick, "Igniting the Light Elements," p. 276, citing Draft Memorandum to the chairman of the AEC, "Notes on the AEC-MLC, LASL Conference on Tuesday, November 14, 1950," November 17, 1950 (Secret-RD); and p. 221, citing Bradbury to Tyler, November 17, 1950, "LASL Technical Program of Calendar Year 1951 and Fiscal Year 1952" (Secret-RD), box 4944, Los Alamos folder 7, RG 326, NARA.

CHAPTER EIGHT: **Teller**

1. Teller to Maria Goeppert Mayer, letters of October 9 and October undated, 1948. Mandeville Department of Special Collections, UCSD.

2. Kathleen Mark, interview with author, October 4, 1999; Carson Mark, interview with author, October 18, 1987.

3. Five undated letters from Edward Teller to Maria Goeppert Mayer, August–November 1950.

4. Undated letter of Edward Teller to Maria Goeppert Mayer from Norman, Oklahoma, probably written after November 25, 1950.

5. Luis Alvarez testimony, *IMJRO*, p. 789.

6. The other members were former AEC commissioner Robert F. Bacher, Luis Alvarez, Charles C. Lauritsen, Mervin J. Kelly, Walter G. Whitman, Major General Kenneth D. Nichols, Rear Admiral William S. Parsons, Major General Roscoe C. Wilson, and Brigadier General James McCormack Jr.

7. JCAE meeting on "H-Bomb Personnel," March 3, 1950, RG 128, NARA.

8. Borden to file, March 2, 1950. "Give It Back to the Indians" was a hit song from a 1939 Rodgers and Hart musical and was still popular in 1946, when Oppenheimer allegedly made this remark. With his talent for the vernacular, Oppenheimer might well have taken the expression from the song.

9. Borden memorandum to Sterling Cole, "The Hydrogen Bomb in Relation to the Atomic Bomb," July 24, 1950, app. III, box 62, doc. no. CLXXXVIII, RG 128, NARA; "Conversation with Dr. Enrico Fermi on September 4, 1951," memo of J. K. Mansfield, October 2, 1951, RG 128, NARA.

10. Borden to Teller, May 3, 1950, RG 128, NARA.

11. The first such suggestion appears in Oppenheimer's FBI file for July 5, 1949; Bergman to Borden, May 7, 1950, app. III, box 41, doc. no. 1531, classified general subject file, RG 128, NARA.

12. Borden memo to McMahon, May 11, 1950, app. III, box 50, doc. no. 1516, RG 128, NARA; those whose terms were expiring were Fermi, Hartley Rowe, and Glenn Seaborg.

13. Borden memo to McMahon, November 24, 1950, RG 128, NARA.

CHAPTER NINE: **Ulam**

1. Ulam, *Adventures of a Mathematician*, p. 10.

2. Galison, *Image and Logic*, pp. 724–725.

3. Carson Mark to Garrett Birkhoff, February 13, 1990. In an interview with the author on March 8, 2000, George Bell noted that the "compression"

being talked about here was extreme compression, much greater than that produced by ordinary high explosives.

4. Françoise Ulam, *From Paris to Santa Fe,* AIP.

5. Carson Mark, interviews with author, August 19, 1986; September 11–12 and November 3, 1989; private memo by Françoise Ulam, August 20, 1988, "How My Conversation with Carson Came About." Mark was working on the Ranger series in Nevada, as well as the Greenhouse tests. Greenhouse included two fission tests, "Dog," detonated at Eniwetok on April 8 at 82 kilotons, and "Easy," April 21 at 47 kilotons. The others were "George," May 9 at 225 kilotons, which included a new type of fission device, and "Item," June 2 at 45.5 kilotons. He later called Item, a boosted device with both fission and fusion components, "particularly dear to my heart." Teller had not been enthusiastic about Item and at one point sought to have it canceled. Today, every U.S. nuclear weapon is boosted.

6. Ulam, *Adventures of a Mathematician,* p. 220; Françoise Ulam to the author, September 18, 1989.

7. Stanislaw Ulam to Glenn Seaborg, March 16, 1962, LANL; Arnold Kramish to Samuel B. Ballen, April 4, 2000.

8. Richard Rhodes is almost certainly correct in saying in *Dark Sun,* p. 467, that Ulam's " 'following days' comprised most of a month," since the diary indicates that Ulam wrote his part of the paper in mid-February and wrote to von Neumann informing him of his new ideas only on February 23. Ulam's diary on February 15 contains this entry: "Wrote Lenses (jointly with Teller). Heterocatalytic Detonation: Radiation Lenses and Hydrogenous Lenses" (Galison, *Image and Logic,* p. 725).

9. George Bell, interview with author, March 8, 2000; Hugh DeWitt, interview with author, March 1, 1992; e-mails from Hugh DeWitt, July 28, August 8 and 21, 2000; Hugh DeWitt, telephone interview with author, August 21, 2000; Hans Bethe, who came to the lab in June 1951 to do calculations for the new scheme, relied on what he was told at that time, and did not read the Ulam-Teller paper until August 11, 1989. After reading the paper, he said that his May 28, 1952, letter to Gordon Dean had been "wrong" and that Ulam deserved more credit than he had given him in that letter and in his essay "Comments on the History of the H-Bomb," published in 1982 (Bethe to Samuel B. Ballen, September 28, 1988). Richard Slansky, then head of the T Division, who also read the Ulam-Teller paper for the first time in the summer of 1989, believed the paper should remain classified.

10. Bethe, "Comments on the History of the H-Bomb," p. 48; Rhodes, *Dark Sun,* pp. 471–472.

11. Norris Bradbury, interview with Arthur Norberg, February 11, 1976.

Opinions differ to this day as to whether Teller or Ulam deserves chief credit. The lab designation is "Teller-Ulam," for alphabetical reasons, but because Ulam contributed two of the three critical ideas, I have called it "Ulam-Teller," as Bradbury did at his September 24, 1954, press conference.

12. *Science,* February 25, 1955, pp. 267–275; Teller with Brown, *The Legacy of Hiroshima,* pp. 48–50; Ulam's offending remark appeared in a letter of February 23, 1951, to von Neumann, in which he said that "Edward is full of enthusiasm about these possibilities, this is perhaps an indication that they will not work." Someone has attributed to Ulam a comment after the George test of May 1951, that its "failure" showed that radiation implosion would not work. But most of Ulam's colleagues doubt that he said this, since it was known within a few days after George that the tritium-deuterium package had emitted neutrons and that the experiment had been successful. Teller told Stanley Goldberg, Gregg Herken, Richard Rhodes, and the author on June 7, 1993, that Ulam deserved no credit because of his skepticism. But Ulam's remark to Françoise over lunch in January, and his February 23 letter to von Neumann, make clear that he knew that radiation implosion would work.

13. Bradbury press conference, September 24, 1954 (LANL).

14. Carson Mark, who served on the Committee of Senior Reviewers, did not think the system was intentionally manipulated to elevate Teller's stature, and Hugh DeWitt, a onetime whistleblower at the Lawrence Livermore Laboratory, agrees. In a charitable moment, Mark suggested that Teller's followers were more responsible than Teller himself for Teller's inflated reputation, and that the sobriquet "Father of the H-bomb" was to some extent forced on him.

15. Carson Mark, interview with author, November 3, 1987; Françoise Ulam, private memorandum of August 20, 1988.

16. Françoise Ulam, *From Paris to Santa Fe,* AIP.

17. Françoise Ulam and David Hawkins, telephone interviews with author, August 19, 2000. Françoise Ulam said that her husband stood up to Teller, as younger members of their wartime TN group did not. During this period Ulam did mathematics on his own with Oppenheimer's assistant, David Hawkins, who happened to work in an adjoining office. The two of them produced a paper on branching processes.

18. U.S. District Court, District of Minnesota, Fourth Division, Honeywell Inc. v. Sperry Rand Corp. and Illinois Scientific Developments Inc., 4-67 Civil 1138, transcript of proceedings, vol. 47, p. 7408; Stanislaw Ulam, *Adventures of a Mathematician,* p. 220.

19. Carson Mark, interview with author, September 26, 1989; Carson Mark, telephone interview with author, February 15, 1990; George Bell, in an interview with the author on March 8, 2000, agreed with Bethe that the

Teller-Ulam concept was surprising, and with Mark that the T Division would have thought of radiation implosion if Teller hadn't thought of it first.

20. Philip Morrison, conversations with author, July 25, 1990, and August 18, 2000.

21. Kathleen Mark, interview with author, October 4, 1999; Leon Heller, interview with author, October 9, 1999; Carson Mark, interview with author, June 14, 1993. The mathematician Paul Stein, who also worked closely with Ulam, said, "Stan's mind was always brimming with ideas, most of them good. It was the collaborator's job to fill in the details." Quoted by Carson Mark in notes for speech given on publication of *Los Alamos Science,* no. 15, 1987.

22. Françoise Ulam, *From Paris to Santa Fe,* chapter 6, AIP; Anna Auerbach Ulam, mother of Adam and Stan, died of cancer in 1938. After the war the student, George Volsky, wrote to Adam Ulam, describing his father's fate.

23. Françoise Ulam, conversation with author, 1993.

24. Françoise Ulam, "Fragments of Taped Conversation with M. Kac and D. Mauldin," June 8, 1984, and undated biographical profile by Françoise Ulam, AIP.

25. Samuel B. Ballen, conversation with author, November 9, 1987; Françoise Ulam, conversation with author, October 7, 1987; Gian-Carlo Rota, "Wheel of Fortune," unpublished draft of March 28, 1986; comment by Seymour Papert, July 1997; Rota, "The Lost Cafe," *Contention,* 2, no. 2 (Winter 1993).

26. Françoise Ulam, "Fragments of Taped Conversation with M. Kac and D. Mauldin"; Rota, "Wheel of Fortune," March 28, 1986; Dolores Everett and Mollie Rodriguez, interviews with author, October 17 and 19, 1991; in a telephone interview on July 23, 2000, William Everett said that within the family, he heard that "Dad did all the work and Ulam got all the credit." Françoise Ulam responded that her husband did not conceal Everett's role, as Teller concealed Ulam's. To the contrary, he frequently spoke of Everett's contribution and lamented not having more opportunities to talk with him. Still another collaborator of Ulam's confirmed the fact of Everett's bitterness and said that he, too, felt used by Ulam. "Ulam had great ideas, and expected his underlings to work them out" (William Beyer, conversation with author, February 14, 2001).

27. Françoise Ulam, interview with author, April 6, 1986; Stanislaw Ulam, *Adventures of a Mathematician,* pp. 76, 79–80, 107–111; Rota, "The Lost Cafe," pp. 48–49.

28. According to David Hawkins, Ulam during the war was able to solve linear equations much faster than other scientists because he was already, in his head, doing statistical sampling. In 1947, playing solitaire with his head

still bandaged from his encephalitis operation, he thought of the Monte Carlo method and the uses to which it might be put. On his return to Los Alamos he firmed it up in his mind in letters to von Neumann and Robert Richtmyer, then head of the T Division.

29. Transcript of H-bomb symposium sponsored by Sloan Foundation at Princeton, NJ, 1982, part 1, p. 13, and part 2, p. 14; Françoise Ulam, interview with author, November 22, 1987; Carson Mark, interview with author, September 12, 1989; Stanislaw Ulam, *Adventures of a Mathematician,* p. 80, refers to Kurt Godel's discovery of undecidability; Heims, *John von Neumann and Norbert Weiner,* pp. 143–144.

30. Françoise Ulam, interview with author, November 22, 1987; Françoise Ulam memoranda February 1, 1987, and December 8, 1988, AIP.

CHAPTER TEN: **Teller's Choice**

1. Pfau, *No Sacrifice Too Great,* pp. 131–132.

2. Dean, "Memorandum of Conversation with Lewis Strauss," note of February 12, 1951, in Anders, ed., *Forging the Atomic Shield,* pp. 117–118; Pfau, *No Sacrifice Too Great,* pp. 132–133; Herken, *Brotherhood of the Bomb,* p. 241.

3. Diary of Thomas E. Murray, vol. 2, part 2, pp. 8–9, TEM. The quotations are Murray's.

4. Anders, ed., *Forging the Atomic Shield,* p. 117; Borden to file, "Conversation with Dr. Edward Teller," February 9, 1951, JCAE doc. no. CCLXXXIII, RG 128, NARA.

5. "The Reminiscences of Gordon Dean," COHP, 1959.

6. Carson Mark later explained: "There was one outfit that handled calculations. Was it to work only on the thermonuclear? The same thing was true of the chemists. And they were working well as it was. . . . In addition to the computing, there was the Experimental Physics Division. It had machines, a Cockroft-Walton, a Van de Graaff, and so on. The work of the machines could be directed toward either fission or fusion. There was no sense saying that a given machine will work only on one and not the other." Carson Mark, interview with author, October 18, 1991. Darol Froman made another objection: "What do we do with people who insist on having ideas . . . in both fields, e.g., Ulam?" He termed the duplication of effort involved in creation of a separate division "time-consuming, wasteful, costly, geographically inappropriate . . . absurd" and added, "I believe we have, entering this reorganizational picture from both sides, a lack of faith either in the motivation of others or in their ability to carry out their parts"; Froman, memos of March 20 and March 22, 1951, LANL. In a memo of March 28, Froman offered to

mediate between Teller and the rest of the lab, adding that in case of a stand-off, Bradbury would make the decision. Teller would not accept Bradbury's having the final say. Bradbury's March 6 proposal was ultimately sidetracked, in Carson Mark's words, "because there was no way you could have a sensible way of working and please Teller." Carson Mark, interview with author, October 18, 1991.

7. A month after his February 9 visit to AEC general manager Marion Boyer, Teller told Bradbury: "You know that I am not pressing at present for any reorganization or change because that might disturb the harmony of the laboratory at a time when united effort is badly needed." Teller to Bradbury, March 7, 1951, LANL.

8. Anders, ed., *Forging the Atomic Shield,* pp. 106–107, 120–126. Dean was unaware that the government's case against the Rosenbergs was mostly based on the decrypted Soviet wartime cable traffic known as "Venona." The secret that the United States had decoded a portion of the Soviet intelligence cables was so tightly held that it has been claimed, probably erroneously, that even President Truman did not know of it. Existence of the decryptions was acknowledged by the U.S. government, and texts were published, only in 1995 and 1996.

9. Dean met with Truman on April 6, 1951, to discuss the JCS request, and the transfer was authorized, a decision that marked the end of exclusive civilian control over the atomic stockpile as mandated by the Atomic Energy Act. Anders, "The Atomic Bomb and the Korean War: Gordon Dean and the Issue of Civilian Control," *Military Affairs,* January 1988; Hamby, *Man of the People,* pp. 555–556.

10. *AS,* p. 541.

11. Anders, ed., *Forging the Atomic Shield,* pp. 106–107, 131–134; Teller with Brown, *The Legacy of Hiroshima,* p. 51.

12. Teller to Dean, April 20, 1951, from "ET" Files, LANL; Anders, ed., *Forging the Atomic Shield,* p. 108.

13. Hansen, *Swords of Armageddon,* vol. 3, p. 251; Anders, ed., *Forging the Atomic Shield,* pp. 143–145.

14. Actually, the hydrogen fuel did not account for much of George's power, nor had it been expected to: of the total yield of 225 kilotons, an esti-mated 160 to 200 were produced by the fission trigger and the rest by the fu-sion component, prompting a young theoretician who worked on it, Robert Jastrow, to compare the test with "using a blast furnace to light a match." Jas-trow, "Why Strategic Superiority Matters," *Commentary,* March 1983, p. 27.

15. Less than an ounce in weight, the tritium-deuterium mixture ac-counted for an estimated yield of 25 kilotons. *Race for the Superbomb,* shown on the PBS television series *The American Experience,* January 1999.

16. Carson Mark, interviews with author, September 26, 1989, and October 17, 1991; Mark to Hansen, September 18, 1989; *IMJRO*, p. 952; *AS*, p. 541.

17. York, *Making Weapons, Talking Peace*, pp. 57–58.

18. Total cost of the conference, said to have been the turning point in the H-bomb program, was $166.07 (including lunch for twenty-five on June 16 at $56, for twenty-seven on June 17 at $68, beer at $11.19, plus labor and equipment). The expense was borne by the Institute for Advanced Study after the AEC refused to pay (Smyth Professional Correspondence Series One, box 5, see Katherine Russell to Evelyn McQuown in "Boyer 1950–1953" file).

19. *AS*, pp. 542–545; Bradbury to Froman and Mark, June 6, 1951, LANL; Bradbury to Oppenheimer, June 1, 1951, LANL; Bradbury to Froman and Mark, June 6, 1951, LANL; Bethe, "Comments on the History of the H-Bomb," p. 48; "Partial Statement Made by Hans Bethe at Princeton Meeting," June 16–17, 1951, LANL; Bradbury to Tyler, July 13, 1951, LANL; Bethe to Joseph and Stewart Alsop, October 1, 1954, Joseph Alsop Papers, LC.

20. Bradbury to Oppenheimer, June 1, 1951, LANL. Oppenheimer later ascribed differences that emerged at the conference to the fact that the leading personalities represented "polar psychological types." Mansfield to file, October 3, 1951, doc. no. C 7404, RG 128, NARA.

21. Teller with Brown, *The Legacy of Hiroshima*, pp. 52–53. In his memo to Froman and Mark of June 6, Bradbury explained that their role as consultants to GAC would enable Teller, Wheeler, and Lothar Nordheim "to speak as freely as they wish . . . without any laboratory strings or restraints attached." The memo had been sent to Teller beforehand.

22. Nicholas Metropolis, interview with Silvan Schweber, August 20, 1990; *AS*, p. 545. Wheeler and Bethe both knew in advance that the Ulam-Teller ideas were to be discussed; both postponed visits to Europe in order to be present.

23. Norris Bradbury, interview with author, August 27, 1986; Anders, ed., *Forging the Atomic Shield*, p. 156.

24. Richard Garwin, interview with author, February 9, 2000.

25. Anders, ed., *Forging the Atomic Shield*, p. 164; Carson Mark, interviews with author, September 26, 1989, and June 12, 1990.

26. Bradbury to Dean teletype, September 26, 1951, LANL. Robert Serber and one or two others later speculated that Bradbury provoked Teller into leaving because he suspected that Teller had deliberately falsified his tritium estimates for the Super.

27. Anders, ed., *Forging the Atomic Shield*, p. 164; Carson Mark, interview with author, June 12, 1990.

28. JCAE, Walker-Borden Chronology, entry for September 18, 1951, RG 128,

NARA. Pressure for a major expansion was heightened by the announcement during the autumn of 1951 of the Soviet Union's second and third atomic tests.

29. John S. Walker memo, "Lunch Meeting with Dr. Teller," October 3, 1951, RG 128, NARA.

30. Mansfield to file, "Conversation with Dr. Oppenheimer," October 3, 1951, RG 128, NARA; Teller to GAC, December 13, 1951, AEC Secretariat Files, RG 326, NARA.

31. Kenneth Pitzer was also mentioned for the job, and Bradbury was said, additionally, to have considered Fred Seitz.

32. Bradbury to Fields, October 11, 1951, LANL Folder 635, "Laboratory Program 1951–1957."

33. Carson Mark, interview with Silvan Schweber, July 19, 1990. Mark added that if Bradbury "let down his hair" with anyone, it would have been with his associate director, Darol Froman.

34. Raemer Schreiber, interview with author, November 19, 1987; J. K. Mansfield memo for record, August 29, 1951, RG 128, NARA; J. Carson Mark, "A Short Account of Los Alamos Theoretical Work," LASL, 1974; Jacob Wechsler, interview with author, July 25, 2001.

35. Silvan Schweber with Marshall Rosenbluth, July 18, 1990; Max Roy, interview with author, October 11, 1991.

CHAPTER ELEVEN: **The Second Lab**

1. Murray, Thermonuclear Chronology, vol. 2, part 1, p. 10; part 2, pp. 27, 31–32, TEM.

2. Murray, Thermonuclear Chronology, vol. 2, part 2, pp. 44–45, TEM.

3. York, *Making Weapons, Talking Peace,* pp. 62–67.

4. Ibid.; Teller and Brown, *The Legacy of Hiroshima,* p. 60.

5. Oppenheimer to Dean, February 17, 1952, AEC Secretariat Files, box 1275, RG 326, NARA.

6. Teller to Murray, February 7, 1952, enclosed in Murray Diary, vol. 2, part 2, TEM; Teller to Borden, February 18, 1952, TN box 59, doc. 2646, RG 128, NARA.

7. A key here was Rowan Gaither, president of RAND and assistant to Paul Hoffman, president of the Ford Foundation (Murray Diary, vol. 2, part 2, p. 59, TEM). In a letter to Murray on March 17, Lawrence said he had mentioned Murray's idea to Gaither, and perhaps RAND could "accomplish the desired objectives."

8. Murray Diary, vol. 2, part 1, p. 15, and part 2, pp. 57–58, TEM. Bradbury added that nothing would provoke him into a protest resignation except

Pentagon takeover of key civilian jobs in atomic energy, and even that might not be sufficient.

9. Ivan Getting, interview with author, October 6, 1989; Walker to Borden, April 3, 1952, RG 128, NARA; *AS,* p. 583; in a draft memo of March 15, 1952, Griggs warned Finletter that the Russians might already possess the radiation-implosion idea thanks to Fuchs. Finletter's assistant, William A. M. Burden, a New York investment banker, later said he had "recommended to Finletter, on Teller's advice, that we set up a separate laboratory . . . to work solely on the hydrogen bomb" (COHP interview with William A. M. Burden, p. 72). About the second-lab proposal and details of the thermonuclear work, two congressional aides said of the Air Force at this time: "They have bought Teller hook, line and sinker" (Walker and Borden to McMahon, April 4, 1952, CD XCIX, RG 128, NARA; Dwayne A. Day, *Lightning Rod* [my thanks to Stan Norris for this document]).

10. At Los Alamos, Bradbury refused to allow one of Finletter's party, Sidney Plesset, to attend the briefing, and the briefer, Carson Mark, no doubt disgusted by still another inspection visit by Washington bigwigs, gave an exceptionally lackluster performance.

11. Blumberg and Owens, *Energy and Conflict,* p. 289; Teller with Shoolery, *Memoirs,* pp. 336–338.

12. The briefings took place between March 6 and April 15, 1952, Walker-Borden Chronology, January 1, 1953, p. 76, RG 128, NARA; Walker to file, "Thermonuclear Background Information—Air Force," December 1952, CD DLXXXVII, TN box 59, app. 3, RG 128, NARA; Anders, ed., *Forging the Atomic Shield,* pp. 206–207; Gordon Dean memorandum, April 1, 1952, AEC Secretariat Files, box 4930, RG 326, NARA; Murray Diary, vol. 2, part 2, p. 68. The Air Force threat was effective despite the fact that its establishment of a nuclear weapons laboratory would have been a violation of the Atomic Energy Act.

13. Borden and Walker memorandum to McMahon, May 7, 1952, p. 6, doc. DXXIX, RG 128, NARA; Anders, ed., *Forging the Atomic Shield,* pp. 209–212.

14. Minutes of thirtieth GAC meeting, AEC Secretariat Files, box 1272, RG 326, NARA; Oppenheimer to Dean, April 30, 1952, AEC Secretariat Files, box 1275, RG 326, NARA; Norris Bradbury, interview with author, August 27, 1986.

15. Walker-Borden Chronology, entry for June 10, 1952, June 16, 1952, draft, doc. 3257, RG 128, NARA.

16. Murray Diary, vol. 2, part 1, pp. 18–19, and vol. 2, part 2, pp. 73–74, plus attachment to p. 74, TEM; Walker to file, "Thermonuclear Program," June

19, 1952, doc. no. 2890, RG 128, NARA; Borden and Walker to file, "Second Laboratory—Dr. Teller," June 19, 1952, doc. no. 2899, RG 128, NARA; Teller to Murray, June 20, 1952; Dean to Bethe, June 23, 1952, RG 326, NARA; LeBaron to Borden, June 30, 1952, doc. no. DXXXVII, RG 128, NARA; Walker and Hamilton, "Denver Meeting," July 1, 1952, RG 128, NARA.

17. York, *Making Weapons, Talking Peace,* pp. 67–68; Blumberg and Owens, *Energy and Conflict,* p. 291; Childs, *An American Genius,* pp. 444–445; Walker to file, "Project Whitney," November 10, 1952, TN box 60, doc. no. DCVII, RG 128, NARA.

18. Edward L. Heller to file, "Project Whitney," October 7, 1952, doc. no. 8055, RG 128, NARA; Charles Critchfield, interview with author, October 28, 1987; Francis Low, interview with author, March 4, 1999. Gell-Mann was already committed to going to Chicago. By September 1952, Lawrence had recruited 123 scientists and technicians. The Materials Testing Accelerator was originally set up to produce uranium-235, but plentiful sources had subsequently been discovered in Colorado and elsewhere in the United States.

19. This chapter also owes much to Sybil Francis, "Warhead Politics"; and Sybil Francis, "Between Science and Politics"; and Sybil Francis, Lecture at the Air and Space Museum, Smithsonian Institution, Washington, DC, February 18, 1999; Barton Bernstein, "The Struggle for the Second Laboratory"; Herbert York, interview with Chuck Hansen, September 29, 1993; Robert Seidel, "Ernest Lawrence"; and Robert Seidel, interviews with author, June 8, 1993, and May 11 and May 30, 2001.

CHAPTER TWELVE: **A New Era**

1. Hansen, *Swords of Armageddon,* vol. 4, pp. 40–59; Jacob Wechsler, interviews with author, July 25 and October 10, 2001; Rhodes, *Dark Sun,* pp. 482–512.

2. Hansen, *Swords of Armageddon,* vol. 3, p. 280.

3. Jacob Wechsler, interview with author, October 10, 2001; Carson Mark, interview with author, September 26, 1989.

4. Rhodes, *Dark Sun,* p. 487; George Bell, interview with author, March 8, 2000.

5. George Bell, interview with author, October 7, 1999; Jacob Wechsler, interviews with author, July 25 and October 10, 2001.

6. Hansen, *Swords of Armageddon,* vol. 4, p. 67; Rhodes, *Dark Sun,* p. 503.

7. Bernstein, "Crossing the Rubicon"; Stern with Green, *Oppenheimer Case,* pp. 194–195; *IMJRO,* p. 248.

8. According to a memo of John Ferguson, deputy director of the Policy

Planning Staff, dated September 2, 1952, Bush gave Acheson a paper, but the text has not been found, *FRUS,* 1952–1954, vol. 2, part 2, pp. 992–993; Zachary, *Endless Frontier,* p. 363.

9. Bradbury to Oppenheimer, June 11, 1952.

10. Bethe oral history interview with Charles Weiner, session 3, May 1972, p. 27, AIP; Bethe to Dean, May 23, 1952, CD 471.6, RG 330, NARA; Dean in his reply agreed about the danger of intensifying the effort "in public." Dean to Bethe, June 23, 1952, Dean's unclassified reader file, RG 326, NARA. At this point, Bethe himself fell victim to secrecy: on August 14, 1952, Teller wrote a reply to Bethe's memorandum for Air Force Secretary Finletter and enclosed carbon copies for Bethe and Dean. In response to a July 25, 1990, query from the author as to whether he had written a classified response, Bethe wrote, "I did not know about Teller's memorandum until today, so I did not write a rejoinder."

11. Bethe to Dean, September 9, 1952, RG 326, NARA.

12. "Timing of the Thermonuclear Test," *FRUS,* 1952–1954, vol. 2, part 2, pp. 994–1008; an unsigned memorandum with the penciled notation "9/5/52" is apparently the substance of the panel's remarks to Acheson. At his security hearing, Oppenheimer testified that the panel had made its points orally, not in a written memorandum. The panel's proposal rested on an argument that a test by either side could not escape detection by the other, a premise that was undercut by Luis Alvarez's incorrectly informing Finletter that the hydrogen bomb could be developed without testing.

13. *AS,* pp. 591–592; Anders, ed., *Forging the Atomic Shield,* pp. 218–230; Deborah Gore Dean, interview with author, June 11, 2001; Eugene Zuckert, interview with author, November 28, 1990. Deborah Dean must have been reporting what her mother told her, since she was not yet born in 1952.

14. Hansen, *Swords of Armageddon,* vol. 4, pp. 70–77; Rhodes, *Dark Sun,* p. 509.

15. York, *Making Weapons, Talking Peace,* p. 69.

16. *IMJRO,* p. 562.

CHAPTER THIRTEEN: **Sailing Close to the Wind**

1. Ladd to Hoover, January 23, 1952, JRO/FBI; Hoover to Souers, March 26, 1952, JRO/FBI; Hoover to Souers, April 16, 1952, JRO/FBI. Pitzer asked to have his identity kept secret, and the FBI complied.

2. Washington Field Office 100-12253, enclosing FBI summaries of May 14 and May 27, 1952, and letter of Teller to Department of Justice, June 19, 1977.

3. FBI, Summary of May 1, 1954, "to Director FBI re JRO." The document quotes Teller as telling a JCAE staff member in 1950 that Robert Oppenheimer was "far to the left," that Frank would not have joined the Party without his brother's approval, and that if Robert were found to have given information to the Russians, "he could, of course, do more damage than any other single individual." Teller had also answered FBI questions about Oppenheimer, Robert Serber, and Philip Morrison on July 5, 1949. NLH, 90-4/32:14, FBI, April 18, 1952.

4. Gordon Dean memorandum, May 19, 1952, RG 326, NARA.

5. Kenneth Pitzer, interview with author, March 2, 1992. Pitzer's animosity apparently had an additional source: Joseph Volpe was present at a GAC meeting at which Oppenheimer subjected Pitzer, the AEC's director of research, to withering treatment. Volpe to author, December 4, 2000.

6. Pitzer to Truman, April 4, 1952; Latimer to Truman, May 29, 1952; and Urey to Truman, June 2, 1952, all at HSTPL; Kenneth Pitzer, interview with author, March 2, 1992; Walker to file, October 3, 1952, TN box 41, doc. no. 3049, RG 128; Borden to McMahon, May 28, 1952, TN box 41, doc. no. 3831, RG 128; Walker to file, May 28, 1952, TN box 41, doc. no. DXIII, RG 128, all at NARA.

7. Keay to Belmont, April 28, 1952, JRO/FBI; Borden to McMahon, May 28, 1952, TN box 41, doc. no. 3831, RG 128, NARA; Walker to file, May 28, 1952, doc. no. DXIII, RG 128, NARA.

8. Nichols to Tolson, May 29, 1952, JRO/FBI; Dean diary entries for May 16, 17, 19–23, and June 5, 11–13, 27, 1952; Dean to file, May 19, 1952; Dean to Oppenheimer, June 14, 1952, all in Dean papers, RG 326, NARA. Dean and McInerny had collaborated in framing the charges against Julius and Ethel Rosenberg in 1951 and evidently trusted each other. McMahon's staff had been relaying Griggs's reports that the Air Force believed there had been "literally criminal negligence" in the H-bomb program (Walker and Borden to McMahon, April 4, 1952, JCAE doc. no. CDXCIX, RG 128, NARA). Griggs's queries as to what they were "doing to get Oppenheimer off the GAC" (Walker to Borden, "Thermonuclear Program," April 7, 1952, JCAE doc. no. CDXCIV, RG 128, NARA) and Teller's comment, " 'Three men, one soul.' He felt very strongly that it would be an extreme mistake to reappoint Dr. Oppenheimer" (John S. Walker, memo to file, "Conversation with Dr. Edward Teller," April 17, 1952, RG 128, NARA). Dean to Oppenheimer, June 14, 1952. In an interview on February 21, 1984, Harold Green told the author that the Justice Department had informed the AEC that it was prepared to indict Oppenheimer and bring him to trial.

9. William Hillman and David M. Noyes oral history with Sidney W. Souers, December 16, 1954, HSTPL.

10. Joseph Volpe, interviews with author, November 19 and 21, 1985; Deborah Gore Dean, interview with author, June 11, 2001; and Roger Anders, interview with author, July 19, 1989; Dean diary entries for May 16 and June 5, 1952, Dean papers, RG 326, NARA; Joseph Volpe to author, December 4, 2000.

11. Dean to Truman, August 25, 1952, and Truman to Dean, August 26, 1952, doc. no. 7693, President's Secretary's Files, HSTPL. The charge mentioning Oppenheimer was temporarily dropped at Dean's request in May 1952. The Justice Department had other reasons for its reluctance to put Oppenheimer on the stand: it would have had to reveal that it was using a paid FBI informer and possibly also that its best evidence against Weinberg was based on wiretaps.

12. McCarthy got wind of what had happened and held an executive session on September 15, 1953, at which Crouch described Truman's intervention in the Weinberg case. The transcript was released on May 5, 2003, by the Senate Permanent Subcommittee on Investigations.

13. Lovett had other informants besides Dean. According to Philip Stern, Lovett told his assistant, James Perkins, that Oppenheimer's security file was "a nightmare" and that "the quicker we get Oppenheimer out of the country, the better off we'll be." Perkins added that Lovett had mentioned the names of people who had expressed doubt to him about Oppenheimer: one of them was Lewis Strauss. Stern with Green, *Oppenheimer Case,* pp. 195–196.

14. Acheson had asked McGeorge Bundy, then dean of Harvard, to act as recording secretary, and the report was written by Bundy with Oppenheimer's participation. A slightly edited version appears as "Early Thoughts on Controlling the Nuclear Arms Race" (ed. McGeorge Bundy), *International Security* 7, no. 2 (Fall 1982).

15. *IMJRO,* pp. 751–752; Walker to file, October 3, 1952, p. 3, CD 3049, TN box 59, app. 3, RG 128, NARA; Walker to file, December 1952, "Thermonuclear Background Information—Air Force," TN box 59, app. 3, CD DLXXXVII, pp. 4–5, RG 128, NARA; Stern with Green, *Oppenheimer Case,* pp. 187–188.

16. Stern with Green, *Oppenheimer Case,* pp. 188–189. The accusation was that Oppenheimer had implied that the leaders of the Pentagon were madmen.

17. Borden to file, November 16, 1951, RG 128, NARA; Elliot, "Project Vista," pp. 163–183; Stern with Green, *Oppenheimer Case,* pp. 180–181.

18. Walker to file, "Thermonuclear Program," May 28, 1952, doc. no. DXIII, RG 128, NARA.

19. Stern with Green, *Oppenheimer Case,* pp. 189–190. Finletter's assistants, William A. M. Burden and Garrison Norton, attended the lunch, while the exchange between Finletter and Oppenheimer was described to Charles J. V.

Murphy in interviews with Gilpatric and Finletter on April 1 and April 11, 1953, respectively. CJVM.

20. Charles J. V. Murphy interviews with Charles Lauritsen and Lee DuBridge, March 18, 1953. CJVM.

21. A fairly complete account by Hanson W. Baldwin did appear in the *New York Times* on June 5, 1952: "Experts Urge Tactical Air Might; Score Stress on Big Atomic Bomber"; Elliot, "Project Vista."

22. In a memo, "Project Vista," November 15, 1951, addressed to William A. M. Burden, Garrison Norton said Finletter's word was "subversive." RG 340 (records of the Office of the Secretary of the Air Force), NARA, College Park, MD. My thanks to Gregg Herken for this document. Walker to file, July 2, 1952, doc. no. 2925, RG 128, NARA. According to his Columbia oral history, Burden did not share Finletter's suspicions. Norton confined himself in a 1990 interview with the author to extolling Oppenheimer's intellect.

23. McMahon did not send either draft and told Borden that he preferred to take the matter up with the president in person, TN box 41, app. 3, doc. no. DCXXXVII, RG 128, NARA. He failed to do so, however, and because of illness or for some other reason canceled a long-standing appointment with the president. Herken, *Brotherhood of the Bomb,* p. 250, and Borden to file, May 30, 1952, RG 128, NARA.

24. Francis P. Cotter, interviews with author, November 21, 1989, and May 2, 1990.

25. The coded messages Taylor dealt with were almost certainly the "Venona" cables, existence of which was a tightly held U.S. government secret until the mid-1990s. Walters and Lyons were instructed to conduct physical surveillance of Oppenheimer from the moment his train arrived in Union Station from Princeton. In later years, Walters assured Joseph Volpe that Oppenheimer was not merely discreet but "very, very discreet." Taylor, whom Volpe saw also in later years, at their golf club, said that "no matter what you think of Oppenheimer, he wasn't a spy." Joseph Volpe, interview with author, November 21, 1985.

26. Walker and Mansfield to file, August 25, 1952, RG 128, NARA; Walker memo for file, January 13, 1953, doc. no. 3344, RG 128, NARA. The latter document contains part of what Teller told committee staffers.

27. Memo of March 2, 1953, for the commissioners from Bethe, Bradbury, Teller, and von Neumann, doc. no. DCXV, RG 326, NARA. Hansen, *Swords of Armageddon,* vol. 4, pp. 99–102.

28. Transcript of JCAE executive session, February 18, 1953, doc. no. 3281, RG 128, NARA. My thanks to Gregg Herken for this document.

CHAPTER FOURTEEN: **Strauss Returns**

1. Strauss to Hickenlooper, September 19, 1952; Hickenlooper to Eisenhower, September 26, 1952; Ralph Cake to Hickenlooper, October 10, 1952. Hickenlooper papers, HHPL. Strauss's sponsor was Herbert Hoover.

2. Walker and Borden to McMahon, April 4, 1952, doc. no. CDXCIX, RG 128, NARA. The memo continues, "It seems further that the Air Force feels that the removal of Dr. Oppenheimer [from the GAC] is an urgent and immediate necessity."

3. Murphy's work diaries for February 12, March 18, and April 8, 1953, and his interviews with Charles Lauritsen and Lee DuBridge, March 18, 1953. CJVM.

4. John Holbrook, interview with author, November 8, 1993.

5. Notes of Murphy's interview with Finletter, April 11, 1953; Murphy's work diaries for December 15, 1952, and January 15 and 23, February 6, and April 9, 14, and 16, 1953, reflect meetings with Finletter. CJVM.

6. Notes of Murphy's interview with Gilpatric, April 1, 1953; other dates when Murphy discussed the story with Gilpatric include January 23, March 31, April 14 and 16, 1953. CJVM.

7. Roswell Gilpatric, interview with author, November 30, 1993; notes of Murphy interview with Gilpatric, April 1, 1953; other dates when Murphy discussed story with Gilpatric include January 23, March 31, April 14 and 16, 1953. CJVM.

8. Murphy's interview with Lewis L. Strauss, March 12, 1953. CJVM.

9. Joseph Alsop to Murphy, October 18, 1954. Joseph Alsop Papers, LC.

10. Undated notes of Murphy's interviews with Walkowicz and Doolittle, Murphy Papers. "It is Murphy's recollection that Teddy Walkowicz . . . was Murphy's main and perhaps only source of information relative to ZORC." Hoover to Waters, June 18, 1954, FBI report 100-17828-1760, FBI/JRO. See also Hoover to Waters, June 3, 1954, FBI report 100-17828-1739, FBI/JRO; and FBI field report of June 21, 1954, by SA Joe R. Craig, FBI/JRO.

11. Notes of Murphy interview with Walkowicz, undated, CJVM. A correct way of putting it would be to say that it was an experiment to determine whether you can use a fission bomb as a match to light a small amount of thermonuclear material.

12. Blumberg and Owens, *Energy and Conflict,* pp. 265–267; work diaries for March 24 and 31, 1953. CJVM.

13. Work diaries for April 14 and 16, 1953. CJVM.

14. On December 20, 1950, Hawkins, appearing before HUAC, took the

"diminished Fifth." Schrecker, *No Ivory Tower,* p. 249. Hawkins's lawyer, Joseph Fanelli, was recommended to him by Oppenheimer.

15. Schrecker, *No Ivory Tower,* p. 157; Philip Morrison, interview with author, March 4, 2003. Morrison's interpretation was that because of Oppenheimer's stature, if he were to be attacked, it would have had to be done by the committee that was most in the public eye, the McCarthy committee, rather than the Jenner committee.

16. Killian, *Sputnik, Scientists, and Eisenhower,* p. 67. Killian says that he, Rabi, and others discussed reports that the Air Force was about to remove Oppenheimer's access to classified material, a step it had already taken in May 1951. Gregg Herken has written that it was Oppenheimer's Q clearance, for access to classified nuclear data, and not his Air Force clearance, that was in question. Herken, *Brotherhood of the Bomb,* p. 257.

17. Joseph Volpe, interviews with author, November 19 and 21, 1985; July 7 and 8, 1989; May 12, 1994.

18. Joseph Volpe, interviews with author, November 19 and 21, 1985; July 7 and 8, 1989; May 12, 1994; Stern and Green, *Oppenheimer Case,* pp. 129–130.

19. Joseph Volpe, interviews with author, November 19 and 21, 1985; July 7 and 8, 1989; May 12, 1994; Volpe to author, June 28, 2001. Contents of the "Isotopes" folder in Strauss's papers in the Hoover presidential library in West Branch, Iowa, bear out the importance of this episode to Strauss.

20. Louis and Eleanor Hempelmann, interviews with author, December 7 and 10, 1987.

CHAPTER FIFTEEN: **Two Wild Horses**

1. Gertrude Samuels, "A Plea for 'Candor' About the Atom."

2. Robert Oppenheimer, "Atomic Weapons and American Policy."

3. Belmont to Ladd, June 5, 1953, sec. 14, JRO/FBI; Bernstein, "The Oppenheimer Loyalty-Security Case Reconsidered," p. 1433.

4. Hewlett and Holl, *Atoms for Peace and War,* pp. 52–55; Deborah Gore Dean, interview with author, June 11, 2001.

5. Strauss appointment diary, 1953/1: June 1, 23, and July 10, 23, LLS; Joanne Callahan to Strauss, July 16, Strauss memo to John Mackenzie, July 15, July 13 draft article, Murphy to Strauss, July 21, with final proof, all 1953, Murphy folder, LLS. The editor of the *Bulletin of the Atomic Scientists,* Eugene Rabinowich, later criticized a series of articles by Murphy, starting with the anonymous piece of May 1953, for violating security: Rabinowich, "Fortune's Own Operation Candor," BAS, December 1953.

6. John Holbrook, interview with author, November 8, 1993; Hewlett and

Holl, *Atoms for Peace and War*, p. 47. Strauss saw Captain Hyman Rickover, Trevor Gardner of the Air Force, Willard Libby of the GAC, Kenneth Pitzer, and Luis Alvarez. Strauss tried to reach Ernest Lawrence and Leslie R. Groves, and was called by Robert Bacher and Kenneth D. Nichols. Some of them were in Washington for a meeting of the National Academy of Sciences, and their conversations with Strauss may have had nothing to do with the impending attack on Oppenheimer.

7. "Questions Raised in My Mind by JRO file—WLB," May 29, 1953, TN box 41, doc. no. DCXXXVIII, RG 128, NARA; "Comment and Recommendations," June 1, 1953, TN box 41, doc. no. DCXXXIX, RG 128, NARA.

8. William L. Borden, interview with Jack M. Holl, February 11, 1975.

9. Borden to file, August 13, 1951, app. III, JCAE doc. no. 3464, RG 128, NARA. I have dated the possible Strauss-Borden conspiracy to the late summer or early fall of 1951, when Borden drafted a letter for McMahon to Walter Bedell Smith of the State Department, inquiring about Teller's relatives. McMahon to Smith, September 28, 1951, RG 128, NARA. As for Strauss's possibly "cooling" toward Borden, Borden had asked Strauss for a job in the AEC before leaving the congressional committee. Strauss did not oblige: instead it was Hyman Rickover and Representative Chet Holifield of California who found him his job at Westinghouse. Strauss's failure to find room for Borden at the AEC may have had to do with the pending Oppenheimer affair but could also have been related to Democratic-Republican differences over the issue of public versus private power.

10. J. Kenneth Mansfield, interviews with author, May 29, May 31, and June 1, 1986; according to the *BAS*, November–December 2002, p. 103, the number of warheads, not assembled weapons, was 32 in 1947, 110 in 1948, and 236 in 1949.

11. Karl Haar, interview with author, July 11, 1990; J. K. Mansfield, interview with author, May 31, 1986; Courts Oulahan, interview with author, July 13, 1990; Frank Cotter, interviews with author, November 21, 1989, and May 2, 1990.

12. Frank Cotter, interview with author, November 21, 1989.

13. JCAE executive transcript, February 18, 1953, CD 3281, RG 128, NARA, courtesy of Gregg Herken; Harold Green, interview with author, February 21, 1984. The author was told on excellent authority that a folder of correspondence between Borden and Strauss had been removed from Strauss's papers. This source believed that the two men worked together up to a point, but that Strauss did not have advance knowledge of Borden's letter.

14. Frank Cotter, interview with author, May 2, 1990.

CHAPTER SIXTEEN: **The Blank Wall**

1. Although most historians have said that the letter was sent by registered mail, the FBI ascertained that it came by regular mail. Nichols to Tolson, January 12, 1954, JRO/FBI; Hoover to Brownell, January 19, 1954, JRO/FBI.

2. Hoover to Tolson and Ladd, November 25, 1953, JRO/FBI; Hoover to Tolson, Ladd, and Nichols, December 3, 1953, FBI doc. no. 17828-418. Although Hoover had discouraged McCarthy from holding hearings on Oppenheimer earlier in 1953, McCarthy did hold an executive session on September 15 at which Paul Crouch described Truman's role in squelching the Weinberg prosecution.

3. Dwight D. Eisenhower, "Note for Diary," December 2, 1953, typed by Ann Whitman, Gordon Gray Papers, DDEPL.

4. Martha Burroughs's telephone conversations with author in 1985; Clarissa Parsons Fuller, interview with author, September 17, 1986; Peggy Parsons Bowditch, interview with author, July 22, 1992; Stern with Green, *Oppenheimer Case,* p. 222.

5. Bernstein, "The Oppenheimer Loyalty-Security Case Reconsidered," pp. 1383–1447.

6. Strauss got away with his deception until publication in 1989 of *Atoms for Peace and War,* the AEC's official history, by Hewlett and Holl.

7. Lewis H. Strauss, interview with author, July 6, 1989. Among those who believe that it was Strauss who urged Eisenhower to lower a "blank wall" is Strauss's son, Lewis H. Strauss, who points out that "blank wall" is the sort of expression his father would have coined. Further evidence exists in handwritten notes exchanged between Strauss and C. D. Jackson at an NSC meeting of December 18, 1953, in which Strauss wrote that "the P. himself had been consulted and had (ordered) or (concurred)." LLS, C. D. Jackson folder, HHPL. A memo by AEC security officer Bryan LaPlante, titled "J. R. Oppenheimer" and dated December 3, 1953, describes a meeting with Strauss, Nichols, and AEC general counsel William Mitchell at 3:30 p.m. that day, at which Strauss displayed a copy of the presidential order, Secretariat Files, RG 326, NARA. Thus it is clear that the president did not first consider his decision "in the chill of late afternoon" on that day, as Strauss later wrote. By 1963, when Strauss published his book, the term "blank wall" had acquired the ring of opprobrium, as typifying the folly of the proceeding. He would logically have wanted to dissociate himself from it and deny his own role.

8. Strauss to Teller, December 3, 1953, LLS, "J. Robert Oppenheimer" folder, HHPL; Bryan LaPlante diary memo, December 3, 1953, Secretariat Files, RG 326, NARA; Teller interview of June 4, 1993, with Stanley Goldberg, Gregg Herken, Priscilla McMillan, and Richard Rhodes. During the same

interview, Teller said that he had discussed the Oppenheimer situation with JCAE chairman Sterling Cole on December 2. In fact, according to Cole's 1978 oral history interview at Cornell, they discussed Atoms for Peace. This means that Strauss discussed the Atoms for Peace proposal with Teller before he told his fellow commissioners about it.

9. Blumberg and Owens, *Energy and Conflict,* p. 332; Teller interview of June 4, 1993, with Goldberg, Herken, McMillan, and Rhodes; William S. Golden, interview with author, January 3, 1990; Victor and Donna Mitchell, interview with author, November 13, 1990.

10. John MacKenzie, interview with author, February 13, 1985; Frank Cotter, interview with author, November 21, 1988.

CHAPTER SEVENTEEN: **Hoover**

1. Ladd to Hoover, March 27, 1953, sec. 14, JRO/FBI; Belmont to Ladd, April 13, 1953, sec. 14, JRO/FBI; Hoover to Tolson and Ladd, June 24, 1953, sec. 14, JRO/FBI; Belmont to Ladd, December 2, 1953, sec. 14, JRO/FBI; Green, "The Oppenheimer Case"; Lee Hancock, interviews with author, August 22, September 22, and December 13, 1983, and January 16, 1985; Hancock to Harold Green, January 22, 1966, in author's possession. The individuals Strauss had offered to purge were Carroll Wilson, former general manager of the AEC; Carroll Tyler, the AEC's former director of Santa Fe operations; Oppenheimer; and Francis Hammack of the AEC's Security Division. Strauss made the promise in March 1953, after he was appointed special White House adviser; Hoover's memo of June 24, 1953, can be read as signifying that Strauss knew the purge of Hammack was a precondition of Hoover's help in getting rid of Oppenheimer. In an interview on March 7, 1984, Harold Green told the author that he had learned of Strauss's promise to Hoover directly from AEC security officer Bryan LaPlante and indirectly, via Lee Hancock, from Francis Hammack, Charles Bates, and C. A. Rolander.

2. Mitchell did not tell Green that he had given up an attempt to do the job himself after two commissioners criticized his inclusion of charges about the H-bomb. Hewlett and Holl, *Atoms for Peace and War,* pp. 75–76; Stern with Green, *Oppenheimer Case,* pp. 223–225.

3. Harold Green, interview with author, May 14, 1984; Stern with Green, *Oppenheimer Case,* pp. 225–226; Hewlett and Holl, *Atoms for Peace and War,* p. 76.

4. Harold Green to John Manley, January 24, 1984, Manley Papers, LANL.

5. Green, "The Oppenheimer Case"; Harold Green, interview with author,

May 14, 1984. Green believed that the FBI official who called him was William C. Sullivan, later head of domestic counterintelligence in the FBI.

6. Gerard Smith writes that Smyth "had a clearer idea of the dangers of the plan and its implications for nuclear proliferation than the rest of us" (Gerard Smith, *Disarming Diplomat*, p. 29). See also Mary Smyth diary entry for December 8, 1953, Smyth Papers, APS.

7. Mary Smyth's "Summary on Strauss Data," p. 2; Henry D. Smyth to Strauss, "Dr. X. Case," February 23, 1954; Henry D. Smyth to the Chairman and Commissioners, May 20, 1954; Henry D. Smyth to Cole, May 20 and June 22, 1954; Henry D. Smyth to [A. L.] Christman, August 15, 1967, all in Smyth Papers, APS; Strauss to file, December 10, 1953; Strauss memo for Smyth, December 17, 1953; Strauss memo for Snapp, December 22, 1953; Strauss memo, undated, all LLS; Hewlett and Holl, *Atoms for Peace and War*, pp. 71–72. Smyth did not learn until April 1954 that Strauss had met with the president on December 3, 1953, or that he had ordered the AEC general manager in July 1953 to discourage consultation with Oppenheimer.

8. Minutes of 957th AEC meeting (NARA), courtesy of Gregg Herken; Bernstein, "The Oppenheimer Loyalty-Security Case Reconsidered"; Mary Smyth diary entries for December 20–26, 1953, and February 3, 1954, Smyth Papers, APS. Smyth made his objections on December 18 and December 21, and was told by AEC general counsel William Mitchell that his colleagues had agreed to inclusion of the H-bomb count. He later realized that this was not the case: Zuckert had not agreed to it and there was a question as to whether Murray had agreed. Smyth, draft memo to Strauss, "Dr. X. Case," February 2, 1954; Smyth to Strauss, "Dr. X Case," April 5, 1954; Smyth to Chairman and Commissioners, May 20, 1954, Smyth Papers, APS.

9. Hoover to Tolson, Ladd, Belmont, Clavin, and Nichols, December 15, 1953, JRO/FBI. The other officials in attendance were Arthur Flemming, head of the Office of Defense Mobilization, and Robert Cutler, national security adviser to the president.

10. Hoover to Tolson, Ladd, Belmont, Clavin, and Nichols, December 15, 1953, JRO/FBI; File number 77-47503-2, Lewis L. Strauss, FBI.

11. Frank Cotter, interview with author, May 2, 1990.

12. Stern with Green, *Oppenheimer Case*, pp. 211–213 and 229–232.

13. Anne W. Marks, interview with author, August 2, 1986; Alice H. Strauss, interview with author, November 28, 1990.

14. Stern with Green, *Oppenheimer Case*, pp. 229–231; Hewlett and Holl, *Atoms for Peace and War*, pp. 78–80; Belmont to Ladd, December 21, 1953, JRO/FBI; Strauss to file, April 15, 1954, LLS.

15. Hewlett and Holl, *Atoms for Peace and War*, pp. 79–80; Stern with Green,

Oppenheimer Case, pp. 231–232. Herbert Marks's widow, Anne, remembers the day differently: she recalls picking up Oppenheimer by car at the AEC building, his coming out white as a sheet and telling her what had happened, and her driving him home to the Markses' house, where they were joined by Volpe and Marks (Anne Wilson Marks, interview with author, August 2, 1986). But the recorded conversation in Volpe's office appears to confirm the version given here. Volpe and his partner discovered that their offices were tapped when something came up the next day in the Dixon-Yates matter that showed advance knowledge by the AEC. Harold Green reports having seen wiretapped reports for that day from Marks's and Volpe's offices (author interview of May 14, 1984). Knowing that Oppenheimer would go to either Marks or Volpe, the FBI had placed wiretaps in both offices.

16. Hoover to Brownell, December 21, 1953, JRO/FBI; Hoover to SAC Newark, December 28, 1953, JRO/FBI; Brownell to the author, September 9, 1993.

17. Belmont to Ladd, December 23, 1953, JRO/FBI. Oppenheimer's attorneys represented him free of charge throughout the hearings, and he had to pay only their out-of-pocket expenses, which, in the case of Garrison's firm, amounted to about twenty-five thousand dollars.

18. Stern with Green, *Oppenheimer Case,* pp. 235–236; Louis and Eleanor Hempelmann, interview with author, December 7, 1987. Mrs. Hempelmann's observation could have occurred either on Snapp's first visit, on Christmas Eve, or on his second visit, on New Year's Eve, when he actually retrieved the documents.

19. Stern with Green, *Oppenheimer Case,* pp. 240–241; Anne Wilson Marks, interview with author, August 2, 1986; Charles Horsky, interview with author, December 19, 1986; "Re: Dr. J. Robert Oppenheimer," January 14, 1954, an FBI field office report, quotes a "reliable confidential informant" to the effect that O'Brian told Herbert Marks that he wanted to take the case but could not do so "because of the disapproval of his partners." Covington and Burling was Acheson's law firm as well.

20. Belmont to Ladd, January 5, 1954, JRO/FBI.

21. Strauss to Hoover, February 1, 1954, LLS; Strauss to Bates, February 8, 1954, JRO/FBI. Of the 110 reports on Oppenheimer sent by the FBI between December 22 and April 12, more than 50 were disguised as personal letters from Hoover to Strauss. Hewlett and Holl, *Atoms for Peace and War,* p. 85.

22. Charles W. Bates, interview with author, October 12, 1983; Joan Harrington, interview with author, November 26, 1990.

23. Charles W. Bates, interview with author, October 12, 1983; Harold

Green, interview with author, May 14, 1984; Green, "The Oppenheimer Case"; Belmont to Ladd, February 2, 1954, p. 2, JRO/FBI.

24. Hoover to Tolson, Ladd, and Nichols, February 1, 1954, JRO/FBI.

25. Lee Hancock, interview with author, August 22, 1983; Lee Hancock to Harold Green, January 22, 1966 (courtesy of Lee Hancock).

26. Hancock to Green, January 22, 1966; Belmont to Ladd, January 26, 1954, JRO/FBI.

27. *IMJRO,* pp. 3–7; Joseph Volpe, interview with author, November 19, 1985.

28. Pfau, *No Sacrifice Too Great,* pp. 163–167; Rhodes, *Dark Sun,* pp. 541–543.

29. Rhodes, *Dark Sun,* pp. 524–526. Joe Four's yield was four hundred kilotons.

CHAPTER EIGHTEEN: **The Hearing Begins**

1. Reston, *Deadline,* p. 221.

2. Hewlett and Holl, *Atoms for Peace and War,* pp. 89–91; a story by Joseph and Stewart Alsop, also sympathetic to Oppenheimer, appeared the same day on page one of the *Times*'s competitor, the *New York Herald-Tribune;* notes of James C. Hagerty, April 8–11, 1954, Hagerty Papers, DDEPL. The strategy was developed at meetings attended by Sherman Adams, Hagerty, Murray Snyder, and Wilton Persons for the White House, and Commissioners Strauss and Campbell of the AEC.

3. Oppenheimer had been cleared informally by Gordon Dean in 1950, and by Walter Whitman, chairman of the Research and Development Board of DoD, in July 1953, under the Eisenhower executive order.

4. Samuel J. Silverman, interview with author, October 5, 1989.

5. James G. Beckerley, interview with author, June 6, 1987; Arnold with Pyne, *Britain and the H-Bomb,* p. 92. At a meeting of commissioners the following summer, Smyth put his finger on the problem when he said he had been worried about "rate and scale and direction of thinking information, and specifically . . . the question of the change in the thermonuclear program and the time it occurred." Minutes of 1,017th AEC meeting, July 23, 1954, NARA. My thanks to Gregg Herken for this document.

6. Samuel J. Silverman, interview with author, October 5, 1989.

7. Charles W. Bates, interviews with author, October 5, 12, and 17, 1983; FBI file dated December 14, 1959, titled "J. Robert Oppenheimer." This file lists 428 documents, mostly wiretapped conversations, transmitted by the FBI to the Atomic Energy Commission between 1947 and 1958. General

Correspondence series, JRO file/RG 128, NARA. My thanks to Gregg Herken for this document. Strauss memo to Robb, February 23, 1954, suggesting questions for Bradbury, Rabi, and Groves, LLS AEC, JRO file.

8. Roger Robb to Samuel B. Ballen, December 1, 1976; Irene Rice Robb, interview with author, November 11, 1988; Harold Tyler, interview with author, October 24, 1989; Patrick Raher, interview with author, November 11, 1991; Judge Oliver Gasch, interview with author, November 13, 1991; Mrs. Ruth Luff, interview with author, January 4, 1992; Judge Paul Friedman, interview with author, May 31, 1986.

9. Manchester, *The Glory and the Dream,* pp. 697–698.

10. *IMJRO,* p. 137.

11. *IMJRO,* p. 146. What neither Oppenheimer, Chevalier, nor Army security seems to have known then or later was that Eltenton was a physicist, not an engineer, and that he worked from 1934 to 1937 in Leningrad under Yuli Khariton, an important figure in Soviet nuclear research and later director of the Soviet H-bomb program. He was also close to Shalnikov, another prominent Soviet nuclear physicist.

12. *IMJRO,* p. 149.

13. Stern with Green, *Oppenheimer Case,* p. 280.

14. Samuel J. Silverman, interview with author, October 5, 1989.

15. Joseph Volpe, interviews with author, November 19, 1985, and July 7, 1989; Stern with Green, *Oppenheimer Case,* pp. 305–309; Goodchild, *J. Robert Oppenheimer: Shatterer of Worlds,* p. 244.

16. Samuel J. Silverman, interviews with author, October 5, 1989, and July 2, 1998.

17. *IMJRO,* pp. 649–650, 656.

18. *IMJRO,* pp. 306, 322, and 517.

19. *IMJRO,* pp. 356–357, 365.

20. *IMJRO,* pp. 566–567.

21. *IMJRO,* p. 468.

22. "Dates and times of appointments Dr. Rabi had with Mr. Strauss at AEC building during month of April, 1954," and Strauss to "Joe" [Campbell], undated, but probably April 16, 1954, in Rabi folder, LLS. Belmont to Boardman, April 17, 1954, JRO/FBI; Strauss to Robb, April 16, 1954, in Oppenheimer folder, LLS. See also James Reston, "Oppenheimer Case Stirs Resentment Among Scientists," *New York Times,* April 15, 1954; Walter Lippmann, "The Oppenheimer Case," *New York Herald-Tribune,* April 15, 1954; and Drew Pearson, "Admiral Strauss Sorry He Started Fuss, Oppenheimer Made Him Look Foolish," *New Mexican,* April 20, 1954.

23. Belmont to Ladd, January 7 and 15, 1954, JRO/FBI.

24. Strauss to file, January 22, 1954, LLS; Belmont to Ladd, January 26, 1954, JRO/FBI.

25. I. I. Rabi, interviews with author, July 22, 1985, and January 31, 1986.

26. In an interview of December 11, 1985, George Kennan used almost the same words: "Oppenheimer had a brain that was outsize and too much for his physical and emotional frame."

27. Ruth and Harold Cherniss, interviews with author, December 13, 1985.

CHAPTER NINETEEN: Smyth

1. "M's Summary on Strauss Data," from Mary Smyth's diary, Smyth Papers, APS. Smyth learned on May 8, 1953, that he would not be appointed chairman, and on May 9 he heard, via radio, of the *Fortune* attack on Oppenheimer.

2. Mary Smyth diary entry of May 25, 1954, Smyth Papers, APS.

3. Times of visits and calls are from Strauss's appointment calendar and telephone log, April 26–30, 1954, LLS.

4. Roger Robb, memo for file, July 24, 1967, LLS; John Wheeler, interview with author, November 14, 1985; Hans and Rose Bethe, interview with author, December 3, 1986; Hans Bethe, interview with Charles Weiner, part 3, April 1972, AIP.

5. Teller's testimony appears on pp. 709–727 of *IMJRO,* this remark on p. 710.

6. Memo of Charter Heslep to Lewis L. Strauss, May 3, 1954. Years afterward, defense attorney Silverman said he had no doubt that Teller's testimony had been the result of a deal, with Robb asking, "Will you say that?" and Teller saying, "so far and no farther," and Robb knowing exactly how far Teller was willing to go. Samuel Silverman, interview with author, October 5, 1989.

7. *IMJRO,* p. 726.

8. Stern with Green, *Oppenheimer Case,* p. 340.

9. Herbert Childs, *An American Genius,* pp. 466–473; Molly B. Lawrence, interview with author, February 24, 1992. Mrs. Lawrence said that her husband was "horribly torn," did not know what he was going to say, and felt relief when he did not have to testify. She attributed his feeling of betrayal to an incident over Frank, to passages in Oppenheimer's testimony in which he admitted lying about the Chevalier episode, and to having heard from a neighbor at Balboa Island that Oppenheimer had allegedly had a long love affair with Ruth Tolman, wife of his colleague Richard Tolman.

10. Childs, *An American Genius,* p. 473. The men he summoned to his room were Leland J. Haworth, Thomas H. Johnson, and Clarence E. Larson. Mrs. Lawrence vouched for Childs's accuracy and added that her husband was not pretending to be sicker than he was.

11. Alvarez, *The Adventures of a Physicist,* p. 180. Lawrence's defection deprived the Berkeley contingent of its heaviest heavyweight: Oppenheimer's old, old friend and one with whom he had worked closely in the 1930s.

CHAPTER TWENTY: **Borden**

1. Allan B. Ecker, interview with author, June 18, 1989. Ecker concluded that Robb had been playing a recording of the August 26, 1943, conversation between Oppenheimer, Pash, and Lyall Johnson. In his questioning of Pash on April 30, Robb asked: "Have you recently refreshed your recollection about this interview by looking over a copy of that transcript?" Pash said: "I have." *IMJRO,* p. 814.

2. Alvarez, *IMJRO,* pp. 770–805; Latimer, *IMJRO,* pp. 656–667; Pitzer, *IMJRO,* pp. 697–709.

3. For Wilson's testimony, see *IMJRO,* pp. 679–697; for the information about Vandenberg, see Meilinger, *Hoyt S. Vandenberg,* p. 155.

4. Interview of Lieutenant General Roscoe C. Wilson by Lieutenant Colonel Dennis A. Smith, December 1–2, 1983, Air Force Oral History Program.

5. Getting to author, March 2, 1990.

6. "To Whom It May Concern" letter of Dr. Allen F. Donovan, dated November 19, 1989, and sent to the author by Ivan Getting; FBI Report 100-17828-1739, "Hoover to Waters via Liaison," June 3, 1954, reports the denials by Piore and Overhage, as well as the remarks by Griggs cited here.

7. Guyford Stever, telephone interview with author, April 27, 1990.

8. FBI Report 100-17828-1760, "Hoover to Waters via Liaison," and marked "attention Rolander," reads in part: "On June 12, Mr. Charles J. V. Murphy was interviewed. . . . [H]e stated that he had no direct or firsthand knowledge relative to the origin of the term ZORC. It is Murphy's recollection that Teddy Walcowicz [*sic*], former Air Force officer, was Murphy's main and possibly only source of information relative to ZORC."

9. *IMJRO,* pp. 834 and 839; Courts Oulahan, interview with author, July 13, 1990.

10. Samuel J. Silverman, interviews with author, October 5, 1989, and July 2, 1998.

11. *IMJRO,* pp. 971–990; Stern with Green, *Oppenheimer Case,* p. 367.

12. Hennrich to Belmont, May 20, 1954, JRO/FBI.

13. Goodchild, *J. Robert Oppenheimer,* pp. 260–261.

14. Charles W. Bates, interviews with author, October 5 and 17, 1983.

CHAPTER TWENTY-ONE: **Caesar's Wife**

1. President Eisenhower told Philip Stern on July 19, 1967, that he "believes he talked with Mr. Gray, and asked him to serve in that capacity" (Stern to Schulz, July 21, 1967, Stern Papers, JFKPL.

2. Green, "The Oppenheimer Case."

3. Harold P. Green, interview with author, May 14, 1984; Polly Wisner Fritchey, interview with author, June 16, 1989; Mrs. Gordon Gray, interview with author, June 14, 1989; Boyden Gray, interview with author, May 3, 1991; Gordon Gray Jr., interview with author, April 4, 1989; and Joan Harrington, interview with author, November 26, 1990. Gray did try to end the hearing, but the person to whom he appealed was not, as he later told Boyden, Lloyd Garrison, but Roger Robb. Gray also gave his family the impression that he and Morgan had gone into the case expecting to clear Oppenheimer, but his notes at the time indicate that he, Morgan, and Evans all were inclined against clearance from the start and that the inclination grew stronger during their immersion in the prosecution's documents before the hearing. Notes dictated by Gray to Ardith Johnson, May 7–14, Gray Papers, DDEPL.

4. Lee Hancock, interview with author, September 22, 1983; Lee Hancock to Harold Green, January 22, 1966, author's files. Some witnesses were told that their testimony was being released and others were asked for permission. One, Jerrold Zacharias, told the author that he refused permission. His testimony was published nevertheless.

5. James Hagerty diary entry for June 15, 1954, Hagerty Papers, DDEPL; Strauss to Gray, June 11, 1954, Gray Papers, DDEPL. According to a memo by Strauss, Garrison may have talked to a public relations adviser about representing the defense in March, but there is no evidence that he did so later. Strauss to file, May 18, 1954, LLS.

6. Murphy's work diaries, June 8, 10, 14, 17, 18, 19, 1954, CJVM. Reid immediately called a high-ranking FBI official, Louis B. Nichols, for advice on how to handle Gray. Nichols to Tolson, June 18, 1954, FBI.

7. Kalven, "The Case of J. Robert Oppenheimer Before the Atomic Energy Commission."

8. Ambrose, *Eisenhower, the President,* pp. 476–477.

9. Murphy's work diaries, CJVM.

10. Mary Smyth diary, June 20–July 10, 1954; "From M's Diary: M's Summary on Strauss Data 1954"; and "Answers to Questions from Philip Stern," August 7, 1967. All in Smyth Papers, APS.

11. H. D. Smyth, interview with author, December 10, 1985; "Answers to Questions from Philip Stern," August 7, 1967, Smyth Papers, APS. Farley did not consider Nichols's warning a threat. Moreover, he was planning to leave the AEC to become assistant to Gerard Smith, chief atomic energy adviser to the Department of State. Philip Farley, telephone interview with author, February 2, 1987.

12. *IMJRO*, pp. 1049–1052.

13. *IMJRO*, pp. 1058–1061.

14. Henry DeWolf Smyth, interview with author, December 10, 1985; Philip Farley, telephone interview with author, February 2, 1987.

15. *IMJRO*, pp. 1061–1065.

16. Mary Smyth diary entry for June 30, 1954, Smyth Papers, APS; "Answers to Questions from Philip Stern," August 7, 1967, Smyth Papers, APS; H. D. Smyth, interview with author, December 10, 1985.

17. Father Daniel Bradley Murray, interview with author, November 12, 1990. John Courtney Murray's papers at the Georgetown University library document his close friendships with Thomas Murray, Henry R. Luce, and Clare Boothe Luce, whom he catechized upon her conversion to Catholicism.

18. Lewis H. Strauss, interview with author, July 6, 1989.

19. Eugene Zuckert, interview with author, November 28, 1990.

20. Harold Green, interview with author, November 13, 1991; Philip Farley, telephone interview with author, October 20, 1983.

21. Eugene Zuckert, interview with author, November 28, 1990.

CHAPTER TWENTY-TWO: **Do We Really Need Scientists?**

1. Hagerty diary entry, June 29, 1954, DDEPL.

2. Hagerty diary entry, May 29, 1954 (Strauss was considering Kenneth Pitzer as Zuckert's replacement). Between April 9 and June 30, Hagerty's diary records contacts with Strauss in person or by telephone on at least fifteen days, including one day when they spoke about the Oppenheimer case four or five times; Strauss's diary records at least four solo visits with the president and numerous other occasions when the two men saw each other in the presence of others.

3. Brownell to author, September 9, 1993.

4. Jerry Hannifin, telephone conversation with author, July 19, 2003. The author's guess is Robb.

5. Murphy work diaries, October 5, 1953, and August 18, 1954, CJVM.

6. Clay Blair, interview with author, February 22, 1993; Borden to Allardice, March 22, 1954, NND 902010, TN box 58, RG 128, NARA. Before leaving the JCAE on June 1, Borden, who wished to remain in Washington, asked Strauss whether he had a place for him at the AEC. But Strauss apparently did not want Borden in Washington, and it was Rickover and Representative Chet Holifield of California who found him his job at Westinghouse.

7. Clay Blair, interviews with author, February 22, 1993, and March 20, 1994. The author's conjecture that Borden and Strauss made such a plan in the autumn of 1951 is based on the August 13, 1951, conversation between the two men and on Borden's letter in late September 1951, to Walter Bedell Smith of the State Department, seeking help in getting Teller's relatives out of Hungary.

8. Clay Blair, interview with author, February 22, 1993.

9. Clay Blair, interviews with author, February 22, 1993, and March 20, 1994. Leach was also consulted about air strategy in Europe by James B. Conant while he was president of Harvard.

10. In an interview with the author on February 22, 1993, Blair described accompanying Shepley to Strauss's office, while Shepley, on the NBC television program *Comment,* on September 26, 1954, said Strauss had summoned him but made no mention of Blair's presence (from an unpublished article on the Shepley-Blair book by Chuck Hansen). Blair told the author that there had been a fire burning in Strauss's office at the time of his visit with Shepley. Since the meeting took place in mid-June, one wonders whether Blair's memory may have slipped and whether the fire might have been lit earlier, during one of his interviews with Strauss for the book.

11. Vannevar Bush, "If We Alienate Our Scientists."

12. Carson Mark letter of June 29, 1954, *BAS,* September 1954; excerpt from Drew Pearson broadcast, October 23, 1954, Teeple folder, LLS; minutes of forty-first GAC meeting, p. 54, box 4932, RG 326, NARA. Three members of Strauss's staff at the AEC were thought to be "gumshoeing": two of them, McKay Donkin and Bryan LaPlante, together with Strauss's secretary, Virginia Walker, reported on Smyth's activities throughout the summer of 1954.

13. Teller with Shoolery, *Memoirs,* p. 401.

14. Bradbury actually answered the charges from the condensed version in *U.S. News & World Report,* September 21, 1954, prior to the book's publication on September 28. Livermore's first successful large-scale fusion test took place only in 1956, and its first design, the W-27, did not go into production until 1958, six years after the lab was founded.

15. Gordon Dean press release of September 28, 1954, with review at-

tached, from David Lilienthal Papers, Princeton University Library; Dean to Strauss, September 10, 1954, LLS; Froman et al. to Strauss, September 28, 1954, RG 326, LANL; Strauss to Froman, October 12, 1954, RG 326, LANL. Strauss reviewed at least two drafts of the Shepley-Blair book: first in early June, prior to his attempt to purchase the manuscript, and second in early July. Chuck Hansen's unpublished article on the book cites a letter from Strauss to Pearl Carroll of Time Inc., dated July 10, 1954, with questions and suggested changes, in Strauss's handwriting. Strauss saw Shepley at least six times during May and June of 1954, most of these meetings lasting more than an hour and at least three of them with no one else present. During those visits Strauss may also have helped with *Time*'s June 14, 1954, cover story on Oppenheimer. In addition to Blair's several hours with Borden in January 1954, Shepley and Blair had been coached by Murphy, had had personal access to his sources, and had read the notes for his stories in *Fortune*.

16. Joseph and Stewart Alsop, "Do We Need Scientists?" *New York Herald-Tribune*, October 1, 1954; Elie Abel, "The Attack on Oppenheimer Continues," *Reporter*, October 21, 1954.

17. All in LLS, Teller folder, HHPL: Teller to Strauss, July 2, 1954; Strauss to Teller, July 6, 1954; Robb to Teller, July 8, 1954, with enclosure; Teller to Robb, July 30, 1954.

18. Teller to Strauss, July 2, 1954; Strauss to Dulles, July 27, 1954. In LLS, Teller folder, HHPL. After his meeting with Blair in February, Borden wrote to his successor at the JCAE and asked him to follow up a 1951 inquiry he himself had made about the relatives. Borden to Allardice, March 22, 1954, NND902010, RG 128, NARA; McMahon to [W. Bedell] Smith, September 28, 1951, doc. no. CDVII, RG 128, NARA.

19. Teller with Shoolery, *Memoirs*, p. 405. In his autobiography, the Italian-born physicist Emilio Segrè wrote that Fermi considered Teller's testimony at the Oppenheimer hearing "unethical." Segrè, *A Mind Always in Motion*.

20. Teller, "The Work of Many People," *Science*, February 25, 1955.

21. Murphy to Teller, May 17, 1961, LLS, Murphy folder, HHPL.

CHAPTER TWENTY-THREE: **Oppenheimer**

1. Peter Oppenheimer, interview with author, November 16, 1987.

2. George Kennan, interview with author, December 11, 1985.

3. Verna Hobson, interview with author, September 20, 1986.

4. Anne Marks, interview with author, November 11, 1986. (The prize money was fifty thousand dollars.)

CHAPTER TWENTY-FOUR: **We Made It—and We Gave It Away**

1. Gerard Smith, *Disarming Diplomat,* p. 37; Leonard Weiss, "Atoms for Peace," *BAS,* November–December 2003.

2. James Killian, interview with Stephen White, 1969, pp. 225–228, COHP. The author is indebted to David Holloway for the insight that the Air Force held us back.

3. Charles Bates, interview with author, October 12, 1983.

4. I. I. Rabi, interview with Chauncey Olinger, 1983, box 3, pp. 759–760 and 827–828, COHP.

Postlude

1. H. D. Smyth, interview with author, December 10, 1985.

2. Mary Smyth Papers, APS.

3. JRO to Smyth, July 5, 1954, Smyth folder, JRO Papers, LC.

SELECTED BIBLIOGRAPHY

Books

Acheson, Dean. *Morning and Noon*. Boston: Houghton Mifflin, 1965.
———. *Present at the Creation: My Years in the State Department*. New York: Norton, 1969.
———. *Sketches From Life*. New York: Harper & Bros., 1959.
Albright, Joseph, and Marcia Kunstel. *Bombshell: The Secret Story of America's Unknown Atomic Spy Conspiracy*. New York: Times Books, 1997.
Alperovitz, Gar. *The Decision to Use the Atomic Bomb and the Architecture of an American Myth*. New York: Knopf, 1995.
Alsop, Joseph W., with Adam Platt. *I've Seen the Best of It*. New York: Norton, 1992.
Altshuler, B. L., B. M. Bolotovsky, I. M. Dremin, V. Y. Fainberg, and L. V. Keldysh, eds. *Andrei Sakharov: Facets of a Life*. Gif-sur-Yvette, France: Editions Frontières, 1991.
Alvarez, Luis W. *The Adventures of a Physicist*. New York: Basic Books, 1987.
Ambrose, Stephen E. *Eisenhower, the President*. New York: Simon & Schuster, 1984.
Anders, Roger M., ed. *Forging the Atomic Shield: Excerpts from the Office Diary of Gordon E. Dean*. Chapel Hill: University of North Carolina Press, 1987.
Andrew, Christopher, and Vasili Mitrokhin. *The Sword and the Shield: The Mitrokhin Archive and the Secret History of the KGB*. New York: Basic Books, 1999.
Arnold, Lorna, with Katherine Pyne. *Britain and the H-Bomb*. Houndmills, UK: Palgrave, 2001.
Badash, Lawrence. *Scientists and the Development of Nuclear Weapons: From Fission to the Limited Test Ban Treaty, 1939–1963*. Atlantic Highlands, NJ: Humanities Press International, 1995.
Badash, Lawrence, Joseph O. Hirschfelder, and Herbert P. Broida, eds. *Reminiscences of Los Alamos, 1943–1945*. Dordrecht, the Netherlands: Reidel, 1980.
Benson, Robert Louis, and Michael Warner, eds. *VENONA: Soviet Espionage*

and the American Response, 1939–1957. Washington, DC: Central Intelligence Agency, 1996.

Bernstein, Jeremy. *Hans Bethe: Prophet of Energy.* New York: Dutton, 1981.

———. *The Life It Brings: One Physicist's Beginnings.* New York: Ticknor and Fields, 1987.

———. *Oppenheimer: Portrait of an Enigma.* Chicago: Ivan Dee, 2004.

Bix, Herbert P. *Hirohito and the Making of Modern Japan.* New York: Harper-Collins, 2000.

Blackett, P. M. S. *Fear, War, and the Bomb.* New York: McGraw-Hill, 1948.

Blumberg, Stanley, and Gwinn Owens. *Energy and Conflict: The Life and Times of Edward Teller.* New York: Putnam, 1976.

Blumberg, Stanley, and Louis Panos. *Edward Teller: Giant of the Golden Age of Physics.* New York: Scribner's, 1990.

Borden, William L. *There Will Be No Time: The Revolution in Strategy.* New York: Macmillan, 1946.

Bowen, Lee, and Robert D. Little. *A History of the Air Force Atomic Energy Program, 1943–1953.* 5 vols. Washington, DC: Air University Historical Liaison Office, Bolling Air Force Base.

Bowie, Robert R., and Richard H. Immerman. *Waging Peace.* New York: Oxford University Press, 1998.

Boyer, Paul. *By the Bomb's Early Light.* Chapel Hill: University of North Carolina Press, 1994.

Bradley, Omar N., and Clay Blair Jr. *A General's Life.* New York: Simon & Schuster, 1983.

Broad, William. *Star Warriors.* New York: Simon & Schuster, 1985.

———. *Teller's War: The Top Secret Story Behind the Star Wars Deception.* New York: Simon & Schuster, 1992.

Brower, Kenneth. *The Starship and the Canoe.* New York: Harper & Row, 1983.

Brown, Andrew. *The Neutron and the Bomb: A Biography of Sir James Chadwick.* Oxford: Oxford University Press, 1997.

Brown, John Mason. *Through These Men.* New York: Harper, 1956.

Brownell, Herbert, with John P. Burke. *Advising Ike.* Lawrence: University Press of Kansas, 1993.

Bundy, McGeorge. *Danger and Survival: Choices About the Bomb in the First Fifty Years.* New York: Random House, 1988.

Bush, Vannevar. *Modern Arms and Free Men.* New York: Simon & Schuster, 1949.

———. *Pieces of the Action.* New York: Morrow, 1970.

Butow, Robert J. C. *Japan's Decision to Surrender.* Stanford, CA: Stanford University Press, 1954.

Byrnes, James F. *All in One Lifetime.* New York: Harper & Row, 1958.

————. *Speaking Frankly.* New York: Harper & Bros., 1947.

Cassidy, David C. *Uncertainty: The Life and Science of Werner Heisenberg.* New York: Freeman, 1991.

Chevalier, Haakon. *The Man Who Would Be God.* New York: Putnam, 1959.

————. *Oppenheimer: The Story of a Friendship.* New York: Braziller, 1965.

Childs, Herbert. *An American Genius: The Life of Ernest Orlando Lawrence, Father of the Cyclotron.* New York: Dutton, 1968.

Christman, Al. *Target Hiroshima: Deak Parsons and the Creation of the Atomic Bomb.* Annapolis, MD: Naval Institute Press, 1998.

Cohen, Sam. *Shame: Confessions of the Father of the Neutron Bomb.* Xlibris, 2000.

Compton, Arthur. *Atomic Quest.* New York: Oxford University Press, 1956.

Conant, Jennet. *Tuxedo Park.* New York: Simon & Schuster, 2002.

Craig, William. *The Fall of Japan.* New York: Dial, 1967.

Curtis, Charles P., Jr. *The Oppenheimer Case: The Trial of a Security System.* New York: Simon & Schuster, 1955.

Davis, Hope Hale. *Great Day Coming.* South Royalton, VT: Steerforth, 1994.

Davis, Nuell Pharr. *Lawrence and Oppenheimer.* New York: Simon & Schuster, 1968.

Day, Dwayne A. *Lightning Rod: A History of the Air Force Chief Scientist's Office.* Washington, DC: Chief Scientist's Office, U.S. Air Force, 2000.

Divine, Robert. *Blowing on the Wind: The Nuclear Test Ban Debate, 1954–1960.* New York: Oxford University Press, 1978.

Donovan, Robert J. *The Presidency of Harry S. Truman, 1945–1948: Conflict and Crisis.* New York: Norton, 1977.

————. *The Presidency of Harry S. Truman, 1949–1953: The Tumultuous Years.* New York: Norton, 1982.

Dorwart, Jeffery M. *Eberstadt and Forrestal.* College Station: Texas A & M Press, 1991.

Drell, Sidney D., and Sergei P. Kapitsa. *Sakharov Remembered.* Woodbury, NY: American Institute of Physics, 1991.

Dyson, Freeman. *Disturbing the Universe.* New York: Harper & Row, 1979.

————. *Weapons and Hope.* New York: Harper & Row, 1984.

Eltenton, Dorothea. *Laughter in Leningrad: An English Family in Russia, 1933–1938.* Privately published, 1998.

Evangelista, Matthew. *Innovation and the Arms Race.* Ithaca, NY: Cornell University Press, 1988.

————. *Unarmed Forces.* Ithaca, NY: Cornell University Press, 1999.

Feis, Herbert. *Between War and Peace.* Princeton, NJ: Princeton University Press, 1960.

————. *Japan Subdued: The Atomic Bomb and the End of the War in the Pacific*. Princeton, NJ: Princeton University Press, 1961.

Fermi, Laura. *Atoms in the Family*. Chicago: University of Chicago Press, 1954.

————. *Illustrious Immigrants*. Chicago: University of Chicago Press, 1968.

Ferrell, Robert H. *The Diary of James C. Hagerty: Eisenhower in Mid-Course, 1954–1955*. Bloomington: Indiana University Press, 1983.

————, ed. *Harry S. Truman: A Life*. Columbia, MO: University of Missouri Press, 1994.

Fitzgerald, Frances. *Way Out There in the Blue*. New York: Simon & Schuster, 2000.

Ford, Daniel. *The Cult of the Atom*. New York: Simon & Schuster, 1982.

Frayn, Michael. *Copenhagen*. New York: Random House, 1998.

Furman, Necah Stewart. *Sandia National Laboratories: The Postwar Decade*. Albuquerque: University of New Mexico Press, 1989.

Gaddis, John Lewis. *The Long Peace*. Oxford: Oxford University Press, 1987.

————. *Strategies of Containment*. Oxford: Oxford University Press, 1982.

————. *The United States and the End of the Cold War*. New York: Oxford University Press, 1992.

————. *We Now Know: Rethinking Cold War History*. Oxford: Oxford University Press, 1997.

Gaddis, John Lewis, Philip Gordon, Ernest R. May, and Jonathan Rosenberg, eds. *Cold War Statesmen Confront the Bomb: Nuclear Diplomacy Since 1945*. Oxford: Oxford University Press, 1999.

Galison, Peter. *Image and Logic: A Material Culture of Microphysics*. Chicago: University of Chicago Press, 1997.

Galison, Peter, and David J. Stump, eds. *The Disunity of Science: Boundaries, Contexts, and Power*. Stanford, CA: Stanford University Press, 1996.

Gamow, George. *My World Line*. New York: Viking, 1970.

————. *Thirty Years That Shook Physics*. New York: Dover Publications, 1996.

Garthoff, Raymond L. *Détente and Confrontation*. Washington, DC: Brookings, 1985.

————. *The Great Transition*. Washington, DC: Brookings, 1994.

————. *A Journey Through the Cold War*. Washington, DC: Brookings, 2001.

Gerhart, Eugene C. *America's Advocate: Robert H. Jackson*. Indianapolis, IN: Bobbs-Merrill, 1958.

Getting, Ivan. *All in a Lifetime: Science in the Defense of Democracy*. New York: Vantage Press, 1989.

Gilpin, Robert. *American Scientists and Nuclear Weapons Policy*. Princeton, NJ: Princeton University Press, 1962.

Ginsberg, Vitaly. *On Physics and Astrophysics*. Moscow: Bureau Quantum, 1995.

Golden, William T., ed. *Science and Technology Advice to the President, Congress, and Judiciary.* New York: Pergamon Books, 1988.

Goldfischer, David. *The Best Defense.* Ithaca, NY: Cornell University Press, 1993.

Goldstein, Jack S. *A Different Sort of Time: The Life of Jerrold R. Zacharias.* Cambridge, MA: MIT Press, 1992.

Goodchild, Peter. *Edward Teller: The Real Dr. Strangelove.* London: Weidenfeld & Nicolson, 2004.

———. *J. Robert Oppenheimer: Shatterer of Worlds.* Boston: Houghton Mifflin, 1981.

Gorelik, Gennady. *Andrei Sakharov: Science and Freedom.* Moscow: RkhD, 2000.

Goudsmit, Samuel A. *Alsos.* New York: Henry Schuman, 1947.

Gowing, Margaret. *Britain and Atomic Energy, 1939–1945.* Vol. 1. London: Macmillan, 1964.

———. *Britain and Atomic Energy, 1945–1952.* Vol. 2. London: Macmillan, 1974.

Greenstein, Fred I. *The Hidden-Hand Presidency.* New York: Basic Books, 1982.

Groves, Leslie R. *Now It Can Be Told.* New York: Harper & Row, 1962.

Gusterson, Hugh. *Nuclear Rites.* Berkeley: University of California Press, 1996.

Hamby, Alonzo L. *Man of the People: A Life of Harry S. Truman.* New York: Oxford University Press, 1995.

Hansen, Chuck. *The Swords of Armageddon: U.S. Nuclear Weapons Development Since 1945.* CD-ROM. 8 vols. Chukelea Publications, 1995.

———. *U.S. Nuclear Weapons: The Secret History.* New York: Orion Books, 1988.

Hawkins, David. *Project Y: The Los Alamos Story.* Part 1, *Toward Trinity.* Woodbury, NY: American Institute of Physics, Tomash, 1983.

Haynes, John Earl, and Harvey Klehr. *Venona: Decoding Soviet Espionage in America.* New Haven, CT: Yale University Press, 1999.

Heilbron, J. L., and Robert Seidel. *Lawrence and His Laboratory: A History of the Lawrence Berkeley Laboratory.* Berkeley: University of California Press, 1989.

Heims, Steve J. *John von Neumann and Norbert Wiener.* Cambridge, MA: MIT Press, 1980.

Heisenberg, Elisabeth. *Inner Exile: Recollection of a Life with Werner Heisenberg.* Boston: Birkhauser, 1984.

Heisenberg, Werner. *Physics and Beyond.* New York: Harper & Row, 1972.

Herken, Gregg. *Brotherhood of the Bomb.* New York: Holt, 2002.

———. *Cardinal Choices: Presidential Science Advising from the Atomic Bomb to SDI.* New York: Oxford University Press, 1992.

———. *Counsels of War.* New York: Knopf, 1985.

———. *The Winning Weapon: The Atomic Bomb in the Cold War.* New York: Knopf, 1980.

Hershberg, James. *James B. Conant: Harvard to Hiroshima and the Making of the Nuclear Age.* New York: Knopf, 1993.

Hewlett, Richard G., and Oscar E. Anderson Jr. *The New World: A History of the United States Atomic Energy Commission.* Vol. 1, *1939–1946.* Washington, DC: U.S. Atomic Energy Commission, 1972.

Hewlett, Richard G., and Francis Duncan. *Atomic Shield: A History of the United States Atomic Energy Commission.* Vol. 2, *1947–1952.* Washington, DC: U.S. Atomic Energy Commission, 1972.

Hewlett, Richard G., and Jack M. Holl. *Atoms for Peace and War: Eisenhower and the Atomic Energy Commission, 1953–1961.* Vol. 3. Berkeley: University of California Press, 1989.

Hoddeson, Lillian, Paul W. Henriksen, Roger A. Meade, and Catherine Westfall. *Critical Assembly.* Cambridge: Cambridge University Press, 1993.

Holloway, David. *The Soviet Union and the Arms Race.* New Haven, CT: Yale University Press, 1983.

———. *Stalin and the Bomb: The Soviet Union and Atomic Energy, 1939–1956.* New Haven, CT: Yale University Press, 1994.

Holton, Gerald. *The Advancement of Science, and Its Burdens.* Cambridge: Cambridge University Press, 1986.

Holton, Gerald, and Robert S. Morison, eds. *Limits of Scientific Inquiry.* New York: Norton, 1978.

Hoopes, Townsend, and Douglas Brinkley. *Driven Patriot: The Life and Times of James Forrestal.* New York: Knopf, 1992.

Hughes, Emmet John. *The Ordeal of Power.* New York: Atheneum, 1963.

Immerman, Richard H. *John Foster Dulles: Piety, Pragmatism and Power in U.S. Foreign Policy.* Wilmington, DE: Scholarly Resources, 1999.

Iriye, Akira. *Power and Culture: The Japanese-American War, 1941–1945.* Cambridge, MA: Harvard University Press, 1981.

Irving, David. *The German Atomic Bomb.* New York: Simon & Schuster, 1967.

Jackson, Robert H. *That Man: An Insider's Portrait of Franklin D. Roosevelt.* Edited by John Q. Barrett. Oxford: Oxford University Press, 2003.

Jenkins, Edith. *Against a Field Sinister: Memoirs and Stories.* San Francisco: City Lights Books, 1991.

Jones, Vincent C. *U.S. Army in World War II, Special Studies, Manhattan: The Army and the Atomic Bomb.* Washington, DC: U.S. Government Printing Office, 1985.

Jungk, Robert. *Brighter Than a Thousand Suns.* New York: Harcourt Brace, 1958.

Kac, Mark. *Enigmas of Chance.* New York: Harper & Row, 1985.

Kamen, Martin. *Radiant Science, Dark Politics: A Memoir of the Nuclear Age.* Berkeley: University of California Press, 1986.

Kaplan, Fred. *The Wizards of Armageddon*. New York: Simon & Schuster, 1983.

Kennan, George F. *The Cloud of Danger*. Boston: Little, Brown, 1977.

———. *Memoirs*. Vol. 1, *1925–1950*. Boston: Little, Brown, 1967.

———. *Memoirs*. Vol. 2, *1950–1963*. Boston: Little, Brown, 1972.

———. *The Nuclear Delusion*. New York: Pantheon, 1976.

———. *Russia and the West Under Lenin and Stalin*. Boston: Little, Brown, 1960.

Kevles, Daniel. *The Physicists: The History of a Scientific Community in Modern America*. New York: Vintage, 1979.

Khariton, Yuli B., and Yury N. Smirnov. *Myths and Reality of the Soviet Atomic Project*. Arzamas 16: Russian Federal Nuclear Center, 1994.

Killian, James R. *The Education of a College President*. Cambridge, MA: MIT Press, 1985.

———. *Sputnik, Scientists, and Eisenhower*. Cambridge, MA: MIT Press, 1977.

Kipphardt, Heinar. *In the Matter of J. Robert Oppenheimer*. Trans. by Ruth Speirs. New York: Hill and Wang, 1985.

Kistiakowsky, George. *A Scientist at the White House*. Cambridge, MA: Harvard University Press, 1976.

Klehr, Harvey, John Earl Haynes, and Fridrikh I. Firsow. *The Secret World of American Communism*. New Haven, CT: Yale University Press, 1995.

Krock, Arthur. *Memoirs*. New York: Funk & Wagnalls, 1968.

Kuhns, Woodrow J., ed. *Assessing the Soviet Threat: The Early Cold War Years*. Washington, DC: Center for the Study of Intelligence, CIA, 1997.

Kunetka, James. *City of Fire*. Albuquerque: University of New Mexico Press, 1979.

———. *Oppenheimer: The Years of Risk*. Englewood, NJ: Prentice-Hall, 1969.

Lamont, Lansing. *Day of Trinity*. New York: Atheneum, 1965.

Lamphere, Robert, and Tom Shachtman. *The FBI-KGB War: A Special Agent's Story*. New York: Random House, 1986.

Lanouette, William, with Bela Szilard. *Genius in the Shadows: A Biography of Leo Szilard, the Man Behind the Bomb*. New York: Scribner's, 1992.

Lansdale, John, Jr. *John Lansdale, Jr., Military Service Record*. Privately printed, 1987.

Lapp, Ralph E. *My Life with Radiation: The Truth About Hiroshima*. Madison, WI: Cogito Books, 1985.

———. *The Weapons Culture*. New York: Norton, 1968.

Leffler, Melvyn P. *A Preponderance of Power*. Stanford, CA: Stanford University Press, 1992.

Libby, Leona M. *The Uranium People*. New York: Scribner's, 1979.

Lichtenstein, Alice. *The Genius of the World*. Cambridge, MA: Zoland Books, 2000.

Lilienthal, David E. *The Journals of David E. Lilienthal.* Vol. 2, *The Atomic Energy Years, 1945–1950.* New York: Harper & Row, 1964.

———. *The Journals of David E. Lilienthal.* Vol. 4, *The Road to Change, 1955–1959.* New York: Harper & Row, 1969.

———. *The Journals of David E. Lilienthal.* Vol. 5, *The Harvest Years, 1959–1963.* New York: Harper & Row, 1971.

MacEachin, Douglas J. *The Final Months of the War with Japan.* Washington, DC: Central Intelligence Agency, Center for the Study of Intelligence, 1998.

Macrae, Norman. *John von Neumann: The Scientific Genius Who Pioneered the Modern Computer, Game Theory, Nuclear Deterrence, and Much More.* New York: Pantheon, 1992.

Major, John. *The Oppenheimer Hearing.* New York: Stein and Day, 1971.

Malkov, Viktor. *The Manhattan Project: Intelligence and Diplomacy.* Moscow: Nauka Publishing House, 1995.

Manchester, William. *The Glory and the Dream: A Narrative History of America, 1932–1972.* New York: Bantam, 1984.

Mark, Hans, and Lowell Wood. *Energy in Physics, War and Peace: A Festschrift Celebrating Edward Teller's 80th Birthday.* Dordrecht, the Netherlands: Kluwer Academic Publishers, 1988.

McMahon, Thomas. *Principles of American Nuclear Chemistry.* Boston: Little, Brown, 1970.

McPhee, John. *The Curve of Binding Energy: A Journey into the Awesome and Alarming World of Theodore B. Taylor.* New York: Farrar, Straus & Giroux, 1973.

Meilinger, Phillip S. *Hoyt S. Vandenberg: The Life of a General.* Bloomington: Indiana University Press, 1989.

Merry, Robert W. *Taking on the World.* New York: Viking, 1996.

Michelmore, Peter. *The Swift Years: The Robert Oppenheimer Story.* New York: Dodd, Mead, 1969.

Millis, Walter, ed. *The Forrestal Diaries.* New York: Putnam, 1952.

Morland, Howard. *The Secret That Exploded.* New York: Random House, 1979.

Morrison, Philip. *Nothing Is Too Wonderful to Be True.* Woodbury, NY: American Institute of Physics, 1995.

Morse, Philip. *In at the Beginnings.* Cambridge, MA: MIT Press, 1977.

Moss, Norman. *Klaus Fuchs.* New York: St. Martin's, 1987.

———. *Men Who Play God.* New York: Harper & Row, 1968.

Moynihan, Daniel Patrick. *Secrecy.* New Haven, CT: Yale University Press, 1998.

Murray, Thomas E. *Nuclear Policy for War and Peace.* Cleveland: World Publishing, 1960.

————. *The Predicament of Our Age*. New York: Privately printed, 1955.

Nelson, Steve, James R. Barrett, and Rob Ruck. *Steve Nelson, American Radical*. Pittsburgh: University of Pittsburgh Press, 1981.

Newhouse, John. *War and Peace in the Nuclear Age*. New York: Knopf, 1989.

Nichols, K. D. *The Road to Trinity: A Personal Account of How America's Nuclear Policies Were Made*. New York: Morrow, 1987.

Nolan, Janne E. *Guardians of the Arsenal*. New York: Basic Books, 1989.

Norris, R. Standish. *Racing for the Bomb*. South Royalton, VT: Steerforth, 2002.

Nuclear Weapons Databook. Vol. 1, *U.S. Nuclear Forces and Capabilities*. Thomas B. Cochran, William B. Arkin, and Milton M. Hoenig. Cambridge, MA: Ballinger, 1984.

Nuclear Weapons Databook. Vol. 2, *U.S. Nuclear Warhead Production*. Thomas B. Cochran, William B. Arkin, Robert S. Norris, and Milton M. Hoenig. Cambridge, MA: Ballinger, 1987.

Nuclear Weapons Databook. Vol. 3, *U.S. Nuclear Warhead Facility Profiles*. Thomas B. Cochran, William B. Arkin, Robert S. Norris, and Milton M. Hoenig. Cambridge, MA: Ballinger, 1987.

Nuclear Weapons Databook. Vol. 4, *Soviet Nuclear Weapons*. Thomas B. Cochran, William B. Arkin, Robert S. Norris, and Jeffrey I. Sands. New York: Harper & Row, 1989.

Nuclear Weapons Databook. Vol. 5, *British, French, and Chinese Nuclear Weapons*. Robert S. Norris, Andrew S. Burrows, and Richard W. Fieldhouse. Boulder, CO: Westview Press, 1994.

Nuclear Weapons Databook, Working Paper. U.S.–USSR/Russian Strategic Offensive Nuclear Forces, 1945–1996. Robert S. Norris and Thomas B. Cochran. Washington, DC: Natural Resources Defense Council, 1997.

Oppenheimer, J. Robert. *Atom and Void: Essays on Science and Community*. Princeton, NJ: Princeton University Press, 1989.

————. *The Flying Trapeze: Three Crises for Physicists*. London: Oxford University Press, 1964.

————. *The Open Mind*. New York: Simon & Schuster, 1955.

————. *Science and the Common Understanding*. New York: Simon & Schuster, 1953.

————. *Uncommon Sense*. Boston: Birkhauser, 1984.

Oshinsky, David M. *A Conspiracy So Immense*. New York: Free Press, 1983.

Pais, Abraham. *Einstein Lived Here*. New York: Oxford University Press, 1994.

————. *Niels Bohr's Times*. New York: Oxford University Press, 1991.

————. *"Subtle Is the Lord."* New York: Oxford University Press, 1982.

————. *A Tale of Two Continents: A Physicist's Life in a Turbulent World*. Princeton, NJ: Princeton University Press, 1997.

Palevsky, Mary. *Atomic Fragments.* Berkeley: University of California Press, 2000.

Pape, Robert A. *Bombing to Win.* Ithaca, NY: Cornell University Press, 1996.

Peat, F. David. *Infinite Potential: The Life and Times of David Bohm.* Reading, MA: Addison-Wesley, 1997.

Peierls, Rudolph. *Bird of Passage.* Princeton, NJ: Princeton University Press, 1985.

Pfau, Richard. *No Sacrifice Too Great: The Life of Lewis L. Strauss.* Charlottesville: University Press of Virginia, 1984.

Polenberg, Richard, ed. *In the Matter of Robert J. Oppenheimer: The Security Clearance Hearing.* Ithaca, NY: Cornell University Press, 2002.

Powers, Thomas. *Heisenberg's War: The Secret History of the German Bomb.* New York: Knopf, 1993.

Rabi, I. I., Robert Serber, Victor F. Weisskopf, Abraham Pais, and Glenn T. Seaborg. *Oppenheimer.* New York: Scribner's, 1969.

Regis, Ed. *Who Got Einstein's Office?* Reading, MA: Addison-Wesley, 1987.

Reston, James. *Deadline.* New York: Random House, 1991.

Rhodes, Richard. *Dark Sun: The Making of the Hydrogen Bomb.* New York: Simon & Schuster, 1995.

———. *The Making of the Atomic Bomb.* New York: Simon & Schuster, 1986.

Rigden, John S. *Rabi.* New York: Basic Books, 1987.

Rogow, Arnold A. *James Forrestal.* New York: Macmillan, 1963.

Romerstein, Herbert, and Eric Breindel. *The Venona Secrets: Exposing Soviet Espionage and America's Traitors.* Washington, DC: Regnery, 2000.

Rosenthal, Debra. *At the Heart of the Bomb.* Reading, MA: Addison-Wesley, 1990.

Rossi, Bruno. *Moments in the Life of a Scientist.* Cambridge: Cambridge University Press, 1990.

Rota, Gian-Carlo. *Indiscrete Thoughts.* Boston: Birkhauser, 1997.

Rouze, Michel. *Robert Oppenheimer: The Man and His Theories.* Greenwich, CT: Fawcett, 1965.

Rovere, Richard H. *Senator Joe McCarthy.* New York: Harcourt Brace, 1959.

Rowny, Edward L. *It Takes One to Tango.* Washington, DC: Brassey's, 1992.

Royal, Denise. *The Story of J. Robert Oppenheimer.* New York: St. Martin's, 1969.

Sakharov, Andrei. *Memoirs.* New York: Knopf, 1990.

Schecter, Jerrold L., and Leona P. Schecter. *Sacred Secrets: How Soviet Intelligence Operations Changed American History.* Washington, DC: Brassey's, 2002.

Schrecker, Ellen W. *No Ivory Tower: McCarthyism and the Universities.* New York: Oxford University Press, 1986.

Schwartz, Stephen I. *Atomic Audit.* Washington, DC: Brookings, 1998.

Schweber, Silvan. *In the Shadow of the Bomb: Bethe, Oppenheimer, and the Moral Responsibility of the Scientist.* Princeton, NJ: Princeton University Press, 2000.

————. *QED and the Men Who Made It*. Princeton, NJ: Princeton University Press, 1994.

Seaborg, Glenn. *Kennedy, Khrushchev, and the Test Ban*. Berkeley: University of California Press, 1981.

Seaborg, Glenn T., with Eric Seaborg. *Adventures in the Atomic Age: From Watts to Washington*. New York: Farrar, Straus & Giroux, 2001.

Segrè, Emilio. *Enrico Fermi: Physicist*. Chicago: University of Chicago Press, 1970.

————. *A Mind Always in Motion*. Berkeley: University of California Press, 1993.

Seidel, Robert W. *Los Alamos and the Development of the Atomic Bomb*. Los Alamos, NM: Otowi Crossing Press, 1995.

Serber, Robert. *The Los Alamos Primer: The First Lectures on How to Build an Atomic Bomb*. Berkeley: University of California Press, 1992.

Serber, Robert, with Robert P. Crease. *Peace and War*. New York: Columbia University Press, 1998.

Shepley, James, and Clay Blair Jr. *The Hydrogen Bomb: The Men, the Menace, the Mechanism*. New York: David McKay, 1954.

Sherwin, Martin. *A World Destroyed: The Atomic Bomb and the Grand Alliance*. New York: Knopf, 1975.

Smith, Alice Kimball. *A Peril and a Hope: The Scientists' Movement in America, 1945–47*. Cambridge, MA: MIT Press, 1971.

Smith, Alice Kimball, and Charles Weiner, eds. *Robert Oppenheimer, Letters and Recollections*. Cambridge, MA: Harvard University Press, 1980.

Smith, Gerard C. *Disarming Diplomat*. Lanham, MD: Madison Books, 1996.

Smyth, Henry DeWolf. *Atomic Energy for Military Purposes: The Official Report on the Development of the Atomic Bomb Under the Auspices of the United States Government, 1940–1945*. Princeton, NJ: Princeton University Press, 1989.

Stein, Jonathan B. *From H-Bomb to Star Wars*. Lexington, MA: D.C. Heath, 1984.

Stern, Philip M., with Harold P. Green. *The Oppenheimer Case: Security on Trial*. New York: Harper & Row, 1969.

Straight, Michael. *After Long Silence*. New York: Norton, 1983.

Strauss, Lewis L. *Men and Decisions*. New York: Macmillan, 1962.

Swanberg, W. A. *Luce and His Empire*. New York: Scribner's, 1972.

Sudoplatov, Pavel, and Anatoli Sudoplatov, with Jerrold L. Schecter and Leona P. Schecter. *Special Tasks: The Memoirs of an Unwanted Witness— A Soviet Spymaster*. Boston: Little, Brown, 1994.

Sylves, Richard T. *The Nuclear Oracles: A Political History of the General Advisory Committee of the Atomic Energy Commission, 1947–1977*. Ames: Iowa State University Press, 1987.

Szasz, Ferenc Morton. *The Day the Sun Rose Twice*. Albuquerque: University of New Mexico Press, 1984.

Talbott, Strobe. *The Master of the Game: Paul Nitze and the Nuclear Peace*. New York: Knopf, 1988.

Teller, Edward. *Better a Shield Than a Sword: Perspectives on Defense and Technology*. New York: Free Press, 1987.

———. *Energy from Heaven and Earth*. San Francisco: Freeman, 1979.

———. *The Pursuit of Simplicity*. Malibu, CA: Pepperdine University Press, 1981.

Teller, Edward, and Albert Latter. *Our Nuclear Future: Facts, Dangers, and Opportunities*. New York: Criterion Books, 1958.

Teller, Edward, with Allen Brown. *The Legacy of Hiroshima*. New York: Doubleday, 1962.

Teller, Edward, with Judith Shoolery. *Memoirs: A Twentieth-Century Journey in Science and Politics*. New York: Perseus Press, 2001.

Thackara, James. *America's Children*. Woodstock, NY: Overlook Press, 2001.

Thorne, Kip S. *Black Holes and Time Warps*. New York: Norton, 1994.

Toulmin, Stephen. *Foresight and Understanding*. New York: Harper & Row, 1961.

Trachtenberg, Marc. *A Constructed Peace*. Princeton, NJ: Princeton University Press, 1999.

———. *History and Strategy*. Princeton, NJ: Princeton University Press, 1991.

Truman, Harry S. *Memoirs*. Vol. 1, *Year of Decisions*. Garden City, NY: Doubleday, 1955.

———. *Memoirs*. Vol. 2, *Years of Trial and Hope*. Garden City, NY: Doubleday, 1956.

Udall, Stewart. *The Myths of August*. New York: Pantheon, 1994.

Ulam, S. M. *Adventures of a Mathematician*. Berkeley: University of California Press, 1991.

United States Atomic Energy Commission. *In the Matter of J. Robert Oppenheimer: Transcript of Hearing Before Personnel Security Board and Texts of Principal Documents and Letters*. Cambridge, MA: MIT Press, 1971.

Van DeMark, Brian. *Pandora's Keepers*. Boston: Little, Brown, 2003.

Van der Post, Laurens. *The Night of the New Moon*. London: Hogarth Press, 1970.

von Hippel, Frank. *Citizen Scientist*. New York: Simon & Schuster, 1991.

Walker, Samuel J. *Prompt and Utter Destruction*. Chapel Hill: University of North Carolina Press, 1997.

Weart, Spencer, and Gertrude W. Szilard, eds. *Leo Szilard: His Version of the Facts*. Vol. 2. Cambridge, MA: MIT Press, 1978.

Weinstein, Allen. *Perjury: The Hiss-Chambers Case*. New York: Random House, 1997.

Weinstein, Allen, and Alexander Vassiliev. *The Haunted Wood: Soviet Espionage in America—The Stalin Era*. New York: Random House, 1999.

Weisgall, Jonathan M. *Operation Crossroads: The Atomic Tests at Bikini Atoll*. Annapolis, MD: Naval Institute Press, 1994.

Wheeler, John Archibald, with Kenneth Ford. *Geons, Black Holes, and Quantum Foam: A Life in Physics*. New York: Norton, 1998.

Wicker, Tom. *Dwight D. Eisenhower*. New York: Times Books, 2002.

Wiesner, Jerome B. *Where Science and Politics Meet*. New York: McGraw-Hill, 1961.

Wigner, Eugene. *The Recollections of Eugene Wigner*. As told to Andrew Szanton. New York: Plenum Press, 1992.

Williams, Robert C. *Klaus Fuchs, Atom Spy*. Cambridge, MA: Harvard University Press, 1987.

Williams, Robert C., and Philip L. Cantelon, eds. *The American Atom: A Documentary History of Nuclear Policies from the Discovery of Fission to the Present, 1939–1984*. Philadelphia: University of Pennsylvania Press, 1984.

Wittner, Lawrence S. *One World or None*. Stanford, CA: Stanford University Press, 1993.

Wyden, Peter. *Day One: Before Hiroshima and After*. New York: Simon & Schuster, 1984.

York, Herbert F. *The Advisors: Oppenheimer, Teller, and the Superbomb*. San Francisco: Freeman, 1976.

———. *Arms and the Physicist*. Woodbury, NY: American Institute of Physics, 1995.

———. *Making Weapons, Talking Peace: A Physicist's Odyssey from Hiroshima to Geneva*. New York: Basic Books, 1987.

———. *Race to Oblivion: A Participant's View of the Arms Race*. New York: Simon & Schuster, 1970.

Zachary, G. Pascal. *Endless Frontier: Vannevar Bush, Engineer of the American Century*. New York: Free Press, 1997.

Ziegler, Charles A., and David Jacobson. *Spying Without Spies: Origins of America's Secret Nuclear Surveillance System*. Westport, CT: Praeger, 1995.

Articles

Alsop, Joseph, and Stewart Alsop. "We Accuse!" *Harper's*, October 1954, 24–25.

Arneson, R. Gordon. "The H-Bomb Decision." *Foreign Service Journal* 46 (May 1969): 27–29; (June 1969): 24.

Baker, Richard Allen. "A Slap at the 'Hidden-Hand Presidency': The Senate and the Lewis Strauss Affair." *Congress and the Presidency* 14, no. 1 (Spring 1987): 1–16.

Bernstein, Barton J. "The Atomic Bombings Reconsidered." *Foreign Affairs,* January–February 1995, 137–152.

———. "Crossing the Rubicon." *International Security* 14, no. 2 (Fall 1989): 132–160.

———. "Eclipsed by Hiroshima and Nagasaki: Early Thinking About Tactical Nuclear Weapons." *International Security,* Spring 1991, 149–173.

———. "Four Physicists and the Bomb." *Historical Studies in the Physical and Biological Sciences* 18, part two (1988): 231–261.

———. "The H-Bomb Decisions: Were They Inevitable?" In *National Security and International Stability,* ed. B. Brodie, M. D. Intriligator, and R. Kolkowicz. Boston: Oelgeschlager, Gunn, 1983, 327–356.

———. "Oppenheimer and the Radioactive Poison Plan." *Technology Review,* May/June 1985, 14–17.

———. "The Oppenheimer Conspiracy." *Discover,* March 1985, 22–32.

———. "The Oppenheimer Loyalty-Security Case Reconsidered." *Stanford Law Review* 42 (July 1990): 1383–1484.

———. "Truman and the H-Bomb." *Bulletin of the Atomic Scientists,* March 1984, 12–18.

Bernstein, Barton J., and Peter Galison. "In Any Light: Scientists and the Decision to Build the Superbomb, 1952–1954." *Historical Studies in the Physical and Biological Sciences* 19, part 2 (1989): 328.

Bethe, Hans A. "Biographical Memoirs of the Fellows of the Royal Society" 14 (1968): 391–416.

———. "Comments on the History of the H-Bomb," *Los Alamos Science,* Fall 1982, 43–53.

———. "Rewriting the History of the H-Bomb." *Science,* November 19, 1982, 769–772.

Bix, Herbert P. "Japan's Delayed Surrender: A Reinterpretation." *Diplomatic History* 19, no. 2 (Spring 1995): 197–225.

Bliven, Naomi. "Ike." *New Yorker,* July 1, 1985, 95–97.

Brands, H. W. "The Age of Vulnerability: Eisenhower and the National Insecurity State." *American Historical Review,* Fall 1989, 963–989.

Broad, William J. "Soviets Shown to Have Lagged on H-Bomb in 50's." *New York Times,* October 7, 1990.

Bundy, McGeorge. "The Missed Chance to Stop the H-Bomb." *New York Review of Books* 29, no. 8 (May 13, 1982): 19.

Burr, William, and Hector L. Montford. "The Making of the Limited Test

Ban Treaty, 1958–1963." www2.gwu.edu/~nsarchiv/nsa/NC/nuchis/html. Posting for August 8, 2003.

Bush, Vannevar. "If We Alienate Our Scientists." *New York Times Magazine,* June 13, 1954, 9.

Chace, James. "Sharing the Atom Bomb." *Foreign Affairs,* January–February 1996.

Coughlin, Robert. "Dr. Edward Teller's Magnificent Obsession." *Life,* September 1954, 60.

————. "The Tangled Drama and Private Hells of Two Famous Scientists." *Life,* December 13, 1963, 87.

Day, Michael A. "Oppenheimer on the Nature of Science." *Centaurus* 43 (2001): 73–112.

"The Decade of Innovation: Los Alamos, Livermore, and National Security Decision-Making in the 1950s." Workshop at Pleasanton, California, February 19–21, 1992, published by the Center for Security and Technology Studies.

De Santillana, Georgio. "Galileo and J. Robert Oppenheimer." *Reporter,* December 26, 1957, 10–18.

DeWitt, Hugh E. "Labs Drive the Arms Race." *Bulletin of the Atomic Scientists,* November 1984.

DeWitt, Hugh E., and Gerald E. Marsh. "Stockpile Reliability and Nuclear Testing." *Bulletin of the Atomic Scientists,* April 1984.

Dingman, Roger. "Atomic Diplomacy During the Korean War." *International Security* 13, no. 3 (Winter 1988/1989): 50–91.

Elliot, David C. "Project Vista and Nuclear Weapons in Europe." *International Security* 2, no. 1 (Summer 1986): 163–183.

Feld, Bernard. "The Oppenheimer Case." *American Scientist,* July 1970.

Gaddis, John Lewis. "The Tragedy of Cold War History." *Foreign Affairs,* January–February 1994, 142–154.

Garthoff, Raymond L. "Assessing the Adversary: Estimates by the Eisenhower Administration of Soviet Intentions and Capabilities." Washington, DC: Brookings Institution Press, 1991.

Goncharov, German A. "Thermonuclear Milestones." *Physics Today,* November 1996, 44–61.

Goodman, Michael S. "The Grandfather of the Atomic Bomb? Anglo-American Intelligence and Klaus Fuchs." *Historical Studies in the Physical Sciences* 32, part 1: 1–22.

Gorelik, Gennady. "The Metamorphosis of Andrei Sakharov." *Scientific American,* March 1999.

Green, Harold P. "The Oppenheimer Case: A Study in the Abuse of Law." *Bulletin of the Atomic Scientists,* September 1977: 12.

————. "Q-Clearance: The Development of a Personnel Security Program." *Bulletin of the Atomic Scientists,* May 1964.

Hammond, Thomas T. "Did the United States Use Atomic Diplomacy Against Russia in 1945?" In *From the Cold War to Détente,* ed. Peter J. Potichnyi and Jane P. Shapiro. Boulder, CO: Praeger, 1976.

Hersey, John. "Hiroshima." *New Yorker,* August 31, 1946.

Hershberg, James G. "Where the Buck Stopped: Harry Truman and the Cold War." *Diplomatic History* 27, no. 5 (November 2003): 735–739.

Hoddeson, Lillian, Adrienne Kolb, and Roger Meade. "Extending the Master's Vision: Bradbury at Los Alamos and Lederman at Fermilab." Los Alamos Technical Release, Los Alamos National Laboratory, 1999.

Holloway, David. "New Light on Early Soviet Bomb Secrets." *Physics Today,* November 1996, 26–27.

————. "Soviet Scientists Speak Out." *Bulletin of the Atomic Scientists,* May 1996, 18–19.

Holton, Gerald. "The Migration of Physicists to the United States." *Bulletin of the Atomic Scientists,* April 1984, 18–24.

————. "Success Sanctifies the Means: Heisenberg, Oppenheimer, and the Transition to Modern Physics." *Transformation and Tradition in the Sciences,* 1984, 155–173.

————. "Young Man Oppenheimer." *Partisan Review,* July 1981, 380–388.

Holtzman, Franklyn D. "Politics and Guesswork: CIA and DIA Estimates of Soviet Military Spending." *International Security* 14, no. 2 (Fall 1989): 101–113.

Jastrow, Robert. "Why Strategic Superiority Matters." *Commentary,* March 1983.

Joravsky, David. "Sin and the Scientist." *New York Review of Books,* July 17, 1980, 7–10.

Kalven, Harry, Jr. "The Case of J. Robert Oppenheimer Before the Atomic Energy Commission." *Bulletin of the Atomic Scientists,* September 1954, 259–269.

Kempton, Murray. "The Ambivalence of J. Robert Oppenheimer." *Esquire,* December 1983, 236–248.

Khariton, Yuli. "USSR Nuclear Weapons: Did They Come from America or Were They Built Independently?" *Izvestia,* December 8, 1992.

Khariton, Yuli, and Yuri Smirnov. "The Khariton Version." *Bulletin of the Atomic Scientists,* May 1993, 20–31.

Lapp, Ralph E. "Atomic Candor." *Bulletin of the Atomic Scientists,* October 1954.

Leffler, Melvyn P. "The American Conception of National Security and the Beginnings of the Cold War, 1945–48." *American Historical Review* 89, no. 2 (April 1984): 346–400.

Leskov, Sergei. "Dividing the Glory of the Fathers." *Bulletin of the Atomic Scientists,* May 1993, 37–39.

Mayers, David. "Containment and the Primacy of Diplomacy: George Kennan's Views, 1947–1948." *International Security* 11, no. 1 (Summer 1986): 124–162.

Miles, Rufus E., Jr. "Hiroshima: The Strange Myth of Half a Million American Lives Saved." *International Security* 10, no. 2 (Fall 1985): 121–140.

Morland, Howard. "Errata." *Progressive,* December 1979.

Murray, Thomas E. "Morality and the H-Bomb." *National Catholic Weekly Review,* December 1, 1956.

Norris, Robert S., and William M. Arkin. "Russian/Soviet Weapons Secrets Revealed." *Bulletin of the Atomic Scientists,* April 1993, 48.

Norton-Taylor, Duncan. "The Controversial Mr. Strauss." *Fortune,* January 1955.

Oppenheimer, J. Robert. "The Atomic Bomb as a Great Force for Peace." *New York Times Magazine,* June 9, 1946.

———. "Atomic Weapons and American Policy." *Foreign Affairs* 31:4, July 1953, 526–535.

———. "International Control of Atomic Energy." *Foreign Affairs,* January 1948.

Pape, Robert A. "Why Japan Surrendered." *International Security* 18:2 (Fall 1993): 154–201.

Rabinowich, Eugene. "Fortune's Own Operation Candor." *Bulletin of the Atomic Scientists,* December 1953.

Rhodes, Richard. "I Am Become Death: The Agony of J. Robert Oppenheimer." *American Heritage,* October 1977, 72.

Rigden, John S. "J. Robert Oppenheimer Before the War." *Scientific American,* July 1995, 76–81.

Ritus, V. I. "If Not Me, Then Who?" *Priroda,* August 1990.

Rosenberg, David Alan. "American Atomic Strategy and the Hydrogen Bomb Decision." *Journal of American History* 66 (June 1979): 62–87.

———. "The Origins of Overkill: Nuclear Weapons and American Strategy, 1945–1960." *International Security* 7, no. 4 (Spring 1983): 3–71.

———. "A Smoking Radiating Ruin at the End of Two Hours: Documents on American Plans for Nuclear War with the Soviet Union, 1954–1955." *International Security* 6, no. 3 (Winter 1981–82): 3–38.

———. "U.S. Nuclear Stockpile, 1945 to 1950." *Bulletin of the Atomic Scientists,* May 1982, 25–30.

———. "U.S. Nuclear Strategy: Theory vs. Practice." *Bulletin of the Atomic Scientists,* March 1987, 20–26.

Rota, Gian-Carlo. "The Lost Cafe." *Contention* 2, no. 2 (Winter 1993): 41–61.

Sagdeev, Roald. "Russian Scientists Save American Secrets." *Bulletin of the Atomic Scientists,* May 1993, 32–36.

Samuels, Gertrude. "A Plea for 'Candor' About the Atom." *New York Times Magazine,* June 21, 1953.

Schilling, Warner. "The H-Bomb Decision: How to Decide Without Actually Choosing." *Political Science Quarterly,* March 1961, 24–46.

Schlesinger, Arthur M., Jr. "The Oppenheimer Case." *Atlantic Monthly,* October 1954.

Seidel, Robert W. "A Home for Big Science: AEC's Lab System." *Historical Studies in the Physical and Biological Sciences* 16, part 1 (1986): 135–175.

———. "The DOE Weapons Laboratories." *Los Alamos National Laboratory,* July 26, 1992.

Smith, Alice Kimball. "Scientists and Public Issues." *Bulletin of the Atomic Scientists,* December 1982, 38–45.

Smith-Norris, Martha. "The Eisenhower Administration and the Nuclear Test Ban Talks, 1958–1960." *Diplomatic History* 27, no. 4 (September 2003): 503–541.

Stimson, Henry L. "The Decision to Use the Bomb." *Harper's,* February 1947.

Suri, Jeremy. "The Surprise Attack Conference of 1958." *Diplomatic History* 21, no. 3 (Summer 1997): 417–451.

Teller, Edward. "The Work of Many People." *Science,* February 25, 1955.

Trachtenberg, Marc. "Truman, Eisenhower, and the Uses of Atomic Superiority." *International Security* 13, no. 3 (Winter 1988–89): 4–49.

Trilling, Diana. "The Oppenheimer Case: A Reading of the Testimony." *Partisan Review,* November–December 1954, 105–142.

Ulam, S. M. "Thermonuclear Devices." In *Perspectives in Modern Physics: Essays in Honor of Hans A. Bethe,* ed. R. E. Marshak. New York: John Wiley and Sons, 1966.

Ulam, S., H. W. Kuhn, and Claude E. Shannon. "John von Neumann, 1903–1957." *Perspectives in American History* no. 2 (1968): 235–269.

Unna, Warren. "Dissension in the AEC." *Atlantic Monthly,* May 1957.

Wampler, Robert A. "NATO Strategic Planning and Nuclear Weapons, 1950–1957." Occasional Paper no. 6, Nuclear History Program, University of Maryland.

Weiss, Leonard. "Atoms for Peace." *Bulletin of the Atomic Scientists,* November–December 2003, 34–44.

Ziegler, Charles, and David Jacobson. "Intelligence Assessments of Soviet Atomic Capability, 1945–1949: Myths, Monopolies, and Maskirovka." *Intelligence and National Security* 12, no. 4 (1997).

Unpublished Materials

―――. "The Struggle for the Second Laboratory, 1951–54." Paper prepared for American Historical Association, 1999.

Bethe, Hans A. Letter to Messrs. Joseph and Stewart Alsop, October 1, 1954, Joseph Alsop Papers, LC.

―――. "Memorandum on the History of Thermonuclear Program." May 28, 1952. Assembled by Chuck Hansen transcription of May 12, 1990.

Borden, William Liscum. "Springtime of the Nuclear Debate." Copy of manuscript, given to author by J. K. Mansfield.

Fitzpatrick, Anne. "Igniting the Light Elements: The Los Alamos Thermonuclear Weapons Project, 1942–1952." Ph.D. diss., Virginia Polytechnic Institute, 1998.

Francis, Sybil. "Between Science and Politics: Edward Teller and the Lawrence Livermore National Laboratory." Paper prepared for "The Martians: Hungarian Emigré Scientists," a workshop held at Eotvos University, Budapest, 1997.

―――. "Race Horses vs. Work Horses: Competition Between the Nuclear Weapons Labs in the 1950's." Paper prepared for workshop on the weapons laboratories at Pleasanton, CA, February 19–21, 1992.

―――. "Warhead Politics: Livermore and the Competitive System of Nuclear Weapon Design." Ph.D. diss., MIT, 1995.

Getting, Ivan A., and John M. Christie. "David Tressel Griggs." Paper given to author by Ivan Getting.

Holloway, David. "The Hydrogen Bomb." From a manuscript dated April 2002.

Hughes, Emmet J. Memorial speech for John Courtney Murray, January 16, 1969, Georgetown University Special Collections.

"In Memoriam: A Celebration of Thanksgiving for the Life of I. I. Rabi." Privately published.

Kuchment, Mark. "The Rosenberg Case and the Sarant-Barr Story." Paper.

Mark, Carson. "A Short Account of Los Alamos Theoretical Work on Thermonuclear Weapons, 1946–1950." Los Alamos Scientific Laboratory, 1974. LA-5647-MS, Los Alamos National Laboratory.

Messer, Robert L. "America's 'Sacred Trust': Truman and the Bomb, 1945–1949." Paper prepared for American Historical Association meeting, December 30, 1987.

Murphy, Charles J. V. Correspondence and papers, property of Edythe M. Holbrook.

Murray, Thomas E. Diary and notes, in the possession of the Murray family.

Operation Epsilon: The Farm Hall Transcripts, August 8–22, 1945. RG 77, NARA.

Oppenheimer, J. Robert. "Atomic Weapons and American Policy." Speech and discussion at Council on Foreign Relations, New York City, February 17, 1953.

———. Speech at meeting of the Association of Los Alamos Scientists, November 2, 1945, LANL.

———. Speech at Seven Springs Farm, NY, June 1963, JRO, LC.

———. Speech on Niels Bohr at Los Alamos, 1967, LANL.

Schilling, Warner. "Interview with Robert Oppenheimer." June 12, 1957. J. Robert Oppenheimer Papers, Library of Congress.

Seidel, Robert W. "Ernest Lawrence and the Founding of a Second Nuclear Weapons Laboratory at Livermore," paper presented at the Institute on Global Conflict and Cooperation Colloquium, University of California at Irvine, May 17, 1984.

Sherwin, Martin. "Policing Science in Cold War America: The U.S. Government and the Conspiracy to Destroy J. Robert Oppenheimer." Speech at Symposium on Science and Technology with a Human Face, MIT, 1992.

Smith, Cyril. Letters to Ralph Lapp, June 23, 1965; Margaret Gowing, July 16, 1965; Richard G. Hewlett, April 27, 1967. Gift of the author.

———. "Los Alamos Reminiscences." August 17, 1964. Gift of the author.

Stern, Beatrice M. "A History of the Institute for Advanced Study, 1930–1950." 2 vols. 1964, Institute for Advanced Study. Gift of Ed Regis.

Ulam, Françoise. "Stanislaw Ulam, 1909–1984: A Biographical Profile." American Institute of Physics.

Walker, John S., and William L. Borden. "Policy and Progress in the H-Bomb Program: A Chronology of Leading Events." Called the Walker-Borden Chronology in the notes. RG 128, NARA.

Weisskopf, Victor F. "Banquet Speech at the Fortieth Anniversary Conference of the Los Alamos National Laboratory," April 15, 1983, Los Alamos National Laboratory.

Author's Correspondence

Samuel B. Ballen
Hans A. Bethe
Herbert Brownell
Charles Critchfield
Lloyd K. Garrison
Ivan Getting

Barry Goldwater
Harold P. Green
Lee Hancock
John H. Manley
J. Carson Mark
Kathleen Mark
John Nuckolls
Abraham Pais
Joseph Volpe

Libraries and Oral History Collections

American Philosophical Society Library: Edward U. Condon Papers, H. D. Smyth Papers, Stanislaw Ulam Papers

Columbia University Oral History Collection: Kenneth Bainbridge, Edward L. Beach, Herbert Brownell, William A. M. Burden, Charles Coryell, Gordon Dean, Dwight D. Eisenhower, Lloyd K. Garrison, Gordon Gray, Edward S. Greenbaum, James Killian, Kenneth D. Nichols, Isidor Isaac Rabi, Norman Ramsey

Cornell University Library: Hans Bethe Papers, Sterling Cole Papers

Dwight D. Eisenhower Presidential Library: Dwight D. Eisenhower Papers, Gordon Gray Papers, James Hagerty Papers

Georgetown University Library, Special Collections: John Courtney Murray Papers

Harvard University Libraries:

    Houghton Library: Time Inc. files

    Langdell Law Library: Lloyd Garrison Papers, Walter Barton Leach Papers

    Pusey Library: James B. Conant Papers

Herbert Hoover Presidential Library: Bourke B. Hickenlooper Papers, Lewis L. Strauss Papers

John F. Kennedy Presidential Library: McGeorge Bundy Papers, Glenn Seaborg Papers, Philip M. Stern Papers

Lawrence Berkeley Laboratory Archives: Edwin McMillan Papers

Library of Congress: Joseph Alsop Papers, Vannevar Bush Papers, J. Robert Oppenheimer Papers, William S. Parsons Papers, Isidor Isaac Rabi Papers, Hoyt S. Vandenberg Papers

Los Alamos National Laboratory: Norris Bradbury Papers, John Manley Papers, Carson Mark Papers

Massachusetts Institute of Technology, Special Collections: J. Robert

Oppenheimer Oral History Collection, Philip Morrison Papers, Cyril Smith Papers, Victor Weisskopf Papers, Carroll Wilson Papers

Seeley Mudd Manuscript Library, Princeton University: Emmet Hughes Papers, David E. Lilienthal Papers, George F. Kennan Papers

National Archive and Records Administration: Joint Congressional Committee on Atomic Energy Files, RG 128, in Washington, DC; Records of the U.S. Atomic Energy Commission, RG 326, at College Park, Maryland: AEC Secretariat Files; Gordon Dean Files; J. Robert Oppenheimer Personnel Security Board Files; Henry D. Smyth Files; Lewis L. Strauss Files; Records of the U.S. Atomic Energy Commission, RG 326, at Coordination and Information Center (CIC), Las Vegas, Nevada

Harry S. Truman Presidential Library: Dean Acheson Papers, Gordon Arneson Papers, Gordon Dean Papers, Sidney Souers Papers, Harry S. Truman Papers, Eugene Zuckert Oral History

University of California, Berkeley, Bancroft Library: Herbert Childs Papers, Ernest O. Lawrence Papers

University of California, San Diego, Mandeville Special Collections: Maria Goeppert Mayer Papers

University of Illinois: Louis Ridenour Papers

University of Maryland, Center for International Security Studies, Nuclear History Program: Oral History with Theodore Taylor

University of Wyoming: Clay Blair Papers

U.S. Air Force Oral History Program: Interview of Lieutenant General Roscoe C. Wilson

U.S. Federal Bureau of Investigation Files: William Liscum Borden no. 77-37709; Lewis L. Strauss no. 77-47503-2; J. Robert Oppenheimer no. 100-17828, at FBI Reading Room, Washington, DC

Interviews

The author is indebted to these individuals, each of whom she interviewed or talked with at least six times: Gennady Gorelik, Kay and John Manley, Carson and Kay Mark, David and Frances Hawkins, Emily Morrison, Philip Morrison, and Françoise Ulam.

Adams, Ruth. April 29, 1985
Alsop, Joseph. May 28, 1986
Anderson, Grace. June 9, 1987
Appel, Leonard. Nov. 14, 1985
Arneson, Gordon. Nov. 23, 1985
Bacher, Robert F. Feb. 3 and 4, 1987

Bainbridge, Kenneth. Oct. 29, 1986

Barnett, Henry and Shirley. Feb. 19, 1985

Bates, Charles W. Oct. 5, 1983; Oct. 12, 1983; Oct. 17, 1983

Beach, Commander Edward L. Nov. 1986

Beckerley, James. June 6, 1987

Bell, Daniel. Jan. 13, 1986

Bell, George. Oct. 7, 1999; March 8, 2000

Bethe, Hans. Dec. 3, 1986; Feb. 2, 1987; Aug. 11, 1997

Beyer, William. April 28, 2001; Oct. 20, 2001

Blair, Clay, Jr. Feb. 22, 1993; March 3, 1993; March 20, 1994 (telephone)

Bowditch, Margaret Parsons. July 22, 1992

Bradbury, Norris. Jan. 8, 1985; Aug. 27, 1986

Brooks, Harvey. May 22, 1986

Bundy, McGeorge. April 22, 1986

Bunkin, Irving. Dec. 4, 1987

Burroughs, Martha Parsons. March 12, 1985; April 8, 1985; May 24, 1985; May
    27, 1985; June 10, 1985 (all by telephone)

Carlsson, Bengt. Oct. 8, 2001

Carothers, James. Feb. 26, 1992 (telephone)

Carter, Ashton. June 4, 1985

Chalk, Rosemary. May 13, 1987

Cherniss, Harold. Dec. 13, 1985

Cherniss, Ruth Meyer. Dec. 13, 1985; Feb. 10, 1986

Conant, Theodore. Nov. 1993

Cooper, Necia. Aug. 27, 1986

Corbett, Peggy Felt. Nov. 6, 1987

Cotter, Francis P. Nov. 21, 1985; May 2, 1990

Cowan, George. Sept. 28, 1997

Crawford, Jack. Nov. 28 and 30, 1990

Critchfield, Charles. Sept. 22, 1983; Oct. 28, 1987; Nov. 5, 1987

Davis, Robert Raymond. Jan. 10, 1985

Day, Michael. Feb. 26, 2000

Dean, Deborah Gore. June 11, 2001

Deutsch, Martin and Suzanne. Oct. 14, 1998

DeWitt, Hugh. March 1, 1992

Diamond, Luna. May 1, 1991

Dow, Sterling. Feb. 15, 1985

Drell, Sidney. Jan. 30, 1987

Duffield, Priscilla Greene. Jan. 16, 1985; Nov. 13, 1987

Durgin, Charlotte Warner Davis. Nov. 5, 1985; Jan. 14, 1986

Dyson, Freeman. Dec. 13, 1985

Ecker, Allan B. June 15 and 18, 1989

Edsall, John. July 3, 1988

Elliot, David C. Feb. 4, 1987

Erdmann, Andrew. April 29, 1999

Erikson, Erik and Joan. Feb. 6, 1987

Everett, Dolores. Oct. 17 and 19, 1991

Everett, William. July 23, 2000 (telephone)

Fanton, Jonathan. Dec. 28, 1989

Farley, Philip. Oct. 20, 1983; Feb. 2, 1987 (telephone)

Feld, Bernard. Feb. 28, 1985

Fergusson, Peggy. Aug. 9 and 10, 1993

Feshbach, Herman. Feb. 14, 1990

Fowler, William A. Feb. 2, 1987

Friedman, Paul L. May 31, 1986

Fritchey, Polly (Polly Wisner). June 16, 1989

Fuller, Clarissa Parsons. Sept. 17, 1986

Garwin, Richard. Dec. 9, 1986; Feb. 15, 2000

Gasch, Judge Oliver. Nov. 13, 1991

Gavin, General James M. June 10, 1986

Getting, Ivan. June 24, 1986; Oct. 6, 1989

Gilpatric, Roswell. Nov. 30, 1993

Gingerich, Owen. Feb. 12, 1990

Glauber, Roy. Sept. 12, 1985; Nov. 7, 1985; Jan. 29, 1986; Feb. 18, 1987; Dec.
1, 1988

Goldberger, Marvin. Nov. 15, 1988

Golden, William T. Jan. 3, 1990

Goldstein, Jack. June 20, 1989

Goodwin, Guy. June 15, 1989; July 21, 1989; Dec. 18, 1989

Gorelik, Gennady. April 28, 1993; Nov. 6, 1998; Jan. 20, 1999; Sept. 10, 2001

Graham, Loren. Feb. 1, 1988

Gray, Boyden. May 3, 1991

Gray, Gordon, Jr. April 4, 1989

Gray, Nancy (Mrs. Gordon Gray). June 14, 1989

Green, Harold P. Jan. 25, 1984; Feb. 21, 1984; March 7, 1984; April 27, 1984;
May 7, 14, 22, 1984; June 18, 1984; Nov. 13, 1991

Haar, Karl. July 11, 1990

Hancock, Lee. Aug. 22, 1983; Sept. 22, 1983; Dec. 13, 1983; Jan. 16, 1985

Hancock, William. Sept. 25, 1990

Hannifin, Jerry. July 19, 2003 (telephone)

Harrington, Joan (Mrs. David Harrington). Nov. 26–27, 1990

Hawkins, David and Frances. Jan. 30–31, 1985; Feb. 2, 1985; Oct. 4, 1991; May 1, 1994; Jan. 1, 1997; Oct. 12, 1997; Jan. 28, 1999; May 20, 2000

Hein, Hilde Stern. March 7, 1987

Heller, Leon. Oct. 9, 1999

Hempelmann, Louis and Eleanor. Dec. 7, 1987; Dec. 10, 1987

Hewlett, Richard G. May 3, 1990

Hobson, Verna (Mrs. Wilder Hobson). Sept. 20, 1986

Hoffman, Stanley. July 18, 1985

Holbrook, Edythe M. Dec. 17, 1992

Holbrook, John. Nov. 8, 1993

Horsky, Charles. Dec. 19, 1986 (telephone)

Hunt, John. June 26, 1986

Johnson, Lyall. June 14, 1997 (telephone)

Kaufman, William W. Feb. 12, 1996

Kaysen, Carl. March 30, 1999

Keeler, Norris. July 8, 1989

Kempton, Mina. May 7, 1988

Kennan, George F. Dec. 11, 1985

Kerr, Walter. Jan. 5, 1985

Kerst, Don. Oct. 29, 1987

King, Percival L. D. P. Nov. 20, 1983; Dec. 20, 1983; Oct. 12, 1987; Nov. 5, 1987

Kuchment, Mark. May 5, 1985; May 9, 1985; May 27, 1985; Oct. 26, 1985

Lamphere, Robert J. February 1996 (telephone)

Lansdale, John. Nov. 12, 1991

Lawrence, Molly. Feb. 24, 1992

Leva, Marx. Nov. 29, 1990

Lichtenstein, Alice. Jan. 23, 1986

Lichtenstein, Immanuel. Feb. 21, 1987

Lichtenstein, Nancy R. March 3, 1985; Dec. 10, 1985; Feb. 24, 1987; May 7, 1988; Nov. 14, 1988

Lilienthal, James and Betty. Jan. 17–18, 1985; Oct. 28–29, 1987; Nov. 20, 1987

Livingston, Lois. Oct. 31, 1987

Livingston, M. Stanley. Sept. 23, 1983

Lofgren, Edward J. July 19, 1988; Feb. 27, 1992

Luff, Ruth. Jan. 4, 1992 (telephone)

MacKenzie, John. Feb. 13, 1985

MacKinnon, Judge George E. Nov. 13, 1991

Malkov, Viktor. April 29, 1993

Manley, John. Jan. 9, 1985; Jan. 18, 1985; Jan. 23, 1985; March 26, 1986; March 28, 1986; March 29, 1986; April 28, 1986; Oct. 17, 1987; Nov. 1, 1987

Mansfield, J. Kenneth. March 9, 1984; May 27, 1986; May 28, 1986; May 29, 1986; May 31, 1986; June 1, 1986

Mark, Carson. Jan. 6, 1985; Jan. 17, 1985; April 2, 1986; April 3, 1986; Aug. 19, 1986; Aug. 20, 1986; Aug. 21, 1986; Aug. 25, 1986; Aug. 26, 1986; Oct. 17, 1987; Nov. 3, 1987; Dec. 10, 1988; Nov. 17, 1991 (telephone); Dec. 9, 1991 (telephone); June 14, 1993

Marks, Anne Wilson. Aug. 2, 1986; Nov. 11, 1986; June 18, 1994; June 3, 1998; July 21, 1998

McKibbin, Dorothy. Jan. 6, 1985

Meade, Roger. Aug. 22, 1986

Meyer, Cord, Jr. Nov. 7, 1986

Meyner, Robert and Helen. Nov. 4, 1984

Mitchell, John F. B. June 29, 1998 (telephone)

Mitchell, Victor S. and Donna R. Nov. 13, 1990; Nov. 15, 1990

Murray, Daniel Bradley. Nov. 12, 1990

Nabokov, Dominique. June 16, 1986

Nagle, Darragh. July 23, 2001

Nagle, William J. April 30, 1990; May 1, 1990

Nekrich, Alexander M. March 11, 1991

Nelson, Steve. Aug. 28, 1985

Neumann, Honora Fergusson. May 5, 1988; Nov. 14–15, 1988

Nitze, Paul. July 20, 1989

Norton, Garrison. Sept. 28, 1992

O'Keefe, Bernard J. March 27, 1985

Olinger, Chauncey. April 14, 1989; Nov. 11, 2003

Oppenheimer, Frank. Sept. 1, 1983

Oppenheimer, Dr. Judith. Feb. 7, 1987

Oppenheimer, Peter. Jan. 28, 1985; Nov. 16, 1987

Oulahan, Courts. July 13, 1990

Pais, Abraham. April 22, 1986 (telephone); Nov. 18, 1986

Parkinson, Kenneth Wells. Nov. 14, 1991

Peierls, Rudolph. March 6, 1986

Pfau, Richard. July 11, 1989 (telephone); Aug. 4, 1989 (telephone); Nov. 3, 1993 (telephone)

Piel, Gerard. Oct. 4, 1989

Pitzer, Kenneth. March 2, 1992

Pound, John. Nov. 10, 1987

Quesada, Elwood R. Sept. 26, 1992 (telephone)

Rabi, Helen. Aug. 13, 1985; Nov. 13, 1985; April 14, 1989; April 28, 1989; Oct. 5, 1989; April 20, 1991

Rabi, Isidor Isaac. Aug. 13, 1985; Jan. 30, 1986; Jan. 31, 1986; Feb. 21, 1987

Raher, Patrick M. Nov. 11, 1991

Ramsey, Norman. June 7, 1986 (telephone); June 5, 1989

Redman, Leslie. Nov. 20, 1987; Dec. 10, 1987

Robb, Irene Rice. Nov. 11, 1988

Rosen, Louis. April 3, 1986; July 26, 2001

Rosenfeld, Susan F. July 1, 1985

Rota, Gian-Carlo. Sept. 15, 1986; Nov. 1, 1986

Roy, Max. Oct. 11, 1991

Rubel, John. Oct. 9, 1987

Schlesinger, Arthur M., Jr. Dec. 2, 1985

Schreiber, Raemer. Nov. 19, 1987

Seidel, Robert. April 8, 1986; June 8, 1993; March 16, 2001; May 12, 2001

Serber, Robert. Feb. 18, 1985; April 22, 1986

Sherr, Pat. May 5, 1988

Sherwin, Martin. March 1, 1985

Shurcliff, William A. June 29, 1994

Silverman, Samuel J. Oct. 5, 1989; July 2, 1998

Singer, Louise Oppenheimer. June 18, 1986 (telephone)

Slansky, Richard. Jan. 25, 1985; October 1991

Sloss, Leon. March 2, 1998

Smith, Alice K. and Cyril S. March 6, 1985; Nov. 29, 1985; May 20, 1986; Feb. 25, 1987; March 5, 1987; Nov. 3, 1990

Smyth, Henry DeWolf. Dec. 10, 1985

Stern, Philip. Nov. 14, 1986

Stever, Guyford. April 27, 1990 (telephone)

Straus, Donald B. Jan. 18, 1986 (telephone)

Strauss, Alice H. Nov. 28, 1990

Strauss, Lewis H. July 6, 1989

Suid, Larry. April 29, 1985; June 17, 1985; Nov. 23, 1985

Sylves, Richard. Aug. 5–6, 1986; March 30, 1987

Teller, Edward. July 18, 1988; May 8, 1990; June 7, 1993

Thorn, Robert. Nov. 23, 1987

Topkis, Jay. July 1–2, 1998

Tyler, Judge Harold R. Oct. 24, 1989 (telephone)

Unna, Warren. Dec. 20, 1989

Volpe, Joseph, Jr. Nov. 19, 1985; Nov. 21, 1985; July 6–7, 1989; May 12, 1994

Wald, Judge Patricia. Nov. 14, 1991 (telephone)

Walkowicz, Christian Anne. Nov. 9, 1993

Wechsler, Jacob. July 25, 2001; Oct. 19, 2001

Weiner, Charles. Nov. 4, 1985

Weisskopf, Victor. Feb. 25, 1985; Oct. 28, 1986

Wheeler, John Archibald. Nov. 14, 1985

Wheeler, Michael. March 24, 1998

White, Stephen. Aug. 14, 1985; Aug. 24, 1985; Aug. 27, 1985; July 28, 1986; May 1987

Wiesner, Jerome. May 28, 1987 (telephone)

Wilson, Robert R. and Jane. Dec. 3, 1986; June 24, 1987

Woodruff, Roy. June 9, 1993

Wyzanski, Charles. Dec. 27, 1985

Zacharias, Jerrold. Dec. 31, 1985; May 1, 1986

Zuckert, Eugene. Nov. 28, 1990

Interviews by Others

Stanley Goldberg with John Lansdale, Feb. 7, 1990
      Fred "Dusty" Rhodes, Sept. 17, 1991

Jack Holl with Lee Hancock, c. 1972, at Albuquerque Airport motel

Bill Moyers with I. I. Rabi, *A Walk Through the Twentieth Century,* shown on PBS, June 26, 1983

Arthur Lawrence Norberg, for the University of California, Berkeley (Bancroft Library), with Norris E. Bradbury, Feb. 11, 1976
      Darol K. Froman, June 7, 1976
      John H. Manley, July 9 and 11, 1976
      J. Carson Mark, June 8, 1976
      Raemer H. Schreiber, Feb. 13, 1976

Silvan Schweber with George Bell, July 19, 1990
      Norris Bradbury, July 19, 1990
      Charles Critchfield, July 17 and 19, 1990
      Carson Mark, July 16 and 19, 1990
      Nicholas Metropolis, Aug. 20, 1990
      Edward Teller, July 21, 1990

Garry Sturgess with K. D. Nichols, Oct. 30, 1989

INDEX

PHOTOGRAPH CREDITS

Insert page 1: Courtesy of LANL Archives; **page 2,** *all:* Courtesy of AP Wide World Photos; **page 3:** Niels Bohr Archive, courtesy of AIP Emilio Segrè Visual Archives; **page 4,** *top:* Photograph by Percival King, courtesy of Nicholas King; *bottom:* Courtesy of Kathleen Mark; **page 5:** AIP Emilio Segrè Visual Archives, W. F. Meggers Gallery of Nobel Laureates; **page 6,** *top:* AIP Emilio Segrè Visual Archives; *bottom:* Courtesy of LANL Archives; **page 7:** Photograph by Frances Simon, courtesy of AIP Emilio Segrè Visual Archives, Frances Simon Collections; **page 8:** Courtesy of Edythe Holbrook; **page 9,** *top:* Courtesy of Herbert Hoover Library; *bottom:* Harris and Ewing, News Service, Massachusetts Institute of Technology, courtesy of AIP Emilio Segrè Visual Archives; **page 10,** *top:* Courtesy of Françoise Ulam; *bottom:* Courtesy of Dolores Everett; **page 11,** *all:* Courtesy of Françoise Ulam; **page 12:** National Archives and Records Administration, courtesy of AIP Emilio Segrè Visual Archives; **page 13,** *top:* Dennis Galloway, courtesy of Emilio Segrè Visual Archives, Physics Today Collection; *bottom:* AIP Emilio Segrè Visual Archives, Physics Today Collection; **page 14:** Photograph by Kenneth Bainbridge, courtesy of AIP Emilio Segrè Visual Archives; **page 15:** Photograph by Fernand Gignon, courtesy of AIP Emilio Segrè Visual Archives, Physics Today Collection; **page 16:** Ulli Steltzer.

THE RED EMINENCE

A Biography of Mikhail A. Suslov

by SERGE PETROFF

The Kingston Press, Inc.
Clifton, N.J. 07015

ISBN 0-940670-13-5

LC 87-081055

Published by

The Kingston Press, Inc.
P.O. Box 2759
Clifton, N.J. 07015

Printed in the United States of America

CONTENTS

FOREWORD

After thirty years in the world of business I took early retirement in January 1983 to return to college and pursue a life-long interest in Russian and Soviet history. *The Red Eminence* is the product of these years in retirement. It grew out of a Master's thesis in history whose primary objective was to examine the role played by Mikhail A. Suslov during the Stalin, Khrushchev and Brezhnev administrations.

Writing a biography is a perilous task. Writing one of a Soviet political figure—let alone of someone as secretive and elusive as Suslov—is even more precarious, because there are so few social and psychological cues to go on. There is almost a complete absence of the usual memoir literature, letters, diaries, dispatches, and pertinent documents that are so much a part of the biographer's *metier*. One has to sift, instead, through the writings of others, through scholarly journals, newspapers, official Soviet tracts, *samizdat* and émigré writings, and miscellaneous other publications that, at best, give only a partial and often one-dimensional view of the man one is writing about. One also has to evaluate the "odds" that the rumors, speculations and impressions are genuine rather than false, and, in the end, hope to glean out of them enough salient facts to draw a fair portrait of the protagonist. Under such circumstances, the best one can do is to write a meta-biography in which the personality is largely revealed through the writings of others, through historical inference, and through an analysis of the protagonist's own official writings and speeches. *The Red Eminence* is such a biography. It traces Suslov's activities from the time of his birth in a remote "middle-Volga" hamlet in 1902 to his death in Moscow in 1982. It does this against the background of the Bolshevik revolution, its aftermath, World War II, Stalin's twilight years, and through the labyrinth of the Khrushchev and Brezhnev eras. In a larger sense, it is a chronicle of Soviet history from its beginning in 1917 to 1982, depicted in the interplay of Mikhail A. Suslov with the Soviet political system.

Many people have assisted me in this undertaking. I am especially indebted to Professor Anthony W. D'Agostino of San Francisco State University who first whetted my interest in Suslov and helped me sort out a storehouse of often disjointed information on Russian and Soviet history that I had absorbed in my lifetime. I am grateful to two other scholars of Soviet life and politics, John B. Dunlop of the Hoover Institution and Kenneth Jowitt of the University of

California, Berkeley. Dr. Dunlop's advice that I make use of the Red Archive at Radio Liberty in Munich saved months of tedious work and greatly facilitated the search of Soviet newspapers and journals. Professor Jowitt's suggestion that I familiarize myself with the existing literature on Father Joseph du Tremblay, the prototype of all future *éminences grises*—proved to be an indispensable intellectual exercise without which I could not have found a coherent approach to a story of Suslov and his relationship to Soviet politics and ideology. I was also privileged in sharing my preliminary thoughts on Suslov in a panel devoted to Soviet ideology at the 1986 meeting of the Western Slavic Association in Portland, Oregon. The questions raised there and the dialogue that they engendered provided important guidelines for the chapters on the Khrushchev and Brezhnev periods.

I have benefited likewise from the work of such specialists as the late Boris I. Nicolaevsky, A. A. Avtorkhanov, Roy Medvedev, Michel Tatu, Robert Conquest, George Urban, Grey Hodnett, Carl A. Linden, Werner G. Hahn, Boris Meissner, Sidney I. Ploss, Robert M. Slusser, R. H. Rigby, John B. Dunlop, Mikhail Agursky, Martin Ebon, Elizabeth Teague and the late Christian Duevel, who had all shown an early interest in Suslov in their writings. Their contribution and my analysis of their views will be very evident in the pages of my study. Dennis A. Pluchinsky's 1978 master's thesis "Mikhail A. Suslov: The Last Stalinist, 1902–1964"—especially, the very extensive appendices to the thesis—also played a significant role in the design and execution of the project.

No study of so illusive and complex an individual as Suslov could have been attempted without a multi-disciplinary framework. The thoughts of Max Weber, Nicolas Berdyaev, Erik H. Erikson, H. J. Eysenck, Claude Levi-Strauss, Clyde Kluckhohn, Henry V. Dicks, and Umberto Eco established important parameters of multi-disciplinary inquiry. So did the explorations of Nathan Leites, Alex Inkeles, Daniel Bell, Frederic J. Fleron, Rita Mae Kelly, Raymond A. Bauer, Nicholas Vakar, and many others who had targeted their writings more specifically to the study of Soviet personal and social behavior. Two practicing California internists, an ophthamologist and a psychiatrist, Martin H. Long, M.D., Arthur L. Walker M.D., Ernest K. Goodner, M.D., and James Spaulding, M.D., were kind enough to review Suslov's medical history and provide a semblance of order out of the conflicting press reports and official medical records on Suslov's illnesses and periodic absences. These insights from medicine and the behavioral sciences have made it possible to offer a more balanced assessment of Suslov, and not just to write a political biography.

The major portion of the research was conducted at the Hoover Institution Library at Stanford, and I am grateful to its staff, especially to Hilja Kukj, who has been most helpful in identifying and locating many essential materials. The libraries at the University of California, Berkeley, the San Francisco State University in San Francisco, and the University of Illinois in Urbana also provided meaningful support during the entire project. The time that I spent at the archive of Radio Liberty- Radio Free Europe yielded an unusually rich harvest of critical information. Keith Bush and his staff provided valuable support and assistance during my stay in Munich, and I am very much in their obligation.

In the brave new age of electronics and information storage technology, I am indebted to three other professionals who made the project more inclusive and immensely simpler. I am grateful to Richard Frewin, Associate Librarian of the J. Paul Leonard Library at San Francisco State University, for convincing me to make use of an on-line political science and world affairs data base, and to his associate, Anne Kennedy, for her help in designing the search. I am grateful to my son, Paul S. Petroff, an actuarial consultant and computer expert, for convincing me to invest in a word processing system and for supervising the work through the early floundering.

Lastly and most importantly, my thanks go to my wife, Jane Amidon Petroff, whose encouragement and participation made the undertaking a most satisfying experience. Her enthusiastic support of the project sustained me during nearly three years of research and writing.

Mill Valley, California
November 1987

The most disturbing thing we know about
the latest mystery in the Soviet Union is that
we know so little. This is the hard fact that
all the hundreds of thousands of words of
intelligent speculation on the current clash
of policy or personality in the Soviet Union
cannot remove.

James Reston, *The New York Times*[1]

God sees the truth, but is slow in revealing it.

Old Russian Proverb[2]

PROLOGUE

Joseph Stalin died on March 5, 1953. Of all his heirs and their political
offspring, no one held power so long or so securely as Mikhail Andreyevich
Suslov. He was elected to the Secretariat of the Central Committee in 1947 and
to the Presidium* in 1952, losing the latter position briefly after Stalin's death,
only to regain it in 1955 and hold it until his death in 1982. He participated in
every major Soviet power play, policy debate, political crisis, and Party dogfight
since 1955. Often perceived as the inflexible dogmatist and hardliner, he had
been called "chief ideologue," "Grand Inquisitor," "kingmaker," "second secretary," and a score of other titles suggesting his preeminence in the Soviet
political hierarchy. "Rigid," "doctrinaire," "sinister" is what the Western press
called him, painting an unflattering picture of a stern and unyielding bureaucrat
whose life and actions were somehow always shrouded in mystery.

He was all that, but he was also—as Elizabeth Teague had perceptively
observed—a "paradoxical figure whose personal skills were as much political as
narrowly ideological."[3] Somehow, he managed to avoid the narrow confines of
factional strife, working behind the scenes and apart from the crude and soaring
machinations of his power-hungry colleagues. He took sides reluctantly and
only when it was crucial to the maintenance of the Party's inner balance and to
the continued purity of the Marxist-Leninist doctrine at home and abroad.

He approved the invasion of Hungary in 1956, but opposed the Soviet
occupation of Czechoslovakia in 1968. As Khrushchev tersely observed, "He
was adamant in resisting the idea of trying to relieve the tension between (the
Soviet Union) and the Yugoslavs,"[4] but he persisted in taking a more moderate
line against China. Favoring strict control in the arts, literature and media, he

---

*The Politburo and the Organization Bureau were abolished by Stalin in 1952 and re-
placed by the Presidium which was but another name for the Politburo. The name Politburo was restored in 1966 at the XXIIIrd Congress of the CPSU.

1

was reputed to have opposed the publication of Solzhenitsyn's *One Day in the Life of Ivan Denisovich* only to express a genuine feeling of approval when he met Solzhenitsyn later at a Kremlin reception. "He took me firmly by the hand," Solzhenitsyn wrote, "and shook it vigorously as he told me how very much he had enjoyed *Ivan Denisovich,* shook it as though from now on I would never have a closer friend."[5] He was often rude, despotic, and devoid of emotion, but he could also be disarmingly beguiling and polite. Enver Hoxha, Albania's venerable dictator and uncompromising Stalinist, thought him to be a bore and a tyrant.[6] Yugoslav Ambassador Veljko Micunovic was appalled by his rudeness when he presented the draft program of the Yugoslav Communist Party to the Soviets in 1958.[7] U.S. Ambassador Jacob Beam, on the other hand, found him to be "most courtly and pleasant" when he and Senator Hugh Scott paid him a visit in 1971.[8] Reputed to be a closet nationalist committed to the preservation of Russia's heritage and ethnic identity,[9] he did not hesitate to admonish Sergei Trapeznikov, that arch Great Russian chauvinist and Stalinist, for his jingoism and zeal, blocking his candidacy to the Soviet Academy of Pedagogical Sciences.[10] There were also other baffling contradictions—contradictions that made Suslov even more of an anomaly. Supervising the liquidation of the Lithuanian resistance movement during the last year of World War II, he thought nothing of using brute force, ruthlessly disregarding the expenditure of human life on both sides of the power struggle.[11] Twenty-one years later, he was reputed to have opposed the prosecution of Sinyavsky and Daniel,"[12] a course of action that precipitated the rise of a powerful dissident movement and opened the eyes of the Western world to the persisting violation of human rights in the Soviet Union. At the XXth Party Congress in 1956 he had joined Khrushchev in censuring the "cult of Stalin," only to go on record a year later with a reaffirmation of Stalin's thesis that the consolidation of communist rule cannot be achieved without a sharpening of class struggle.[13] His most contradictory act followed the ouster of Khrushchev. Having masterminded Khrushchev's fall in 1964 and standing at the apex of Party power, he chose not to seek the ultimate prize. Instead, he took a backseat to Leonid Brezhnev, a relative newcomer to the Kremlin and the Party's Olympus.

A purveyor of Communist orthodoxy and neo-Stalinism, Suslov was also patron to two reformist General Secretaries who followed in Brezhnev's wake. In their rise to power, both Yurii Andropov and Mikhail Gorbachev owed a great deal to Suslov's commanding influence, especially to his backing of their candidacies to the Politburo. He was not, in fact, as predictable as everyone thought. Nor was he always the dour and hidebound *apparatchik* that the press made him out to be. In many ways, he was a supreme realist who carefully calculated the risks and cautiously moved towards the least painful solution. He was convinced that his power and influence in the Soviet leadership rested almost exclusively on the Party's state of health, and he devoted himself completely and relentlessly to the goal of preserving its well-being. The prospect of potential embarrassment to the Party and the international Communist movement horrified him, and he did everything he could to sanctify them. He would have preferred the security of the Communist version of the *Bull Unigenitus*. But this was not to be—Moscow was not Rome, and the 1950s and 1960s were not 1715.

There was also something else that made him appear contradictory to his milieu. Tall, gaunt, and ascetic in appearance, he stood out like a sore thumb among the other heavy-bodied and square-jawed Politburo colleagues who looked more like they had just stepped out of a XXth century adaptation of a Pieter Brugel canvass than out of their modern Kremlin offices. He would have made a better subject in his later years for El Greco or Russia's own iconographic master of the XIIIth and XIVth centuries, Andrei Rublev. Favoring loosely-hanging double-breasted Soviet-made suits, a carelessly knotted flowered tie that tended to sag from the collar, and wearing a *pince-nez* or horn-rimmed glasses, he gave the appearance, as Theodore Shabad had so adroitly observed, of a "XIXth century Chekhovian intellectual"[14] rather than the number two man of a XXth century super-power.

Shy and retiring, he shunned limelight and avoided contact with the non-Communist world. Western statesmen had virtually no access to him, catching only a glimpse of him at rare diplomatic receptions in Moscow. Soviet and Eastern politicians also found it difficult to meet with him other than on formal occasions. He deplored ostentation and excessive display of power, often escaping from the hustle and bustle of Moscow's high life to his suburban *dacha*. His lack of pretentiousness and his blind respect for law and order spilled over even to his driving. Unlike most of his Politburo associates barreling through Moscow on their way to the Kremlin at top speed, he kept his black limousine to the obligatory sixty kilometers per hour speed limit, often choosing the hard-backed resting place of the jump seat instead of the luxurious comfort of the back seat.[15] Despite frequent bouts with illness in his later years, he somehow always managed to exhibit a store of nervous energy often lacking in his hardier and younger colleagues. This was especially noticeable at congresses and public meetings. While they sat staidly in prim self-restraint, applauding only perfunctorily, he threw his heart and soul into the occasion, vigorously clapping his hands and showing his obvious satisfaction and approval.[16] When he spoke, everyone listened, even Brezhnev. He, alone, could talk to him as an equal, and sometimes even as a political senior, using his influence freely and forcefully to slow down ideologically-suspect proposals and programs.

As the chief ideologue of a society where even trivial decisions have ideological ramifications, he held enormous power over the different Soviet factions vying for primacy and recognition. He was not an innovator, however, despite the glowing praise of the Soviet press about his contributions to Marxist thought. As Roy Medvedev and A. A. Avtorkhanov have properly observed, he never proposed anything really original.[17] He merely repackaged Marx and

Lenin to fit the changing circumstances and developments in the USSR. What was even more remarkable was the manner in which he dispensed his countless pronouncements. Holding his text almost to his nose, with a lock of hair down on the right side of his bespectacled visage,[18] he delivered his messages in a monotonous but resonant voice that recalled days gone by when Russian patriarchs spoke to the faithful from the steps of St. Basil's the Blessed. The substance was dull and tedious, but one could not help being impressed by the incredible optimism and unfailing faith in the Communist idea. The form reminded of those long and often obtuse benedictions delivered on feast and saints' days. The occasions were different, of course. Instead of Christmas, Easter, or St. Nicholas Day, these were new Soviet holy days commemorating the birth of Lenin, the October Revolution, or the completion of a new Soviet industrial miracle. But the solemnity and style remained the same. *Nasha Pravoslavnaia Rus'* (Our Orthodox Russia) was replaced by *Nasha Sovetskaia Rodina* (Our Soviet Fatherland), *Pravoslavnye Ludi* (Orthodox Populace) by *Sovetskie Ludi* (Soviet people), and other themes devoted to the myth of the new "Soviet people."[19] He spoke to Party congresses and local electoral meetings, to professional groups and scientific conventions, to gatherings of workers and international communists. It is not accidental that Abraham Brumberg, writing about Suslov in *The New Leader,* named him the "Party's supreme Toastmaster" whose function was not only to deliver the latest Party line, but also "impart a note of solemnity to any important social, cultural or political event in the life of his country."[20]

His more important pronouncements and writings on major Soviet policy positions—often running thirty to forty pages of print—were equally listless and tiresome tirades. Covering a broad array of subjects from relations with China to the education of the Soviet youth and the doctrine of mature socialism, Suslov's papers, invariably, called for the strengthening of Party discipline to achieve a higher level of stability at home and influence abroad. Published in *Kommunist* and *Partiinaia zhizn'** or reprinted in *Pravda,* they were not unlike Papal bulls to be heard and adhered to as infallible truths and precepts of moral and political behavior. Blind to the growing problems at home and abroad, they portrayed to the world an undivided brotherhood of Communist states and a Soviet society of milk and honey. Such optimism did not fade with the years. A "true believer" all his life, Suslov remained a guardian of Communist faith to the end, uncompromisingly defending the fundamentals of the Marxist-Leninist system against the encroaching rationality of Western-style autonomy and freedom.

---

*Kommunist and *Partiinaia zhizn'* are theoretical journals published by the Communist Party of the Soviet Union.

He was seventy-nine when he died. A solitary figure frequently disappearing without any notice from the Moscow political scene, his life had always been couched in riddle and mystery. This long established pattern was not to be broken even in death. The official medical bulletin stated that "he had suffered from general arteriosclerosis brought about by diabetes," and that death occurred on January 25, 1982, five days after he had suffered a severe and disabling stroke.[21] He had been in poor health for sometime, and his death was not unexpected. But the Moscow rumor mill insisted that he had suffered a sudden heart attack in an argument with Andropov, who was getting ready to taint the Brezhnev name with corruption. If there is any truth to this, then Suslov had rallied again to the defense of the Party and its General Secretary, succumbing in the final hour of his life to what had been his lifetime obsession.

He was buried on January 29 under the Kremlin wall next to Stalin in one of the most elaborate state funerals witnessed in Moscow. Resting on a gun carriage and followed by a military band playing the now familiar Chopin funeral march, his open casket was conveyed to the nation's most hallowed ground in front of the Lenin Mausoleum. Red Square was jammed. A dozen heavy-bodied generals in dress uniform, carrying red cushions with his most prized decorations, stood at attention while the Party notables and the public paid their last respects. The mood was solemn, dignified, but there was no grief, no tears, no public expression of emotion. The Moscow public appeared almost apathetic.[22] The official Soviet obituary described Suslov as a man with a "vast soul, crystal clear morals, exceptional industry, who earned the profound respect of the Party and people,"[23] but to the majority of those present he was but another faceless leader—perhaps more mysterious and awe-inspiring than the others—but not very different from the rest of those distant and potent "authorities" that ordinary Russians have known all their lives. In the biting cold of a January midday, with the full Politburo arrayed at his side atop the mausoleum, somewhat flustered but obviously moved by the solemnity of the occasion, Brezhnev paraphrased Alexander Pushkin's famed passage from *The Lay of the Wise Oleg.* "Sleep in peace, dear friend. You lived a great and glorious life," Brezhnev intoned, ignoring the poet's warning that Oleg's "old friend" was his faithful mount and that it was from the "courser's skull" that the viper had "crept forth" to deliver the deadly sting to the prince.[24]

Who was he? Who was this "true believer" who for more than thirty years influenced the course of Soviet life and politics? What were the social and psychological bases of his political behavior, and how did he rise to the top of the Soviet power pyramid? How did he serve Stalin and how did he manage to emerge unscathed from his regime? What was his relationship to the Khrushchev and Brezhnev eras? Were they, indeed, Khrushchev and Brezhnev eras, or were they one single epoch dominated by one man's dedication to foster the stability of a system left intrinsically unstable by Stalin's death? If one dispenses with the details, with Khrushchev's wild experimentation and bungling, with

5

Brezhnev's indifference and inability to innovate, with the highs and lows of the de-Stalinization campaign, with the international crises, with the zig-zagging course of Soviet-American relations, one has to admit that there may have been something inherently cohesive about the thirty years after Stalin's death. The evidence is not all in. The new Soviet leadership has not played all its cards, but there are strong signs that the winds of change are finally beginning to blow. If that is the case, the post-Stalin years were years of painful transition—years during which the traditional forces of anti-reform had coalesced around one man whose fierce devotion to the slowing down of the process of change had contributed to nearly thirty years of post-Stalinist conservatism barely touched by the political and cultural thaw of the Khrushchev years. That man is now dead, but will the viper of Pushkin's epic poem "twine its black ring around (the) legs" of the new men in the Kremlin, will Suslov's ghost come to haunt the new generation of Soviet leaders? That is the "accursed question" of Soviet politics today. Just as serfdom in the 1860s and the growing rupture between the town and the village in the 1920s were the "accursed" problems of their times, so is the future of reform the major problem in the Soviet Union of today. Everything depends on how the new leadership will stand to the tenets of the past, and how it will respond to the growing pressures for reform.

PART ONE

PASSAGE FROM OBSCURITY

Each new being is received into a style of
life prepared by tradition and held together
by tradition, and at the same time disinte-
grating because of the very nature of tradition.

Erik Erikson, *Young Man Luther*

> (Communism) has its own dogmatic system, obligatory for all, and its catechism; it exposes heresies and excommunicates heretics. This religious character of Communism finds a congenial ground in the religious psychology and character of the Russian people.
>
> Nicolas Berdyaev,
> *The Russian Revolution*

Chapter I

ROOTS

Mikhail Andreyevich Suslov was born on November 21, 1902 in Shakhovskoe, a small village in Saratov province[1] not far from the right bank of the Volga. Situated approximately thirty-five miles, as the crow flies, north of Vol'sk and thirty miles west of Khvalynsk—two obscure river towns north of Saratov—Shakhovskoe could not have been much larger than twenty-five households at the turn of the century.[2] Today it is part of a large collective farm, symbolically named *Put' Ilyicha* (The Way of Ilyich) in honor of no other than Lenin himself.*

The Volga flows quietly between Ulianovsk** and Saratov, meandering first east and then southwest for almost five hundred miles through the Russian heartland. Made famous by the novels of Melnikov-Pechersky[3] and affectionately referred to as "The Hills," the right bank stretches for nearly three hundred miles to the west in an undulating chain of low hilltops, deep ravines, and broad meadows that are washed by a network of rushing streams and lesser rivers feeding the mighty Volga. There is a contrasting harshness about the land. In the summer, the grass on the hills is dry, and the oak and maple leaves are stiff as if they are made of tin. It is a land parched by a hot summer sun, and dust is everywhere, in the air and along the village pathways. In the winter, a cold wind blows across the Volga from the eastern steppe. The sky is leaden, and the air is crisp and pure, but the frozen waste of ice and snow is unforgiving.[4] It is a land known for its generous harvests and its sudden outbursts of drought and severe famine.[5]

---

*Lenin's full name, including the patronymic, was Vladimir Ilyich Ulianov (Lenin). He was often affectionately referred to as Ilyich.
**Prior to the Revolution, Ulianovsk was called Simbirsk. It was renamed in honor of the Ulianov family who lived there when Lenin was born.

At the turn of the century, hundreds of small villages and hamlets were scattered through "The Hills." Taken over now by large state and collective farms, they were eking out at the time of Suslov's birth a meager existence, raising wheat and barley, cutting wood, and distilling pitch. Originally populated by the Finnish-speaking Mordva in the north and the Volga Bulgars and Tartars in the south, the right bank saw a succession of runaway serfs, religious dissenters, and adventurers moving up and down the river as the Great Russian people, driven by geography and politics, pressed eastward in the XVIth, XVIIth and XVIIIth centuries. The Volga was the first real obstacle, a major artery connecting the deep forests of the north and the arid steppe of the south. Here, on the right bank of the Volga, thousands stopped, put out roots and built new settlements. Saratov was founded in 1590, Khvalynsk in 1606, Ulianovsk in 1648. Originally built as military outposts to protect the settlers against the Tartars, they grew to become centers of trade, lumbering, and river traffic on the Volga. No one knows exactly when Shakhovskoe was settled or who were its first owners. The name Shakhovskoe is probably derived from the Princes Shakhovskie, descendants of Prince Grigorii Shakhovskoi, Tsar Vasilii Shuiskii's arch rival during the Time of Troubles.* Prince Grigorii raised a large army in support of the Bolotnikov uprising in 1606 and marched north together with Ivan Bolotnikov,[6] only to be stopped at the gates of Moscow.

Political and social unrest were endemic to the middle Volga region. Barely touched by the Bolotnikov uprising in 1606 and 1607, the middle Volga saw full scale violence and rebellion in 1670 and again a century later. Remembered to this day in song and tale, Stepan (Sten'ka) Razin raised a large army in 1670, and proclaimed a new order along the entire stretch of the middle Volga. Protesting against social injustice, his cossacks moved north massacring officials and landlords in the outposts and towns of the right bank. In 1773, spurred by a rebellion among the Ural cossacks and Russia's involvement in a major war with Turkey, Emilian Pugachev launched a massive uprising that engulfed the entire middle Volga basin, threatening Moscow and sounding a full-scale alarm in St. Petersburg. Alleging that Peter III had escaped alive and that the palace plot which brought Catherine to the throne was a conspiracy of the upper classes against the common folk, he proclaimed himself tsar and established an imperial court on the Volga. The great uprising raged until late 1774 when Pugachev was finally betrayed and executed in Moscow.

How much of this history was actually part of the Suslov family background and how much a common heritage passed from one generation to another and shared by all peasants of the middle Volga basin, is not known. Like the rest of the rural youth from "The Hills," young Suslov must have listened to

---

*The period of Russian history from 1598 to 1613 known as *Smutnoe Vremia* (Time of Troubles) and characterized by dynastic, social and national struggle.

the Razin and Pugachev legends fantasizing and acting out their exploits and achievements. Whether or not he understood fully the social implications of the Razin and Pugachev rebellions is doubtful, but he could not have been totally blind to the iniquities of village life, and to the lesson learned from these uprisings. Nor could he have been unaware of the purpose and meaning of his own life. Russia's peasants were poor, backward, and superstitious, but they were also human beings with passion and ambition, creators of a distinctive culture, rising at times above the limitations of their birth to become prominent churchmen, statesmen, and military leaders.[7] As a bright young village lad, Suslov must have thought about his future, about his chances of escaping the abject poverty and inadequacy of village life, about a career. No one really knows if there were adult models with whom he could identify, or if he was compelled to seek one in fantasy. One thing is clear, however. The social and psychological foundations of his adult life must have been laid in Shakhovskoe.

There is unfortunately a total black-out on information about the Suslov family background. We know absolutely nothing about his parents, his religious training, his early schooling, and his life in Shakhovskoe.[8] The probability is very high, however, that Suslov was born into a family of Old Believers.[9] The middle Volga region, and Saratov province particularly, have always been a seat of the Old Faith. The Old Believers moved and settled there in the first decades of the XVIIIth century, seeking a sanctuary from reprisals by Peter the Great. A number of American scholars and journalists have referred to Suslov's Old Believer roots;[10] further acceptance of this heritage is also found in the works of prominent Russian and Soviet specialists,[11] who have pointed out that the Khvalynsk district of Saratov province, where Suslov was born, had always been an important scene of Old Believer activity. There is also the authority of the *Great Soviet Encyclopedia* which confirms this, stating that "Khvalnynsk was," indeed, "one of the centers of the Old Belief."[12]

Suslov's Old Believer heritage may be open to question, but his peasant origin is a matter of certainty. "(He) was born to a peasant family,"[13] states the official Soviet biography, reporting his social origin with a predictable display of proletarian pride. There is also confirmation from Suslov himself. "The son of a poor peasant, I gained my first life experience when the Revolution had just thrown off the yoke of centuries of oppression," he notes in the only autobiography that we have available.[14] It would be a mistake to conclude from this that his life in Shakhovskoe was all sweat and heartbreak. Despite its harsh reality, Russian village life has always had its moments of peace and joy. It was not always the "coarse, dishonest, filthy and drunken" existence that Chekhov claimed,[15] nor was it the simple and idealized life portrayed by Tolstoy and Turgenev.[16] Each village had its own uniqueness, its share of successful husbands and devoted wives, its allotment of drunkards and bullies, its grief and joy, its particular level of economic conflict and social dysfunction. Where exactly Shakhovskoe stood, we do not know, but we do know that villages in the

11

Russian heartland displayed certain general characteristics at the time of Suslov's birth and early upbringing, certain modalities of behavior and view of the world, certain distinctive traits of "national character" that must have left an imprint on young Suslov.[17]

Like all peasants of the Russian heartland, the villagers from "The Hills" led a stern life governed by the rhythm of the seasons and the age-old habit of toiling in the fields. Work was hard and unrelenting. Farming methods were so archaic and inefficient that it was often difficult to subsist, let alone make a profit. Boris Pilniak, the Soviet author who died under strange circumstances in 1937 at the height of the "great terror," described the peasantry of northern Saratov province with artful perception. "From Spring to Autumn they slaved," he wrote, "from sunup to sundown, old and young, burned by the sun and by sweat. And from Autumn to Spring they worked, burned by wood smoke, in cottages like henhouses, cold, half-starved. . . . Life was hard and fierce—and yet they loved that life fiercely with all its hunger, its cold, its heat and its weariness."[18] Life was a matter of survival, and there was little time for idle play or tenderness. Everyone in the family had to work, and women and children toiled side by side with the men.

Peasant society was patriarchal. A family of three generations was often unified under one roof with the family elder holding absolute authority over family life. Nowhere was the authority of the family head more oppressive than in the power to regulate the free movement of individual family members. Despite increased industrialization and demand for urban labor, young and ambitious village lads found it extremely difficult to leave for the greater advantages of the city. Rural life did not encourage individualism. On the contrary, expressions of personal freedom were systematically stifled by the village council and the family elders. Housing was cramped, uncomfortable, and without privacy, and the conditions of domestic life demanded a defensive attitude from birth. The outside environment was also hostile, conspiring against the personal aspirations of individual family members. Interaction with the authorities called for caution, shrewdness, and even treachery. Village folklore glorified cunning.[19] It is no accident that peasant children often grew up to play the double role of an accommodating and angry adult who would rather lead the life of a demanding master.

The village view of the world was a vision of a single religious-temporal community—a view from which the more urbanized West had been emancipated a long time ago by the Renaissance and the Industrial Revolution. The faith was deeply rooted, but it was stimulated more by superstition than by real religious belief. Literacy was minimal. The vast majority—especially the older generation and women—remained illiterate. The social and economic structure of the village stayed frozen and unresponsive to change throughout the XIXth century. Even the emancipation of the serfs did not introduce any substantive changes in peasant society. The concept of the *Mir** remained relatively intact. The peasants continued to regard land not as property, but as sustenance to which each man must have access through what was in reality a village commune.[20] The courts attempted to deprive the *Mir* of its communal prerogatives, but the less efficient peasants resisted this stubbornly, often with violence and deliberate subversion of the law.[21] To them, the *Mir* was the means of resolving the unavoidable conflict between the villagers' selfish and community interests, between those who tried to enrich themselves at the expense of others and the greater good of all.

By the time of Suslov's childhood, important changes were beginning to creep into village life. The Third Duma** in 1908 made substantial improvements in the primary education of peasant children.[22] Primary schools were opened in the more remote regions of the empire and, by 1913, seventy-three percent of the recruits called for military service were reported to have been literate.[23] Indeed, it would have been very unlikely for young Suslov not to have attended a district village school, completing at least the required four years of primary education. The social and economic structure was also undergoing modification. The continuance of the communal form of agriculture was not in the interest of the nation. In the wake of the abortive 1905 revolution, Russia's conservative but capable premier Pyotr Stolypin introduced a series of reforms to transform Russia's land-poor peasants into conservative farmers. The Stolypin reform program was enacted between 1906 and 1911, giving millions of Russian peasants private land previously held in common by the entire village.[24] It also put on the market large tracts of crown land for individual purchase. Almost three million families applied to exchange the tracts that they held in common for land of their own, and many enterprising peasants began to buy more land from other peasants and the government. Working their own land, the peasants made rapid improvements in productivity, raising Russia's gross national product and adding considerable impetus to increased production of cloth and other consumer goods.

The Stolypin program was not without its share of accompanying problems. Prior to the reform, the peasant's primary motivation was subsistence.

---

*Literally meaning order, the *Mir* was an ancient village organization of peasant households, exercising collective authority before the Emancipation in matters of land reapportionment, military service, marriage, and other matters of concern to villagers living in close relationships with each other.
**The term *duma* in Russian means a council or an assembly. The October 1905 Manifesto called for the election of a consultative assembly to act as a lower legislative house. This assembly became known as the *Duma*. The First *Duma* met from April to July 1906, the Second *Duma* from February 1907 to June 3, 1907, and the Third *Duma* replaced the Second *Duma* when the latter was prorogued on June 3, 1907.

Each peasant was interested in having as much land as he and his family could work to support themselves. Now profit became the real objective. The more successful peasant entrepreneurs began buying larger tracts of land, expanding their farms, and hiring others to work them. They had been doing this even before the reform, but the *Mir* limited their freedom of activity. With the elimination of the *Mir,* the restrictions gave way to the demands of the market place. Through superior industry, thrift and *kustar'** production, the new peasant entrepreneurs accumulated substantial holdings. With increased wealth came grubstaking and money-lending. It was not uncommon for the wealthier peasants to offer needed food to carry the poor through the winter, provided the latter pledged repayment in crops or labor, often three or four times the original loan.[25] Nor was it unusual for them to lend money at interest rates that ruined the borrowers and brought the lender the land that was pledged as collateral.[26] It did not take long for the village to become polarized into "haves" and "have-nots." In the decade after the first reform in 1906, a new class of landowners emerged in the Russian countryside. The *kulaks,*** as they became known later, gradually imposed on the peasantry a system of land tenure that was even more cruel than that of the *pomeshchiki.**** Self-made, uneducated, and often thoroughly unscrupulous, they squeezed out the less fortunate and poorer peasants, extracting from them the last *kopek*. Their behavior was even more distasteful than that of the *pomeshchiki* because it was directed against their own people, against the men and women with whom they often grew up in the same village. The government was not entirely innocent, of course. The new class of peasant landowners was the government's creation, and the government protected it through laws and patronage that gave the *kulaks* considerable power in the countryside.

Growing up in Shakhovskoe after the reform, young Suslov must have soaked up every last bit of the unpleasantness that accompanied the extension of *kulak* authority in the countryside. The middle Volga region witnessed serious peasant disturbances after the war with Japan. The villages of Saratov province were especially affected by the agrarian reform as the struggle between the Social Revolutionaries (SRs) and Stolypin, the province's former governor, transformed them into a hotbed of social strife. Young Suslov must have witnessed frequent outbursts of resentment against the new agrarian policies. He must have heard stories about how heavily-indebted peasants were being manipulated in the village councils. He must have also listened to village rumors—

---

*Home industry which often included tailoring, needlework, and other handicrafts produced at home during the winter months.
**Literally translated, a *kulak* is a fist. The word was used to identify the most prosperous peasants in the village wielding economic and political power.
***Estate owners.

often maliciously spread—about secret agreements of the wealthier peasants with government agents and estate owners. How much of an impact this left on him is not known, but it is not unrealistic to assume that his life-long preoccupation with the idea of class struggle—however spurious this idea may actually be on closer examination—had resulted from the early impressions of harsh village life, colored by the struggle with the estate owners and the newly emerging bosses of the Russian countryside.

It would be a dangerous mistake to conclude, nevertheless, that this early experience had somehow frozen his psycho-social development, making the older Suslov a slave of a past that he could not escape. This would be far too deterministic a view of life, especially of someone like Suslov who had surpassed in his adult life the most extravagant fantasies of early childhood. But the child is invariably the father of the man. To overlook this is an equally dangerous mistake. Each human life finds itself molded to a large extent by the experience and environment of childhood and young adulthood, and so it must have been with Suslov. The village continued to be, however tenuous this may seem, an important social and psychological foundation of his adult life.

> . . . On they march with sovereign
> tread. . . . Who else goes there? Come out!
> I said come out! It is the wind and the red
> flag plunging gaily at their head.
>
> Aleksandr Blok, *The Twelve*

Chapter II

INITIATION

Young Suslov was nearly fifteen when the October Revolution* put an end to Russia's fragile and short-lived democracy. The Bolsheviks had seized power in Petrograd and Moscow, but the political future of the new Soviet government remained dubious. The November elections for the Constituent Assembly gave them only twenty-four percent of the vote. The majority—fifty-eight percent—polled for the Social Revolutionary party whose political roots were predominantly rural.[1] Lenin declared the Constituent Assembly counter-revolutionary, and the Congress of Soviets dissolved it on January 18, 1918. By the end of January, the first round of the Civil War exploded in the Ukraine and on the Don, where locally established governments proclaimed their independence from Petrograd.

The situation on the Volga, where Suslov lived, was even more precarious for the new government. The June 28th uprising of the Czechoslovak Legion[2] near Samara** spawned the outbreak of a full-scale civil war along the middle Volga from Kazan to Saratov and, by the middle of August, the combined forces of the Czechoslovak Legion and the Peoples' Army*** were posing a serious threat to Moscow. Although Khvalynsk was occupied by the Whites on July 10th,[3] the fighting in its environs was exceptionally heavy throughout the summer as the White command attempted to link up with the Ural and Orenburg cossacks in the east and Denikin's army in the south.[4] It is unlikely that Shakhovskoe remained untouched by the civil war, although the vast majority of the peasants stayed away from it, remaining passively fickle shifting their alle-

---

*The Bolshevik uprising occurred on Wednesday, November 7, 1917, according to the Western calendar. Because Russia was on the old Julian calendar prior to the revolution (13 days behind the Western calendar), it became known as the October Revolution. The Western calendar will be used throughout this work.

**A large city on the Volga, now called Kuibyshev.

***The White Army on the Volga was called Narodnaia Armiia (Peoples' Army) to reflect its populist origin and connection with KOMUCH (Russian abbreviation for the Committee of Members of the Consitutent Assembly), a local anti-Bolshevik government in Samara.

16

giance from one side to the other. Young Suslov also stayed away. Instead, he joined a local Committee of the Poor, obviously preferring to pursue the revolution at the local level, against the *kulaks* and the landowners, against the iniquities of village life that he knew so well and understood far better than what seemed to him like an abstruse war between two distant forces vying for political power on a national level.

Officially referred to as the *kombedy,** the Committees of the Poor were called into action throughout rural Russia in the summer of 1918 by Lenin himself. Despite Bolshevik successes in the cities, rural Russia remained suspicious of the new authority. The village *soviets* (assemblies) were dominated by the wealthier and more industrious peasants whose sympathies remained with the Provisional Government and the Social Revolutionary party. Food shortages in the cities were widespread, and peasants were beginning to hoard grain and other essential supplies. The practical function of the committees of the Poor was to ensure that the wealthier peasants shared their food surpluses with the rest of the population, but the doctrinal objective was to politicize and polarize the village. The leadership of the Communist Party** was convinced that the prosperous peasants—the *kulaks*—controlled village life and exploited the poor and middle-rung peasants. The purpose of the *kombedy* was to put an end to this by dislodging the *kulaks* permanently from their position of social and political power. Membership in the *kombedy* was accessible, therefore, only to the poor and middle peasants, while recruitment, training, and organization were handled by the Party. In the first half of 1918, more than four hundred communist instructors and propaganda specialists were dispatched to set up local *kombed* organizations in Saratov province.[5] Attracted by the opportunity to even out old scores with the *kulaks* and the estate owners, the village poor—particularly, the raw youth—streamed into the *kombedy* in large numbers. Suslov was no exception. As the son of poor peasants, he was both eligible and sought after.

The decree for the organization of the *kombedy* called for careful screening and training of the new cadres, but expediency and the threat of spreading civil war demanded action. More often than not, the rank and file were nothing more than self-appointed vigilantes acting in their own interest against the more prosperous peasants and landowners. Julius Martov, the leader of the Mensheviks, claimed that the Bolshevik insistence on class struggle in the village "contradicted the entire course of the revolution."[6] Nikolai Sukhanov, the revolution's principal historian and eyewitness, considered the *kombedy,* "organs of village police power."[7] With predictable contempt, the *kulaks* and landowners called the Committees of the Poor, a "union of loafers." The *kombed*

---

*Russian acronym for *Komitety Bednoty* (Committees of the Poor). *Kombed* is singular; *kombedy* is plural.

**Communist Party of the Soviet Union (b), sometimes also designated as CPSU (b) or VKP (b). Hereafter it will be referred to as "the Party" with a capital "P".

cadres were often alienated village bullies who ran roughshod over everything that came in their path. They seized food supplies, confiscated private property, and inventoried the grain stores. They knew what everyone had and what everyone did. They were the new guardians of law and order in the village.

The *kombedy* did more than just alleviate the food shortages. By the end of 1918, they were actively competing for political power with the local soviets.[8] The relations became so strained that the Party leadership began to think seriously about how it would be best to merge the *kombedy* with the village and district soviets.[9] The central government could not tolerate more than one source of power in the countryside anymore than it could in the cities. The solution proposed by Lenin was to phase out the *kombedy,* and call for new elections. On December 4, 1918, the All-Union Congress of Soviets laid down the rules for the elections and, during the following winter and spring months, the local soviets replaced their old members with the newly recruited cadres from the Committees of the Poor.[10]

In Khvalynsk and the surrounding countryside, the establishment of the *kombedy* moved at a slower pace.[11] Northern Saratov province remained in the war zone throughout the winter of 1918–1919. The White Army had evacuated Khvalynsk in early October,[12] but the Bolsheviks did not consolidate their power in the city and the surrounding areas until February.[13] Thus, it was probably not until the early spring of 1919 that young Suslov actually began working in a local Committee of the Poor.[14] There, he learned to work with others and to recognize that the use of power was an indispensable tool of the new regime. It may have been even there that he first discovered his preference for anonymity and behind-the-scenes politicking that became a trademark of his long political career. The Committees of the Poor served as a training ground for hundreds of thousands of young communists. Through them the nation's future leaders learned the fundamentals of political organization and cut their first teeth on the realities of the struggle for political power. There, amongst the under-privileged peasants of the Khvalynsk district, Suslov must have first learned to give and take orders. There, he was introduced to the basics of Marxist-Leninist practice, laying the foundation for his life-time obsession with the inevitability of class struggle. There, he must have also experienced the crisis of young adulthood, a crisis that led him eventually to supplant the faith of his forefathers for a new orthodoxy that was equally intense and self-sustaining.

The political situation in the Russian countryside underwent a rapid change between 1918–1921. In the fall of 1918, Trotsky had fashioned and deployed a powerful Red Army against the Whites and the interventionists. Kazan was retaken in September, and by the year-end the White Army was in retreat. The much publicized 1919 White Army spring offensive failed, and by 1920 military action on the Volga front ground down to a complete halt.[15] There were still pockets of strife in Siberia and the south, but for all intents and purposes the Civil War was ended. Lack of cooperation among the White Army commanders and the political insensitivity of the Kolchak government[16] sealed the fate of the White movement and gave a decisive victory to the Bolsheviks.

It is not entirely clear how and when the elections to the soviets were conducted in the Khvalynsk district. The Civil War had hardly ended when serious peasant disturbances broke out spontaneously throughout the Volga basin. Growing food shortages, the threat of famine, increasing bureaucracy, and the violation of civil rights produced an explosive climate in the countryside, while punitive measures undertaken by the central government only increased peasant resistance to the establishment of the new order. The Sapozhkov peasant army at one time had as many as eighteen hundred fully armed fighters operating in the middle Volga area.[17] Khvalynsk was not spared by them—it was occupied by the insurgent peasants in March 1921.[18] The political situation in central Russia and on the Volga was so unstable that some historians have named the peasant uprisings of the early 1920s, the Second Civil War.[19]

In March 1921, the Soviet government suffered its most serious setback. An uprising at the Kronstadt naval base sent reverberations around the world. Kronstadt was sacred ground to the revolution, and the signal it sent could no longer be ignored. The very same sailors who played so prominent a role in the Bolshevik seizure of power in 1917 now rose against the Soviet government and its bankrupt policies of War Communism.* The rebellion was a response to the growing mood that was sweeping the nation. The wave of food riots in the cities, the disturbances in the countryside, the intense misery and poverty of the people, sooner or later, were bound to bring forth a government crisis. The mutiny of the sailors merely hastened it. The insurrection was violently suppressed, but not before it sounded a clear warning that the government could not ignore if it wanted to remain in power. On March 21, 1921, in an attempt to alleviate the crisis and in opposition to the left wing of the Party, Lenin proclaimed the New Economic Policy. NEP, as it became known later, scrapped War Communism, relaxed economic life, reallowed the growth of trade unions and foreign trade, and reestablished a degree of free enterprise in the cities and the villages.

The announcement of NEP had its immediate effect on the political situation in Khvalynsk. By the end of 1921, order was established throughout the district. Suslov was nineteen and it was now time for him to move ahead. He had been a member of the Komsomol** since 1918, and he was now ready to become a full fledged member of the Communist Party. It is not clear if he took

---

*The term "War Communism" is used to identify the period of Soviet history lasting from the spring of 1918 to March 1921. During this period, the government nationalized industry and land, introduced compulsory labor and rationing, suspended private trade, forcefully requisitioned food supplies, and actively pursued war against the White Army, the interventionists, and the rebellious peasants.

**Young Communist League.

this step independently or in compact with the *kombed* in which he served. It was not unusual for the newly elected soviets—especially in provinces where their reorganization was delayed by the Civil War and the peasant uprisings—to demonstrate their loyalty to the Soviet regime by petitioning the District Central Committee for admission to the Party on a group basis. In the middle Volga basin, such mass conversions were quite common, as the entire soviet and its members literally "crossed over into the Communist party"[20] in what was in effect a mass recruitment campaign to bring new blood into the Party. Suslov could have refused, of course, but the Party was part of his life now. More than three years of apprenticeship in Khvalynsk had given him a feeling of belonging. By his own admission, the Party "was the main choice of (his) life,"[21] and he committed himself to it completely and with devotion.[22]

One could speculate on the motivation and circumstances responsible for Suslov's conversion. After all, the appeal of communism is many-faceted. Poverty without any hope of betterment remains high on the scale of circumstances leading to greater susceptibility to communist ideas. Adverse social relations likewise provide a cause for affiliation with the communist movement. Alienation and social dysfunction during periods of profound social change often lead to feelings of isolation and resentment. Communism's appeal as a secular religion also cannot be discounted. Communism provides a deep psychological fulfillment and a substitute solution for those who have broken away from traditional religions. Nicolas Berdyaev pinpointed the applicability of this appeal to the Russian case.[23] There is also, as Gabriel A. Almond has suggested, a high degree of correlation between conversion to communism and emotional involvement.[24] Existing psychological studies have shown that there is a relatively high incidence of persons in the Communist movement who were chronically rebellious and antagonistic.[25] There are also the self-oriented interests of career and educational advancement. Lenin referred to this when he said that a "ruling party invariably attracts careerists,"[26] and Trotsky, in an even less kind observation, noted that people after the revolution no longer joined the Party to support an ideal but to secure for themselves a position of authority in a vast bureaucracy.[27]

All of these inducements could be applied to Suslov's case. The abject poverty of peasant life, the intense social dislocation brought about by the revolution, the conscious and unconscious search for a new faith to replace the outdated religiosity inherited from the past were all causes in themselves to have turned young Suslov toward Communism. A case could even be made for emotional maladjustment. He was, after all, only fifteen in 1918, an emotionally confused adolescent readily susceptible to the ritualization of a new ideology. In the final analysis, he was probably also attracted by the inherent aggressiveness of the Party, an organized militancy that transcended all the other causes. His career pattern, his behavior as a leader, his lifetime obsession with the notion of class struggle attest to the inducement of Party militancy as an appeal of communism. The Party satisfied his unconscious needs. It emancipated him from the pattern of life to which he was born and from the feelings of aggression that he had repressed. Under the Party's protection he could now be aggressive without fear, ruthless without guilt, and dogmatic without the stain of arrogance. He could be all that and, at the same time, pursue the interest of personal career advancement.

> I must say that the tasks of the youth in general, and of the youth Communist Leagues and all other organizations in particular, might be summed up in a single word: learn.
>
> Lenin

> Education is a weapon, whose effects depend on who holds it in his hands and at whom it is aimed.
>
> Stalin

Chapter III

GROOMING

In the fall of 1921, with a party card in his pocket, Suslov arrived in Moscow to begin what turned out to be ten years of intensive education and political grooming.

Higher educational institutions were opened to all who wished to enter in 1918, and the requirement of a secondary school diploma was abolished. The majority of the workers and peasants who sought a higher education were poorly qualified, however, and the People's Commissariat of Enlightenment (Narcompros) was compelled to create special worker faculties (*Rabfaks*) to prepare the applicants for entry to institutions of higher learning.[1] Pursuant to a decree of December 2, 1918, *rabfaks* were organized in Moscow, Leningrad and most of the larger provincial centers in the Russian republic.[2] They were essentially secondary schools for adults, and academic standards were usually low. The Prechistensky *rabfak* to which Suslov was assigned occupied a unique position. Its predecessor, the Prechistensky Classes for Workers[3] was founded in 1897 and, in the twenty years between 1897 and the revolution, tens of thousands of workers had matriculated from it. It was the oldest proletarian institution of learning in Russia, and the model for all *rabfaks*. There, between 1921 and 1924, Suslov received as fine a secondary education as any in early post-revolutionary Russia.

No one knows why Suslov wound up in Moscow and the Prechistensky. He could have been assigned to a nearby *rabfak* in Saratov, Samara, Penza, or a dozen other provincial capitals of the RSFSR. Nor can we speculate how his political life would have unfolded if he had not ventured out to Moscow. Someone must have recognized his potential and urged him to go to Moscow, or it may have been Suslov himself trying to make a clean break with his roots on the right bank of the middle Volga. In the end, it was probably a combination of causes, aggravated by the fact that the provincial *rabfaks* were even more swamped with applications than Moscow and Leningrad. It was not unusual for the more enterprising aspirants to arrive in Moscow without reservation and demand to be admitted.[4]

The years between 1921 and 1924 were years of extreme hardship and tiresome readjustment. Civil War, War Communism, and the droughts of 1920 and 1921 exhausted and ruined the Soviet economy. Millions perished during the Civil War and the famine that followed it.[5] The New Economic Policy attempted to make life more bearable, but for most people life remained conspicuously disagreeable and even menacing. Living in Moscow and Leningrad was better than in the provinces, but it was never easy. Recalling many years later his first days at a Leningrad *rabfak,* a new arrival described his situation with the laconic statement: "We have no bread, I live in the dormitory kitchen, and you say everything is fine."[6] The situation in Moscow was not much better, and Suslov must have also suffered intense privation during this period. Like all students in the *rabfaks,* he received a government subsidy—a pittance which made part-time cutting and hauling of wood, or working on a construction gang, a necessity. As a Party member still on probation he also had to attend countless Party meetings, help with the transmission of propaganda, and periodically submit himself to exhaustive questioning about his own state of mind and that of his fellow students.

Except for the *Cheka** and the repression of the anti-Bolshevik groups, everyday life in the Soviet Union remained relatively free in the early 1920s. After the establishment of the NEP, food and consumer goods became more plentiful. In the arts, a refreshing mood of cultural revival swept the nation again. Under the influence of the NEP and the *Smena Vekh* movement** émigré intellectuals were returning to the Soviet Union in 1921. Literature, particularly poetry, picked up the trends of the "silver age," and such writers as Blok, Esenin, Maiakovsky, Pasternak, Brusov were again publishing poetry and prose. Open political debate outside the Party had ceased to exist, but within it there was still freedom of expression under Lenin's leadership. Despite his fanatical commitment to the new order, he tolerated differences of opinion, preferring to use his superior reasoning powers to resolve controversy and factionalism within the Party.

---

*Russian acronym for Extraordinary Commission to Combat Counter-revolution, Sabotage, and Speculation. The commission was established on December 20, 1917, and was the predecessor of NKVD and now KGB.

**Smena Vekh,* literally meaning "those who changed the sign posts," was an émigré organization of intellectuals who reversed their previous position of hostility to the Soviet government, and proclaimed their willingness to support the new regime in the interest of protecting the traditional Russian national objectives.

Suslov had neither the time nor the interest for cultural diversions, and his political views were still of limited perspective. For him the early 1920s were years of getting up with the sun and plowing through Kiselev's *Algebra,* Kistiakovsky's *Economic Geography* and Volume I of Marx's *Capital.* They were also years when he had to cement his affiliation with the Party—years of tedious and unimaginative work at the Prechistensky student Party committee. He was, after all, only a peasant lad from the right bank of the Volga, alert, motivated, and willing to learn new ways, but still intimidated by the sophistication of the capital and its intelligentsia. Suspicious, excessively cautious, and somewhat unsure of himself, he preferred to refrain from involvement in doctrinal debates that could compromise him politically and foil his chances of getting ahead.

Lenin's death in January 1924 and the first salvos of the struggle for power that followed it took place about the time of Suslov's graduation from the Prechistensky *rabfak* and his admission to the prestigious Plekhanov Institute of National Economy in Moscow.[7] Suslov's area of specialization remains unknown, but at the time he was there, the institute's primary objective was to prepare its graduates for higher positions in Gosplan* and other government bureaus dealing with the nation's economy. It is not improbable, therefore, that it was economics, and that his penchant for production statistics in his speeches and writings went back to his student days at the Plekhanov Institute.

The struggle for power after Lenin's death was dominated by both personal ambition and policy issues. In the end, Stalin's superior control of the Party organization triumphed. Maintaining a centrist position at first, Stalin outmaneuvered Trotsky by showing that the latter's emphasis on heavy industry underestimated the importance of the partnership between the proletariat and the peasantry, and placed too much stress on the notion that the ultimate success of the Russian revolution depended on the outbreak of revolution in other countries. Admitting the failure of a Communist victory in the West— especially after the German Communist fiasco—and basing his conclusion on an obscure quotation from Lenin, Stalin postulated instead that socialism would be built in one country, and that the Soviet Union's enormous population and natural resources would make this a reality.[8]

The first round of the struggle coincided with the 1924 student purges precipitated by the Party's growing concern that the "proletarization" of the student body at institutions of higher learning was not moving fast enough. Social and cultural changes which followed the revolution were not keeping up with the political changes.[9] The majority of the lower classes continued to question the need for a higher education, while the intelligentsia and their children rushed in to take advantage of the free education. In the year that Suslov entered

---

*State Planning Board.

the Plekhanov Institute almost forty-four percent of VUZ* students still came from the intelligentsia and their children.[10] Disagreement between the Party and the more liberal Narcompros directorate regarding admission policy had been going on since 1920, and the new Party leadership now decided to change the make-up of the student body. The purge began in May 1924 and continued through the rest of the year, reducing the number of "socially undesirable" students in Russian *VUZy* by 33,000.[11]

The 1924 student purge was not unrelated to the power struggle between Trotsky and the Central Committee dominated by Stalin, Zinoviev and Kamenev. Throughout 1924, students at institutions of higher learning took an active interest in it, and generally supported Trotsky against the triumvirate. This choice was strongly influenced by Trotsky's outstanding performance during the Civil War, his tough and implacable position against the bureaucratization of the Party, and his direct appeal to the Soviet youth. Trotsky's letter on "The New Course"[12] and his essay published under the name of *Lessons of October*[13] were widely read. Pro-Trotsky speakers were received with applause while such prominent members of the Central Committee as Kalinin and Kuibyshev were often subjected to heckling and ridicule. The most telling sign of the students' mood was the 1923–1924 winter vote of VUZ party cells. Forty VUZ party cells with 6,594 members polled for Trotsky and only thirty-two cells with 2,790 members voted for the Stalin-dominated Central Committee.[14]

Suslov could not have been unaware of what was happening in 1924. He must have known that the purge was the direct result of the pro-Trotsky feeling among students and that this feeling was a reflection of the composition of the student body. There was no question about where Suslov's sympathies lay. As a *kombed* veteran and Party activist, he supported the anti-Trotsky faction at the Plekhanov Institute. It was probably at the Plekhanov Institute that he first began to find personal gratification in identifying with Stalin and his strong commitment to rid Soviet society of its bourgeois and intelligentsia influences. This preference went beyond the cold analysis of the issues at stake. Stalin, Kalinin and most of the other stalwarts of the *apparat* were much closer to Suslov's own cultural and psychological roots than the more urbane and intellectually sophisticated opposition. Stalin's strong desire to eliminate the "Old Guard" did not become a reality until the next decade, but the symptoms were already there. Suslov must have sensed this. Indeed, it is not unrealistic to assume that his lifetime preoccupation with class struggle, nurtured by his experience in the Committees of the Poor, was born out of this realization in 1924.

The XIVth Party Congress in December 1925 sealed Zinoviev's and Kamenev's fate, and Stalin emerged as the leader of the Party *apparat*. In the spring and early summer of 1926, Zinoviev made peace with Trotsky, and out of

---

*Russian acronym for Higher Educational Institution.

this reconciliation came the "United Opposition"—Trotsky's and Zinoviev's unsuccessful joint attempt to dislodge Stalin. Using both domestic and foreign policy issues as the thrust of their accusation,[15] the Trotsky-Zinoviev forces appealed for support directly to the public, beyond the borders of the Party organization and in total disregard of the Party's unwritten rule to confine its internal disputes within Party debate. The campaign backfired among the rank and file, and Stalin retained his firm grip of the Party *apparat*. Final victory came to Stalin at the XVth Party Congress. In December 1927, the leaders of the "United Opposition" were condemned as deviationists from the general Party line and expelled from the Party. Zinoviev and Kamenev recanted and petitioned for readmission. Trotsky, refusing to sink that low, was exiled from Moscow in January 1928, and from the Soviet Union in 1929.

Suslov took an active part in the campaign against the "United Opposition."[16] Throughout 1926 and 1927 he defended Stalin in the lecture rooms and dormitories of the Plekhanov Institute and other Moscow *VUZy*. Thanks to the favorable student response, the Plekhanov Institute remained a bastion of solid support for Stalin.[17] Suslov also played an active role in the campaign against *Eseninshchina*.* Sergei Malakshin's 1926 novel, *Luna s pravoi starony* (The Right Side of the Moon),[18] sensationalized student corruption, drugs, promiscuity and disillusionment with the revolution. Its message was inescapable. Moral degeneracy of the student youth was the work of the Trotsky-Zinoviev opposition, dominated by Jewish intellectuals and obscured by all kinds of ideas foreign to the spirit of communism.[19] The suppression of *Eseninshchina* made sense to Suslov. The revolution had changed his political views, but the cultural and psychological bases of his childhood remained intact. There was no room for cultural and social avantgardism in the rudiments of his peasant upbringing and religious training. He loathed intemperate living then, just as he did in later life. As far as he was concerned, the Revolution did not grant license to moral laxity. On the contrary, it called for the exorcism of "petty bourgeois" behavior. On a personal level, Suslov never felt comfortable in the big city; nor did he find self-gratification in the extracurricular activities of his fellow students. He had always been somewhat of a loner; now he turned even more inward and away from what he considered the nonessential conventions of student life.

Suslov graduated from the Plekhanov Institute in 1928 as Stalin was getting ready to scrap the NEP and launch his massive collectivization and industrialization programs. Rumors of a change in industrial and agricultural policy circulated openly during the early spring, but there was nothing conclusive about them. In March, the State Prosecutor announced the discovery of a

---

*After Sergei Esenin, an outstanding peasant poet who committed suicide at the end of 1925. The label *Eseninshchina* was used by the Party to describe manifestations of youthful departure from acceptable behavior—hooliganism, sexual promiscuity, drunkenness, suicide.

"counter-revolutionary plot" by non-communist engineering specialists in the Shakhty region of the Donnets Basin. The engineers were put on trial not as individuals but as representatives of a class of specialists of the old regime. The ten year alliance between the Party and the non-communist experts started by Trotsky and sanctioned by Lenin had come to an end, marking the "Great Turning-point"* in Soviet policy toward the intelligentsia, and the beginning of a conservative cultural orthodoxy that gripped the entire nation. The Shakhty trial was not directly related to the industrialization and collectivization debates, but it came at a time when Stalin was desperately searching for an excuse to intensify the vigilance of the Party in order to speed up the cultural and social revolutions that were bound to follow the political revolution.[20] The trial precipitated a sweeping purge of the non-communist specialists employed by the Soviet government. It galvanized the debate, widened the disagreement in the Central Committee, and ultimately allowed Stalin to scrap the NEP and launch a relentless collectivization program in the countryside.[21]

Stalin's decision to reverse the NEP did not pass unopposed. During the summer, Nikolai Bukharin, Aleksei Rykov and Mikhail Tomsky[22] allied themselves against Stalin and his new policies. That same summer, Suslov became a research fellow in economics[23] at the Institute of the Red Professoriat.[24] The Institute of the Red Professoriat was organized in 1921 as a research institute for Marxist specialists in the social sciences. It included a variety of different departments, but its primary function was to prepare a cadre of dedicated future professors and specialists in the social sciences.[25] Mikhail N. Pokrovsky, the iron man of Soviet historiography, served as its first rector from its inception in 1921 to his death in 1932. Other Party notables on the Institute's faculty during Suslov's time were Anatoly V. Lunacharsky, Marxist cultural theorist and Commissar for Education from 1921 to 1929, Eugene Varga, the Hungarian émigré economist and later author of the controversial *Changes in the Economy of Capitalism Resulting from the Second World War,*[26] V. V. Adoratsky, V. M. Friche, and many other luminaries of the Soviet social sciences.[27] No less famous were Suslov's colleagues at the Institute. Nikolai A. Voznesensky, wartime chairman of the State Planning commission and 1947–1950 Politburo member, was at the Institute together with Suslov from 1928 to 1931.[28] Pyotr N. Pospelov, one of Suslov's chief competitors for the job of party ideologist under Khrushchev, was also a fellow from 1927 to 1930.[29] Molotov and Kalinin were frequent outside lecturers, and Bukharin's influence was felt in almost every department. Even Stalin came to the Institute. It was here, on May 28, 1928, that he delivered his lecture on the "The Grain Front,"[30] that forecast the end of the NEP and the beginning of a massive industrialization and collectivization

---

*In Russian, "Velikii perelom" (The Great Break). Most western scholars have translated it as the "Great Turning-point."

drive. The academic life of the Institute went beyond research, lectures and seminars. Many of its outstanding fellows taught in nearby institutes and universities. Suslov was for several years an instructor at the Moscow State University and the Stalin Academy of Industry where two of his more famous students in Marxist theory were Nikita Khrushchev and Nadezhda Allilueva-Stalina, Stalin's second wife and mother of Svetlana Allilueva.[31] The Institute was also a center of political discourse. New policies were fiercely debated, and Soviet authors were either eulogized or defamed. Suslov participated in the debates, but refrained from publishing his views. He had developed already then a healthy respect for circumspection and anonymity that became the future trademark of his career.

The opposition of Bukharin, Rykov and Tomsky, usually referred to as the "Right-wing Opposition" in contrast to the "Left-wing Opposition" of Trotsky, coalesced in the fall of 1928 into a powerful challenge to Stalin. It had a two-pronged goal: to end the Party's arbitrary and autocratic leadership, and to slow down the course of industrial expansion. Stalin had decided to dismantle the NEP and, instead, collectivize agriculture, reallocating its surplus resources to develop industry at a rapid pace. Bukharin and his supporters were opposed to this. They were convinced that the future of the Soviet regime lay in an equal and balanced development of industry and agriculture, and that the free peasantry could not be forced to pay the heavy cost of rapid industrialization. With his usual proclivity for maneuvering, Stalin did everything he could to discredit the opposition leaders. Bukharin made a last emotional attempt to compromise Stalin in a speech on the anniversary of Lenin's death in January 1929,[32] but the die was already cast. In April, the Central Committee acting on instructions of the Politburo and the Central Control Commission* indicted Bukharin and his allies for factionalism and support of the *kulaks*. Bukharin was discharged from his post as editor of *Pravda*. Tomsky was forced out of his position as head of the Trade Unions. Rykov was allowed to stay on as Chairman of the Council of People's Commissars, but was later also ousted. All three were removed from the Politburo, and Stalin's victory was complete by the end of 1929. On January 5, 1930, the Party formally approved the full collectivization of the farmlands,[33] and a social revolution of immense proportions was unleashed.

The Institute of the Red Professoriat was an enclave of Bukharin Sympathizers. Bukharin had been both a faculty member and a frequent guest lecturer. A. A. Avtorkhanov, who was himself a fellow at the Institute, said that "in the sphere of theory, the Institute was considered Bukharin's patrimony, given to him by the grateful Stalin for his help in the struggle against the Trotskyites and the Zinovievites."[34] The Institute was also the medium of party

---

*Originally, an impartial arbiter of intra-Party conflicts, the Central Control Commission was a Stalinist stronghold and a militant tool of Stalinist policy.

wisdom and Marxist-Leninist theory, and Stalin had every reason to worry about what was going on there. Suslov played a critical role in rallying the pro-Stalin forces at the Institute against Bukharin and his allies. Together with Voznesensky, Pospelov, Ponomarev, Mitin, Yudin, Mekhlis, Ponkratova and others— many of whom later became members of Suslov's conservative brain trust—he fought energetically against Bukharin and his right-wing deviation.[35] Indeed, the likelihood is that it was here at the Institute of the Red Professoriat that Suslov was first marked by Stalin as an aggressive Party "comer" and future member of his team.

By the time he left the Institute of the Red Professoriat in 1931,[36] Suslov had spent ten whole years in Moscow. During this period, he had married a young dental student and fathered a son and daughter.[37] He had worked personally with a broad spectrum of future Soviet leaders. However, it is unlikely that he had formed any close political relationships. Forming intimate connections was, for the most part, not what Suslov liked. There were also definite long-range benefits to standing apart from the rest of the Party workers at a time when Stalin was beginning to eliminate not only his competitors, but also their subordinates, and the subordinates' subordinates within the Party *apparat*. In this respect, Suslov's natural aloofness, his inherent peasant caution, his desire for anonymity were a saving grace that others often lacked. He had climbed onto the Stalinist bandwagon cautiously and deliberately, without any outside aid, using his skills as a grass roots propagandist and ideologist, skills that were to become most desirable as Stalin's social and cultural revolution unfolded itself in the 1930s. He had also matured politically. 1929 was a "Great Turning-point" for Suslov, as well as the nation. He had become fully convinced that his future lay with Stalin and the coming social revolution.

Like Stalin, he felt no scruples about what had to be done to achieve a total transformation. Boris Nicolaevsky—perhaps, the most perceptive early interpreter of Soviet politics—was first to recognize Suslov's motivation. "The fact that Suslov's political career began (with the movement of the Committees of the Village Poor) is almost symbolic: his whole life has been marked by an intensification of the class struggle in the countryside," he noted in the *Power and the Soviet Elite*.[38] He was right. Suslov's fanatic devotion to the principle of class struggle was a genuinely distinctive and permanent mark of his career. The other was his aloofness, his circumspection, his inaccessibility. Together, these two characteristics became his distinguishing feature and the symbol of his future political power and success. He had acquired them by way of his early experience in Shakhovskoe and Khvalynsk, but he also nurtured and developed them. In this respect, the years between 1921 and 1931 were watershed years in his passage from obscurity.

PART TWO

THE STALIN YEARS:
The Time of Tempering and Compliance

Eighty percent of our people live under the
constant fear of the knock on the door. The
milkmaid fears the loss of her cow, the
peasants—forced collectivization, the Soviet
worker is terrorized by the purges, the Party
worker is afraid of being called a deviationist, the scientist of being charged with idealism, the technician of being a wrecker. We
live in an epoch of the great fear.

A. N. Afinogenov, *Fear*

Brother killers with sweaty hands. . . .
Their hearts, like ordinary soot are black
Anonymously, they scribble libelous notes at
night
And forge their way through them to rank.

M. Ryl'skii, *Winter Sketches*

The Revolution's not over
Homely mooing time's
drowned by the approaching
final combat . . .
Through your samovar funnels,
Messrs. Philistines,
it roars
the oncoming foe
no comeback.

Maiakovsky, *The Idyll*

Chapter IV

APPRENTICESHIP

In 1931 Suslov gave up being a Red Professor and accepted a post in the Party's Central Control Commission. Why he decided to leave teaching is not known. Nor is it known whether he actually sought out a position in the Central Control Commission, or was co-opted into it as a result of his outstanding performance as a Stalinist at the Institute of the Red Professoriat. The significant observation is that he did not take a government post, but remained instead in the Party machine. Describing his Party career, Roy Medvedev speculates that Suslov "did not chase after prominent state posts. . . . (occupying) only the modest post of chairman of the Commission of Foreign Affairs" in the Supreme Soviet.[1] Thus, the likelihood is that Suslov decided to make a career in the Party very early in his life.

The Central Control Commission was established by Lenin in 1920 as an adjunct to the Party's Central Committee to act as an independent and impartial arbiter of intra-Party conflicts and disputes.[2] Unlike the NKVD, it did not concern itself with the general populace, supervising only the Party *apparat* and the government bureaus. Its primary function was the maintenance of Party discipline and the purging of ideologically "harmful and demoralizing elements." Although its duties were clearly defined, expediency and the infusion of officials who owed their careers to the Secretariat caused the Commission to lose its previously established detachment and independence.[3] It was no accident, therefore, that by the end of the 1920s it had become a militant tool of narrow Stalinist policy.

Describing Suslov's work in the Commission, Roy Medvedev suggests that "his primary task in this post was to sort out countless 'personal cases'—that is, infringements of Party discipline and the Party statutes, and appeals by people who had been expelled."[4] While this may have been the case in some instances, Medvedev's description does not provide an entirely adequate explanation of Suslov's work. Better educated and more qualified than the majority of the Commission's staff, Suslov must have been assigned to the Central Control Commission for other purposes, particularly in the light of the existing shortage of technically competent cadres in 1931. It is more likely that his work on the Commission's staff during the early years was related to the preparation of analytical and statistical studies of cadres' problems for the joint plenum of the Central Committee and the Central Control Commission that Stalin had improvised to implement his policies in the late 1920s and early 1930s. Purging and raising the quality of the cadres were two inseparable sides of the same problem dealing with the Party's campaign to speed up the slow tempo of cadres' development throughout 1931 and 1932. Suslov was trained as a Marxist economist, and it is more probable that he was originally assigned to the Central Control Commission staff to direct research, rather than become a rank-and-file inspector of Party expulsion indictments and petitions for readmission. Seeing no future in a staff position, Suslov must have then sought a more promising career assignment which catapulted him into the administrative work of the commission.

The early 1930s were years of continued agitation against Stalin. Stalin had put an end to organized opposition, but he did not succeed yet in silencing the voices of individual Party members. In the fall of 1929, in response to the declining output of foodstuffs, the Party launched a full-scale drive to "disgorge" the grain surpluses of the peasants. The campaign was directed mainly against the well-to-do peasants—the *kulaks*. The grain collection campaign was merely a prelude to the far more drastic operation of collectivization. At the end of 1929 and beginning of 1930, tens of thousands of trusted Communist activists were dispatched to the countryside to organize *kolkhozes** and establish socialism in the villages. The peasants met this onslaught with open resistance, and the Party responded with troops and concentration camps to force the peasants into the collectives. The massive collectivization program uprooted millions of peasants, producing immeasurable suffering and loss of life.[5] Famine made it even more horrific as millions faced starvation in 1931 and 1932. Stalin himself began to see the weakness of the rapid collectivization program, and ordered a slowdown, spilling his wrath on the collectivizers in his "Dizzy with Success" speech in March 1930.[6] In the fall of 1930, S. I. Syrtsev, a candidate member of the Politiburo, and V. V. Lominadze, another prominent Bolshevik who represented Stalin in China during the Comintern's abortive attempt to revitalize the Chinese revolution, openly defied Stalin, holding him responsible for the horrors of collectivization.[7] Disturbed by the growing violence in the countryside, M. N. Riutin, a prominent member of the Central Committee, authored a one hundred and sixty page proposal in the summer of 1932 urging a retreat from collectivization, a reinstatement of Party democracy, and the immediate removal

---

*Collective farms.

34

of Stalin.[8] Stalin took Riutin's denouncement as a personal attack against him, demanding the reinstatement of the death penalty and the execution of Riutin. To his embarrassment, his demand was struck down by the Presidium of the Central Control Commission. In November, Stalin suffered a personal tragedy and an intense insult to his political prestige. Doubting the wisdom of her husband's policies and reputedly no longer able to bear the pain of the horror in the countryside, Nadezhda Allilueva, Stalin's devoted second wife, committed suicide after an argument witnessed by friends at the home of Marshal Klementii Voroshilov.

Criticism of Stalin continued throughout 1933, with the literary community joining the dissenting Party officials. Demian Bedny, a leading proletarian poet, wrote "Bez poshchady" (Without Mercy), a poem highly critical of the collectivization drive and, by implication, of Stalin's policies. A. N. Afinogenov's popular play *Strakh* (Fear) played to vast theatre audiences portraying the life of fear in the early 1930s. "We live in an epoch of the great fear," declared Borodin, the play's principal character and hero, describing the life of the Soviet citizen.[9] The XVIIth Congress which convened on January 26, 1934 unleashed not only criticism of Stalin on domestic issues, but added the more serious censure on foreign policy—against Stalin's insensitivity to the rise of Hitler and in favor of closer cooperation with the democracies of the West. To avoid confrontation, Stalin affected a tactical retreat. The result was a new Soviet policy hammered out, on the surface, in a spirit of Party solidarity and support for Stalin but, in reality, in an atmosphere of reservation and censure. Domestically, the new policy meant a reduction of terror in the countryside and the fostering of military preparations against the Nazi threat. The turn-around was linked to Sergei Kirov, the head of the Leningrad Party organization. The prevailing view was that the early difficulties of the Revolution had been overcome and that it was now time to replace terror and vigilance at home with "proletarian humanism," and join abroad with the Western democracies against Nazi Germany.

The concessions made during the XVIIth Party Congress[10] and the wave of mounting criticism convinced Stalin that the only alternative to continued opposition was the destruction of all remaining pockets of resistance, especially the Old Guard who persisted in subverting his authority within the Party. No one knows for certain how Stalin decided to accomplish this. Some scholars have maintained that he had conceived a single coherent plan to rid Soviet society of all those hostile to him and his policies.[11] Others have said that he took advantage of separate and unrelated events to initiate a series of independent and often vicariously motivated purges.[12] Relying on the evidence from the Smolensk Archive, one historian has suggested that the repression and terror of the 1930s had their origin in different Party agencies seeking different targets, and without Stalin's direct participation as planner and initiator.[13] Which of these explanations best describes the outbreak of the purges remains an unresolved controversy. What is notable, however, is that Stalin created the climate and momentum for repression, and orchestrated the purges for his own benefit.

The 1933 *chistka** in which Suslov participated as a staff member of the Central Control Commission was relatively benign in comparison to what happened from 1936 to 1938. Directed against those who had "wormed their way" into the Party, the 1933 *chistka* was hardest on the rank-and-file, particularly on those who entered the Party by way of the mass recruitment drive during the First Five Year Plan from October 1928 to December 1932.[14] Its principal effect was that it set the stage for escalation, for a growing outpouring of accusations and betrayals that later evolved into the full-blown hysteria of the Great Purge. The 1933 *chistka* represented the flip side of Stalin's other policy to create a new elite through the promotion of workers and peasants into positions of responsibility. Both the 1933 *chistka* and the *vydvizhenstvo*** had the same objective: to reduce the influence of the old intelligentsia and eliminate the services of the experts inherited from the Tsarist regime. Between 1930 and 1932, more than two hundred thousand young people from the working class and the peasantry were enrolled in higher military schools, engineering colleges and other higher secondary and technical schools.[15] In the years to come *vydvizhenstvo* would represent the "Who's Who" of the new Soviet elite. Brezhnev, Kosygin, Gromyko, Ustinov were all products of Stalin's cadres policy of 1930–1932. Suslov himself was also an early *vydvizhenits,* preceding the formal commencement of the program by five years.

Suslov remained unconditionally loyal to Stalin during the early 1930s. The grain collection campaign, the collectivization program, the promotion of the new cadres, and the 1933 *chistka* were measures for which he had great respect. Directly or indirectly, they contributed to the sharpening of the class struggle and the destruction of the old social order. They fulfilled his intense desire to rid Soviet society of the "class alien"[16] elements inherited from the past, and to bestow power and influence on a new group of beneficiaries recruited from the least advantaged strata of the pre-revolutionary society.

In 1933 and 1934, Suslov was placed in charge of the purges in the Ural and Chernigov *obkoms,**** traveling periodically to distant Ural'sk in the Caspian steppe, and to Chernigov, Kievan Russia's ancient citadel in northern Ukraine.[17] There, he examined Party records and helped to rectify the bureaucratic confusion wrought by the influx of new membership during the industrialization and collectivization drives in 1930 and 1931. The 1933 *chistka* had a

---

*Literally meaning a cleansing in Russian, the word *chistka* has been loosely translated as a "purge." *Chistka* is singular and *chistki* is plural.

**Derived from the Russian word *vydvizhenie* (promotion), *vydvizhenstvo* has been used to explain the promotion of workers and peasants during the period of 1930–1935, and *vydvizhenits* to include those so promoted.

***Abbreviation for Regional Committee of the Communist Party of the Soviet Union.

limited effect on the outlying regions,[18] and Suslov's impact on the Ural and Chernigov *obkoms* could not have been too substantive. Of greater significance to his career in the early 1930s was his exposure to the various police, security and control agencies and their executive and administrative officers. During this period, he became personally acquainted with Yezhov, Malenkov, Shkiryatov, Agronov and numerous other officials who played key roles in the purges of 1936–1938. It is unlikely that he formed any close political associations with them, preferring to remain uncommitted and free of any obligations. This was a behavior pattern that had worked for him before, and he saw no reason to change it now.

By the summer of 1934, the terror and violence of the previous years had gradually subsided. For the first time in many years, all levels of the Soviet populace were beginning to experience a lapse of revolutionary passion. But the newly gained domestic peace did not last. On December 1, a disgruntled young Party member named Nikolaev made his way into the Smol'nyi Institute* in Leningrad, gained admission to Kirov's office and fired a revolver. Kirov was killed instantaneously. This was Nikolaev's second attempt—he had been apprehended two weeks earlier with a loaded revolver in Kirov's presence but for some unknown reason was released. The circumstances surrounding Kirov's death and the investigation that followed it raised serious doubts about Nikolaev's motives. Speaking many years later at the XXth Party Congress, Nikita Khrushchev strongly implied that there were inexplicable and mysterious aspects to Kirov's murder.[19] It remains to this day an unsolved mystery and, probably, will remain unsolved forever, although some historians have presented a circumstantial case for Stalin's direct involvement, arguing that Stalin had actually organized the murder.[20]

It is really unimportant whether or not Stalin was directly involved in the assassination or was merely its beneficiary. The significant fact is that Nikolaev's bullet removed Kirov from the scene of action, eliminating the only man in the Soviet Union who could have stood up to Stalin. As in the Shakhty case, the assassination gave Stalin and the radicals the justification to rekindle the fires of revolutionary zeal. Kirov's murder, they claimed, was the result of a vast conspiracy involving all of the opposing forces threatening the integrity of the Soviet state. Trotskyites, Zinovievites, Anti-Party Right Deviationists, Nazi collaborators, and dissenters of all shades and color could now be swept in a new wave of repression to cleanse the Party and secure Stalin's uncontested leadership for the years to come. No one will know for certain what was Stalin's principal motivation in allowing the excesses of the next five years. Were they caused, as some have suggested, by his insatiable appetite for domination, his

---

*The fashionable former girl's school in St. Petersburg, made famous in 1917 as the headquarters of the October Revolution and later used as the headquarters of the Party Organization in Leningrad region.

paranoia, his Georgian penchant for the vendetta? Or were they the result of his equally fanatic commitment to the building of a new society legitimized by the aspirations and prodding of a radicalized new elite recruited only recently from the disadvantaged strata of a class society? Or did the motivation arise, perhaps, from both his personal drive for power and his ideological commitment to accelerate the social transformation that was still lagging behind the political revolution? The motivation for personal power is always easier to identify, and it is not surprising that Western scholars have on the whole adopted a Stalin-centered model to explain the holocaust that evolved out of Kirov's murder. Motivation for social change finds expression in more complex mental and psychological processes that are infinitely more difficult to isolate and analyze. Stalin's personal drive for domination may have been, therefore, only the starter and the steering wheel of what happened in the 1930s, the engine being the unspent revolution itself. If this is the case, the personal, political and social motivations were not incompatible. There was, as the Marxists say, a dialectical relationship among them; they interacted with each other in a continuum of escalating "action-reaction purges"[21] conducted in a climate of growing fear, recrimination and betrayal.

In terms of our twentieth century values, what happened in the Soviet Union was perverse, inhuman, and morally untenable. This should not prevent anyone, nevertheless, from recognizing that Stalin did succeed in building a new society—however distasteful and illogical it may seem to us—and that he did this with the help of an approving new elite that saw in the purges not only his personal desire to grasp power, but also an opportunity to become the purge's permanent beneficiaries. For every Trotsky, Zinoviev, Bukharin and Piatakov, for every Tukhachevsky, Yakir and Blyukher, for all the Rudzhutaks, Chubars and Krestinskys that Stalin destroyed, there were thousands of Ivanovs, Petrovs and Sidorovs.* They also fell on the "butcher block" of one of history's more brutal upheavals, but they fell not at the hands of Joseph Stalin, but at the hands of other radicalized Ivans, Peters and Pavels who betrayed them in the name of the Revolution. Not to recognize this is to commit a mistake almost as unpardonable as Chateaubriand and De Maistre made when they attributed the terror of the French revolution solely to the work of a few Jacobins with a "criminal mentality."[22] The blood bath in the Soviet Union was the direct result of the social upheaval triggered by the Revolution. For more than three hundred years, two separate, incompatible and often conflicting Russias—the Russia of the educated and westernized upper classes, and the dark backward, neglected and superstitious Russia of the village—lived side by side hardly conscious of having

---

*Ivanov, Petrov and Sidorov are the most common Russian names roughly equivalent to Smith, Jones, and Brown. The assertion suggests that a large number of Soviet citizens perished in the 1930s as a result of denunciations and betrayals by other ordinary Soviet citizens.

a single national origin. The Revolution changed this. In the new Soviet state, the two Russias became one again, as the westernized upper strata of Russian society either fled abroad, perished in the Civil War and the purges, or simply became superannuated, retreating from the locus of power and politics to private lives and internal exile. The majority of those who remained in the political mainstream were men and women of the village and the newly invested proletariat whose historical background was rooted in the Muscovite state and its medieval psychology of orthodoxy, violence, and inhumanity from which most of Europe had been emancipated. The extreme excesses of the 1930s were the product of that consciousness, raised to its limit by the semi-hypnotic and cathartic upsurge of emotion and revolutionary zeal, and exacerbated by the newly imposed revolutionary ethic of political vigilance and betrayal.

The repression and terror after Kirov's death went through a series of interrelated stages of escalating intensity. Starting with the 1935 documents verification campaign,[23] they ripened into a round of unrelenting purges that included a wide circle of targets previously untouched by the Revolution: senior Party and government officials, industrial managers, the Bolshevik Old Guard, the intelligentsia and the clergy, the military, the foreign communists, and even the families of the unfortunate victims.[24] Stalin's manifesto of July 29, 1936 became the slogan of the new purges. Authored by Stalin himself, it reminded the Party activists that "the inalienable quality of every Bolshevik must be the ability to detect the enemy of the Party, however well he may be masked."[25] In August 1936, Zinoviev, Kamenev and fourteen associates were put on trial and convicted on the basis of trumped up testimony prepared by Genrikh Yagoda, the head of the NKVD. All were executed, while thousands of less prominent figures throughout the Soviet Union were also either shot or sent to concentrations camps for their support of the alleged conspiracy. Pursuant to Stalin's telegram expressing his dissatisfaction with Yagoda's slow pace of progress, Yagoda was replaced in September 1936 by Yezhov.[26] The reign of terror initiated by Yezhov defies description. In January 1937, seventeen members of the so-called Anti-Soviet Trotskyite Center faced the dock in Moscow. The trial was as much directed against Trotsky, whose reputation had to be destroyed permanently *in absentia,* as against the major participants—Piatakov, Radek, Sokolnikov and Muralov. In June 1937, Marshal Tukhachevsky, the hero of the Civil War, and seven other prominent generals were summarily executed without a public trial, allegedly for conspiring to bring about the downfall of the government with the help of exiled White Army generals and the Nazis.[27] The 1936 and 1937 purges were followed with the 1938 trial of Bukharin and twenty other Bolsheviks. They, too, were executed after a long and messy interrogation that led to their public trial. The cleansing had reached a crescendo in what became known as the *Yezhovshchina**—a period of unparalleled terror in European his-

---

*The period of extreme terror associated with Yezhov's reign over the secret police.

tory. Millions of innocent Soviet citizens were implicated in the alleged conspiracies of the principal victims of the purges. They either faced the firing squad or were sent to distant concentration camps in Siberia and the north. Sixty percent of the delegates to the XVIIth Party Congress in 1934 perished in the purges of 1936–1938. No exact estimates of total executions are available, but most experts agree that the number exceeded one million,[28] while another ten to twelve million probably died in prisons and concentration camps as a result of the purges.[29] In a final stroke of irony, Yezhov himself became a victim of the terror, disappearing in 1939 in a mass liquidation of former NKVD officers and collaborators.[30]

Suslov continued to work in the Party Control Commission* throughout 1935 supervising phases of the Party Documents Verification program and the early stages of the Party Documents Exchange drive, but his participation in the purges of 1936 and 1937 remains doubtful. The official Soviet biography states that he "worked until 1936 in the Control Commission attached to the Council of the People's Commissariat of the USSR . . . (and) from 1937 to 1939 was a department head in the Secretariat of the Rostov Obkom in the VKP (b)."[31] The most detailed and authoritative biography, prepared by the Central Research Division of Radio Liberty in Munich, based on reports periodically appearing in the Soviet press, outlines his career from 1936 to 1939 as follows: "From 1934 to 1937 (Suslov) held a post in the Soviet Control Commission of the USSR Council of Commissars and possibly also attended the Moscow Institute of the Red Professoriat . . . From 1937 to 1939 (he) was Department Chief, later Secretary of the Rostov Obkom in the All Union CP (b)."[32] The Soviet biography gives no information about what he did in 1936, and the Radio Liberty biography lumps his activity in the Control Commission for the entire period of 1936 to 1937. Clearly, Suslov's activity in 1936 and 1937 is clouded by serious contradictions. Soviet sources generally tend to give only scant information about the period of the Great Purge. It is entirely possible, therefore, that the year 1936 has been purposely exhumed from Suslov's biography, but why also obfuscate his tenure in the Rostov *Obkom* when it is clear from Suslov's own speech at the Rostov *Obkom* Party Conference on June 9, 1938 that he was responsible for Party cadres in Rostov *oblast'* in June 1938?[33] Is it possible that Suslov may have somehow dropped out of Soviet political life during 1937 and parts of 1936 and 1938—the most intense period of the reign of terror? The idea is intriguing and not as preposterous as it may seem. Other Soviet officials had succeeded in doing this.[34]

Suslov may have decided to distance himself from the purges for a number of reasons. He may have felt that the cleansing had gone too far, and that the purges were now subverting the very integrity of the Party. Stalin's

---

*The Central Control Commission was reorganized by Stalin in 1934 and the name was changed to Party Control Commission.

tactical response to the purges was characterized by his usual strategy of zigzag-ging between alternating positions championed by his adversaries and senior lieutenants. As in the 1920s and early 1930s, he kept his options open siding occasionally with Zhdanov to restrain the zealots in the prosecution of the cleansing.[35] At other times, he would back Yezhov and Malenkov, demanding sterner measures and greater results.[36] As a perceptive tactician himself, Suslov must have grasped the full significance of Stalin's maneuvering. It was inesca-pingly clear what Stalin was trying to accomplish. Stalin had created out of the NKVD and his personally managed State Security Committee[37] an *Oprichnina**—a separate government, not unlike that of Ivan the Terrible—that stood apart from the Party and the state ready to destroy everything in its path. Suslov had been an enthusiastic supporter of the class struggle and the levelling of Soviet society, but Stalin's *Oprichnina* went beyond that. It was directed toward the exaltation of Stalin's own authority, towards the destruction of the entire revolutionary tradition without which the Party was bound to become an empty shell. As an orthodox Marxist and life-long purist he could not have condoned what was happening in 1936. He was in his middle thirties, and it is not inconceivable that he may have even suffered as a result of this an identity crisis that forced him to withdraw temporarily from the political arena.

Suslov may have also belatedly discovered that he could no longer work with Yezhov. It was becoming obvious that Yezhov was more than just a Jacobin dedicated to the principle of class struggle; he was a blood-thirsty deviant who used terror to satisfy the sadistic cravings of his own perverse personality. This is not to say that Suslov can be completely absolved from what happened in 1936 to 1938. His appointment many years later to the chairmanship of the funeral commissions for L. Z. Mekhlis and M. F. Shkiryatov[38]—Yezhov's prin-cipal assistants in 1936 and 1937—clearly indicates that he had a close relation-ship with them. Nor can it be said that he was against the use of violence. Lenin had sanctified violence, making it an important instrument of the class strug-gle.[39] But this was a different kind of violence. It was the most repugnant form of terror characterized by torture, confessions, unprecedented degradation and outright murder. Exercising his usual sense of caution and his strong instinct for self-preservation, Suslov may have simply decided to drop out, to distance him-self from the purges before he was consumed by them himself. Such withdrawal behavior was totally consistent with his psychological orientation. Suspicious, cautious, "puritanical," and endowed with an over-developed super ego nur-tured by his early religious upbringing and Marxist commitment to socialist

---

*Derived from the word *oprich,* meaning separate in medieval Russian, *oprichnina* liter-ally meant the husband's separate estate, set apart from his widow. It is believed that Ivan the Terrible chose this word for his special service of XVIth century "storm troopers" because it suggested both separation and bereavement. The *Oprichnina* was for all intents and purposes a separate government dedicated to the savage destruction of all enemies.

legality, he would have found it extremely difficult to identify with the *Yezhovsh-china*. It was too threatening, too violent, too vicious, too unlawful for him. Withdrawal was Suslov's preferred strategy of handling conflict, allowing him to resurface unscathed over and over again. It is entirely conceivable that he chose this option also in 1937. Indeed, Radio Liberty's claim that Suslov had returned to the Institute of the Red Professoriat may be quite plausible.[40] In early 1937, Stalin warned the Central Committee that Party officials had become preoccupied with "economic work" and were neglecting "political work." To deal with this problem, he called for the renewal of theoretical education.[41] As a result of this, special "refresher" schools were organized in Moscow for the senior *obkom,* republic and All-Union officials. It is not improbable, therefore, that Suslov may have returned to the Institute, serving again as a Red Professor on the faculty of these special Party political schools.

Describing Suslov's career during the 1930s, A. A. Avtorkhanov has linked Suslov to the *Yezhovshchina* solely on the basis of his connection with the Party Control Commission. "Under Yezhov's personal direction," Avtorkhanov asserts, "Suslov took part in one of the biggest operations undertaken by the Soviet regime, known as the "Great Purge" or *yezhovshchina*. How many persons in the USSR fell victim to this operation has always been a secret well guarded by the Kremlin, even under the loquacious Khrushchev."[42] Avtorkhanov does not offer any details, nor does he give any dates, but on the basis of this statement Suslov has been linked to the Great Purge and held accountable for the severe repression in the Rostov region."[43] Roy Medvedev disagrees with this assessment, suggesting that:

> Many people are convinced that Suslov was responsible for the repression that took place in Rostov, but their assumption is based only on the fact that Suslov happened to be engaged in important Party work there during the years of the terror . . . The fact is, we have no evidence of his personal involvement in the repressive campaigns of 1937–1938, though they certainly paved the way for his rapid rise.[44]

The course of events also contradicts Avtorkhanov's assertion. By the time Suslov was assigned to the Rostov *Obkom,* the terror was beginning to abate even though the Bukharin trial and the liquidation of Yezhov and his lieutenants did not take place until 1938 and 1939. In January 1938, the plenum of the Central Committee passed a resolution to put an end to the expulsions and executions, giving detailed instructions on the need to begin the rehabilitation of former Party members who had been wronged. The New *ukase* was distributed to all Party organizations throughout the Soviet Union.[45] Stalin himself had begun to feel that the terror had gone too far. Suslov's speech to the Rostov *Obkom* Party Conference in June 1938 confirms this and exonerates him from any association with the repression in Rostov. Speaking of the repression, Suslov announced that:

> In 1937 in Rostov *Oblast* more than twenty-five hundred Communists were expelled from the Party. In most cases, as it is now completely clear, these expulsions were carried out without justification, motivated by considerations of careerism and reinsurance. The previous leadership of the *Obkom* left to us an inheritance of two thousand appeals that have not been investigated.[46]

Suslov remained in Rostov through 1938. By the end of the year, he had completely rebuilt the Rostov Party organization rehabilitating much of the old membership and, according to Medvedev, also recruiting three thousand new members.[47] In March 1939, Suslov was appointed First Secretary of the Stavropol Territory,[48] and, at the XVIIIth Party Congress which convened in Moscow on March 10, 1939, he was elected to the All-Union Auditing Committee. The Stavropol assignment brought a major change to Suslov's life. At age thirty-six he had bridged the wide chasm existing in the USSR between junior and senior officialdom. As First Secretary, he had become the chief executive officer of an important geographical entity, while the appointment to the Central Auditing Committee gave him direct access to Moscow and its power elite.

Chapter V

PROCONSULSHIP

The appointment to the Stavropol Territorial Party Committee was an important step in the chain of promotions that marked Suslov's rise to the top of the Soviet power pyramid. As First Secretary, he now became Stalin's resident proconsul of a vast and strategically important area north of the great Caucasus mountain chain, an area bordering four autonomous republics[1] inhabited predominantly by non-Slavic Moslem peoples who first came under Russian domination in the XIXth century after the Russian conquest of the Caucasus. The Stavropol Territory was also multinational in its composition. Although populated mostly by Russians and Ukrainians, it contained sizable pockets of indigenous peoples—Karachai, Chechen, Circassian, Osetin, and other smaller national groups from the northern slope of the Caucasus mountains.[1] Administratively, the area constituted one of those large geographic units which the central government in Moscow had named *krai* (territory), incorporating into it for political reasons one or more autonomous national regions or republics. At the time of Suslov's appointment, the Stavropol Territory included one such semi-independent grouping—the Karachai-Cherkess ASSR with dual capitals in Mikoyan-Shakhar and Cherkessk. The territory was an important agricultural and industrial base, but its principal significance was strategic. It was the gateway to the Caucasus and its rich oil reserves.

The Party organization of the Stavropol Territory had also experienced a series of purges and repressions, and Suslov's primary task in 1939 was to reestablish order and rebuild the ravaged Party *apparat*. Details of Suslov's early administration are not known, but it is obvious from his promotion two years later that he fulfilled his responsibilities in Stavropol to the Party's full satisfaction. It was no accident that he was made a full member of the All-Union Party

Central Committee in February 1941, joining at the age of thirty-eight the most prestigious and politically powerful group of Party officials in the USSR.

The routine work of a territorial First Secretary did not last long. The German invasion drastically altered Suslov's normal responsibilities. On June 22, 1941, Molotov broke the grim news of the German attack to the startled nation. Stalin was too embarrassed to face the people and admit that the 1939 Non-Aggression Pact with Hitler was a failure. The nation was caught unprepared, and the Red Army crumbled as the Germans advanced east, taking a vast number of prisoners of war. By the end of October, Leningrad was under blockade and the advance patrols of the Wehrmacht's Army Group Centre were within twenty miles of the capital. In November, the German high command launched an all-out attack on Moscow, as Party and government officials prepared for evacuation of the government to Kuibyshev. Stalin had recovered his self-confidence, however. Refusing to leave the Kremlin, he went public urging the Russian populace to emulate their ancient saints and warriors and fight the Nazi host.[2] During the first week of December a massive Russian counteroffensive under Zhukov's command stopped the German advance. Hitler had lost his chance of capturing Moscow, but the next ten months saw the German Army extending its tentacles beyond the Dnieper and the Don, all the way to the Volga. Russia was again trading space for time, hoping to reverse Germany's gains during the first year of the war.

The Stavropol Territory was not immediately affected by the German advance, and Suslov's energies during the early phase of the invasion were directed largely to the conversion of local industry and agriculture to the needs of a war economy.[3] However, in the spring of 1942, tempted by the vast oil reserves of the Caucasus and motivated by political considerations of establishing a Near East springboard for a link with the Japanese in India, Hitler decided to seize the North Caucasus. The German offensive got off to a late start in June, meeting only sporadic resistance as the Red Army fell back to the Caucasus, preparing to defend key positions along the Black Sea, the Georgian Military Highway, and the cities along the Caspian coastal road to Baku. To the Soviet command this meant the German occupation of the entire North Caucasus area, including the Stavropol *Krai,* and the accompanying risk of having to face increasing opposition from the politically vulnerable Moslem groups seeking independence and escape from communism. Moscow's orders were to prepare for the occupation by establishing partisan units and promoting a program of winning the loyalty of the ethnic groups. Of the two tasks, the first was clearly less difficult. During the early summer of 1942 a territorial partisan command was organized in Stavropol, with Suslov himself acting as the chief of staff.[5] Party officials, members of the NKVD and the militia, firemen, and members of the Komsomol formed the main body of the partisan movement. Soviet sources acknowledge Suslov's contribution, and give him full credit for the establishment of a well-thought out system of utilizing all segments of the population in the partisan movement—including the nationalities.[6]

Rostov was occupied by the Germans on July 23rd and Stavropol on August 3rd. By the end of August, all of Stavropol *Krai* and a good part of the autonomous regions to the south of it were under German control. In contrast to the harsh attitude towards the Slavs, Berlin adopted a more farsighted policy toward the Moslem population. The German Army entered the North Caucasus not as victors but as liberators, promising independence and autonomy under German rule. The occupation remained almost completely under the military control of well-qualified German experts who played down racial dogma and recognized the national aspirations of the indigenous peoples, offering them a constructive program of economic, agricultural and political reform.[7]

The German occupation of the North Caucasus lasted less than six months. The breakthrough to Baku and Batumi never materialized as the over-extended German forces got bogged down in the face of increasingly stubborn resistance by the Red Army and the locally recruited troops. Faced with the threat of encirclement at Stalingrad and the possibility of a greater disaster on the suddenly exposed North Caucasus front, Hitler reluctantly ordered a full-scale withdrawal from the Caucasus. In the meantime, Suslov's responsibilities had broadened considerably. As the senior party official in the area, he was appointed a member of the Military Council for the North Caucasus front,[8] frantically shuttling between Grozny and Ordzhonikidze to raise reinforcements among the indigenous civilian population. The Russian offensive at Stalingrad called for a coordinated effort in the North Caucasus, and Suslov now also began to take part in the military planning for the coming counter-attack. During this period, Suslov must have stayed in close communication with Stalin who had a special interest in the Caucasus. As a native Georgian, Stalin was acutely aware of the Caucasus' strategic importance to the war effort. Never completely trustful of his military commanders' reports, Stalin often called the First Secretaries in the war zone for details of military operations and morale. Opening his conversation with the customary "Kak u Vas dela?" (What is the situation?)[9] Stalin must have spoken with Suslov a number of times, expecting a concise but clear assessment of the situation at the front. The Russian offensive was scheduled for December 30, and Suslov was at army headquarters on that day. A copy of an order in the Stavropol archive, signed by Suslov on December 30, 1942 and addressed to the partisan units in the North Caucasus, anticipates the start of the German retreat and calls for the "intensification of the decisive struggle."[10] The German Army began its withdrawal on January 1, 1943, swinging northeast toward Rostov and the Kuban Peninsula. By January 20th, the Germans were already in the Stavropol uplands, and Stavropol itself was evacuated by them on January 21st. Marshal Andrei Grechko speaks warmly of Suslov in his memoirs,[11] stating that "the partisans of the Stavropol Territory liberated seventy villages and towns and inflicted heavy losses on the enemy, greatly helping the 347th Division of the 44th Army in liberating the territory."[12]

The much feared massive rising of the Moslem nationality groups never materialized. The Soviet government had instituted a more realistic policy in 1941, giving the Moslem youth greater motivation to continue the maintenance of the communist order in the North Caucasus. Only the Karachai established a firm relationship with the occupation authorities that eventually blossomed out into the formation of an independent self government under German protection.[17] The more assimilated Kabardins, Osetins and Circassians were least inclined to collaborate, preferring to stay uncommitted throughout the occupation.[13] Many communities also refused to help the Germans because they were not certain how long they would stay and, fearing reprisals, remained on the side lines until the Germans left. The occupation did not last long enough to allow pro-German sentiment to become diffused enough to precipitate a massive uprising, and Stalin remained genuinely satisfied with the outcome. This did not prevent him, however, from taking revenge against the Karachai, the Balkars, the Chechen and the Ingush, liquidating their autonomous regions and deporting their entire populations to Central Asia and Kazakhstan after the Red Army reoccupied the North Caucasus.

Suslov has been unceremoniously implicated in the deportation proceedings by both émigré and Western commentators.[14] An often cited quotation continues to emphasize how Suslov "helped to supervise the mass deportation of various North Caucasus nationalities, including the Chechen-Ingush, conducted in 1944 by NKVD troops under General Serov, an affair that has since been repudiated by the Soviet government as a criminal act."[15] As First Secretary of the Stavropol *Krai,* Suslov could hardly have avoided participating in this scandalous affair, but it is a mistake to place the blame on him without qualification. This is not to say that he was somehow innocent of what happened to the deported peoples. He had always tended to see life's values in terms of black and white, and he undoubtedly must have done so in this case. The German occupation was a trying and ugly experience to live through, and emotions ran high among the Russian patriots. Even if he had some reservations, it is doubtful that he would have raised them. This would not have been consistent with his personality, or with the spirit of the times. In the final analysis, the punishment imposed on the Karachai, the Balkars, the Chechen and the Ingush was the result of a more inclusive decision that involved also the Kalmyks, the Crimean Tartars, and the Volga Germans—a decision initiated by Stalin not out of military considerations but solely out of his vindictiveness and stubborn commitment to continue the repression of all those whom he considered oppositionists and traitors. At the XXth Party Congress, Nikita Khrushchev placed the responsibility for the deportation squarely on Stalin's shoulders, facetiously suggesting that the "Ukrainians avoided meeting this fate only because there were too many of them and there was no place to deport them."[17] Stalin dealt with the Ukrainians and Russians individually, sending tens of thousands of collaborators and returning forced-labor workers and prisoners of war to concentration camps from which many never returned.

The city of Stavropol did not sustain heavy damage. The Red Army's 347th Division succeeded in retaking it before the retreating Germans were able to inflict serious harm to it,[18] but the destruction in the surrounding areas was extensive, particularly to the flour mills and the munitions factories.[19] Suslov returned to Stavropol, remaining there through 1943 and most of 1944 as First Secretary, managing the reconstruction of the devastated economy.[20] The war was going well for the Soviet Union. By the fall of 1944, its most westerly forces were in East Prussia. Lithuania was reoccupied during the summer, and Suslov was now transferred there to direct a new Bureau of Lithuanian Affairs, especially created in November 1944 to reorganize Lithuania's economy and government and rebuild her Communist Party.[21] Stalin was convinced that Suslov was the right person to handle this assignment because of his specialized experience with nationality and partisan problems in the North Caucasus.

The situation in Lithuania on Suslov's arrival in Vilnius was decidedly threatening to the Soviet Union.[22] The Lithuanians had been resisting Russian domination for centuries.[23] During their short period of independence from 1918 to 1940 they had made a concerted effort to move politically and economically toward Western Europe, exhibiting a strong anti-Soviet bias in all their policies. In 1940, Stalin had again reincorporated Lithuania into the Soviet Union, forcibly communizing the unhappy nation and alienating a broad spectrum of its population. The German attack on the Soviet Union brought Lithuania under German occupation, but not before the Soviet-Lithuanian relationship had suffered another serious rupture. A massive armed insurrection against the Soviets on the day the Germans attacked the Soviet Union[24] accelerated significantly the German advance during the first week of the war. The rebellion was motivated by nationalist sentiment for an independent Lithuania, but its result was direct military aid to the advancing German Army. Exacerbating the Russian-Lithuania relationship even more was the attitude of the Lithuanians during the German occupation. The majority pursued a policy of neither collaborating actively with the Germans nor supporting the pro-Soviet communist underground. There were also outright collaborators who actively supported the Germans against the partisans and the underground. The return of the Red Army rekindled the nationalist sentiment and reopened the wounds inflicted by the Russian and German occupations. The middle class, the peasants and the intelligentsia continued to harbor strong nationalist feelings against a reunion with the USSR. The pro-Soviet communist underground, on the other hand, demanded a major role in the new government, insisting that all those who cooperated with the Germans should be removed from the government and punished. The situation was made even more critical by the resistance of the landowners and the peasants to the hastily decreed Soviet policy of forceful collectivization in August 1944. The result was civil war—a hard and bloody struggle in which a smaller pro-Soviet segment of the Lithuanian population supported by the Red Army and the NKVD fought a bitter war against the Lithuanian patriots and "forest brethren"—a mixed bunch that often included both independence fighters and former German collaborators.

Invested with full power to end the Civil War, Suslov moved decisively to reestablish Soviet rule. First of all, he reduced the existing armed conflict to a predictable ideological formula of a class struggle between the working class and the exploiting forces of domestic reaction and foreign interference. The Lithuanian patriots—many of whom came from the ranks of the pre-war Lithuanian leadership—now became "kulak-nationalists" fighting for an allegedly obsolescent political and economic order that Suslov claimed no one wanted in Lithuania. There was some justification in Suslov's analysis. The inter-war years in Lithuania were years of persisting political turbulence precipitated by Polish and German provocation, and the ever changing governments were, as a general rule, notoriously anti-labor. To resolve the conflict, Suslov devised a four-pronged strategy. With the help of the Red Army and the NKVD, pro-Soviet native units were organized into a militia of "people's defenders" to fight the partisans and the "forest brethren." To demoralize the Lithuanian partisans, the new government enlisted the aid of the Catholic clergy, promising amnesty to all those who laid down their arms and came out of the forests. German collaborators and oppositionists of all shades and color were summarily deported to the Soviet Union and incarcerated in prisons and concentration camps. The Lithuanian Communist Party was overhauled from top to bottom, its membership replaced by younger and politically loyal supporters of Soviet policy. Tactically, the program was placed under the command of General Sergei N. Kruglov, a tough and coldblooded former deputy director of *Smersh,** who followed Suslov's orders to the letter, using all means at his disposal to suppress any activity harmful to the consolidation of Soviet power in Lithuania. The struggle was marked by widespread violence and savagery on both sides, but by the end of 1945 the pro-Soviet forces had the upper hand. A Soviet offensive in February 1946 severely crippled the nationalist movement, sending thousands of sympathizers and activists to the concentration camps. Armed resistance did not end in 1946, continuing sporadically until it finally died out in the 1950s, but its back had been broken. It was no longer the threat it was in 1944. Stalin was completely satisfied with Suslov's progress and, in March 1946, summoned him to Moscow where he was rewarded a year later with membership in the Secretariat of the Party's Central Committee.[25]

---

*Russian acronym for death to spies. *Smersh* was a special intelligence agency set up during World War II to deal with the uncovering of foreign spies.

It would be interesting to speculate what went through Suslov's mind as he returned to Moscow after nearly ten years of absence. The war had brought great changes, and nothing was really the same as before. Suslov's personal life had been dramatically affected too. During the past five years he had to endure long and frequent separations from his family, and there were even rumors that he had abandoned the family, having become infatuated with the young widow of General Ivan D. Chernyakhovsky, the popular commander of the Bellorussian front killed in action in East Prussia.[26] That Suslov had some connection with the Chernyakhovskys is evident from the stirring eulogy that he delivered at the memorial meeting in honor of the general in February 1945.[27] No one will ever know, however, if there really was an affair or how serious it was, although the Moscow rumor mill insisted that Stalin had to intervene. There were no political repercussions, and shortly thereafter Suslov was reunited with his family in Moscow where he later also moved his mother, displaying singular attention to her until her death in the early 1970s.[28]

The nation and the Party had also changed. The war brought unprecedented losses in human life. Close to twenty million people died during the dreadful conflict.[29] The physical devastation to the nation was enormous—nearly two-thirds of its material wealth was destroyed in the areas occupied by the German army.[30] But there were other changes that troubled Suslov—less perceptible changes that went to the core of the system to which he had dedicated his entire life. In an attempt to bolster patriotism, Stalin had made substantial concessions to religion, and religious revival was now sweeping the nation. To generate goodwill in the West, Stalin had dissolved the Comintern, watering down the Soviet commitment to communism abroad. Collectivization also underwent a decline. In many regions, the occupation brought the collapse of the *kolkhozes,* and peasants were again farming as private landowners. The army, too, was beginning to flex its muscles. Fresh from recent successes on the battlefield, the generals were seeking greater autonomy from the control of the political commissars. The war had loosened too many controls, too many prohibitions, too many standards of personal and political behavior. Those who survived the war were now looking for more tolerance, more freedom, more personal comforts. Even more threatening to Suslov was what had happened to the Party. Stalin had emasculated it in the 1930s, but the war had disabled it completely. There had been no significant party activity since the last Party Congress in 1939.

Stalin had emerged from the war as the all-powerful *vozhd'* and savior, elevated by the cult of personality to an exalted position no longer subject to the Party's rules and restraints. This was not how Lenin perceived the role of the Party and its leadership, nor was it how Suslov saw it. This did not mean that he was losing confidence in Stalin. The process of climbing to the top does not demand complete confidence in the leader's ability to satisfy the personal needs and aspiration of the climber. It does not even call for complete loyalty. Men like

Suslov are rarely loyal to other men, however exalted. It is not in their make-up. Their loyalty is not to other men, but to concepts and ideologies that they subsume to rationalize their life's goals. And so it was with Suslov, as he thought about his future. The unconditional loyalty that he had held for Stalin had been strained and somewhat diminished, but not enough to opt for withdrawal from what he had conceived as his role in the Party.[31] Temporarily, he was quite willing to ignore the glaring contradictions caused by Stalin and the war. What really mattered was his career, and he chose, instead, to rise as high as possible in the Soviet political hierarchy.

> The world in which the Soviet leaders lived . . . was slowly taking on a new appearance to me: horrible unceasing struggle on all sides. Everything was being stripped bare and reduced to strife which changed only in form and in which only the stronger and the more adroit survived.
>
> Djilas, *Conversations with Stalin*

Chapter VI

VEILED ASSIGNMENT

By the end of World War II Stalin had become a suspicious and aging autocrat ruling the Soviet Union from the comfort of his *dacha* in Kuntsevo and his vacation retreats on the Black Sea. This did not mean that Stalin's authority was reduced. On the contrary, he emerged from the war with supreme authority. But power cannot subsist on authority alone.[1] "A wise prince should rely on what he controls, not what he cannot control," Machiavelli advised centuries ago,[2] and complete and unrestricted control Stalin did not have. He was no longer able to maintain a firm grip over the command structure that he had so carefully built and nurtured during the prewar years. The wartime relaxation of freedom and privileges at home, the emergence of the Soviet Union as a major power in a polarized world on the brink of the Cold War, the complexity of managing a modern bureaucratic state, and the rise of a new civilian and military elite led by impatient satraps waiting to seize power at the death of the *vozhd'*,* narrowed his span of control. The result was that the eight years between the end of the war and Stalin's death in March 1953 were years of unprecedented intrigue, wholesale repression, Byzantine domestic and satellite politics, and unbridled antagonisms within what appeared to be on the surface a monolithic Party and state organization.[3]

It was into this political and cultural inferno that Suslov was suddenly thrust when he returned to Moscow in March 1946. Central Committee Secretary Andrei Zhdanov had established himself as Stalin's protégé and heir apparent, largely at the expense of Georgii Malenkov, another Central Committee secretary with whom he had been feuding since the 1930s.[4] He had accomplished this by convincing Stalin that it was Malenkov who was responsible for the ideological and administrative laxity in the Party. Malenkov was removed from the Secretariat, temporarily losing his grip over the Party *apparat,* but remained in the Politburo where he had been raised to full membership earlier

---

*Chief or leader.

in 1946. Zhdanov's ascendance over Malenkov produced a realignment in a number of important Party and state organs, including the crucial government security agencies. In 1946, the Party reassumed its responsibility for the supervision of the police activity, and A. A. Kuznetsov, one of Zhdanov's principal associates from Leningrad, took over the overall supervision of police activity as Secretary of the Central Committee in charge of internal security affairs. Kuznetsov's promotion reduced the influence of Lavrentii Beria, another crafty Politburo member and former Minister of Internal Affairs. Demoted and downgraded in political stature,[5] Malenkov and Beria now allied themselves in a joint vendetta against Zhdanov.

In less senior positions, but exercising considerable influence, were Nikita Khrushchev, a full member of the Politburo from the Ukraine, and Nikolai Bulganin, the Minister of Defense and candidate member of the Politburo. The main protagonists were surrounded by a menagerie of lesser senior *apparatchiks* with Party memberships dating to the days before the Civil War: Viacheslav Molotov, Lazar Kaganovich, Andrei Andreyev, Klement Voroshilov. The primary contenders remained Zhdanov and Malenkov and, to a lesser degree, Khrushchev, Bulganin and Beria, but the postwar years also saw the emergence of a new loosely organized political force of younger *apparatchiks* from the *obkoms,* the *kraikoms,* and the state apparatus.[6] They were the *vydvizhentsy* who had gradually risen to power in the 1930s, and were now occupying important positions in the Party and state apparatus. Suslov was one of them, but there were also others: Andrianov, Brezhnev, Kosygin, Kozlov, Mikhailov, Patolichev, Pegov, Ponomarev, Voznesensky. The principal contenders were becoming too powerful, and Stalin was again constructing a new political reserve to counterbalance their ambitions. This had always been Stalin's strategy. He had rehabilitated and promoted Zhdanov in 1944 to neutralize Malenkov. He was now establishing a new power base by packing the most crucial Party institutions with the new men from the provinces and the state ministries. A few years later he would use the same maneuver in recalling Khrushchev from the Ukraine to counterbalance the resurging influence of Malenkov and Beria.

The majority of the new men had risen to the top through patronage. Patolichev, for example, owed his promotion to Andreyev, Brezhnev to Khrushchev, Andrianov to Malenkov, and Kosygin and Voznesensky to Zhdanov. Suslov, alone, remained untouched by patronage. He owed his rise neither to Zhdanov nor Malenkov, nor to any of the other senior Party leaders.[7] His career was almost exclusively the result of his own capacity for hard work and his devotion to the Party and the Communist movement. If anyone was accountable for Suslov's rise, it was Stalin himself. He had recognized Suslov's potential in the 1930s, and gradually had saddled him with greater responsibility. His recall to the capital in 1946 was another such promotion, even though the immediate purpose of this move remains a mystery that has not been satisfactorily solved to this day.

According to the usually reliable Institute for the Study of the USSR, "Suslov was transferred to the staff of the CPSU Central Committee in 1946 as head of the Agitation and Propaganda Department,"[8] an assertion that cannot be taken seriously as G. F. Aleksandrov continued to head the Agitation and Propaganda Administration (*Agitprop*) throughout 1946 and the first half of 1947. The eight page biography in *Soviet Leaders* states that "Suslov went to Moscow in March 1946 to work in the Central Committee apparatus and served as a member of the Orgburo, but his specific position (was) unknown, though probably it was connected with Party propaganda and ideological activities."[9] The Central Research Department of Radio Liberty describes his activities in 1946 with the laconic statement that Suslov "assumed responsibilities in the apparatus of the Central Committee."[10] The official Soviet biography, also using a minimum of words, simply states that in 1946, "Suslov worked in the apparatus of the Central Committee."[11] A twelve page biographical sketch in the influential *Leaders of the Communist World* reports that "in March (Suslov) was made a member of the Central Committee's all powerful Organization Bureau, and was later appointed to a lectureship at the Soviet Academy of Science."[12] A. A. Avtorkhanov suggests that Stalin recalled Suslov to Moscow to "help with the preparation of a second great purge."[13] Roy Medvedev overlooks any reference to 1946, and suggests that Suslov was transferred to Moscow in 1947 and not 1946.[14] A short 1953 biography by an English journalist suggests that Suslov may have been a private secretary of Stalin in 1946, presumably together with Poskrebyshev in Stalin's personal chancellory.[15] Newspaper articles, obituaries and other background studies offer varying explanations of Suslov's 1946 duties, depending on their sources.[16] No explanation provides a sufficiently clear picture of Suslov's activity in 1946 and early 1947, but the absence of clarity should not lead to the assumption that Suslov was recalled to Moscow to vegetate in the back rooms of the Central Committee. His transfer must have been prompted by something of vital importance to Stalin. It must have also involved a highly sensitive operation—sensitive enough to warrant a substantial promotion for Suslov after its successful completion. No one will probably know the full story, as the lack of primary sources continues to be a serious obstacle, but there is enough circumstantial evidence to suggest a hypothesis.

Zhdanov assumed responsibility for the revival of the Party about the same time as World War II was coming to its end. General A. S. Shcherbakov's sudden death in May 1945 and the growing hostility of the Soviet dogmatists to Aleksandrov, the wartime head of *Agitprop,* could not have passed by without making Stalin aware that something had to be done to put the Soviet propaganda machinery on a more sound footing after the war. As head of the Political Directorate of the Red Army, Shcherbakov was the undisputed propaganda chief of the Soviet Union during the war.[17] Like Goebbels in Germany, he had his fingers in every propaganda scheme that was hatched in Moscow for the conduct of psychological war against the Nazis. *Agitprop,* on the other hand, lost most of its influence during the war. By 1945, it was engaged only in such routine work as the publishing of Party journals, the supervision of Party schools that were almost non-existent, and the control of the patriotic domestic press that had become largely non-ideological. The important functions were usurped by Shcherbakov or by other Party leaders working directly with Stalin. This state of affairs could not continue indefinitely after the war. The Party's propaganda machinery had to be rebuilt and its functions centralized again. In short, a new and activist leader had to be appointed to give *Agitprop* a new life. A number of Party stalwarts would have jumped at this opportunity, but Suslov's practical experience combined with his theoretical training and political independence within the Party's power structure made him an especially desirable candidate. Stalin needed someone he could depend on to help him formulate the theoretical basis for his postwar foreign and domestic policies. Whether or not he actually planned to replace Aleksandrov immediately with Suslov is not known. Zhdanov had overall responsibility for ideology, and the likelihood is that Stalin agreed to let him make the decision. Aleksandrov was Zhdanov's protégé, and Zhdanov did not want to have an outsider in charge of *Agitprop*. In the end, Zhdanov decided to keep Aleksandrov, giving him his full support by replacing his dogmatist critics with a more flexible group of younger ideologists.

Stalin was considerably more devious. In 1934, he had utilized Yezhov's and Malenkov's services to spawn an *ad hoc* Purge Commission in order to circumvent Rudzhutak and the Central Control Commission. It made sense to him now to repeat the maneuver. Bypassing Aleksandrov and *Agitprop,* Stalin gave Suslov the secret and unpublicized assignment of working out a new ideological platform for the reorganization of the Party. Such an arrangement also gave Stalin the added protection of waiting to see how Suslov would fare in the capital's rarefied climate of intrigue before making the official appointment. Accordingly, Suslov was discreetly attached to the General Department of the Central Committee on his arrival in Moscow.[18] As a full member of the Central Committee and the Orgburo he had no problem in settling down to work. He knew Poskrebyshev personally and, through him, could easily communicate with Stalin.

The Central Committee apparatus was undergoing its first serious postwar reorganization. Stalin had actually started this already in 1944 when it became obvious that a revival of the Party was absolutely necessary to counteract the growing laxity in the arts and the social sciences.[19] The 1946 reorganization was the extension of this early effort to reestablish Party discipline. Moscow was swarming with former *obkom* and *kraikom* secretaries summoned by Stalin and Zhdanov to help with the reorganization of the Party. Nikolai Patolichev, former First Secretary of the Cheliabinsk *obkom,* was appointed head of the newly formed Administration for Checking Party Organs, a special department charged with the tightening of control over local Party organs. Patolichev's autobiography describes his meeting with Stalin and his appointment to the new post, bearing witness to Stalin's personal involvement and his great concern over the lack of discipline and control in the Party.[20] There was also a tightening of agricultural policy. In September 1946, a joint decree of the Central Committee and the Council of Ministers condemned the expansion of private lots, and created the Council of Kolkhoz Affairs to supervise the recollectivization of agriculture. The crackdown extended to the sphere of ideology. On August 14, 1946, a decree of the Central Committee condemned Mikhail Zoshchenko, a talented Soviet satirist, for his "ideologically harmful" works, fired a salvo against Anna Akhmatova, the much admired poetess and doyenne of Russian literature, and replaced the editorial staff of *Zvesda*, the Leningrad journal that published their writings.[21] Given the name of *Zhdanovshchina,** the drive for greater Party control of ideology gathered momentum in the fall, alienating the intelligentsia and promoting strong feelings of dislike for Zhdanov.

Throughout 1946 and early 1947, Zhdanov extended his newly acquired influence to the promotion of his allies and protégés. A. A. Kuznetsov became a member of the Secretariat in March 1946, Alexei Kosygin became a candidate member of the Politburo in early 1946,[22] and N. A. Voznesensky was elected to the Politburo in February 1947. There were corresponding promotions in the republic and *oblast* committees. But the primacy of the Zhdanov clique remained tenuous. Malenkov and Beria continued to chip away at Zhdanov's political influence by characterizing him as a moderate who was lenient to the "bourgeois" West and incapable of dealing decisively with the reorganization of the Party. As usual, Stalin remained detached, carefully weighing the debate between the conservatives and the moderate ideologues. He had never been particularly happy with the way Zhdanov had handled the controversy over Aleksandrov's publishing of his *History of Western Philosophy,*[23] and now a new debate was heating up over Lysenko's pseudoscientific theories[24]—a debate on which Zhdanov was again taking a moderate position without due regard for the controversy's repercussion on the achievements of Russian science. It was time to take a more radical position and turn against the moderates. It was a situation not unlike that in 1937 when Stalin, displeased with the slow progress of the campaign against the alleged Trotskyite-Zinovievite conspiracy, fired Yagoda and replaced him with Yezhov. It is not entirely clear when Stalin removed Aleksandrov and replaced him with Suslov. The probability is that he did this sometime in May or June of 1947, even though Suslov's appointment to the *Agitprop* and the Secretariat was not confirmed officially until November 23, 1947.[25]

A photograph in *Pravda* identified Suslov among the members of the Politburo and the Secretariat as early as June 21. Subsequent stories in the

---

*After Zhdanov who launched the campaign for ideological purity and Party discipline in 1946.

Soviet press continued to recognize Suslov as a member of the top leadership. A July 21 photograph, with an accompanying caption, listed him twelfth out of fourteen senior leaders attending the All Union parade for physical culture in Moscow.[26] An August 4 photograph showed him as one of twelve leaders on the reviewing stand of the Air Force Day celebration.[27] A large photograph of the October Revolution parade identified Suslov as the thirteenth of fifteen senior Soviet officials on top of the Lenin mausoleum in Red Square.[28] There was no evidence of Suslov's preeminence in the Soviet pantheon before June 21. As a matter of fact, only a few months prior, he was still listed on the back pages of *Pravda*—eighteenth in a delegation of nineteen Soviet functionaries visiting Great Britain from March 10 to April 11.[29] A March 28 story described his visit to Oxford University, the university library, and the university publishing facilities. It, too, said nothing that could be construed to identify him as a new head of *Agitprop* or secretary of the Central Committee. Nor was he among the leaders photographed on the reviewing stand at the 1947 May Day parade.[30] The sacking of Aleksandrov and the appointment of Suslov to the *Agitprop* and the Secretariat must have taken place, therefore, sometime between May and June 21, 1947. The pinning down of Suslov's appointment date is more than just a question of academic precision. It is crucial to the understanding of when Zhdanov's political career had crested and when it began to break up on the shoals of the conservative reaction and the Malenkov-Beria counterattack.

On the surface, Zhdanov appeared to be still riding high, but the real situation was different. Stalin allowed Zhdanov to continue his official duties, playing a deadly game of "cat and mouse" for almost a whole year.[31] Zhdanov, on the other hand, tried everything he could to reverse the irrevocable course of his accelerating fall. In June, he even changed his position on Aleksandrov, calling him a "toothless vegetarian" afraid of criticizing the philosophies of the West.[32] By then he had lost his influence and was sinking fast into political oblivion that finally ended in his death on August 31, 1948. Svetlana Allilueva's comment about a harsh exchange of words at the Black Sea resort in the fall of 1947 throws an interesting light on the deterioration of the Stalin-Zhdanov relationship. "Angered by Zhdanov's silence at the table," she observed, "father suddenly turned on him viciously: 'Look at him sitting like Christ, as if nothing was of any concern to him!' "[33] According to her, Stalin was constitutionally incapable of reversing his mind about people,[34] and was now waiting for Zhdanov to make his final mistake. The heavy drinking Zhdanov continued to appear at Party functions and international meetings for another nine months, but almost never alone, and usually in the company of Malenkov and Suslov. Stalin was afraid to let him loose without someone watching him closely.

Stalin's turnaround in 1947 did not result from domestic pressures alone. The Communist seizure of power in eastern Europe created serious problems for Stalin in the field of foreign relations. By the fall of 1947, his postwar foreign policy was being severely tested on a number of fronts. Churchill's

Fulton, Missouri speech in March 1946 started a chain reaction of Western counter measures against Soviet expansion in eastern Europe. In the spring of 1947, President Truman proclaimed what became known as the Truman Doctrine when he appealed to Congress for funds to provide military aid to Greece and Turkey whose independence was being threatened by Communism. In June 1947, the Marshall Plan was introduced to rebuild the war-devastated economies of the West. On the surface, Tito was still a loyal ally, but rumblings of things to come were already audible—the civil war in Greece was straining the Soviet-Yugoslav relationship. Clearly, a more activist and hardline policy was needed to obviate the political instability at home and abroad. Always cautious, Stalin did not want to rush into a new policy, preferring to wait for a propitious moment to play his hand. This was his *modus operandi* in 1928 when he used the Shakhty incident to launch a social revolution at home and, again in 1935, when Kirov's assassination provided the pretext for the purges. Suslov's recall to Moscow was a calculated step to coopt a reliable and competent outsider—not a reigning member of his immediate entourage—for the express purpose of helping him formulate and put in force a new policy of national vigilance at home and abroad.

In the fifteen months between March 1946 and June 1947, shuttling from the offices of the Central Committee on Staraia Ploshchad' to the inner sanctum of Stalin's personal chancellory, Suslov rejuvenated ideology and worked out a new Soviet formula suitable for the postwar reconstruction of the Communist world. It included a reinforced commitment to class struggle, the renewal of collectivization, the declaration of a doctrine of Soviet political and economic dominance in the satellite nations, the establishment of a new form of Comintern, and the revitalization of the Party. Much of the new formula was Stalin's, but there were elements in it that were distinctly Suslovian. The emphasis on class struggle and the primacy of the Party, the concept of the new Soviet man, the idea of strict control in the arts and sciences, and the notion of a binding community of interest among the Communist parties outside the Soviet Union with Moscow acting as the Third Rome, came from Suslov.[35] He was discreet enough, however, to circumscribe these elements in a framework that was acceptable to Stalin, recognizing that time was on his side to make appropriate adjustments later. Unlike Aleksandrov, Varga, and Voznesensky, who got carried away with revisionism and their own importance, he refrained from postulating views that could be misinterpreted or construed to be in opposition to those of Stalin. He did this quietly, without publicity, in consultation with Stalin, and with the backing of the conservative ideologists. He recognized that Stalin was both chief and high priest guarding a "sacred" cult created by him out of Marxism-Leninism and his personal predilection for Russian statism. There were differences of view, but this was not the time to voice them. He was perfectly willing to remain the sorcerer's apprentice, a high priest, but not the highest priest in the land. Like all suspicious politicians, he did not want to rush into a dangerous relationship until he was certain that he could manage it on his own terms. He was interested in influence and leverage, not in building an empire of his own. As two émigré historians have astutely observed, "in contrast to Zhdanov, who loved to pontificate in front of large audiences, Suslov preferred to keep his distance, acting behind the scenes through the *apparat,* allowing others to do the dirty work."[36]

Chapter VII

HIGH OFFICE

With the appointment of Suslov to *Agitprop* and the Secretariat, his
leadership role in the Party expanded into the open. *Zhdanovshchina* now
blended into a new form of more intense political and cultural repression targeted toward the rooting out of cultural dissent at home and political noncon-
formity in the satellite states of eastern Europe. Unlike Zhdanov, who tended to
react spasmodically to manifestations of cultural dissent among the Soviet intelligentsia, Suslov approached the problem of restoring ideological conformity in
the Soviet Union with the same kind of systematic planning that he had always
shown in his work.

The academies, the universities and the scholarly press were first to
feel the brunt of this new policy. In 1947, using the momentum established by
the reaction of the conservatives to G. F. Aleksandrov's *History of Western Philosophy*[1] and Ye. S. Varga's *Changes in the Economy of Capitalism as a result of
the Second World War*,[2] Suslov brought the academies and the universities under
his control by instituting rigid censorship standards in the scholarly press. In
February 1948, together with Zhdanov, he attended a Central Committee conference on music. Under attack for formalism was Muradeli's opera "The Great
Friendship," presented by the Bolshoi Theater during the celebration of the
thirtieth anniversary of the October Revolution in 1947, and the works of
other Soviet composers, including Dimitri Shostokovich's "Lady Macbeth of
Mtsensk." Zhdanov delivered the official indictment,[3] but the presence of Suslov's heavy hand was inescapable. The consensus was that he was the real author
of Zhdanov's speech.[4] In March 1948, Suslov laid down the new publishing
rules at a conference of *Agitprop* administrators.[5] In April and May, he spoke at
a meeting of *oblast'* and *krai* newspaper editors, and at a conference of publishing establishments.[6] The April speech to the newspaper editors criticized the
failure of the local papers to address what Suslov called the "basic questions"
dealing with the need to intensify the struggle against imperialism, the warmongers, and the tendencies of the petty bourgeiosie to oppose the development of a
socialist society.[7] Together with his injunction to emphasize the accomplishments of the Soviet society and the "Soviet people," these were to become the
major themes of many of his public addresses in the years to come. During

1949, the editorial staffs of *Bolshevik, Pravda,* and *Kul'tura i zhizn'* were purged and replaced with new and more tractable officials. The biology debate which erupted in 1947 over T. D. Lysenko's theories of genetics brought forth a crackdown on *Voprosy filosofii* and its editorial staff, indirectly contributing also to changes in the editorial board of *Literaturnaia gazeta* which took on the main task of attacking Lysenko's critics.[8]

During 1947 and 1948, Suslov reorganized *Agitprop.* All of the deputy chiefs inherited from the previous administration were replaced, and its departments restructured along functional lines to deal directly with the various media, educational, and artistic segments of Soviet life. The status of *Agitprop* was downgraded by changing it from a *"upravlenie"* (administration) to an *"otdel"* (division). Finally, in 1948, Suslov turned over the management of *Agitprop* to Dimitri T. Shepilov, one of his deputy chiefs, providing thereafter only overall supervision from his position as Central Committee Secretary in charge of Ideology and Inter-party Affairs.

Suslov's involvement in foreign affairs was equally damaging to the moderates. The Communist Information Bureau (Cominform) which replaced the disbanded Comintern was conceptualized by Suslov as a vehicle of bringing together the foreign Communist parties within the framework of Soviet control after World War II. It was created in September 1947 with Zhdanov and Malenkov representing the USSR at its first meeting.[9] Suslov was careful not to attend. What appeared at first to be a hard foreign policy line in response to the Marshall Plan turned out to be an ambiguous and cautious policy formulated by Zhdanov, a policy of continuing with the moderate line of "coalition governments" followed by Stalin after the war. The idea of transforming coalition governments into socialist states by peaceful means never really caught on. The communists in China, Vietnam and Greece had been in open rebellion since 1946, and the Yugoslavs were also urging insurrection instead of coalition. There were also significant differences of opinion between the Poles and the Yugoslavs. The Poles rejected the revival of Comintern while the Yugoslavs saw a need for a coordinated effort. The conference was another setback for Zhdanov. It was no accident that the official confirmation of Suslov's appointment and the announcement that he was responsible for relations with the East Germans was revealed while the Cominform meeting was still in session.[10] The announcement made it clear that relations with foreign Communist parties was not Zhdanov's bailiwick alone, but was also Suslov's.

Between October 1947 and September 1948, Soviet-Yugoslav relations became seriously strained by the unexpected announcement that the Bulgarians and the Rumanians were drafting with Tito's blessing an agreement to form a Balkan Federation without prior approval from Stalin. The Bulgarians and the Yugoslavs were summoned to Moscow and severely chastised by Stalin at a February meeting attended by Stalin, Malenkov, Molotov, Zorin, Zhdanov and Suslov.[11] In the next four months, Soviet-Yugoslav relations turned from bad to worse. At the end of February the Soviet Union informed the Yugoslavs that the trade agreement expiring at the end of 1948 would not be renewed and, in March, all Soviet civilian and military specialists were recalled from Yugoslavia. Everything was now orchestrated for a final showdown. Suslov's invitation to the Yugoslav Central Committee to attend the June meeting of the Cominform was rejected by Tito.[12] The Yugoslav position threatened Moscow's claim to primacy, and challenged her self-asserted hegemony over the Communist world. Yugoslavia was the first Communist state to oppose the Soviet Union openly and, according to Suslov, it deserved to be anathemized. On June 28, at the Cominform meeting in Sofia, in the presence of Malenkov and Suslov, Zhdanov read the resolution which expelled Yugoslavia from the Cominform. The resolution symbolized Stalin's final break with Tito and the end of Zhdanov's cascading political career. Malenkov now officially became Secretary in charge of Cadre Administration, and Suslov, Secretary in charge of Ideology and Inter-party Affairs. The resolution for the expulsion of Yugoslavia was a joint resolution of the Cominform nations, but its author was reputed to be Suslov.[13] The expulsion of Yugoslavia from the Cominform was a bitter pill to swallow for Suslov, and its memory continued to haunt him for many years despite Khrushchev's attempt to make peace.[14]

Suslov's promotion to the Secretariat increased his political stature and expanded his influence beyond the Party's inner circle into the public arena of Soviet life. In 1948, he was picked to give the traditional Lenin Day speech. Glorifying Lenin and reciting the Soviet accomplishments of the postwar years, Suslov delivered on January 21 a "fire and brimstone" indictment of capitalism and the West. Calling the United States "the gendarme of imperialism," he attacked it directly, painting a gloomy picture of a "decomposing society" trying to assert its dominance on the rest of the world.[15] The Lenin Day speech reflected the changing climate in U.S.-Soviet relations, establishing Suslov in the eyes of the world as the foremost hardliner among the younger Soviet leaders coming out of World War II. But there was more to the Lenin Day speech than just the ranting of anti-capitalist propaganda. It included an important Suslovian innovation that was still in its embryonic stage. Using a carefully chosen phraseology, Suslov introduced the concept of *"Sovetskii narod"** and a new interpretation of Soviet patriotism:

> Socialism was built in our country by the Soviet people under the supervision of Bolshevism. It is the embodiment of the all victorious idea of Lenin . . . An integral characteristic of Soviet culture is socialist patriotism. Lenin taught that the interest of national pride coincides with the socialist interest of workers. This idea of Lenin lies as a foundation of Soviet culture.[16]

---

*Soviet people or Soviet nation.

Suslov had replaced the historical *"Russian patria"* by the revolutionary *"Soviet patria,"* committing it to the establishment of a Soviet-led proletarian world.[17] In the post-Stalin years a more polished and expanded version of this interpretation would become a crucial ingredient of Soviet foreign policy.

The Malenkov-Zhdanov struggle did not affect Suslov's posture within the Party hierarchy. Suslov resolutely refused to play a part in the power struggle. He remained conspicuously detached, sending a clear signal to everyone that his interest lay in ideology and relations with the Communist states, not in political infighting for personal aggrandizement. He was carving out for himself a unique but strategic position in the Party, a position of a dispassionate interpreter of Marx and Lenin, an objective Communist practioner and future Soviet elder statesman. Whether he knew it or not, he was following in the footsteps of a succession of Russian ideologues who had faithfully served the Romanov dynasty. Best known for his formula of "Orthodoxy, Autocracy and Nationality," Count Sergei Uvarov acted as chief counselor and ideologue to Nicholas I. From his bastion of *Ober-Prokuror** of the Most Holy Synod of the Russian Orthodox Church, the reactionary Constantin Pobedonovtsev was another *éminence grise* who exercised an immense influence on Alexander III and Nicholas II for nearly twenty-five years. The resemblance often extended beyond the political issues to striking similarities in form and style. There was an especially close resemblance between Suslov's and Uvarov's styles. Suslov's relationship with Stalin was one of shrewd and flattering submission to the dictator's will and prejudices.[18] So was Uvarov's. He also avoided confrontation, presenting his views to the headstrong autocrat as reflections of the sovereign's own will, so much so that it is still difficult for historians to separate his ideas from those of Nicholas I.[19] Most Russian ideologues, including Suslov, were high priests of sorts, serving their chiefs in a variety of ways. The times were different, of course. So was the character and content of their programs. But, in a changing world, all exercised a reactionary influence, on the side of political stability, tradition, dogma, and precedent. All had an implacable fear of subversive ideas, and all were convinced that they were enlightened guardians of their nation's interests.

Malenkov was the principal winner of Zhdanov's downfall, regaining his position in the Secretariat and his control over the Party cadres. Zhdanov's rout also contributed to the rise of Beria who reasserted his dominance over the police and the security apparatus. With the rise of Malenkov and Beria came the unfolding of the two most notorious and far-reaching purges of Stalin's twilight years: the campaign against cosmopolitanism and the Leningrad affair. The anti-cosmopolitanism campaign was a landmark of Stalinist repression against the intelligentsia, while the Leningrad affair caused a new decimation of the Party.

---

*Derived from German and meaning Director General in Russian.

The term "cosmopolitan" was a euphemism that applied primarily to Jews, although it could also refer to anyone who was considered "internationalist," "unpatriotic," and pro-Western by the Party zealots. The campaign had its roots in the 1947–1948 debates on biology, economics, and philosophy. Pervasive criticism was levelled at the publicists and editorial staffs of *Voprosy filosofii, Literaturnaia gazeta,* and *Vestnik.** Spearheaded by editorial articles in *Pravda* and *Kul'tura i Zhizn',* the criticism exploded into a full-fledged witch hunt in January 1949 denouncing the "rootless cosmopolitanism" of four prominent theater critics, all of whom were Jewish. In March, several leading articles under the authorship of Mitin and Maksimov in *Literaturnaia gazeta* demanded that Soviet philosophy also be cleansed of such "rootless cosmopolitans" as B. M. Kedrov, the prominent Soviet liberal philosopher, and many others. By June the campaign spread to other areas of the arts and sciences, causing extensive arrests as a result of which thousands of innocent victims were sent to concentration camps on fabricated charges of treason, including Molotov's Jewish wife Polina Zhemchuzhina.[20] The drive against cosmopolitanism had distinct anti-semitic overtones arising partly out of the anti-semitism among the Soviet elite, and partly as a reaction against the much-publicized request of the Jewish Anti-Fascist Committee to give the Jews a national homeland in the Crimea.[21] The campaign was launched by Stalin, but Suslov must also bear his share of responsibility for the early attacks on the arts and sciences which set the stage for the anti-cosmopolitanism campaign. The purge affected all segments of the professional, academic, and artistic communities, touching Jews and non-Jews alike, and snatching along many others only remotely connected with the targeted field.

The Leningrad case was equally devastating. It was directed primarily against Zhdanov's former associates from Leningrad. Under Zhdanov's patronage, the Leningraders prospered after the war, exercising considerable influence in the top echelons of the Party *apparat.*[22] The heavy presence of the Leningraders in the top decision making strata of the Party *apparat* did not go unnoticed by Stalin. In March 1949, with Stalin's and Malenkov's approval, Beria and Minister of State Security Abakumov set in motion a large scale purge that liquidated the Leningraders.[23] The charges against the Leningraders were Russian nationalism and opposition to the Central Committee,[24] but the real reasons were more devious. The Leningrad affair was first of all a consequence of Malenkov's and Beria's struggle for power against Zhdanov. Having deposed Zhdanov, they now tried to eliminate his protégés and their political supporters. Leningrad's position vis-a-vis Moscow also played a role. As the former capital and seat of the October Revolution, Leningrad had for some time entertained the hope of becoming the capital of the Russian republic. The realization of this

---

*Official journal of the Soviet Academy of Science.

plan would have watered down Moscow's stranglehold of the All-Union Party organization, but there was more to it than just Stalin's fear of losing control. Stalin saw in the Leningrader's desire to raise the prestige of the old capital an attempt to reorient the Soviet Union towards closer relations with the West. This was a replay of the age-old struggle between Russia's two largest cities— Westernized Leningrad looking towards Europe, and ancient Moscow seeking solace in its medieval past. The Leningrad case allowed Stalin to smash the Leningrad Party organization and destroy the city's striving to recover its lost prestige.[25]

N. A. Voznesensky's growing influence in the capital also had something to do with the Leningrad case. As a member of the Politburo and head of central planning, he had established himself after the war as the undisputed authority in the field of economics. His book on the war economy of the USSR[26] received the Stalin prize in 1948, and his influence at the Institute of Economics was spreading fast throughout the entire government establishment. He had risen too fast and too precipitously from his political base in Leningrad, alienating a broad sector of the Party *apparat,* particularly those Party theorists who resented Voznesensky's recruitment of academics for government posts. Voznesensky also had a running conflict with Beria, who resented Voznesensky's financial meddling in the vast police empire under his control.[27] Voznesensky was reputed to have refused signing a list of condemned persons, when it was presented to him by Beria for his approval as a member of the Politburo.[28] Stalin was apparently also jealous of his popularity, especially when he discovered that Voznesensky was working on a second book about the Soviet economy.[29] He could not allow someone else to usurp his authority in Communist theory. No one really knows the precise reason for Voznesensky's downfall but, on March 5, 1949, he was unexpectedly removed from all his responsibilities, and later arrested and sentenced to death, lending even greater notoriety to the Leningrad affair.[30]

Suslov's connection to the Leningrad case was only peripheral. He was not involved in the preparation of the charges or the staging of the trials. As usual, he remained behind the scenes, pursuing his duties in ideology and foreign affairs. Although he never liked Beria and Malenkov, his sympathies were probably with them and the Party dogmatists who resented the influence of the Leningraders—especially Voznesensky's growing influence. However, it is unlikely that he would have agreed to go as far as Beria and Malenkov did. Some indication of Suslov's position in 1949 may be gained from his 1952 article in *Pravda* in which he accused Voznesensky of "anti-Marxist and unscientific" views.[31] Entitled "On the articles by P. Fedoseev in *Izvestia,*"[32] Suslov's diatribe in *Pravda* referred to a secret 1949 Central Committee resolution that criticized P. N. Fedoseev for giving "fawning praise" to Voznesensky's book on the Soviet economy during World War II.[33] Published for the first time as part of Suslov's article, the resolution remains to this day the only known official document from which the existence of the Leningrad case may be deduced. Suslov's 1952 article was a reaffirmation of the 1949 resolution, presumably echoing his own sentiments toward Voznesensky and the prosecution of the Leningrad case. Some analysts have theorized that Suslov had written the 1952 article on Stalin's behest, pointing out that the unusually cautious Suslov would not have done this on his own.[34] Stalin had just published his *Economic Problems of Socialism in the USSR,* and a condemnation of Voznesensky was necessary, they argued, to justify the ideological pronouncement in his book. Suslov may have consulted Stalin, but the suggestion that it was written solely to reinforce Stalin's authority in the field of economic theory seems far fetched. *Economic Problems of Socialism* was prepared by Stalin for the XIXth Party Congress which took place between October 5 and October 14. At the congress, Stalin's opus received widespread recognition and flowery praise. If Stalin wanted to remonstrate against Voznesensky in 1952, he did not have to wait for Fedoseev's articles in December—the time to have done this would have been earlier, as part of the publicity released during the congress, or immediately thereafter. Suslov's response to Fedoseev, with whom he had a long-lasting feud, was as much a censure of Fedoseev as a condemnation of Voznesensky whose lingering influence he also continued to resent.[35]

Suslov's official status in the Party was enhanced during the last years of Stalin's life. In September 1949, he replaced P. N. Pospelov as chief editor of *Pravda,* holding this important position through 1950 and part of 1951.[36] There were no substantive changes in *Pravda*'s editorial policy during this period, although some commentators have detected the first signs of spreading anti-semitism.[37] In June 1950, he was elected to the Presidium of the Supreme Soviet. His official ranking remained constant—from 1950 to 1951, his name was consistently listed immediately after the twelve top-ranking members of the Politburo and the Secretariat—but somehow he seemed to have faded away from the Moscow limelight. Except for the usual Lenin Day ceremony, the May Day parade, the October Revolution celebration, and the sessions of the Supreme Soviet, Suslov's name disappeared from the Soviet press until the XIXth Party Congress in October 1952. This has lead some émigré analysts to speculate that Suslov may have been working during this time with Stalin in the preparation of his *Economic Problems of Socialism.* According to Avtorkhanov, a secret meeting of leading Party theoreticians was convened by Suslov in November 1951 to discuss Voznesensky's work on the Soviet economy during the war, and the conclusions reached at this meeting reputedly determined the framework of Stalin's treatise.[38] If this is true, Suslov's criticism of Fedoseev's article becomes even less abstruse. As the anonymous editor of Stalin's economic treatise, Suslov must have found Fedoseev's restrained praise of Stalin and implicit reference to Voznesensky a direct affront not only to himself, but also to all the Party theoreticians who participated with him in the November 1951 meeting.

The early 1950s saw the emergence of Nikita Khrushchev as a new contender in the struggle for dominance in the Central Committee. Stalin had transferred him to Moscow in December 1949 to check Malenkov's and Beria's growing power, appointing him First Secretary of the Moscow Party organization and member of the Secretariat. Khrushchev's political credentials were impressive. He had been a member of the Politburo since World War II, and he also had the full backing of the Ukrainian Party apparatus, his bailiwick during the war and the immediate postwar years. Malenkov remained the primary contender, delivering the prestigious opening address at the XIXth Party Congress, but his power in the Party had been restrained by recent personnel changes in the critical cadres department of the Central Committee.[39] Beria's position was even more uncertain. In late 1952, Beria's protégé Abakumov was dismissed from the MGB and replaced by S. D. Ignatiev who was clearly hostile to Beria. The XIXth Party Congress saw the elimination of the Orgburo and the expansion of the Politburo into a twenty-five member Presidium which now included Suslov and a number of younger *apparatchiks* selected by Stalin personally without consulting the older Politburo members. 1952 also witnessed the decline of several other political careers. A. A. Andreyev was not reelected to the new Presidium, and Molotov, Mikoyan and Voroshilov were being harassed in a campaign of disparagement by Stalin. On January 13, 1953, *Pravda* announced the uncovering of the Doctor's plot, a case fabricated under Stalin's personal direction by Ignatiev against a group of mostly Jewish doctors arrested in late 1952 and accused of murdering Zhdanov and plotting to kill a number of senior military leaders.[40] The threat to Beria was now real as *Pravda* criticized the state security organs for failing to uncover the plot at an earlier date. The Doctor's Plot bore the unmistakable signs of another forthcoming purge that could easily sweep away thousands of innocent victims in its wake. A forbidding sense of gloom and suspense hung over the Kremlin as Party officials and ordinary citizens waited for what looked like a repeat of the 1930s.

Suslov's political stature in the Party *apparat* remained unchanged in 1952, despite the speculation that Stalin may have chosen him to lead the forthcoming purge.[41] The appointment to the Presidium improved his official status, but it did not increase his power. The Party's leadership remained in the hands of a nine-man smaller "bureau" consisting of Stalin, Malenkov, Beria, Khrushchev, Voroshilov, Kaganovich, Saburov, Pervukhin, and Bulganin. Real power resided with Stalin; the Presidium never convened, and all decisions continued to be made by Stalin in consultation with those who remained in his favor.

On November 21, Suslov celebrated his fiftieth birthday, and was awarded his first Order of Lenin. He had come a long way in the past thirty years. Caution, aloofness, and a keen sense of survival helped him reach high office without any significant political liabilities. He had never really succeeded in becoming a regular member of the drinking and story-swapping inner group that joined Stalin for dinner at his *dacha* in Kuntsevo, but this did not mean that he had no access to Stalin. Describing her meeting with Suslov in 1967, Svetlana Allilueva recalled that she "had seen Suslov several times" with her father during those rare and painful visits in the last years of Stalin's life.[42] Nor did this mean that he did not have a following of his own. On the contrary, he had built a lasting relationship with the security organs, the dogmatist wing of the intelligentsia, and the more conservative members of the Party *apparat*. He had accomplished this, furthermore, without posing a threat to Stalin and his other lieutenants. He had constructed for himself a very special niche in the Party *apparat* that set him apart from the rest of the power-hungry men who coveted Stalin's office. Never a true "man of action" like Khrushchev or Malenkov, nor a confirmed theoretician like Ponomarev or Yudin, Suslov had emerged during Stalin's twilight years as an indispensable intermediary, an ideological "honest broker" and *éminence grise,* a Marxist-Leninist guru helping decision makers to bridge the gap between theory and practice in Soviet politics. He had been a dedicated purist all his life, tenaciously pursuing a new faith. Now, under Stalin's protection, he had become a stern and unyielding spokesman of orthodoxy at home and communist expansion abroad. As a Party dogmatist, he remained firmly committed to the ideological conceptions of the Stalin regime, but as a practitioner and "true believer" in the Party's primacy, he could never completely come to terms with Stalin's autocratic rule. Stalin had reduced the Party to a position of complete dependence, mercilessly exploiting it for his own sake. Suslov was convinced that the restoration of socialist legality and Party rule was an absolute necessity, and he waited for the day that this could come to pass. He was also enough of a realist to recognize that the sluice-gates of change could not be raised until Stalin was gone.

PART THREE

INTERREGNUM:
The Time of Adaptation and Survival

I did not know whether things would be
worse or better, but they were going to be
different.

Ilya Ehrenburg, *Post War Years*

I feel that we are at the threshold of new days, and I think I detect signs of new attitudes. They are few and far between—indeed almost imperceptible—but they are nevertheless there.

Nadezhda Mandelstam,
Hope against Hope

Chapter VIII

REVERSAL

Stalin died on March 5, 1953 after suffering a brain hemorrhage and a stroke six days earlier. Fortuituously, he had lingered on long enough before dying to allow his successors sufficient time to agree on an assignment of responsibilities in the Party and the state, and to consider how to break the news to the nation. Malenkov, Beria and Khrushchev had been keeping an almost continuous vigil by his side, and had worked out a tolerable redistribution of power. Malenkov was to become Chairman of the Council of Ministers, Beria was to take charge of the combined Ministries of Internal Affairs and State Security, and Khrushev was to concentrate on the work of the Secretariat.[1] The distribution of responsibilities reflected each man's perception of how it was best to gain control in his search for power.

The immediate reaction of the nation to Stalin's death was ambiguous. Some wept in anguish, others sighed with relief, while the majority expressed considerable anxiety about the future course of the nation. Stalin had been the undisputed *khoziain** and *vozhd'* for so long that they could not conceive how they would live without him. As a precaution, extra MVD troops were moved to Moscow under the pretext of keeping order during the funeral.[2] The capital stayed calm, however, and the much feared military *coup d'etat* never materialized. The generals acquiesced and no Russian Bonaparte rose to challenge the nearly thirty-five years of Communist rule. The new leaders abstained from any overt political maneuvering, presenting a united team ready to take over the reigns of the Party and the government.

While Stalin's body was still lying in state in the Hall of Columns, the senior leaders of the Party and the government[3] approved the arrangement reached by Malenkov, Beria and Khrushchev, and also passed a resolution to abolish the enlarged Presidium that was created after the XIXth Party Congress in October 1952. The new Presidium was to include Malenkov, Beria, Molotov, Voroshilov, Khrushchev, Bulganin, Kaganovich, Mikoyan, Saburov, and Per-

---

*Russian for master. Ordinary Soviet citizens often referred to Stalin as *khoziain*.

vukhin. Except for Shvernik,[4] who was excluded from the new Presidium, the new makeup was a carbon copy of Stalin's "inner bureau." It retained the majority of Stalin's trusted drinking companions and loyal colleagues from the 1930's. Four other senior members of the Central Committee were elected alternate members: Shvernik, Ponomarenko, Melnikov, and Bagirov.[5] Bulganin, the Army's political marshal, was appointed Minister of the Armed Forces, and Molotov became Minister of Foreign Affairs again. Molotov, Bulganin, Kaganovich and Mikoyan also joined Beria as vice-chairmen of the Council of Ministers, and Voroshilov was appointed Chairman of the Presidium of the Supreme Soviet. The new distribution of responsibilities represented an uneasy and fragile compromise. It was not surprising, therefore, that the rival heirs began plotting almost immediately to destroy what they had agreed upon only a few days before.

The reorganization of the Presidium and the Secretariat did not pass without a demotion for Suslov. Some observers went so far as to say that "the ground was cut from under (his) feet and for a whole week he was virtually without a job."[6] In the new configuration of forces he was no longer a member of the Presidium, not even a candidate member. Much more threatening was the uncertainty of his position in the Secretariat. The new leadership had reached an understanding on the Presidium and the government assignments, but it was stymied in its agreement on the new Secretariat. As far as Suslov was concerned everything now depended on Khrushchev and whether or not he would back him in his effort to retain his position as Secretary in charge of Ideology and inter-Party affairs. He could not expect Malenkov's support, as his relations with him were not amicable. Malenkov tended to underrate the importance of ideology in the administration of Party affairs, and Suslov resented this. Nor could he expect any backing from Beria. He had never really approved of Beria's methods and was certain that Beria knew this. The only one among the new leaders who carried enough weight to oppose Beria and Malenkov was Khrushchev.

On the surface nothing seemed to have changed. Despite the uncertainty of his position, Suslov did not lose any ground in the leadership's official ranking. At the mourning ceremonies for Stalin, he was still being listed by the press among the first named officials in the group that followed immediately after the full members of the Presidium. On March 8, he was listed first among a group consisting of himself, Ponomarenko, Mikhailov, S. D. Ignatiev, Aristov, and Shatalin, and on March 10, second after Shvernik, in a group of candidate members of the Presidium and other senior Party *apparatchiks*.[7] The uncertainty persisted until March 14 when the new leadership finally agreed on the new makeup for the Secretariat. On March 21, *Pravda* announced that Malenkov had been released from his duties as Secretary of the Central Committee and that the new Secretariat now consisted of Khrushchev, Suslov, Pospelov, Shatalin, and S. D. Ignatiev.[8] Ignatiev's appointment to the Secretariat did not last; in April, he was removed after being accused of promoting the Doctor's plot.

Suslov had obviously weathered the storm. Malenkov had withdrawn from the Secretariat convinced that power should rest in the government organs, not the Party. In the event of an emergency, Malenkov felt certain that he could continue wielding sufficient influence in the Secretariat through his protégé Shatalin, who had taken charge of the Cadres Department.[9] Malenkov's preference for the state apparatus was based on Stalin's experience. He was convinced that it was easier to hold on to power by maintaining control over the state machinery. He had overlooked, however, that Suslov and Pospelov would ally with Khrushchev to oppose the submission of the Party to the state. Khrushchev's decision to back Suslov, on the other hand, was an impressive strategic move to solidify his control over the Central Committee and the Party *apparat*. Despite the marked differences in their personalities and outlook, Khrushchev and Suslov had much in common in 1953. Both were products of the Russian village, and both had spent their entire adult lives in the Party apparatus. Unlike Malenkov and Beria, who were essentially careerists, both also had a deep and enduring commitment to communism. Suslov's dedication to communism subsisted on dogma and fanaticism; he even named his son and daughter, Revolii and Maya, in honor of the Revolution and May Day.[10] Khrushchev's was more idyllic. He had never succeeded in mastering Marx, but his attachment to the practice of communism was consuming. "In our eyes, there was something romantic about our task. Everyone lived to see the day when Lenin's words would come true," he observed many years later, recalling the early days after the Revolution.[11] Both were also certain that the construction of socialism in the Soviet Union was an achievement of the Party, and not, as Stalin had maintained, his personal accomplishment.[12] From the Village Committees of the Poor to the top of the Party pyramid they had both risen without any detours, absolutely convinced that the future of the nation depended on the restoration of the Party to its position of primacy.

For entirely different reasons, Suslov probably also had the backing of Molotov, Kaganovich, and Bulganin, the hardline Stalinists in the Presidium. To them Suslov was the conservative high priest of Marxist-Leninist orthodoxy and the dedicated watchdog of ideological dissent. The old guard did not want to see him replaced by someone who would take a more flexible position during the crucial period of transition from Stalinism to a new and still unproved regime under Malenkov. Their expectations did not materialize, however, at least, not in the way that they had hoped. By the end of March, Suslov was facing opposition from a new and unexpected quarter. In an attempt to expand the power of the state machinery and undercut the influence of *Agitprop*, Malenkov formed the Ministry of Culture and appointed Ponomarenko to head this new government organ.[13] Malenkov had obviously decided to strengthen the state machinery by taking a plunge into the "sacred" confines of ideology and culture, confines jealously guarded by Communism's high priests and their acolytes. For Suslov, this was a symbolic act, a threat and an insult that could not be ignored. *Agit-*

prop was the seat of Suslov's personal influence since 1947. He had rescued it from obscurity after World War II, and now his influence was being challenged by an intruder who had neither the experience nor the education for the job. P. K. Ponomarenko was trained to be a transportation engineer, and had spent his entire career in administrative assignments, most recently as the First Secretary in Belorussia.[14] Appointed to the Secretariat one year after Suslov in 1948, Ponomarenko continuously competed with Suslov for recognition in the Soviet press. Ponomarenko's appointment to the new Ministry of Culture heightened the competition and also created a serious conflict at the organizational level. A joint meeting of *Agitprop* and the Ministry of Culture in January 1954, attended by Suslov, Pospelov and Ponomarenko resolved the crisis. The Ministry of Culture was retained, but its responsibilities were reduced. It was agreed that the Party and its ideological organs would continue formulating policy, while the Ministry of Culture would be responsible primarily for the promotion and execution of policy. This was a clear victory for Suslov and the Party—a victory that vindicated Suslov's senior position in the Party *apparat*. Ponomarenko was removed form his post as Minister of Culture, and transferred to Kazakhstan as First Secretary of the Kazakh Republic,[15] an important area of cattle production and the future site of the "virgin lands" project. The newly appointed Minister of Culture was the very same G. F. Aleksandrov whom Suslov had superseded as head of *Agitprop* in 1947. Ponomarenko's replacement with Aleksandrov constituted a definite downgrading for the Ministry of Culture.[16] As a candidate member of the Presidium, Ponomarenko had both prestige and contacts; Aleksandrov, on the other hand, plagued by scandal and eventually removed from the post, was a virtual nonentity in 1954.[17]

The Suslov-Ponomarenko conflict was only a sideshow. The real struggle for the top job had begun much earlier, and Beria was the first member of the triumvirate to fall. On April 4, 1953, the Soviet press announced that the Doctor's Plot was a provocation and that the men responsible for the arrest of the doctors had been arrested themselves. The case that was aimed at Beria was resolved, but the criticism of Beria now took on a new complexion. The press began a campaign to expose the "arbitrary" abuses of the security services and, indirectly, to embarrass Beria and his lieutenants in the MVD and MGB.[18] Under Stalin, the Party had become a captive to the state security services, unable to exercise its normal supervisory and investigative functions. As the new Minister of State Security (MGB) and Internal Affairs (MVD), Beria now presented an even greater threat to the Party and the state. Khrushchev had never cared much for Beria, and he convinced Malenkov that he had to be removed. It is not entirely clear how and when Beria was actually arrested and executed; according to *Pravda* the decision to remove him was made as early as June 16.[19] He was accused of a number of crimes, but the decisive issue was the misuse of power. Despite persistent warnings, Beria had continued to manipulate the internal security forces for the purpose of achieving his own goals.[20] Beria's execution was followed by other arrests in the Ministry of Internal Affairs and by sweeping changes in the Soviet legal system. In the next twelve months, the monster that Beria had created was hacked in pieces. The Ministry of Internal Affairs (MVD) was reorganized to handle only criminal cases. The Ministry of State Security (MGB) was transformed into the new State Security Committee (KGB), reporting directly to the All Union Council of Ministers. The legal system was overhauled to include a network of legally-constituted semi-autonomous courts handling criminal and political cases.[21] The new system was still a far cry from the justice of the West, but it was a step in the right direction. Beria's removal marked the end of a terrible epoch in Soviet history. It emancipated the Party from the clutch of the secret police, and restored a degree of legality unknown in the Soviet Union since the 1920s.

In the summer of 1954, Suslov gave up his direct responsibility for ideology and culture in order to concentrate his efforts on liaison with the foreign communist parties and to participate more actively in foreign affairs. This realignment in the Secretariat temporarily transferred the responsibility for ideology and culture to Pospelov. It is not clear if Suslov made this change voluntarily or at Khrushchev's bidding. In either case he had good reason to do it. The domestic climate was changing rapidly in the direction of more liberalism in literature and the arts. A carefully phrased critique of the "cult of personality" published in the domestic press during the fiftieth anniversary celebration of the founding of the Bolshevik Party legitimized the spontaneous outpouring of anti-Stalinist feelings that was building up momentum since Stalin's death. The Party's May 1954 campaign to put a stop to the spread of liberalism in literature was, at best, a standoff.[22] The liberal writers accepted the criticism of the Writers' Union, but refused to be silenced. The surge of pent-up emotion had grown beyond the stage where it could be completely controlled, short of going back to the methods of the past. This was a new experience for Suslov. He had been accustomed to strict regimentation and the prompt and expedient acceptance of his *ukases,* not to criticism or obstruction. In the face of this new development, withdrawal from the ideological arena made sense, at least until the domestic situation had clarified itself. He did not want to become known as another Zhdanov; nor did he want to run the opposite risk of being criticized for leniency. A withdrawal was also expedient because it removed Suslov from the more substantive domestic issues that had to do with agriculture, productivity, worker discipline, and education and welfare. Discretion is the better part of valor. In Suslov's case, discretion was the guiding principle of his life. His keen sense of preservation told him that he should move away from the domestic scene until there was a more stable political climate, until Communist theory and practice could be repackaged to meet the reality of the new mood.

In April, Suslov was appointed Chairman of the Foreign Affairs Commission of the Supreme Soviet.[23] Whether or not this was Khrushchev's way of appeasing Suslov at a time when he was giving up his domestic duties is not known, but the new position gave Suslov a perfect excuse to bow out gracefully from the domestic arena and his responsibilities in ideology and culture. He had already begun to allot more time to inter-party affairs. During the first week of April, together with Bulganin and Shepilov, he had travelled to Berlin to attend the Fourth Congress of the East German Communist Party.[24] Throughout the rest of 1954 and 1955 he was intimately involved with interparty affairs, playing host to an increasing number of foreign Communist Party delegations visiting Moscow. In 1955, he chaired the debates of the Foreign Affairs Commission, and made another trip to Berlin, ostensibly to attend the Sixth Anniversary of the German Democratic Republic, but, in fact, to help defuse the explosive situation growing out of the Cold War.

The domestic climate was definitely changing. Stalin's name was disappearing from the Soviet press. Vladimir Pomerantsev's article "Ob iskrennosti v literature" (On Sincerity in Literature) in *Novyi Mir* precipitated an unprecedented expression of solidarity for freedom and honest feelings.[25] 1954 witnessed the return of the first rehabilitated victims of the repression, including Molotov's wife, Polina Zhemchuzhina. Ilya Ehrenburg's *The Thaw*,[26] cautiously but sympathetically portrayed an anti-establishment painter in one of its conspicuously more provocative sub-plots. Vera Panova's *The Seasons* and Leonid Zorin's play *The Guests* criticized the Soviet bureaucracy, creating a furor among the conservatives in the Union of Writers.[27] Like the 1855 "unbinding" after the reign of Nicholas I, the word "thaw" became overnight a symbol of hope and a new awakening, allowing Soviet writers and publicists to breathe more freely for the first time in many years.[28] A week before the opening of the XXth Party Congress in February 1956, the Soviet Union paid tribute to Fyodr Dostoevsky, whose works had been under a strict ban since the Revolution. The gala meeting honoring the seventy-fifth anniversary of the author's death took place in the Hall of Columns in Moscow in the presence of his grandson and hundreds of Soviet and foreign writers.[29] "We have gathered here to assert before the whole world the great significance of Dostoevsky's writings in the life of our people," were the opening words of the welcoming address.[30] The rehabilitation of Dostoevsky was followed by the publishing of more than a million copies of his works, each volume carefully circumscribed with a *caveat* advising the Soviet readership that the author was an ideologist of reaction. The long arm of ideological control was still there, but it was less direct, more circumspect, and no longer typical of the kind of regimentation that constituted the unpardonable abuses of *Stalinshchina*.* Despite the new constraints and regulations, Soviet literature had become more honest, more open, and less obsessed with the axioms and standards of "socialist realism." In a very short period of time, it had travelled miles from where it had been for almost twenty-five years.

---

*Time of Stalin, usually associated with the dictator's last and most repressive years of his life.

On the domestic political scene, the last months of 1954 saw the final stage of the struggle for power between Khrushchev and Malenkov. Beria's indictment had seriously damaged Malenkov's reputation. It was becoming increasingly clear that Malenkov had participated in many of the crimes ascribed to Beria, including the Leningrad affair. Khrushchev also did not remain silent. Throughout 1954, he continued to criticize the inadequacy of Malenkov's policies, striking out at his agricultural and consumer goods programs and the related reduction in heavy industry. The generals had always been critical of Malenkov's economic policy and, as the production of tanks and rockets plummeted, they became increasingly hostile and restless. The political climate was clearly tipping in favor of Khrushchev. Malenkov sat paralyzed unable to reverse the trend. Khrushchev, on the other hand, dashed about the country "packing" the Party's key posts with loyal allies, extolling the Virgin Lands project, and selling panacea to the gullible public. The situation finally reached a crisis at the February 1955 plenum of the Central Committee. Malenkov tried to defend himself, but it was too late. On February 8, 1955, at the meeting of the Supreme Soviet, Malenkov officially resigned from his position of Chairman of the Council of Ministers, asking that he be replaced, of all things, "by another comrade with greater administrative experience,"[31] obviously referring to Khrushchev who was by then the undisputed leader of the Party *apparat*. He was named Minister of Electric Power Stations, a post of no significance, but remained a member of the Presidium and the Council of Ministers, the latter in the capacity of Deputy Chairman. Bulganin was confirmed as the new Chairman while Marshal Zhukov took over the Ministry of Defense. Bulganin had never been a real power in Soviet politics, and his appointment as Prime Minister was clearly cosmetic. Acting through the Central Committee, Khrushchev had wrested the control of the government from the state, returning it to the Party, but the dethronement of Malenkov raised another question. What were to be the limits of Khrushchev's power? In the following months, a series of leading articles in *Pravda* and *Kommunist** stressed the importance of "collective leadership in the Party," urging Khrushchev to constrain the exercise of his newly won power.[32] It is not clear if Suslov had anything to do with these articles—his position in the Soviet leadership was still too precarious—but the likelihood is that he did not disagree. His subsequent speeches and writings confirm this. "The Party started to restore Leninist standards immediately after Stalin's death," he reported to a meeting of social science professors on January 30, 1962, "It revived the principles of collective leadership, increased the creative activity of the Party organizations and took decisive steps to restore social legality."[33] True to the dictates of his self-interest, Suslov must have purposely chosen to be silent at the time of

---

Kommunist is the name of the official theoretical journal of the Party previously published under the name of *Bolshevik*.

Malenkov's ouster to escape the suspicion of being branded a backer of either Khrushchev or Malenkov.

In fact, Suslov's support for Khrushchev remained unwavering, despite his consistently independent stand within the Party leadership. In July, he was rewarded with a reappointment to the Presidium,[34] from which he had been removed in 1953. He was now fifty-two, a full member of the Presidium and the Secretariat, and the most senior member in the Secretariat, having been named Secretary two full years before Khrushchev. The appointment to the Presidium gave him another distinction. Except for Khrushchev, he was the only other Soviet leader whose portfolio now included both the Secretariat and the Presidium. Throughout 1954 and 1955, Suslov also enhanced his stature *vis a vis* the state organs. He had expanded his power base to foreign affairs, vastly improving his relations with the professionals in the Ministry of Foreign Affairs. Suslov's appointment to the Presidium was part of a more extensive realignment of forces meant to strengthen Khrushchev's position in the Presidium and the Secretariat. It included the appointment of Alexei Kirichenko, Khrushchev's energetic protégé and successor in the Ukrainian Communist Party, and three other Khrushchev protégés, Aristov, Beliaev, and Shepilov who joined Khrushchev, Suslov and Pospelov in the Secretariat. The likelihood, therefore, is that Suslov's election to the Presidium was supported not only by Khrushchev, but, as Michel Tatu has suggested,[35] also by the Molotov-Kaganovich faction as a means of maintaining the balance of power under a collective leadership to which most of the Presidium membership was unequivocally committed. This conclusion was confirmed by Suslov himself who made a clear differentiation between 1955 and 1956, emphasizing many years later that the formation of the "anti-Party group did not take place until 1956."[36] Real power continued to be concentrated in the Presidium where Khrushchev now counted on Kirichenko's loyal and unqualified support, Suslov's selective backing, and the more restricted support of Bulganin, Molotov and Kaganovich, who disapproved Malenkov's attempt to regain control of the state organs.

The first nine months of 1955 were characterized by an unusually busy schedule of activity for Suslov on the international scene. The month of May saw the emergence of the Warsaw Pact Organization. Suslov played an active part in the events that led to the signing of the alliance that counter-balanced NATO, travelling to Warsaw in July where he delivered the principal speech at the ceremonies celebrating the revival of Poland after World War II.[37] In July, on Khrushchev's initiative, the Soviet Union established diplomatic relations with the Federal Republic of Germany after long and difficult negotiations with Chancellor Adenauer. This was perceived as a definite threat by Walter Ulbricht. To relieve the fears of the German Democratic Republic that the Soviet Union was not trying to bring both parts of Germany together, Suslov had to make several trips to Berlin as well as entertain Ulbright at home.[38] Ulbright's anxiety about the possibility of a rapprochement between the two Germanies went back to July 1953 when it was first disclosed after Beria's fall that Beria was in favor of abandoning East Germany. It persisted to be a sore point in Soviet-East German relations until September 20, 1955, when a treaty was finally signed in Moscow.[39]

In the broader scope of Soviet politics, Suslov's appointment to the Presidium marked the beginning of a new chapter in his life. With a vote in the highest decision making organ of the Soviet Union, Suslov now prepared to become the second most influential man in the Party *apparat*. His functional area of responsibility continued to be relations with other communist nations, but this was not to last forever. After a hiatus of almost two years, he was again ready to assert his influence in what had always been his main interest—ideology. The political instability of the early years after Stalin's death demanded that he withdraw temporarily from his post as the Party's chief idealogue to recalibrate and readjust himself to a new set of realities at home and abroad. This was a period of intense tension for Suslov during which he had to overcome a number of challenges to his career. It was also a period of new learning and assimilation characterized by nearly two years of close association with the more westernized satellite nations of eastern Europe. The old Suslov did not disappear entirely, but a more mature and time-mellowed man did take his place. This did not mean that he had somehow undergone a conversion that changed his devotion to communism. On the contrary, he had become even more convinced of the efficacy of communism and the growing hostility of the western world to the Soviet Union, particularly the United States.[40]

It was not theory that Suslov sought to modify, but practice. He was not questioning the soundness of Marxist-Leninist dogma, but the effectiveness of its practice in the past. He had often experienced doubts about Stalin's harsh and arbitrary methods, but ambition and a strong instinct for self preservation precluded a shift to a different approach. The political climate demanded that he accept Stalin's use of force as the only effective tool to impose conformity on the intelligentsia. The times had changed, however. It was now more expedient to steer a new course, one that would be less autocratic and more adaptable to persuasion than the aggressive use of force. There was nothing unusual about this change of heart. Other political leaders had made similar turnarounds without sacrificing the consistency of their purpose. The Lenin of *''Left-Wing'' Communism—An Infantile Disorder* was very different from the Lenin of *What is to be Done*,[41] and that most consistent of XIXth century politicians, von Bismark, had changed his tactics twice during his long political career, once in 1851 and the second time in 1877.[42] Suslov was not just a conservative ideologue, but a practical politician whose personal motivation and skills were as much political as ideological, problem-solving as arbitrary. He was a dedicated communist purist—in many respects more like the first generation of communists than his own career-oriented contemporaries who had survived the *Stalinschina*—but he was also a consummate opportunist who understood that means and methods must be changed to fit the times.

> The revenge of history is greater than that of the most powerful secretary-general, I dare to take consolation from this.
>
> Leon Trotsky, *Stalin*

Chapter IX

PLAYING SAFE

By the fall of 1955, Khrushchev had gained almost complete dominance over the Party's central apparatus and its affiliates in the republics and the provinces. However, he had not succeeded in acquiring full control in the Presidium. Molotov continued to offer opposition on foreign policy, Kaganovich and Voroshilov remained cool to his administrative reform, and Malenkov was still a power to be reckoned with. The interregnum had not run its full course. All things considered, Khrushchev had not won the war yet. Throughout 1956 and the first part of 1957, he was still facing formidable setbacks and opposition.

Suslov also faced his share of new challenges in 1955 and 1956. He had to consolidate his new position in the Presidium, reassert control over ideology and culture, and help stabilize the Party's reacquired dominance in the affairs of the state. To complicate matters, there was also the XXth Party Congress—the first post-Stalinist Party Congress—lurking in the months ahead, together with the controversial debate over the future course of de-Stalinization. During the first week of October Suslov had gone to Berlin for the celebration of the Sixth Anniversary of the German Democratic Republic,[1] returned home and, after October 23, dropped out of sight until November 26.[2] He already had one extended absence from press coverage when he was on vacation in August 1955, and now there was a second one in the same year. Falling during the highly visible October Revolution ceremonies which he had always attended in the past, the November 1955 absence became the first of Suslov's many future unexplained absences leading to rumors that he was either ill or in political trouble.[3]

A careful analysis of Suslov's press coverage contradicts the thesis that these absences were always related to illness or political trouble.[4] The consensus among American physicians, who have examined Suslov's medical data within the framework of his record of absences from 1955 to 1975, is that "adult onset" diabetes probably began to attest itself sometime during his late fifties or early sixties, contributing to a gradual development of coronary heart disease that resulted in the myocardial infarction in 1976 at age 73. According to this view, Suslov would have sustained a largely imperceptible and steady decline in his health that would not have resulted in the number and duration of extended absences in the 1950s and 1960s.[5] Barring the existence of pathology missing in the available medical reports, it is the unanimous opinion of the American experts that Suslov's physical condition should have remained relatively stable through the 1950s and 1960s, beginning to deteriorate only in the 1970s as he approached the age of seventy.[6]

An examination of Suslov's political standing against the events and mood of this period also does not give any clues about his extended absences in the 1950s and 1960s. There is simply no evidence that he was in serious political trouble after 1955. On the contrary, the absences generally coincided with periods of political crisis affecting other members of the leadership, or a time of intense debate on policies that Suslov did not approve. It is during these periods that Suslov's name would consistently disappear from the Soviet press.[7] Retreat was Suslov's principal strategy during periods of indecision or crisis, invariably causing him to withdraw from the center of activity. In retrospect, there is every indication that his ego may have been sufficiently bruised in childhood to embrace a lifetime defense strategy of distancing itself from conflict and uncertainty.

There were many reasons why Suslov would have preferred to distance himself from the debates that were consuming the leadership in 1955. In addition to the newness of his Presidium appointment, there was the troublesome question of the coming XXth Party Congress, and the debate over how it was best to handle de-Stalinization. Also, under consideration was the problem of future relations with Yugoslavia, an issue on which Suslov had exceptionally strong feelings that went back to 1948 when he personally supervised Tito's expulsion from the Cominform. Suslov was not against de-Stalinization per se. He recognized the desirability of doing away with the excesses of the Stalin years, but he was concerned about how far and how fast the process of de-Stalinization should be allowed to proceed. Above all, he was disturbed about Khrushchev's impatience to patch up relations with Tito. Suslov was categorically opposed to Khrushchev's trip to Belgrade,[8] and even more disturbed by Tito's conditions for a new agreement, conditions that called for a public vilification of Stalin and the admission by the Kremlin of the trumped-up charges against the alleged "Titoist traitors" in eastern Europe. From his point of view, the reestablishment of relations with Yugoslavia and de-Stalinization were part and parcel of the same problem. The rehabilitation of Tito and the Titoists could raise havoc among the foreign communist parties in eastern Europe and create irreparable damage to the world communist movement, just as the uncontrolled condemnation of Stalin at home could produce confusion and embarrassment to the Party and its leadership. At a more personal and self-serving level, he was probably also intensely distressed about how this would affect his prestige in eastern Europe and his political standing at home. He was, after all, one of the principal instigators of Stalin's anti-Titoist purge that decimated the ranks of the Polish, Hungarian, Rumanian and Bulgarians Communist parties in 1948 and

1949. His address "The Defense of Peace and the Struggle with the Warmongers" at the November 1949 meeting of the Cominform in Hungary was a blistering apologia of the purge.[9] An admission by Moscow that Stalin's purge of the eastern European leaders in 1948 and 1949 was a mistake and a gross miscarriage of Communist justice could be a fatal blow to his future career.

The problem of de-Stalinization was being studied by the Pospelov commission,[10] and Suslov felt confident that there was still time to resolve it to his satisfaction. The Yugoslavian question, on the other hand, called for more immediate reaction, as Khrushchev was pressing hard to bring Tito back into the fold.[11] Suslov did not feel sufficiently secure, however, to speak out authoritatively on these issues in the fall of 1955. The struggle for power in the Presidium was still not over, and taking a position on such controversial issues as Yugoslavia and de-Stalinization could become a serious liability later. It was more expedient to play safe and let Khrushchev and his opposition fight it out among themselves. Suslov felt confident that he could rouse enough obstruction later to temper Khrushchev's impatience, and bring about a more gradual and moderate censure of the Stalin regime. Despite the obvious discomfort and anxiety that unresolved political turmoil always brought to his personal life, he had learned to live with it and use it successfully to achieve his needs.

In the interval between the July 1955 plenum and the XXth Party Congress in February 1956, a number of important events took place in the Soviet Union. More than ten thousand Party functionaries were amnestied and allowed to return home, while thousands of former Party leaders, writers, and scientists were rehabilitated posthumously.[12] There was also a new outpouring of anti-Stalinist criticism in the arts and sciences. The scholarly press assailed Stalin's atrociously ornate and pompous architecture, his predilection for Russian nationalism, and his treatment of Voznesensky and the Leningraders in 1949.

The XXth Party Congress opened on February 14, 1956. The criticism of Stalin dominated the proceedings, but equally important was the recognition that "different roads to socialism" did exist. Not only Khrushchev, but Suslov, Shepilov, Kuusinen, and even Molotov expressed their views on this. Khrushchev went so far as to suggest the possibility of reaching socialism by the parliamentary road, only to be corrected by Suslov's abstruse statement that "the capitalist class *(must) be deprived of ownership* of the means of production and that the means of production (must) be made public property, *that all attempts by the overthrown exploiting class to restore their rule be repulsed** and the socialist construction be organized."[13] The principle of "different roads to socialism" was further qualified by another important doctrinal modification, the acceptance of the view that wars were no longer inevitable and co-existence could be achieved.[14]

---

*Italicized by the author to show Suslov's qualification of Khrushchev's view on reaching socialism by peaceful parliamentary means.

The criticism of Stalin took a number of forms at the Congress. Khrushchev's opening speech was relatively mild. Even Suslov had more to say. In his ideological report on February 16, Suslov carefully inventoried the principal negative effects of Stalin's practice of "the cult of personality."

(They) caused considerable harm to both organizational and ideological Party work. They belittled the role of the masses and the role of the Party, disparaged collective leadership, undermined inner-Party democracy, suppressed the activeness of Party members, their initiative and enterprise, led to lack of control, irresponsibility and even arbitrariness in the work of individuals, prevented the development of criticism and self-criticism, and gave rise to one-sided and at times mistaken decisions.[15]

Suslov's report was clearly critical of Stalin's practices, but it did not offer details or produce new disclosures. Couched in generalities, it acknowledged the existence of the cult of personality, and condemned it tangentially by urging the delegates to return to Leninism. It was Mikoyan who took the first step toward a more direct and unambiguous criticism of Stalin. "In the course of nearly twenty years," he said, "we had no collective leadership; the cult of personality flourished."[16] Mikoyan made no bones about Stalin's shortcomings. He criticized Stalin's Yugoslavia policy, the apocrypha in the *Short History of the All-Union Communist Party,* Stalin's *Economic Problems of Socialism in the USSR,* and the inadequacy of ideological work by *Agitprop.* Mikoyan went far beyond the issues and policies discussed at earlier sessions of the Congress. He reminded the audience of the inexcusable treatment of Party members, recalling particularly Kosior and Antonov-Ovseyenko who were executed in the 1930's.[17] Suslov was actively involved in at least three of the spheres criticized by Mikoyan—Stalin's policy toward Tito, his economic opus, and the disgraceful behavior of *Agitprop* in 1947 and 1948. No one really knows how Suslov reacted to Mikoyan's criticism, but it is worth while noting that Soviet biographies of Suslov, on the whole, say very little about his participation in what Mikoyan chose to castigate. As a matter of fact, Suslov's 1952–1953 membership in the enlarged Presidium is more often than not completely excluded from his official biographies.[18]

The speakers who followed Mikoyan added very little to what had already been said. The majority continued to follow the general line of mild criticism started by Khrushchev and Suslov. The exception came on the evening of February 25.[19] At a closed session requiring special passes, Khrushchev dropped the bomb that startled the entire world. Speaking for nearly five hours and sparing no detail, Khrushchev presented a comprehensive condemnation of Stalin that brought amazement and indignation from the entire audience. He spoke of the conflict between Lenin and Stalin in the last months of Lenin's life, and of Lenin's "last will and testament" to remove Stalin as General Secretary.[20]

He alluded to the dubious circumstances surrounding Kirov's death, implying that Stalin may have been involved in his murder. He referred to the *Yezhovsh-china,* to the mass exterminations of the Old Bolsheviks and the military. He described Stalin's confusion during the early days of World War II, and placed the blame for the severe military losses on Stalin. He denounced the Leningrad Affair, the repression in the Caucasus, the Doctor's Plot. He spoke about Stalin's mania for greatness, and about his victims. He conjured the ghosts out of the long forgotten past and, to the applause of the audience, restored their good names.[21]

It would be a mistake to think that Khrushchev's speech was not self-serving; some of the passages were clearly aimed at Malenkov, Kaganovich, Molotov, and Voroshilov, obliquely associating them with Stalin's worse abuses of power. But its force and courage outweighed its weaknesses, and no amount of formal and theoretical demagoguery could have aroused the kind of emotion that it did. It sent a clear and explicit signal to the audience to break with the past and to participate in a national catharsis that would offer respite from the torment of the Stalin years. It was an emotional outpouring of a man who had already done this himself and was now trying to have others do the same.

No one has really been able to explain fully why Khrushchev gave his secret speech. Some have suggested that Khrushchev took on the "role of the prosecutor" at the request of his Presidium colleagues.[22] Others have made the argument that he had decided to do it on his own, to reinforce his hold over the Party and not to be outdone by Mikoyan.[23] According to Khrushchev's own testimony—self-serving and moralistic though it may be—he did it after a long and heated debate with the rest of the Presidium members, out of respect for all those who had suffered under Stalin's wrath.[24]

Several other reasons also demand consideration. The origins of the Secret Speech went back to the July 1955 plenum when the special Pospelov commission was established to investigate Stalin's abuse of power.[25] Working together with Suslov, who was Pospelov's senior after Suslov had been reelected to the Presidium, Pospelov prepared a comprehensive report for the XXth Party Congress. Shortly before the opening of the Congress, the report was reviewed at a meeting of the Presidium, and an agreement was reached among the leaders to confine the censure of Stalin to a theoretical criticism of the cult of personality, without revealing the specific details of the Pospelov report.[26] Khrushchev's opening address and Suslov's speech on February 16 followed those guidelines. Why then did Khrushchev break the agreement? The likelihood is that there was a contingency plan and that Khrushchev's speech was part of it. Mikoyan's address certainly served as an impetus, but it took more than just Mikoyan's remarks to precipitate a change in plans. It is generally agreed that the level of anti-Stalinist feelings had reached a point of grave concern to the leadership by the time of the XXth Party Congress. The extent of Stalin's crimes had become generally known to the public from thousands of former Party members returning from prison and the Gulags. Indeed, the corridors and back rooms during the Congress were buzzing with rumors and stories of the Stalin years. The military may have also had something to do with it. According to Wolfgang Leonhard, a special meeting of the army delegates on February 23, under the chairmanship of Marshal Zhukov, may have been convened specifically to demand the rehabilitation of the military leaders imprisoned and executed during the Stalin regime.[27] The fear of having to face massive spontaneous demonstrations should also not be discounted. Khrushchev's decision to share the details of the Pospelov report with the delegates was, therefore, as much a preemptive measure against things getting out of hand as it was a personal commitment to rehabilitate the Party's "old comrades." This is not to say that Khrushchev did not exhibit a considerable amount of determination and courage in forcing the Presidium to agree.[28]

This conclusion is supported by other important considerations. Despite its sensationalism, the speech set certain precise limitations on the process of de-Stalinization. To begin with, criticism of Stalin was confined only to the period after 1934. The excesses of collectivization, the campaign against Trotsky and Zinoviev, and the early purges were specifically excluded. No censure of the terror imposed on the ordinary Soviet citizen was incorporated into the criticism of the Stalin regime. The Secret Speech painstakingly avoided the inclusion of any reference to the nation as a whole, leaving the impression that Stalin was not an enemy of the people, but only of the Party. The implication was obvious—Stalin had sinned against the Party and not the people, and only the Party could criticize him. What was needed was a return to Leninism and social legality to bring the Party back to its original state of supremacy and primeval virtue. The influence of Suslov's heavy hand was inescapable. Some commentators have even gone so far as to suggest that the entire theoretical portion of Khrushchev's speech was written by him.[29] As the high priest of Marxism-Leninism—a position that he had fully recovered by 1956—Suslov obviously had a great deal to do with the contents of Khrushchev's speech and with the decision, reached during the Congress, to go ahead with it. He would have preferred, of course, to adhere to the original agreement reached at the meeting in January, but the general mood of the Congress convinced him that it made sense for Khrushchev to seize the initiative and turn Pospelov's report into the Secret Speech.[30] Once the decision was made, it was clearly in Suslov's interest to set the parameters of Khrushchev's speech and retain control over the escalating process of de-Stalinization wholly within the ideological apparatus of the Party. Not only did this make sense in terms of the functional division of responsibilities but, more importantly, it was the only way that he could continue maintaining the unique position of independence that he had forged for himself within the essentially unstable process of Soviet politics.

The notion of Suslov's unique position in Soviet politics calls for clarification. Ever since it was established that conflict was a continuous aspect of Soviet political life—especially during the Khrushchev years—students of Soviet politics have identified well-defined political factions within the Soviet body polity.[31] Some have interpreted this conflict in terms of pure power struggle, others have emphasized the struggle over policy, and a growing majority have fittingly recognized that political conflict in the Soviet Union is the product of the struggle for both power and policy, and that the two are irrevocably linked together. They have failed to recognize, nevertheless, that in a society where even trivial decisions have ideological ramifications, the chief ideologue plays a very unique role, a role usually detached from the scene of factional strife, a role that has to be viewed on its own merits without any reference to the political preference of its high priest. Ideologically motivated societies have always had chiefs and high priests to control and conciliate an atomized populace. Ancient Egypt had its pharaohs and high priests, primitive societies their tribal chiefs and medicine men. Lenin was chief and high priest by virtue of being the new society's founder. Stalin had succeeded to both positions in the 1930's through a combination of terror and the "personality cult." Robert C. Tucker has very astutely noted that power alone was not enough to establish Stalin as the Party's *vozhd'*. To become one he also had to project an image of a Marxist philosopher and high priest.[32] In their struggle for leadership, neither Malenkov nor Khrushchev aspired to the position of high priest; as a matter of fact, neither of them was particularly interested in ideology at first. Captivated by economics and the pursuit of political power, they failed to see the indispensableness of the high priest in a society dominated by the tenets of Marxist-Leninist teaching and the historical traditions of the Russian past. It was not surprising, therefore, that they created an ideological vacuum which Suslov cautiously filled almost unchallenged as the new ideologue and high priest of Soviet society. For the first time since the Revolution, the combined function of chief and high priest was separated into its component parts, creating an inherently adversary relationship between the chief and the high priest and, during the interregnum created by Stalin's death, between the competing chiefs and the high priest. Aloof, circumspect, inaccessible, and better educated than his Presidium colleagues, Suslov projected a distant and feared image of a senior statesman without whose pronouncements the Soviet leadership could not survive. Using esoteric language and incantations couched in generalities, he held himself out as someone who was above the narrow confines of factional strife, someone who had to be courted and conciliated lest he cast a spell or pronounce a curse on whatever the contending rivals were trying to achieve or promote.[33] This is not to say that Suslov was without rivals. Pospelov was one, and so was Dimitri Shepilov.[34] Khrushchev tried to become one himself when he finally recognized his folly and, having failed to achieve this, endeavored to promote Leonid Ilyichev as a counterweight to Suslov.[35] By 1963, it was too late, however. Suslov had entrenched himself too firmly to be dislodged even by Khrushchev.

Khrushchev's Secret Speech did not remain secret very long. Fifteen hundred delegates and dozens of visitors quickly spread the news about Stalin's sins. What had been only speculation and rumors now became the substance of an official report, circulated widely in the USSR and, some weeks later, reprinted in full and distributed by the United States State Department. At least four separate repercussions emanated from the speech.

Domestically, the thaw that had been temporarily restrained by the publishing regulations of 1954 and 1955 now burst out into a full scale flood of anti-Stalinist criticism. The returning prisoners from the Gulag camps told tales of incredible horror and personal fortitude. There was a general relaxation in literature that applied to foreign writers as well as to such well known and long proscribed Soviet authors and publicists as Boris Pilnyak, Anna Akhmatova, Mikhail Kol'tsov. The literary periodicals—*Novyi Mir, Neva, Moskva, Nash Sovremennik*—began publishing short stories and poetry on subjects that had been forbidden since the purges in the 1930's. In September, the much discussed poem of Semyon Kirsanov, "The Seven Days of the Week" eulogized an innovative Soviet hero who had invented a new and feeling heart to replace the iron and inhuman heart of the bureaucrats.[36] During the months of August to October, *Novy Mir* serialized Vladimir Dudintsev's *Not by Bread Alone*,[37] a powerful political novel that praised the exploits of a resourceful inventor in his struggle with a cold, domineering and contemptuous bureaucrat. The criticism went beyond the censure of Stalin alone, extending itself to the Party leaders and *apparatchiks,* raising for the ideological apparatus of the Party the question of socialist propriety again. The divisions in the Presidium were also sharpened. The Secret Speech widened the existing gap on policy issues between the more liberal Khrushchev-Mikoyan-Kirichenko alignment and the conservative forces represented by Molotov, Kaganovich, and Malenkov, laying the groundwork for one more decisive encounter between Khrushchev and the ripening "anti-Party" group. This division in the leadership was especially invidious to Suslov who knew that the time was not far off when he would have to make a choice, or at least give his blessing to one or the other of the feuding groups.

In the realm of foreign relations, the consequences were even more threatening. On the positive side, Khrushchev's censure of Stalin seemed to have satisfied Tito, paving the way for his state visit in June 1956. Tito's triumphant visit to Moscow—his first since 1946—produced one unexpected result. It brought Molotov down from his position of Foreign Minister. Just as Stalin had replaced the highly respected Litvinov with Molotov in preparation for Ribbentrop's visit in August 1938, Molotov was removed in June 1956 and replaced with Shepilov, sending Tito a clear signal that Moscow was ready to restore relations with Belgrade. Suslov participated in the official reception for Tito, but once the formalities were dispensed with, Suslov mysteriously disappeared from the central stage. This was not a vacation, but another unexplained absence, followed by an official vacation in August of the same year.[38] The likelihood is that he was again following his long-established practice of distancing himself from what could be a liability in the years to come, and from the reshuffling of responsibilities that took place during the first week of Tito's visit.

On the negative side, was the growing unrest in the Soviet satellite nations. Triggered by Khrushchev's de-Stalinization speech and the internal demands for greater democratization, the Soviet-bloc nations were beginning to experience dangerous political convulsions that were bound to test the already strained relations with the Soviet Union.

In July, an uprising in Poznan, Poland precipitated Khrushchev's emergency trip to Warsaw to defuse what was becoming a serious threat to the pro-Soviet leadership in Poland. Despite the demands of the hardliners, Khrushchev agreed not to intervene in Poland's internal affairs, allowing the Polish leadership to make concessions to the unhappy workers and peasants. The Poznan rising was for the most part a spontaneous rebellion—not an uprising provoked by factionalism within the Polish United Workers' Party itself. Moscow was confident that it would pass without any serious repercussions, particularly after Wladislaw Gomulka, Poland's trusted Party chief, had convinced Khrushchev that there would be no break with the "socialist order," and that Poland would remain a reliable ally of the USSR.

The situation in Hungary was more complex. De-Stalinization generated unrest not only in the nation, but also within the government and the leadership of the Hungarian Communist Party itself. Premier Imre Nagy openly challenged Erno Gero and the established Party leadership that continued the repressive Rakosi policies without any significant reform. To complicate the situation, the Hungarian Communist Party was clearly losing its hold over the government organs as the new cabinet would show when it was finally formed on October 30.[39] The Hungarian army command was also unreliable. It was rapidly losing control over its forces, while the security apparatus simply disintegrated as the insurgency spread. What started as a drive for a more democratic government turned into an uncontrollable movement for severing all political and military ties with the Soviet Union. To halt what was beginning to look like another defection from the Soviet camp, Suslov and Mikoyan arrived in Budapest on October 24. Both men had been following the Hungarian situation closely since the first signs of trouble began appearing in May when the spreading surge of de-Stalinization threatened Matyas Rakosi's leadership of the Hungarian Communist Party. Suslov attended the May 18 meeting of the Hungarian Communist Party in Budapest, and his support was crucial to Rakosi's remaining in office. Mikoyan was in Budapest in July to oversee Rakosi's replacement by Erno Gero. Both men had met again in Moscow with Gero and Janos Kadar on October 6. Both undoubtedly leaned toward an amicable solution, despite the persisting rumor in the West that Suslov represented the tougher line of the Molotov-Kaganovich faction.[40] As secretary responsible for Inter-Party affairs, Suslov clearly did not want to alienate the other European communist parties with which he had to deal on a day to day basis by taking a hardline position in favor of military intervention. The ideal solution as far as he was concerned was an accommodation, a return to an acceptable form of "socialist order" and subservience, within the framework of a Soviet version of the "cordon sanitaire" in Eastern Europe. To achieve this, Suslov was prepared to make minor concessions that would enhance Nagy's political standing with his supporters. The decision to replace Gero with Kadar was such a concession. Unfortunately, its announcement came too late to prevent Kadar and Nagy from taking immediate control of a situation that was rapidly escalating into an open rebellion. As a final attempt at conciliation, Suslov and Mikoyan made another visit to Budapest on October 29, bringing with them an official statement of the Soviet Union's newly charted relations with the Communist countries in Eastern Europe. Bolstered by the promise to withdraw Soviet troops from Hungarian cities, the statement lessened the tensions somewhat, but not enough to satisfy the insurgents who provided Nagy's political base. On October 30, Nagy announced that Hungary was returning to a government "based on the democratic cooperation of all coalition parties," while the insurgents and workers' councils publicly demanded the withdrawal of all Soviet troops, the denunciation of the Warsaw Pact, and the proclamation of Hungarian neutrality.

It is not clear when the Soviet leadership decided to commence military operations. They had been preparing for this contingency at least since October 21,[41] but the likelihood is that they had to wait for Suslov's and Mikoyan's return to Moscow. The demands of the insurgents and Suslov's and Mikoyan's report were undoubtedly the crucial information that changed the Kremlin's mood from conciliation to repression. Janos Kadar's defection during the night of November 1 sealed the fate, although the actual decision to intervene militarily was probably taken before then, as Soviet behavior after October 31 became clearly more deceptive.[42] The decision was apparently unanimous, despite previous differences. No Presidium member would have dared to vote against intervention after it became clear that Hungary was going to withdraw from the Soviet bloc.

Six days later, while Soviet armor was still crushing the short-lived Hungarian independence, Suslov delivered the traditional October Revolution anniversary address in Moscow. Khrushchev's de-Stalinization speech and the uprisings in Poland and Hungary demanded the establishment of new guidelines in Soviet-East European relations. Speaking in the new Palace of Sports, Suslov conceded the possibility of different roads to socialism, but reminded the audience that there could be no compromise on the question of "defending the gains of the socialist revolution against attempts of former dominating and exploiting classes."[43] If Hungary had seceded from the Communist camp, "it would have presented a threat to other socialist countries," he said, "because it would have brought the capitalist base nearer to their borders."[44] Some analysts have wondered why Suslov was picked to give the October Revolution anniversary address, speculating that his selection signalled the victory of the hardliners in the Presidium. The fact of the matter is that he was clearly the most logical person to do this. He had been involved in the Hungarian dilemma from the very beginning. He was the author of the October 30 "new charter" statement on relations between the Soviet Union and the communist bloc countries, a statement which served as the basis for the anniversary address.[45] He was Secretary in charge of Ideology and Inter-Party affairs, and it was his responsibility to set the guidelines for future Soviet-satellite relations. The anniversary of the October Revolution offered a perfect opportunity for this.

The Hungarian revolution and its aftermath catapulted Suslov to the international stage of news making. Largely unnoticed until then, he had suddenly emerged as the insensitive and ruthless "butcher of Budapest,"[46] the Soviet Union's foremost hardliner and conservative. In protest to the Soviet military intervention in Hungary, the Italian government cancelled Suslov's previously approved visa to attend the Eight Congress of the Italian Communist Party in December 1956.[47] Protests from the Soviet Union and the Italian Communist Party kept Suslov's name in the limelight throughout December, permanently associating him with the suppression of the Hungarian revolution and, contrary to his uniquely independent position in Soviet politics, with the hardline faction of the Soviet leadership. Suslov had tried to play it safe, and had obviously succeeded within the narrow sphere of the Soviet leadership, but on the broader arena of international public opinion, he had suddenly become the Soviet Union's chief ogre and executioner.

PART FOUR

THE KHRUSHCHEV YEARS:
The Time of Accord and Conflict

And I, appealing to our government.
petition them
to double,
and treble
the sentries guarding his slab,
and stop Stalin from ever rising again
and, with Stalin
the past.
Yevgeny Yevtushenko, *The Heirs of Stalin*

We are all servants of the state.[1]

Georgii Malenkov

Lenin created our Communist Party . . .
and the entire people followed the Party.[2]

Nikita Khrushchev

Chapter X

PARTY VICTORY

What started as a year of hope and new resolve to erase the stain of the
Stalinist past, turned into a political boomerang. The intervention in Hungary
precipitated a wave of anti-Soviet criticism, mass resignations from the ranks of
the western European communist parties, and a proliferation of reformist programs in the communist world. Although mild by comparison to previous de-
nouncements of counter-revolution, Suslov's speech[3] on the anniversary of the
October Revolution did not defuse the festering anti-Moscow feelings in the
Soviet bloc countries. The declaration that national characteristics may create
different methods of building socialism did not mollify European communists.
It was clear to everyone that the basic principles of Soviet development were to
continue applying to all communist parties. Within the international community
of communist nations, Tito endorsed the spirit of the XXth Party Congress, but
strongly condemned the Soviet handling of the Hungarian revolution, especially
after he discovered that the Russians reneged on their promise to free Nagy after
his release from the sanctuary of the Yugoslavian Embassy in Budapest.[4] The
Soviet Union, too, did not escape the backlash. Liberal Soviet writers joined in
the criticism of the military intervention in Hungary, while student protests and
*samizdat** manifestos became a common occurrence in the larger cities during
the winter of 1956–1957.[5]

For different reasons, Soviet conservatives also responded critically.
The Hungarian rising and its aftermath brought a new stream of criticism from
Molotov, Kaganovich, and Malenkov, forcing Khrushchev to halt the course of
de-Stalinization, despite the success of his virgin lands project and the record
harvest. Throughout December and January, *Pravda* called for renewed vigilance against the dissenting writers and students, categorically denying that
Stalinism was still rampant in the Soviet Union.[6] At a more theoretical level, a
lead piece in *Partiinaia Zhizn'* underscored the existence of class struggle in

---

*Underground literature. Literally meaning "self-published" in Russian, *samizdat* includes illegally distributed leaflets, journals, and books often appearing in mimeo-
graphed form.

Soviet society, declaring that the Party must not "allow any leniency towards bourgeois ideology and its influence on individuals."[7] Suslov was again asserting his influence on the ideological and propaganda organs. The opposition was also becoming more vocal. Molotov, Malenkov, and Kaganovich continued to campaign for an end to the de-Stalinization process, forcing Khrushchev to make new concessions in order to push through his economic reforms.

Economic questions dominated the Central Committee's December and February plenary sessions. At the February plenum, Khrushchev had proposed to reduce centralization by dividing the nation into economic regions under the authority of the *sovnarkhozy,** and abolishing all specialized ministries for industry and construction. The idea of shifting management responsibility to local industrial organizations was not unsound. The Soviet economy had become too bulky and complex to be directed from a single center in Moscow. However, the political implications of the proposal were momentous. Local economic management appealed to the republic and *obkom* secretaries, but was very unpopular with the central planning agencies, and the heads of ministries and their staffs. Without exception the men in Moscow did not want to lose the political leverage that came with centralized control. Regional management, on the other hand, expanded the Party's power, giving Khrushchev direct access to the republic and *oblast'* leadership where he had always enjoyed strong support. The armed services were also in favor of local management.[8] It was not accidental, therefore, that the Party, the military, and the provincial *apparatchiks* joined forces to push the economic reforms through.

The closing down of the Moscow ministries caused an immediate reaction. Personal political ambitions, ideological differences, and diverging opinions on policies and issues suddenly merged to create a tangible coalition between the pro-Stalinist forces led by Molotov and Kaganovich and the central planners under Malenkov, Pervukhin, and Saburov. The coalition's primary objective was to depose Khrushchev, but its platform went beyond the mere struggle for power. Contrary to Khrushchev's more dynamic program of modernization in foreign policy and industrial organization, the Molotov-Malenkov forces sought the perpetuation of Stalin's strategy of international tension, unrestrained control of ideology, and centralized economic rule.[9]

Suslov remained obstinately neutral, fastidiously avoiding any involvement in the ripening struggle for power. Shepilov, who was removed from the Secretariat during the December plenum, was reappointed at the February session, and Suslov was again put in the precarious position of having to share his responsibility in the field of ideology with him. Shepilov's reappointment to the Secretariat was accompanied by his removal from the post of the Foreign Affairs Minister, allowing him more time and freedom to wield his influence in the

---

*Russian acronym for People's Economic Councils, territorial industrial administrations patterned on the industrial councils originally set up during Lenin's time.

Party's Central Committee.[10] An important result of this was the gradual setting of Pospelov's star. By the spring of 1957, the more aggressive Shepilov had almost completely replaced Pospelov, giving rise to rumors that Khrushchev was grooming him as a counterweight to Suslov.[11] Suslov's and Shepilov's vying for primacy in the spring of 1957 lacks confirmation, but the likelihood that there was a struggle in the Secretariat is not altogether groundless, especially in the light of Shepilov's unexpected backing of Malenkov and Molotov during the June anti-Party crisis.

What is clear, nonetheless, is that Suslov avoided a decisive clash with Shepilov, maintaining throughout the spring of 1957 a heavy schedule of meetings and appearances with foreign communist party delegations. In February, he met with the Bulgarian and Finnish delegations; in March, with the Hungarian and Austrian delegations; in April with the Albanians and the Poles; and in May, with a deputation of West German communists and the Mongolians.[12] These meetings supplemented other activities—attendance at Supreme Soviet sessions, conferences with cultural workers, domestic rallies, and formal ceremonies. Suslov's name hogged the domestic press from February 5, to May 19,[13] appearing occasionally also in the international press, particularly after Tito had singled him out as the principal spokesman of neo-Stalinism.[14] This situation did not last beyond spring. After May 19 Suslov's name mysteriously disappeared from press coverage, generating rumors that he was either taking an extended vacation or was on a tour of the provinces until his return in June.[15] Whatever the reasons may have been for this absence, the fact remains that Suslov had again conveniently withdrawn from the political arena at a time when the confrontation of the Stalinists and the revisionists was about to take place.

Khrushchev was also away from Moscow; he was on an official visit to Finland from June 5 to June 14. During his absence the opposition scheduled a special meeting of the Presidium for June 18, allegedly in connection with the celebration of the 250th anniversary of Leningrad[16]—a celebration that seemed suspiciously out of place in 1957, as the official founding of St. Petersburg has generally been attributed to 1703. Despite the absence of Suslov, Kirichenko and Saburov, who arrived in Moscow later, the Presidium met as originally scheduled, remaining in session until June 22. The Leningrad anniversary was a clumsy smoke screen. Molotov and Malenkov had called the meeting for one reason only—to remove Khrushchev from his position of First Secretary. They had prepared in advance a long list of charges which Khrushchev refused to recognize, aggressively justifying his policies and actions by reference to his domestic and foreign successes. Minutes of Presidium meetings are not published, and no one really knows how the vote went, but it has been generally conceded on the basis of Soviet, Polish and Italian accounts[17] that only Mikoyan and Kirichenko gave Khrushchev their unqualified support. Molotov, Malenkov, Kaganovich, Voroshilov, Bulganin, and Pervukhin definitely favored his removal.[18] Saburov apparently equivocated,[19] while Suslov remained predictably neutral, throwing his support for Khrushchev only at the Central Committee plenum, which followed the Presidium meeting.[20] Whether or not a vote was actually taken is also not certain. The notion that the Presidium was operating like a Western board of directors in 1957 is an unverified hypothesis. A convincing case can be built for an opposing view according to which the Soviet leadership was still acting by consensus in 1957. The procedure used by the Central Committee and the Politburo in its decision-making process had undergone a number of changes since the Revolution. Lenin eschewed factionalism and favored a collegiate form of decision-making by consensus that strived for unanimity. He even allowed the non-voting candidate members to have a consultative voice. By the mid 1930s, Stalin had enslaved the Soviet leadership, reserving the right to make decisions almost exclusively to himself. After his death, the Lenin tradition was restored by the new leadership, but Khrushchev tried to circumvent it with a formal voting procedure in the Presidium. However, the new voting statues were introduced only after the confrontation with the "anti-Party" group. Indeed, it is more probable that the Presidium was still operating on a consensus basis at the time of the "anti-Party" crisis. Nor is it entirely clear if the conspirators had a contingency plan to remove Khrushchev by force. No evidence has been uncovered to indicate that any substantive preparations were made by Malenkov, Molotov and Kaganovich to use force of arms, to say nothing of the fact that the success of such an operation would have been very doubtful, as the Army and the KGB remained overwhelmingly loyal to Khrushchev.

News that the Presidium meeting was convened to consider Khrushchev's fate and not the Leningrad anniversary was leaked out to the members of the Central Committee—perhaps, by Khrushchev himself, or, as Roy Medvedev suggests,[21] by KGB General I. A. Serov and Secretary Frol Kozlov. Khrushchev's demand that the question of his leadership be referred to the Central Committee resulted in the summoning of a Central Committee plenum attended, according to *Trybuna Ludu,* by a total of 309 senior Party *apparatchiks,* consisting of members, candidate members, and members of the Central Auditing Committee,[22] many of whom were urgently flown to Moscow in military aircraft specially provided by Marshal Zhukov. According to *L'Unita,* the plenum was opened by Suslov who "gave a brief review of the facts to those present."[23] There is a degree of ambiguity to the *L'Unita* statement that makes a conclusive identification of Suslov's function at the plenum difficult. The statement conveys the impression that Suslov acted as an impartial chairman, briefing the audience on the arguments and positions of the competing factions. Roger Pethybridge, whose book on the June 1957 crisis remains to this day the most thorough study of the intended coup, agrees with this view. "Suslov was evidently chosen to be the chairman," he observes, "it was he (who) gave information on the quarrel in the Presidium."[24] The selection of Suslov to act as an intermediary is not improbable. Unlike the rest of his Presidium colleagues, Suslov had always maintained a position of non-alignment. He had been away from Moscow, probably intentionally, to escape any suggestion that he had been a participant in a conspiracy that was unfolding during Khrushchev's absence. He had refrained from taking a firm position during the Presidium session, and he was also the most logical person for another significant reason. As the chief ideologist and senior Central Committee Secretary, he had always been looked upon by the Party bureaucracy as their own representative—even more than Khrushchev.[25] He was, as one American correspondent said many years later, "the keeper of the Party's conscience."[26]

No record of Suslov's opening remarks is available, and no one really knows if he remained impartial. All that is known is that the Molotov-Malenkov forces suffered a defeat. The concluding resolution was clearly in support of Khrushchev and against the "anti-Party" group. Voroshilov, Bulganin, Pervukhin, Saburov, and Malenkov all admitted that they had been wrong—only Molotov remained stubborn to the end.[27] Their confessions were not unqualified, however. Bulganin, Voroshilov, Pervukhin, Saburov, and Shepilov admitted their faults, but refused to concede unconditional surrender.[28] There is also some doubt about Malenkov's confession. Malenkov apparently remained silent, electing neither to admit his errors nor defend himself as Molotov did.[29]

The June plenum brought a significant victory to the Party and the Khrushchev forces. Malenkov, Molotov, Kaganovich, and Saburov were expelled from the Presidium, while Pervukhin was demoted to the rank of a candidate member. Shepilov, who had switched during the Presidium meeting in favor of the "anti-Party" coalition—probably because he thought the new alignment would offer him a better chance of replacing Suslov as the Party's chief ideologist—was removed from the Secretariat and from his position as candidate member of the Presidium. Nine new senior officials, six of them loyal Party *apparatchiks*—Aristov, Beliaev, Brezhnev, Furtseva, Ignatov, and Kozlov—the Finnish veteran Otto Kuusinen, Chairman of the Soviet trade unions Nikolai Shvernik, and Marshal Giorgii Zhukov were raised to full Presidium status. Molotov, Kaganovich, Pervukhin, and Saburov were dismissed from their positions as First Deputy Prime Ministers of the USSR, Molotov becoming Ambassador in Outer Mongolia, Kaganovich, director of an industrial complex in the Urals, and Malenkov, who was only a Deputy Prime Minister, director of a power station in Kazakhstan. On the surface, the removal and demotion of the main conspirators looked like an all-inclusive triumph for the Khrushchev forces. In reality, it was a compromise, probably engineered by Suslov. It was only a partial victory—a triumph for the Party, but an incomplete victory for Khrushchev. It rested on a new alignment of forces that continued to stand in the way of Khrushchev's effort to bring de-Stalinization to its full fruition.

Suslov's role in the June crisis has been a subject of frequent debate, and it is worthwhile to appraise it carefully. Without the participation of the

Central Committee under Suslov's chairmanship, the "anti-Party" coup would have undoubtedly reversed the course of reform started by Khrushchev. If successful, it would have probably degenerated into the proverbial *"kto-kogo"** confrontation that was bound to follow the initial transfer of power. The repercussions on Soviet foreign and domestic policy would have been also highly disturbing.

Like all political struggles, the challenge posed by Molotov, Malenkov, and Kaganovich was the result of an escalating conflict between men of enormous and consummate ambitions, men who sought power for themselves, to the exclusion of others, men who had built their own loyalties and had forged the loyalties of others. It may have even been partly motivated by the unconscious awareness of their unmistakably different social and psychological heritages. It should not be overlooked that Molotov and Malenkov were city-bred sons of well-to-do townsmen—the *ancien regime*'s emerging new middle class—while Khrushchev, like the majority of the Party apparat, came from the lowliest of Russia's estates—the impoverished peasantry. The Revolution may have broken the old social framework, but it did not succeed in erasing its social prejudices and psychological predilections. Whether or not Suslov had actually a sense of social solidarity with Khrushchev remains an unanswered question, but it is a well known fact that Malenkov never cared for Suslov, and the feeling was reciprocal. It is a safe bet to suggest that Suslov did not have any strong personal attachments. He had always considered himself above the narrow confines of factional strife, and it would have been very unlikely for him to change this behavior pattern solely out of loyalty or social solidarity for Khrushchev. His loyalty was invariably to ideas and policies, and it was here—in the company of impassioned beliefs and displaced biases—that Suslov had to choose between the proverbial Scylla and Charybdes.

There were at least two major questions on which Suslov was genuinely closer to the Molotov-Malenkov position than to that of Khrushchev—the question of de-Stalinization and the conduct of foreign policy. While Khrushchev wanted to rush ahead and blame Stalin for all of the excesses suffered under Stalin's rule, Suslov preferred a more gradual, selective, and controlled approach of dealing with the "contradictions" of the Stalin era. Like all conservative politicians, he was certain that society—Russian society especially—longed for order, and that rapid de-Stalinization could bring a devouring conflagration to the Soviet political system. He was not quite as unyielding as Malenkov and Molotov, who were Stalin's faithful tribunes during the massive repressions of the 1930's and 1940's, and now stood to be implicated in Stalin's sins. Nevertheless, his opposition to rapid de-Stalinization remained an essential and central

---

*Literally meaning "who-whom," the expression *'kto-kogo''* takes its origin from Lenin's famous quotation "Vopros stoit: kto kogo," usually translated as "The question is: Who shall prevail?"

element of his approach to change in Soviet society. He was even more disturbed about the effect of rapid de-Stalinization on the integrity of the Party and the international communist movement. He was not alone in this. Even Palmiro Togliatti was apprehensive of what was happening in the Soviet Union. "It is true that today they are criticizing," he said, in his interview with *Nuovi Arguamenti* in 1956, "and this is their great merit, but in the criticism there is no doubt that some of their own prestige has been lost."[30] Suslov was also closer to the Molotov position on relations with the United States and Yugoslavia. Convinced that the United States was engaged in an "opportunistic" game of "cultural and territorial imperialism," Suslov resented Khrushchev's flirting with the West, especially in the face of the Eisenhower Doctrine which he considered a direct threat to international Communism. He was also consistently uncompromising in his attitude towards Tito and Yugoslavia, perhaps even less conciliatory than Molotov. The Soviet Union's conflict with Yugoslavia had turned into a bitter personal feud between Suslov and Tito, clouding Suslov's political judgment beyond his usual display of political shrewdness. Certain that Tito could not be trusted, he was categorically opposed to Khrushchev's policy of allowing Tito to drift into what he felt was an alliance with the West.

These were serious concerns, but his principal apprehension went beyond de-Stalinization and foreign policy. Khrushchev's confrontation with the "anti-Party" group was a reflection of two diverging tendencies in Soviet political theory. Molotov and Malenkov represented the resurging spirit of the *Gosudarstvo**, an old notion rediscovered by Stalin in the 1930's, glorified during the war, and molded by him out of Marxism and Russia's historical tradition into a new form of Soviet statism. The leaders of the "anti-Party" group had spent a good part of their active lives in responsible positions of the state apparatus, had fully assimilated the "statist" perception of political organization, and had actually helped Stalin break the back of the Party. They were the technocrats, the state-oriented men, who rose under Stalin, to exploit the human and material resources of Stalin's absolute autocracy.[31] Pitted against them was Khrushchev and his political allies. They, too, had risen to the top during Stalin's time, but unlike the "statist," they had somehow succeeded in preserving Lenin's unbridled optimism for the construction of socialism under the rule of an infallible and benevolent Party. No one really knows how and why they survived during nearly twenty-five years of expanding state power. Perhaps this was because they had spent their entire lives in the Party apparatus, often in distant Party posts jealously guarded against the encroaching power of the state, or because, as the vanguard of the new order, they had succeeded in saving some of the initial enthusiasm inherited from the Bolshevik old guard. To the Party's rank-and-file, they were the guardians of a new consciousness, a consciousness recently acquired and fashioned out of Lenin's legacy of one-party dictatorship and Marxist

---

*State as in *Sovetskoe Gosudarstvo* (Soviet State).

utopia. They were the Party *apparatchiks,* the dedicated Party men utterly convinced that it was they who had built socialism in the Soviet Union and that it was now up to them to rejuvenate the Party and, through it, sustain the interests of the Soviet state.

The two diverging tendencies had a long history of conflict, and the June 1957 crisis was merely the culmination of that surging clash. There was no uncertainty on Suslov's part about where his priorities were. The Party was his entire life, and his commitment to it was total. All of the viewpoints shared with the Molotov-Malenkov group paled before the overriding goal of rejuvenating the Party. It is most unlikely, therefore, that Suslov gave serious consideration to the support of the "anti-Party" group on the basis of his preference for slower de-Stalinization and a tougher foreign policy.

It is also improbable that Suslov ever contemplated backing the "anti-Party" group solely on the basis of pure power politics. His support of the Molotov-Malenkov coalition would have inevitably led to a decline of his career, and logic and caution clearly warned against such an undertaking. Had he done this, and the "anti-Party" coup had failed, it would have been merely a matter of time before Suslov would have been ousted like Bulganin and Voroshilov. If the coup had succeeded, on the other hand, he would have found himself isolated and without any support, at the mercy of a powerful anti-Party alignment in which the turn-coat Shepilov would have undoubtedly forced him out of his long-standing position as the Party's chief ideologist. It was a hopeless "no win" situation for Suslov, regardless of the outcome. Backing of Khrushchev, on the other hand, presented a threat only in the event of his defeat. A Khrushchev victory clearly guaranteed the continuance of Suslov's unchallenged preeminence in Soviet leadership. Everything that seemed important to Suslov—his devotion to the Party, the injunction of power politics, even his personal and social affinities—called for the support of Khrushchev, not the "anti-Party" group. Waiting to make his position clear until the plenum was but a reassertion of his customary pattern of behavior at the time of Party factional strife. It may have even been taken with the approval of Khrushchev, who knew perfectly well that once the resolution of the conflict was transferred to the Central Committee plenum under Suslov's chairmanship he could count on the defeat of the "anti-Party" group. Molotov and Malenkov also recognized the threat of Central Committee action and fought doggedly against the convening of the Central Committee plenum. Using the prestige of their high government offices, Bulganin and Voroshilov tried unsuccessfully to persuade the arriving delegates that the conflict was being resolved in the Presidium and that there was no need for a Central Committee plenum.[32] The opposition knew perfectly well that their game would be over once the Presidium conflict was submitted to an assembly of Party leaders where Khrushchev enjoyed a clear majority among the republic and *obkom apparatchiks.*

The plenum resolution was a compromise, settled largely on Suslov's own terms as the Party's "honest broker." It removed the opposition leaders and reestablished the Party's dominance, but it did not satisfy Khrushchev. The preservation and protection of Khrushchev's political enemies denied Khrushchev the unlimited power he needed to initiate an unrestricted reform policy free of orthodoxy and precedent. Suslov had established the framework within which the Party was to assert its dominance, much as he had done a year earlier when he set the parameters for Khrushchev's secret speech at the XXth Party Congress. As one American analyst had suggested, the settlement "was inherently unstable,"[33] but that is what Suslov wanted in order to maintain his influence over the competing factions in the Presidium and the Secretariat. The Party's victory was, therefore, Suslov's victory, and his prestige and influence soared among the Party *apparatchiks*. According to the official protocol, Suslov now became the fifth most important Soviet dignitary after Khrushchev, Bulganin, Voroshilov, and Mikoyan. Voroshilov and Bulganin were, of course, tarnished carry-overs without real power, and would soon be permanently retired from Soviet leadership. The appointment of Aristov, Beliaev, Brezhnev, Furtseva, and Kuusinen to the Presidium ended Suslov's short-held distinction of being the only leader to possess dual membership in the Presidium and the Secretariat aside from Khrushchev, but this did not dilute Suslov's ability to maneuver. The new appointees did not wield any real power yet. Within the Secretariat, Suslov continued to maintain his position of "second secretary"—it would take another six months before Khrushchev would succeed in placing Kirichenko in that post.[34] Far more significant was Suslov's unofficial standing that rested on his prestige in the Party *apparat* and his control over the ideological organs of the Party bureaucracy.

With the removal of Shepilov, Suslov emerged from the June crisis as the undisputed overlord and high priest of Communist ideology, regaining full control over both ideology and inter-Party relations. He now supervised the activities of Pospelov and Kuusinen, Pospelov again heading ideology and culture, while Kuusinen was placed in charge of inter-Party relations. Neither Kuusinen nor Pospelov presented a serious threat to Suslov's authority, despite later speculations that Khrushchev may have been grooming Pospelov to replace Suslov. Suslov and Pospelov had known each other since the 1930's when they were fellows at the Institute of the Red Professoriat. They had collaborated after Stalin's death in neutralizing Malenkov's and Ponomarenko's efforts to raise the prestige of the Ministry of Culture above that of the Party ideological organs. They were co-authors of the report that became the basis of Khrushchev's secret speech, and they both held approximately the same views on the subject of domestic control of culture. Otto Kuusinen was also an old friend and colleague. A Party member since 1905, Kuusinen was a seventy-six-year-old Communist leader and former candidate for the presidency of the puppet Finnish republic during the war with Finland. More recently Chairman of the Supreme Soviet of the Karelo-Finnish Republic, Kuusinen had excellent contacts and long years of experience in inter-Party work. Assisting Suslov, Pospelov, and Kuusinen were two younger senior Party *apparatchiks:* Boris Ponomarev and Yurii Andropov. Ponomarev, a theoretician who also studied at the Institute of the Red Professoriat and later served on the Comintern Executive Committee, was in charge of relations with the non-ruling Communist parties. Andropov, a protégé of both Kuusinen and Suslov, had headed the Komsomol of the Karelo-Finnish Republic during the war, and enjoyed a long standing relationship with Kuusinen. Suslov had met him during the Hungarian crisis, when the latter was Ambassador in Budapest, liked his analytical approach, and brought him to Moscow in 1957, where he assumed responsibility for liaison with the ruling Communist parties. This was a formidable team of able theoreticians and practitioners whom even Khrushchev could not afford to alienate. Working under Suslov's direction, they now laid down the foundation for a powerful Party ideological apparatus that remained largely unchallenged until the XXIInd Party Congress in October 1961, when Khrushchev promoted Leonid Ilyichev to the Secretariat.[35]

The first thing that the Party had to attend to after the June crisis was cultural policy. The Soviet leadership had been trying to regain control over the writers and artists since 1956, but foreign and domestic crises had somehow always intervened, creating the impression among the intelligentsia that de-Stalinization would be allowed to continue indefinitely without any interference by the Party. A notable aspect of the 1957 drive to curb the spreading liberalism of the writers and artists was that Khrushchev himself became its principal spokesman. Whether he decided to do this to assert his leadership, or to satisfy the demands of a concerned Presidium that new direction in the arts and literature had to come from the First Secretary himself, has not been determined. What is certain, however, is that Suslov's conservative influence was clearly behind Khrushchev's new cultural policy, giving additional credence to the speculation that Khrushchev may have been more heavily obligated to Suslov for the June victory than was usually believed. Throughout the summer and fall of 1957 Khrushchev condemned the writers' and artists' struggle for creative freedom, demanding that *"partiinost'"** again be given precedence and not be sacrificed for "misguided and unruly criticism."[36] Khrushchev did not deny the right to criticize the Stalinist past, but insisted that it was appropriate only when it was in the interest of the Party. The primary goal of socialist creativity remained the same—to emphasize the positive side of the Soviet accomplishment. Less repressive than Zhdanov's and Suslov's directives during the *Stalinshchina*, Khrushchev's speeches carried the unmistakable touch of the new post-Stalinist Suslov who did not denounce artistic freedom, but insisted that it conform to the

---

*Party-mindedness, or party loyalty.

rigid standards laid down by the Party. The main result was that free flowing criticism of the Stalinist past became again less prevalent, eventually disappearing completely in the official press.

Having defeated the "statists" and restrained the intelligentsia, the Party was now ready to take on the last and, in some respects, the most menacing rival—the military. On October 26, Defense Minister Marshal Georgii Zhukov was peremptorily summoned from his visit to Albania, and relieved of his post as Defense Minister and member of the Presidium. Three days later a Central Committee plenum confirmed the decision of the Presidium,[37] stripping Zhukov of his Party posts and passing a resolution indicting him on charges of Bonapartism, policy disagreement with the civilian leadership, promotion of his own personality cult, transgressions against other military officers, and attack on the Main Political Administration (MPA) of the armed forces. The charges against Zhukov were delivered by Suslov.[38]

The reasons for Zhukov's indictment and removal have never been fully clarified. Most Western scholars have interpreted Zhukov's removal in institutional terms, as the outcome of the Party's effort to reestablish its dominance over the military.[39] Contending that Zhukov had assumed a political role which could endanger the Party's primacy, and that the charges brought against him— whether real or fabricated—reflected the attitude of the Party toward the military establishment, they have generally concluded that Zhukov's dismissal was the result of the struggle between the professional military cadres and the Party bureaucracy. An exception to this view has been Timothy J. Colton, who has argued convincingly that personal factors—Zhukov's abrasiveness and lack of tact, his status as a national hero, Khrushchev's anxiety about Zhukov's popularity, and the resentment and jealousy of other Soviet marshals and generals— played a far more important role in Zhukov's ouster than the institutional conflict between the Party and the military.[40] This assessment was especially constraining because it contained the admonition that the institutional view of Zhukov's firing failed to "distinguish conflict between leaders and conflict among groups and institutions."[41]

Both interpretations failed to provide a complete answer. Invariably, they saw the conflict in terms of one view to the exclusion of the other, ignoring the crucial connection that linked the personal factors influencing the conflict with the historical intransigence of the Party to the emancipation of the military from its control. Above all, both interpretations also failed to see that the expulsion of Zhukov was not the work of Khrushchev alone, but that Suslov, too, played a determining role in this affair.

After the June political crisis, Suslov committed the entire resources of the ideological apparatus toward the consolidation of the Party's dominance in all spheres of Soviet life, including the military. The rewriting of war history had been a subject of frequent controversy since 1955, especially after Zhukov had challenged Khrushchev's claims that the success of the Stalingrad offensive was the result of Khrushchev's and the Party's direction.[42] Throughout 1957, the question of Zhukov's cult of personality and war history became even more interrelated. In June, *Voprosy istorii* was censured and its editorial board purged for its refusal to give the Party more credit for organizing the defense of Moscow. On July 15, Marshal Zhukov gave a speech to the workers of the "Bolshevik Plant" in Leningrad stressing the people's and his contribution to the defense of the city, without paying the required obeisance to the Party.[43] Zhukov's speech did not go by unnoticed, producing a widespread reaction among the civilian leadership and the Party-oriented generals of the MPA. The next day, the Red Army paper *Krasnaia zvesda* listed the instructions of the Central Committee's April plenum and, a few days later, cited that "it is necessary . . . to eliminate entirely the harmful effects of the cult of the individual on military affairs."[44] In September, the Central Committee announced its decision to publish an official history of the war in order to emphasize "the role of the Communist Party as the organizer of the nationwide struggle against the enemy."[45] The campaign to contain the growing independence of the military was clearly gaining momentum. Zhukov's attitude on de-Stalinization also did not help. His statements urging that Stalin's role in the repression be brought out in greater detail, particularly with respect to the 1937 purge of the military, ran contrary to Suslov's more minimal and controlled policy of de-Stalinization.,[46] According to the Party stalwarts and the resentful generals, Zhukov was openly subverting the unity of the Party, and it was up to Suslov to put an end to this.

Zhukov left for Yugoslavia and Albania on October 4, and Suslov started immediate preparations for his removal. The preparations included the drafting of the indictment, a series of consultations with Khrushchev and other senior Party members to reach a consensus in the Presidium, and the careful staging of a Central Committee plenum. Relying on the briefings of the Soviet Ministry of Foreign Affairs, Yugoslav Ambassador Micunovic later recalled that it was during this period that the Presidium had ordered an inquiry of military operations in certain regions of the USSR.[47] There is no doubt but that this was done to strengthen the Party's case against Zhukov. To insure that everything went as planned, Suslov took on the job of the prosecuting attorney himself, sending a clear signal to the nation and the military that Zhukov's ouster was more than just a removal of a dissident and uncouth general, but a manifestation of the Party's policy to control the military. It was no accident that shortly after Zhukov's dismissal, the Central Committee began implementing a military reform specifically directed toward the limitation of authority among the professionals, and the strengthening of the Party's control within the military establishment itself.[48]

Suslov's participation in the Zhukov Affair had all the markings of a finale in the Party's struggle against the military, a finale during which the Party permanently curbed the power of the armed forces and subordinated the military to the Party *apparat*. "We were dealing in this case not with isolated mistakes but with a system of mistakes . . . that was leading to a dangerous isolation of the armed forces from the Party . . . tending to keep the Central Committee out of the decision-making on crucial matters affecting the affairs of the army and the navy," Suslov reported, explaining the indictment of Zhukov to the October plenum.[49] From Suslov's viewpoint, institutional factors provided the only basis of the conflict with Zhukov. They were not powerful enough, however, to precipitate by themselves the reassertion of Party rule. Khrushchev's intense feelings of political vulnerability, and the hostility of the Party-minded generals provided the necessary trigger to remove Zhukov, helping Suslov in taming the military and eliminating the potential menace to Party rule. Without Khrushchev's blessing and the participation of the generals, the Party could not have won the conflict and imposed the controls that followed Zhukov's dismissal. Clearly, both institutional and personal factors played a crucial role, the former as a basis of the deep-rooted struggle, the latter, as a catalyst to deliver the control that the Party sought.

The Western press continued to speculate about Suslov's role in Zhukov's removal,[50] but it was not until the XXIInd Party Congress in October 1961 that Marshal Golikov, head of the Main Political Administration (MPA) of the armed forces, confirmed that Suslov played the key role.[51] Why Suslov's participation in Zhukov's ouster was concealed from the public until 1961 has never been fully explained. One Western analyst has suggested that this was done at the request of Khrushchev, to "prevent Suslov from acquiring the reputation of foremost defender of the prerogatives of the Party bureaucracy against the encroachment of military and state interests."[52] Whatever the reasons may have been, Golikov's statement cleared up the mystery, confirming that Suslov was, indeed, the Party's self-appointed protector who took advantage of the existing personal conflicts to reestablish Party rule over another crucial sphere of Soviet life.

> It is not correct to refer to the Socialist countries, including the Soviet Union, as if everything were always going well in them.[1]
>
> Palmiro Togliatti

Chapter XI

FIRST SKIRMISH

The defeat of the "anti-Party" group and the dismissal of Zhukov signified an overwhelming triumph for the Party apparatus. In the face of powerful opposition, the Party's victory had confirmed Khrushchev's dominant position, but it did not bestow unlimited power on him. A semblance of collective leadership continued to prevail, despite Khrushchev's clear majority in the Presidium and the Secretariat. Bulganin and Voroshilov had become largely figureheads, but the remaining old guard—Mikoyan, Suslov, Pospelov and Kuusinen—still exercised considerable influence over Khrushchev's efforts to consolidate his rule. In eastern Europe, the removal of Malenkov, Molotov, and Zhukov passed without serious repercussions. Even the more conservative East German, Czechoslovakian, Bulgarian and Albanian parties saw no reason for alarm. The reaction of the influential Yugoslavian and Chinese parties was also favorable. The Yugoslavs seized the opportunity to improve their relations with the Soviet Union, hoping to receive more Soviet economic aid, while Mao Tse-tung endorsed the Soviet action, temporarily refraining from questioning Khrushchev's new policies. The consensus was that Khrushchev had solid backing in China.[2] On the international scene, Soviet prestige was also never better. The October launching of Sputnik overshadowed the negative publicity resulting from Zhukov's ouster and Khrushchev's attack on the liberal artists and writers, contributing to an unusually calm winter for the Soviet leadership.

For Suslov the settling of the June crisis was a gratifying personal experience. He had emerged from the June plenum as the Party's senior statesman and rapporteur who had presided over seven days of intense and largely unconstrained hearings from which the Party had emerged unscathed by the challenge of the "anti-Party" group. Despite the emotional and political disequilibrium, everything worked out to Suslov's satisfaction. The Party—the central heroic element of his personal emotional commitment—had regained its position of preeminence, and Khrushchev's tendencies toward single leader dominance had been temporarily restrained, if not by doctrinal allegiance to collective leadership, at least by the internal structure of the new political alignment.

The year 1957 marked the fortieth anniversary of the October Revolution. The week after the gala celebration on November 7 was set aside for an international communist conference in Moscow, a global gathering of Communist parties that Suslov wanted to pattern on the World Congress of the Communist International. The Moscow conference was Suslov's show; he had been working on it since 1956, and everything now depended on whether or not he would succeed in gaining sufficient consensus among some sixty Communist Parties sending delegates to the conference.[2] Suslov's concern about the success of the conference was legitimate. The Communist movement was no longer monolithic; political and doctrinal differences made inter-party dealings progressively more difficult, and the question of the "leading role" of the Russian Party in the international movement was becoming a delicate issue for the Soviet Union. During the interval between the June plenum and November 7, Suslov and his close associates had lobbied energetically for the recognition of Soviet supremacy in the Communist movement.[3] The Yugoslavian and Chinese Communist parties presented the biggest problem for the Soviet Union. Because of their mutually exclusive positions on reform and de-Stalinization, the Yugoslavs and the Chinese required very different handling to gain their collaboration. The reform-oriented Yugoslavs refused to make concessions that would compromise their hard-won independence from the Stalinist past. Mao, on the other hand, remained strongly pro-Stalinist, critizing Soviet attempts at de-Stalinization and urging all Communist parties to resist the Yugoslav policy of reform. Conceived by the Soviet Union as a conflict between "revisionism" and "dogmatism," Moscow had to decide which of the two deviations presented the greater danger to its "correct line." Suslov's conservative leanings were clearly against "revisionism," especially the Yugoslav variety, while Khrushchev's campaign against "dogmatism" was tied to his policy of rapprochement with Yugoslavia. In the weeks before the conference, Suslov's emphasis on the dangers of "revisionism" won Mao to the Soviet cause, forcing Tito to cancel his trip to Moscow, and sending Kardelj and Rancovik in his place. Speaking at the first session of the conference, Mao obligingly set the tone by recognizing that the world Communist movement could not exist without a head. "The Chinese Communist Party is not worthy of this position," he remarked, pointing out that the Soviet Union had greater experience in building socialism. "China does not even have a quarter of a sputnik*," he noted with a certain amount of levity, "while the Soviet Union has two."[4] Mao's backing of the "leading role" of the Soviet party was endorsed by Ho Chi Minh, Kim Il-sung, Enver Hoxha, and most of the Communist parties of the eastern bloc. The resolution of this delicate problem did not lead to a wholesale acceptance of Suslov's proposals. The conference turned his request for future global conferences down, and the language on

---

*A clever play on words, as "Sputnik" means companion, fellow traveller, or help-mate in Russian. "Sputnik" was, of course, also the name given to the first Soviet artificial Earth satellite launched in October 1957.

Moscow's "leading role" was also watered down in a compromise resolution that assigned this role to the Soviet Union, not to the Communist Party of the Soviet Union, as Suslov wanted. On the question of reform and de-Stalinization, "revisionism" was officially declared "the main danger," while the definition of "dogmatism" was scaled down to permit its condemnation without causing embarrassment to China.[5] Despite these concessions, the final declaration was an undisputed success for Suslov and the Soviet Union, raising Suslov's stature to the very top of the Soviet leadership, and causing the Western press to take notice of his accomplishments. In November, *Newsweek* proclaimed that "Suslov Could Threaten Khrushchev,"[6] and a month later, it followed through with another article, using the slick title "The Name is Suslov—and He's an Egghead to Watch."[7]

It is most unlikely that Suslov intended to challenge Khrushchev for the leadership of the Soviet Union in the fall of 1957. The risk of taking such a threatening and hazardous step in the absence of full and uncontested support made such a move out of the question. Besides, this was not how Suslov perceived his role. Lacking personal charisma, Suslov saw himself primarily as the dispassionate and impersonal mentor of an ideological movement, claiming leadership through the Party on the basis of dogma and the primacy of the "correct line," not as a charismatic secular ruler responsible for the political reality of the Soviet state. In his perception, his duty was to stress the continued relevance of the Marxist-Leninist tradition, and to protect the Party and its authority from being again usurped by a charismatic leader. He was convinced that his relationship with Khrushchev was a firm one, and he had no interest in dislodging him from the position of First Secretary in 1957.

This was not the way Khrushchev perceived Suslov's position in the Party. Power-motivated and concerned with Marxist-Leninist dogma only to the extent that it legitimized what he perceived as the Communist experience, Khrushchev saw in Suslov's increasing prestige a potential threat to his leadership. As far as he was concerned, Suslov had become too powerful, and had to be somehow stripped of his influence as the Party's undisputed ideologue, or at least isolated from his power base. As a first step toward the scaling down of Suslov's influence, Khrushchev was successful in bringing about several important changes in the Secretariat and the Presidium during the December Central Committee plenum. Khrushchev's protégé Mukhitdinov was appointed to both the Secretariat and the Presidium, while Presidium members Kirichenko and Ignatov joined the Secretariat, raising the number of secretaries in the Presidium to nine and seriously diluting Suslov's influence in both bodies. With at least eight of the nine Secretaries in the Presidium sharing a common view with him, Khrushchev now proceeded to consolidate his power to its full limit. In March 1958, Bulganin was forced to resign from the chairmanship of the Council of Ministers, allowing Khrushchev— like Stalin—to become head of both the state and Party apparatus. To cement his newly acquired power, Khrushchev also wasted no time in implementing a series of reforms in agriculture, education, and procurement.

The agricultural reform involved the dissolution of the Machine and Tractor Stations (MTS), a cornerstone of Soviet agriculture since 1927. The MTS were state organizations that provided organizational and mechanized aid to all of Soviet collective agriculture. They plowed the fields, harvested the grain, and acted as technical and organizational specialists who helped the government to maintain control over the collective economy of the farm. The MTS enjoyed a singularly exclusive status in Soviet agriculture. Their directors and deputy directors were employees of the Ministry of Agriculture exercising both functional and political control over the tractor stations and the entire countryside, including the collective farmers themselves. The idea of being subordinated to the *apparatchiks* of the MTS was never popular with the collective farmers, nor were the MTS always profitable. There was even an attempt to discontinue the MTS. In 1952, two Soviet economists suggested the dissolution of the MTS and the selling off of the equipment to the collective farms.[8] Stalin turned the proposal down, declaring that this would be "taking a retrograde step and attempting to turn back the wheel of history."[9] Khrushchev had been championing the dissolution of the MTS since 1956, but was unable to bring it about until he had consolidated his power in the Presidium. Having accomplished this, Khrushchev was ready to implement the program that Stalin refused to consider. In a speech on January 22, 1958 to the agricultural experts in Minsk, Khrushchev officially proposed to dissolve the MTS.[10]

The MTS reform had a particular salience for Soviet ideology. In a socialist society, co-operative ownership of property—ownership by farm collectives and artisans' cooperatives—was considered a "lower" form of public property than state ownership. Khrushchev's proposal to hand the "higher" form of MTS equipment to the farm collectives, a "lower" form of economic organization whose ultimate elimination was the objective of communist society, ran contrary to the entire teaching of Marxist theory as interpreted by Stalin. Stalin had aired this subject in his *Economic Problems of Socialism,*[11] and Suslov, as the probable editor of Stalin's economic opus, found Khrushchev's proposal also unacceptable on theoretical grounds. To him the sale of MTS to the *kolkhozes* meant the expansion of a "lower" form of production—a symbolic retreat from the socialist goal of full state or public ownership.

In the next three months, an extensive debate broke out in the Soviet Union. Using the sacred language of Marxism-Leninism but, in fact, targeting his remarks at his political rivals, Khrushchev energetically defended his proposal. In the end, the dissolution of the MTS and the sale of its equipment went through as proposed, but not without a certain amount of political damage to Suslov. Like his denouncement of Voznesensky in 1952 and his feud with Tito, Suslov's reaction to the MTS proposal became another stumbling block, an *idée fixe* carried over from the Stalin years that threatened to subvert his political standing. Following his usual pattern of handling conflict, Suslov refrained from a direct attack on Khrushchev, but he could not resist taking a theoretical stand on the issue. In a Supreme Soviet election speech in March, Suslov refused to recognize the theoretical significance of Khrushchev's reform, praising the sale of the MTS equipment only as a "practical" measure to increase productivity.[12] Unlike the rest of the Party leaders who participated in the discussion, Suslov also conspicuously refrained from mentioning Khrushchev as the initiator of the MTS reform. Adding even more oil to the fire was Pospelov's rebuttal a few days later. Speaking also as a candidate for the Supreme Soviet, Pospelov condemned Suslov's treatment of the MTS reform, stating that it was "incorrect" to view the MTS sale only as a "practical" measure unrelated to the established Marxist-Leninist theory of transition to communism.[13] Pospelov had been a loyal Suslov supporter, and his defection was obviously a reflection of the changing "correlation of forces" at the very top of the Soviet political pyramid.[14]

The scaling down of Suslov's authority did not stop with the expansion of the Secretariat and the critique of his position on the MTS reform. Kirichenko's appointment to the Secretariat was also a calculated attempt by Khrushchev to reduce Suslov's stature. Aleksei I. Kirichenko had been a loyal protégé of Khrushchev since the time they had served together in the Ukraine, and Khrushchev was now grooming him to become his *dauphin*. By the end of March, Kirichenko had clearly displaced Suslov as the number two man in the carefully orchestrated Party protocol.[15] Continuing his bid to counterbalance Suslov's influence in the sphere of ideology, Khrushchev made another tactical move. In May 1958 he appointed Leonid Ilyichev, a long-standing critic of Suslov, as head of *Agitprop*. Shortly thereafter, *Pravda* published a Central Committee decree exonerating Muradeli and Shostokovich whose operas were denounced by Zhdanov in 1948 and again attacked in *Pravda* in 1951.[17] Suslov was reputed to have been the author of the Zhdanov's denouncement,[18] while the *Pravda* editorial reflected even more directly on Suslov as editor of *Pravda* in 1951. A disclosure by a Central Committee *apparatchik* after the XXIInd Party Congress in 1962 revealed that the May 1958 decree had been issued on the "initiative of N. S. Khrushchev," who wanted to make "an example of how we overcome mistakes which are connected with the personality cult of Stalin and the *activities of conservatives and dogmatists.**"[19] The May 1958 decree was clearly another attempt by Khrushchev to compromise Suslov.

Suslov's decline in domestic and Party stature was somewhat counterbalanced by his activities in inter-Party affairs. Despite Yugoslav efforts to conciliate the Soviet-Yugoslav rift, Suslov had convinced Khrushchev and the Presidium that it was in the Soviet interest to continue the criticism of Tito and his "revisionist" policies. The hardening of the Soviet position toward Yugo-

---

*Italicized by the author for emphasis.

slavia was connected with the growing threat of rupturing ties with China. To preserve its relations with Mao, the Soviet Union had to yield to Chinese demands for a formal censure of Tito and his experimentation with a free market economy. In a penetrating appraisal of Suslov's intransigence, Yugoslavian Ambassador Micunovic described his meeting with Suslov on April 16, 1958. Having been instructed by Tito to show Khrushchev the amendments and additions to the draft program of the League of Communists of Yugoslavia,* Micunovic sought an audience with Khrushchev, but was referred to Suslov. Apparently the Soviet leadership had already decided to escalate its attack on Yugoslavia, and Khrushchev saw no reason for a meeting with Micunovic.

> I found (Suslov) in his office barely visible behind the mass of papers and books on his desk. As soon as we had greeted each other he started to raise his voice and to criticize our program in sharp terms. At the beginning I was unable to get a word in edgewise. Suslov appeared to be so angry and furious that he was unable to restrain himself. It didn't occur to him even to offer me a seat; he stood behind his desk and I stood opposite him and listened to the bitter attacks on our program. He behaved so angrily that it was not in fact a conversation; I listened to his attacks on Yugoslavia . . ., spoken as though I or some other Yugoslav had insulted Suslov or his family personally.[19]

Nothing constructive came out of the meeting. After a further exchange of unpleasantness, Suslov promised to show the draft to the Presidium, but the die had already been cast. On April 18, a lead article in *Kommunist* launched a heavy-handed campaign against the Yugoslavs and their party program.[20] The Yugoslav Party Congress was boycotted, and a flood of anti-Yugoslav propaganda was unleashed after the Congress, with China taking a particularly sharp position against the Yugoslav program. Soviet backing of the Chinese did not improve Chinese-Soviet relations. Peking had proclaimed the "great leap forward," and a deep and dangerous ideological dispute broke out between the Soviet and Chinese Communist parties in the summer of 1958 in connection with the formation of people's communes in China. Using a long forgotten quotation from the *Communist Manifesto,* the Chinese proclaimed that the communes were a sign of China's "transition to communism," contrary to the established principle that only the Soviet Union had reached that advanced stage, and that all the other Communist countries were still only "building socialism." After months of bickering, the Chinese withdrew their claim of "transition to communism" and the Soviets recognized the communes as a legitimate form of Chinese communism,[22] but the controversy had gone beyond mere differences in

---

*The Communist Party in Yugoslavia is officially called the League of Communists of Yugoslavia (LCY).

ideology, despite Suslov's efforts to moderate the expanding rift. It was clear to everyone that Peking, like Belgrade, had become a center of a new and more radical communist movement opposed to Soviet communism.

On the domestic scene, the end of 1958 marked the final phase of Khrushchev's attempt to consolidate his position in the Soviet leadership. Bulganin was removed from the Presidium in September, leaving only three voting members from the Stalinist regime: Voroshilov, Suslov, and Mikoyan. Suslov continued to exercise his independence, but his political influence had been greatly reduced. He had lost ground on two counts. The expanded membership in the Presidium and the Secretariat jeopardized his facility to maneuver successfully at the very highest level of Soviet power, while Khrushchev's strategy of limiting his authority in the ideological sphere diminished his capacity to dominate Soviet cultural life.

The retention of Malenkov, Molotov, and Kaganovich in party ranks remained a sore point for Khrushchev throughout 1958. He continued to depict Malenkov and Molotov as the disruptive elements in the Party, accusing them of open opposition, especially to his agricultural program. Although demoted, they persisted in questioning his schemes and practices until it was absolutely clear to him that they had to be permanently restrained. Khrushchev had been working on a new reform program throughout 1958, and the possibility of employing it as a vehicle for resolving the festering "anti-Party" group issue made good sense. In September, using it as a principal reason to justify the need for an early conclave of the Party, Khrushchev announced the convening of the XXIst Party Congress in January 1959, nearly two full years earlier than called for by Party statutes—an unprecedented action in the Party's annals. Billed as an "Extraordinary Congress" to consider the draft of the new Seven-Year Plan, the XXIst Party Congress convened on January 27, 1959. It became apparent almost immediately that the First Secretary had personal reasons for convening the Congress. What he really wanted to do was to establish a platform that would allow him to put an end to the "anti-Party" opposition and to dramatize his claim as leader and theoretician of the Party and the international Communist movement.[23] Speaker after speaker attacked Malenkov, Molotov, Kaganovich, Bulganin, and Shepilov for their stubborn commitment "to destroy the unity of the Party," and some even added Saburov's and Pervukhin's name to the list. Particularly fierce were the attacks of Ivan Spiridonov, the head of the Leningrad Party organization, and Alexander Shelepin, the newly appointed head of the KGB. They went farther than anyone else by describing the "anti-Party" leadership as "conspirators," "miserable bankrupts," and "people who behaved like Trotskyists and Rightists." In the area of Communist theory, Khrushchev boldly proclaimed that the Soviet Union was moving from "socialism" to the higher stage of "communism," and that the notion of the "dictatorship of the proletariat" no longer applied to the USSR.

Assuming the role of a doctrinal adversary and leader of the more moderate block, Suslov addressed the Congress on January 30. "The XXIst Party Congress," he warned, "is not a regular Party Congress, which explains why no Central Committee report has been heard at the Congress. . . . Only three years have elapsed since the XXth Party Congress," he continued, "this is a short time."[24] The implication was obvious: Khrushchev's account to the Congress was a personal report and not a formal presentation reflecting the consensus of the Central Committee, nor was there any real reason to convene the XXIst Party Congress. Suslov did mention the "anti-Party" group, but his remarks were short and conciliatory, and he omitted Bulganin's, Saburov's, and Pervukhin's name. Suslov also suggested that there was no purpose in bringing up the "anti-Party" case again, and counseled the delegates to be tolerant, indicating that the group's mistakes were political, not criminal, and that there were no real grounds for their expulsion from the Party. The Party's chief ideologist did not stop with this. Countering Khrushchev's assertion that the USSR was moving from "socialism" to the higher stage of "communist" development, Suslov cautiously demonstrated that Khrushchev's view of "transition from socialism to communism" was seriously flawed, and that it did not have the official stamp of Party approval. To belittle Khrushchev's optimistic assertion that the Soviet Union was moving toward full communism and would soon reach it, Suslov deferred to Marx and Lenin, emphasizing that:

> Marx and Lenin teach us that communism does not appear suddenly, but comes into existence, matures, develops, passes in its development through definite stages or phases . . . The new period in the development of Soviet society will be marked by the gradual drawing together of two forms of socialist property—state and kolkhoz. . . . The process of these social changes will be long, and understandably, cannot end in the course of a seven year period.[25]

Mikoyan's address followed in the same vein. Reminding the delegates that the purpose of the Congress was to discuss the Seven-Year Plan and not the "anti-Party" group, Mikoyan backed Suslov's recommendation to exclude the discussion of the "anti-Party" group from the agenda. Khrushchev's loyal retainers also failed to give him their full support. The majority of the full Presidium members—Kirichenko, Kozlov, Furtseva, Brezhnev, Mukhitdinov, Kuusinen, and Shvernik—compromised by condemning the "anti-Party" group, but refrained from recommending prosecution or expulsion from the Party's ranks.

On balance, the XXIst Party Congress ended in a draw. Khrushchev had succeeded in resurrecting the "anti-Party" case, and adding Bulganin, Saburov, and Pervukhin to the list of "anti-Party" conspirators, but failed in having the opposition's leadership expelled form the Party. Bulganin and Saburov remained members of the Central Committee, and Pervukhin retained his position as candidate member of the Presidium. Suslov, on the other hand, with the help of Mikoyan, managed to halt Khrushchev's bid for unopposed leadership, diffusing at the same time the conflict between the moderates and the more militant supporters of Khrushchev. A further indication that the Congress ended in an unmistakable draw was provided by the decision not to elect a new Central Committee. Neither side wanted to run the risk of upsetting the compromise.

The XXIst Party Congress brought an icy chill to the already cooling Suslov-Khrushchev relationship. The conflict over the handling of the "anti-Party" leadership obscured a more delicate issue. Using the forum of the XXIst Party Congress, Khrushchev had made an explicit bid to play the role of both the political and ideological leader of the Party. Suslov, on the other hand, reacted to this with a more open and forceful political disapproval of the First Secretary than he had ever made publicly before. The result was a stalemate, a venturing out for both adversaries into dangerous and unfamiliar territory that called for coexistence and cautious ploy. It was no accident, therefore, that the next five years evolved into a period of intense contention between Khrushchev and Suslov, a time when the First Secretary and his chief ideologist tried unsuccessfully to reconcile their differences in order to maintain a semblance of unity in the Party *apparat*.

> Let the storm rage even stronger.
>
> Maxim Gorky,
> *Song of a Stormy Petrel*

Chapter XII

COEXISTENCE

The ambiguity of the XXI Party Congress did not prevent Khrushchev from launching a full-scale foreign relations blitzkrieg in its aftermath. 1959 saw the beginning of a new phase of East-West coexistence distinguished by hastily organized ministerial conferences and summit meetings, the opening of the American exhibition in Moscow's Sokolniki park, and Khrushchev's historic visit to the United States. Soviet foreign policy turned toward a Soviet-American *rapprochement,* a new form of friendlier coexistence that marked what became known later as Phase I of Detente.[1]

At a different and more personal level of Soviet domestic relations, 1959 also saw the beginning of another form of coexistence—less friendly, more threatening, and marked by increasing conflict rather than *rapprochement*—the coexistence of the First Secretary and the Party's chief ideologue. They had emerged from the XXIst Party Congress in greater opposition to each other than they had ever been before. Obsessed with the idea that Suslov was a political rival, Khrushchev had been trying to reduce Suslov's authority and influence since the Moscow International Communist Conference in November 1957. Suslov, on the other hand, was becoming progressively more critical of Khrushchev's theoretical pronouncements, his political intransigence, and his campaign to eliminate what was left of the old Stalinist guard. There were also deep-seated divergences in foreign and domestic policy between the First Secretary and the Party's chief ideologue. Suslov was convinced that the United States was the cause of most Soviet domestic and foreign difficulties, and was against Khrushchev's attempts at *rapprochement* with Yugoslavia and the West. Khrushchev's China policy was likewise a bone of contention. Suslov did not share Khrushchev's hardline attitude toward Mao and, in the interest of inter-Party solidarity, was in favor of appeasement and moderation in Sino-Soviet relations. On the domestic arena, Suslov was opposed to Khrushchev's policy of rapid and uncontrolled de-Stalinization, his views on economic decentralization, and his determined endeavor to lift the restrictions in literature and the arts.

Especially disturbing to Suslov were Khrushchev's doctrinal innovations presented at the XXIst Party Congress.[2] The notion that the "class struggle was on the wane" in the Soviet Union, that "the withering of the state process" was leading to a permanent relaxation in domestic societal relations, and that the Soviet Union had been freed of "capitalist encirclement" and was no longer in danger of being overthrown, were antithetical to the dogma of the Stalin years.[3] So was Khrushchev's suggestion that the "dictatorship of the proletariat" was being replaced by a "state of the whole people"[4]—a populist thesis to be fully developed only in 1961. Suslov was particularly concerned about the direction of this last proposition. Despite Khrushchev's carefully worded qualification that the Party was to remain a "permanent institution,"[5] Suslov found something distinctly threatening in Khrushchev's emphasis on the magnified role of the people in a society that was still a long way from reaching communism. As a conservative Marxist-Leninist and the Party's self-appointed guardian he had great misgivings about Khrushchev's suggestion that the Soviet Union should be moving toward a more populist form of government. The legitimacy of the Party, as far as he was concerned, was derived from Marxist-Leninist ideology and the "objective laws of history," not from the Soviet people. The idea that the Party may be made subservient to the nation or its people, instead of the loftier objectives of communist doctrine, was heresy that could not be condoned even in its least virulent form. These reservations were not new. They had always been there, but they had been somehow deemphasized, temporarily submerged in the exhilaration of reinstating the Party's dominance, and even partially excluded from consciousness. Khrushchev's hostile maneuvering in 1958 and during the XXIst Party Congress brought them again to the forefront. It was apparent to Suslov that Khrushchev's attack on Stalinism went far beyond the criticism and the removal of Stalin's excesses, to a more extensive and organic restructuring of the Soviet society and its political process.

On the strength of these differences, news stories were circulating in Belgrade and Warsaw about a Stalinist challenge to Khrushchev, allegedly under Suslov's sponsorship.[6] It is highly improbable that there was any authenticity to the Belgrade and Warsaw rumors. They were apparently prompted by speculations of over-anxious Kremlin watchers who saw in Kirichenko's downgrading at the May Day ceremony the beginning of a newly developing opposition in the Presidium led by Suslov.[7] The real situation in Moscow was very different, indeed. The months after the XXIst Party Congress represented a low point in Suslov's political life. He had again withdrawn from participation in domestic affairs, concentrating his enormous energy on the politically safer foreign and inter-Party relations. Throughout February, *Pravda* reported at least seven meetings and receptions, involving the Hungarian, Chinese, German, Bulgarian, Italian, Japanese, and French delegations, attended by Suslov.[8] From March 14 to 24, Suslov toured the United Kingdom as head of a Supreme Soviet delegation, delivering, by comparison to his usual pronouncements, relatively mild and conciliatory speeches to various corporate bodies in England.[9] Suslov's activities during the rest of 1959 were also largely divorced from domestic participation. Except for the May 18–23 Writers' Congress, which he attended but did not address, Suslov's responsibilities continued to be focused on foreign and inter-Party relations, including a June 25 to July 3 trip to France where he spoke to the 15th Congress of the French Communist Party in Paris.[11]

On September 27, accompanied by Shelepin and Andropov, Suslov left for Peking and the summit conference with Mao. Khrushchev was still in the United States, and Suslov's departure received top billing in the Soviet press.[12] The occasion was the tenth anniversary of the Chinese People's Republic, but the primary purpose of Suslov's early departure was to prepare the way for Khrushchev's meeting with Mao Tse-tung on September 30. Suslov's efforts to pave the way for a successful meeting of Khrushchev and Mao turned out to be fruitless. Peking's coverage of Khrushchev's visit was subdued and unenthusiastic, and Khrushchev's speech was more like a "lecture than a celebration address."[13] In his speech to the Chinese communists the First Secretary emphasized peaceful competition, the lessening of international tension, and even praised President Eisenhower for his contribution to world peace. The Chinese remained unimpressed, and only a brief statement of the negotiations appeared in the Chinese press after the meeting. Throughout the spring of 1960 a hardening of both Soviet and Chinese positions became obvious, and on April 22—Lenin's birthday—the ideological controversy burst out in the open. In preparation for Khrushchev's scheduled May summit meeting with Eisenhower in Paris, Otto Kuusinen stressed, in his official Lenin Day address, the avoidance of war and the policy of coexistence as the "only correct course" for relations with the "burgeois world."[13] In opposition to this, *Jen-min Ji-pao* announced on the same day that "to forget that wars were inevitable was to become a victim of extreme opportunism."[14] Sino-Soviet rivalry had clearly reached a state of open conflict as Suslov's search for ideological harmony with China was being conspicuously preempted by Khrushchev to achieve the more immediate goal of enhancing the political climate for the Paris conference. Using the arguments of Lenin's *"Left-wing" Communism-an infantile disorder,*[15] Party ideologists, with Khrushchev connections, released a barrage of criticism to refute the Chinese position on the inevitability of war.

Khrushchev's attempt at *rapprochement* with the United States ended abruptly on May 1, 1960, when an American U-2 aircraft was brought down after having penetrated about 1,250 miles into Soviet territory. Aerial intrusion into Soviet air space had been part of a U.S. surveillance program since 1956, but Moscow was officially following a cautious policy of refraining from making protests, despite strong internal opposition from some of its leaders.[16] Initially sensitized by an American denial and later aggravated by Eisenhower's decision to accept full responsibility for the flight, the bringing down of the U-2 on the eve of the Paris summit conference created an extremely embarrassing situation for Khrushchev and his policy of East-West *rapprochement.*[17] In the end, Khrushchev was forced to walk out of the Paris conference, cancel Eisenhower's proposed visit to the Soviet Union, and substantially curtail his pro-American policy of détente. The exact position of individual Soviet leaders during the crisis remains a speculation, but Suslov's strong opposition to Khrushchev's unilaterally initiated peace policy,[18] the waning of Kirichenko's influence in 1959,[19] and Suslov's 1960 entry into military affairs[20] suggest that it was probably Suslov—with the help of Frol Kozlov—who acted as the ideological helmsman of the anti-*rapprochement* faction during the crucial Central Committee plenum following the U-2 incident. Ever since Kirichenko's demotion in January 1960,[21] Suslov had been regaining his political influence, appearing again at domestic conferences, and devoting more time to internal affairs.[22] At the April 22 Lenin Day meeting, he had even substituted for the absent Khrushchev, opening the ceremony and introducing Otto Kuusinen, who delivered the main address.

The May plenum that followed the U-2 incident was an important short-term victory for the conservatives and the military. Its immediate repercussion was the undermining of Khrushchev's influence among the leadership and the slowing down of détente. Its more long-term consequence was the gradual build-up of anti-Khrushchev sentiment and the reinstatement of collective leadership which Khrushchev never stopped trying to erode. The changes that took place in the Presidium and the Secretariat after the U-2 incident showed conclusively that support for Khrushchev was not quite as stable and resolute as most people believed it to be. Aristov, Furtseva, Ignatov, Kirichenko, and Pospelov were removed from the Secretariat, and the long-expected dismissal of Kirichenko and Beliaev from the Presidium was also approved. Frol Kozlov was added to the Secretariat, becoming with Khrushchev and Suslov the only other Party leader holding membership in both the Presidium and the Secretariat. Alexei Kosygin joined the Presidium and also became Khrushchev's first deputy in the Soviet government. The May 1960 changes did not upset Khrushchev's overall predominance in the leadership, but the reduction of the Secretariat* and the addition of Kozlov and Kosygin to the Presidium vastly improved Suslov's capacity to obstruct Khrushchev's predisposition to autocratic rule.

By June, the seesawing relationship of coexistence between Suslov and Khrushchev had swung clearly in favor of Suslov. Even Khrushchev recognized this. On June 13, a front-page article in *Pravda* described a June 11 ceremony at a Pitsunda tourist camp on the Black Sea attended by Khrushchev, Suslov, and Voroshilov. Suslov had been on vacation since May 30, while Khrushchev had left Moscow sometime during the first week of June.[23] Khrushchev often invited various Presidium members to his summer villa in Pitsunda—most notably Mikoyan—but he had never played host to Suslov. Whether the Pitsunda communique was deliberately given special handling to demonstrate to the Party faithful that rumors of a Khrushchev-Suslov rift were groundless, as Michel

---

*The May 4 realignment resulted in the reduction of the Secretariat to five full members: Khrushchev, Suslov, Kozlov, Kuusinen, and Mukhitdinov.

Tatu had suggested,[24] or it simply mirrored the reality of Soviet vacation living, is not the crucial element. Far more important was the obvious implication that Khrushchev was either trying to patch up his relationship with Suslov, or had felt that it was necessary to consult with him prior to the June 24–28 Communist party meeting in Bucharest. The staging of the Pitsunda meeting was for all intents and purposes an open admission by Khrushchev that ideological considerations in Soviet foreign and domestic policy could not be disregarded if he wished to maintain peace in the Presidium. The extent of their discussions at Pitsunda is not known, but it is not unreasonable to assume that it covered a broad scope of subjects on which they differed, including the question of Sino-Soviet relations.

Suslov had decided not to attend the Bucharest meeting. He had serious reservations about its success, and preferred to distance himself from what he believed would be its repercussions. Khrushchev, on the other hand, felt that he could not go to Bucharest without projecting at least a modicum of Soviet solidarity on relations with China and the West. The Suslov-Khrushchev meeting at Pitsunda was, therefore, a necessary business session during which the First Secretary and the Party ideologist worked out an acceptable compromise for the Soviet position in Bucharest. The fact that Khrushchev did not go to Bucharest unattended, but was accompanied by a support team consisting of not only Pospelov and Ilyichev, but also Ponomarev and Andropov, Suslov's two principal lieutenants, tends to confirm the view that some kind of a framework must have been imposed on Khrushchev.

The Bucharest conference turned into a fiasco, just as Suslov had expected. Hoping to exploit Khrushchev's vulnerability in the aftermath of the U-2 incident, the Chinese mounted a powerful attack against the Soviet party. Khrushchev lost his self-control and accused the Chinese of being not only "ultra-leftist" and "ultra-dogmatist," but also insinuated that Mao was a war monger "who did not know anything about modern war."[26] The ideological quarrel in Bucharest destroyed the last opportunity for practical diplomacy. Khrushchev returned home in no mood for further debate and, at the July 13–16 plenary session, rammed through the withdrawal of Soviet technicians from China, the cancellation of almost all cultural exchanges, and the termination of negotiations on nuclear weapons. The Chinese, in turn, accused the Soviet Union of undermining Chinese prestige in Asia, sabotaging the liberation movement in the developing countries, and of joining the Western imperialist camp.[27] Khruschev had clearly gone beyond what had been originally agreed upon at previous consultations.

On the surface, the leadership presented a united front, but later developments raised some doubt about the unity of the Soviet decision. According to Michel Tatu, Suslov returned from his long vacation on July 9, snubbed Khrushchev by failing to attend a briefing session at which the latter gave a report on his recent travels abroad, and showed up a few hours later at a reception for the

Indonesian Prime Minister, making his presence conspicuously noticeable by "sporting a Ukrainian peasant shirt without a tie."[28] Details of the report on the Bucharest meeting have never been released,[29] and there is no concrete evidence available on Suslov's reaction to Khrushchev's behavior in Bucharest. Some Western analysts have speculated, however, that Suslov did not take the floor at the July plenary session because he was still smarting over Khrushchev's behavior in Bucharest.[30] There is also a difference of opinion on his conduct after the plenum. On July 26 and 27, Suslov delivered two major addresses to the Moscow and Leningrad Party organizations. Both addresses remained unpublished, but according to unofficial sources, Suslov did not depart from the established anti-Chinese line adopted at the plenum. Stressing the unity of Soviet leadership, Suslov accused the Chinese of bellicose behavior, intimating that future "relations with Peking would be restricted to government channels, while relations between the parties would cease."[31] A more subtle distinction has been suggested by Carl Linden. According to him, Suslov may have been more accommodating to the Chinese after the July plenum. Restricting his analysis to Sino-Soviet doctrinal differences, Linden has pointed out that Suslov saw the " 'dictatorship of the proletariat' turn(ing) from a 'national force, meaning a force existing only in one country, and therefore unable to determine world politics, into an international force, that is, a dictatorship of the proletariat in many countries, . . . and one able to exercise a decisive influence on world politics,' " clearly a more militant position that was closer to the Chinese formula of revolution.[32] Suslov's commitment to the mending of the Sino-Soviet cleavage was also evident in the official Soviet declaration submitted at the November 1960 international Communist Conference in Moscow,[33] in the manifesto signed by the participants at the end of that conference,[34] and in Suslov's later pronouncements.[35] Despite the violence of the Sino-Soviet debate and Khrushchev's forceful plea for disarmament and coexistence with the West, justified by the inescapable danger of atomic war, the doctrine of coexistence was watered down at the Moscow conference, and made inseparable from the aims of international communism and the national liberation movements. The United States was designated as the "center of world reaction." The notion of the struggle against Yugoslav "revisionism" was given more prominence, and the Soviet Communist Party was explicitly recognized as the "vanguard of the communist world movement."[36] Suslov's influence in drafting a program acceptable to the Chinese was inescapable. Two years later the Chinese themselves recognized Suslov's accommodating position,[37] confirming that their complaint at the time of the November 1960 Conference was with Khrushchev and not with the Soviet leadership as a whole.[38]

After the International Communist Party conference Khrushchev was noticeably absent from all ceremonial meetings with the Chinese. Suslov, Kozlov, and Kosygin continued to act as hosts and senior representatives of the Party and the government. Khrushchev missed the gala performance at the Bolshoi theater on December 6.[38] He was also conspicuously missing at the Kremlin reception for the Chinese delegation on December 7, and at the farewell ceremony on December 8,[39] sending a strong signal that he was displeased with the results of the conference. He had every reason to be unhappy. In 1960, any improvement in Sino-Soviet *rapprochement*—even a trivial one—pointed toward weaknesses in Khrushchev's own political position and in his policies of détente and reform at home. The accursed relationship between Soviet foreign and domestic policy had asserted itself again in disallowing Soviet development to move in the direction of greater economic and cultural latitude at home.

1961 brought a new set of problems. Party activity was now centered on the XXIInd Party Congress and the doctrinal controversy over the new Party program. At stake was Khrushchev's "withering away" thesis and attempt to reduce the massive administrative apparatus inherited from the Stalin regime. In foreign relations, the leadership was preoccupied with the Berlin crisis, with negotiations on the nuclear test ban, and the expanding Sino-Soviet conflict. Suslov remained steadfastly on the conservative side of the leadership alignment, backing Frol Kozlov, the Party's conservative opposition leader in the Presidium, on almost all domestic and foreign issues. There was one exception, however. A slight but nevertheless significant change was beginning to take shape in Suslov's outlook on the Chinese question. Prompted by Mao's persisting hostility and Kozlov's alarmingly inflexible and undiscerning support of the Chinese, Suslov was moving slowly but surely toward Khrushchev's more restrictive policy on relations with Peking. This did not mean that Suslov had suddenly reversed his overall position on China. As secretary responsible for the supervision of the international communist community, he was still a long way from indicting Mao and advocating a break with China. However, as a Russian patriot, he was beginning to recognize that Mao's increasingly defying posture was endangering the Soviet Union's strategic position in the Far East. There was nothing unusual about this change in Suslov's thinking. Despite his devotion to international communism and his penchant for doctrinal interpretations, Suslov was a supreme realist who almost always chose caution and moderation to the taking of unnecessary and ill-advised risks. His stance on de-Stalinization and economic reform was largely motivated by caution, and his attitude toward China was to follow the same pattern. In contrast to Kozlov, he favored greater discretion in Sino-Soviet relations. The border clash at Damansky island on the Ussuri river was still years off,[41] but the exigencies of realpolitik could not be overlooked already in 1961. Particularly disturbing was Kozlov's justification for the Chinese development of the atomic bomb.[42] As the Party's impartial senior leader and arbiter, Suslov did not feel comfortable any longer in backing Kozlov's Chinese policy and, therefore, threw his support to Khrushchev and the anti-Kozlov majority in the Presidium.

This conclusion is based on circumstantial evidence, but in the absence of hard data, there is simply no other plausible explanation for Khrushchev's

September victory in the Presidium.[43] For the most part, it is substantiated by Suslov's own subsequent behavior, the gradual hardening of his position on China, and that most intense and caustic attack of his on China that produced the final break in Sino-Soviet relations on February 14, 1964.[43] It is also supported by the Soviet Union's sudden lifting of the 1961 deadline on the peace treaty with Germany, and by the ensuing political setback of Kozlov. That Kozlov had indeed suffered a temporary loss of influence in September 1961 is now a carefully documented episode.[44] In the accepted Soviet ritual of a defeated leader forced to preserve collective unity, Kozlov was not only required to announce the shift of Soviet foreign policy on September 12, 1961, but he was also ordered to do this from distant Pyongyang where he was hastily dispatched by the leadership while the Berlin problem was being aired in Moscow. Suslov's failure to back Kozlov's vociferously anti-Western and pro-Chinese stand spilled over to other issues, to the debate on the economy and the new Party program, to the planned agenda of the XXIInd Party Congress, and to a temporary *rapprochement* between Khrushchev and Suslov. It was not accidental that Soviet press reports in September 1961 often featured Khrushchev and Suslov appearing together at public ceremonies and state dinners in the capital.[45]

No previous congress had been as carefully planned as the Twenty-Second. The reorganization which ended with the July 1960 plenum strengthened collective leadership, trimmed down the bureaucracy, and launched a massive recruitment program for new Party cadres, but it did not resolve the differences among the leadership. At issue were the neglected economic problems, détente, and the drafting of a new Party program based on Khrushchev's doctrinal formulations inherited from the XXI Party Congress. The Seven Year Plan, which got off to a good start in 1959, was running into serious difficulties. The production of consumer goods was still lagging, despite the reallocation of resources. There was also a substantial increase in private enterprise. Khrushchev's promise to catch up with and overtake the United States was not living up to expectations, and the development of the economy continued to be the most substantive domestic problem facing the Soviet leadership. To extricate themselves from the economic quagmire, the Soviet leaders had to either change their foreign policy, consenting to a higher level of disarmament and improved relations with the West, or try to reach the nation's economic goals independently by making even a more drastic reallocation of resources at the expense of defense and heavy industry. The drafting of the new Party program was also steeped in controversy. Khrushchev's "withering away" thesis involved the disposal of the massive state apparatus and the rethinking of the Soviet political process. In practice, this meant that the Soviet leaders had to reach agreement not only on the theoretical interpretation of the "withering away" thesis, but also decide on the future levels of military and police power, on the soundness of soviet political institutions, and on the future function of the Party itself. Because of the intertwining nature of Soviet domestic and foreign policy, the controversy spilled over into the supercharged realm of détente, relations with China, and Soviet backing of international communism, splitting the leadership between the more reform-minded forces led by Khrushchev, and the conservative and orthodox elements rooted in the Stalinist past, including the ousted but nevertheless still active "anti-Party" groupings.

The debate continued throughout most of 1961 reaching an uneasy accommodation by mid-September. Aided by the temporary decline of Kozlov's influence and the unexpected backing of Khrushchev by Suslov, the Soviet leadership struck a compromise on the allocation of resources, on détente, and on Khrushchev's controversial notion of the "withering away of the state." Khrushchev's "withering away" thesis was a particularly irritating stumbling block, but the leadership managed to circumvent it by agreeing on a new formula that was acceptable to both Khrushchev and Suslov. To satisfy Khrushchev, the notion of the "dictatorship of the proletariat" was replaced by the new concept of the "state of the whole people" that deemphasized the coercive and repressive functions of the state apparatus, but legitimized its retention "until the complete victory of communism."[46] Khrushchev appeared genuinely satisfied and even chose to absent himself from Moscow after September 21 to avoid risking any further discussions that might heighten the underlying controversy before the opening of XXIInd Party Congress.[47] The rest of the leadership also seemed gratified that they had reached a consensus on the proposed reform. Despite their ideological differences, there was a feeling of accomplishment and almost naive belief that they were going to the XXIInd Party Congress doctrinally united and ready to put in force a new blueprint that would set the USSR on its long-awaited course of socialist happiness and abundance.

The euphoria was not long lasting. On October 14, three days prior to the opening of the Congress, an unscheduled Central Committee plenary session was convened, reputedly to approve the drafts of the new Party program and Party statutes to be delivered by Khrushchev and Kozlov at the opening session of the Congress.[48] The convocation of the unscheduled plenum on the eve of the XXIInd Party Congress was unprecedented. The Soviet press gave no concrete details,[49] and subsequent analyses by Western scholars have been conflicting.[50] Judging by what transpired at the Congress, the likelihood is that it was called to reopen the festering issue of de-Stalinization and the status of the "anti-Party" group. Why Khrushchev waited until the last minute to resurrect the anti-Stalin campaign remains an unsolved mystery. It is possible that he postponed it purposely knowing that an earlier debate would have polarized the Presidium and precluded agreement on the new Party program. It is also conceivable that the issue of continued de-Stalinization may have reerupted on its own during the weeks immediately preceding the Congress. Despite the unseating and demotion of the "anti-Party" group in 1957, the Molotov-Malenkov forces had never been completely isolated or repressed, continuing to undermine Khrushchev's authority and reform program, particularly in the more conservative circles of the

Party and state apparatus. Molotov's letter to the October 14 plenum was an example of such subversion. According to Michel Tatu, Molotov had distributed his letter to all the delegates as a "congress document," criticizing the draft of the new Party program and condemning it for failing "to link the building of communism in the USSR with the prospects for the revolutionary struggle of the working class in the capitalist countries and for socialist revolution on the international scale."[51] Whatever the reasons for the unprecedented plenum may have been, by the time XXIInd Party Congress had opened, the Party's leaders had shifted their focus from the new Party Program to a renewed and more frenzied damning of the Stalinist past.

The Congress opened on October 17. Khrushchev's six hour report on the first day was confined largely to the new Party program, expressing the leadership's hard-won consensus of the past months. Except for a surprise attack on Voroshilov and a sweeping but somewhat restrained accusation of the "anti-Party" group, Khrushchev refrained from any direct condemnation of Stalin and his surviving lieutenants. This was performed by the pro-Khrushchev delegates themselves. One after another—junior Presidium members, government officials, and republic and regional party secretaries—rose during the first ten days of the Congress to vilify Stalin, Molotov, Kaganovich, Malenkov, and Voroshilov.

Podgorny was first to open a full-scale attack against the "anti-Party" group. Recalling his experience in the Ukraine after World War II, he denounced Kaganovich for his allegedly "sadist" and "degenerate" behavior in 1947, when the latter was First Secretary of the Ukrainian Republic. Brezhnev attacked Molotov and Kaganovich for their opposition to Khrushchev's agricultural policy. I. V. Spiridonov, the head of the Leningrad party organization, condemned Malenkov for his participation in the Leningrad affair, and K. T. Mazurov, First Secretary of the Byelorussian Republic, demanded his expulsion from the Party. P. A. Satiukov, the editor of *Pravda,* and L. F. Ilyichev, Suslov's perennial competitor for the position of chief ideologue, criticized Molotov for his bullheaded opposition to Khrushchev's policy of coexistence. The assault on the "anti-Party" group gained momentum with each day, involving an ever expanding number of conspirators: Bulganin, Pervukhin, Saburov, Shepilov. It reached its climax on October 27 in Khrushchev's dramatic summation—his second speech to the XXIInd Party Congress. Khrushchev again enumerated Stalin's lurid crimes, this time more poignantly and unequivocally than in 1957, demanding the indictment of the "anti-Party" group. Khrushchev's violent attack on Stalin was not unintentional. In the ranks of the Party's higher and middle strata there were still thousands of unrepentant Stalinists who continued to sympathize with the "anti-Party" group. By establishing a link between the "anti-Party" group and the abuses of the Stalinist past, Khrushchev now attempted to eliminate, in one final swoop, the remaining opposition to his leadership.

Suslov's response to this was cautious, deliberate, and notably lacking in enthusiasm for any drastic action against the "anti-Party" leaders. Mikoyan had already laid the groundwork by suggesting that the Party refrain from any further punishment of the "anti-Party" group.[52] Suslov's remarks at the Congress repeated Mikoyan's admonition. Omitting Pervukhin, Saburov, and Shepilov, and following the same line of thinking that he had used at the XXIst Party Congress, Suslov picked Molotov, Kaganovich, Malenkov, Voroshilov, and Bulganin as the principal oppositionists. Without identifying their specific crimes and referring to them as a group, not as individuals, Suslov implied that the struggle against the "anti-Party" group was a closed chapter in the Party's history.[53] The careful phraseology, the ambiguity of the indictment, the perfunctoriness with which he delivered this part of his address were inescapable. It was clear to everyone that he found the attack on the "anti-Party" group not only distasteful but also grossly exaggerated.

His remarks on the new Party Program, on the other hand, appeared genuine and tangible. Leaving no doubt to the delegates that he was still the chief ideologist and senior arbiter of the Party, Suslov gave the program his stamp of approval, but cautiously offered important points of clarification. Implying that there were sharp conflicts among the leadership, he admitted that the task of drafting the program was "not simple" and that there were "theoretical difficulties," that had to be first resolved. These difficulties were "brilliantly overcome," he said, intimating that it was he who was successful in resolving them without making any concessions in Marxist-Leninist theory. In his opening speech on October 17 Khrushchev had glossed over the fact that the new Program was a compromise between his reformist views and the more orthodox positions championed by the conservatives. Suslov corrected the impression left by Khrushchev. Singling out the most important doctrinal assumption of the new Program, Suslov reminded the delegates that the replacement of the "dictatorship of the proletariat" by the notion of the "state of the whole people" did not mean that the prosecution of the class struggle was coming to an end. On the contrary, "the tasks of strengthening socialist legality," he declared, "increase in the period of full-scale building of communism."[55] "The state of the entire people, must unwaveringly apply the means of coercion," he said "against malicious and dangerous criminals, hooligans, plunderers of socialist property, loafers, parasites and other anti-social elements that hinder the people from building communism."[56] The notion of "class struggle" dominated Suslov's speech. He even predicted the expansion of the class struggle on a world scale,[57] dampening Khrushchev's enthusiasm for détente and world peace. He also attacked the Yugoslav "revisionists," labeling them "anti-Marxist" for demanding the "withering away" of the state, prior to the establishment of communism.[58] He was noticeably more accommodating on the question of Sino-Soviet relations. He overlooked Chou En-lai's unmistakable coolness to the new Soviet Party Program and, instead, condemned only the Albanian leadership for their refusal to fall in step with the rest of the Communist parties throughout the world.[58]

The coupling of the campaign against the "anti-Party" group with the more substantive agenda on the new Party Program brought the internal contradictions of the Soviet leadership out in the open. Khrushchev did not succeed in obtaining the mandate that he sought. Nor was there any consensus on the crucial question of what should be done with the leaders of the "anti-Party" group. As Michel Tatu had painstakingly shown, thirty-three delegates favored the expulsion of one or more members of the "anti-Party" group, while thirty-two—including Suslov, Kosygin, and Mikoyan—refrained from mentioning punishment. A third group, consisting of such prominent delegates as Kozlov, Brezhnev, and Polyanski, purposely remained ambiguous, refraining from specific statements for or against expulsion.[59] Khrushchev's disappointment was perhaps best portrayed in his response to Tatu when the latter asked him a few weeks later if Molotov was still a member of the Party. "Why don't you ask Shvernik? He's taking care of it," he responded, obviously annoyed by Tatu's question.[60] As head of the Party Control Commission, Shvernik was officially in charge of initiating expulsions, but was clearly dragging his feet and doing very little about it.

Khrushchev also failed to secure support for his Sino-Soviet policy. The XXIInd Party Congress refused to indorse his condemnation of the Chinese-Albanian alliance on charges of "sectarianism" and "dogmatism." Suslov's and Kozlov's more restrained views on relations with China apparently left a more lasting influence on the delegates. The realignment of the Secretariat created problems too. The dropping of Mukhitdinov and the addition of five young secretaries left Khrushchev a working majority of five to four,[61] a majority that he later found difficult to manipulate, especially on domestic issues. Finally, in a typical application of Gresham's Law, the emotional and dramatic debate over the future of Stalinism and the "anti-Party" group drove out and sidetracked the more substantive issues before the Congress. Delegates spent more time damning Stalin and his loyal survivors than hailing the vision of a bountiful communist society. It was not surprising that Khrushchev's economic and political reform did not get off the ground as planned.

Suslov, too, was unhappy with the results of the XXIInd Party Congress. Stripped of all the ideological abstractions, his speech was a classic lament of a tired and disillusioned conservative who felt that he had been somehow outmaneuvered by the radicals. His reference to "theoretical difficulties," his long critique of the "withering away" thesis, and his unmistakingly uncompromising statement that full "withering away" can occur only when Communist society has been fully built in the USSR and when socialism has won a world victory,[62] in contrast to Khrushchev's more optimistic assertion that radical reorganization was possible in a "state of the whole people," were tacit reminders that Khrushchev had gone beyond what was agreed prior to the Congress. In the past, Suslov had somehow always managed to avoid the risks of open conflict at Party congresses and Central Committee plenums, preferring to work behind the scenes in providing the necessary inner balance within the leadership of the Party. Even in his critical statement to the XXIInd Party Congress, he had tried to conceal the full extent of his disagreement with the First Secretary. This time, he was clearly too angry to remain silent or uncommitted. Despite all the niceties and abstractions of his speech, the message was unmistakable. The chief ideologist and the First Secretary had obviously reached an impasse on the future course of the Party.

In fact, no one was really happy with what transpired at the XXIInd Party Congress—not even those who emerged from it with more power. In a final symbolic act delineating the end of an unhappy era and the beginning of a new stage in Soviet society, Stalin's remains were removed from the Lenin mausoleum, but the antagonisms lingered on. The debate over the fate of the "anti-Party" group had created a permanent breach in the higher ranks of the Soviet leadership. It is no accident that at least two historians intimately familiar with Soviet institutions have suggested that the plot against Khrushchev had germinated in the "corridors of the XXIInd Congress."[63]

Chapter XIII

DELAYED OFFENSIVE

The XXIInd Party Congress severely undermined Suslov's confidence in Khrushchev's willingness to comply with the principle of "collective leadership." He had experienced strong feelings of apprehension before about Khrushchev, but had somehow continued to make allowances and excuses. This time it was different. The First Secretary's obsession with the prosecution of "anti-Party" group convinced him that there was more to Khrushchev's intransigence than just a divergence of views and philosophies. It became patently clear to him during the XXIInd Party Congress that Khrushchev—like Stalin before him—was also trying to eliminate all opposition, but unlike his former master, was being restricted by a reformist regime that he had himself championed. Nothing made this more obvious than the appointment of Leonid Ilyichev to the Secretariat.

Suslov and Ilyichev had their first differences of opinion when they were with *Pravda* in 1949 to 1951, Suslov as editor-in-chief and Ilyichev as deputy editor. Suslov's ill-advised attack in 1952 on Fedoseev and the members of the editorial board of *Bolshevik** for praising Voznesensky's book damaged their relationship permanently,[1] and Ilyichev had never forgiven Suslov for the severity of that attack. It had come at a time when the entire Party *apparat* was nervously waiting for a new Stalinist purge that could have easily ended Ilyichev's career solely on the grounds of Suslov's censure. In the years that followed, their stormy relationship was strained even more seriously by frequent theoretical disputes, especially when Ilyichev became head of *Agitprop* and again at the XXIInd Party Congress when Ilyichev took another disdainful swipe at Suslov for his censure of Voznesensky.[2]

The demotion of editor-in-chief of *Kommunist* F. V. Konstantinov, director of TASS N. G. Palgunov, director of the Marx-Engels Institute K. A. Gubin, and editor-in-chief of *Voprosy filosofii* P. F. Yudin—four prominent purveyors of orthodoxy with close ties to the conservatives—was also a distressing sign.[3] They had been Suslov's loyal supporters and collaborators since 1947, and Suslov was clearly annoyed that they were dislodged from his power base in the Party's Auditing and Central Committees. The appointment to the Central Committee of P. N. Fedoseev was even a more ominous sign. The least orthodox of

---

*Leonid Ilyichev was a member of the editorial board of *Bolshevik* in 1952.

the Party's ideologists, Fedoseev was Suslov's nemesis since 1952, when Suslov had attacked him for praising Voznesensky.

Another sure sign that the battle was escalating was the appearance on November 21 of an unsigned article in *Pravda*. Attacking "certain people who now look ludicrous and pitiful" for failing to "enrich" Communist theory,[4] the *Pravda* piece had the unmistakable markings of Khrushchev's approval. With the word "enrich" conspicuously set off in quotation marks, the article took an explicit dig at Suslov's repeated use of this term to defend the accomplishments of the Stalin period and to justify his own conservative conviction that Marxist-Leninist theory could not be created, but only "enriched."[5] The employment of the phrase "ludicrous and pitiful" was also not accidental. Ilyichev had used this expression in his speech to the XXIInd Party Congress,[6] and its inclusion in the *Pravda* article was an open admission that the poorly disguised polemic had come from his pen. As Carl Linden had succinctly noted, Ilyichev was in effect accusing Suslov of being a Stalinist who had only recently climbed "on the anti-Stalinist bandwagon."[7] In the light of the ripening conflict, this was a serious accusation, and Suslov could not allow it to pass unchallenged. Exactly one month later, he counterattacked, also in an unsigned article in *Pravda,* insisting that the Party had "tirelessly developed and enriched" theory and that without this enrichment the Soviet Union could not have built socialism or survived World War II. Without mentioning Ilyichev by name, Suslov charged him with gross misrepresentation and blamed him for deviating from Marxist-Leninist theory.[8] A month later, Ilyichev made a partial retraction, but the full significance of this exchange of rhetoric remained obvious. It heralded the beginning of a new stage in the Khrushchev-Suslov relationship, a stage in which the First Secretary and the Party's chief "theoretician" had suddenly become dangerous adversaries, vying for influence in the Party's ideological *apparat.* Suslov had been challenged before—by Ponomarenko, Shepilov, and Pospelov—but previous confrontations had never extended beyond organizational and doctrinal issues. The new challenge was infinitely more menacing. For the first time Suslov was being openly stigmatized as a former "Stalinist."

United in a common cause to rejuvenate the Party and establish a less autocratic foundation for Soviet polity after the death of Stalin, Suslov and Khrushchev had carried on a stormy relationship from the very beginning of their collaboration. Causing this were important theoretical and practical differences that divided them on Soviet policy toward China and Yugoslavia, on détente, on the course of de-Stalinization, on domestic political and economic reform, and on the treatment of the "anti-Party" group. There were also frequent and serious disagreements on Party standards, and on how it was best to achieve them.

These disagreements exacerbated the stormy relationship of the First Secretary and the chief ideologue, but even more fundamental to their conflict were certain behavioral disparities that exhibited themselves in deep-seated differences in personality and diametrically opposing styles of leadership. Almost everyone who knew them agreed that Khrushchev and Suslov represented the two opposing extremes of the personality spectrum so meticulously described in the psychological novels of Dostoevsky and Saltykov-Shchedrin—the primitive aggressiveness of the Russian peasantry and the more compulsive passivity of the educated elite. Khrushchev's overflowing vitality, his tendency to rush ahead, his spells of manic omnipotence, his spontaneity, his optimistic belief in unlimited achievement, and his anarchic commitment to the eradication of restrictions were pitted against Suslov's melancholy, his caution and suspicion, his moral and doctrinal masochism, and his grudging idealization of a strong and arbitrary authority as the only safeguard against the excesses of what has been loosely characterized as the anarchic Russian nature. No two men working together could have been more different than Suslov and Khrushchev. Compulsive, analytical, introspective, enamored with channels of authority, and distressingly slow in making decisions, Suslov found it extremely difficult to work with Khrushchev whose directness, informality, intolerance for protocol, and preference for face-to-face improvisations ran contrary to everything he had always considered as a prerequisite of public life. As if this were not enough there were also glaring conflicts in their life styles. A shy and retiring teetotaler whose family remained largely anonymous, Suslov shunned limelight, deplored ostentation, and preferred to spend his weekends and long vacations in the protected isolation of his *dacha* or his Black sea retreat. A heavy drinker and an avowed merrymaker, Khrushchev, on the other hand, took short vacations almost always accompanied by his cronies, promoted nepotism, and enjoyed the hustle and bustle of Moscow's high life. How they coexisted this long without cannibalizing each other politically can be explained only by the security of their entrenched positions and their common dedication to the Communist cause. But even entrenched positions and common causes fall prey to the ravages of time; theirs were no exception. By 1962, both Suslov and Khrushchev had obviously tired of each other and were looking for ways to disengage.

In the unfolding confrontation, Khrushchev clearly assumed the more militant position—especially during 1962. Suslov again withdrew from the home political arena, concentrating on inter-Party relations,[9] and venturing only occasionally into domestic affairs. It was Ilyichev, for example—not Suslov— who delivered the key address to the All-Union Conference on Ideological Work on December 24.[10] Suslov attended the meeting, but did not participate, and the *Pravda* photograph of the conference's principals showed a grim looking Suslov sitting next to Ilyichev.[11] Suslov did make one foray into the field of ideology in 1962. On January 30, 1962, he delivered an important address on "the problems in the social sciences."[12] Khrushchev did not attend, and the introduction was made by Kozlov. The address resembled Ilyichev's speech given one month earlier, but there were two notable statements on de-Stalinization and the Sino-Soviet dispute. Suslov absolved the present leaders from any complicity in Stalin's crimes, emphasizing that Stalin's crimes had been "hidden from the Party" until the purge of Beria in 1953, and that the new leadership began correcting the abuses "immediately" after Stalin's death.[13] He also offered a new and less hospitable critique of the Chinese position on Communist doctrine. In a section entitled "Struggle against the bourgeois ideology during the present stage," he admitted that "dogmatism" was as dangerous as "revisionism.*" Never mentioning Mao or the Chinese by name, Suslov asserted that "dogmatism is a most dangerous form of isolation of theory from practice," indicating that the Chinese form of communism was, indeed, a dangerous aberration.[14] This statement was particularly significant when viewed against an earlier comment in the same address, which lessened the danger of "revisionism." "Several years back revisionism acquired an especially dangerous character," Suslov declared, "however, as the result of powerful blows struck against it first of all by the CPSU and the other fraternal parties, it suffered ideological defeat. But the danger of revisionism remains . . . "[15] Suslov's thinking on the Sino-Soviet dispute was clearly undergoing an important transformation in the direction of a harder line toward Mao and the Chinese Communists, and its implication was obvious. While Tito and the Yugoslav Communists continued to present a problem, Mao and the Chinese Communists were also becoming a great danger to continued Soviet control of the international Communist movement.[16] There was another notable innovation in Suslov's address, an innovation that became more obvious only many years later. Admonishing the audience to standardize the teaching of social sciences, Suslov suggested that the basic course should "also include an examination of the fundamental historical stages, the theory of the international labor movement, and the practice of building socialism, but that the central theme of the course should be the problems of building communism."[17] Suslov's discussion of the "problems of building communism" was still years away from the development of Brezhnev's theory of "mature socialism," but it was clear that the Chief Ideologist was thinking already in 1961 how it was best to adapt Lenin's scheme of reaching communism to existing Soviet conditions.

The January 1962 speech was Suslov's last known direct public involvement in Party ideology and domestic cultural affairs until the fall of Khrushchev. Throughout 1962 and 1963, Suslov maintained a generally low profile as a Party leader, avoiding speaking engagements even on questions of inter-Party relations. Except for the November 6, 1962 address to the VIII Congress of the Bulgarian Communist Party in Sofia, he remained unusually silent until February 14, 1964 when he delivered the Party's crushing attack on the Chinese at the February Central Committee plenum.[18] This did not mean that he had

---

*As used in this context, "dogmatism" refers to Mao Tse-tung and the more dogmatic Chinese practice of Communism in the 1950's and 1960's, and "revisionism" to Tito and the more reform-minded Yugoslav variety of Communism.

somehow suddenly faded away from the Soviet scene. Press reports of this period portray a flurry of appearances by Suslov at receptions, concerts, ceremonies, public rallies, and meetings with foreign delegations,[19] but a strange silence had apparently set itself on any public pronouncements.

No one will probably ever know for certain why Suslov chose to declare a moratorium on his speaking engagements, but the likelihood is that he had simply decided to keep silent until the domestic political climate had improved sufficiently and he had again rebuilt his political fences in the Party *apparat*. Kozlov had largely taken over the duties of the opposition leader, and Suslov was satisfied that the latter would continue throwing roadblocks in Khrushchev's path to slow down the First Secretary's enthusiasm for unlimited reform. The past five years had been especially taxing for Suslov. He had never been particularly strong, and the physical and psychological strain of frequent travel, long hours, and emotionally exhausting confrontations was showing in his health. A reduction in activity was obviously warranted before it was too late. The years 1962 and 1963 were also an immensely turbulent and momentous period in Soviet history, and discretion seemed to be again the best line of defense.

On the cultural scene, in the wake of the XXIInd Party Congress, Yevgenii Yevtushenko had published his "Stalin's Heirs," calling upon the Soviet government "to double, to triple" the guard at Stalin's grave indirectly pointing a finger at Suslov and Kozlov as the remaining Stalinists in the Soviet leadership.[20] In January, *Novyi Mir* unleashed its attack on Kochetov's *The Obkom Secretary,* labeling it a "camouflaged neo-Stalinist plot,"[21] and in September, Khrushchev approved the publication of Solzhenitsyn's *One Day in the Life of Ivan Denisovich.* In the field of art, the venerable critic Mikhail Alpatov broke new ground in February 1962 by defending modern art, and especially abstractionism.[22] Unfortunately, the liberal flowering of the arts did not last and, in the winter of 1962–1963, the Party launched an enormous public campaign to bring the writers and artists again under its rigid control. Nikita Khrushchev had made a surprise visit to the Manezh gallery in December 1962, found the abstract exhibit "degenerate," and, in an outburst of profanity, ordered Ilyichev and Furtseva to put an end to the unwanted "liberalism."[23]

In the political arena, the years 1962 and 1963 were especially consequential. The U.S.-Soviet confrontation over the Cuban Missile crisis left Khrushchev with an immense political liability at home, forcing him to curtail the pace of his domestic reform and to reverse himself on the issue of de-Stalinization. In February 1963 there were even rumors that his resignation was being considered in the Presidium.[24] The Sino-Soviet conflict was also not scaling down. On the contrary, it was escalating, despite Kozlov's efforts to appease Mao. On April 10, Kozlov suffered a serious stroke, permanently withdrawing from the day-to-day activity in the Presidium.[25] Kozlov's misfortune was Khrushchev's gain. By the middle of 1963 Khrushchev had largely regained his prestige, and was again pushing through the recently approved program for the bifurcation of the Party. Kozlov's illness had another consequence. It catapulted Brezhnev and Podgorny into the ranks of the senior leadership, positioning them as Khrushchev's rival heirs. In East-West relations, July witnessed the negotiations of the United States, Great Britain, and the Soviet Union that led to the July 25 limited test ban agreement, and to the final break with China over her insistence to acquire nuclear weapons.

These were, indeed, momentous events, and Suslov could not have refused to participate in them, even if he wanted. The much publicized Soviet military defector Oleg Penkovsky had identified him as a member of the Supreme Military Council,[26] intimating that he had probably taken part in the Soviet discussions during the Cuban crisis. Suslov was on vacation until September 23, but must have caught the most crucial phase of the crisis on his return to Moscow. Kozlov's illness was also a source of concern. Some Western analysts have even suggested that Suslov may have contemplated a coup against Khrushchev on the advice of the ailing Kozlov.[27] Khrushchev's Party bifurcation plan must have also been a sore point. The notion of dividing the Party apparatus into two separate components with footing in agriculture and industry was highly controversial from a theoretical point of view, and it was probably no accident that the chief ideologist was conveniently absent from Moscow during the November 1962 plenum that considered this question. Suslov knew perfectly well that a strict Marxist-Leninist interpretation of Khrushchev's plan would have labeled it a violation of Lenin's principle of "the alliance of workers and peasants." Whether or not he had actually endorsed it remains unclear to this day, although there is some indication that he may have gone along with it. His November 7, 1962 speech to the Bulgarian Party Congress is the only hard evidence available on this question. In it Suslov acknowledged the existence of the Party bifurcation program, but did not elaborate on its legitimacy and merits.[28] His reaction to the oscillating de-Stalinization and re-Stalinization campaigns in literature and the arts was equally cautious. He had conspicuously avoided these campaigns, allowing Ilyichev to spearhead the 1963 repression of the artists and writers. One action that he was reputed to have taken in 1962 was to have opposed the approval of Solzhenitsyn's *One Day in the Life of Ivan Denisovich,* inspiring numerous stories about how Khrushchev had castigated him for his Stalinism.[29] One story is particularly suggestive of the growing hostility between Suslov and Khrushchev. Pointing his finger at the chief ideologist, Khrushchev is reputed to have cried out in anger: "How can we fight against remnants of the cult of personality if Stalinists of this type are still in our midst?"[30]

Very little else can be added to the rather sparse inventory of Suslov's activities from 1962 to early 1964. Even if we concede that Suslov's unprecedented restraint may have been partially brought about by his long and unexplained illness in the fall of 1963,[31] it is hard to conceive how the Secretariat's most senior official could have been that insulated from the official Soviet press unless he had devised this himself or was being purposely excluded from coverage. That his influence may have been deliberately subverted is brought out by a noteworthy occurrence in early 1964. On February 12, 1964, Suslov delivered a report to the Central Committee plenum on the unity of the International Communist movement.[32] Short of outright excommunication, the report was a devastating condemnation of Chinese communism and its leaders who, according to Suslov, now "represented the main danger" to the world Communist movement.[33] Because of its fiercely anti-Chinese formulation and Suslov's record of moderation on relations with China, the report became immediately an object of considerable doubt and conjecture. It did not take much to convince the Moscow rumor mill that it was not written by Suslov, but by someone else in Khrushchev's office.[34] The profusion of compliments paid to Khrushchev, the sharpness of the attack on the "anti-Party" group, the detailed reference to Stalin's crimes, the writing style, and the absence of those unmistakably Suslovian abstractions seemed entirely out of character, suspiciously pointing to someone else's authorship. This commentary was completely sound, of course, but it did not take into consideration that Suslov's view on Sino-Soviet relations had gone through a long evolutionary process since the 1957 Moscow International Conference. From an undisputedly hospitable view of the Chinese position in 1957, Suslov had gradually moved through a more cautious posture of withholding his support for Kozlov's strongly pro-Chinese policy during the debates preceding the XXIInd Party Congress, to his January 1962 admission that "dogmatism" was at least as dangerous as "revisionism," and finally to the February 14, 1964 acknowledgment that it was the "main danger" to world Communism. Like Father Joseph who had only gradually acquiesced in Richelieu's political claim that in the pursuit of France's divine mission it was more important to break the power of Hapsburg Spain and Austria than to uphold the unity of the Counter Reformation, Suslov, too, came to recognize that Soviet geopolitical considerations outweighed the demands of world Communist solidarity. Had he presented his own report—true to his innate preference for equivocation—his phraseology would have been probably more ambiguous, more moderate, and more extensively couched in abstractions to allow for a greater scope of possible interpretations. It would not have lacked, however, the fundamental affirmation it contained that Chinese intransigence was posing a threat to the Soviet union and the Soviet-inspired Communist movement. By 1964, Suslov had definitely reached the conclusion that the Chinese could no longer be conciliated. Whether or not the report was actually written by him has never been fully established, and Suslov has apparently never made an effort to deny it. What is clear though is that he had obviously fallen victim to the Soviet leadership's accepted practice of selecting the opposition leader to deliver the majority report in the interest of projecting Party unity. But even in this there was a touch of irony and typical Suslovian aversion to the risk of harmful publicity. It was rumored that he had agreed to accept responsibility for the report only on the condition that it would remain unpublished.[35]

If there is a conclusion to be derived from the scrutiny of Suslov's activities after the XXIInd Party Congress, it is that he had again resolved to exercise extreme caution, avoiding thereby any possibility of an open confrontation with Khrushchev. This was born out by almost everything that he did from 1962 to 1964—his more than usual restraint in dealing with the other members of the Presidium and the Secretariat, his increased cautiousness in doctrinal matters, his avoidance of speaking engagements, and the reduction in his press coverage. It was even born out by the official listings in the Soviet press. Suslov's name had gradually slipped one or two notches in the official Soviet protocol lineup from second or third position after Khrushchev to fourth or fifth place.[36] The years 1962 to 1963 were 1937 and 1953 all over again. Prompted by the insecurity of the escalating conflict with Khrushchev and the reality of an increasingly energy-draining illness,[37] he had again pulled his horns in, distancing himself—as much as his official position allowed him—from the day to day activities of Soviet political life. It is even possible that he had used this time— especially the period of his illness in 1963—for the express purpose of developing a scheme of action to reduce Khrushchev's expanding authority, or even to remove him altogether.

The story of Khrushchev's removal from Soviet leadership has been told countless times,[38] but no one has really succeeded so far in establishing the exact time frame or cause of his fall. Some analysts have gone back as far as the XXIInd Party Congress to discover the origins of the anti-Khrushchev plot,[39] others have looked back to Kozlov's illness, intimating that it was Kozlov who counseled Suslov to remove the First Secretary from his post. Roy Medvedev has suggested that a discussion of Khrushchev's removal took place in September 1964 while a group of Presidium and Central Committee members were on a hunting and fishing trip as guests of Stavropol Kraikom First Secretary F. D. Kulakov.[40] Confining their analysis mainly to Khrushchev's last days in power, the majority of Western analysts have concluded that the plot could not have succeeded unless it had suddenly materialized during Khrushchev's absence in October 1964.[41] The analysis of the causes has been equally diverging. In their search for an all-embracing explanation, some scholars have attributed Khrushchev's fall to his China and German policies, or looked to the anticipated November reform and the Party purge that was rumored to follow it. Others, delving into the entire post-Stalin period, have itemized a succession of Khrushchev's blunders suggesting that he was toppled for a combination of reasons— among them, his China and German policy, the Cuban missile crisis, the inefficiency of his agricultural scheme, his policy of down-grading the military, his persistent flirting with the United States, and his policy toward the Third World. To a lesser degree they have also blamed the Penkovsky trial, the disastrous 1963 harvest, and the widespread outbreak of rioting—especially the intense rioting in Novocherkassk. There was likewise a difference of opinion on who was the initiator and coordinator of the plot. At least two Western analysts have ascribed the primary responsibility for Khrushchev's ouster to Brezhnev, arguing that the coup could not have succeeded without his solid connections with the Army and the KGB.[42] Michel Tatu, on the other hand, using a variety of sources, has generally concluded that it was Suslov who was the guiding spirit behind the plot.[43]

The full story will probably never be known. The principal participants have died leaving no personal memoirs or last minute confessions of their roles. Even Khrushchev has remained silent. Maintaining Lenin's stricture on Party secrecy, he has dutifully chosen to end his memoirs with 1962, escaping thereby the painful discussion of how and why he was deposed two years later.[44] To piece the full story one has to rely, therefore, almost exclusively on fragmentary evidence. Few events in history just happen unexpectedly or as a result of some immediate and suddenly compelling causes. Even natural disasters—floods, storms, and earthquakes—find their origins in more distant and elemental causes that often take a long time to evolve. Exploring the causes of the Russian revolution, Edward H. Carr has convincingly noted "that the historian deals in a multiplicity of causes."[45] This admonition applies equally to Khrushchev's ouster. It, too, was bound in a multiplicity of causes that conspired together to erode Khrushchev's authority, causes that often transcended power politics and specific issues, and originated in personal conflicts and the unique character of Khrushchev's style of leadership.

In this connection, of particular significance were Khrushchev's appalling crudeness and tactless relations with his colleagues, his lack of discretion, his insatiable tendency to exaggerate, and his persistent attempts to subvert the leadership's search for the holy grail of collectivity in decision-making. As if this were not enough, there was also a consensus building up among the leadership that a new cult of personality, shamelessly blown out of proportion by a growing number of eulogizers of Khrushchev, was turning itself into an unwanted repetition of the same kind of adulation that was paid to Stalin. Khrushchev did not discourage this outpouring of excessive veneration, and there is every indication that he actually thrived on it.

The First Secretary's penchant for meddling and direct diplomacy through his own kitchen cabinet was also a source of constant dissatisfaction. The senior Party *apparatchiks* and technocrats strongly resented the interference of his son-in-law A. I. Adzhubei, the editor-in-chief of *Izvestia,* P. A. Satiukov, the editor-in-chief of *Pravda,* M. A. Kharlmanov, the director of Soviet radio-television, and V. I. Polyakov, the zealous and highly controversial agricultural expert. Khrushchev had his supporters, of course—in the Presidium and the Central Committee, and in the republic and regional organizations—but a powerful opposition momentum was building up among the higher levels of Soviet leadership, especially after the Cuban missile crisis. With each new year and each new blunder the list of grievances multiplied, as a growing number of important officials found themselves increasingly frustrated by the oscillating instability and antics of the First Secretary. Thus, it is not surprising that, by 1964, a loosely-knit but clearly defined coalition began to form under the leadership of Suslov, Brezhnev, and Kosygin.

Each of these men had his own particular reasons for seeing Khrushchev's authority reduced. Suslov was profoundly disturbed by Khrushchev's unwillingness to pursue a uniform foreign policy that would promote international communism and openly oppose the Western coalition in Europe and the Third World. As the defender of the Party's ideological purity, he was convinced that the First Secretary was corrupting Marxism-Leninism. He was also genuinely concerned about the direction of the domestic changes, especially the reorganization of the Party and the economic reforms. But his disappointment with Khrushchev went beyond these issues, to ten years of see-sawing political relations and intense personal conflicts, to the bitter realization that he and Khrushchev could not coexist any longer, and that the First Secretary wanted to discard him in favor of a more pliable and opportunistic chief ideologue who would endorse his programs and not act as an adversary. The appointment of Ilyichev to the directorship of the newly created Ideological Commission* was, as far as he was concerned, the final *coup de grace* administered by Khrushchev against his long-standing preeminence in the field of Soviet ideology. Brezhnev's disillusionment with the First Secretary arose from disagreements over defense policy. Brezhnev was strongly against the signing of an agreement with West Germany, and against the reallocation of resources from the "steel eaters" to consumer goods. He was in favor of a more comprehensive Soviet defense posture, and his speeches often reflected this. He was also seriously disturbed by the promotion of Podgorny whose range of responsibilities continued to expand in 1964. Especially galling to Brezhnev was Khrushchev's demotion of Vladimir Shcherbitsky, Brezhnev's old colleague and protégé in the Ukraine. By rights, Shcherbitsky should have been made chief of the Ukrainian party to replace Podgorny when the latter was transferred to Moscow, but Khrushchev appointed instead Pyotr Shelest, stripping Shcherbitsky of his candidate membership in the Presidium and depriving Brezhnev of an important supporter in the Ukraine. At a more intimate and psychological level, Brezhnev may have also experienced a heightening of hostility against Khrushchev for another reason. The First Secretary was his political father and mentor, and it would not have been unusual for Brezhnev to have developed out of this relationship strong feelings of intensified rivalry over the years. Kosygin's disenchantment with Khrushchev resulted from less subtle causes. Although he often supported Khru-

---

*The Ideological Commission of the Central Committee was created in 1963 to assist the recently bifurcated Party in supervising the ideological development and education of its workers and peasant cadres.

shchev's economic schemes—particularly the market-oriented economic programs recommended by Liberman—he was the Soviet Union's consummate technocrat. His primary interest was to improve Soviet productivity and long term planning—two cardinal objectives that almost always were foiled by Khrushchev's "harebrained" method of management.

The "troika" must have also had the support of Marshal Malinovsky, the Soviet Union's formidable Minister of Defense and Khrushchev's old friend from the days of World War II. In recent years Malinovsky had been increasingly critical of Khrushchev's radical views on modern war, and often indicated his displeasure publicly about how little support he received for the building of the conventional ground forces. The trio could probably also count on the help of Aleksandr Shelepin, the recently appointed candidate member in the Presidium, who still exercised considerable influence on the KGB through his former colleague Vladimir Semichastny, the new head of the secret police. Moreover, Brezhnev had extensive personal control over both the KGB and the military through patronage, and could bring considerable pressure on a number of key professionals in the uniformed services.

Of Khrushchev's three principal faultfinders, Suslov was least interested in taking on the job of the First Secretary. He had never envisaged himself as a charismatic leader, and was not motivated at this stage of his life in taking on the heavy responsibilities of the chief executive. Although only two years Kosygin's senior and four years older than Brezhnev, he had only recently returned to a full schedule of work after what was probably a case of complete exhaustion or the first episode of cardiac heart disease. A less cautious person might have been willing to take the risk, but not Suslov. He had more than three months to think about it during his illness, and he was thoroughly convinced that it was not for him, not even as a caretaker. As a younger man he had spent nearly ten years in responsible field assignments in Rostov, Stavropol, and Vilnius, but his administrative experience at the central level of Party and state government was, at best, very limited. Taking on the Party's top job was clearly out of the question; his Kremlin colleagues probably would not have supported him anyway, even if he wanted it. His objective was to recapture his old position of preeminence and, like Father Joseph,[46] the classic prototype of all future grey eminences, to continue acting out his political career as the Party's chief ideologist, senior statesman, and confidant to a mutually compatible First Secretary. Kosygin was also not an ideal candidate. He had spent almost his entire career in the state government, without developing enough influence in the various levels of the Party *apparat*. He was Deputy Chairman of the Council of Ministers, and and was the most eligible senior technocrat to become Chairman on Khrushchev's retirement. Brezhnev was clearly the best connected and most qualified of the three. The youngest and most versatile of the trio, he had developed important organizational and administrative skills at the very top level of the Soviet command structure, and his extensive connections with the military and the KGB made him an even more acceptable candidate. Furthermore, he was ambitious enough to have wanted the job, and probably had no compunction about toppling Khrushchev if it also meant the political demotion of his rival Podgorny. Affable, easy-going, and an accomplished coalition builder, he was probably also Suslov's choice; the two of them complemented each other and did not have any serious and far-reaching differences on major issues.

By the middle of 1964, the disillusionment with Khrushchev had reached alarming proportions, engulfing a broad spectrum of the Soviet leadership. In the Presidium, Khrushchev continued to have the solid backing of Podgorny and Voronov, but Mikoyan and Shvernik, despite their close association with the First Secretary, could be convinced to vote against him, especially if they were assured that the idea of retiring Khrushchev had the blessing of the majority in the Central Committee, and the Army and the KGB. The remaining full members were solidly anti-Khrushchev. Dmitri Polyansky, a tough but well educated expert on agriculture, would have undoubtedly voted with Suslov, Brezhnev, and Kosygin. He had become highly critical of Khrushchev's agricultural policy, and was most unhappy about Khrushchev's promotion of V. I. Polyakov whom he considered an agricultural charlatan. So would Andrei Kirilenko, another Ukrainian, who recently had a fall-out with the First Secretary. Kuusinen was dead,[47] but Kozlov—terminally ill and completely disabled—was still a member of the Presidium. The "correlation of forces," to use a Soviet expression, was clearly in favor of the anti-Khrushchev coalition. Khrushchev himself must have been aware of this. His remark to Gaston Palewski, the last foreign visitor to see him before his removal, that "only death can wrest a statesman from his work,"[48] was a prophetic admission that all was not well. What was at first only a loosely-knit inchoate movement was beginning to look like a conspiracy. As it is often the case with an impending political upheaval, a series of developments that may have been in themselves inconsequential now propelled the anti-Khrushchev forces to more drastic action.

The rationale for urgent and immediate action came from a number of directions during the summer and early fall of 1964. Of particular significance to the course of future events was the "Togliatti Memorandum."[49] Written during the Italian Communist leader's visit to the Soviet Union in the early summer of 1964, the memorandum painted a gloomy picture of Soviet progress under Khrushchev. Togliatti was highly critical of Khrushchev's pet programs and achievements—especially his handling of the de-Stalinization campaign—and strongly suggested the need for fundamental changes in the Soviet system. First published in the Soviet Union in September,[50] the Togliatti testament made a strong impact on a wide circle of the Soviet leadership, creating a powerful momentum for the anti-Khrushchev coalition. Adding more fuel to the fire were two other unrelated incidents arising out of Khrushchev's German policy. The First Secretary was being severely criticized by the conservatives for his attempted *rapprochement* with West Germany, but what really triggered a general outcry was his decision to entrust the early phase of the negotiations to his son-in-law Adzhubei. The Soviet establishment had always been critical of Khrushchev's penchant for informal channels of diplomacy, and the dispatch of Adzhubei to Bonn in July 1964 aroused widespread unrest among the professionals. Asked some time later about why Khrushchev was overthrown, Gromyko is reputed to have bluntly answered: "Because he sent Adzhubei to Bonn, of course."[51] Khrushchev's telegram of apology to Bonn in connection with the infamous "Schwirkmann incident"[52] also created an uproar among the leadership. Sent by Khrushchev, apparently without the approval of the collective leadership only a few days prior to the coup in order to pave the way for his intended visit to Bonn, the telegram angered the KGB and gravely undermined Suslov's and Brezhnev's efforts to conciliate the German Democratic Republic. There was also a rising tide of anxiety over the prospects of the November 1964 plenary session. Summoned by Khrushchev supposedly to deal with agricultural problems, the plenum was widely rumored in Moscow circles to have been called by the First Secretary for the purpose of purging the collective leadership of its anti-Khrushchev elements. Basing his conclusion on reliable Moscow sources, Michel Tatu has convincingly argued that this was the "last straw. . . . that drove Suslov and the collective leadership to take action."[53]

The timing was also in favor of decisive action. Khrushchev was on vacation at his Black Sea resort, cut off from the immediate sources of his power. Podgorny was in Kishenev attending a celebration of the Moldavian republic. Except for Adzhubei, most of Khrushchev's kitchen cabinet was also away—Satiukov was in Paris and Kharlamov was touring Scandinavia. The absence of the editor-in-chief of *Pravda* and the national director of radio and television precluded the possibility of Khrushchev making a direct appeal through them to the broader strata of the Party apparatus. Their absence from the capital provided an extra margin of safety.

What happened during those four crucial days between October 11 and 14 is now history, masterfully chronicled by an assortment of Soviet scholars and reporters.[54] The coup that unseated Nikita Khrushchev was carried out with great precision and in a manner that vindicated the lesson of the abortive "anti-Party" coup in 1957. On October 13, the First Secretary was summarily recalled to Moscow for a meeting of the Presidium, and offered an opportunity to resign "honorably." Khrushchev confidently refused this offer, and the unpleasant confrontation was moved the next day to a prearranged plenum of the Central Committee. The support that he had expected from the Central Committee plenum did not materialize. During the crucial three days prior to Khrushchev's return to Moscow an exerted effort was launched by the opposition to make sure that enough anti-Khrushchev members of the Central Committee were in Moscow to form a quorum that would endorse the decision of the Presidium. As in 1957, Suslov had again assumed the position of the senior Party leader and protector of the Party's incorruptibility, this time not as an impartial arbiter, but as an aggressive and ominous prosecutor. Reading a carefully prepared report, he accused Khrushchev of a wide range of serious errors and misdemeanors which, apart from specific issues and policies, narrowed down to the condemnation of Khrushchev himself. The First Secretary was indicted for his precipitate judgment, his persistent flouting of authority, his penchant for using informal channels and close personal connections in diplomacy, his disregard for collective leadership, his lack of tact and discretion, and his promotion of a new cult of personality.[55] It was clear that he was being deposed not so much for what he had done, but for the style in which he had been acting. There was no debate, no provision for rebuttal, only more accusations and hostile innuendos. Suslov had correctly assessed the mood of the Central Committee, and it did not take long to pronounce the final judgment. On October 14, 1964, the Central Committee plenum approved the decision of the Presidium, confirming "that N. S. Khrushchev (should) be released from his duties because of his advanced age and poor state of health."[56]

Although often described as another palace revolution,[57] the October 1964 coup had widespread support in the Soviet leadership. In the end, it was endorsed by all of the important segments of the Soviet polity: the Party leadership, the state apparatus, the military, and the KGB. Suslov's role in it was unequivocal. After almost two and one half years of political hibernation, he had emerged in the summer of 1964 to play a crucial role in Khrushchev's ouster. He had completely recovered his confidence, and was again speaking out and getting top press coverage. Khrushchev's prestige, on the other hand, was again declining, this time more precipitously than before. After ten years of zig-zagging achievement and oscillating leadership, he had alienated and angered enough of the Soviet leaders to create a broad consensus favoring his immediate removal. Suslov's genius was in recognizing this trend and assessing the degree of its unanimity. He had been unhappy with Khrushchev's leadership for a long time, and was waiting for an appropriate opportunity to mount a powerful offensive against him. As the arbiter of the 1957 power struggle, he had personally supervised the settlement that saved Khrushchev and defeated the "anti-Party" group. No one understood better than he did how critical it was for everything to fall in place before another attempt could be made, this time with success.

It is inconceivable to imagine a man of Suslov's cautiousness taking this drastic a step without being certain of its success. The unanimity that he was looking for was clearly the crucial criterium, but it was also important to have a favorable setting. Everything was emphatically pointing toward a successful enterprise during the second week of October—the long term build-up of grievances, the intensity of the new criticism engendered by the events of the summer and early fall, Khrushchev's absence from the capital, and the probable efficacy of the timing. Suslov was clearly not alone in putting the plan into action. A *modus operandi* had probably been discussed earlier—perhaps as early as mid-summer. Brezhnev had to secure unequivocal assurance from the military and the KGB that they would back the opposing leadership. Kosygin probably also had to obtain a similar guarantee from the principal state ministers. A nose count also had to be made of the anti-Khrushchev bandwagon in the Central Committee. But these were mostly precautions taken to improve the margin of success. The anti-Khrushchev bandwagon had been building throughout the summer, and Suslov must have felt absolutely certain that the coup would succeed. Brezhnev returned from his secret talks with Ulbricht on October 11 even more convinced that Khrushchev's German policy was a mistake. The probability, therefore, is that the machinery for the coup was set in motion on the eve of October 11, after Suslov and Brezhnev had taken a final count of everything. Michel Tatu's analysis of Moscow activity on October 11, 12, and 13 tends to confirm this. In a final effort to maximize the success of the coup, several less reliable generals were conveniently sent to Poland for the annual Polish Army Day celebration,[58] a sizable number of Central Committee members who could be counted on for support returned urgently to Moscow,[59] and there is every indication that the KGB had cut off Khrushchev's access to his supporters by changing their telephone numbers during the night of October 12. Suslov may not have been directly responsible for the execution of these moves, but he was clearly the coordinator of the coup.

Khrushchev had obviously failed to realize how deeply disillusioned his Kremlin colleagues had become. For the past ten years he had been manipulating the balance of forces in the Presidium and the other centers of Soviet power, playing one against the other and constantly shifting his own position on both issues and people. In the process he had offended nearly every sphere of Soviet society—the Party apparatus, the military and their heavy industry allies, the state technocrats, the KGB, and most importantly, the orthodox ideologues. In a society where even trivial decisions have ideological implications, this was a mistake of immense proportions, and it is not surprising at all that his political demise came at the hands of the chief ideologue himself.

PART FIVE

THE BREZHNEV YEARS:
The Time of Orthodoxy and Stagnation

What awaits our country if a course of democratization is not taken? We will fall behind the capitalist countries in the course of the second industrial revolution and be gradually transformed into a second-rate provincial power.

Andrei Sakharov, *Sakharov Speaks*

The nature of the state machine was also changing: the early revolutionary zeal and fervor had been wiped out by Stalin . . . , and the apparatus was growing more sclerotic, overtaken by bureaucratic intertia—fear of responsibility, fear of superiors—and by bureaucratic indifference.

Vladimair Bukovsky,
To Build a Castle

Only collective leadership provides a guarantee to our further successes.[1]

Mikhail A. Suslov

Chapter XIV

KINGMAKER

By the afternoon of the fourteenth it was all over for Khrushchev. Having deposed him, the Central Committee Plenum chose Brezhnev First Secretary and, in a bid to eliminate the future misuse of power, agreed that the First Secretary could not serve again as the Chairman of the Council of Ministers.*[2] The Presidium of the Supreme Soviet took care of that the next day, electing Kosygin the new Chairman of the Council of Ministers. The unseating of Khrushchev and the election of Brezhnev and Kosygin marked a new milestone in the history of the Soviet Union. One Western observer succinctly noted that "in a way it was (Khrushchev's) finest hour; ten years earlier no one would even have imagined that Stalin's successor would be removed by so simple and gentle a process as a vote."[3]

Moscow took Khrushchev's dismissal in stride, remaining calm and outwardly unaffected. Except for increased security at government buildings, there were no visible signs of any impending political upheaval. There were unconfirmed rumors of Khrushchev's ouster—especially after *Izvestia* had failed to appear that evening and angry citizens calling its editorial offices were told that it would not come out until the following morning.[4] The world had to wait one more day to learn that Khrushchev had been removed and a new team was being installed. On October 16, *Pravda* and *Izvestia* officially informed the Soviet people that Brezhnev and Kosygin were their new leaders.[5]

The dismissal of Khrushchev did not bring about an immediate restructuring of his domestic and foreign policies. Despite his many personal shortcomings, he had been a genuine innovator who had launched widespread changes in Soviet society, and the newly installed leadership was reluctant to initiate new programs hastily. Nor were there any immediate summary firings or far-reaching purges. Except for Khrushchev's kitchen cabinet—Adzhubei, Satiuikov, Kharlamov, and a small number of liberal philosophers and ideologists—the Party's princes and barons remained temporarily unscathed. Khrushchev's disdain for collective leadership was a major reason for his fall, and "collectivity" now became the *raison d'etre* of the newly established leadership, giving rise overnight to a new Soviet cult of enforced collectivity. Everything in the Soviet Union suddenly became "collective." The returning *Voskhod*

---

*Prime Minister.

147

cosmonauts were referred to as the new "cosmic collective," the TV crew that filmed them was described as the "television collective," and the Soviet Olympic team at the 1964 Tokyo Olympiad became "our Olympic collective."[6] But behind the facade of collectivity which the new leadership had vowed to uphold in the interest of a stable oligarchy, a struggle for power began unfolding itself almost instantly among the major contenders.

With Suslov's blessing Brezhnev had emerged from the plenum as *primus inter pares* empowered to guide and direct the Party and exert great influence on the administration of the state and government organs, but he was by no means in full control of the new leadership. Kosygin, the nation's most qualified professional manager, took charge of the formal execution of policy as Chairman of the Council of Ministers. Decisive, pragmatic, and highly self-confident, he had been struggling for some time under Khrushchev to secure greater freedom of action and now saw his opportunity to move swiftly in asserting his authority in the state apparatus. Khrushchev's loyal backer and protégé Nikolai Podgorny also remained a power to deal with. At the last moment he decided to withdraw his support from Khrushchev, emerging together with Suslov, Brezhnev and Kosygin as a ruling member of the collective leadership. As the Secretary in charge of the Party machine, he was a formidable counterweight to Brezhnev in the Secretariat.[7] At a lower level of decision making, but also wielding considerable power, was Aleksandr Shelepin, the ambitious and versatile former head of the KGB and the Comsomol. He had provided the security "muscle" for the coup, and was now waiting to collect the debt owed to him. Clearly, Brezhnev was being threatened from a number of directions in the first weeks after Khrushchev's fall. His conflict with Kosygin was both jurisdictional and over differences in policy— especially economic policy. With Podgorny, he was vying for the control of the Secretariat. It was no accident that Podgorny, rather than Brezhnev, was chosen to deliver the Presidium's report to the November 1964 Central Committee plenum, giving the assembled Party *apparatchiks* the good news about the abandonment of Khrushchev's highly unpopular Party bifurcation policy.[8] Shelepin was Deputy Chairman under Kosygin and had a foothold in both the Council of Ministers and the Secretariat. Young, intelligent and very ambitious, he openly encouraged factional conflict by spreading the word among his political supporters—the Komsomol, the uniformed police, and the KGB—that he would take over the First Secretary's post as soon as Brezhnev made his first serious political blunder, a strategy that backfired against him later.[9] The old timers—Mikoyan and Shvernik—as well as a variety of junior members in the Presidium and the Secretariat sat uncommitted, discreetly waiting to support the man who looked most likely to gain full control. Despite the salience of Brezhnev's favorable position, it was by no means obvious during the early months of the collective leadership who would emerge as the undisputed chief executive.

The unseating of Khrushchev and the ensuing struggle did not alter the uniqueness of Suslov's position. He had always considered himself the Party's ideological defender, and he now emerged from the plenum in an even more powerful position to demand that the leadership of the Party adhere to the essential rules prescribed by Lenin. During the past seven years he had fought tenaciously against Khrushchev's intermittent attempts to subvert the principle of "collectivity." Now that Khrushchev was dethroned and a new First Secretary had assumed his post, the restoration of collective leadership loomed even higher among his priorities. The Presidium—like almost all oligarchies—could easily dissolve itself again into a pattern of individual rule, creating another despotic autocrat. The Russian historical tradition had favored this pattern since the XVth century, and the Soviet experience followed the same trend. Despite Lenin's dictum that "the dictatorship of the proletariat" was to assert itself through a collective leadership, the Soviet government had recast itself in varying degrees both during Stalin's and Khrushchev's regimes into an autocratic rule of one dominant individual who had usurped the powers of the ruling group. Khrushchev's dismissal did not automatically eliminate this tendency, and a new start had to be made to infuse the notion of collective leadership permanently into the Soviet polity.

The procedure used by the Central Committee and the Politburo to arrive at decisions has never been fully understood in the West. As already noted,[10] Lenin adopted a consensual form of decision-making and preferred to abstain from the process of formal voting, deferring the vote and the rule of majority to the most obdurate problems only. Stalin made a mockery of both forms of decision-making. After the 1957 attempt of the "anti-Party" group to oust him, Khrushchev established a formal voting procedure in the Presidium and the Central Committee, and even started to publish digests of the Central Committee meetings. The more structured approach favored by Khrushchev came about, of course, as a result of the sharp devisions within the leadership and Khrushchev's desire to circumvent Lenin's adherence to the notion of unanimity by the outcome of a formal vote. After Khrushchev's fall, Suslov inisted on a return to collective leadership, to decision by consensus, and to the strict adherence of Lenin's rules. It is not clear how he restored the Lenin tradition, but the fact is that the Khrushchev statutes were scrapped almost immediately after the election of Brezhnev and Kosygin, and the Politburo and the Central Committee reverted to decision-making by consensus, employing the vote and the rule of majority only when everything else had failed and there seemed no other way left to reach a decision.[11]

The times also favored the enhancement of Suslov's improved standing. On the international scene, the continuing ideological, political, and economic diversification of the world communist movement made dealings with the foreign Communist parties an ever more complex and demanding problem for the

Soviet government, calling for the expansion of Suslov's responsibilities in inter-Party relations. At home, the gradual post-World War II secularization and westernization of the Soviet society increased the importance of the Party's ideological apparatus. To maintain discipline and to legitimize the regime's existence, the Soviet Union was compelled to intensify the political indoctrination of not only the Party cadres, but also the entire people. These developments, increased decisively Suslov's standing at home and abroad, propelling him to the very top echelon of the Soviet leadership after Khrushchev's fall.[12]

Having satisfied himself that the initial transfer of power had been accomplished smoothly, Suslov now retreated again into the background, venturing out only occasionally to protect his investment in Brezhnev and to restore decorum in Party affairs. There was nothing unusual about this. He had done this previously, and he was following the same pattern again.[13] Suslov's withdrawal from the mainstream of Soviet politics did not go by unnoticed. He was too important a person—especially after the role he had played during the coup—to be left alone for long. By the third week of October persisting rumors began spreading that he was again suffering from either an "authentic or diplomatic illness."[14] There was also an unconfirmed report that he had flown on a secret mission to Peking to familiarize Mao with the details of Khrushchev's ouster, and to submit to him a proposal for friendlier relations.[15] How much truth there was in these reports is anyone's guess. There is every reason to believe, however, that Suslov had survived the coup without any serious physical after-effects, despite the anxieties and added pressures of the past weeks. Indira Ghandi, who had spoken with him during the last week of October, reported that he had a cold, but had not changed physically since she had seen him sixteen months earlier. T. N. Kaul, the Indian Ambassador, who was also present at the interview with Mrs. Ghandi, said that he had noticed a cough, but when he asked Suslov how he felt, Suslov had facetiously replied: "When I cough, the Western press magnifies it into thunder."[16] Whatever the reasons may have been for the silence that suddenly settled over Suslov's name in the Soviet press, it did not mean that he stopped attending meetings and receptions for foreign diplomats, appearing in a ceremonial capacity, and meeting with the leaders of the Communist world. Apparently, he had stepped behind the scenes for good reasons: to allow Brezhnev to fight his own battles, and to escape the publicity emanating from the controversial debate taking place in the Politburo.

History has always had its religious eccentrics and trailblazers, its high priests and ideologues. Their actions have generally been marked by disinterestedness and serenity, creating a special mystique about them, and giving them a strange kind of uncoercive but compelling authority over fellow men. An even more significant circumstance was that the essence of their authority was usually divorced from the ordinary social sanctions of power, position, or wealth. Invariably, their authority drew its strength from how they led their lives, how they interacted with their surroundings, the doctrines they preached, and how they built their prestige. Social anthropologists studying primitive cultures have also noted this quality, and have argued conclusively that shamans and high priests often played more important roles in the "war and peace" of their societies than the "great chiefs and their tribal councils."[17] Aloof, dignified, circumspect, and distinctive in diet, language, and way of living, they invariably exerted great political and social influence on their milieu. In the economically modern, but politically and socially traditional and ideocratic setting of the Soviet society, Suslov's behavior exhibited many of the same traits. His aloofness, his circumspection, the esoteric language of his doctrinal pronouncements, and his continuous disregard for the attributes of political power, also made him into a kind of a modern-day tribal shaman who dispensed charms, condemned heretics, resolved quarrels, invested new chiefs with the markings of their power and authority, and watched over them lest they stray from the teachings of established dogma. Beginning with the XXth Party Congress, he had consistently conciliated Party differences, helped expose and eliminate dangerous rivals, and moderated the First Secretary's enthusiasm for policies and programs that diverged from the Party line. In the process, he had gained the recognition and respect of a wide spectrum of Party officials, but had somehow failed to tame the intractable Great Chief himself.

In Brezhnev, Suslov saw a different kind of leader, a more tolerant and discreet ruler, a man who would probably respect the prerogatives of collective leadership, and respond positively to the nation's paramount need for stability and doctrinal discipline after more than ten years of internal political crises and experimentation. Prudent, cautious, conservative, a compromiser with a strong preference for negotiation rather than force or manipulation, Brezhnev showed many of the same character traits that Suslov nurtured. The new First Secretary and the chief ideologist also held similar views on the major issues facing the new government. To begin with, they were remarkably close in their attitudes toward de-Stalinization. Both were convinced that it had already gone too far and that it was time to stop the escalating denigration of Soviet history. Both favored a limited restoration of Stalin's prestige and a crack down on literary dissent and factional strife. Brezhnev probably also saw in "re-Stalinization" a political tool to neutralize Podgorny who had been advocating a more flexible policy in tune with Khrushchev's liberalism. Their positions on détente and Soviet military power were likewise comparable. Both were in favor of reallocating a larger share of the nation's economic resources to the defense industry, and both were highly critical of Khrushchev's sporadic attempts to improve relations with West Germany and the United States. They were especially concerned about an unconditional *rapprochement* with Bonn. A week before the coup, Suslov took an unusually strong stand against improved relations with the Bonn government in the absence of a clear understanding first on how this would affect the status of the German Democratic Republic. In a speech made in Moscow on October 6, Suslov said:

> The treaty between the USSR and GDR puts a stop to the foolish illusion of West German revanchist circles about the possibility of a deal with the Soviet union at the expense of the GDR. 'If the USSR wants good relations with West Germany,' it is being said in those circles, 'let it give in on the interests of the GDR.' It is an understatement to say that such plans are a provocation. . . . In the first place, the GDR is a sovereign state, and no one, except its own people, is entitled to bargain with its interests; in the second place, the fraternal amity and socialist solidarity which link the USSR and the GDR are not to be bought and sold, even for all the gold in the world.[18]

Brezhnev's speech in East Berlin a day later was more moderate in tone, but its substance was similar. He, too, made it clear that the Soviet Union was not going to make "deals . . . at the expense of the GDR and its security."[19] They may have held somewhat different views on Sino-Soviet policy, but both were in agreement that the removal of Khrushchev gave the Soviet Union a new opportunity to improve relations with Mao. Never since the death of Stalin had the First Secretary and the chief ideologist been of equal mind on so many different issues.

During the next eighteen months Brezhnev undertook a series of tactical operations that "cleansed" the senior levels of the Party leadership and brought the Secretariat and the Presidium under his control. Among the first to go were Suslov's ideological nemesis Leonid Ilyichev and Khrushchev's agricultural expert V. I. Polyakov. Both were removed from the Secretariat, giving Suslov a free hand in doctrinal and cultural matters and freeing Brezhnev to pursue his own agricultural policies without Polyakov's interference. Nikolai Shvernik and Anastas Mikoyan were retired in March 1966, and Podgorny was removed from the Secretariat and kicked upstairs to take over Mikoyan's position as Chairman of the Presidium of the USSR Supreme Soviet.*[20] The chairmanship of the Party Control Commission—Shvernik's job—was handed to Arvid Pel'she, Suslov's brother-in-law.[21]

Paralleling the dismissals and retirements, a number of important victims of Khrushchev's ire were restored to positions of responsibility. In February 1965, Vladimir Matskevich, a much maligned former Minister of Agriculture, was reinstated in his old job. Kunaev and Shcherbitsky were also rescued from oblivion, Shcherbitsky becoming the Chairman of the Council of Ministers of the Ukrainian republic. Dimitri Ustinov, Stalin's armaments minister and spokesman for the defense industry, was elected to the Secretariat and made a candidate member of the Presidium. In recognition of his support during the coup and breaking all precedent, Shelepin was elected almost immediately after Khrushchev's removal to full membership in the Presidium without having to

---

*President of the USSR.

serve as a candidate member. Shelepin's rapid rise to power was short lived. In December of 1965, he lost two of his more important sources of influence—his deputy premiership and his chairmanship of the Party-State Control Committee[22] which was disbanded after the repeal of the Party bifurcation scheme. Finally, in a decisive victory for Brezhnev, Andrei Kirilinko was appointed to the Secretariat in April 1966, becoming, together with Brezhnev, Suslov, and Shelepin, the fourth Party official holding a portfolio in both the Secretariat and the Politburo.*

Thus, by the XXIIIrd Party Congress, Brezhnev had more or less consolidated his power in the collective leadership. He had accomplished this largely on his own, but not without an occasional assist from Suslov. Despite his aversion to factional conflict, the kingmaker had to step into the ring on several occasions to support Brezhnev and to neutralize the opposition. The most important incident occurred in May 1965 during the crisis created by the debate over the industrial reform.

In January 1965, apparently without the approval of the Presidium, Kosygin ordered the extension of the Bolshevichka-Mayak experiment to four hundred enterprises in light industry. Bolshevichka in Moscow and Mayak in Gor'kii were large plants manufacturing clothing and footwear under a production system organized in the fall of 1964 on the basis of actual orders placed, without any interference from central planning. This was a new experiment encouraged by Kosygin, approved by Khrushchev, and evolving out of the market-oriented thinking formulated by Professor Yevsei Liberman, a liberal Soviet economist popular during the 1960s. There were no serious objections to the experiment, but a wider application of the new system raised an immediate protest. Conservative central planners and orthodox Party *apparatchiks* steeped in more than thirty-five years of unimaginative central planning and production, based on quantity rather than quality, raised strong opposition to the reform initiated by Kosygin. The Prime Minister defended himself by pointing out that the government organs should be able to manage the economy without any outside interference. "We have to free ourselves," he said "from everything that used to tie down the planning officials and obliged them to draft plans otherwise than in accordance with the interests of the economy."[23] Because the new system of production was less affected by central planning, the debate had definite ideological overtones. Central planning and command-initiated production were an integral part of the Soviet economic system since the 1920s, and it was not surprising, therefore, that the debate over the Mayak-Bolshevichka experiment spilled over into the public press.[24] On May 17, Vasilii Stepanov, the editor-in-chief of *Kommunist,* undoubtedly with the blessing of Brezhnev and Suslov, published a blistering article in *Pravda* attacking Kosygin for departing from the

---

*The name Presidium was dropped and the name Politburo was restored at the XXIIIrd Party Congress in 1966.

established principles of socialist production.[25] The criticism of Kosygin did not go by unchallenged. A few days later, Vladimir Stepakov, a spokesman for the government, responded in *Izvestia* with an equally caustic article, attacking Brezhnev for his opposition to the government reform. "An engineering diploma is not everything," said *Izvestia*. "The diploma must be supplemented by a talent for organization, by a correct understanding of the leader's political role, and by an ability to motivate people."[26] Podgorny also did not sit still. In a speech in Baku he came to the assistance of the reformers and against the heavy industry lobby by emphasizing the efficacy of industrial reform and the nation's demand for increased consumer goods production. Taking the argument even further than Stepakov, he praised the more drastic reforms undertaken by the other countries of the eastern bloc. "Our friends are at present carrying out the plan of the Czechoslovak Communist Party for improving the organization and management of the economy. A great creative impetus reigns in that country. The same tireless pursuit of new ways . . . is going on in Poland, in the German Democratic Republic, in Bulgaria, in Hungary, and in other lands of socialism."[27] On the subject of consumer goods production, he recalled Khrushchev's views, reminding the audience that "there was a time when the Soviet people consciously accepted material restrictions for the sake . . . of heavy industry and the strengthening of our defense capacity . . . but now collective wealth is multiplying year by year, while conditions are emerging that make it easier to satisfy the workers' ever-growing domestic and cultural needs."[28]

Working behind the scenes, Suslov had been trying to diffuse the conflict, but the debate had developed its own momentum, seriously undermining Brezhnev's newly won authority. Suslov had hoped that the conflict would resolve itself without becoming public, but by the end of May it was clear that a serious crisis had developed within the Soviet leadership, threatening the unity of the Party and contributing to a general loss of Party decorum at home and abroad. On June 2, in a major speech in Sofia, Bulgaria, Suslov finally broke his long silence, undercutting both the pro-Kosygin forces and Podgorny. "We have been deeply interested in the new system of planning and economic management that you have worked out, which, *we have been told,** makes it possible to raise substantially the efficiency of production," he noted, referring the the Bulgarian economic reforms already in operation.[29] The phraseology of Suslov's comment left no doubt about what he thought of the much touted new economic reforms. But Suslov did not stop with that. The stampede for economic reform needed a more formal doctrinal admonishment. "Even though material conditions play a large part in the life of society," he emphasized, "the problem of the building of communism is not fully resolved by the abundance of material goods. *It is also necessary that communist social relationships should establish themselves in all aspects of life.'*[30]**

---

*Italicized by the author to indicate Suslov's obvious skepticism of the "new system."
**Italicized for emphasis.

His rebuke of Podgorny was even more unequivocal and stinging. Referring to Podgorny's advocacy for increased production of consumer goods, Suslov sharply reprimanded him by saying:

> We would like the life of the Soviet people to improve at a faster rate. But we have to take into account objective reality that forces us to make considerable expenses for the defense of our country. . . . At a time when the imperialist powers are pursuing the arms race and unleashing military aggression . . . , our Party and our Government have to maintain the country's defense at the highest level and improve constantly . . . All this naturally demands considerable material sacrifices from the Soviet people and the appropriation of a major part of the national revenue for defense.[31]

The Party sage had spoken, and in the following months the conflict over the economic reform gradually died down in a series of compromises worked out between the Party and the government. The Kosygin reforms, as they became known, were approved at the September 27 Central Committee plenum. Some decentralization was introduced by getting away from the purely quantitative goals and the deterioration of quality that these goals encouraged. Interest and rent charges were included in the pricing of consumer goods, and plant managers were empowered to hire and fire employees and to use their profits in local projects. However, the central planners continued to exercise control over the expansion of plant capacity, and the central distribution system was strengthened through the creation of a special ministry in charge of disbursing raw materials and finished products. The *sovnarkhozes* introduced by Khrushchev in 1957 were eliminated and many of the abandoned ministries were restored. After a long and dangerous conflict, Kosygin had won some autonomy for his managers and technocrats, but only at the expense of a greatly strengthened Party administrative power held by Brezhnev and his *apparatchiks*. Kosygin was too important a political figure to be censured openly for his rebellion against the rigid direction of the Party. The complex compromise—which was more administrative than economic—was all that Brezhnev and Suslov could devise in their attempt to constrain Kosygin. Podgorny's case was different. His political standing was not as privileged as Kosygin's, and he had to be castigated publicly for questioning one of the Soviet Union's most sacred cows. The force of Suslov's criticism was so devastating that Podgorny was reputed to have cancelled all public appearances and meetings on his doctor's orders, remaining in political seclusion for almost two months until the end of July.[32] The Baku address seriously damaged Podgorny's position in the collective leadership *vis a vis* Brezhnev, leading eventually to his dismissal from the Secretariat and to his appointment in 1966 to the largely ceremonial post of President.

Interacting with the economic debate was a growing consensus among the leadership for a more centrist, *albeit* orthodox, position on the question of the de-Stalinization. The approach of the twentieth anniversary of the end of

World War II in May 1965 spawned a profusion of articles, memoirs, and historical papers extolling the role played by Stalin during the war. For the first time in many years, Stalin's name reappeared in the press, and a documentary film about the war actually showed him in a positive light as the supreme commander of the Soviet armed forces. There were, of course, the usual arguments and recriminations of the military, who sought a more objective and balanced interpretation of the war, but they did not thwart the rehabilitation of Stalin. Brezhnev, himself, was partially responsible for the reinstatement of Stalin as a competent war leader. He undoubtedly saw in Stalin's restoration the possibility of improving his own position within the collective leadership, and may have even contributed to the trend by legitimizing it when he first praised Stalin's war accomplishments at the Twentieth Anniversary Victory celebration in May, 1965.[33] The renaming of the Presidium as the Politburo, and of the First Secretary as the General Secretary, also must have had a salutary effect on Stalinist attitudes. There may have been justification for these changes on the basis that they enhanced the dignity and authority of the Party, but Brezhnev's association of these titles with Stalin's personal authority, raised some questions about how far re-Stalinization should be allowed to proceed.

The rehabilitation of Stalin did not stop with the exaltation of his war record. What started only as a partial restoration in the spring of 1965 transformed itself in the next ten months into a full-blown upsurge of extravagant neo-Stalinism. A series of articles in *Pravda* and *Izvestia*[34] during March and April of 1965 attacked sharply a well-balanced earlier editorial in *Pravda,* written by editor-in-chief Aleksei Rumyantsev, for its lack of fidelity to Lenin's sacred principle of "party-mindedness."[35] In April, a Moscow district court ruled against Lydia Chukovskaya, a well-known and revered Soviet writer,[36] in a suit brought by her against a publishing house that reneged on a contract to publish her anti-Stalinist novella *Sofia Petrovna.*[37] The court ruling was an affirmation of the Party's decision to stop further revelations about the Stalinist past. Also in April, a highly caustic article in *Izvestia* directed against A. T. Tvardovsky, the liberal editor of *Novyi Mir,* took him to task for "losing his sense of proportion" in criticizing Stalinist literature, and for his excessive promotion of Solzhenitsyn's works.[38] It was becoming obvious that increased censorship and a resurgence of Stalinist attitudes were again becoming a part of Soviet life. In mid-September, the KGB arrested Andrei Sinyavsky and Yuly Daniel, two prominent members of the Soviet intelligentsia, on charges that they had published treasonable anti-Soviet works abroad under a pseudonym. Their trial and sentencing provoked a powerful anti-Soviet reaction in the West and among the intelligentsia of the Communist world. An open conflict was also breaking out between the more liberal ideologues and the Party hardliners. A few weeks before the Sinyavsky-Daniel trial, the First Secretary of the Komsomol, Sergei Pavlov upbraided certain "theoreticians and writers who view entire stages in the history of socialist society exclusively through the prism of the adverse consequences of the cult of personality," calling for a rewriting of the history of the thirties in a more favorable light.[39] An article in the October 8 issue of *Pravda* by Sergei Trapeznikov, the head of the Science and Education Department of the Central Committee and one of the most ardent reactionary spokesmen in the Soviet Union, went even further by calling the thirties "one of the most brilliant (periods) in the history of the Party and of the Soviet State."[40] The neo-Stalinist rhetoric continued to surge through the winter of 1965–1966, reaching a sudden impasse in the January 30 statement of three prominent historians—E. Zhukov, V. Trukhanovsky, and V. Shunkov. Asserting that the continued use of the phrase "the cult of personality" had "minimized the heroic efforts of the Party and the people in their struggle for socialism," they announced that "it was time to stop using it altogether."[41] As Michel Tatu had appropriately noted, "the order" to bury any further discussion of the "cult of personality" "must have come from a very high quarter, since the phrase disappeared from the press overnight."[42]

Suslov had been urging the Party to stop the discussion of Stalin's crimes and to tighten the ideological diversity in literature and the arts since 1961, but it is unlikely that he favored a runaway resurgence of Stalinism.[43] As a conservative and orthodox ideologue, Suslov was clearly in favor of putting an end to the flood of anti-Stalinist manuscripts that had come to Soviet publishers after the XXIInd Party Congress. He was also opposed to what he considered was a deliberate attempt by some liberal intellectuals to discredit the Party's role in Soviet history. He was for stricter Party discipline, for more rigorous Communist indoctrination, and for a tougher foreign policy against the West, but he was not for an unbridled restoration of Stalinism. His primary allegiance had always been to the Party—not to the leader—and he was not about to condone a return to the excesses of the Stalinist past that were inherent in the extravagant and almost idolatrous veneration of the leader. His attitude toward Sergei Trapeznikov was an indication of how far he was willing to proceed with re-Stalinization. There is every indication that he considered Trapeznikov a crass and dangerous Stalinist who had warmed himself into the inner circle of the Brezhnev entourage, and it is almost certain that it was Suslov who blocked Trapeznikov's candidacy to the Soviet Academy of Pedagogical Sciences.[44] The chief ideologue was also reputed to have opposed the prosecution of Sinyavsky and Daniel, arguing that they should have been punished only by "political means," by expulsion from the Writer's Union as Pasternak was in 1958, and not condemned to seven and five years of forced labor.[45] The Sinyavsky-Daniel trial unleashed an unprecedented volume of criticism at home and abroad, causing considerable discomfort for the Politburo and triggering the formation of a powerful dissident movement as a counterforce to the upsurge of rabid Stalinism. Perhaps the most convincing signal of the movement's strength was the petition to the Central Committee on the eve of the XXIIIrd Party Congress for the release of Sinyavsky and Daniel. Signed by twenty-seven prominent academicians, writers and artists, representing a cross section of the Soviet intelligentsia, it included such world-known figures as Kapitsa, Sakharov, Nekrasov, Chukovsky, and Plisetskaia.

The Stalinist bandwagon had created a dangerous situation for the Soviet leadership. There were still a large number of hardcore Stalinists in the Central Committee, in the state apparatus, and in the republic and *obkom* organizations, and there was also a fairly solid nucleus of senior *apparatchiks* with previous Khrushchev connections who had not completely embraced the policies and leadership championed by Brezhnev. The political and ideological sniping within the literary community and among the ideological workers could easily spill over into the higher echelons of the Soviet political leadership, transforming the XXIIIrd Party Congress into another confrontation over Stalinism. The risk of this happening again was high enough to discourage the Party's leaders from bringing the issue officially out in the open. Indeed, it was more expedient to remain silent than to reopen the gates of controversy on Stalin's role in Soviet history.

This is exactly what happened on March 29. The XXIIIrd Party Congress opened with a distinctly Suslovian touch to its proceedings. Caution, covertness, and the deliberate attempt to sidestep the pressures of making a formal statement on Stalin or the "cult of personality" dominated the Congress proceedings. There was something almost surrealistic about the whole event. Despite all the "pomp and circumstance" and the verbiage placed on record, it was as if it had never taken place. Suslov remained conspicuously silent on the subject of the "cult of personality," confining his remarks solely to Vietnam and the condemnation of the United States.[46] So did Shelepin and a score of other senior Party stalwarts who would have normally brought up the subject. Brezhnev, who addressed the Congress at its opening session, reaffirmed the positions of the XXth and XXIInd Party Congresses and assumed an explicitly centrist position, circumventing completely any reference to Stalin or anything else that may have been even remotely considered controversial in the months before the Congress. The only direct and substantive reference to Stalinism and the "cult of personality" came from Nikolai Yegorychev, the First Secretary of the Moscow city organization.[47] Evidently picked by the leadership to deliver the official Party line, Yegorychev promised that "the cult of personality, the violation of Leninist standards and principles . . . everything in short that impeded (the Party's) forward movement, has been decisively rejected by our Party, *and there will never be any return to that Past!*"*[48] The warning to remove any mention of "the cult of personality" from the Soviet lexicon was obviously taken seriously. The junior Party *apparatchiks* who followed Yegorychev confined their remarks to regional economic achievements and the administrative modifications of the

---

*Italicized by the author for emphasis.

past eighteen months. No one among them even attempted to touch the subject. Who was behind the January order remains a mystery to this day. But it is not unrealistic to assume that Suslov may have had something to do with it. As far as he was concerned the issue had been settled ten years earlier at the XXth Party Congress, and there was no need to bring it up again.

Isolated incidents of ardent Stalinism continued to occur occasionally, as hard-core Stalinists persisted in testing the waters. In October 1966, Devi Sturia, Secretary of the Georgian Party Central Committee, boldly proclaimed at a nationwide seminar of Party ideologists that he was a Stalinist and that there was no reason to be ashamed of this.[49] But to all intents and purposes the resurgence of strong pro-Stalinist attitudes had peaked in 1966, and—except for the families of Stalin's victims and the liberal intelligentsia—the whole nation settled on the formula offered by Suslov in 1956. Hereafter, Stalin's accomplishments were to be considered more important than his errors, despite the serious mistakes of his later years.

Chapter XV

PARTY GUARDIAN

With the XXIIIrd Party Congress out of the way and the Politburo
reacting more favorably to his new policies, Brezhnev assumed full and unham-
pered responsibility for the reconstituted leadership of the Soviet Union. Suslov's standing and influence also became magnified. Together with Brezhnev,
Kosygin, Podgorny and Kirilenko, he now became a permanent member of the
policy-making inner core of the Politburo.[1] Playing the silent role of protector of
the faith and defender of the rights of the oligarchy against the leader, Suslov
now could exert great influence over the entire leadership. Nothing made this
more explicit than the protocol-conscious seating arrangements at the XXIIIrd
Party Congress. Instead of Podgorny sitting next to Brezhnev as one might have
normally expected, the General Secretary was flanked on one side by Kosygin,
and on the other by Suslov. In addition to the increased executive authority there
was also a substantial expansion of Suslov's functional responsibilities. Andropov's appointment to the chairmanship of the KGB in 1967 concentrated in Suslov's hands what T. H. Rigby has correctly labeled as the "convergence of the
ideological, Party discipline and security concerns of the regime."[2] Pel'she's and
Andropov's careers were inseparably linked to Suslov's patronage—Pel'she was
his brother-in-law, and Andropov a well-ensconced protégé since the days of the
Hungarian revolution when Andropov was Ambassador in Budapest. With Andropov heading the KGB and Pel'she the Party Control Commission, Suslov
wielded enormous power in the smaller upper echelon of the Politburo. This
power was further amplified by two other critical positions held by the chief
ideologue. Suslov was a member of the Defense Council[3] and chairman of the
prestigious Foreign Affairs Commission of the Supreme Soviet, a collegiate
body that reviewed the decisions of the Supreme Soviet and scrutinized foreign
treaties.[4] The full significance of Suslov's "converging concerns" is perhaps
best exemplified in Arkady Shevchenko's description of his appointment interview[5] with Suslov prior to his departure in 1973 for New York as Under Secretary General of the United Nations.

"In Suslov's office, I found an imperious man whose gray-blue eyes peered through thick-lensed glasses under a shock of graying blond hair that seemed in permanent disarray. Skin taut over sharp, high cheekbones, he looked tired. He went quickly from a handshake and congratulations to the business of indoctrinating me in his views of the UN. . . . Slowly drumming his long, bony fingers on his desk, he declared that in assuming my new post I should look upon the United Nations as he did, as a setting to be used to the maximum extent for propagating progressive ideas. To make sure I understood him, he expressed this thought three times. Since the majority of the UN members were now developing countries, he said, there was the danger that they might fall victim to neocolonialist and bourgeois ideology. The Soviet Union's task, the responsibility of all dedicated Communists, was to prevent such an occurrence.[6]

Suslov's involvement in Shevchenko's appointment corroborates the importance assigned by the Party to Shevchenko's new post, but more importantly, it is to this day the only positive confirmation available in the West of Suslov's converging responsibilities in the field of ideology, Party discipline, internal security, and foreign affairs.

Nineteen Sixty-Seven saw a number of developments in foreign affairs that left a permanent impact on Soviet domestic relations. The Arab-Israeli Six-Day War precipitated Brezhnev's confrontation with Shelepin and his removal from the Secretariat,[7] giving Suslov a virtual monopoly within the leadership as the only remaining senior secretary with a penetrating intelligence. Kosygin's June conference with President Johnson at the height of the Vietnam war in Glassboro also had a regrettable consequence. Suslov was reputed to have opposed it vehemently, arguing that it would be misunderstood by the Communist parties of the world, and would alienate the emerging nations struggling for liberation. Although there were no immediate repercussions, Suslov's and Kosygin's working relationship in the Politburo sustained a serious setback in the long run.

Nineteen Sixty-Seven also saw a heightened display of activity by Suslov and his staff to rejuvenate the international Communist movement, and recapture the position that the Soviet Union lost during the Khrushchev era. During the celebration of the Fifty Years Anniversary of the Revolution in November, Suslov acted as host to a large number of foreign Communist delegations in preparation for a Soviet sponsored International Conference to discuss "the revolutionary revival of the world."[8] The consultative conference took place in Budapest in February 1968, and Suslov delivered an impassioned key note address calling for a rekindling of "international solidarity among the working class."[9] In the months that followed, the campaign to revitalize the international Communist movement became even more intensified. At the celebration of the

150th Anniversary of the birth of Karl Marx in Moscow on May 5, Suslov gave a major speech that touched on a broad spectrum of world problems being then discussed by a preparatory committee working on a new platform for the World Communist Conference scheduled for later in the year.[10] The lengthy address zeroed in on two new developments affecting the Soviet Union's relations with the rest of the Communist world: the growing disarray of the Communist movement itself, and the need for a more revolutionary policy arising out of the political and military consequence of the Vietnam War. The new formula contrasted sharply with Khrushchev's thesis of "simultaneous transition to communism"[11] and its corollary of Soviet economic assistance to the underdeveloped countries in the Third World. It emphasized the need for a more aggressive strategy of supporting revolutions, instead of trying to construct socialism by example and economic aid. Suslov's address was also noteworthy for another reason. In its analysis of international communism, the speech raised the question of "mature socialism"

> The terms for solving the socialist tasks and, particularly, *the terms for the formation of mature socialism** . . . are not identical for different countries. Those among them that embarked upon the new road while being economically developed, find it relatively easier to secure the construction of socialism. The countries, which in the beginning of socialist relations had an underdeveloped material-technological base, will have to pass through a great historical road and solve great problems.[12]

While this statement may have been inserted by Suslov to provide a theoretical framework for a new Soviet policy of reduced economic aid to less developed countries, the significant observation is that Suslov had used the term "mature socialism" four years before it entered officially the Soviet lexicon as Brezhnev's doctrine of "mature or developed socialism."

The World Communist Conference did not take place in 1968. Instead, a potentially far more troublesome question began occupying the Soviet leadership during that year. In December 1967, Brezhnev had traveled to Prague to deal with an increasingly intractable Czechoslovak Central Committee that wanted to remove Antonin Novotny, its unpopular and doctrinaire First Secretary. Brezhnev was unable to resolve the impasse, and Novotny was replaced by Alexander Dubcek who proceeded almost immediately with a series of political and economic reforms that created in the eyes of the Soviet hardliners a threat to the Soviet hegemony in eastern Europe. The "Action Program" adopted by the Dubcek government in April 1968 specified new guarantees of freedom, new

---

*Italicized for emphasis by the author.

electoral laws, the lifting of censorship, widespread economic reforms, and an independent foreign policy. The developments in Czechoslovakia generated a strong reaction in the Soviet Union, especially among the Soviet military who feared that Czechoslovakia's shift to a more pluralistic Western form of government and economy would imperil the integrity of the Warsaw Pact. Czechoslovakia was an integral part of the Soviet defense system, they argued, and Moscow obviously could not allow its withdrawal from the Warsaw Pact.

The Czechoslovak situation resembled the Hungarian crisis in 1956, but there were also important differences that prevented Moscow from taking immediate and decisive action. Unlike Hungary, there were no violent riots or demonstrations. The Czechoslovak Communist Party had not lost control, and the changes that were taking place within the Party were following an orderly process in conformity with existing Party statutes. Furthermore, the Soviet Union had no troops in Czechoslovakia as it did in Hungary and could not interfere internally without creating a serious international diplomatic crisis. The military tried to correct this situation in May 1968 by deploying troops in Czechoslovakia under the pretext of Warsaw Pact maneuvers, but their number was limited and their effectiveness as a deterrent questionable. There were also ideological considerations. To the Soviet leadership, Czechoslovakia was an industrial socialist nation that did not seek to alter its economic policies, while Hungary had not yet shed all of its feudal traditions and could easily lapse into a nationalist counterrevolution. All things considered, the rationale for a negotiated settlement clearly outweighed the use of military force, and it is not surprising that Brezhnev opted for negotiations that precipitated a series of summit conferences in the spring and summer of 1968.

This did not mean that there was no opposition to Brezhnev's policy of caution. Strong recommendations for more drastic measures came from at least four directions: from the military, from Pyotr Shelest of the Ukrainian Party, and from the Polish and East German parties. Suslov did not participate in the crucial Warsaw conference on July 14, attended by Poland, Hungary, Bulgaria, the GDR, and the USSR. Because relations with eastern Europe were his responsibility in the Politburo, his absence was sufficiently conspicuous to start speculation that he was again ill, a rumor that was highly unlikely as he was at the airport on July 16 together with many other senior officials who met Brezhnev returning from Warsaw.[13] The more probable explanation for his absence is that he had decided to keep his options open and not participate in a formal accusation of Czechoslovakia, as the "Warsaw letter" would later reveal.[14] He had been involved in the planning of the World Communist Conference and obviously did not want any adverse publicity that could impair the already very difficult task of organizing a viable international meeting of Communist parties in November 1968. The threatening "Warsaw letter" did not resolve the crisis, and a new Soviet-Czechoslovak bilateral conference took place at Cierna nad Tisou from July 29 to August 1.

The highly charged Cierna meeting was unprecedented in Soviet history. Except for Kirilenko and Polyansky, who were left in Moscow to mind the store, nearly a full Soviet Politburo met the Czechoslovak Presidium at a railroad siding in a small Slovak village on the Soviet border.[15] According Pavel Tigrid, whose study of the crisis is based largely on Czechoslovak sources, Suslov took a distinctly conciliatory position at Cierna. "The Czechoslovak question must be settled by agreement," he said, "if great harm is not to ensue to the international communist movement and its unity."[16] Kosygin, Shelepin, Ponomarev, and Katushev apparently also counselled for moderation, influencing Brezhnev to strike a compromise. In the end, the Czechoslovaks made several minor concessions without yielding on the essential reforms, while the Soviets promised that they would withdraw the troops that remained in Czechoslovakia after the maneuvers. The Bratislava conference on August 4 followed the same pattern, easing the crisis and affirming the principle of solving conflicts by negotiation. But Cierna and Bratislava did not settle the Soviet-Czechoslovak differences, despite the external appearance of good will. On August 20, assisted by troops from the Warsaw Pact allies, ten Soviet divisions crossed into Czechoslovakia terminating the short-lived Czechoslovak experiment and putting an end to "Communism with a human face." The hardliners and the military had obviously prevailed in their views. An especially aggressive opponent of the Prague spring was Pyotr Shelest who had great misgivings about liberal ideas spreading across the border to the Ukraine. Emigré sources later suggested that the Cierna-Bratislava compromise was a deceptive maneuver to lure Czechoslovakia and the West into a false sense of security. Most Western experts who have investigated carefully the Czechoslovak crisis disagree with this view, pointing out that the Soviet decision did not come easily and that the lack of unanimity prevented the Soviet leadership from making a hasty decision.[17] Suslov was reported to express serious reservations during the entire debate, contending that "in spite of the undeniable upsurge of counterrevolutionary forces," it was still "possible to settle the affair by political means."[18] Czechoslovak Prime Minister Oldrich Cernik is reputed to have confirmed this in private conversation on his return from Moscow after the invasion, emphasizing that Suslov had strong reservations about a military intervention.[19]

Those who opposed the invasion did not escape criticism. An unsigned editorial in *Pravda* on August 22, criticized obliquely the non-interventionists for their "compromising approach" and the "conscious belittling of the danger of counterrevolution."[20] Suslov, Kosygin and Ponomarev were also reported to have been censured in a special memorandum distributed by the Party in the fall of 1968.[21]

The Soviet invasion of Czechoslovakia generated an enormous amount of criticism and ill will. In the Soviet Union, protests came from Party organizations, the intelligentsia, and the Soviet youth. Abroad, there was was an unprecedented outpouring of uncontrollable anger and disappointment. President

Johnson cancelled his planned visit to Leningrad, and the SALT talks were also postponed indefinitely. Eighteen West European Communist parties remonstrated against the Soviet intervention, and the Chinese, the Yugoslavs, the Rumanians, and the Albanians condemned the Soviet Union and its leadership for their failure to have resolved the crisis peacefully.

An intimidating consequence of the Czechoslovak crisis was what became known as Brezhnev Doctrine. The reform movement in Czechoslovakia presented a double challenge to the Soviet Union. The notion of "socialism with a human face" created a powerful threat to the one-party authoritarian rule championed by the Soviet leadership. It also stimulated the forces of independence among the Communist nations, forcing the Soviet Union to become more aware of the dangers inherent in the United States policy of "bridge building" to the no longer monolithic socialist world. Foreign Minister Gromyko had warned two months earlier that the "strengthening of the commonwealth of socialist countries" was the Soviet Union's "primary duty in foreign policy."[22] The "Warsaw letter" to the Czechoslovaks clarified this by stating that the frontiers of the socialist world had shifted to the center of Europe, to the Elbe and the Bohemian Forest, and that the Soviet Union "would never allow imperialism, by peaceful or nonpeaceful means, from within or without, to make a breach in the socialist system and change the balance of power in Europe in its favor."[23] In the months between the Soviet intervention in Czechoslovakia and the World Communist Conference in Moscow, a series of articles written by S. Kovalev, a Party ideologist working under Ponomarev, further amplified the declarations made during the Czechoslovak crisis, bringing them in line with the essential theoretical positions on "the different roads to socialism" enunciated by Suslov since the XXth Party Congress.[24] In its final form, the Brezhnev Doctrine, as it became universally known, stipulated that all attempts at the restoration of overthrown prerevolutionary political systems in socialist countries were to be opposed vigorously with organized resistance, and that future socialist development had to follow the Soviet experience and be carried out with Soviet help. Stripped of the high-sounding verbiage that promoted the concept of "collective socialist sovereignty," the Brezhnev doctrine was actually a Soviet proclamation of "limited sovereignty" for the satellite nations in Eastern Europe. Suslov had been urging the adoption of this policy on ideological grounds since 1957,[25] and Brezhnev finally acquiesced in it after the Czechoslovak crisis out of considerations that were more geopolitical and strategic than ideological.

The World Communist Conference did not meet in November 1968 as originally planned. The Czechoslovak crisis and its aftermath forced the Soviet Union to defer it in the hope that the passions aroused by the intervention would subside in 1969, but the postponement did not wipe the slate clean. When the conference finally convened in Moscow from June 5 to 19, 1969, it failed to reunite the parties, despite Suslov's efforts to develop a consensus. Of the fourteen ruling parties, five were absent; China, Albania, Yugoslavia, North Korea and North Vietnam chose not to participate, and Cuba sent only an observer. Even more embarrassing was that the parties that sent delegations proved to be unusually outspoken in their criticism of the Soviet Union. In preparation for the Moscow conference, Suslov presented a detailed argument for the universality of the Soviet revolutionary experience. Citing Lenin's experience in the struggle for a socialist Russia, he offered a comprehensive three point explanation of the relevance of Lenin's experience, concluding it with the statement that "Leninism arose not only out of the Russian, but also out of the world-wide workers' movement and of the national liberation, and anti-colonialist movements."[26] To confirm Leninism's Marxist heritage and preclude a discussion of the uniqueness of the Russian experience, he also added a fourth point:

> Leninism arose not in a vacuum but on the foundation of Marxism, and its (further) development. Not a single tenet of Marx and Engels on the important questions of theory and practice of the international revolutionary movement has been omitted from Leninism. Lenin developed and enriched Marxism, on the basis of the fundamental positive studies of Karl Marx and Friedrich Engels.[27]

This did not prevent the foreign parties at the conference from taking a critical stand against the Soviet Union. The majority—especially, the Italian, the Spanish and the Australian delegations—insisted that the tendency of one party to dominate the others was alien to the spirit of Communism, and violated the principles of sovereignty, equality, and non-interference of sovereign states. Only the Eastern European satellite countries and Mongolia supported the "Brezhnev doctrine" and agreed that the Soviet action in Czechoslovakia was warranted by the anti-socialist threat of counterrevolution.[28] In the end, the final resolution of the Conference was nothing but a litany of worn out anti-imperialist slogans and prevailing Communist views on the abolition of war, the approval of the non-proliferation treaty, Israel's withdrawal from the Arab territories, and other generally accepted Communist positions.[29] For Suslov the conference was an unmitigated embarrassment; for Brezhnev, it was a political failure that the Soviet Union could not afford.

The Moscow Conference of Communist Parties was not the only embarrassment for the Soviet Union in 1969. Before the Soviet leaders had fully consolidated their position in Czechoslovakia by removing Dubcek and reconstituting the Czechoslovak leadership on terms satisfactory to them,[30] a serious emergency occurred on the Chinese border. In March, a series of armed skirmishes between the Chinese and Soviet border guards on the Ussuri river created a dangerous new crisis in the Soviet Far East that lasted through the summer of 1969. There was even talk in the West—much of it encouraged by the bellicose statements of the Soviet military—that the USSR was contemplating a "surgical strike" against China. In the end, no such drastic action was undertaken and, instead, a fragile truce was negotiated with the Chinese government. The reality of the Chinese threat made a profound impact on Soviet military thinking. It convinced the Soviet leadership that a permanent settlement of the German question could no longer be postponed indefinitely. The election of Willy Brandt as West German chancellor in October 1969 created the long overdue opening for new negotiations which culminated in the August 1970 treaty with the Federal Republic of Germany. After many years of uncertainty and tension, the Soviet-FRG treaty recognized the division of Germany, validated the Oder-Neisse line and the *status quo* in Berlin, and removed the risk of war in eastern Europe.

Important changes were also taking place in the Soviet Union itself. After years of domestic instability during the Stalin and Khrushchev regimes, the Party *apparatchiks* and the people of the Soviet Union finally began to see the unfolding of a more secure and calm life for themselves. Personnel turn-over in the Party and government organs was trimmed to the minimum. The compulsory rotation of assignments introduced by Khrushchev was revoked, insuring a higher degree of security for the Party *apparatchiks* and the government officials. Repression of dissent and non-conformity continued—perhaps even with greater intensity than during the Khrushchev era—but it was now less accidental, and more institutionalized and orderly in its enforcement, so that everyone knew within reasonable limits what was permitted or tolerated. The *Nomenklatura,** which had always been an integral part of Soviet life, became more entrenched, more bureaucratized, more self-perpetuating—a privileged "class" that fulfilled with almost an inconceivable irony Nekrasov's politically inspired poem "Who Lives Happily in Russia?"[31] All of these changes carried Brezhnev's and Suslov's trademarks, especially Suslov's, whose thirst for order, decorum, and moderation had finally brought a level of modest satisfaction to the majority of the Party and government *apparatchiks*. Indeed, life became more predictable and relaxing for all those whose overriding objective was the maintenance of the newly established *status quo*. Only the liberal intelligentsia continued to feel left out by the lack of impartial and comprehensive reform.

Important changes were also taking place in the field of Soviet ideology—especially with regards to how it interpreted Soviet "peaceful coexistence" with the West. The *rapprochement* with West Germany aroused considerable anxiety among the more conservative Soviet ideologists that the Moscow-Bonn treaty could lead to a reduced Soviet commitment to revolution

---

*Strictly speaking, *Nomenklatura* is a list of positions whose ranks require the confirmation of higher authorities. In practice, it encompasses the privileged Soviet social stratum that is responsible for the administration and running of the Party, the government, and the various industrial, agricultural, research, academic, and service facilities in the Soviet Union.

abroad. According to them, a reinterpretation of "peaceful coexistence" was clearly called for, and Suslov soon came out with one. In October 1969, the chief ideologist proclaimed that "peaceful coexistence" did not just mean peaceful economic competition as it did under Khrushchev, but that it implied a more activist policy of international revolutionary activity. "An analysis of new present-day social phenomena," he said, "shows that the present stage is characterized by growing possibilities for the further advancement of revolutionary and progressive forces."[32] This pronouncement was soon followed with a more explicit statement by Boris Ponomarev, another Central Committee Secretary and loyal supporter of Suslov. "The policy of peaceful coexistence," Ponomarev wrote, is a particular form of class warfare in the international arena. It not only does not restrain revolutionary warfare but helps to boost it."[33] That Suslov and Ponomarev were speaking for the entire Soviet establishment was obvious from other statements appearing in the Soviet press.[34] The new interpretation of "peaceful coexistence" did not put a complete stop to Soviet efforts of reaching détente with the West, but it circumscribed it in a new Soviet policy of Communist expansion that took the West nearly ten years to understand.

As 1969 moved to a close it became clear that the year would end in serious food shortages as a result of a floundering economy and extremely unfavorable weather conditions throughout the year. Under attack from a variety of directions, Brezhnev chose to place the blame on the government organs, insisting that the poor economic performance was due to the inefficiency of the government administration and the faulty economic reforms of 1965. In December, Brezhnev delivered an extremely harsh speech to the Central Committee plenum, implicitly attacking Kosygin for the continued shortcomings of the Soviet economy and charging the government team with irresponsibility and dishonesty.[35] This was a serious accusation, and it is not improbable that Brezhnev may have even been flexing his muscles to ease Kosygin out of his position as Chairman of the Council of Ministers.

That a struggle for power was indeed taking place within the Soviet leadership was evident from the unusual degree of secrecy that suddenly fell on the activities of the Politburo. It was also confirmed by a significant increase in the number of important dismissals. Four heads of republican governments—in Kazakhstan, Moldavia, Azerbaijan and Latvia—were dismissed in the spring of 1970. A number of *obkom* First Secretaries in the Ukraine—Brezhnev's old stronghold—were also replaced, and there were comparable firings in the ideological sector and the central state administration. Even more mystifying was the fact that the XXIVth Party Congress, which was to convene in 1970, was suddenly postponed to 1971, despite Brezhnev's continued assurances that it would be held in 1970.[36] The postponement was attributed to the difficulties encountered in the preparation of a new five-year plan, but it was clear that other reasons must have been the cause, as most of the decisions pertaining to the allocation of resources in industry and agriculture had already been made and announced. To lend more mystery to the conflict, a profusion of rumors and speculations circulated in Moscow and the eastern capitals. According to one account, Suslov, Shelepin and K. T. Mazurov had sent a letter to Brezhnev criticizing him severely for his speech at the December 1969 plenum.[37] The alleged addressing of such a letter seems highly improbable, despite the usually reliable record of its source.[38] In retrospect, it is very unlikely that Suslov would have joined forces with Shelepin in such a risky enterprise. Even more significant, however, is that this was not Suslov's style of reacting to a power struggle in the Politburo. He would have characteristically used caution, discretion and a circuitous maneuver instead of a frontal attack, to say nothing of the fact that such an open display of factionalism was simply not in keeping with his long-established commitment of avoiding factional strife. Another version claimed that the crisis in leadership was precipitated by an attack on Brezhnev by the "super Stalinists" and "ultra-reactionaries," Shelepin and Shelest.[39] In the final analysis, the postponement of the XXIVth Party Congress was probably the most telling sign that a crucial struggle for power was actually taking place in the Politburo and the Secretariat. It would have been a mistake of immense proportions to have convened the Congress without settling the crisis first.

The "Mini Crisis," as it became known among Sovietologists, remains an unsolved mystery to this day, even though the probability is high that Brezhnev's attack on Kosygin in December 1969 was its primary cause. The attack provoked an intense political confrontation within the leadership during the first half of 1970. The confrontation probably reached its most crucial period in April when a significant number of leaders suddenly dropped out of sight. Not surprisingly, the Moscow grapevine immediately concluded that Kosygin was again ill and had been admitted to a hospital for "unspecified complications resulting from a bout with influenza," Podgorny was at home recuperating from a "feverish cold," Suslov was suffering from one of his "recurring tubercular attacks," and Shelepin was "in the hospital undergoing a gall bladder operation."[40] To the surprise of the entire diplomatic corps, the rumors were proven false on Lenin's birthday. Looking mysteriously fit,[41] the entire Politburo reappeared briefly on April 21 to celebrate Lenin's one hundredth anniversary, vanishing from sight again until the Supreme Soviet elections at the end of May. Brezhnev's pointed reference, at the gala ceremony, to Lenin's disapproval of "factionalism" mystified the dissention even more.[42] Invariably, it reinforced the persisting rumor that Kosygin was tired of getting Brezhnev out of trouble and would soon retire to be replaced by Polyansky or, perhaps, even Brezhnev himself.[43]

The primary struggle for power was undoubtedly between Brezhnev and Kosygin, but Shelepin was probably also peripherally involved. He had never completely accepted the erosion of his position, and now used the occasion of the crisis to make another bid for Brezhnev's job. The struggle was also a reflection of the continuing impasse in the Party's approach to the management of the economy. The leadership was hopelessly divided on the economic reform established in 1965, with the Party *apparatchiks* insisting on increased centralization and heightened Party discipline, and Kosygin promoting greater economic flexibility and decentralization. The confrontation apparently came to a head during the last days of June, resolving itself completely in the July 13 plenary session. Kosygin was given a vote of confidence, and the XXIVth Party Congress was postponed to March 1971. On the next day, the Supreme Soviet reaffirmed Kosygin as the Chairman of the Council of Ministers, taking the unprecedented step of not replacing a single member of his cabinet.

The West will probably never know the full story, but the probability is high that Suslov was again the one who played the role of the mediator and power broker. Only he could have kept Brezhnev from seizing Kosygin's post in the government and restraining the majority from falling prey to the power play contrived by Shelepin. The confrontation had clearly gone far enough, and a patching-up was badly needed to restore the *status quo* negotiated after the fall of Khrushchev. No one else but Suslov had enough prestige and influence in the Politburo to restore the collective leadership without reducing Brezhnev's authority as General Secretary. That collectivity was indeed reestablished by the end of June is revealed by an interesting incident described by Mohamed Heikel. During a June 29 meeting with Nasser in the Kremlin, a telegram was brought in and delivered to Minister of Foreign Affairs Gromyko for his approval. Heikel was present at this meeting, and recalls in minute detail the Soviet handling of this communication.

> Gromyko . . . read it, got up, and took it to Kosygin. Kosygin read it, and gave it to Brezhnev. Brezhnev read it, and gave it back to Kosygin. Kosygin than gave it to Podgorny. Podgorny read it, and gave it back to Kosygin, who gave it back to Brezhnev. Then Brezhnev signed, and gave it to Kosygin, who signed it too. Then Podgorny signed. Then Podgorny gave it to Gromyko, who gave it to Vinogradov, who gave it back to the Foreign Office official. The official then left the room.[44]

The communication turned out to be a telegram warning General Siad in Somalia that a *coup d'etat* was expected to take place against him that evening. "Did you see what happened," Nasser said to Heikel later. "It is too bureaucratic. If a telegram to General Siad . . . needs the signature of those three, then we are in trouble. Now I understand why our requests take such a long time to produce results."[45] Nasser was obviously not aware that the Soviet leaders were still smarting from the recently resolved "Mini Crisis" and that its resolution had imposed on them again a most rigidly structured demand for the exercise of collective leadership.

The importance of ideology for the Soviet leadership—any Soviet leadership—is seldom understood in the West . . . Their rule is anchored in ideology, as the divine rights of kings was in Christianity.[1]

Milovan Djilas

Chapter XVI

PARTY THEORETICIAN

The Soviet leadership had emerged from the July plenum outwardly reconciled, but internally lacking in confidence and unity. Suslov had negotiated a compromise that was more a stalemate than a settlement, a state of near-equilibrium between the more progressive economic reformers and the politically conservative Party *apparatchiks* seeking a higher level of Party participation in the economic life of the nation. Brezhnev and Kosygin had retained their dominant positions, but at the expense of long-overdue reform. The result was sterility, a *status-quo* that recognized the need for economic and social advances, but could not agree on what was precisely needed and how it was to be achieved.

The XXIVth Party Congress that finally opened on March 30, 1971 revealed most vividly the continuity of this impasse, accomplishing almost nothing to solve the pressing social and economic problems with which the Party and the Soviet society were faced. The Congress approved a new program for the exchange of Party documents and the extension of Party control to a wide range of government, research, and service institutions. The tightening of supervision and the strengthening of the Party's direct role at the primary level of production were counter-balanced by the decision to move ahead with the formation of production associations that were to act as intermediaries between the ministries and the industrial complexes. By agreeing to take power away from individual enterprises and giving it to the production associations, the Party had, in effect, decided to give up on decentralization as a means of improving the performance of individual production plants. In the end, the changes announced at the Congress were clearly administrative—not economic—and the balancing act was but another reflection of the delicate equilibrium struck by Suslov during the previous year.

Suslov attended the Congress and performed his traditional duty of chairing the second morning session on March 31. However, he did not address the XXIVth Party Congress. In the transitional climate of expanding détente the chief ideologist had decided not to make any ideological statements that might reduce the Soviet Union's options in dealing with the Communist nations and the countries of the Third World.

An important innovation coming out of the XXIVth Party Congress was the expansion of the Politburo to a total of fifteen voting members. Four new members—three of them close supporters of Brezhnev—enhanced the relative weight of the Party apparatus, vastly improving Brezhnev's long-term influence in the Politburo.[2] The expansion of the Politburo insured a better distribution of the functional responsibilities at the very top of the Soviet leadership, but its immediate effect was unsettling. Especially confusing was the order of the new leadership line-up. The initial announcement on the radio provided an ordered ranking of the new Politburo as Brezhnev, Podgorny, Kosygin, Suslov, Kirilenko, Pel'she, Mazurov, Polyansky, Shelest, Voronov, Shelepin, Grishin, Kunayev, Shcherbitsky, and Kulakov, while a press follow-up on the next day set a new precedent, listing the members in alphabetical order in what appeared to be a deliberate effort to promote equality and discourage rank.[3]

Although the practical outcome of the XXIVth Party Congress was negligible, an important new theoretical concept was added to the official canons of Soviet doctrine.[4] Speaking at the opening session, Brezhnev proudly announced that the "developed socialist society about which Lenin spoke in 1918 had already been built in the Soviet Union."[5] Brezhnev did not give any details, but the implication was obvious. According to the resolution of the Central Committee,[6] Soviet society had apparently reached a new period of development, the stage of "developed socialism."[7]

Suslov had been pondering the question of how it was best to reconcile Lenin's notion of "transition from socialism to communism" with the Soviet experience since the early 1960s. He had referred to this problem in his January 1962 address to the Conference of the Heads of Social Science Faculties,[8] and had actually used the term "mature socialism"[9] several times in 1968 in his speech at the celebration of the 150th anniversary of the birth of Karl Marx.[10] Beginning with the late 1950s, he had consistently lowered Soviet expectations and emphasized the very slow and gradual development of Soviet society on its way to full communism. Perhaps the best example of his early thinking on this subject came from his address to the XXIst Party Congress. "Communism does not appear suddenly," he said, "but comes into existence, matures, develops, passes in its development through definite stages or phases."[11] There were also other references in his speeches and writings to the slow transition of socialism to communism in the Soviet Union.[12] Whether or not he actually thought of replacing Lenin's periodization with a new and more realistic timetable remains debatable. As the Party's chief theoretician and defender of the faith, he was probably more interested in bolstering morale and conveying a sense of progress in the face of the Soviet failure to achieve an early construction of full communism, than in a reformulation of Lenin's theory. He had always insisted that Marxist-Leninist theory could not be altered, but only enriched, and he probably had serious misgivings about a formal reperiodization of Soviet history. The works of Marx and Lenin were sacred writings, and he could never take that crucial step himself. He was too much of a conservative and "true believer" to propose a new scheme. It was Brezhnev who recognized the symbolic value of the new concept, and decided to construct out of it a new interpretation of Soviet development.

Lenin had visualized three stages of Soviet history—an initial period of "building socialism," a period of "established socialism," and a final period of "full communism" during which a classless and stateless society would supplant socialism.[13] According to Khrushchev, Soviet society had reached Lenin's stage of "established socialism" in 1960, but its progress to "communism" had been extremely slow since then, despite Khrushchev's extravagant promises that the Soviet Union would achieve full communism in the 1970s. The insertion of a transitional stage between "socialism" and full "communism" rationalized the slowing down of social and economic development in the Soviet Union during the 1960s. Both Brezhnev and Suslov recognized the practical benefits of this, but it was far more tempting and beneficial for Brezhnev to take the crucial step. For him it was not just a matter of reconciling theory with practice, but a once in a lifetime opportunity to rise beyond the executive and administrative framework of his position as General Secretary to the more sublime status of a Marxist theoretician. Stalin had achieved this posture with his notion of "socialism in one country" and with his economic writings after the war. Khrushchev tried to do the same with his "withering away" thesis and his theory that the "whole people" had replaced the "dictatorship of the proletariat." Brezhnev saw a similar opportunity in Suslov's notion of "mature socialism."

The Russian term for "mature socialism," *"zrelyi sotsializm"* could easily acquire a negative connotation,* and Brezhnev decided to call it *"razvitoi sotsializm,"* "developed socialism," a term that was semantically safer and had a better ring to it. Obliging Marxist political scientists and philosophers adopted the new concept without any reservations, giving Brezhnev full credit for the conceptualization of a new framework of Soviet development. Beginning with Boris Sukhachevsky's article "The Economy of the USSR: An Economy of Developed Socialism" in the December 1971 issue of *Kommunist,*[14] a steady flow of essays and monographs began appearing on the subject of "developed socialism" in the Soviet press.[15]

Suslov had actually set the stage for a more detailed and specialized analysis of "developed socialism" with his seminal essay on the Party's role, "KPSS—Partiia tvorcheskogo Marksizma" (CPSU, The Party of Creative Marxism). Using Marx's often vulgarized and oversimplified Preface to the *Contribution to The Critique of Political Economy*[16] as a guide, Suslov gave the

---

*The first and most common meaning of the Russian word *"zrelyi"* is "ripe" rather than "mature." Moscow wits wasted no time in renaming *"zrelyi sotsializm"* as *"perezrelyi sotsializm,"* or "over-ripe socialism," an obviously disparaging term.

first complete definition of "developed socialism" in the September 1971 issue of the *Kommunist,* three full months before Sukhachevsky's article appeared in the same journal.[17]

> Mature socialism presupposes all-round and harmonious development of the economic, socio-political, and cultural conditions of life. At this stage society has a powerful material and technological potential built up on the basis of comprehensive development of the national economy and application of the latest scientific and technological achievements in production. . . . Developed socialism is distinguished by mature social relations which have taken shape on the basis of unchallenged socialist ownership of the means of production, the eradication of all exploiter elements, and the establishment of the socio-political and ideological unity of society. Developed socialist society has a corresponding political super-structure— the state of the whole people embodying profound democratism. Among its distinctive features are the broad development of public education and the universal spread and assertion of the Marxist-Leninist world outlook.[18]

Suslov's definition was essentially an economic formulation. It precipitated a revision of Khrushchev's time table of rapid building of communism and postponed the ultimate attainment of a fully communist society to an undisclosed future date. It did not alter the leadership's commitment to centralized administration. Consistent with his previous critique of Khrushchev's thesis of the "state of the whole people,"[19] it did not say anything about the abatement or termination of political and ideological control during the long and transitional stage of "mature socialism." The fact that the Soviet leadership recognized a new stage of "mature socialism" did not signify that the class struggle had come to an end. On the contrary, it reinforced Suslov's pessimistic view that the complete elimination of class distinctions was still years away and that a need for a conscious and centralized organization of society under the aegis of the Party and the state continued to exist in the Soviet Union despite the attainments of the "developed socialist society."

The obvious question arising out of the new prescription for Soviet development is how sincere are the Soviet leaders about Marxist-Leninist doctrine when it can be revised so painlessly to meet the reality of the Soviet ethos. This is an old question convincingly argued by a succession of Western experts trying to determine the relationship between Soviet ideology and Soviet reality.[20] The spectrum of opinion ranges from those who contend that Marxism-Leninism functions as a rigidly imposed precept of political, economic and social action, to those who consider it nothing but a cynical smokescreen used to legitimize the inadequacies of Soviet life. The real answer is probably somewhere in between these two assertions. Even though the primary function of ideology is to define how men should think and act, in varying degrees, all ideologies justify reality, and Soviet ideology is not an exception to this rule. As a matter of fact, Soviet ideology is unquestionably more compulsive and dogmatic than the established ideologies of the West. Because of its revolutionary tradition and newness, it is so completely obsessed with the idea of building a new system of thinking and living that it often defeats the more pragmatic interests of the Soviet nation state. It is also not as constant and homogeneous as it is generally believed to be. The intensity of faith and commitment shifts back and forth with the times, with political crises, and with the intrinsic and extrinsic pressures against the regime. To a large extent, it depends on the objectives of the General Secretary, and the methods he chooses to achieve the Party's goals. His temperament and motivation have a great deal to do with whether ideology becomes the determining plan of action or a cynical public relations device. Stalin, for example was clearly more dogmatic than Khrushchev, but it is highly unlikely that he believed in everything he did and said. Brezhnev, on the other hand, was probably least dogmatic, but the constraints placed on him by Suslov and the collective leadership forced him to conform to the official ideology more often than Khrushchev did.

Suslov's attitude towards ideology was explicitly defined. Marxism-Leninism was the dominant and motivating force of his entire life. This is not to say that he never used ideology as a polemical and political tool. As a matter of fact, his secret—like that of the original *éminence grise*—was that he had learned to compartmentalize his political behavior without restructuring his ideological beliefs. Invariably, he remained a "true believer" even when he chose to compromise. This was reflected in his attitude to Khrushchev's decision to scrap the Machine Tractor Stations and to the Party bifurcation plan. In both instances, Suslov accepted the reforms as practical measures, refusing to recognize them on theoretical grounds. His roots, his preference for Party work, his pursuit of a career in ideology rather than in the administrative field, his personal attitudes and values were all witnesses to a love affair with Marxism-Leninism that lasted an entire lifetime, sustaining his ego even when he was forced to take a back seat to someone else.[21]

The circumstances surrounding Brezhnev's announcement of the achievement of "developed socialism" certainly attest to this. No matter how strongly Suslov felt about the need for the reperiodization of the Soviet experience, he could not take that crucial step himself. The acceptance of a fourth and intermediate period of Soviet development embodied only a peripheral alteration in Leninist theory, but Suslov could not bring himself to embrace what had been stamped in his mind as a heretical act. "Thou shall have no other gods before thee" was too strongly imprinted to allow even a minor variation of the Soviet "holy writ." It took six full months for him to approve Brezhnev's declaration. Despite earlier attempts to come to grips with it, it was not until December 21,

1971, that Suslov finally endorsed the concept of "mature socialism" as an official doctrine. Speaking to the All-Union Conference of the Heads of Social Science Departments, Suslov finally acknowledged that "the main guideline the XXIVth CPSU Congress set for our social scientists is the theoretical elaboration of the fundamental problems of a developed socialist society and the scientific substantiation of the ways and means of its gradual development into communism."[22]

In the sphere of foreign relations, the years 1971 and 1972 witnessed a dramatic change in Soviet foreign policy. The Soviet Union began scaling down its military and economic commitments throughout the world, working systematically to reduce the explosive situation in the Middle East, and collaborating more actively with the United States to prevent the proliferation of nuclear weapons. Economic difficulties at home compelled the Soviet Union to seek a reduction in its armaments expenditures, while the growing fear of the Chinese threat—especially after the improvement of Sino-American relations initiated by Kissinger and Nixon—lead to a less aggressive Soviet foreign policy. The winding down of the Vietnam War was also a positive development, allowing the Soviet Union to reduce its anti-American propaganda and engage in more open negotiations with the United States. The net result of all this was a feverish expansion of diplomatic activity with the United States, resulting in the May 26, 1972 Nixon-Brezhnev Interim Agreement to stabilize the level of the two superpowers' nuclear armaments, leading eventually to SALT I and the US-Soviet Trade Agreement.

At home, the year 1970 witnessed an escalation in the Party's campaign against a new wave of Russian nationalist and Orthodox religious activism. Despite numerous attempts to tone Russian nationalism down or integrate it with Marxism-Leninism, the Party never really succeeded in suppressing Great Russian chauvinism. Nikolai Danilevsky, Konstantin Leontiev,[23] and a procession of early and latter-day Slavophiles had left a permanent mark on the Russian psyche and the stride of Soviet history. The Revolution had temporarily muffled Russian nationalism, but it did not succeed in silencing it permanently. After the Civil War, Russian nationalism gained a new lease on life through the émigré *Smena vekh* movement and Nikolai Ustrialov's doctrine of "national bolshevism,"[24] which exerted a considerable influence on Stalin's thinking by downgrading the internationlist component of Marxism-Leninism. In 1924, Stalin partially legitimized Ustrialov's views in his policy of "socialism in one country," turning the Soviet Union inward and away from the Revolution's internationalist roots.[25] The next ten years saw a series of unsuccessful maneuvers by what was essentially a pro-internationalist opposition to Stalin's Russian nationalist leanings, followed by the repression and purges of the 1930s that permanently demolished what remained of the internationalist old guard. World War II gave Russian nationalism a new impetus, raising it from the obscurity of Stalin's camouflaged policy to the level of individual patriotism and reawakened national consciousness. The emergence of the Soviet Union as a major world power after the war precipitated a new interest in Communist internationalism and in a new ideology that suppressed nationalism and promoted proletarian internationalism as a vehicle of Soviet expansion and post-war reconstruction of the Communist world. Despite the new ideological injunction, the internationalist idea was never fully assimilated in the multinational Soviet state, and nationalist strivings have continued to surface in the post-Stalin era. Rooted in Russian history and stimulated by Khrushchev's anti-religious assault on ancient Russian churches and national monuments, Russian nationalism reemerged in the 1960s and early 1970s as a powerful challenge to the official Soviet ideology of proletarian supra-nationalism. It appeared in the spontaneous forming of patriotic organizations for the preservation of neglected monuments and churches, in the revival of Russian Orthodox Christianity, in the rise and popularity of the *Derevensh-chiki,** in the reawakening of Russian chauvinism and anti-Semitism, and in the emergence within the democratic movement itself of a distinctly Russian species of patriotic and religious dissent.

Soviet nationality policy instinctively adapted itself to the course of history, displaying clearly defined fluctuations in its programs and goals. During the 1920s its primary goal remained predominantly Leninist. With the help of the radical intelligentsia and the non-Russian elements who made up the early Soviet leadership, Soviet nationality policy continued to suppress Great Russian nationalism and promote revolution at home and abroad. Under Stalin's policy of socialism in one country, the non-Russian leadership was gradually exterminated and new Russian cadres were hurriedly recruited to produce a resurgence of Russian nationalist tendencies in Soviet nationality policy. In the Khrushchev and Brezhnev periods, the integration of the "socialist bloc" into a Soviet commonwealth of nations caused the Soviet leadership to reverse Stalinist policies and initiate, instead, a new foreign and domestic policy that restrained nationalism and maximized the proletarian unity of the Communist world.[26] Throughout these zigzagging fluctuations, Suslov remained intensely faithful to the Marxist-Leninist view of a supra-national proletarian fatherland. His love affair with the concept of the "Soviet nation" and the "new Soviet man" went back to the early 1940s.[27] Expressions such as "Sovetskie ludi" (Soviet people), "Sovetskii narod" (Soviet nation), "nasha Sotsialisticheskaia rodina" (our socialist fatherland), "nasha mnogonatsional'naia Sotsialisticheskaia rodina" (our multi-national Socialist fatherland) have been a constant feature in all his speeches and writings since his May 25, 1940 address at the meeting commemorating the completion of the Nevinnomyskii canal in Stavropol *oblast'*.[28] Even during World War II, when everyone else in the Soviet Union was bowing in deference to the "Rus-

---

*Ruralist writers who criticized the course of Soviet industrialization and urbanization and, indirectly, belittled the whole Soviet system.

sian people," Suslov continued to single out the "Soviet people" as the "loyal and brave fighters" of the Great Patriotic War for the Fatherland.[29]

After the war, Suslov helped Stalin formulate a new foreign policy that reaffirmed the concept of class struggle and reintroduced the idea of a binding international community of Communist states under Soviet leadership. In his Lenin Day speech in 1948, he defined the essentials of Soviet patriotism and unfolded a general theory of the Soviet nation-state and Soviet man.[30] Since then, he had gradually expanded the original concept, dispensing a range of closely related views on Soviet nationalism which placed him into the category of a Marxist-Leninist universalist in direct opposition to Russian nationalism.

It was probably Suslov who pressed for the censure of *Molodaia gvardiia* in 1971. The journal had become too outspoken in its promotion of Russian nationalism, and the Politburo had no other alternative but to purge it of its nationalist influence.[31] With the sacking of the *Molodaia gvardiia* editorial board, Russian nationalism turned to *samizdat* and other clandestine activities,[32] forcing the Party to wage a far-reaching campaign of repression against the *samizdat* writers, whose ranks included a wide spectrum of Russophile intellectuals, including such internationally known authors as Aleksandr Solzhenitsyn.

During the first half of the 1970s Suslov remained an intractable foe of the Russian nationalists, steering the Soviet ideological *apparat* against all political orientations of nationalism that did not have the approval of the Party. A. N. Yakovlev's lengthy article "Against Anti-Historicism" in the November 15, 1972 issue of *Literaturnaia gazeta* was a clear confirmation of this.[33] In his capacity as acting head of *Agitprop,* Yakovlev lambasted Russian nationalism for its "single stream" interpretation of Russian history and for the "unfailingly reactionary" ideology of the Russian Orthodox Church. It is inconceivable that Yakovlev could have taken such a drastic step without the encouragement of the Party's ideological leadership, perhaps even Suslov himself. There was a rejoinder in the *samizdat* press and the debate continued to sputter for another year,[34] but to all intents and purposes Yakovlev's powerful attack on Russian nationalism put an end to further public manifestations of extreme nationalism.

In the meantime, the chief ideologist systematically glorified the notions of the "Soviet party state" and "Soviet man," sometimes even overstepping the framework of Lenin's nationality policy and his prescription for a multi-national communist state. Lenin's thoughts on world internationalism and domestic nationality questions remained strikingly constant, even after 1917 when he had to face the practical problems of building a new state.[35] He had a profound distaste for Great Russian nationalism, but considered it on the whole a transient problem—a by-product of capitalism—which, like all manifestations of nationalism, was doomed to die out once capitalism was replaced by socialism. He recognized the reality of the non-Russian nationalist feelings and looked upon the various national and ethnic groups in the multinational Russian empire as allies that could be mobilized to support the revolution and promote proletarian liberation movements against the "imperialist nations" of the world. He conceded the right to national self-determination, but was convinced that in the interest of international integration and proletarian unity, it was a mistake to split up multinational states into their component parts. Thus, nationalism had only an instrumental and transitory value for Lenin, a value that he thought would lose its stimulus with the abolishment of oppression and imperialist rule. While Lenin tended to underestimate the power of nationalist feelings, Suslov learned the hard way how durable and pernicious they were. He never lost faith in the ultimate demise of nationalism, but the growing discrepancy between Soviet ideology and reality convinced him that the disappearance of national feelings would not take place spontaneously without a concerted effort to stifle them. It was no accident, therefore, that he used every opportunity possible—especially in the 1970s—to alert the Party and its leadership to the dangers of persisting nationalism in the Soviet Union and throughout the world. Invariably, he called for the integration of the various nations and ethnic groups in the Soviet Union within the "nonnational" and "ideological" framework of the Soviet party state drawing its authority from the Marxist interpretation of history and the 1917 Revolution. The most explicit formulation of this doctrine may be found in his November 28, 1973 address in Vilnius, "Friendship and Brotherhood of the Free Nations of the USSR:"

> The socio-political relations of developed socialism are characterized by the further unity of all classes and social groups, all nations and nationalities in one mighty collective of builders of communism . . . The principal tendency of the future perfection of the relations of developed socialist society is the steadfast striving toward the socialist homogeneity and national *rapprochement* (*sblizhenie*). This tendency is expressed in the strengthening of the moral and political unity of Soviet society . . . The general lines that bind and unite the (socialist nations) into a single indivisible Soviet nation came into existence and developed on the socio-economic basis of socialism, proletarian internationalism, and the massive educational work of the Party.[36]

Suslov's Vilnius speech was important for another reason. It contained significant comments on the question of Soviet inter-Republic boundaries. In late 1972, Victor Kistanov, a respected Soviet economist, proposed in the authoritative *Voprosy ekonomiki* that existing Soviet boundaries between union republics be redrawn to maximize the economic activity of the USSR as a whole.[37] Several months later, a rebuttal to this proposal appeared in the Lithuanian edition of the *Kommunist*.[38] The rebuttal was written by Al'gimantas Lebedinscas, a Soviet official of Lithuanian origin, who insisted that the boundaries of the Soviet constituent republics must be maintained along strict ethnic lines. Suslov categorically rejected Lebedinscas' view, and instead endorsed Kistanov's thesis with the statement that "the raising of the efficiency of our socialist production and the creation of the material-technological basis of communism are possible only within the framework of an all-union economic complex."[39] Suslov's commentary did not resolve the controversy, and other senior Soviet officials joined the debate. Kiril Mazurov, a Politburo member and First Deputy Chairman of the All-Union Council of Ministers, even went so far as to suggest that the existing boundaries were drafted along ethnic lines specifically at Lenin's behest.[40] The debate petered out in 1973, and the existing borders were left untouched, but it became very apparent from it that Suslov favored a national *rapprochement* of the union republics not only out of ideological considerations but also on the basis of an economic and perhaps even political rationale,[41] a position that clearly transcended Lenin's prescription of spontaneous proletarian integration. Suslov obviously had no hesitation to use more drastic measures that would hasten the national *rapprochement* of the various nationalities in the union republics.

The spread of Russian nationalist activism was by no means the only domestic issue that troubled the Soviet authorities in the early 1970s. By 1973, dissent within the Soviet Union had reached vast proportions, affecting a broad spectrum of the Soviet intelligentsia. Literally hundreds of leading intellectuals and disaffected nationalist and religious spokesmen rose up under the impetus of détente and the Helsinki civil rights accords to question the regime's persisting unwillingness in democratizing Soviet society and relaxing the internal tensions that had built up since the ouster of Khrushchev.

In July 1973, Andrei D. Sakharov, the Soviet Union's leading physicist and father of the Soviet hydrogen bomb, published a scathing attack on the one-party system in the Soviet Union, calling it antidemocratic and vindictive.[42] In August, Aleksandr I. Solzhenitsyn gave an interview to two Western correspondents in which he spoke of threats against his life and, in December, further outraged the Party leadership by publishing in Paris *The Gulag Archipelago,* a stirring account of police oppression and terror in the USSR from 1919 to 1956.[43] The Jewish emigration issue was also heating up. The adverse publicity generated by Moscow's refusal to grant an exit permit to Valery Panov, a Jewish dancer with the Bolshoi Ballet, and by the increasing anxiety over the reduction in the number of emigration permits issued in 1974, caused widespread concern over the treatment of Jews in the Soviet Union.[44] The *Chronicle of Current Events,* an outlawed *samizdat* publications monitoring civil rights violations, again appeared in Moscow, despite a widely publicized campaign to discourage the dissemination of underground literature. Avant-garde artists were also testing the patience of the authorities. A Moscow exhibition of unauthorized works in September 1974 was bulldozed into the ground, and a large number of the works were completely ruined.

As usual, the leadership responded with a vigorous press campaign against the principal challengers, followed by a stepped-up police drive to silence the dissident publishers, writers, artists, and churchmen. But, this time, the Party's reaction seemed more cautious, more pliable, more temperate. There was almost a kind of a schizophrenic incongruence to the campaign. On the one hand, the regime deployed all its resources to silence the leading figures in the struggle for civil rights, using every possible means of pressure—arrests, harassment, intimidation, termination of employment, cancellation of travel permits and exit visas, and even physical force. On the other, it avoided extreme measures and, on the whole, handed out relatively light sentences to those whom it chose to incarcerate.

In September 1973, Pyotr Yakir and Victor Krasin, who were arrested in 1972 and pleaded guilty to charges of working with foreign correspondents in Moscow, received sentences of three years in prison and three years in internal exile, only to be subsequently released from prison. The Ukrainian literary critic Ivan Dzyuba, sentenced to five years of imprisonment and five years of internal exile for "anti-Soviet agitation," was pardoned in November 1973, and Andrei Amalrik's sentence for "slandering the Soviet Union" was reduced from imprisonment in a labor camp to exile. Some protesters were simply deprived of their Soviet citizenship and expelled from the Soviet Union. Aleksandr Solzhenitsyn, the Soviet Union's most famous dissenter and novelist, was so expelled. So were the dissident writer Vladimir Maksimov and Pavel Litvinov, grandson of Maxim Litvinov, the former Commissar of Foreign Affairs. Zhores A. Medvedev and Valery N. Chalidze were given permission to pursue their scientific work abroad, but were deprived of their citizenship and denied the right to return to the Soviet Union after they had left. In June 1974, former Major General Pyotr Grigorenko, who had been incarcerated in insane asylums for five years, was suddenly released. Permission was also granted for the closed-down art exhibit in a park on the outskirts of Moscow, and more than ten thousand curious Russians viewed the avant-garde pictures. It was as if the Politburo had suddenly discovered that moderation, lighter sentences, clemency, and exile served its domestic objectives better in neutralizing the new wave of political protest.

A number of developments contributed to the adoption of the new policy. The Soviet determination to pursue détente played an important role in moderating the leadership's attitude toward domestic dissent. The Party leaders were obviously concerned about world public opinion, especially during Brezhnev's visit to the United States and the Western European capitals in 1973. The reconstitution of the Politburo in April 1973 also had a salutary effect on domestic policy. The retirement of Pyotr Shelest and Gennadii Voronov, the two principal hardliners in the Politburo, and the addition of Andrei Gromyko, Yuri Andropov, and Marshal Grechko altered the internal dynamics of the Soviet collective leadership, moving it in the direction of a more rational and pragmatic behavior on both foreign and domestic issues. The expansion of Suslov's influence was also not unimportant. The chief ideologue was at the peak of his career in 1973, exerting tremendous influence on all Soviet policies. He had not given up yet completely Moscow's quest to rejuvenate the international communist movement, and was desperately trying to promote a more favorable opinion of the Soviet Union among the European communist leaders.

Suslov's preference for moderation in dealing with the dissident movement probably went beyond the pragmatic prerequisites of appeasing the European communists. With his strong commitment to socialist legality and his unremitting faith in Communism's power to reeducate even the most recalcitrant of political protestors, Suslov was never really in favor of extreme measures of punishment. He was for closer Party vigilance, and for a more vigorous and uncompromising pursuit of discrediting the various manifestations of dissent in the Soviet Union.[45] But his stance on punishment appeared to be more restrained. He had endorsed the rather lenient handling of Pasternak in 1958, and he was also reputed to have opposed the severe sentences inflicted on Sinyavsky and Daniel.[46] On the whole, he preferred more tolerant methods of disciplinary action—exile, forfeiture of citizenship, expulsion from the Party, public and professional ostracism, and compulsory reindoctrination. It is not improbable, therefore, that the seeming incongruence of the 1970s campaign was at least partially the result of his influence. Indeed, Suslov's primary objective remained always the same—to reinforce the vigilance of the Party faithful and to discredit the dissidents in the eyes of the largely apathetic Soviet people. Once this was achieved, he was quite willing to tolerate a relatively lenient form of punishment, and acquiesce to a sentence of exile in the interest of minimizing repercussions at home and abroad. Originally applying primarily to internal exile, this quintessentially Russian form of penance suffered by thousands of Russian liberals and radicals since the XIXth century was conveniently converted to foreign exile, providing a sensible and functional solution for the hard-pressed Soviet leadership of the 1970s. But for a few exceptions, it isolated the dissident from his partisan audience and from his source of protest, allowing time and distance to blur the controversy and muffle the voices of the critics. Andrei Amalrik's poignant remark on this subject is especially relevant. In an interview with Radio Liberty in Amsterdam, Amalrik perceptively noted that there are "some individualistic people in the Soviet Union whom the authorities can not convert to their way of thinking and, having understood that there is no place for them in Soviet society, send them abroad."[47]

The early 1970s brought both tragedy and recognition to Suslov's personal life. In September 1972, Elizaveta Suslova, Suslov's wife of many years, died after a long and grave illness.[48] A communist member since 1928 and Director of the Moscow Dental Institute, Suslova was given a ceremonial funeral, including a lying in state at the Central Committee headquarters, attended by Brezhnev and a host of Soviet dignitaries who came to pay their last respects.[48] On a more pleasant note, Suslov celebrated his seventieth birthday on November 21, and was awarded another Order of Lenin and his second Sickle and Hammer Medal in ceremonies staged in the Kremlin specially for the occasion. "I consider my whole life belonging to the Party,"[49] Suslov said, reaffirming fifty years of loyal service to Communism in his reply to the commendation address. The past ten years had propelled him to the very top of the Party pyramid, but not without paying for it with increasingly failing health. In contrast to the rest of his fleshy and heavy-bodied colleagues, he had become at seventy a gaunt, angular and ascetic-looking skeleton of a man who looked more like a beardless version of an ancient Russian prelate than a successful senior *apparatchik,* a living reminder of the role that he had been playing most of his adult life.

The summit conferences of May 1972 and June 1973 evoked in the Soviet Union—just as they did in the United States—a feeling that détente would lead to the negotiation of Soviet-American differences and bring about a significant improvement in Soviet-American relations. Fearing that the uncontrolled expansion of this outlook could undermine the basic tenets of international communism, Suslov adamantly denied that détente could lead to an eventual reconciliation of the two systems. He had opposed an unrestricted policy of détente during Khrushchev's administration, and he was against a similar attempt by Brezhnev. In January 1973, he and Ponomarev launched a powerful campaign in the Soviet press to clarify that "peaceful coexistence" between communism and capitalism did not mean that the Soviet Union was looking toward an eventual reconciliation with the West. To Suslov détente meant the avoidance of a military confrontation in an environment of continued conflict and competition for the liberation of the oppressed peoples of the world. "Our Party," he said in an address fittingly entitled "The Great Science of Victory," "regards as its international duty . . . the continued pursuit of a socialist foreign policy aimed at consolidating world peace, and ensuring new successes in the struggle of people for social and national liberations."[50] The 1973 speech was actually an abridged version of a more comprehensive statement made by Suslov in his 1967 article in *Great October,* a commemorative book specially issued to observe the fiftieth anniversary of the October Revolution.[51]

Since the death of Stalin, there had always been two factions within the Soviet leadership debating the efficacy of détente. In the early 1970s, the moderates were headed by Brezhnev and Kosygin, and the hard-liners by Suslov and Ponomarev. The moderates were clearly in the majority, but this did not mean that Suslov was entirely without support. He had the backing of the KGB, the military and the ideological apparatus of the Party, and he was convinced that détente was, in fact, a newly induced form of conflict that would lead to the ultimate victory of communism over capitalism because the "correlation of world forces" had shifted in favor of the Communist world.[52] Arguing that the "correlation of world forces" had gradually shifted from capitalism to communism in three successive stages that included the collapse of the intervention during the Civil War, the defeat of Nazi Germany and the rise of communism in Eastern Europe, and the 1969–1970 attainment of strategic military parity with the United States, Suslov consistently maintained that the conflict and competition between the two systems had become economic, political, and ideological, and that the Soviet Union had now surpassed the West in strength. A succession of Soviet political and military authors followed in Suslov's footsteps expressing the same view,[53] and Suslov went even beyond that to argue that, owing to the new correlation of forces, it was the "capitalist states" that were forced to accept "peaceful coexistence" with the communist states.[54] This view was closely associated with his unremitting faith in the power and vitality of "proletarian internationalism." "The Communist parties," he said "challenge the cunning strategy of imperialism and its ideological sabotage with *proletarian internationalism,** the determined struggle against imperialism and its accomplices."[55] One Western expert on Soviet politics has correctly noted that of all the Soviet leaders since Stalin, Suslov, more than anyone else had "stressed the party's world mission and its role as a vanguard of the international proletariat."[56] With the help of Ponomarev and a bevy of orthodox theoreticians in the Party's ideological apparatus, Suslov continued to remind the leadership that the Soviet Union had an ideological rather than a national basis for its existence and, therefore, had a sacred duty and responsibility of supporting world revolution, despite détente and the negotiations with the West. "The communist movement," he insisted, "derives its strength from its loyalty to the great Marxist-Leninist teaching—the ideals of proletarian internationalism."[57] In another equally internationalist statement, he affirmed with an even greater degree of emphasis that "proletarian internationalism, which expresses the common position and interests of the working people in all countries, has always been and remains the guiding principle in the theoretical and practical activities of Marxist-Leninists."[58] And in the summer of 1975, as Soviet transport aircraft began airlifting armaments to Brazzaville for the MPLA,[59] Suslov boldly proclaimed that "the principle of peaceful coexistence between states with different social systems . . . has nothing in common with class peace between the exploiters and the exploited, the colonialists and the victims of colonial oppression, or between the oppressors and the oppressed."[60]

Despite Suslov's crusade to encourage the export of revolution, several factors militated against a more aggressive Soviet position in 1973. Détente was only a year old, and Brezhnev was still hesitant about taking a more vociferous stand on national liberation movements in the Third World. The instability in the Middle East and Southeast Asia, and the Sino-American *rapprochement* also called for a more cautious approach. This state of uncertainty was short-lived, however. Watergate and the anticipated Communist victory in Vietnam radically changed the Soviet stance *vis a vis* the United States, especially as the Soviets saw their position in Egypt slipping away to the United States. In June 1974,

---

*Italicized by the author for emphasis.

Suslov again reminded his listeners that détente was "based on the change in the world correlation of forces in favor of socialism," and that Soviet diplomacy was again fostering "more possible prospects for pushing revolution further ahead."[61] Soviet statements in favor of détente continued through the rest of 1974, but they were becoming increasingly less conciliatory and in favor of more aggressive support of revolution in the Third World. By the end of 1974, the Soviet Union began to reassess it policies toward the Third World, gradually stepping up again its support for revolutionary regimes and movements throughout the world. This had been the policy during the Khrushchev era when the Soviet Union did not hesitate to take advantage of favorable situations, openly providing support for the civil war in Zaire[62] and the radicalized governments in Indonesia, Ghana, and Guinea. During the early years of the Brezhnev administration, swayed by Kosygin's influence and the adverse outcome of the confrontations in Cuba, the Soviet Union had scaled down its support of revolution, concentrating primarily on projects of economic benefit to the Soviet Union and countries along the southern border where there was a clearly defined strategic interest. After 1974, the Soviet Union again expanded it activities throughout the Third World—this time with the help of a built up navy and newly developed military power—leading eventually to Soviet involvement in Angola and Ethiopia and to the undermining of détente to which Suslov had always remained only lukewarm.

While Suslov's prodding had succeeded in influencing Soviet foreign policy, it had failed miserably in stimulating the interests of the international communist movement itself. Claiming its authenticity from Marx and the *Communist Manifesto*, and vicariously interpreted by a succession of communists as the struggle of the progressive forces of society against capitalist nationalism and imperialism, "proletarian internationalism" had acquired a distinctly Soviet coloring by the end of the 1960s. It had become primarily a euphemism for Soviet rule, a strategic tool in the hands of the Soviet leaders to help them maintain control over the rapidly crumbling world Communist movement. The defection of Yugoslavia in 1948, the Sino-Soviet split in 1962, and the rise of strong anti-Soviet feelings after the Soviet invasion of Czechoslovakia diminished Soviet prestige, contributing to the questioning of the doctrine of proletarian internationalism as a fundamental tenet of world communism. As a result of this, Suslov's call for increased participation in the international revolutionary movement fell on deaf ears. The warning that peaceful coexistence in international affairs did not mean the weakening of the class struggle on a world-wide scale and that socialism and capitalism were "irreconcilable"[63] did not provide a sufficient motive for the Communist parties of the West, nor did the suggestion that the Soviet Union was the innocent victim of deliberate "bourgeois propaganda."[64] The emergence of what later became known as Eurocommunism[65] raised increasing apprehension in the sincerity of the Soviet intentions, stymieing Soviet efforts to regain the stewardship of the communist movement, and leading to the eventual collapse of proletarian internationalism, despite Soviet prodding to the contrary.

The recalibration of the official Soviet doctrine was not the only change affecting the Soviet leadership during the first half of the 1970s. There were also important changes within the Politburo. In May 1973, KGB Chairman Andropov, Defense Minister Grechko, and Foreign Minister Gromyko—the three functional heads of the national security bureaucracies—became full members of the Politburo. In elevating them to the highest decision-making body of the Party Brezhnev was undoubtedly looking for a new source of political support. Accountable to the Politburo for their actions, they had been organizationally subordinate to Kosygin and the Council of Ministers, and Brezhnev probably wanted to put an end to this by bringing them under his direct control. Nineteen Seventy-five saw the expulsion of Aleksandr Shelepin from the Politburo. In April, after nearly ten years of gradual political decline, the *enfant terrible* of Soviet politics was finally cashiered by a nervous collective leadership fearful that he may make another attempt to seize power during Brezhnev's recovery after his heart attack.[66]

The first part of the 1970s was marked by persisting friction within the Soviet leadership. A close reading of Suslov's address to the RSDRP Congress on July 13, 1973 gives a distinct impression of a renewed attack by Suslov against the imposition of one-man rule.[68] Suslov's call for the continuance of collectivity was clearly another oblique reminder to Brezhnev, Shelepin or anyone else attempting to seize unrestricted power that only "collective leadership" provided "a guarantee of our further successes," and that a return to one-man rule was contrary to the "Leninist norm of Party leadership."[69] This admonition was especially meaningful because it was directed to Brezhnev's role in foreign policy and to his management of détente and relations with the Third World. Whether or not this meant that a serious breach was developing between the General Secretary and the chief ideologist is not known. The likelihood that this was actually happening is not too high. What is obvious is that Suslov was again using the prestige of his office to reinforce the principle of collective leadership in an attempt to undermine Brezhneve's continued bid to monopolize the decision-making process in the Politburo.

'Tis time, my friend, 'tis time!
The heart for rest is crying.

Alexander Pushkin
'Tis Time, My Friend

CHAPTER XVII

ELDER STATESMAN

Ninety-six communist, socialist and liberationist parties from around the world sent delegates to the XXVth Party Congress that convened in Moscow on February 24, 1976. Swelled by the presence of many delegations from the noncommunist liberation movements of Africa and the Middle East—many of whom came on Soviet invitation for the first time—the XXVth Party Congress was host to more foreign delegates than any previous congress. In his welcoming speech to the foreign delegates, Suslov recognized the high level of participation, remarking that:

> There have never been so many fraternal delegations at one of our Party congresses . . . This is evidence of the further expansion and strengthening of the life-giving bonds of internationalism . . . The Party of Lenin carries high and will continue steadfastly to carry the sacred banner of proletarian internationalism.[1]

Suslov's optimism turned out to be premature. For the first time in Soviet history, a party congress became an open and controversial forum that revealed deep cracks in the ranks of the world communist movement. The Soviet leadership had expected problems, but they did not anticipate anything quite as devastating as the speeches of the West European Communist leaders. Enrico Berlinguer, the leader of the Italian Communist party, Gaston Plissonier of the French party,[2] Gordon McLennan, the General Secretary of the Communist Party of Great Britain, all went to the podium demanding not only "independence," "sovereignty," and "respect for the autonomy of all parties," but also proclaimed their support for religious and cultural freedoms, pluralistic democracy, national—rather than international—socialism, free trade unions, and freedom for artistic and scientific activities.[3] Suslov had tried to arrange an all-European communist conference before the congress to pacify the European leadership, but his efforts failed. The XXVth Party Congress turned into a condemnation of Soviet-style socialism, exposing to the world and the Soviet delegates a new schism in international communism that was potentially as momentous as the Soviet rift with China and Yugoslavia.

The harsh outcry against Soviet ideological orthodoxy and international coercion was an agonizing and bitter pill to swallow for the Soviet leaders, distressing enough to force Brezhnev into signing a joint statement with Berlinguer after the congress pledging respect for the "independence" of each other's party.[4] Brezhnev's attempt to diffuse the confrontation did not prevent Suslov from issuing a formal rejoinder to the Eurocommunists. In a major speech at the annual meeting of the USSR Academy of Science two weeks later, Suslov emphasized the central role of the Soviet party and denounced the Eurocommunists as "enemies of Marxism." "They slander real socialism," he said, and "try to wash out the revolutionary essence of Marxist-Leninist teaching, and substitute bourgeois liberalism for Marxism."[5] Suslov's statement about the European parties was sufficiently critical for *Pravda* to censor his remarks,[6] in what Western observers claimed was as much an attempt "to stop Soviet readers learning about the growing independence of Italian and French communists as sparing the feelings of the Western communists."[7] In the end, Brezhnev had to play down Suslov's ideological intransigence and make a tactical concession in order to salvage the long-sought conference of European communist parties that finally took place in June 1976.

Suslov did not attend the conference of the European communist parties. Sometime in June he had suffered a myocardial infarction—a serious heart attack that put him out of commission until mid-September.[8] The past two years had been years of especially hectic activity and it is entirely possible that he may have exceeded the careful regimen prescribed for him nearly thirteen years ago. The ideological conflict over the backing of liberation movements may have also been a contributing cause. Since the publishing of Konstantin Zarodov's polemic article in August, 1975, urging Soviet support for direct and violent revolutionary action,[9] an intense debate had erupted in the Politburo, a debate that required close monitoring by Suslov to insure that the Zarodov doctrine was properly integrated with his own view of proletarian internationalism.[10] With the support of the military and the KGB, the Politburo eventually sanctioned the application of Zarodov's thesis, but the result of this decision weighed heavily on Suslov. It left him and Ponomarev in the precarious position of having to defend the rationale of increased Soviet military involvement in the Third World while trying to avoid, at the same time, a complete break with the more peacefully inclined European parties. What kind of an effect this had on the already over-extended physical resources of the chief ideologue is not known, but it is not inappropriate to suggest that the stress of being caught in the middle may have added further insult to injury.

Acute and life-threatening illness invariably spawns reminiscence, self-absorption and introspective reflection about the past. No one really knows what went through Suslov's mind as he was being nursed back to health during the summer of 1976, but it is not unrealistic to assume that he used the occasion to review the Party's accomplishments, especially the record of the post-Stalin years during which he had played such an important role in Soviet politics.

Despite the growing economic problems and the continuing weakness of its agriculture, the Soviet Union had made rapid strides in the twenty-three years after Stalin's death. The Soviet Gross National Product increased at an impressive rate during the post-Stalin period, averaging in excess of 5 percent through 1970, and declining to 3.7 percent from 1971 to 1975.[11] Although still painfully deficient by Western standards, consumer goods had become more plentiful and so did urban housing, increasing from the incredibly low 4.9 square meters per person in 1950 to 8.2 square meters.[12] The quality of life in rural areas was brought up almost to urban norms, while health care, education, and cultural and leisure opportunities were expanded to provide a vastly improved standard of living. Periodic detours and purges notwithstanding, literature and the arts progressed beyond the "Boy Meets Tractor" mentality of the 1920s–1930s to such sophisticated works as Mikhail Bulgakov's *The Master and Margarita,* a Faustian morality play that caricatured Stalin's Moscow in the 1930s.[13] Soviet science had also largely cleansed itself of its ideological aberrations, eliminating Lysenko's influence after the fall of Nikita Khrushchev. Life became easier for the average citizen, and Soviet society, despite the zigzagging swings of de-Stalinization, grew more orderly, less repressive, and more harmonious than it had been before. There were, of course, notable contradictions. The relaxation of restrictions in literature was more than matched by a tightening of political controls, forcing many dissident writers to emigrate to the West. Although freed from the interference of the ideologists in technical work, Soviet scientists could still get in trouble because of their political views, as the case of Andrei Sakharov, the eminent Soviet physicist, so well illustrates. Soviet society had become more stratified, more bureaucratic, and politically and morally more corrupt. The internal contradictions had become more accentuated and more visible, and Suslov must have recognized that not all was well in Soviet society.

Suslov returned to work in the fall, and on September 17 awarded the Order of Friendship to the workers' union of the Kirov factory in Leningrad, delivering a ceremonial address fittingly entitled "Loyalty to the Ideals of the Socialist Revolution."[14] Despite his continuing display of optimism in the future of the Marxist-Leninist agenda, the September address was the first of a series of increasingly discerning speeches indicating that he was not unaware of the contradictions of Soviet life. That he found the contradictions disturbing was clear from the increased attention he now assigned to domestic societal problems in his post-1975 speeches. Especially notable was his October 16, 1979 address "A Task for the Whole Party" in which he carefully inventoried the major deficiencies of Soviet life and prescribed a palliative program of greater self-control for the Party and the nation[15]—a program of discipline and vigilance that Andropov adopted four years later almost in its entirety.

The second half of the 1970s brought with it subtle but significant changes in the configuration of the Soviet leadership, changes that eventually played an important role in the factional strife and the final realignment of forces that took place after Suslov's death. On the surface, everything pointed to the expansion of Brezhnev's influence and power in the Politburo and the Secretariat. At a special meeting of the Supreme Soviet on June 16, 1977 he was unanimously elected, on Suslov's nomination, Chairman of the Presidium of the USSR Supreme Soviet,* replacing his old rival Podgorny and finally ousting him from the Politburo.[16] To improve his overall position in the leadership, he was also successful in appointing Konstantin Chernenko candidate member of the Politburo in October 1977 and a full member in November 1978. An old and loyal retainer since their joint assignment in Moldavia, Chernenko now substituted for the out-of-favor Kirilenko,[17] strengthening considerably Brezhnev's eroding position within the Secretariat.

In practice, the situation was very different. It had become quite obvious from the procedural changes approved at the April 17, 1979 Central Committee plenum that a deliberate policy of burden sharing had been agreed upon by the Politburo earlier in the year as a result of Brezhnev's advanced age and poor health.[18] Of particular concern to the leadership of the Party were the fulfillment of Brezhnev's dual functions as General Secretary of the Party and Chairman of the Supreme Soviet.[19] Suslov played a leading role at the April plenum and at the Supreme Soviet session that followed it to assure the delegates that Brezhnev was not being left alone to shoulder the heavy responsibilities of both the Party and the state. While it was not generally admitted, Western observers had already noted that Brezhnev had fallen into the habit of skipping the weekly meetings of the Politburo to let the chief ideologue chair them in his place.[20] But beyond the purely procedural changes, a far more crucial political realignment was also taking place. One Western analyst has fittingly called it the "estrangement of the Andropov-Ustinov-Gromyko phalanx."[21] Brezhnev had brought the functional heads of the "national security" triumvirate into the Politburo in 1973 to create a new source of support for his policies. As his health failed and his political power became more diffused, they turned away from him, positioning themselves—probably with the blessing of Suslov—for a more independent stance in the inevitable succession that was bound to take place in the future.

The summer of 1979 ended in an explosion of rumors, speculations and false reports about the health of Leonid Brezhnev. The arrival of a team of American eye specialists in Moscow in the third week of October raised the rumors to a high pitch. The Associated Press reported that Brezhnev was suffering from a "serious illness," and some Western reports even claimed that he was "dead."[22] The mystery was finally cleared up on October 20, when it was discovered that the Politburo member operated on by the Americans was not Brezhnev

---

*President of the USSR.

but Suslov. A later report confirmed that a vitrectomy,* was performed on Suslov by Dr. Fedorov, a world known Soviet opthamologist with the help of three American eye surgeons specially invited from the Johns Hopkins University in Baltimore to demonstrate the newest American methods of treating diabetes-related eye diseases.[22] The operation was successful, and Suslov was reported to be back in his office shortly thereafter.

Almost seventy-seven, in dangerously poor health, and severely restricted by the regimen imposed upon him by his physicians to control the further march of diabetes and its complications, Suslov was unquestionably at the very height of his power in 1979—exercising perhaps even a greater level of influence than the General Secretary. He had become not only the Chief ideologist and senior member of the Politburo and the Secretariat, but an elder statesman and power broker without whose participation and counsel the Soviet gerontocracy remained paralyzed and politically unstable. During the 1970s he had thrust himself into almost every phase of Soviet political and private life. As Roy Medvedev has aptly noted, Suslov had complete control over ideology, *Agitprop,* civilian and military political education, the media, the State Publishing Committee, the Comsomol, inter-Party relations, and even Soviet foreign policy.[23] Through Andropov and Pel'she he also exercised immense influence on the KGB and the Party Control Committee. In his rise to power, he had surpassed the influence of all previously rising stars in the Politburo. He had become a permanent "Second Secretary" in the full sense of that rather ambiguous and evasive title attributed at one time to Aleksei Kirichenko and Andrei Kirilenko.

The expansion of Suslov's political influence and functional responsibilities did not curtail the output of his ideological pronouncements. Since his heart attack in 1976, he had actually stepped up the level and frequency of his ideological writings and addresses, especially on such subjects as international proletarianism, socialist solidarity, Soviet patriotism, and ethnic nationalism. Although the recent wave of Russian nationalism had been largely contained, he continued to maintain pressure on any new manifestations of nationalistic feelings in the Soviet Union. In his speech at the conference dedicated to the 60th anniversary of the October Revolution on November 10, 1977, Suslov reaffirmed the Soviet commitment to national consolidation. "Among the major theoretical problems are those connected with the progress towards homogeneity of the social structure of our society, its increasing unity, and ever greater cohesion of all the country's large and small nations," he said, reconfirming that the "working class" will continue to play the "leading role" in this process.[25] This

---

*A delicate surgical procedure for removing blood from the vitreous fluids of the eyeball, an operation associated with a common complication of diabetes.

optimistic view of national *rapprochement* dovetailed with his posture on national liberation and proletarian internationalism. Proletarian internationalism, he maintained expresses "the common interests of the working people in all countries," and is, therefore, the guiding principle for the construction of a socialist society throughout the world. Paraphrasing Marx and Lenin, Suslov insisted that "relations of national hostility, distrust, and suspicion (were) not innate qualities of man," but developed only in "conditions of class-antagonistic society" that fostered "the exploitation and oppression of man by man in the sphere of relations between nations as well."[26] "The implementation of the Leninist nationality policy," he concluded would invariably "remove the hostility of the Soviet peoples," serving as an example for the coming international brotherhood of all men.[27]

Some Sovietologists have questioned the sincerity of Suslov's official pronouncements, arguing that his crusade against nationalism was in reality a subterfuge contrived by him to legitimize Russia's traditional striving for unbridled territorial expansion. Others have hinted that Suslov may have remained a Russian nationalist all his life, but made his real feelings public only in his twilight years, after he had fully secured his power within the Soviet leadership.

Mikhail Agursky has suggested, for instance, that Suslov had fashioned out of two conflicting tendencies in Russian nationalism a new form of Soviet nationalism. Arguing convincingly that Russian nationalism is not monolithic, and that two opposing orientations of "isolationist conservative Russian nationalism" and "aggressive Russian imperial nationalism" continue to be in constant contention with each other, Agursky has credited Suslov with the construction of a new form of "imperial Russian nationalism," which he insists has been "deprived of any national and cultural foundation and supported only by the external might of the state."[28] Agursky's analysis is not implausible. Contemporary Russian nationalism encompasses a broad spectrum of nationalist tendencies ranging all the way from the liberal and isolationist nationalism of Solzhenitsyn rooted in the psycho-historical traditions of Russian Orthodoxy and culture, to the dogmatic and expansionist statism of national bolshevism. However, his conclusion is not appropriate.

Agursky's interpretation implies that the Soviet commitment to world Communist expansion is but an extension, under a different name, of the foreign policy of the *ancien regime*. Soviet interests in eastern Europe, the Baltic, the Far East and Central Asia may in fact be very similar to those of Tsarist Russia, but the achievement of a world community of Communist nations under the aegis of the Soviet Union is clearly an element of only Soviet policy. To suggest that Soviet expansionary nationalism had evolved out of a generalized Russian predilection for "the might of the state" does not make sense when it is clear that the driving force behind the periodic outbursts of Russian territorial expansion has not always been the same. Early Russian expansion had its roots in the "gathering" of the Russian lands after the Mongol invasion and in the sweeping ideology of "Holy Russia," while the Russian advance in Europe in the seventeenth, eighteenth, and nineteenth centuries was to a large extent aroused by recurring military incursions of the western European powers. The surge to Siberia and the Kazakh steppe, on the other hand, pursued a very different course. It followed much the same pattern as the American settlement of the Indian lands—a spontaneous movement of peasants, cossacks, traders and adventurers who drove east in search of a better life and new wealth. Other instances of Russian expansionism also had their distinct causes and motivations.[29] To overlook the specificity of the multifarious causes and phases of Russian expansion and to lump them under one rubric of Russian bias for the "might of the state" is in itself a bias and a generalization that overemphasizes the continuity of Russian expansion, denies the influence of specific circumstances, and overlooks that more often than not, Russia, like almost every great power, merely took advantage of existing opportunities.

Agursky's view also neglects to see that Soviet foreign policy transcends previous Russian attitudes of universal mission or national security that were confined to the Eurasian land mass and its bordering lands. It conveniently overlooks that Soviet expansion is internationalist, and that it is motivated by Communist ideology which views the world as an arena of relentless conflict between capitalism and communism, a competition for the hearts and minds of the people that rejects the notion of a status quo in the world. Finally, it simply does not agree with what is known about Suslov and his allegiance to Communist internationalism. Carl Linden has carefully identified this commitment, placing Suslov as the spokesman of the most orthodox universalist orientation among Soviet leaders in profound opposition to the particularist ideologies of the prevailing nationalist movements in the Soviet Union and the rest of the world.[30]

Arguing from a different perspective, John Dunlop has also suggested that Suslov may have in his twilight years turned toward a more Russian orientation in his world view. Basing his judgment on reports that Suslov was the "shadowy guarantor" of Il'ya Glazunov, a traditionalist artist, who openly expressed his love for Orthodoxy and Russian culture,[31] and on the possibility that Gennadii Shimanov's *samizdat* almanac *Mnogaia leta* also had Suslov's blessing,[32] Dunlop has implied that Suslov may have at some point in the mid-to-late 1970s become a "sympathizer and protector of the Russian party" in the Soviet Union.[33] Roy Medvedev has questioned this hypothesis, noting that Suslov's "dogmatism would not allow him to become an ally" of the nationalists, and that his support of Glazunov could be more easily explained by recognizing that Suslov probably liked the artist's traditional style and agreed to have his portrait painted by him.[34] There is a lot to be said for Medvedev's unpretentious explanation; Suslov's dogmatism can not be dismissed cavalierly. Throughout his entire life, Suslov had championed the most orthodox form of the universalist party-state, passionately defending it against the assault of both populism and nationalism. The Marxist-Leninist creed had been too rigidly stamped on his consciousness to permit even a minor deviation of doctrine, let alone allow a change of such vast proportion. It is possible, of course, that out of pragmatic considerations he may have been willing, as Dunlop suggests, to tolerate certain Russian nationalist extremists—publicists like Shimanov and Karelin—who were willing to work within the Soviet political system and who, not unlike the Party ideologues themselves, were also lambasting the United States and the West. Such an attitude by Suslov would not have been inconsistent with the growing Soviet leniency to officially accepted literature that, by the end of the 1970s, had contrived to weave into the fabric of social realism numerous illusive and controversial themes of national tradition and ethnic lore.[35] It is inconceivable, however, to posit that Suslov could have found anything in common with National Bolshevism, or, as John Dunlop tends to agree, with the more liberal *vozrozhdentsy** who sought broad and sweeping changes of the Soviet system. What is more probable is that as an ethnic Great Russian, Suslov had never completely lost his affinity for Russian culture and Russian history, and not unlike a Rashidov or Mukhitdinov[36] who also never divorced themselves fully from their Islamic roots, found a certain amount of solace and identification in the Russian ethos and the traditions of his boyhood in Shakhovskoe. It would have been too much to expect otherwise. Even Lenin never completely lost his enthusiasm for Turgenev and the pleasant Russian traditionalism of his boyhood and young adulthood. Rebuking Ol'minsky for his violent and extreme revolutionism during their stay in Geneva, Lenin is reputed to have reminded his friend that there was a limit to ideological and revolutionary zeal. "I too used to live on a country estate," he admonished, "in a sense, I too am a scion of the landed gentry . . . but I still haven't forgotten the pleasant aspects of life on our estate. . . . I have forgotten neither its lime trees nor its flowers. . . . I gather that you consider such memories unworthy of a revolutionary . . . Think it over, aren't you going a bit too far?"[37] Finally, one should also not overlook the fact that by the late 1970s, laxity and the perversion of established Soviet values had penetrated not only into economic and social life, but into all phases of Soviet polity, including censorship and control of the arts. Except for a token display of Party discipline, the super-annuated Soviet leadership had become completely exhausted, and no longer able to enforce in practice what they still professed from the "pulpit." It was not until Andropov became the new General Secretary that Soviet culture was again subjected to the rigors of careful Communist censorship and the new outpouring of Party discipline.

In the meantime, Suslov continued to warn the Party cadres of the dangers that are inherent in all forms of particularist views. Speaking at the All-

---

*From the Russian word for "renaissance," the *vozrozhdentsy* urged the casting off of Marxism-Leninism, and the return to the indigenous traditions of the Orthodox Church and pre-revolutionary Russia.

Union Conference of Ideological workers in October 1979, Suslov instructed his colleagues that "it is necessary to oppose resolutely all advocacy of national exclusivity . . . (and) to struggle against the manifestations of parochialism."[38] Suslov also continued to speak out frequently and forcefully on the subject of proletarian internationalism. After the XXVth Party Congress, Suslov wrote off the deviationist parties of western Europe and China from the list of reliable pro-Soviet supporters, and zeroed in instead on the revolutionary movements of the developing countries. In one of his most programmatic statements for increased revolutionary activity and socialist reorganization of society, Suslov called on Lenin to clarify Soviet goals.

> "V. I. Lenin predicted that the socialist revolution will not be just and mainly a struggle waged by the revolutionary proletariat in each country against its own bourgeoisie. No it would be a struggle by all colonies and countries oppressed by imperialism . . . against international imperialism.' The imperialist colonial system has crumbled and about 100 independent countries, playing an every important role . . . have come to life. Today, when the liberated countries face in their entirety the tasks of eliminating economic backwardness and dependence on imperialism. . . , the Leninist ideas of the possibility of a noncapitalist way of development, on the ways and means for the socialist reorganization of the mixed economy of such countries, have become particularly topical. . . . The experience of the post-October revolutions . . . and the experience in reorganizing life on a new basis in the socialist countries, convincingly prove that many of the essential features of the revolutionary strategy of the Bolsheviks, which brought victory of the October Revolution, have retained their topical significance."[39]

Having legitimized the dominance of the Soviet revolutionary experience and restated the doctrine of proletarian internationalism, Suslov devoted the rest of his article to what might be appropriately called a 1970s version of "What is to be Done"[40] in the Third World. It was a program that stressed the empowering of the working class, the elimination of the capitalist establishment, the gradual reorganization of the economy and agriculture, the creation of modern industry, the establishment of a new socialist discipline and organization, the development of a "socialist democracy," and the mounting of a comprehensive defense against "the counterrevolutionary impulses" of the "overthrown exploiting classes" and the "international bourgeoisie."[41] The *Kommunist* article on "socialist statehood" was Suslov's most comprehensive and sweeping opus, a prescription aimed specifically at the developing nations of the Third World. To profess that he did not believe in it would be to write off more than sixty years of devoted service to the Party and international communism, and to infer that he was a profligate hypocrite who had never fully believed in what he prescribed.

Two climactic events rocked Suslov's last years of service to the Communist Party. The April 1978 Communist coup in Afghanistan toppled the Daoud regime prematurely, before the Afghan communists had actually consolidated their power to form a new communist government without any opposition. Between April and July 1978, the Soviet Union maintained a low profile in its Afghan policy confining itself to the signing of a treaty of friendship and financial support for the new government. In July, increased opposition to the new government and the threat of a full-scale insurgency forced Moscow to expand its activity in Afghanistan with direct military assistance and build-up of Soviet advisors who took over the task of constructing socialism according to the Soviet model. In a speech in Leningrad on February 28, 1979 Suslov named Afghanistan as one of the "new states of socialist orientation that have emerged in the last five years."[42] The possibility that anti-Soviet rebels might take power in Kabul during the fall of 1979 weighed heavily therefore on Suslov's mind. Besides the long-term geopolitical benefit of a socialist Afghanistan on its southern border, Soviet prestige was clearly at stake in the Soviet-bloc nations and other areas of Soviet penetration in the Third World. The December 1979 invasion was thus largely a foreordained operation, dictated by Soviet strategic interests of maintaining a forward deployment in southwest Asia and by the purely ideological considerations related to the expansion of Soviet-style socialism throughout the underdeveloped world. No information is available on Suslov's reaction to the Soviet incursion into Afghanistan, but the likelihood is that, together with the other hardliners in the Politburo, he had not only approved the invasion but may have actually encouraged it. The situation in 1979 was very different from 1968 when Suslov counseled against the occupation of Czechoslovakia. Soviet relations with the European communist parties and China were at their lowest in 1979, and Suslov had given up hope of recovering Soviet control of the world communist movement. From the Soviet point of view, adverse world-wide communist reaction to military intervention was no longer of consequence, and the incentive to guarantee the consolidation of a communist regime on its southern border outweighed all considerations of caution and international diplomacy. No one in the Politburo expected a strong Western reaction, not even those who opposed intervention. Nor was there any fear of a Soviet Vietnam. In the end, the invasion was accepted as an unavoidable *fait accompli*.

A far more menacing development in late 1980 was the rise of the Polish Solidarity movement and the threat of internal reform and growing Polish nationalism. The Polish crisis seemed especially ominous to the Soviet leadership because it held the prospect of an unpopular and internationally dangerous invasion to bring Poland back under Soviet control. Speaking at the 1981 congress of the East German party on April 12, Suslov warned Poland—without mentioning it by name—that deviation from Communist theory would come to no good. "Only consistent implementation of Marxist-Leninist principles guarantees the triumph of our socialist ideals," he said, reminding the delegates that "the atmosphere has been poisoned by attempts of reactionary forces to split our community . . . and undermine the foundations of socialism by interference in the affairs of socialist countries."[43] "There is no other road," Suslov concluded, *"any deviation from our socialist teachings results in fatal consequences."*[*44]

Suslov's warning fell on deaf ears. By April 1981, political and economic turmoil had seriously eroded the authority of the Polish party, forcing the seventy-eight year old Suslov to make a second hurried trip within less than two weeks, this time to Warsaw. Officially billed as a "working visit," the one day surprise trip on April 23 was an indication that the internal political situation in Poland had deteriorated to a point that some kind of an understanding between the Soviet Union and Poland had to be reached before the crucial meeting of the Polish Party Central Committee scheduled for the following week.[45] It was obvious that the ailing Suslov was in Warsaw to secure assurance from Kania and Jaruzelski that Soviet interests would not be sacrificed and that the pace of reform would be slowed down. What exactly Suslov said to the Polish leadership remains a state secret, but it is not improbable that he counseled the Polish leadership to proceed with caution to prevent a repetition of a Hungarian-style intervention in 1981. It would be naive to conclude from this that Suslov's visit to Warsaw provided the only motivation for the crushing of Solidarity and the imposition of martial law. Political conditions in Poland also had a significant effect on the defeat of Solidarity, even though the threat of Soviet occupation remained an overriding influence. The loyalty of the Polish officer corps and the security forces to the Communist regime also contributed to the crackdown of Solidarity. So did the ambiguous role of the Church which supported the workers but exerted a moderating influence on them in fear that continuing resistance to the regime might erupt into violence and civil war. Suslov's initiative was not inconsequential, however. Speaking on October 14 at the All-Union Conference of the Heads of Social Science Departments, Suslov repeated his April warning, this time mentioning Poland by name.

> "For a long time now, imperialism has attempted secretly and openly to undermine the socialist structure in the Polish People's Republic, to exacerbate the crisis phenomena there, to foster anti-socialist counter revolutionary forces and to spur them to greater activity. . . . In this connection, one needs to be reminded that socialist Poland, the Polish Communists and the Polish people can firmly count on the fraternal solidarity and support of the Soviet Union and other Warsaw treaty member countries."[46]

The mention of "fraternal support" and the "Warsaw treaty countries" carried the unmistakable overtones of 1968 when the Warsaw pact forces invaded Czechoslovakia and put down the liberal reforms initiated during the "Prague

---

*Italicized for emphasis by author.

197

Spring." Suslov's threat did not end the crisis, but it did contribute to the coalescing of the Polish Communist leadership around Jaruzelski to avoid a possible Soviet intervention and an international crisis.

The late 1970s witnessed important changes within the Soviet leadership. During the 1970s, Brezhnev had succeeded in gaining a firm grip over the Politburo and the Secretariat, but toward the end of the decade, shifts in personal relationships and perceptions began to alter the power alignment of the Soviet leadership. Especially divisive were differences of opinion on domestic problems. The slowing down of economic growth, the dilemma over resource allocation, and the feeling on the part of the opposition that the country was beset by deteriorating morale and corruption, polarized the leadership. Recent changes in the composition of the Politburo also contributed to the division. Fedor Kulakov, the ambitious Secretary in charge of agriculture and the most likely Politburo member to succeed Brezhnev, died very suddenly in July 1978. There were even rumors that he had committed suicide.[47] The embattled and ailing Kosygin died in October 1980. Brezhnev's protégé and anticipated successor during the early 1970s, A. P. Kirilenko, for reasons never fully explained, had largely lost his influence by 1980 and was finally retired from the Politburo in September 1981. Between 1978 and 1980, in an intricate balancing act brokered and closely watched by Suslov, Brezhnev had promoted to full membership in the Politburo his protégé and loyal chief-of-staff Konstantin Chernenko[48] and another member of the Dnepropetrovsk "clan," Nikolai Tikhonov,[49] who later replaced Kosygin as Chairman of the Council of Ministers. To counter-balance the Brezhnev faction, Suslov brought Mikhail Gorbachev into the Secretariat as secretary in charge of agriculture to replace Kulakov. By the time of the XXVIth Party Congress in February 1981, the Politburo was now neatly divided into two competing factions: the Brezhnev grouping which included Chernenko, Kirilenko, Tikhonov, Shcherbitsky,[50] Kunaev, and probably Moscow chief Victor Grishin, and a potentially opposing faction made up of the governmental phalanx consisting of KGB Chairman Yurii Andropov, Defense Minister Dimitri Ustinov and Foreign Affairs Minister Andrei Gromyko, supported by the still uncommitted but loyal Mikhail Gorbachev, the profligate Leningrad chief Grigorii Romanov, who would have undoubtedly had to back Andropov purely out of self-preservation, and Suslov's brother-in-law, the octogenarian Arvid Pel'she. Maintaining his position as elder statesman and Party arbiter, Suslov alone remained deliberately independent, safeguarding the delicate balance struck in the Politburo.

Suslov's independence was, of course, largely a function of the uniqueness of his position as the Party's disinterested peacemaker. He would have undoubtedly chosen as a matter of personal preference to support the Andropov faction. Andropov was his protégé, a "true believer" who also decried the extravagant life style of the Brezhnev-bred bureaucracy. So was Gorbachev, whom he first met with Andropov while vacationing in Kislovodsk in the 1970s and with whom he toured the Stavropol *krai* in May 1980. Gorbachev had gotten his start under Kulakov in Stavropol *krai,* where he was born in 1931, and, through a slow process of Party promotions and Kulakov's patronage, had successively become Second and First Secretary of the Stavropol *krai.* As a former First Secretary of Stavropol *krai* himself, Suslov continued to maintain a personal interest in the area,[51] and undoubtedly saw in the well-educated, hard working and highly motivated Gorbachev a well-rounded staunch Communist and a little bit of himself as a younger man. Suslov also had another area of communality with the Andropov-Ustinov-Gromyko faction. Unlike the rather low caliber Brezhnev men who had reached high office through patronage and favoritism, Andropov, Ustinov, Gromyko, and Gorbachev, were men of impressive intellect and practical competence who, not unlike Suslov himself, were predisposed to a more analytical and disciplined method of responding to the economic and social problems facing the nation. In the 1970s, corruption, bureaucracy, increased alcoholism, and the expansion of the *Nomenklatura's* privileges had crippled the economic and social progress of the Soviet people, creating a serious domestic crisis that begged to be resolved.

The XXVIth Party Congress that convened on February 23, 1981 did very little to rectify the sorry state of affairs, despite speculation in the Soviet Union and among foreign observers that the leadership would finally face up to the growing social and economic problems. In his Central Committee report, Brezhnev recounted the successes of the past decade, but tempered the Party's projections with guarded statements about the limits of future development. He blamed "inertia, tradition, and the habits that took shape in the period when the quantitative side of things rather than qualitative stood out first and foremost," prescribing a regimen of "greater discipline, exactingness, and responsibility in fulfilling plans" as a means to the solution of the economic and social problems.[52] For the most part, Brezhnev's report offered nothing new that would relieve the growing malaise in the Party and among the general population. The aging Soviet leadership had become inept, and the majority did not want to make the painful choices to overcome the economic and social paralysis which the Brezhnev leadership had brought on itself. Suslov, least of all, wanted to do anything that could impair Party decorum and destroy what he had tried so hard to build during nearly seventeen years of collective leadership under Brezhnev. He was well aware that the administration was riddled with corruption and inefficiency, but he was categorically opposed to baring them out in the open. More than anything else, he feared that a frontal attack on corruption and inefficiency could turn itself, like de-Stalinization, into a factional strife of immense proportions. It is impossible to verify with any degree of certitude what Suslov did to reduce the threat of an open conflict, but the likelihood is that he counseled the opposition against any drastic action, arguing that Brezhnev's end was near and death would set the stage for a new coalition that would initiate, with his blessing, a comprehensive program of reform within the Party.

Power struggles have been a regular aspect of every political succession in the Soviet Union since the death of Lenin, and the long awaited succession of Brezhnev was not an exception to the rule. By 1981 the General Secretary was in such poor health that even Suslov was expected to survive him. Because he had become the second most important figure in the Soviet leadership, often substituting for Brezhnev at Politburo meetings and sensitive foreign conferences, there was even speculation that Suslov might be appointed General Secretary himself to oversee the transition to a new administration. But the wily Brezhnev fooled everyone, and Suslov never succeeded in presiding over the Brezhnev succession. On January 20, 1982—nearly ten months before Brezhnev's death in November—Suslov suffered a fatal stroke from which he never recovered, permanently leaving the Soviet political scene on January 25, 4:05 Moscow time.[53]

Suslov's death came within weeks of an oblique attack on Brezhnev by Andropov and, by implication, on the whole Party and its superannuated leadership. According to one version, a cache of stolen diamonds was found on December 27, 1981 in the flat of Boris Buryatiya, known also as Boris the Gypsy, a popular singer and intimate friend of Brezhnev's high-spirited daughter Galina Churbanova, the wife of the First Deputy Head of the MVD.[54] Because of its political sensitivity, the case was referred to the KGB where General Semyon Tsvigun, First Deputy Chairman of the KGB and Brezhnev's brother-in-law, personally took charge of the investigation and allegedly tried to arrest Buryatia without seeking prior approval from the Party leadership. Andropov, who was still the Head of KGB, apparently refused to hush up the case to the embarrassment of Brezhnev and Suslov. To confound the mystery, General Tsvigun was found dead on January 19 under mysterious circumstances, probably having committed suicide after finding himself in the untenable position of conflict of interest between his responsibilities as a senior KGB officer and member of the Brezhnev family. Even more baffling was the absence of Brezhnev's and Suslov's signatures on Tsvigun's official obituary. The General Secretary normally signs the obituary of every Central Committee member, and the absence of his name on his brother-in-law's obituary was a dead give away that something was dreadfully wrong. The story became even more obscure when reports began to circulate in Moscow that Suslov tried to protect Brezhnev's good name and hush up the incident, and that his stroke on January 20 was brought on by a violent confrontation with Andropov who had decided to make an issue of the case. Details of this murky case remain cloudy to this day. The rumor that the General Secretary's daughter was involved in a spectacular scandal was a sensation that seriously damaged the reputation of the Brezhnev family. Even more shocking was that corruption had penetrated the very highest level of the Soviet elite.

Andropov's attempt to embarrass the administration was merely the first salvo in a campaign against corruption and incompetence that would eventually give him control of the Politburo. In the next four months he would return to the Secretariat after nearly fifteen years of absence, succeed to Suslov's position as chief ideologue, and outmaneuver Chernenko for the job of the Second Secretary. Disabled again in April by a mild stroke, Brezhnev held on to his position as General Secretary for another six months until his death on November 10, but for all intents and purposes the Brezhnev era was already at an end. Suslov's disappearance from the Soviet political scene put an end to the delicate balance that kept the sharply divided soviet leadership under Brezhnev's control. No one really knows what the General Secretary thought in those last six months of his life. But with all the advantages and drawbacks of hind sight, it is not inappropriate to suggest that Brezhnev may have been prone to say about Suslov what Richelieu remarked at the death of Father Joseph du Tremblay, "My support, where is my support?"[55]*

---

*English translation of the French soliloquy "Mon appui, ou est mon appui?" attributed to Richelieu at the death of Father Joseph du Tremblay, the Capuchin friar who became known to history as the Grey Eminence.

To work, then, comrades! We are faced with
a new and difficult task.

Lenin, *The Party Organization and
Party Literature*

Men make their own history, but they do not
make it as they please; they do not make it
under self-selected circumstances, but under
circumstances existing already, given and
transmitted from the past.

Karl Marx, *The Eighteenth Brumaire
of Louis Napoleon*

EPILOGUE

The changes launched by Yurii Andropov in his fifteen months in office
were temporarily halted when Konstantin Chernenko became General Secretary
after Andropov's death. The new interregnum lasted even less than the first. The
ailing Chernenko died on March 11, 1985, and a new and younger leader—a
protégé of Suslov and Andropov—stepped into Chernenko's shoes, bringing
with him an end to a long era that has spanned the post-Stalinist period of Soviet
history. The succession that propelled Mikhail Gorbachev to the helm of the
Soviet leadership brought with it expectations of reform and hope for a new
beginning that everyone had been waiting for since the death of Brezhnev. Since
then, the Soviet Union has held its XXVIIth Party Congress. The Central Committee has had a number of important plenary sessions, and Gorbachev, himself,
has tried to clarify his program. But the future of the Soviet Union still remains
uncertain. No one has been able to assess with accuracy the long-term course
that Gorbachev has charted for the Soviet Union, nor to agree on how well it
will be accepted by the Party *apparat* and the Soviet public at large. So far, he
has made a number of significant changes that bode well for the Soviet people
and for improved international relations, but the specter of Suslov's orthodoxy
within the bureaucracy continues to haunt the Soviet Union.

According to the official Soviet view reflected in a 1982 retrospective
prepared by the Institute of Marxism-Leninism, Suslov made a number of important contributions to the Soviet body politic. In the stilted language of Soviet
ideology, the Institute singled out the "elimination of voluntarism and subjectiv-
ism" and the "strengthening and development of Lenin's norms and principles"
as his principal legacy to future Soviet leadership. In a secondary role, the
article recognized Suslov's "cultivation of improved relations" with other communist parties, the "promotion of proletarian internationalism and national liberation movements," the "strengthening of friendship" among the Soviet
nationalities, and the "formation of the new (Soviet) man."[1] The same analysis

also credited Suslov with "extensive creative ability in approaching contemporary problems" from the "position of Marxism-Leninism."[2]

Self-serving and predictably lenient to Suslov's failures, the Institute's appraisal was not altogether incorrect, especially with respect to Suslov's impact on the primacy of the Party and the construction of a more stable oligarchical form of leadership. Suslov was not the only Politburo member who opposed Khrushchev's and Brezhnev's efforts to impose one-man rule, but he was undoubtedly the single most important force acting as catalyst and umpire to guarantee the dominance of the Party and the continuing maintenance of a self-stabilizing collective leadership. Although it is still too early to assert unequivocally that the Soviet oligarchy will not dissolve itself into another instance of individual dominance, it is becoming increasingly apparent that more than twenty years of collective leadership have created a corporatist tradition that will become progressively harder to discard with each successive generation of Soviet leaders. The institutionalizing of this tradition has not stopped analysts of Soviet politics from questioning the permanency of collective leadership. Basing their conclusions on past experience, Western scholars continue to point out that in the Soviet system there is always a potential for the emergence of a powerful and charismatic leader.[3]

Past experience notwithstanding, this view may be no longer entirely applicable to the Soviet political system. Recent developments in the evolution of Soviet politics indicate that the Soviet system has moved beyond its early stage of charismatic leadership exemplified by Lenin, Stalin and Khrushchev to a new form of conservative and institutional *gestalt* in which the leader's personality now tends to influence interpersonal authority relationships, without enslaving the system itself. The revival of the Party, the restoration of collectivity in decision-making, the growing willingness of the Soviet leadership to satisfy the demands of special interest groups and public opinion, the establishment of rules of redressing grievances, and more than twenty years of uniformly enforced administrative practice have shifted the Soviet political system irrevocably toward what Max Weber had typified as "legal authority," in contrast to the "traditional and charismatic authority" that is usually associated with despotic and charismatic leaders who hold on to power with the help of personal retainers.[4] With its stress on societal rights rather than individual rights and with its emphasis on ideological purity, Soviet "legal authority" is clearly very different from the "legal authority" that protects the rights of individuals in Western forms of political organization. But this distinction does not invalidate the view that Soviet polity is now closer in its form and substance to "legal authority" than to either "traditional" or "charismatic" authority. Despite its many faults, Soviet polity has gradually acquired its own unique form of "legal authority" that is now unanimously endorsed by its leaders and freely supported by the majority of Soviet citizens. Gorbachev may indeed emerge as a strong leader— after years of mediocrity, the Soviet Union thirsts for one—but if he does, he will probably work within the system, employing his position as leader cautiously and judiciously in order to achieve his goals.

Suslov was largely responsible for solidifying another key ingredient of the Soviet political system. In what has become a uniquely Soviet form of political organization, the General Secretary of the Party is now universally accepted as the *de facto* chief executive of the Soviet Union. This has not always been representative of the Soviet political organization. Supreme executive authority did not always rest in the position of the party secretary. Even though he insisted that policy was to derive from the Party, Lenin's authority as chief executive of the Soviet Union came from the *soviets,* from his position as Chairman of the Council of Commissars, and from his enormous stature as founder of the Soviet state, not from the office of the Secretary of the Central Committee. Until his untimely death in 1919, the sole secretary of the Party was Yakov Sverdlov, followed by Nikolai Krestinsky. Stalin's executive authority, on the other hand, never really emanated from the offices that he held. He had assumed supreme executive authority by emasculating the Party and by ruling as a despotic dictator who had captured the combined offices of General Secretary, Premier and President. During his short period of dominance, Malenkov's authority as chief executive was derived from his position as Chairman of the Council of Ministers. Khrushchev's authority sprang from both the Party and the government. With the help of Suslov, he had rejuvenated the Party and returned the policy-making powers to the Central Committee and its Presidium, but his authority as chief executive came from the office of Chairman of the Council of Ministers and from his control of the crucial joint Party-government committees that he had established to maximize his executive powers. It was not until Brezhnev became General Secretary—and only after several years of intermittent struggle for dominance with Premier Kosygin—that executive authority in the Soviet Union was finally vested in the office of the General Secretary. This authority was substantially curtailed, however, by the imposition of the 1964 rule against the simultaneous holding of the office of General Secretary and Chairman of the Council of Ministers, and the gradual expansion of the power and influence of the chief ideologist as the brake-applying "Second Secretary" in charge of anti-reform.

The prohibition against the simultaneous holding of the office of General Secretary and the Chairman of the Council of Ministers now appears to be permanently institutionalized. The appointment of Nikolai Ryzhkov as the new Chairman of the Council of Ministers to replace the aging Tikhonov is a strong indication that Gorbachev intends to continue recognizing the 1964 agreement. Indeed, this practice has now been applied not only to the position of General Secretary, but to all secretaries of the all-Union Central Committee, and to the First Secretaries of the republic and *obkom* Party committees. But the future status of the "Second Secretary" remains problematic. During his short tenure in office, Andropov acted as both General Secretary and chief ideologist.

Chernenko was also his own ideologist, although a plausible argument could be made that Gorbachev was, in fact, "Second Secretary," performing many of the crucial functions of the General Secretary behind the scenes. In the Gorbachev Politburo, Yegor Ligachev has unmistakably assumed the position of chief ideologist, Party arbiter, and defender of the conservative opposition to Gorbachev's more liberal reforms. Thus, the separation and sharing of functional responsibilities initiated by Suslov have been reintroduced into Soviet governance, if not by precendent or decree, at least by the reality of the new political alignment in the Politburo and the Central Committee. It is still early to say with certainty what will be the fate of this innovation, but the probability that it will become permanently institutionalized is not minimal by any means. The unmistakably ideocratic nature of Soviet politics, the inherent frailty of oligarchy, the permanence of factionalism and dissent among the Soviet leadership, and the growing complexity of government itself, all point to the indispensability of the "Second Secretary" as a necessary "honest broker" and elder statesman who can moderate the leaders' inevitable struggle for power, and conciliate their varying points of view.

Succession has likewise become a more orderly and institutionalized process. This is not to say that it is no longer accompanied by the typical struggle for power that is endemic to all hierarchial organizations, but the period of consolidation has been dramatically shortened from what it had been before. Stalin needed nearly ten years to usurp the Party's powers. Khrushchev never really succeeded in gaining full control. With the help of Suslov, Brezhnev had reached the height of power by 1972, while Andropov and Gorbachev attained a high level of authority in less than one year. The circumstances surrounding each succession were different, but on the whole the post-Brezhnev transfers of power proceeded in a more orderly and expeditious manner, without the disparaging manifestations of *"kto kogo,"* and with a certain degree of decorum that had been lacking in the past. Part of this can be explained in terms of the normal maturation process during which the Soviet leadership had gradually moved forward organizationally from a tradition of revolution and *coup d'etat* to the more mundane demands of maintaining an efficient government, but a good part was also the result of Suslov's exhortation that the Soviet leadership adhere to the rules of "collective leadership" laid down by Lenin.

On the other hand, the Institute's conclusion about Suslov's contribution to international communism and national liberation is greatly exaggerated. The idea that he had somehow preserved the solidarity of international communism is simply not born out by its recent history. On the contrary, during his thirty years in high office, Suslov had presided over the gradual fragmentation of international Communism. Disregarding the powerful sway of post-World War II nationalism and history's longer term trend toward political and social diverseness, Suslov tried every possible remedy to hold the Communist movement together but the right one. With Stalin's blessing he excommunicated Tito, forcing the Yugoslavian party to be the first to secede. Having discovered that expulsion does not cure the turmoil, he tried to cajole and mollify Mao, only to find out that appeasement also does not work. Another alternative was to summon a series of international communist conferences, but they too failed to stop the devolution of Moscow's sovereignty. In the end, to save what still remained under Moscow's direct domination, Suslov was forced to invoke the Brezhnev doctrine, and switch his attention from international communism to the promotion of national liberation movements among Communism's still spellbound peoples of the Third World.

The Soviet Union's futile attempt to halt the widening schism in Communism had a striking resemblance to the experience of the Catholic Church during the religious revolt at the end of the XVth and the beginning of the XVIth centuries. Overlooking that they had provoked the Protestant secession themselves, the embattled popes first threatened the heretics with excommunication. When this failed, they summoned General Councils of the church, and finally, in an act of utter folly, excommunicated Luther, casting off nearly half of Europe and permanently shattering western Christianity. There were important distinctions, of course, but the underlying cause was the lack of internal reform and proper understanding of the powerful surge of nationalism that ran in opposition to centralized control. It would be uncharitable to place the entire blame on Suslov for the demise of international communism; much of what happened in the 1950s and 1960s was beyond his control. The interventions in Hungary and Czechoslovakia, the inability of the Politburo to resolve the de-Stalinization issue swiftly and effectively, the predicament of being caught in the middle of a hopeless doctrinal conflict between Belgrade and Peking made it extremely difficult for Suslov to preserve the unity of the Communist movement. The military establishment's obsession with defense also did not help. But these obstacles were not insurmountable. They could have been circumvented if Suslov were willing to tone down the ideological rhetoric, and convince the Politburo that "different roads to socialism" could be followed independently of interference from Moscow or Washington.

To patch up the fragmented Communist movement Gorbachev will have to drastically alter Soviet foreign policy in the direction of greater tolerance for political diversity and recast the sagging image of Soviet-style socialism at home. There is some indication that he is already doing this. In his speech to the foreign delegates attending the commemoration of the seventieth anniversary of the Bolshevik revolution, he has offered a more tolerant and flexible approach to Soviet relations with the rest of the Communist world, stressing that "unity does not mean identity and uniformity . . ., and that there is no single model of socialism to be emulated by everyone."[5] He has also taken a positive step to improve the image of Soviet-style socialism. While the primary purpose of his campaign against widespread corruption, alcoholism, privilege, and lack of discipline is to improve productivity and extricate the Soviet Union from the economic morass that it had fallen into during the Brezhnev era, its collateral function is to cleanse Soviet society of its "contradictions" and, not unlike the Counter Reformation, show to the faithful and the rest of the world a more consistent and virtuous Communist society. He has affirmed this secondary goal on a number of occasions, stating that the most convincing argument in favor of socialism would be the image of an economically and socially viable Soviet Union.[6]

The Institute's observation about Suslov's impact on the "formation of the new Soviet man" also appears to be an exaggeration. Although Suslov may have provided the ideological rationale for the *rapprochement* of Soviet nationalities, no direct evidence exists that the trend toward the formation of a more homogeneous Soviet population developed as a result of pervasive Party propaganda. The more likely explanation is that it was the result of a number of different social forces that impinged on the minds and life styles of the soviet people. Increased industrialization and urbanization, World War II, the expansion of the Communist Party membership, greater social and geographic mobility and higher levels of education, television, and above all, the heightened communality of interests among the very large percentage of the total Soviet population working in the so called "*zakrytyi uchrezhdenii*" (closed establishments)* where security clearances and special privileges are an integral part of employment, all have helped to shape what may be loosely called a new Soviet frame of reference. But even on this, there are differences of opinion. The question of whether or not *Homo Sovieticus* is indeed an evolving reality or merely a myth fabricated by Soviet ideologists in the interest of national *rapprochement* has never been fully resolved. On the whole, anthropologists and political scientists have looked to national and ethnic criteria that place greater emphasis on the cultural and political differences of the Soviet citizens, while sociologists and psychologists have concentrated on social and psychological trends that have led to a congruence of the various national, ethnic, and social components of the Soviet population. The evidence is not all in yet. There is some indication that the new generation of Soviet citizens—except for the rural population and the liberal and nationalist intelligentsias—is beginning to exhibit a supranational Soviet consciousness and an attendant willingness to accept alterations in traditional values that cannot be explained in terms of Russian culture or russification alone. These men and women represent the third and fourth generations of Soviet citizens brought up after the revolution, and it is they who legitimate the Soviet political system, forming Mikhail Gorbachev's most populous political constituency. It is not surprising, therefore, that the General Secretary has gone out of his way in acknowledging the growing sophistication of

---

*Research and industrial enterprises working almost exclusively for defense, the infrastructure, and the production of critical and strategic materials.

their demands for more and better consumer goods and a more gratifying and creative life style.[7]

Perhaps the most threatening Suslovian legacy entirely overlooked by the author of the Institute article is the restricted framework of Suslov's ideological thinking and its impact on future Soviet political reform.[8] Although Suslov was willing to repackage the Marxist-Leninist doctrine to fit the changing needs and circumstances of Soviet society, he always employed the very strictest construction of Marx and Lenin, setting a critical limit beyond which Soviet politicians rarely dared to venture ahead. This is not to say that Soviet ideology had become, as a result of this, a completely unified set of beliefs rigidly professed by all Soviet practitioners of Marxism-Leninism. Since the time of Stalin a lively debate has been waged by Soviet scholars on how the Marxist-Leninist framework should be applied to various policy options. But theory must eventually be brought to action—this is the very essence of Marx's key to the unity of theory and practice—and it is here that Soviet politicians have stumbled over the doctrinal barrier erected by Suslov to protect the central core of the Marxist-Leninist creed. Whether or not Gorbachev will break out of this framework remains an open question. In the end, he may be forced to expand the present economic reform and bring the Marxist component closer to the rational demands of Soviet society. Both conservatives and reformers among the Soviet leadership now agree that there is an urgent need for change because another fifteen years of economic stagnation may be fatal to the Soviet system. But whether or not he will want to initiate political changes that will radically alter the Leninist component is another matter. Of the two, the restructuring of the Leninist component is by far the more hazardous and difficult undertaking. A radical remodeling would require the alteration of the whole Lenin tradition and *Weltanschauung* that has been ritualized and firmly integrated into the Soviet ethos. In the final analysis, it would mean that the Soviet political system would have to exorcise a number of critical Leninist preconceptions and their Stalinist byproducts, leading to a shift from Bolshevism to the more Westernized and humanistic Menshevism—a shift of colossal proportions for the Soviet ruling elite to undertake.

Gorbachev has been moving in that direction, but exercising extreme care not to deviate from the ideological limitations set by Suslov. So far, he has confined the major thrust of his economic policy to the safe domain of promoting labor discipline, improving productivity, and refining incentive mechanisms, without introducing any systemic changes in the structure of the Soviet economy.[9] The same caution and limitations apply to his political reforms. He has restricted them primarily to the partial release of the system from central bureaucratic control, to the encouragement of *glasnost'** and to the liberalization

---

*Russian for "openness" or "willingness to make it public." The word is ambiguous in that it portrays not only frank and open disclosure, but also has the connotation of disclosure for public relations purposes.

of censorship,[10] without making any significant changes in the direction of establishing a genuine participatory democracy. The freeing of Sakharov and other prominent dissidents is encouraging. So are the recent changes in electoral practices affecting the choice of candidates in the Party, the soviets, and the economic enterprises.[11] But neither development has been followed so far by a comprehensive reform of the Soviet political system as a whole.

Where Gorbachev has been far more innovative is in foreign policy. In an attempt to improve the Soviet image in the West, he has drawn away from the simplistic foreign policy rationalized by Suslov and expounded by Gromyko, toward a multipolar course which recognizes that foreign relations do not necessarily fall into two neatly separated camps of "American imperialism" and "peaceful Soviet-style socialism." Professing that the broadening of economic ties with the rest of the world is indispensable for Soviet economic growth, he has been waging a comprehensive public relations campaign for improved relations with Western Europe, China, and Japan. There has also been a reassessment of Soviet foreign policy toward the Third World, although Gorbachev himself has remained surprisingly silent on this subject.[12] In contrast to the ideologically expansive policy advocated by Suslov and supported by Brezhnev during the second half of the 1970s, the Soviet Union has become much more selective in backing Third World socialist-oriented states in achieving socialism.[13] This does not mean that Moscow will back away from existing commitments such as Nicaragua and Angola. However, it reflects the current Soviet position that domestic economic difficulties place a limit on overextended Soviet economic and military aid to nations that are at best only poor candidates for socialism.

With its stress on technological modernization and improved production and distribution of consumer goods, its emphasis on discipline and the curbing of official privilege and corruption, its more flexible foreign policy, and its reduced commitment to the Third World, Gorbachev's economic program bears a functional resemblance to Stalin's policy of industrialization in the 1920s and early 1930s. Instead of the industrial revolution which Stalin launched in his frantic effort to catch up quantitatively with the industrialized West, Gorbachev is directing his program toward the achievement of a second revolution, a post-industrial technological and distributional revolution targeted at the realization of Western levels of productivity and satisfaction of consumer wants. At the same time, he is also trying to rejuvenate Soviet society by eliminating speculation, bribery, theft, and a myriad of other illegal gains euphemistically named "unearned income," and restoring the abandoned moral and social values of the early revolutionaries. In his attempt to accomplish this, Gorbachev does not appear to be making a radical break with the established strategies of central planning, command economy, and heightened Party vigilance, nor with the ideological framework imposed on him by the previous regime. On the contrary his program seems to be a reaffirmation of these strategies adapted to the need for a greater level of humaneness and openness in restructuring an economy that has not kept up with the technological and consumer sophistication of the West and Japan.

Within the broader frame of reference, the Gorbachev program represents an attempt to launch a new and revivalist stage in the long process of the Russian Revolution that began in 1917. Having gone through a millenarian revolt and a Jacobin revolution during which violence, repression and force ran amok, the Russian Revolution had disintegrated, in its post-Stalinist period, into a transitional stage during which security, stability, and routinization became the principal preoccupations of the Party elite. Khrushchev had tried to reverse this process, but the Party conservatives refused to give him their support. In the next twenty years, a conservative and unimaginative team of Party *apparatchiks,* led by Brezhnev and guided by Suslov, dedicated themselves to the achievement of political stability and Party supremacy. Their efforts to bring stability to the Party and the nation were not without cause, of course. After the harsh Stalin years and the Khrushchev roller coaster that followed them, all segments of Soviet society were in search of greater political stability and personal security. Suslov's contribution to the Soviet political system was the attainment of that stability, but at the expense of a new resurgence of political conservatism and unbridled bureaucracy, public apathy and corruption, and unresolved Stalinist legacy that continue to pervade Soviet life. Gorbachev's attempt at a *"perestroika"** is a step in the direction of erasing these afflictions. It is no accident, therefore, that he has gone on record to clarify the meaning of this word by stating that "he would equate the word *'perestroika'* with the word 'revolution,' " a revolution that would touch all phases of Soviet political, economic and cultural life.[14]

Western analysts have responded in different ways to the Gorbachev "revolution." Extrapolating from Russian history, a small minority of incorrigible pessimists have concluded prematurely that the Gorbachev reform is but another short-lasting thaw in the cycle of Russian history that will invariably end in a new phase of repression and economic stagnation.[15] A larger and more eclectic group of practicing Sovietologists have taken a more open-minded approach. In varying degrees, they have accepted the reform for what it is, but not without a certain amount of caution and skepticism. Focusing their attention on the vast Soviet bureaucracy and the traditionally conservative enclaves of Soviet society, they have questioned the efficacy of the reform, arguing that the vested political and economic interests—the central planners, the middle and low level Party *apparatchiks,* the technocrats—will not surrender their power and privileges, nor change their inefficient and obdurate ways.[16]

Reservations have also been voiced by specialists examining the reform from the position of their respective disciplines. Economists have challenged the

---

*Russian for restructuring.

Soviet assumption that a real and permanent turn-around of the Soviet command economy can be achieved without a conversion of the system to a free market.[17] Kremlinologists have questioned the solidarity of the Gorbachev Politburo, arguing that its full members come from different backgrounds, owe their positions of influence not to Gorbachev but to Andropov and Brezhnev, and lack the kind of unanimity that is necessary to carry the reforms through, especially after the honeymoon period is over.[18] Recognizing the intricate relationship of Soviet foreign and domestic policies, at least two political scientists have singled out the slow process of Soviet-American arms negotiations as the bogey that may stall domestic reform. They have pointed out that the combination of a hostile international environment and a reversal in arms negotiations could seriously damage Gorbachev's credibility at home, strengthen the conservative and reactionary force of Soviet society, and plunge the soviet Union into a new phase of sword-rattling and heightened xenophobia.[19] The surge in public demonstrations by an array of nationalist, ethnic and religious groups testing the limits of *glasnost'* has also produced uncertainty, raising new speculation on how long the thaw will continue and how soon the frost will return.[20] The litany of pessimistic and skeptical commentary has not been dwindling. On the contrary, it has escalated in 1987, casting a deep shadow on the likelihood of an early success.

Countering the dirges of the pessimists and skeptics, is an assortment of more optimistic assessments that sees the dawning of a new and more liberal era in the Soviet Union. Influenced by the exhilaration of the new openness in the arts and the media, and by Gorbachev's refreshing style of leadership, the optimists have on the whole tended to overlook the questionable assumptions of the reform program. Two recent biographies of Gorbachev have been partially guilty of this.[21] The hope aroused by the Soviet creative intelligentsia has also played into the hands of the optimists; so has the changing of the guard in the ranks of the top and middle leadership.[22] One supporter of the optimistic view has been especially sanguine about the positive effect of the changing Soviet leadership. Stressing the discontinuity of the Soviet experience, he has argued forcefully that the generational replacement of Party and government officials is bringing a new elite into all levels of Soviet public life, a younger and more pragmatic elite that has grown up without experiencing the war and the terror of the Stalin era. Better educated, less ideological and more self-confident than their predecessors, the new elite, he insists, represents a new generation of Soviet men and women who are committed to the idea of an efficient and peaceful government and to the urgent need for change.[23]

Aired on television, in the newspapers, and in scholarly journals, these views dominate Western discussion of Gorbachev's attempt in restructuring the ailing Soviet society. Partially valid and focusing mostly on selected facets of the Soviet political, social and economic systems, these views fail to offer a comprehensive and holistic analysis of the *perestroika*. The pessimistic view invariably exaggerates the continuity of Russia's historical experience, conveniently disregarding that the Soviet Union of today is no longer the impenetrable totalitarian regime of the Stalin era or the unstable and transitional society of his early successors. The optimistic view also overstates its case. Swayed by the generational change and the increased openness of the new administration, the optimists tend to overlook that the new Soviet leaders have experienced essentially the same process of upbringing and political grooming as their immediate predecessors, despite the new outlook of the Gorbachev regime. They forget that culturally ingrained attitudes exhibit an exceptionally stubborn resistance to change and frequently reinstate themselves in a crisis with the same degree of firmness as they had displayed before.

What are the real prospects for reform then? The most likely answer is that it will be carried through, but it will not have the breadth that the optimists envision. The reallocation of resources from defense to the consumer sector of the economy and the establishment of small privately operated production enterprises and retail sales outlets will provide a new and higher level of consumer satisfaction. The restructuring of the technologically sensitive industries, the streamlining of the cumbersome central planning system, the granting of greater autonomy to regional and local enterprises, and a more efficient utilization of the vast underemployed resources will produce some improvement in productivity. So will the massive campaign against alcoholism, absentism, fraud, and the decline of the work ethic. The retirement and replacement of the old Party and government leaders with younger, more pragmatic and enlightened cadres will temporarily rejuvenate the bureaucracy, but it will not make it more malleable or receptive to the needs of the populace. Like all massive and engulfing bureaucracies it will remain fundamentally authoritarian. The promotion of *glasnost'* and the extension of more liberal censorship will raise the artistic level of the creative arts and the media, and will foster the continued backing of the Gorbachev regime by the Soviet intelligentsia. The international climate will also improve. A less aggressive and more flexible foreign policy, supported by reductions in the military budget, will temporarily ease international tensions and lessen the risk of direct confrontation with the West. The restructuring will be slow, painful and not without periodic outbursts of sabotage from the more conservative segments of the Soviet society. Reform is by its nature a developing process that calls for a certain amount of "give and take" before its component parts can be fully integrated into a newly evolving body politic. "The most perilous moment for a bad government is when it seeks to mend its ways," de Tocqueville noted about the French government on the eve of the French revolution.[25] The prospects for Gorbachev are not very different. He, too, will experience his share of challenges and disappointments, but it is unlikely that the *"perestroika"* will break up on the shoals of a conservative reaction. Almost everyone agrees that the Gorbachev reform has a better chance of succeeding than that of Khrushchev. Paradoxically, Suslov's stewardship has also been consequential to the success of the *perestroika*. Suslov had worked harder than anyone else among Brezhnev's contemporaries to construct a stable Party-sustained oligarchy from which an orderly reform could be initiated without the lingering fear of the previous regimes that the whole government would collapse in the process. The most startling observation often overlooked by students of the Soviet Union may well be that the thirty years after the death of Stalin were, indeed, a time of painful transition during which the contending forces of reform and anti-reform had gradually created a new mold of leaders, a more receptive populace, and a more tolerant environment to bring about an improvement in the lives of the Soviet citizens.

Will the "*perestroika*" broaden beyond Gorbachev's limited objectives to a more fundamental reform of the Soviet system? The evidence is not all in yet, but the likelihood that this will happen is not too encouraging. Gorbachev's motivation for the reform has been mostly pragmatic: to catch up technologically with the West, to expand the production of consumer goods, and to enhance the world image of an economically and socially viable Soviet Union. The recent tendency toward the democratization of Soviet society is in many respects merely an indispensable by-product evolving out of the General Secretary's firm conviction that a turn-around of the Soviet economy can not be achieved without *glastnost'* and social and political reform. The *perestroika* was never meant to be a systemic reform that would lead the Soviet Union toward a fully integrated market economy and a participatory democracy. Neither the XXVIIth Party Congress nor any of the ensuing agenda point to any fundamental changes in Soviet thinking, and Suslov's ghost continues to haunt the deliberations of the Soviet establishment.[26] Indeed, the decision to confine the reform within the administrative and organizational framework of the existing system is a tangible confirmation of how securely Suslov had fused the Marxist-Leninist components into the present Soviet formula.

History has, on the whole, been unkind to Russian attempts at modernization. Except for the Petrine reform, pragmatism and the desire for reform from above have failed to sustain long-term substantive transformations of the Russian society as a whole. At best, they brought only partial transformations that affected different segments of the population, or produced temporary breathing spells between longer periods of lingering political anxiety and economic stagnation. If the Soviet Union is to effect a permanent and fundamental change that affects the whole Soviet society, the reform must go beyond the imperative of economic and technological change to the heart of the Soviet political culture. It must free the Soviet Union from the centuries-old Russian traditionalism that the Revolution had failed to dislodge and from the more recently grafted Leninist-Stalinist framework that has made it even more unyielding. Failing to accomplish that, the Gorbachev "revolution" could easily degenerate into another short-term modernization, a "revolution from without," as one Western scholar has correctly diagnosed Lenin's and Stalin's attempts at modernization,[27] another reform in the interest of eradicating those recurring positions of weakness *vis a vis* the world's major powers that have periodically plagued Russian history.

For the reform to be genuine and permanent, the Soviet Union must stage a "revolution from within," a revolution motivated by the awakening of a new national consciousness, a consciousness that would deliver not only a temporary economic and technological modernization from above, but one that would produce a political and cultural climate to sustain a permanent transformation. To achieve this, ordinary Russians will have to learn to restrain their conservative and orthodox passions, embrace a more pluralistic and pragmatic view of life, and temper their predilection for deterministic philosophy. Agricultural and industrial managers will have to learn to function as entrepreneurs willing to take on greater economic and political risks in pursuit of higher productivity. Journalists, editors, and the media will have to become more experimental, more forthright, and more committed to the tenets of their profession. Digging deep into their long concealed archives and using high academic standards, Soviet scholars will have to document the trauma of Russian and Soviet history, setting the record straight for future generations. To compete in the world, the new Soviet leadership will have to dismantle the political and economic juggernaut that their predecessors had built, and replace it with a new and technologically viable infrastructure suitable for the twenty-first century. The Party will have to acknowledge its shortcomings, fully repudiate Stalinism, and develop a new perception of its responsibilities to the Soviet people. In the final analysis, the entire society will have to expunge what that austere and earnest "true believer" from Shakhovskoe had so resolutely tried to instill in order to legitimate the sanctity of the Party and the security of the Marxist-Leninist tradition. There are faint signs that this is beginning to take place, but whether or not the Soviet society as a whole is ready to go that far still remains an open question. In his speech on the seventieth anniversary of the Bolshevik revolution Gorbachev has urged his countrymen to begin moving in that direction,[28] but the triple-headed ogre of orthodoxy, indifference and resistance to change has not been tamed yet, let alone slain. Indeed, the General Secretary has had to admit publicly that the *perestroika* "has proved more difficult than we at first imagined."[29]

SELECTED CHRONOLOGY

1902

November   Mikhail A. Suslov is born on November 21, in Shakhovskoe
               (now in Pavlovka *raion*, Ul'yanovsk *oblast'*.

1917

February   February Revolution. Tsar Nicholas II abdicates on March 2.

November   October Revolution. Lenin takes power.

1918

November   Young Suslov joins local *Kombed* (Committee for the Relief of
               the Poor).

1919

February   Suslov becomes active in local *Kombed* and Khvalynsk *Komso-
               mol*.

1921

Summer   During the summer or early fall of 1921 Suslov joins the Com-
               munist party.

Fall   Arrives in Moscow and enrolls in Prechistinsky *rabfak* (worker
               faculty, equivalent to a secondary school).

1924

January   Lenin dies on January 24.

Fall   Suslov graduates from Prechistinsky *rabfak*, and is admitted to
               the G. V. Plekhanov Institute of National Economy in Moscow.

1927

December   XVth Party Congress. Trotsky and Zinoviev are condemned as
               deviationists and expelled from the party. Suslov participates ac-
               tively in Stalin's campaign against the "United Opposition."

1928

Summer   Suslov graduates from the Plekhanov Institute and is admitted to the Institute of the Red Professoriat in Moscow.

1929–1931   Suslov becomes an instructor at Moscow State University and the Stalin Academy of Industry, holding these positions through 1931 and continuing research work at the Institute of the Red Professoriat.

Active in campaign against Bukharin and the Party's "right wing deviation."

1931–1934   In 1933, Suslov begins working for the Central Control Commission. Active in the 1933 *chistka* (purge), with special responsibilities for Chernigov and Ural *Obkoms*.

1935–1936   Continues to work in the Central Control Commission, supervising phases of the "documents verification program" and the early stages of the "Party card exchange program."

1937–1938   Stalin's Great Purge.

1938   In the spring of 1938, Suslov surfaces in Rostov *Obkom* in charge of propaganda and cadres departments.

1939

March   Suslov is appointed First Secretary of the Stavropol *Kraikom*.

March   At the XVIIIth Party Congress Suslov is appointed member of the All-Union Central Auditing Commission.

1941–1942   Germany invades the Soviet Union on June 21, 1941.

Suslov becomes a full member of the Party Central Committee.

Becomes chief of staff of the Stavropol *Krai* partisan command and member of the Military Council for the North Caucasus front.

1944

November   Suslov is transferred to Vilnius, Lithuania to direct the newly formed Bureau of Lithuanian affairs. Stalin orders him to reestablish Soviet power in Lithuania.

1946

March   Suslov is recalled to Moscow by Stalin to work in the General Department of the Party Central Committee.

1947

March   Makes his first trip abroad to England as member of a Soviet delegation.

June   Appointed head of *Agitprop* (Agitation and Propaganda Department). Revamps *Agitprop* and launches campaign for more rigid adherence to the doctrine of socialist realism in the arts.

September   Appointed to the Secretariat of the Party Central Committee.

1948

January   Delivers the traditional Lenin Day Speech.

September   After Zhdanov's death, Suslov assumes Zhdanov's responsibilities as Secretary in charge of ideology and inter-Party affairs. Also becomes Chairman of the Cominform.

1949

September   Suslov is appointed editor-in-chief of *Pravda,* serving in this capacity through 1950.

?   Appointed Candidate Member of the Politburo.

1952

October   Appointed Full Member of the expanded Presidium (formerly known as the Politburo).

November   Awarded the Order of Lenin on his fiftieth birthday.

1953

March   Stalin dies on March 5. Suslov loses his membership in the Presidium following Stalin's death, but retains his position in the Secretariat.

1954

April   Suslov is appointed Chairman of the Foreign Affairs Commission of the All-Union Supreme Soviet.

               Transfers responsibilities for ideology to Pospelov in order to concentrate on inter-Party relations.

1955

July   Suslov is reappointed to the Presidium.

July   Delivers key-address in Warsaw at the ceremonies reestablishing the new post-World War II Polish government.

1956

February   Suslov resumes responsibilities for ideology.

	At the XXth Party Congress, inventories the principal negative effects of Stalin's practice of "the cult of personality."
	Khrushchev delivers his "Secret Speech."
October	Together with Mikoyan, Suslov travels to Budapest to resolve the Hungarian crisis. The Soviet Union invades Hungary on November 1 and puts down the Hungarian revolution.
November	Suslov delivers the traditional October Revolution anniversary address on November 6, reminding the world that there cannot be any compromise on the question of "defending the gains of the socialist revolution."

1957

June	An "anti-Party coalition headed by Malenkov, Molotov and Kaganovich attempts to oust Khrushchev. Suslov backs Khrushchev against the "anti-Party" group.
October	Suslov presides at the removal of Marshall Zhukov from the Presidium and from his post as Defense Minister.
November	Suslov chairs the International Communist Conference in Moscow.

1958

March	Experiences his first serious disagreement with Khrushchev over the dismantling of the MTS program.
March	Khrushchev appoints Aleksei I. Kirichenko to the Secretariat as a counterweight to Suslov.

1959

January	Suslov addresses the XXIst Party Congress, obliquely criticizing Khrushchev's intransigent position on the "anti-Party" group.
September	Flies to Peking to pave the way for a meeting of Khrushchev and Mao at the tenth anniversary of the Chinese People's Republic.

1960

May	U-2 incident leading to the cancellation of the Eisenhower- Khrushchev summit.
May	Suslov regains his influence and, together with Frol Kozlov, mounts a campaign against Khrushchev and his attempt at *rapprochement* with the United States.
June	Suslov and Khrushchev meet at Pitsunda in the Crimea to reconcile their differences.

1961

October   Delivers address at the XXIInd Party Congress openly criticizing Khrushchev's position on the "anti-Party" group.

1962

February   Low point in Suslov's career during the Khrushchev regime. After delivering the address to the Heads of the Social Science Departments on January 30, 1962, Suslov virtually drops out of Soviet domestic affairs.

October   Cuban crisis.

1963

September   Suslov drops out of Soviet press coverage until january 1964. The long absence lasting from September 25, 1963 to January 1, 1964 was probably caused by hospitalization and prolonged rest after diagnosis of on-set adult diabetes and coronary heart disease.

1964

February   Suslov delivers a report to the Central Committee plenum condemning Chinese communism and its leaders on February 12.

October   Presides at the Central Committee plenum that approves Khrushchev's ouster, and the appointment of Brezhnev and Kosygin to replace Khrushchev.

1965

June   Suslov delivers a major speech in Sofia, Bulgaria, castigating Podgorny and the pro-Kosygin forces.

1966

March   The XXIIIrd Party Congress opens on March 29, and puts the "cult of personality" issue to rest.

1967

May   Suslov delivers major speech at the 150th anniversary of the birth of Karl Marx, zeroing in on the growing disarray of the world communist movement.

December   Brezhnev travels to Prague to try to resolve the growing Czechoslovakian crisis.

1968

July   Soviet-Czechoslovak bilateral conference at Cierna nad Tisou

	from July 29 to August 1. Suslov counsels against military intervention.
August	Assisted by troops from the Warsaw Pact allies, the Soviet Union invades Czechoslovakia on August 20. World Communist Conference scheduled for November 1968 is cancelled.
1969	
June	Suslov delivers the key address at the World Communist Conference in Moscow, citing relevance of Lenin's experience in the struggle for socialism. The conference ends in a failure.
1970	
January	Brezhnev's condemnation of Kosygin and the government *apparat* for continuing shortcomings of Soviet economy precipitates an internal political crisis.
June	After six months of infighting in the Politburo, Suslov negotiates a settlement.
1971	
March	XXIVth Party Congress opens on March 30. Suslov does not address the congress. Brezhnev announces that the Soviet Union has reached a new stage of "developed socialism."
1972	
May	Policy of détente leads to U.S.-Soviet summit conference and Nixon-Brezhnev Interim agreement, leading eventually to SALT I and U.S.-Soviet Trade Agreement.
September	Elizaveta Suslova, Suslov's wife dies after long and grave illness.
November	Suslov celebrates 70th birthday, and is awarded another Order of Lenin and a second Sickle and Hammer medal.
1973	
January	Suslov launches campaign for a more restricted policy of détente with his speech "The Great Science of Victory" on January 17.
May	Andropov, Gromyko and Grechko become full members of Politburo.
November	Suslov delivers a major speech on the subject of nationalities and the new "Soviet man" on November 28 in Vilnius.
1974	Suslov and Ponamarev continue to promote a more restricted policy of détente, precipitating a reassessment of Soviet policies toward the Third World.

1976

February   The XXVth Party Congress opens on February 24, and turns into a condemnations of Soviet-style socialism by the Eurocommunists.

June   Suslov suffers a heart attack that puts him out of commission until September.

September   Suslov delivers speech in Leningrad on the need to rekindle socialist values, the first of a series of speeches indicating his concern over the growing "contradictions" of Soviet life.

1977   Suslov reaches high point of his political career, exercising influence over ideology, inter-Party relations, civilian and military political education, the media, the State Publishing Committee, the Comsomol, the KGB, and even Soviet foreign policy. Becomes "Second Secretary," often sitting in for Brezhnev at Politburo meetings.

1978   Mikhail Gorbachev, protégé of Suslov and Andropov, is appointed to the Secretariat at the November plenum.

1979

February   Suslov names Afghanistan as one of the "new states of socialist orientation."

1979

November   Gorbachev becomes candidate member of the Politburo.

December   Soviet Union invades Afghanistan.

1980

December   Rise of Polish Solidarity movement.

October   Gorbachev becomes full member of the Politburo.

1981

February   XXVIth Party Congress opens on February 23. No important changes in Soviet domestic or foreign policies, despite prior speculation about anticipated modifications in economic policy.

April   On April 12, in a speech in East Germany, Suslov warns Poland that deviation from Communist theory would come to no good.

            On April 23, Suslov makes trip to Warsaw to secure assurance that Soviet interests will not be sacrificed.

October   On October 14, Suslov repeats his warnings to Poland.

December   Suslov makes his last public appearance at a celebration honoring
            Brezhnev on December 19.

1982

January   Suslov suffers a stroke on January 20 and dies on January 25.
            Andropov replaces him as chief ideologue.

November   Brezhnev dies on November 10.

NOTES TO THE PROLOGUE

1. *New York Times,* February 13, 1955.
2. *"Bog pravdu vidit, da ne skoro skazhet,"* a Russian proverb.
3. Elizabeth Teague, "Mikhail Suslov—The Power Behind the Throne?" *Radio Liberty Research Bulletin,* RL 42/82, January 26, 1982, p.1.
4. Nikita Khrushchev *Khrushchev Remembers* (Boston/Toronto: Little Brown & Co., 1970), p. 377.
5. Aleksandr Solzhenitsyn, *The Oak and the Calf* (New York: Harper and Row, 1979), p. 302.
6. Enver Hoxha, *The Khrushchevites* (Tyrana, Albania: 8 Nantori Publishing House, 1980), pp. 269–272.
7. Veljko Micunovic, *Moscow Diary* (Garden City, N.Y.: Doubleday, 1980), pp. 365–366.
8. Jacob Beam, *Multiple Exposure: An American Ambassador's Unique Perspective on East West Issues* (New York: W. W. Norton, 1978), p. 275.
9. John B. Dunlop, *The Face of Contemporary Russian Nationalism* (Princeton, N.J.: Princeton University Press, 1983), p. 291n; Dan Fisher, *Los Angeles Times,* December 2, 1979.
10. Sergei Trapeznikov, *At the Turning Point of History* (Moscow: Progress Publishers, 1972). For details regarding Suslov's censure of Trapeznikov, see Stephen F. Cohen, Ed. *End of Silence: Uncensored Opinion in the Soviet Union* (New York/London: W. W. Norton, 1982), pp. 170–171.
11. V. Stanley Vardys, "The Partisan Movement in Postwar Lithuania," *Slavic Review,* Vol. XXII (3), September 1963, pp. 499–522; "Samizdat Documents on Suslov's Role in Lithuania," *Lituanus,* Vol. 24 (1), 1978, pp. 67–80.
12. Anatole Shub, *The New Russian Tragedy* (New York: W. W. Norton, 1969), pp. 52–53; Elizabeth Teague, p. 2.
13. Associated Press Release, January 1982 (FFO 69).
14. Theodore Shabad, *New York Times,* January 27, 1982.
15. *New York Times,* February 15, 1980.
16. Theodore Shabad, *New York Times,* January 27, 1982.
17. Roy Medvedev, *All Stalin's Men* (Garden City, N.Y.: Anchor Press, 1984), p. 77; A. A. Avtorkhanov, "Suslov: The Kremlin's Chief Ideologist," *Bulletin of the Institute for the Study of the USSR,* Vol. XV (2), February 1968, p. 3, also *Sila i bessilie Brezhneva* (Frankfurt/Main, 1979), p. 74.
18. *New York Times,* February 15, 1980.
19. Suslov's use of such expressions as *Nasha Sovetskaia rodina, Sovetskii ludi, Sovetskii narod* is pervasive throughout all of his speeches and writings contained in M. A. Suslov, *Marksizm-Leninizm i sovremennaia epokha,* 3 vols. (Moscow: Izpolit, 1982).

20. Abraham Brumberg, "Moscow's Toastmaster," *The New Leader*, November 2, 1981, pp. 11–12.
21. *Pravda*, January 27, 1982.
22. The description of Suslov's funeral is based on Serge Schmeman, *New York Times*, January 30, 1982, and on the Associated Press Release of January 26, 1982, as reported in FI77 and FFO65.
23. *Pravda*, January 27, 1982.
24. Alexander Pushkin, "The Lay of the Wise Oleg," *Poems, Prose and Plays of Alexander Pushkin* (New York: The Modern Library, 1936), pp. 55–58.

NOTES TO CHAPTER I

1. In a 1930s restructuring of the boundaries of Ulianovsk and Saratov provinces, the northern most part of Saratov province was incorporated into Ulianovsk province. The term "province" was eliminated and replaced by the term "*oblast*" (region). Shakhovskoe is now located in the Pavlovka District of Ulianovsk *Oblast*.
2. According to Army Map Service, Corps of Engineers, United States Army, Map. No. *MN38-12 (Vol'sk)*, *G7010 S250 U5*.
3. P. I. Melnikov-Pechersky, for many years superintendent and watchdog of Old Believer Affairs in the XIXth century Russia, and later author of *Na gorakh (In the Hills)* and *V lesakh (In the Forests)*, two epic novels portraying the life of Old Believers on the Volga's right bank. For details, see Thomas H. Hoissington, "Melnikov-Pechersky" The romancer of Provincial and Old Believer Life," *Slavic Review*, Vol. XXXIII (4), December 1974, pp. 679–694.
4. The description of the contrasting harshness of Saratov province is based on Boris Pilnyak, *Mother Earth* (New York: Frederick A. Praeger, 1968), p. 3.
5. Drought and famine were endemic to Saratov province. In the past 100 years, the most devastating were the famines of 1891–1892, the famine of 1911, and the great famine of 1921 that followed the Russian Civil War.
6. Ivan Bolotnikov, leader of the 1606–1607 insurrection south of Moscow that grew into a full-scale rebellion of serfs, slaves, fugitives, and vagabonds against the authority of the central government. In many respects, the Bolotnikov Rebellion was the first manifestation of serious social turmoil in Russia.
7. Beginning with the second half of the XIXth century, ambitious peasant youth, using the medium of the seminaries and the military schools, often rose to play important positions in the government.
8. Official Soviet biographies of Suslov do not contain data about his life in Shakhovskoe. The author's attempt to obtain precise information about Suslov's family background from the Marx-Engels Institute and the *Put' Ilyicha* Archive in Ulianovsk Oblast resulted in failure.
9. *Starovery* (Old Believers) seceded from the Russian Orthodox Church in the middle of the XVIIth century, refusing to accept the new religious ritual introduced by Patriarch Nikon in 1653. What started as a protest against such minor changes in ritual as the use of three fingers instead of two in making the sign of the cross, became a major movement against all reform, against foreign influence, against the

Church's insensitivity to the need for moral rebirth, and against centralized government authority and Church control. Anathemized by the Church and persecuted by the government, the Old Believers fled to the borderlands to escape the reach of the westernizing Tsar Peter. It is estimated that in 1917 approximately one fourth of the Russian populace were Old Believers. For details see: Frederick Conybeare, *Russian Dissenters* (New York, 1962); Nickolas Lupinin, *Religious Revolt in the XVII Century* (Princeton, N.J.: The Kingston Press, 1985); Serge A. Zenkovsky, "The Russian Church Schism, Its Background and Repercussions," *The Russian Review*, Vol. 16 (4), October 1958.

10. James Billington, *The Icon and the Axe* (New York: Vintage Press, 1970), p. 542; Martin Page, *The Day Khrushchev Fell* (New York: Hawthorne Books, 1965), p. 40.

11. S. P. Melgunov, *Staroobriatsy i svoboda sovesti* (Moscow: Zadruga, 1917), pp. 16 and 36; V. E. Milovidov, *Staroobriadstvo v proshlom i nastoiashchem* (Moscow: Izd. Mysl', 1969), pp. 4–5 and 69–85.

12. *Bolshaia Sovetskaia Entsiklopedia*, Vol. 28 (Moscow, 1978), pp. 221–222.

13. *Ibid.*, Vol. 25 (Moscow, 1976), p. 96.

14. M. A. Suslov, *Selected Speeches and Writings* (Oxford: Pergamon Press, 1980), p. 2.

15. Anton Chekhov, *The Peasants and Other Stories* (New York: Anchor Books, 1956), p. 279.

16. Leo Tolstoy, *War and Peace*, Chapters 12 and 13 (Garden City, N.Y.: International Collectors Library, 1949): Ivan Turgenev, *Sportsman Sketches* (New York: Viking Press, 1957).

17. M. Lewin, *Russian Peasants and Soviet Power*, pp. 21–40; Geroid Tanquary Robinson, *Rural Russia under the Old Regime* (Berkeley, Ca.: University of California Press, 1932), pp. 117–118 and 243–265; Theodore Shanin, *The Awkward Class, Political Sociology of Peasantry in a Developing Society: Russia, 1910–1925* (Oxford: Clarendon Press, 1972).

18. Boris Pilniak, *The Naked Year* (New York: Payson & Clark, 1928), pp. 140–141.

19. Nicholas Vakar, *The Taproot of Soviet Society* (New York: Harper and Brothers, 1961), p. 62.

20. Nicholas Vakar, p. 46.

21. William T. Shinn, Jr., "The Law of the Russian Peasant Household," *Slavic Review*, Vol. XX (4), pp. 601–621.

22. Geroid T. Robinson, pp. 256–257.

23. *Ibid.*

24. The majority of the peasants chose not to accept communal tenure after the Emancipation in 1861, and a large portion of the farm land was, therefore, still held in common in 1906.

25. Nicholas Vakar, p. 49.

26. *Ibid.*

NOTES TO CHAPTER II

1. William H. Chamberlin, *The Russian Revolution*, Vol. I (New York: The Universal Library, 1965), p. 365.

2. There were more than two hundred thousand Czech and Slovak prisoners of war in Russia during World War I. As subjects of the multi-national Austro-Hungarian empire, they had been pressed into service against the allies, and had surrendered—often en masse—on the Eastern front. By the middle of 1917, the Provisional Government of Russia had cautiously armed 40,000, forming an independent Czechoslovak Legion that was to be transferred to France via Vladivostok. The October Revolution caught them in transit, but the new Bolshevik leadership agreed to proceed with the original plan provided the Czechs were to travel not as fighting units but as citizens carrying arms to protect themselves against the growing violence in the Russian countryside. By June 1918, the Legion was strung over thousands of miles of rail on its way to be picked up by allied transports in Vladivostok. The movement of the Czechoslovak troops was not without occasional armed clashes with local Bolshevik authorities, as the majority of the troops were strongly anti-Bolshevik. To this day, there is no clear explanation for the Czechoslovak uprising. It is likely that the Legion's decision to take action against the Bolsheviks may have been prompted by rumors that the Soviet government was preparing to disarm it after Lenin had signed the peace treaty with the Germans at Brest-Litovsk. For more details, see David Footman, *Civil War in Russia* (New York: Praeger, 1962), pp. 85–134; George Stewart, *The White Armies of Russia* (New York: Russell & Russell, 1970), pp. 96–125 and 239–335.
3. P. P. Petrov (Paul P. Petroff), *Ot Volgi do Tikhogo Okeana v riadakh Belykh* (Riga, Latvia: Izd. Didkovskogo, 1930), p. 20.
4. *Ibid.*, p. 35.
5. I. Ya Trifonov, *Likvidatsiia eksplotatorskikh klassov v SSSR* (Moscow: Izd. Polit. Lit., 1975), p. 130.
6. I. Ya. Trifonov, p. 131.
7. *Ibid.*
8. A. M. Dedov, *Komitety derevenskoi bednoty i ikh rol' v ukreplenii Sovetskoi vlasti* (Moscow: Izd. Znamia, 1958), pp. 34–46.
9. According to Kommunisticheskaia Akademiia, *Komitety Bednoty,* Vol. I (Moscow), pp. 210–213, minutes of local soviets, resolutions, official party correspondence and telegrams attest to the growing struggle for power between the *kombedy* and the local soviets.
10. A. A. Chernobaev, *Razvitie Sotsialisticheskoi Revolutsii v derevne, October 1917 to 1918–19* (Moscow: Vysshaia Shkola, 1975), p. 87.
11. V. K. Medvedev, *Povolzhskaia derevnia v period kombedov* (Saratov: Izd. Saratovskogo Universiteta, 1966), p. 34.
12. P. P. Petrov, p. 41.
13. The White Army evacuated Khvalynsk, leaving behind a small garrison and three hundred cadets from the local military school together with their officers. By the first week of December, following the same tactics used by Trotsky in Petrograd a year earlier, the Bolsheviks seized control of the Knvalynsk soviet and formed a Military Revolutionary Committee in opposition to the local government. An attempt by the cadets to disarm the Bolsheviks failed during the night of January 1–2 and, by the end of the week, the Bolsheviks had a firm grip on the city, even though resistance in the surrounding areas continued for another month. Semen V. Terekhin, *Gody ognevye: Saratovskaia organizatsiia bolshevikov v period Oktiabr'skoi revolut-*

sii i grazhdanskoi voiny, 1917–1920 (Saratov: Privolzhskoe kn. Izd., 1967), pp. 45–46 and pp. 305–306.

14. The official Soviet biography of Suslov states that he joined a *Kombed* in November 1918.

15. For details on the pursuit of the Civil War on the Volga and in Siberia, see David Footman, p. 114–134 and 211–244; P. P. Petrov, pp. 66–149; G. K. Eikhe, *Ufimskaia avantura Kolchaka* (Moscow: Voennoe Izd., 1960), pp. 45–266.

16. Admiral A. V. Kolchak assumed power as Supreme Ruler at Omsk in mid-November of 1918 by means of a military coup, and began to pursue a policy that was not politically acceptable to many of his more liberal backers and the minorities in the Volga and Urals area.

17. Mikhail Heller and Aleksandr Nekrich, *Utopiia u vlasti,* Vol I (London: Overseas Publications Interchange, 1982), p. 107.

18. *Ibid.,* p. 108.

19. *Ibid.,* p. 102.

20. V. K. Medvedev, p. 55.

21. M. A. Suslov, *Selected Speeches and Writings* (Oxford Pergamon Press, 1980), p. 2.

22. Suslov became a member of the Party in 1921 according to the *Bolshaia Sovetskaia Entsiklopedia,* Vol. 25 (Moscow, 1976), p. 96.

23. Nicolas Berdyaev, *The Russian Revolution* (Ann Arbor, Mich.: University of Michigan Press, 1961), pp. 38–39.

24. Gabriel A. Almond, *The Appeals of Communism* (Princeton, N.J.: Princeton University Press, 1954), pp. 258–294.

25. *Ibid.,* pp. 259–261.

26. Lenin, *"Left Wing" Communism—An Infantile Disorder* (Moscow, 1920).

27. Leon Trotsky, *The Revolution Betrayed* (London, 1957).

NOTES TO CHAPTER III

1. Only a few studies dealing with the early Soviet educational system are available in English. For an overview of *Rabfaks,* see Sheila Fitzpatrick, *The Commissariat of Enlightenment: Soviet Organization of Education and the Arts under Lunacharsky, 1917–1921* (London/New York: Cambridge Univ. Press, 1970) and *Education and Social Mobility in the Soviet Union, 1921–1934* (London/New York: Cambridge University Press, 1970), pp. 42–63; Frederick M. Tanner, *The Workers' Faculty (Rabfak) System in the USSR,* unpublished Ph.D. diss. (Columbia Teachers' College, 1965); David Lane, "The Impact of the Revolution: The Case of Selection of Students for Higher Education in Soviet Russia, 1917–1928," *Sociology* (UK), Vol. 17 (2), May 1972.

2. According to the Leningradskoe Upravlenie VUZOV i Rabfakov, *Itogi i perspektivy Rabochikh Fakultetov* (Leningrad: Izd. KOBUCH, 1925) there were in the Russian republic: 11 daytime *rabfaks* and 11 evening *rabfaks* in Moscow, 11 daytime *rabfaks* and 3 evening *rabfaks* in Leningrad, and a total of 39 *rabfaks* in provincial centers. According to N. V. Vikharev, *Rabochie Fakultety k desiatiletiu Oktiabria* (Moscow:

Gos. Izd., 1927), pp. 10 and 14, 8,000 graduated from a total *Rabfak* enrollment of 32,440 in 1924, the year Suslov graduated.

3. Prechistenskie Rabochie Kursy (Prechistinky Classes for Workers) were founded in 1897 in Moscow, offering day and night classes in a variety of subject to help workers achieve a higher degree of technical competence and allow them to receive a secondary school diploma.

4. *Molodaia Gvardiia,* 1924 (5), pp. 206ff, as cited in Sheila Fitzpatrick, *Education and Mobility in the Soviet Union,* p. 92.

5. The loss of life during the famine following the Civil War has been estimated at five million. The death tolls would have been even greater if assistance had not come from the American Relief Administration, the American Red Cross, and a number of other American and European agencies. George Vernadsky, *A History of Russia* (New Haven: Yale Univ. Press, 1962), p. 332.

6. Leningradskoe Upravlenie VUZOV is Rabfakov, pp. 121-122.

7. Founded in 1907 as the Moscow Institute of Commerce, it was renamed after the Revolution as the Plekhanov (after G. V. Plekhanov, an early Marxist theoretician, who later broke with Lenin) Institute of National Economy (Moskovskii Institut Narodnogo Khoziaistva im. G. V. Plekhanova). Concentrating, at first, only on applied economics, by 1973, it included the following departments: general economics, applied economics, economic planning, economic cybernetics, trade, finance, and technology.

8. Lenin was convinced that socialism could not be achieved in backward Russia without accompanying revolutions in the more advanced nations of western Europe. Nikolai Bukharin was first to suggest that it could be built in the Soviet Union without western European help. For a more comprehensive discussion, see Edward H. Carr, *Socialism in one Country, 1924-1926* 2 vols., Vol II (New York, 1960); Robert C. Tucker, *Stalin as a Revolutionary, 1879-1929* (New York: W. W. Norton, 1973), pp. 368-395.

9. The notion that social and cultural changes following the Russian revolution lagged behind the political changes is argued convincingly in David Lane, "The Impact of Revolution: The Case of Selecting Students for Higher Education in Soviet Russia, 1917-1928," pp. 241-252.

10. David Lane, p. 246.

11. Sheila Fitzpatrick, *Education and Social Mobility in the Soviet Union, 1921-1934,* p. 100.

12. Leon Trotsky, "The New Course," *Pravda,* December 21, 1923.

13. Leon Trotsky, *Lessons of October* (Moscow, 1924).

14. Sheila Fitzpatrick, p. 96.

15. The Soviet Union had suffered serious political reverses in 1926 and 1927. In domestic affairs, the intolerable condition of industrial workers and the growing power of the *kulaks* and the *nepmen* was undermining the morals of the Party *apparat.* In the field of foreign policy, the failure of the 1926 general strike in Great Britain and the 1927 defeat of the communists in China severely tarnished Stalin's reputation at home.

16. *Bolshaia Sovetskaia Entsiklopedia,* Vol. 25 (Moscow, 1976), p. 96.

17. N. Akimov, *Krasnoe studentchistvo, 1927-1928,* No. 6, p. 47, as cited in Sheila Fitzpatrick, p. 104.

18. Sergei Malakshin, *Luna s pravoi starony* (Moscow, 1926).

19. The association of Trotsky with *Eseninshchina* by the pro-Stalin forces may have resulted from Trotsky's emotional essay "In Memory of Sergei Esenin," published in *Pravda,* January 19, 1926.

20. The traditional view is that the Soviet cultural revolution of the late 1920s was launched by Stalin and the central *apparat* from above. A revisionist view rejects the notion that it was engineered solely from above, and suggests that it had developed gradually from below through the efforts of the new intelligentsia that matured after the revolution. See Sheila Fitzpatrick, ed., *Cultural Revolution in Russia, 1928–1931* (Bloomington, Ind.: Indiana Univ. Press, 1978), especially the "Editor's Introduction," and her essay "Cultural Revolution as Class War."

21. For a comprehensive study of Soviet collectivization, see Dorothy Atkinson, *The End of the Russian Land Commune: 1905–1930* (Stanford, California: Hoover Press, 1984); R. W. Davies, *The Socialist Offensive: The Collectivization of Soviet Agriculture 1929–1930* (Cambridge, Mass.: Harvard University Press, 1980); Robert Conquest, *The Harvest of Sorrow* (New York/Oxford: Oxford University Press, 1986).

22. Bukharin was an economic theorist and prominent member of the Politburo, Rykov was Chairman of the Council of People's Commissars (Premier), and Tomsky was head of the trade unions, an important position during the NEP.

23. It is the opinion of the author that the term "research fellow" is more suitable than the more often used term "graduate student." The Institute of the Red Professoriat operated more like a think tank and research institute than a traditional Soviet institution of higher learning at the time when Suslov was there. Many of its research fellows carried other responsibilities besides being graduate students. Some, like Suslov and Pospelov, were instructors in Moscow *VUZy.* Others worked for government bureaus. In the autobiographical introduction to his *Selected Speeches and Writings* (Oxford: Pergamon Press, 1980), Suslov himself refers to his tenure at the Institute of the Red Professoriate by saying: "After graduating from the Plekhanov Institute, a higher educational institution, I took up research and teaching."

24. *Bolshaia Sovetskaia Entsiklopedia,* Vol. 25, p. 96.

25. *Ibid.,* Vol. 10 (Moscow, 1972), p. 293.

26. Eugene S. Varga, *Izmeneniia kapitalizma v itoge Vtoroi Mirovoi Voiny* (Moscow, 1947).

27. *Bolshaia Sovetskaia Entsiklopedia,* Vol. 10, p. 293.

28. *Ibid.,* Vol. 5 (Moscow, 1971), p. 268.

29. *Ibid.,* Vol. 20 (Moscow, 1975), p. 415.

30. A. A. Avtorkhanov, *Stalin and the Communist Party: A Study in the Technology of Power* (New York: Praeger, 1959), pp. 1–10.

31. A. A. Avtorkhanov, *Sila i bessilie Brezhneva* (Frankfurt/Main: Posev Verlag, 1979), p. 77.

32. Bukharin's long speech on January 21, 1929, entitled "Lenin's Political Testament" was later published in *Pravda.* It anathemized Stalin and his plan to scrap the NEP. It also carried a more personal insult to Stalin. From its title it was clear that Bukharin was trying to associate Stalin with Lenin's "Last Testament" in which Lenin clearly recommended that Stalin should be removed from power.

33. The XVIth Party Congress, which dealt with the problem of collectivization during

the summer of 1929, approved the collectivization of only 17.5 percent of farmlands. The January 5, 1930, resolution stated that "the enormous majority" of the peasant households would be collectivized.

34. A. A. Avtorkhanov, *Sila i bessilie Brezhneva*, p. 77.
35. *Ibid.*
36. There is a difference of opinion about whether or not Suslov graduated from the Institute of the Red Professoriat. The official Soviet biography in the *Bolshaia Sovetskaia Entsiklopedia* states that he was at the Institute from 1929 to 1931. A number of western and émigré biographies of Suslov (Grey Hodnett in George W. Simmonds, ed. *Soviet Leaders*, New York: Thomas Y. Crowell, 1967, p. 109, and A. A. Avtorkhanov, "Suslov, The Kremlin's Chief Ideologist," *Bulletin of the Institute for the Study of the USSR*, Vol. XV (2), February 1968, pp. 3–4) suggest that he may not have completed the full program at the Institute, and instead started teaching at the Stalin Academy of Industry. The position of the author is that the official Soviet biography is probably more accurate. This assessment agrees with Roy Medvedev, *All Stalin's Men* (Garden City, N.Y.: Anchor Press, 1975), p. 66.
37. *The Annual Obituary, 1982* (New York: St. Martin's Press, 1983), pp. 33–35.
38. Boris Nicolaevsky, *Power and the Soviet Elite*, p. 254.

NOTES TO CHAPTER IV

1. Roy Medvedev, *All Stalin's Men*, p. 61.
2. The Central Control Commission experienced a number of organizational modifications since its establishment. Lenin merged it with the governments's People's Commissariat of Workers' and Peasants' Inspectorate in the early 1920s. Stalin separated these agencies again and, in 1934, reorganized it into the Party Control Commission.
3. Leonard Shapiro, *The Communist Party of the Soviet Union* (New York: Vintage Books, 1971), pp. 260–262.
4. Roy Medvedev, p. 66.
5. Close to five million people either died or disappeared in concentration camps from 1930 to 1933. Nicholas Riasanovsky, *A History of Russia*, Third Ed. (New York: Oxford Univ. Press, 1977), p. 551.
6. *Ibid.*
7. Syrtsev was demoted from Premier of the Russian republic to director of a phonograph records factory, and Lominadze was transferred to work in the Commissariat of Trade. Syrtsev was later executed and Lominadze committed suicide. Roy Medvedev, *Let History Judge* (New York: Alfred A. Knopf, 1971), p. 142.
8. The Riutin platform actually contained a number of other proposals, but its main thrust was directed toward a retreat from collectivization, a reinstatement of Party democracy, and the removal of Stalin.
9. A. N. Afinogenov, *Strakh* (Moscow, 1931), as cited in Mikhail Heller and Aleksandr Nekrich, *Utopia u vlasti*, Vol. I, p. 279.
10. At the XVII Party Congress, Kirov, Kaganovich and Zhdanov were elected to the Secretariat of the Central Committee to balance Stalin's disproportionate influence

in the Party. Zhdanov was still too much of a newcomer to play a major role, Kaganovich was one of Stalin's men, but Kirov's appointment was a threat to Stalin. Kirov was Russian, decisive, and universally liked and respected by the rank-and-file. Although loyal to Stalin's policies, he could easily become a new force around whom the anti-Stalinist opposition could coalesce. Backed up by the prestige of the Leningrad Party apparatus, he was the most obvious person to oppose Stalin in what Stalin saw as a personal affront to his leadership.

11. The most important works adhering to the thesis of an all-embracing plan by Stalin are: Robert Conquest, *The Great Terror* (London: Macmillan, 1973), Roy Medvedev, *Let History Judge,* and Aleksandr Solzhenitsyn, *The Gulag Archipelago* (New York: Harper & Row, 1973).

12. The works tending to interpret the purges in terms of "action-reaction" responses by Stalin are: T. H. Rigby, *Communist Party Membership in the USSR*, and Merle Fainsod, *How Russia is Ruled* (Cambridge, Mass.: Harvard Univ. Press, 1963).

13. J. Arch Getty, *The Origins of the Great Purges, The Soviet Community Party Reconsidered, 1933–1938* (London: Cambridge University Press, 1985.

14. Merle Fainsod, *Smolensk under Soviet Rule* (Cambridge, Mass.: Harvard Univ., Press), pp. 220–222.

15. Sheila Fitzpatrick, "Stalin and the Making of the New Elite, 1928–1939," *Slavic Review,* Vol. XXXVII (3), September 1979, pp. 384–385.

16. A complete listing of categories affected by the 1933 purge may be found in Merle Fainsod, *Smolensk under Soviet Rule,* p. 221, and in T. H. Rigby, *Communist Party Membership in the USSR,* pp. 201–202.

17. Central Research, Radio Liberty, *Directory of 100 Leading Soviet Officials* (Munich, 1981), pp. 207–210.

18. Merle Fainsod, *Smolensk under Soviet Rule,* p. 222.

19. Nikita Khrushchev, *Khrushchev Remembers* (Boston/Toronto: Little Brown, 1970), pp. 574–575.

20. Robert Conquest, *The Great Terror,* pp. 72–96.

21. After Neils Erik Rosenfeldt who used the expression "action-reaction process" in his critique of J. Arch Getty's article in the *Slavic Review,* Vol. XXXII (1), Spring 1983, pp. 85–91.

22. Francois Rene Chateaubriand, *Essai histoire, politique et moral sur les révolutions* (London, 1797), and Joseph De Maistre, *Considerations sur la France* (1796).

23. There is reason to believe that the decision to conduct the Verification of Party Documents campaign had been taken prior to December 1934, and that Kirov's death merely hastened its implementation. See J. Arch Getty, *The Origins of the Great Purges,* pp. 58–59 and p. 232.

24. Almost immediately after Kirov's assassination, the Central Committee sent a closed letter entitled "Lessons of the Events Bound up with the Evil Murder of Comrade Kirov" to all Party organizations with instruction that it should be discussed at meetings throughout the Soviet Union. A second letter to all regional Party committees, dated February 17, 1935, placed heavy stress on the need of ousting all former supporters of Zinoviev, Kamenev and Trotsky. A second letter of May 13, 1935, initiated a new check-up of Party documents. On December 25, unhappy with the results of the documents verification program, the Central Committee ordered the

exchange of old Party cards for new with the injunction that a "rigorous unmasking of the enemies who survived earlier screenings" was to be followed before the issuance of new Party cards. See: Merle Fainsod, *Smolensk under Soviet Rule,* pp. 222–223.

25. *Pravda,* July 29, 1936.

26. Stalin's and Zhdanov's telegram of September 25, 1936, from Sochi to Kaganovich, Molotov and other members of the Politburo in Moscow: "We deem it absolutely necessary and urgent that Comrade Yezhov be nominated to the post of People's Commissar for Internal Affairs. Yagoda has definitely proved himself to be incapable of unmasking the Trotskyite-Zinoviev bloc. The OGPU is four years behind in this matter. This is noted by all Party workers and by the majority of the representatives of the NKVD," as cited in Nikita Khrushchev, *Khrushchev Remembers,* p. 575.

27. It has been suggested that Tukhachevsky was framed by the Nazis, who allegedly passed false documents, via Euard Benes in Czechoslovakia, implicating him and other Soviet generals in a plot to carry out a coup. For details see: Lev Nikulin, *Marshal Tukhachevsky* (Moscow, 1964), pp. 189–194, and John Ericson, *The Soviet High Command* (London, 1962), p. 433.

28. Robert Conquest, *The Great Terror,* pp. 702–705.

29. *Ibid.,* p. 709–710. The excess mortality attributed to the period of 1929–1938 suggested by Robert Conquest in *The Great Terror* has been questioned by several demographers studying this period. For a comprehensive bibliography of the controversy that has arisen see the Discussion section of the *Slavic Review,* Vol. 44 (3), Fall 1985, pp. 505–536 and Vol 45 (2), Summer 1986, pp. 213–244.

30. Yezhov's fate remains a mystery. As late as 1965, rehabilitated veterans of the concentration camps have reported that Yezhov had gone mad and that they had seen him in a concentration camp in 1939 and 1940. The most probable account is that he was shot in 1939 or 1940.

31. *Bolshaia Sovetskaia Entsiklopedia,* Vol. 25 (Moscow, 1976), p. 96.

32. Central Research, Radio Liberty, *Biographical Directory of 100 Leading Soviet Officials,* pp. 207–210.

33. M. A. Suslov, *Marksizm-Leninizm is sovremennaia epokha,* Vol. I, p. 11.

34. Roy Medvedev, *Let History Judge,* p. 199.

35. Stalin's letter of June 24, 1936 "On Errors in the Examination of Appeals from Persons Expelled from the Party during the Verification and Exchange of Party Documents" criticized the arbitrary treatment of members of the Party.

36. Stalin's letter of July 29, 1936 "On the Terrorist Activities of the Trotskyist-Zinovievist Counterrevolutionary Bloc" is an example of those instances when Stalin took a hard-line position during the purges.

37. It is not clear when Stalin actually created the special State Security Committee. Robert Conquest, basing his conclusion on the writings of emigrés and the *Samizdat,* suggests that this may have been as early as the summer of 1933. Robert Conquest, *The Great Terror,* p. 68.

38. *Pravda,* February 14, 1953, and January 19, 1954.

39. Vladimir Lenin, *Sochinenie,* 4th Ed. (Moscow, 1935), Vol. XXXIX, p. 417.

40. See note 32 of this chapter.

41. I. Stalin, *Sochinenie,* Ed. Robert H. McNeal, Vol. I (14) (Stanford, Ca., 1967), pp. 211–220.

42. A. A. Avtorkhanov, "Suslov, The Kremlin's Chief Ideologist," p. 9.
43. Dennis A. Pluchinsky, "Mikhail A. Suslov: The Last Stalinist," p. 9.
44. Roy Medvedev, p. 67.
45. *Pravda,* January 19, 1938. For full text in English, see: Robe t H. McNeal, Ed. *Resolutions and Decisions of the Communist Party of the Soviet Union, Vol. 3, The Stalin Years: 1929–1953* (Toronto: Univ. of Toronto Press, 1967), pp. 188–195.
46. M. A. Suslov, p. 11.
47. Roy Medvedev, p. 67.
48. The official Soviet biography states that Suslov was First Secretary of the Stavropol *Kraikom* from 1939 to 1944. It does not give the exact date of this appointment. However, it is known that Suslov attended the XVIII Party Congress in march 1939 as a delegate of the Stavropol *Kraikom*. He must have been appointed, therefore, sometime before March 10, 1939 when the Congress opened.

NOTES TO CHAPTER V

1. The Kabardino-Balkar ASSR, the North Osetin ASSR, the Chechen-Ingush ASSR, and the Daghestan ASSR.
2. *Bolshaia Sovetskaia Entsiklopledia,* Vol. 24 (Moscow, 1976), p. 394.
3. *Pravda,* Nov. 6, 1941.
4. P. A. Shatskii and V. N. Muravyov, *Stavropol, A Historical Sketch* (Stavropol: Stavropolskoe Knizhnoe Izd., 1977), pp. 183–184.
5. Central Research, Radio Liberty, p. 208.
6. P. A. Shatskii and V. N. Muravyov, pp. 193–195.
7. Alexander Dallin in John A. Armstrong, Ed., *Soviet Partisans in World War II* (Madison, Wis.: University of Wisconsin Press, 1964), pp. 574–576 and 581–583.
8. Central Research, Radio Liberty, p. 208.
9. A. Chuianov, *Na stremnine veka* (On the Chute of the Century) (Moscow: Izd., Polit., 1976), p. 4.
10. P. A. Shatskii and V. N. Muravyov, p. 197.
11. A. Grechko, *Battle for the Caucasus* (Moscow: Progress Publishing, 1971), pp. 211–212.
12. *Ibid.,* p. 211.
13. Alexander Dallin, p. 567.
14. *Ibid.,* pp. 617–619.
15. A. A. Avtorkhanov, *Narodoubiistvo v SSSR: Ubiistvo Chechenskogo Naroda* (Munich: Svobodnii Kavkaz, 1952). This work by A. A. Avtorkhanov appears to be the basis of all existing references to Suslov's participation in the deportation of nationality groups from the North Caucasus.
16. Grey Hodnett, p. 111.
17. Nikita Khrushchev, *Khrushchev Remembers,* p. 596.
18. P. A. Shatskii and V. N. Muravyov, pp. 198–199.
19. *Ibid.,* pp. 200–201.
20. Institut Marksizma-Leninizma, *Istoriia Velikoi Otechestvennoi Voiny Sovetskago Souza, 1941–1945,* Vol. 3 (Moscow: Voenizdat, 1961), p. 189.

21. *Bolshaia Sovetskaia Entsiklopedia,* Vol. 25 (Moscow, 1976), p. 96.
22. A complete and scholarly study of the German occupation of Lithuania and the partisan struggle that followed it is still to be written. Following is a listing of works and articles consulted by the author: E. J. Harrison, *Luthuania's Fight for Freedom* (New York, 1952); Albert T. Tarulis, *Soviet Policy Toward the Baltic States* (Notre Dame, Ind.: Notre Dame Univ. Press, 1952); K. V. Tauras, Guerilla Warfare on the Amber Coast (New York: Voyager Press, 1962); V. Stanley Vardys, Ed. *Lithuania under the Soviets, 1941–1945* (New York: Praeger, 1965); V. Stanley Vardys, "the Partisan Movement in Postwar Lithuania," *Slavic Review,* Vol. XXII (3), September 1963; "Samizdat Documents on Suslov's Role in Lithuania." *Lituanus,* Vol. 24 (1), 1978; *Radio Liberty Research Bulletin,* RL 3/78 (Munich, January 2, 1978); *Bolshaia Sovetskaia Entsiklopedia* Vol 14 (Moscow, 1973), pp. 535–538; P. Zhugzha and A. Smirnov, *Litovskaia SSR* (Moscow, 1957); Tautavichius, et al, Eds. *Istoriia Litovskoi SSR s drevnikh vremyon do nashikh dnei* (Vilnius: Moklas, 1978), pp. 419–525; A. Sniecku, *Sovetskaia Litva na puti rastsveta* (Vilnius, 1970), pp. 46–63.
23. Although the Grand Duchy of Lithuania was not annexed to Russia until 1795 at the time of the third partition of Poland, Lithuanian resistance to Russian expansion dates back to the XVIth century. Insurrections since the annexation were not uncommon; the last serious rebellion during the Tzarist period took place in 1863.
24. The rising began on the evening of June 22, 1941, growing into a full-scale armed insurrection involving as many as 100,000 Lithuanians on the next day, the day of the German attack.
25. *Bolshaia Sovetskaia Entsiklopedia,* Vol. 25 (Moscow, 1976), p. 96.
26. Roy Medvedev, *All Stalin's Men,* p. 70.
27. M. A. Suslov, *Marksizm-Leninizm i sovremennaia epokha,* Vol. I, pp. 120–121.
28. Roy Medvedev, *All Stalin's Men,* p. 65.
29. Estimates of total Soviet dead (military and civilian) during World War II remain uncertain. Nicholas V. Riasanovsky in his *History of Russia,* p. 585, suggests, on the basis of estimates made by experts, that the total may have been from fourteen to twenty million.
30. Nicholas V. Riasanovsky, p. 585.
31. The author's psychological assessment of Suslov is strongly influenced by the work of Robert C. Carson, *Interaction Concepts of Personality* (Chicago: Alpine Publishing Co., 1969) and by his personal experience as a marketing executive working with Dr. David W. Merrill of Personnel Predictions and Research, Inc. of Denver, Colorado.

NOTES TO CHAPTER VI

1. The author is indebted for this observation and the political analysis that follows it to William O. McCagg, Jr., *Stalin Embattled, 1943–1948* (Detroit, Mich.: Wayne University Press, 1978).
2. Niccolo Machiavelli, *The Prince* (New York: Penguin Books, 1979), p. 98.
3. For other views on the postwar period of high Stalinism see: Werner G. Hahn, *Postwar Soviet Politics: The Defeat of Zhdanov and the Defeat of Moderation, 1946–*

1953 (Ithaca, N.Y.: Cornell University Press, 1982), Gavriel Ra'anan, *International Policy Formation in the USSR: Factional Debates during the Zhdanovshchina* (Hamden, Conn.: Anchor Books, 1983), Robert Conquest, *Power and Policy in the USSR* (London: Macmillan, 1961).

4. For details on Zhdanov's victory over Malenkov, see Werner G. Hahn, pp. 19–60. For information on the prewar Zhdanov-Malenkov feud, see Jonathan Harris, "The Origins of the Conflict between Malenkov and Zhdanov, 1939–1941," *Slavic Review,* Vol.XXXV (2), June 1976, pp. 287–303.

5. Although the Politburo now exercises the dominant position in Soviet politics, in 1946, it was still the Secretariat that had primacy in the Soviet command structure under Stalin.

6. A detailed analysis of the political significance of this new force is found in Arnold Beichman and Mikhail S. Bernstam, *Andropov: New Challenge to the West* (New York: Stein and Day, 1983), pp. 83–134.

7. The argument that Suslov owed his rise neither to Zhdanov nor Malenkov, but to Stalin, is presented in a carefully reasoned conclusion in Denis A. Pluchinsky, "Mikhail A. Suslov: The Last Stalinist, 1902–1964," Unpublished Master's Thesis, George Washington University, May 7, 1978, pp. 22–25.

8. V. Skorodumov, "Suslov, Mikhail Andreevich," *Portraits of Prominent USSR Personalities,* No. 143 (Munich: Institute for the Study of the USSR, April 1967).

9. Grey Hodnett in George W. Simmonds, Ed. *Soviet Leaders,* pp. 108–115.

10. Central Research, Radio Liberty, *A Biographical Directory of 100 Leading Soviet Officials* (1981), pp. 207–210.

11. *Bolshaia Sovetskaia Entsiklopedia,* Vol. 25 (Moscow, 1976), p. 96.

12. George Urban in Roger Swearington, Ed. *Leaders of the Communist World* (New York: Free Press, 1971), pp. 141–152.

13. A. A. Avtorkhanov, *Sila i bessilie Brezhneva,* p. 79, and "Suslov" The Kremlin's Chief Ideologist," *Bulletin of the Institute for the Study of the USSR,* Vol. XV (2), February 1968, p. 6.

14. Roy Medvedev, *All Stalin's Men,* p. 70.

15. George Gordon Young, *Stalin's Heirs* (London: Derek Vershoyle, Ltd., 1953), p. 128.

16. Hans-Jurgen Eitner, "Chefideologue des Kreml—Michail Andrejewitsch Suslov," *Osteuropa* (West Germany) No. 10, June 1960, pp. 404–407; David Floyd, "Suslov" The Power Inside the Kremlin," *Now,* February 20, 1981, pp. 35–37; *Current Biography Yearbook, 1957,* pp. 540–542; *The Annual Obituary, 1982,* p. 33–35; Herwig Kraus, "Mikhail Suslov Dead at Seventy-Nine," Central Research, Radio Liberty RFE/RL 4142, January 26, 1982; *International Herald Tribune,* June 9, 1976; *New York Times,* October 17, 1964, October 21, 1979, October 15, 1980, April 24, 1981, April 25, 1981, January 27, 1982, and March 6, 1982; *The Times* (London), January 27, 1982; *Christian Science Monitor,* April 27, 1981, January 27, 1982, June 30, 1982, and December 30, 1982; *Wall Street Journal,* January 27, 1982, and September 15, 1982.

17. General A. S. Shcherbakov, the First Secretary of the Moscow Party organization, was chief of the Sovinform Bureau and the Political Directorate of the Red Army (GPUKA) during World War II. He was also Deputy Assistant Commissar of Defense.

18. The General Department was, for all intents and purposes, the command post of the Central Committee, maintaining direct connection with Poskrebyshev and Stalin's personal chancellery. For details see: Leonard Shapiro, "the General Department of the CC of the CPSU," *Survey* (UK), Vol. XXI (3), Summer, 1975, pp. 53–66.
19. The 1944 attack on Mikhail Zoshchenko for the "unpatriotic style" of his autobiographical essays was the first salvo fired against the ineptitude of the Party *apparat* during the war. William O. McCagg Jr., pp. 105–106.
20. Nikolai S. Patolichev, *Ispytanie na zrelost'* (Moscow: Izpolit, 1977).
21. For details, see: Werner G. Hahn, pp. 53–59.
22. It is not entirely clear when Kosygin became a candidate member of the Politburo in 1946.
23. The publication of G. F. Aleksandrov's book *Istoriia zapodnoevropeiskoi filosofii* (History of Western European Philosophy) in 1946 started a debate which led to the criticism of Aleksandrov for belittling the role of Russian philosophy. For more information, see: Werner G. Hahn pp. 70–78 and Gavriel Ra'anan, pp. 173–176.
24. Zhores A. Medvedev, *The Rise and Fall of T. D. Lysenko* (New York: Columbia University Press, 1969); David Joravsky, *The Lysenko Affair* (Cambridge, Mass.: Harvard Univ. Press, 1970).
25. First identified in an article in *Bolshevik,* November 23, 1947.
26. *Pravda,* July 21, 1947.
27. *Ibid.,* August 4, 1947.
28. *Ibid.,* November 8, 1947.
29. *Ibid.,* March 10-April 11, 1947.
30. *Ibid.,* May 2, 1947.
31. Throughout 1947, Zhdanov continued to be listed third after Stalin and Molotov in the official protocol line-up. Zhdanov also tried hard to stay visible by delivering speeches throughout the summer and fall of 1947.
32. A. A. Zhdanov, "Vystuplenie na diskusii po knige G. F. Aleksandrova," *Bolshevik,* August 30, 1947. Some Western analysts have suggested that Zhdanov's attack on Aleksandrov was prompted by Zhdanov's concern that Aleksandrov was moving back into Malenkov's good graces. For a discussion of this view, see Gavriel Ra'anan, pp. 171–176. It is the author's opinion that this view is unduly influenced by the "kto-kogo" school of Sovietology without due regard for the positions of the principal adversaries on issues and for the chronology of the actions taken in 1947.
33. Svetlana Allilueva, *Only One Year* (New York: Harper and Row, 1967), pp. 384–385.
34. Svetlana Allilueva, *Twenty Letters to a Friend* (New York: Harper and Row, 1967), p. 59.
35. The notions of a "Soviet people," "continuing class struggle," "strict control in the arts and sciences," and "the collective interests of all Communist parties throughout the world under the aegis of Soviet protection" receive repeated emphasis in many of Suslov's speeches and writings.
36. Mikhail Heller and Aleksandr Nekrich, *Utopia v Vlasti,* Vol. II, p. 229.

NOTES TO CHAPTER VII

1. G. F. Aleksandrov, *Istoriia Zapodnoevropeiskoi filosofii* (Moscow, 1946), a work that was severely criticized by the more conservative Soviet philosophers for its alleged depreciation of Russian philosophers.

2. Ye. S. Varga, *Izmeneniia kapitalizma v itoge Vtoroi Mirovoi Voiny* (Moscow, 1947). Varga argued that the capitalist nations were becoming more like socialist states, because of the influence of central planning on their economies during World War II. This thesis was heresy to the Soviet conservatives who looked for an economic crisis in the capitalist camp after the war, not social and economic stability.

3. Vano Muradeli, a Georgian composer, was accused of having "formalist" sympathies, and his opera "The Great Friendship" was condemned in a resolution of the Central Committee of February 14, 1948. For the text of the resolution, see Robert H. McNeal, Ed. *Resolutions and decisions of the Communist Party of the Soviet Union,* pp. 248–251.

4. Boris Nicolaevsky, *Power and the Soviet Elite,* p. 260.

5. *Kul'tura i zhizn',* March 31, 1948.

6. *Ibid.,* April 11 and 12, 1948.

7. M. A. Suslov, *Marksizm-Leninizm i sovremennaia epokha,* Vol. I, pp. 169–177.

8. The Lysenko debate also had repercussions on Zhdanov by way of criticism of his son, Yurii Zhdanov, the head of the Science section of Agitprop. Zhores A. Medvedev, *The Rise and Fall of T. D. Lysenko,* pp. 78–84 and 94–98.

9. The Communist parties of Bulgaria, Czechoslovakia, Hungary, Poland, Rumania, Yugoslavia, France, and Italy met with the Soviet party from September 22 to 27, 1947 at Sklarska Poreba in Polish Silesia.

10. The September 25, 1947 *Pravda* article identified Suslov as a member of the Secretariat, and noted that "he was sending fraternal greetings in the name of the Communist Party of the Soviet Union (b)" to the Congress of the East German SED, then in session.

11. Milovan Djilas, *Conversations with Stalin* (New York: Harcourt, Brace, and Ward, 1962), pp. 173–184; Vladimir Dedijer, *Tito* (New York: Simon & Schuster, 1953), p. 316.

12. Letter from the Central Committee of CPSU of May 19, 1948, signed by Suslov, according to Vladimir Dedijer, p. 355.

13. Boris Nicolaevsky, p. 260.

14. Nikita Khrushchev, *Khrushchev Remembers,* p. 377.

15. M. A. Suslov, *Marksizm-Leninizm i sovremennaia epokha,* Vol. I, pp. 156–168.

16. *Ibid.*

17. After Carl A. Linden, *The Politics of Ideocratic Despotism* (New York: Praeger, 1983), pp. 95–97.

18. During Stalin's life, Suslov never failed to mention Stalin's name in his speeches and writings. For example, in his short address to the XIX Party Congress in October

1952, Stalin's name is mentioned sixteen times. After Stalin's death, Suslov's speeches were revised and Stalin's name was expunged. For comparison see the original address to the XIX Party Congress, as reported by Radio Liberty, and the same address as reprinted in M. A. Suslov, *Marksizm-Leninizm i sovremennaia epokha*, Vol. I, pp. 193–198.

19. Nicholas Riasanovsky, *Nicholas I and Official Nationality in Russia* (Berkeley, Ca.: Univ. of California Press, 1959), p. 46.

20. Nikita Khrushchev, *Khrushchev Remembers*, pp. 260–261.

21. *Ibid.*, pp. 260–261 and 208–309.

22. After Malenkov's removal from the Secretariat in 1946, A. A. Kuznetsov became Secretary in charge of Cadres and Internal Security, a position of immense power in the Party. M. I. Rodionov became premier of RSFSR, P. S. Popkov, the First Secretary of the Leningrad organization, and A. N. Kosygin, Deputy Premier and Minister of Light Industry. N. A. Voznesensky, who had enjoyed a spectacular rise in the early 1940s, was a member of the Politburo, Chairman of Gosplan, and Deputy Premier of the Soviet Union.

23. Alexei Kosygin was the only one to survive the purge and rise to prominence together with Brezhnev in the post-Khrushchev reorganization of the Party and the government apparatus.

24. Nikita Khrushchev, p. 256.

25. Blair A. Ruble, "The Leningrad Affair and the Provincialization of Leningrad," *The Russian Review*, Vol. 42 (3), July 1983, pp. 318–319; Harrison Salisbury, *The 900 Days: The Siege of Leningrad* (New York, 1969), pp. 577–583.

26. N. A. Voznesensky, *The War Economy of the USSR during the Great Patriotic War* (Moscow, 1947).

27. Nikita Khrushchev, p. 251.

28. Terry McNeil, "The Spector of Voznesensky Stalks Suslov," *Radio Liberty Bulletin*, RL 338/74, October 11, 1974, pp. 3–4.

29. V. V. Kolotov, *Nikolai Alekseevich Voznesensky* (Moscow: Politizdat, 1974), pp. 346–347; Nikita Khrushchev, p. 272.

30. Although released from his responsibilities, Voznesensky was not indicted immediately as the case fabricated against him failed to bring a guilty verdict. He continued working on his new book, but was eventually rearrested and brought to trial for the second time in the fall of 1949. This time he was sentenced to death and executed.

31. *Pravda*, December 24, 1952.

32. *Izvestia*, December 12 and 21, 1952.

33. Robert H. McNeal, Ed. *Resolutions and Decisions of the Communist Party of the Soviet Union*, Vol. 3, pp. 252–253.

34. Terry McNeil, "The Spector of Voznesensky Stalks Suslov," p. 5.

35. P. N. Fedoseev was one of the more moderate and flexible philosophers appointed by Zhdanov to the staff of *Bolshevik* to replace the conservative Yudin and Mitin. He was a carryover from the Aleksandrov administration at *Agitprop*. On July 13, 1949, pursuant to a Central Committee resolution, he was removed from the staff of *Bolshevik*.

36. It is not clear when Suslov was replaced by Leonid Ilyichev as editor of Pravda; Soviet biographies are contradictory on the dates. Basing his conclusion on a careful comparison of existing press reports, Dennis A. Pluchinsky suggests that it was

probably in late 1952. Dennis A Pluchinsky, "Mikhail A. Suslov: The Last Stalinist, 1902–1964," p. 33.

37. Shel'ga, "Suslov, M. A.," *Posev* (émigré journal published in West Germany), January 1968, pp. 12–13.

38. A. A. Avtorkhanov, "Suslov, the Kremlin's Chief Ideologist," *Bulletin of the Institute for the Study of the USSR,* Vol. XV (2), February 1968, p. 6.

39. Malenkov's protégé, N. N. Shatalin, was removed from his post as Chief of the Cadres Department in the Central Committee in 1950. He was first replaced by N. M. Pegov, and later by A. B. Aristov. After Stalin's death in March 1953, Shatalin again took charge of the Cadres Department, remaining in that position until the fall of Malenkov in 1955.

40. The Doctors case was fabricated on the basis of testimony by Lydia Timashuk, a radiologist in the Kremlin Hospital and probably a secret agent of the MGB, who wrote Stalin saying that she had observed many eminent doctors prescribing wrong methods of treatment. Although the MGB tried to hush the matter up, it was brought to Stalin's attention. Stalin dismissed Abakumov, the head of the MGB, appointed Ignatiev in his place, and personally took charge of the investigation. Abakumov was Beria's protégé, and Beria was now being accused of insufficient vigilance.

41. Basing their allegations on Suslov's criticism of Fedoseev and on Suslov's hard-line speech at a meeting of the Soviet Academy of Sciences, Boris Nicolaevsky and A. A. Avtorkhanov have maintained that Stalin had selected Suslov to carry out a massive new purge of the Party after the XIX Party Congress. The purpose and details of the alleged purge remain unclear, and the suggestion that Suslov was to take charge of the purge has never been confirmed. Neither the December 24, 1952 *Pravda* criticism of Fedoseev nor the January 1953 Academy of Sciences speech make reference to a new Party purge. Boris Nicolaevsky, p. 262, and A. A. Avtorkhanov, p. 6.

42. Svetlana Allilueva, *Only One Year,* p. 47.

NOTES TO CHAPTER VIII

1. For details pertaining to Stalin's last days, see: A. Avtorkhanov, *Zagadka smerti Stalina (The Riddle of Stalin's Death* (Frankfurt/Main: Possev, 1976); G. D. Embree, *The Soviet Union between the 19th and 20th Party Congresses, 1952–1956* (The Hague, Holland: Martinus Nijhoff, 1959), pp. 1–18; Wolfgang Leonhard, *The Kremlin since Stalin* (New York: Frederick A. Praeger, 1962), pp. 31–62.

2. Roy Medvedev, *Khrushchev,* (Oxford, U.K.: Basil Blackwell, 1982), p. 59.

3. Members of the Presidium's "inner bureau, the principal members of the Council of Ministers, and the most senior members of the Presidium of the Supreme Soviet.

4. N. M. Shvernik was a member of the enlarged Presidium and, according to Robert Conquest, was probably also a member of its "inner bureau." See Conquest, *Power and Policy in the USSR* (New York: St. Martin's Press, 1961), pp. 1599–161.

5. *Pravda,* March 6, 8, and 10, 1953.

6. Hans-Jurgen Eitner in *Osteuropa,* as cited by Boris Nicolaevsky, *Power and the Soviet Elite,* p. 262.

7. *Pravda,* March 8 and 10, 1953.

8. Malenkov resigned from the Secretariat on March 21, 1953, but it is not clear when the makeup of the Secretariat was officially approved. Most analysts have maintained that the appointment of Khrushchev, Suslov, Pospelov, Shatalin, and S. D. Ignatiev was made on March 14, despite the fact that the official announcement was not made until March 21.

9. Robert Conquest, *Power and Policy in the USSR: The Struggle for Stalin's Succession* (New York: Harper Torchbooks, 1967), pp. 42 and 72.

10. Roy Medvedev, *All Stalin's Men*, p. 77.

11. Nikita Khrushchev, *Khrushchev Remembers*, p. 57.

12. *Ibid.*, p. 612.

13. *Pravda*, March 15, 1953.

14. *Bolshaia Sovetskaia Entsiklopedia*, Vol. 20 (Moscow, 1975), p. 350.

15. *New York Times*, February 8, 1954. One year later, Ponomarenko was replaced by his deputy, Leonid Brezhnev, eventually disappearing from the leadership after Malenkov's final removal in 1957.

16. Robert Conquest, *Power and Policy in the USSR*, p. 247.

17. G. F. Aleksandrov was only a candidate member of the Central Committee in 1954. Regarding the scandal, see: Yuri Glazov, *The Russian Mind since Stalin's Death* (Dordrech, Boston, Lancaster: D. Reidel Publishing Company, 1985), pp. 63–64.

18. *Pravda*. April 6, April 16, and 26, 1953.

19. *Pravda*, August 9, 1953. For details regarding Beria's removal, see: Roy Medvedev, *Khrushchev*, pp. 64–70; Wolfgang Leonhard, *The Kremlin since Stalin*, pp. 68–75; R. Conquest, *Power and Policy in the USSR*, pp. 215–226; G. D. Embree, *The Soviet Union between the 19th and 20th Party Congresses*, pp. 51–65.

20. Dozens of legends, many of them improbable, have been circulating in connection with Beria's arrest and trial. According to a July 10 article in *Pravda*, he was accused of four crimes: (1) disregard of the Party's directives to refrain from "arbitrariness and illegality" in the execution of his duties, (2) hindering of agricultural policy, (3) fostering of disunity among the nationality groups, and (4) pervasive "misuse of the organs of the Ministry of the Interior against the Party."

21. Roy Medvedev, *Khrushchev*, p. 69.

22. *Pravda*, May 15, 1954.

23. *Izvestia*, April 21, 1954.

24. *Pravda*, April 12, 1954.

25. *Novyi Mir*, December 1953.

26. Ilya Ehrenburg, *The Thaw* (Moscow, 1954).

27. *Kommunist*, No. 9 (1954).

28. It is generally acknowledged that the word "thaw" first came into use in 1855 after the death of Czar Nicholas I whose reign of regimentation and state controls was followed by the coming of relaxation and the awakening of hope for a new liberalism.

29. *Pravda*, February 5, 1956.

30. As cited in *Bulletin of the Institute for the Study of the USSR*, Vol. III (3), March 1956, p. 41.

31. *Pravda*, February 9, 1985.

32. *Ibid.*, April 20, 1955; *Kommunist*, Nov. 6, 1955.

33. M. A. Suslov, "The XXII Party Congress and the Problems of the Faculty of Social Sciences," *Marksizm-Leninizm i Soivremennaia epokha*, Vol. I, p. 409.

34. *Pravda,* July 13, 1955.
35. Michel Tatu, *Power in the Kremlin: From Khrushchev to Kosygin* (New York: Viking Press, 1969), pp. 30–31.
36. M. A. Suslov, "Speech at the XXII Party Congress," October 21, 1961.
37. M. A. Suslov, *Marksizm-Leninizm i Sovremennaia epokha,* Vol. I (Moscow, 1982), p. 205.
38. *Pravda,* September 8, 11, 12, 16, and October 6–9, 1955.
39. *Ibid.,* September 20 and 21, 1955.
40. Prior to 1956, Suslov's speeches tended to be more general in their attack on the enemies of communism and the Soviet Union. The enemy was usually identified as "imperialism" or "capitalism." After 1956, Suslov began focusing on the United States as the main enemy.
41. Robert C. Tucker, *The Lenin Anthology* (New York: W. W. Norton, 1975), pp. 550–618 and 3–114.
42. A. J. P. Taylor, *Bismark, The Man and the Statesman* (New York, N.Y.: Vintage Books), pp. 159–193.

NOTES TO CHAPTER IX

1. *Pravda,* October 9, 1955.
2. Suslov was last reported in the Soviet press on October 23 when he attended the performance of a Turkmenian opera (*Pravda,* October 23, 1955). The next press coverage was not until November 26, when *Pravda* reported that Suslov attended an All-Union Congress of Soviet Architects, and again November 27, when it stated that he was present at a reception for a Yugoslavian delegation to Moscow.
3. *New York Times,* October 26, 1964 and April 7, 1970.
4. The analysis of Suslov's press coverage is based on information obtained from Moscow *Pravda* clippings for the period of 1955 to 1975 stored in the Suslov file at the Red Archive of Radio Free Europe/Radio Liberty, Munich, West Germany. During the ten year period from 1955 to 1965, Suslov's name or photograph appeared in the Moscow *Pravda* 826 times—on the average, every fourth day of each month. During the next ten year period, from 1965 to 1975, it appeared 718 times, approximately every fifth day. The frequency of press coverage remained unusually constant during both periods, except during those months when he was on vacation or was conspicuously absent for some other reason. Thus, absences of three or more weeks are readily identifiable, while longer absences of six or more weeks stare the researcher in the face.
5. The author showed the official Soviet "Medical Conclusion regarding the illness and death of M. A. Suslov" (Meditsinskoe zakluchenie o bolezni i prichine smerti Suslova, Mikhaila Andreevicha), signed by Minister of Health E. Chazov and seven other prominent Soviet professors of medicine, to three American internists and cardiologists. Based on the information in that report, they concluded unanimously that Suslov would have had no real medical reason to have been absent as often and as long as he had been in the 1950's and 1960's.
6. *Ibid.*

7. Suslov's name disappeared from the Soviet press in June and July 1956 during Tito's visit to Moscow. After attending a formal reception for Tito on June 4, Suslov dropped out of sight for forty-four days—a period much too long for a vacation—until July 19 when he suddenly reappeared together with Kirichenko and Ponomarev at th 14th Congress of the French Communist Party in Paris to deliver a major address. His name was also missing from the press in June 1957, during the period that preceded the "anti-Party" crisis and again in the summer of 1962, during the early phase of the Cuban crisis and the Party bifurcation debates. A careful examination of Suslov's absences after 1962 also contradicts the view that they were somehow always related to illness or political trouble. Except for 1963 when Suslov was forced to take a prolonged rest from September to the end of the year, and for 1976 when he suffered a myocardial infarction, all his extended and unexplained absences were clearly unrelated to health or political troubles.

8. Together with Bulganin and Mikoyan, Khrushchev travelled to Belgrade in July 1955 to establish a new and improved relationship with Yugoslavia.

9. M. A. Suslov, *Marksizm-Leninizm i sovremennaia epokha,* Vol. I, pp. 178–192.

10. P. N. Pospelov, a member of the Secretariat, was appointed to head a special commission to investigate Stalin's excesses.

11. A special commission was created by Khrushchev in 1955 to determine if Yugoslavia was a socialist country with which the Soviet Union could reestablish "friendly" relations. Despite its favorable recommendation, Suslov remained unyielding in his conviction that Yugoslavia was not a socialist nation, a conviction born out of his experience in 1948 to expel Yugoslavia from the Cominform.

12. Roy Medvedev, *Khrushchev,* p. 83.

13. *Pravda,* February 18, 1956.

14. Unlike the principle of "different roads to socialism," Khrushchev's proposition at the XX Party Congress that "wars are no longer inevitable" is not supportable by quotations from Marx or Lenin. The best that Khrushchev could do was to emphasize that Lenin's thesis on the inevitability of war under imperialism was no longer applicable because of the great diversification of capitalism today.

15. M. A. Suslov, *Marksizm-Leninizm i Sovremennaia epokha,* Vol. I, pp. 213–228.

16. A. I. Mikoyan, "Address to the XX Party Congress," February 16, 1946. For details, see: *XX-y s'ezd KPSS: Stenograficheskii otchet (Stenographic Report of the XX Congress of the CPSU),* Vol. 1, (Moscow, 1956), pp. 302–328.

17. *Ibid.*

18. *Bolshaia Sovetskaia Entsiklopediia,* Vol. 25 (Moscow, 1976), p. 96.

19. There is disagreement about the date of Khrushchev's secret speech. Some analysts have maintained that it was delivered on February 24, others on February 25. Khrushchev started speaking at midnight and finished in the morning. The likelihood is that he started on February 24, but delivered most of the speech on February 25.

20. Between December 24, 1922 and January 4, 1923, Lenin wrote two notes that collectively became known as his last will and testament. In the first note, written between December 24 and 25, he assessed the strengths and weaknesses of the principal leaders in the Party. In the second note—a postscript—he stated that "Stalin is too rude," implying that this quality was insupportable in a General Secretary. The postscript specifically stated: "Therefore, I propose to the comrades to think out some way of removing Stalin from this position."

21. For details of Khrushchev's secret speech, see: *Khrushchev Remembers,* Appendix 4, "Khrushchev's Secret Speech," pp. 559–618.
22. Edward Crankshaw, *Khrushchev: A Career* (New York: The Viking Press, 1966), p. 228.
23. *Ibid.*
24. *Khrushchev Remembers,* pp. 347–351.
25. *Ibid.*, p. 345–345. Pyotr N. Pospelov was a member of the Secretariat together with Suslov. In 1954, Suslov had distanced himself from the ideological apparatus to concentrate on relations with the satellite states and foreign communist parties, and Pospelov took over Suslov's responsibilities for ideology. Suslov continued to exercise considerable influence, however, particularly after he was elected to the Presidium.
26. *Ibid.*, p. 346.
27. Wolfgang Leonhard, *The Kremlin since Stalin,* p. 185.
28. For Khrushchev's description of the events leading to the Secret Speech, see: *Khrushchev Remembers,* pp. 346–351. For other comments, see: Wolfgang Leonhard, *The Kremlin since Stalin,* pp. 167–192; Roy Medvedev, *Khrushchev,* pp. 83–94.
29. A. Avtorkhanov, "Suslov: The Kremlin's Chief Ideologist," *Bulletin of the Institute for the Study of the USSR,* Vol. XV (2), February 1968, p. 9.
30. Khrushchev recalled in his memoirs that "Pospelov was instructed to turn his report into a speech." *Khrushchev Remembers,* p. 350.
31. In the early 1960's, students of Soviet politics began to recognize that Soviet politics no longer followed the stable and totalitarian pattern established during the period of high Stalinism, but instead were characterized by a continuous struggle over power and policy. For a discussion of the "conflict model" of Soviet politics, see: *Problems of Communism,* September-October 1962, November-December 1963, January-February 1965, May-June 1965, and July-August 1965; Carl A. Linden, *Khrushchev and the Soviet Leadership, 1957–1964* (Baltimore, Md.: Johns Hopkins University Press, 1966), pp. 1–21.
32. Robert C. Tucker, "The Rise of Stalin's Personality Cult," *American Historical Review,* Vol. 84, April 1979, pp. 347–366.
33. A number of prominent anthropologists have recognized the universality of the role played by the high priest in ideologically-motivated societies. See: Claude Levi-Strauss, *Structural Anthropology* (New York/London: Basic Books, 1963), and John Lee Maddox, *The Medicine Man: A Sociological Study of the Character and Evolution of Shamanism* (New York: The Macmillan Co., 1923), pp. 2, 92–131, and 292–294.
34. For a discussion of Shepilov's role, see: Robert Conquest, *Power and Policy in the USSR,* pp. 211–218.
35. The 1963 Party reform streamlined the entire Party apparatus into parallel industrial and agricultural units, drastically reducing the powers of the traditional ideological organs by setting up the Ideological Commission headed by Leonid Ilyichev. Suslov continued to exercise overall control over ideology from his position as Secretary in charge of Ideology and Relations with Foreign Communist Parties, but the economic reform and the formation of the Ideological Commission substantially diminished his influence in the day to day control of cultural affairs.
36. *Novyi Mir,* September 1956.

37. Vladimir Dudintsev, *Not by Breat Alone* (Moscow, 1956).
38. *Pravda,* August 1, 1956.
39. Only three members of the Communist party—Janos Kadar, Pal Losonczi, and Nagy himself—were appointed to the cabinet.
40. Stephen S. Kaplan, *Diplomacy of Power* (Washington, D.C.: The Brookings Institute, 1981), p. 216.
41. Noel Barber, *Seven Days of Freedom: the Hungarian Uprising, 1956* (New York, N.Y.: Stein and Day, 1974), p. 46.
42. For more information regarding the Soviet intervention in Hungary, see: Miklos Molnar, *Budapest 1956: A History of the Hungarian Revolution* (Allen and Unwin, 1971); Noel Barber, *Seven Days of Freedom: The Hungarian Uprising, 1956* (New York: Stein and Day, 1974); Tibor Meray, *Thirteen Days that Shook the Kremlin* (New York: Praeger, 1959).
43. M. A. Suslov, *Marksizm-Leninizm i Sovremennaia epokha,* Vol. I, pp. 239–256.
44. *Ibid.*
45. For a comparison of the October 30 "new charter" statement, and Suslov's October Revolution Anniversary speech, see *Pravda,* October 31, 1956 and M. A. Suslov, *Marksizm-Leninizm in Sovremennaia epokha,* Vol. I, pp. 239–256.
46. *Time,* December 17, 1956.
47. *Pravda,* December 9, 1956.

NOTES TO CHAPTER X

1. Georgii Malenkov, *O zadachakh partiinykh organizatsii v oblasti promyshlenosti i transpaorta* (1941).
2. Speech of December 7, 1954 at the All-Union Conference of Builders, Architects and Workers in the Building Materials Industry, in Construction Machinery and Road Machinery Industries, and in Design and Research Organizations. *Pravda,* December 28, 1954.
3. M. A. Suslov, *Marksizm-Leninizm i Sovremennaia epokha,* Vol. I, pp. 239–256.
4. Nagy took refuge in the Yugoslavian Embassy in Budapest but was released to the Russians on the express guarantee that he would not be harmed. He was never heard of since then.
5. *The Blue Flower* in Leningrad, *The Bell* (obviously patterned after Alexander Herzen's revolutionary paper published outside of Russia during mid XIX century) in Moscow, the *Figleaf* in Vilnius, were but a few examples of illegal student publications openly circulating among students during December 1956 and January 1957.
6. *Pravda,* December 23, 1956, and January 19, 1957.
7. *Partiinaia Zhizn',* No. 20 (1956).
8. According to articles appearing in *Red Star,* the army paper, as described in Wolfgang Leonhard, *The Kremlin since Stalin,* p. 241.
9. For an analysis of the competing platforms on the eve of the June 1957 crisis, see: A. A. Avtorkhanov, "The Khrushchev Coup: Its Prospects," *Bulletin of the Institute for the Study of the USSR,* Vol. IV (7), July 1957, pp. 3–7.

10. Shepilov was released from the office of Minister of Foreign Affairs and replaced with Andrei Gromyko.
11. Dennis A. Pluchinsky, "Mikhail A. Suslov: The Last Stalinist," p. 88.
12. *Pravda,* February 18, 27, March 27, 28, April 12, 15, 18, 20, and May 1, 14, 15, 16.
13. From February 5 to May 19, 1957, a period of approximately three and one half months, Suslov's name or photograph appeared in *Pravda* a total of 49 times.
14. Tito's speech at Brioni, originally reported in *Borba,* April 19, 1957.
15. Robert Conquest, *Power and Policy in the USSR,* p. 312; Carl A. Linden, *Khrushchev and the Soviet Leadership,* p. 44; and Michel Tatu, *Power in the Kremlin,* p. 32. An examination of *Pravda* and *Izvestia* for the period of May 19 to June 18, 1957, does not yield any information about Suslov's tour of the provinces. Wolfgang Leonhard's notation in *The Kremlin since Stalin* that Suslov was in Moscow on June 14 to meet the Khrushchev party returning from Finland is also incorrect. A closer examination of the June 15 *Pravda photograph* shows that the welcoming party did not include Suslov, although it did include Pervukhin, who resembled him. The author is indebted for this piece of fine detective work to Dennis A. Pluchinsky, "Mikhail A. Suslov: The Last Stalinist," Unpublished Master's thesis, George Washington University, (1978), p. 81.
16. Robert Conquest, *Power and Policy in the USSR,* p. 310, Wolfgang Leonhard, *The Kremlin since Stalin,* p. 242.
17. *L'Unita,* July 8, 1957, *Trybuna Ludu,* July 9, 1957, and various Soviet accounts as reported in Roger W., Pethybridge, *A Key to Soviet Politics: The June Crisis of 1957* (London: George Allen and Unwin, 1962), pp. 190–195.
18. The most detailed analysis of the June 1957 crisis remains Roger W. Pethybridge, *A Key to Soviet Politics: The June Crisis of 1957.* For specific details on the vote see pp. 190–195. Additional information may also be obtained from Robert Conquest, *Power and Policy in the USSR,* pp. 292–328, Wolfgang Leonhard, *The Kremlin since Stalin,* pp. 242–245. Roy Medvedev, *Khrushchev,* pp. 111–123.
19. At the XXI Party Congress in February 1959, Saburov claimed that he supported the Party line against the Anti-Party group, stating that "maintaining correct positions on the basic questions of the policy of the party, I saw the actual aims of the Anti-Party Group, leading to a change in the leadership of the Central Committee, . . . with the aid of some comrades from the healthy section of members of the Presidium—Comrades Mikoyan and Kirichenko—I broke strongly with the Anti-Party Group."
20. The view that Suslov remained neutral during the Presidium meeting is opposed by Veljko Micunovic, Yugoslav Ambassador to the USSR in 1957. According to him, Suslov and Kirichenko took Khrushchev's side immediately on their return to Moscow. For details see: Veljko Micunovic, *Moscow Diary,* (Garden City, N.Y.: Doubleday, 1980), p. 268.
21. Roy Medvedev, *Khrushchev,* p. 118.
22. *Trybuna Ludu,* July 9, 1957.
23. *L'Unita,* July 8, 1957.
24. Roger Pethybridge, *A Key to Soviet Politics: The June Crisis of 1957,* p. 106.
25. For the view that the Party bureaucracy saw Suslov as their own representative, perhaps even more so than Khrushchev, see: Boris Meissner, "The Soviet Political

Process," in Sidney I. Ploss, Ed. *The Soviet Political Process* (Waltham, Mass.: Ginn & Co., 1971), p. 199.

26. Dan Fisher, *Los Angeles Times,* December 2, 1979.
27. Roy Medvedev, *Khrushchev,* p. 119.
28. The conclusion that the majority of the "anti-Party" group did not suffer an unconditional defeat is born by: (1) they were not expelled from the Party, (2) many of them continued to hold important posts in the Party and the government, and (3) between the June 1957 plenum and the XXII Party Congress in October 1961, they continued to offer strong resistance to Khrushchev's unremitting efforts to purge them completely. For details, see: Carl A. Linden, *Khrushchev and the Soviet Leadership, 1957–1964,* pp. 45–116.
29. *Partiinaia Zhizn',* No. 13, July 1957, as cited in Roger W. Pethybridge, *A Key to Soviet Politics,* p. 194.
30. Palmiro Togliatti, "Interview with *Nuovi Argumenti* (1956) in Palmiro Togliatti, *On Gramsci and Other Writings* (London: Lawrence and Wishart, 1979), p. 129.
31. For a more comprehensive analysis of the notion of *gosudarstvo,* see Robert C. Tucker, *The Soviet Political Mind* (New York: Praeger, 1963), pp. 69–90.
32. Roy Medvedev, *Khrushchev,* pp. 118–119.
33. Carl A. Linden, *Khrushchev and the Soviet Leadership, 1957–1964,* p. 54.
34. According to most analysts, the notion that the "second secretary" was, in fact, the second most important person in the Soviet leadership did not develop until the December 1957 plenum when Kirichenko became a member of the Secretariat and, for all intents and purposes, assumed the position of the "second secretary."
35. Leonid Ilyichev was head of *Agitprop* from 1958 to 1964. Until October 1961, *Agitprop* remained within the general responsibility of Suslov who supervised ideology and inter-Party relations. At the XXII Party Congress in October 1961, Ilyichev was appointed to the Secretariat where, under Khrushchev's protection, he became also the Secretary in charge of Ideology. During the reorganization of the Party in 1963, Khrushchev made him head of the special Ideological Commission.
36. Wolfgang Leonhard, *The Kremlin since Stalin,* pp. 251–253.
37. The Central Committee plenum convened on October 28–29. Zhukov's indictment and removal was on October 29, 1957.
38. Zhukov's release from the Defense Ministry was announced in *Pravda,* October 27, 1957. The decree of the plenary session was published in *Pravda,* November 3, 1957. Suslov's role at the plenary session was not disclosed until the appearance of S. S. Khromov, *Bor'ba KPSS za Pretvorenie v Zhizn' Reshenii XX-go S'yezda Partii, 1956–1958* (CPSU Struggle for the Implementation of Decisions of the XX Party Congress, 1956–1958) (Moscow: Moscow University Publishers, May 1961), later also confirmed by General F. I. Golikov, chief of the MPA at the XXII Party Congress (*Pravda,* October 30, 1961).
39. Carl A. Linden, *Khrushchev and the Soviet Leadership 1957–1964* (Baltimore: Johns Hopkins University Press, 1966), Roman Kolkowicz, *The Soviet Military and the Communist Party* (Princeton, N.J.: Princeton University Press, 1967), Paul M. Cocks, "The Purge of Marshal Zhukov," *Slavic Review,* Vol. XXII (3), September 1963, pp. 483–498.
40. Timothy J. Colton, "The Zhukov Affair Reconsidered," *Soviet Studies,* Vol. XXIX (2), April 1977, pp. 185–213, Timothy J. Colton, *Commissars, Commanders and*

Civilian Authority: The Structure of Soviet Politics (Cambridge, Mass.: Harvard University Press, 1979), pp. 175–195.

41. *Ibid.*, p. 213, based on T. H. Rigby's admonition in his "Crypto-Politics," Frederic J. Fleron, Jr. Ed. *Communist Studies and the Social Sciences* (Chicago, 1969), pp. 122–127.

42. Interview with William Randolph Hearst, Jr. of February 7, 1955, published in the supplement of the *New Times* (Soviet paper published in English), February 19, 1955.

43. *Ibid.*, July 16, 1957.

44. *Krasnaia zvezda*, July 19, 1957.

45. *Pravda*, September 29, 1957. The official history of World War II was published in 1961 as *Istoriia Velikoi Otechestvennoi Voiny 1941–1945* (The History of the Great Patriotic War 1941–1945) (Moscow: Voenizdat, 1961).

46. Carl Linden, *Khrushchev and the Soviet Leadership, 1957–1964*, p. 48; Robert Conquest, *Power and Policy in the USSR*, pp. 337–338.

47. Veljko Micunovic, *Moscow Diary*, p. 309.

48. Roman Kolkowicz in H. Gordon Skilling and Franklyn Griffiths, Eds. *Interest Groups in Soviet Politics* (Princeton, N.J.: Princeton University Press, 1971), pp. 157–158.

49. XXII *Syezd KPSS, stenograficheskii otchet* (Moscow, 1962), Vol. III, p. 67.

50. *New York Times*, November 5, 1957.

51. *XXII S'yezd KPSS, stenograficheskii otchet* (Moscow, 1962), Vol. III, p. 67.

52. Sidney I. Ploss, *Conflict and Decision-Making in Soviet Russia*, p. 115.

NOTES TO CHAPTER XI

1. Palmiro Togliatii, *Memorandum on Questions of the International Working Class Movement and its Unity*, September 5, 1964 (also known as Togliatti's last testament).

2. Roger W. Pethybridge, *A Key to Soviet Politics, the June Crisis of 1957*, pp. 146–151.

3. Sixty-four Communist parties sent delegations to the Moscow conference from November 14 to 19, 1957.

4. According to the press coverage in *Pravda*, almost all of Suslov's time was devoted to meetings with foreign Communist Party delegations from July to November 1957.

5. Wolfgang Leonhard, *The Kremlin since Stalin*, p. 262.

6. *Pravda*, November 17–19, 1957; *Kommunist*, No. 12 (1957). For more details see: Wolfgang Leonhard, *The Kremlin since Stalin*, pp. 260–264, and Carl A. Linden, *Khrushchev and the Soviet Leadership, 1957–1964*, pp. 54–57.

7. *Newsweek*, November 18, 1957.

8. *Ibid.*, December 23, 1957.

9. Two Soviet economists, Zanina and Venzher, suggested in 1952 that the MTS should be dissolved.

10. As cited in Wolfgang Leonhard, *The Kremlin since Stalin*, p. 273.

11. *Pravda*, January 26, 1958.

12. Joseph Stalin, *Economic Problems of Socialism* in L. Gruilow, Ed. *Current Soviet Policies, Documentary Record of the XIX Communist Party Congress* (New York, N.Y.: Praeger, 1953), pp. 1–18, as cited in Carl A. Linden, *Khrushchev and the Soviet Leadership, 1957–1964*, p. 62n.
13. *Pravda*, March 12, 1958.
14. *Ibid.*, March 14, 1958.
15. The analysis of the MTS debate has been based on Carl A. Linden, *Khrushchev and the Soviet Leadership, 1957–1964*, pp. 61–69, and Wolfgang Leonhard, *The Kremlin since Stalin*, pp. 272–276.
16. Dennis A. Pluchinsky, "Mikhail A. Suslov: The Last Stalinist," p. 99.
17. *Pravda*, June 8, 1958.
18. Boris Nicolaevsky, *Power and the Soviet Elite*, p. 260.
19. *Literaturnaia Gazeta*, January 4, 1962, as cited in Carl A. Linden, *Khrushchev and the Soviet Leadership, 1957–1964*, p. 66n.
20. Veljko Micunovic, *Moscow Diary*, p. 365.
21. *Kommunist*, No. 6 (1958).
22. The Chinese decision to reverse its position on "transition to communism" was announced in the middle of December 1958. The resistance of such prominent Chinese Politburo members as Chou En-Lai and Chu-Teh to the "transition" formula, and the acknowledgement that China's transformation to communism depended on the development of an industry that was still fifteen to twenty years in the making, caused the Chinese to reverse their position and recognize that the communization of agriculture did not put them on a par with the Soviet Union.
23. For a more detailed analysis of the XXI Congress of the CPSU, see: Robert Conquest, *Power and Policy in the USSR*, pp. 371–381; Wolfgang Leonhard, *The Kremlin since Stalin*, pp. 310–337; Carl A. Linden, *Khrushchev and the Soviet Leadership, 1957–1964*, pp. 82–89; Roger W. Pethybridge, *A Key to Soviet Politics*, pp. 166–174.
24. KPSS, *Vneocherednei XXI S'ezd KPSS, January 27-February 5, 1959, stenograficheskii otchet, Vol. I* (Moscow, 1959), p. 365.
25. *Ibid.*, pp. 357–358.

NOTES TO CHAPTER XII

1. For an analysis of Soviet foreign policy leading to the 1959 Soviet-American *rapprochment*, see Adam B. Ulam, *Expansion and Coexistence, Soviet Foreign Policy, 1917–73* (New York: Holt, Rinehart and Winston, Inc., 1974), pp. 572–628.
2. Khrushchev's speech to the XXI Party Congress as cited in *Pravda*, January 28, 1959.
3. *Ibid.*
4. *Ibid.*
5. *Ibid.*
6. *Time*, June 19, 1959.
7. The May Day line-up showed Suslov ahead of Kirichenko in the official leadership

listings, indicating that Kirichenko's downfall may have actually begun in May 1959 and not December 1959 as it was generally believed.

8. *Pravda,* February 4, 6, 7, 8, 9, 11, 13, 24, 1959.

9. *Daily Herald,* March 15, 21, 1959; *Pravda,* March 15, 19, 21, 22, 24, 1959.

10. *Pravda,* May 22, 26, 30, 1959; June 25–29, 1959, August 2, 25; September 1, 6, 13, 20, 1959.

11. According to *Pravda* of September 28, 1959, Suslov's departure from Moscow was attended by six full members of the Presidium.

12. Wolfgang Leonhard, *The Kremlin since Stalin,* p. 357.

13. *Pravda,* April 23, 1960.

14. *Jen-min Jih-pao,* April 22, 1960.

15. June 12, 1960 marked the fortieth anniversary of the appearance of Lenin's pamphlet *"Left-wing" Communism-an infantile disorder.*

16. Michel Tatu, *Power in the Kremlin* (New York, N.Y.: The Viking Press, 1967), pp. 53–54.

17. For the analysis of the May 1960 crisis and the stir that it created in Soviet politics, see Michel Tatu, *Power in the Kewemlin,* pp. 52–126.

18. *Pravda,* January 16, 1960.

19. *Ibid.,* May 2, May 18, and November 8, 1959.

20. Oleg Penkovsky's acknowledgement in *The Penkovsky Papers* (New York: Doubleday and Co., 1965), p. 209 that Suslov was a member of the Supreme Military Council since early 1960, and other press reports of meetings with the military (*Pravda,* January 20, May 11–15, 1960) tend to indicate that beginning with 1960 Suslov was expanding his military connections.

21. *Pravda,* January 13, 1960.

22. *Ibid.,* January 26 and 29, 1960; March 6, 8, and 11, 1960; April 23, 1960.

23. According to Michel Tatu, *Power in the Kremlin,* p. 106, Khrushchev and all the Presidium members then in Moscow visited an art exhibit on June 1, 1960.

24. Michel Tatu, *Power in the Kremlin,* pp. 107–108.

25. Edward Crankshaw in the *Observer,* February 12 and 19, 1961, as cited in Wolfgang Leonhard, *The Kremlin since Stalin,* p. 367.

26. For a thoughtful and carefully pieced together analysis of the Sino-Soviet schism and the Bucharest meeting see Edward Crankshaw, *The New Cold War, Moscow v. Peking* (Baltimore, Md.: Penguin, 1963), especially pp. 97–110.

27. Michel Tatu, *Power in the Kremlin,* p. 111.

28. An interesting sidelight is that the report on the Bucharest meeting was given not by Khrushchev, but by Frol Kozlov who never attended the Bucharest meeting.

29. Michel Tatu, *Power in the Kremlin,* p. 111.

30. *Ibid.,* pp. 103–104.

31. Carl A. Linden, *Khrushchev and the Soviet Leadership, 1957–1964,* pp. 99–100.

32. *Pravda,* November 12, 1960.

33. *Ibid,.* December 5, 1960.

34. *Ibid,.* January 23, 1961.

35. *Ibid.*

36. Suslov was not alone in encouraging better Sino-Soviet relations. He was supported by Frol Kozlov, who had assumed by then the leadership of the conservative faction

in Soviet internal politics. The Chinese were aware of this, and did everything they could to promote a split among the Soviet leadership.

37. "The Origin and Development of the Differences between the Leadership of the CPSU and Ourselves, *Hong-chi,*" September 1963.

38. *Pravda,* December 7, 1960.

39. *Ibid,.* December 8 and 9, 1960.

40. The clash between Soviet and Chinese troops at Damasky island on the Ussuri river took place in march 1969.

41. For a discussion of Kozlov's position on the Chinese development of the bomb and the Soviet leadership's reaction to this, see Robert M. Slusser, *The Berlin Crisis* (Baltimore, Md.: Johns Hopkins University Press, 1973), pp. 162, 213, and 269–273.

42. This view is more extensively and carefully developed in Robert M. Slusser, *The Berlin Crisis,* pp. 268–273.

43. *Pravda,* April 3, 1963.

44. Robert M. Slusser, *The Berlin Crisis,* pp. 269–272.

45. *Pravda,* September 6, 7, 1961.

46. For a more detailed analysis of the "withering away" controversy, see Carl A. Linden, *Khrushchev and the Soviet Leadership, 1957–1964,* pp. 108–116.

47. Khrushchev was absent from Moscow between September 22 and October 6, 1961.

48. *Pravda,* October 15, 1961.

49. *Ibid.*

50. Carl A. Linden, *Khrushchev and the Soviet Leadership, 1957–1964,* 119–120, Sidney I. Ploss, "Deadlock in the Party Presidium," in Sidney I. Ploss, Ed. *The Soviet Political Process* (Toronto/London: Ginn & Co., 1971), pp. 231–232. Robert M. Slusser, *The Berlin Crisis,* pp. 286–288.

51. Michel Tatu, *Power in the Kremlin,* p. 146: P. A. Satiukov and P. N. Pospelov, Speeches to the XXII Party Congress *XXII Congress of the CPSU, stenographic report,* Vol II, pp. 355 and 460.

52. *Pravda,* October 21, 1961.

53. *Pravda,* October 23, 1961.

54. *Ibid.*

55. *Ibid.*

56. *Ibid.*

57. *Ibid.*

58. The author's appraisal of the XXII Party Congress is based on the contents of *Pravda* from October 17 to November 1, 1961, and on the analysis contained in A. Avtorkhanov, "the Political Significance of the Twenty-Second Party Congress," *Bulletin of the Institute for the Study of the USSR,* Vol. VIII, November 1961, pp. 3–16; Carl A. Linden, *Khrushchev and the Soviet Leadership, 1957–1964,* pp. 117–145; Robert M. Slusser, *The Berlin Crisis of 1961,* pp. 286–46'; Michel Tatu, *Power in the Kremlin,* pp. 125–175.

59. Michel Tatu, *Power in the Kremlin,* pp. 160–161.

60. *Ibid.,* p. 164.

61. Based on previous loyalties and views on major issues, the Secretariat was probably divided into a pro-Khrushchev grouping consisting of Khrushchev, Demichev, Ilyi-

chev, Shelepin, and Kuusinen, and a Suslov-Kozlov alignment of Suslov, Kozlov, Spiridonov, and Ponomarev.

62. *Pravda,* October 21, 1961.
63. Mikhail Heller and Aleksander Nekrich, *Utopia u vlasti: istoriia Sovetskogo souize s 1917 goda do nashikh dnei* (London: Overseas Publications Interchange, 1982), p. 368.

NOTES TO CHAPTER XIII

1. *Pravda,* December 24, 1952.
2. Michel Tatu, *Power in the Kremlin,* p. 202.
3. Konstantinov lost his candidate membership in the Central Committee, Palgunov and Gubin were removed from the Central Auditing Committee, and Yudin was dropped from full membership in the Central Committee. For details see A. Avtorkhanov, "Political Significance of the Twenty-Second Party Congress," *Bulletin of the Institute for the Study of the USSR,* Vol. VIII (November 1961), p. 12.
4. *Pravda,* November 21, 1961.
5. Suslov had used this expression most recently at the XXII Party Congress when he again said that the party would continue "to enrich and develop the scientific theory of Communism."
6. *Ibid.,* October 26, 1961.
7. Carl Linden, *Khrushchev and the Soviet Leadership,* p. 135.
8. *Pravda,* December 21, 1961.
9. *Ibid.,* November 3, 24, 27, December 3, 1961, January 6, March 23, 1962.
10. *Kommunist,* No. 1 (1962), pp. 11–38.
11. *Ibid.,* December 25, 1961. Picture shows Mikoyan in the center surrounded by Suslov and Ilyichev on one side, and Khrushchev and Kuusinen on the other.
12. Suslov's speech "The XXII Congress of the CPSU and the Problems of the Social Science Faculties" was first carried in an abridged form in *Pravda,* February 4, 1962. It was also reprinted with minor excisions in *Kommunist,* No. 3, 1962, and in M. A. Suslov, *Marksizm-Leninizm i sovremennaia epokha,* Vol. I, pp. 409–425.
13. *Kommunist,* No. 3 (1962), p. 22.
14. *Pravda,* February 4, 1962; *Kommunist,* No. 3 (1962), p. 42.
15. *Ibid.,* p. 41.
16. Suslov's speech was first carried in an abridged form in *Pravda* and later published as a full text in *Kommunist,* where certain parts were removed from the *Pravda* version. Carl A. Linden has suggested that the changes may have been the result of a "provocative ploy of the Khrushchev forces" to identify Suslov as a "Stalinist ideologist" with sympathies to Peking. Although the excisions soften Suslov's leading formulation, they do this only peripherally. The significant assertion that "dogmatism is a most dangerous form of the isolation of theory from practice" remains unexcised in the *Kommunist* text. That it may have been done deliberately is also not likely. It is not born out by the text carried in a newly edited M. A. Suslov, *Markisizm-Leninizm i sovremennaia epokha* published in three volumes in 1982,

when Suslov and his editors could have easily insisted on the *Pravda* version if they felt that the excisions in *Kommunist* were unwarranted. The critical passages in the *Kommunist* text (*Kommunist*, No. 3, 1962, pp. 39, 40, and 43) and in *Marksizm-Leninizm i sovremennaia epokha* (Vol. I, pp. 430–432) are identical, leading the author to the conclusion that the revision in *Kommunist* was probably made with Suslov's approval. For a detailed analysis of the excisions from the original *Pravda* text, see Carl R. Linden, *Khrushchev and the Soviet Leadership*, pp. 138n–139n.

17. M. A. Suslov, *Marksizm-Leninizm i sovremennaia epokha*, p. 417.

18. The contents of this report was not made public until April 3, 1964, when it was published in *Pravda*.

19. Except for the period of illness lasting approximately from September 15, 1963 to January 1, 1964, Suslov's name or photograph appeared in *Pravda* on the average every third day in connection with his attendance at receptions, concerts, ceremonies, rallies, and meetings with foreign delegations.

20. *Pravda*, October 21, 1961.

21. *Novyi Mir*, No. 1, January 1962.

22. *Izvestia*, February 14, 1962.

23. Khrushchev visited the Manezh exhibit on December 1, 1962. The speed with which the "ideological purity" campaign was launched has led a number of Western analysts to suggest that Khrushchev's visit to the Manezh exhibit was purposely staged by conservatives in the Party to provoke a violent reaction by Khrushchev, who was known to detest modern art. This view tends to be substantiated by the mysterious closing of a modern art exhibit in the Yunost Hotel, and the sudden transfer of the Belyutin (Eli Belyutin was a modern art teacher and proprietor of a private Moscow gallery) works to the Manezh gallery a few days before Khrushchev's visit. The Belyutin works represented the most avant-garde example of modern art, sure to be found ideologically harmful by Khrushchev. For details, see Priscilla Johnson, *Khrushchev and the Arts, the Politics of Soviet Culture, 1962–1964* (Cambridge, Mass.: The M.I.T. Press, 1965), pp. 7–10.

24. Michel Tatu, *Power in the Kremlin*, p. 312.

25. Although permanently disabled, Frol Kozlov remained a member of the Presidium and the Secretariat until his death on January 30, 1965.

26. Oleg Penkovsky, *The Penkovsky Papers* (New York: Doubleday & Co., 1965), p. 209.

27. According to Michel Tatu, Suslov reportedly went to see Kozlov in the hospital where the latter argued that "the only way to alleviate the USSR's problems was to get rid of Khrushchev." Michel Tatu, *Power in the Kremlin*, p. 369; also Paul J. Murphy, *Brezhnev, Soviet Politician* (Jefferson, N.C.: McFarland & Co., 1981), p. 209.

28. *Pravda*, November 7, 1982. For a more careful and detailed analysis of Suslov's reaction to the Party bifurcation plan see Barbara Ann Chotiner, *Khrushchev's Party Reform* (Wesport, Conn.: Greenwood Press, 1984), pp. 168–170.

29. Abraham Rothberg, *The Heirs of Stalin* (Ithaca, N.Y.: Cornell University Press, 1972), pp. 56–57, Michel Tatu, *Power in the Kremlin*, p. 248.

30. Michel Tatu, p. 248.

31. Suslov was absent from Moscow and reported ill from the end of September 1963 to January 1, 1964.

32. *Pravda,* April 3, 1964.
33. *Ibid.*
34. Michel Tatu, *Power in the Kremlin,* p. 367.
35. *Ibid.*
36. Usually listed in second or third place immediately after Khrushchev, Suslov's name dropped in 1962–1964 one or two notches beyond that of Mikoyan.
37. According to the opinion of three American physicians who have examined Suslov's medical record, Suslov's long absence in 1963, lasting more than ninety days, from approximately September 25, 1963 to January 1, 1964, was probably brought about by the emergence of more acute symptoms of on-set adult diabetes and coronary heart disease, calling for hospitalization and prolonged rest.
38. William Hyland and Richard W. Shryock, *The Fall of Khrushchev* (New York: Funk and Wagnall's, 1968), Martin Page, *The Day Khrushchev Fell* (New York: Hawthorne Books, 1965), Carl Linen, *Khrushchev and the Soviet Leadership,* pp. 195–235. Roy Medvedev, *Khrushchev,* pp. 235–245, Paul J. Murphy, *Brezhnev,* pp. 200–244, Michel Tatu, *Power in the Kremlin,* pp. 363–423.
39. Mikhail Heller and Aleksandr Nekrich, *Utopiia a vlasti,* p. 368.
40. Roy Medvedev, *Khrushchev,* p. 235.
41. Michel Tatu, *Power in the Kremlin,* pp. 399–423; Peter B. Reddaway, "The Fall of Khrushchev—A Tentative Analysis," *Survey,* No. 56 (July 1965), pp. 11–30, and Sidney I. Ploss, Ed. *The Soviet Political Process* (Toronto/London: Ginn & Col., 1971), p. 241–264; William Hyland & Richard W. Shryock, *The Fall of Khrushchev* (New York: Funk & Wagnall's, 1968), pp. 167–197.
42. Paul J. Murphy, *Brezhnev,* William Hyland & Richard W. Shryock, *The Fall of Khrushchev.*
43. Michel Tatu, *Power in the Kremlin,* pp. 401–418.
44. Neither *Khrushchev Remembers* (Boston/Toronto: Little Brown, 1970), nor any other material available to Western researchers—including the Khrushchev tapes—makes any reference to the 1964 coup.
45. Edward Hallett Carr, *What is History?* (New York: Vintage Books, 1961), p. 116.
46. Father Joseph du Tremblay, monk, diplomat, senior statesman, and confidant of Cardinal Richelieu. Aldous Huxley, *Grey Eminence* (New York/London: Harper & Brothers, 1941).
47. Otto Kuusinen died in May 1964.
48. Michel Tatu, *Power in the Kremlin,* p. 412.
49. Palmiro Togliatti, *Memorandum of Comrade Togliatti on Questions of the International Working Class Movement and its Unity,* (Italy: Foreign Section of the CC of the ICP), August 1964.
50. *Pravda,* September 10, 1964.
51. Michel Tatu, *Power in the Kremlin,* p. 389.
52. On September 6, 1964, Schwirkmann, a West German diplomat, was injected with a toxic gas by an unidentified assailant in Zagorsk monastery near Moscow. The Soviet government has never explained the reason for this foul play, but the speculation is that it was engineered by the KGB in an effort to sabotage Khrushchev's efforts at *rapprochement* with West Germany.
53. *Ibid.,* p. 398.
54. The day by day reportage and analysis in Michel Tatu, *Power in the Kremlin,* pp.

399–423 remains a classic of Khrushchev's last days in power. Other important accounts are: William Hyland & Richard W. Shryock, *The Fall of Khrushchev,* pp. 167–197; Paul J. Murray, *Brezhnev: The Soviet Politician,* pp. 214–244; Martin Page, *The Day Khrushchev Fell,* pp. 33–65; Stephen Rosenfeld, *Washington Post,* October 22, 1964; Harrison E. Salisbury, *The New York Times,* October 17, 1964; Henry Tanner, *The New York Times,* October 22, 1964.

55. For a detailed listing and analysis of the counts on which Khrushchev stood accused see Roy Medvedev. *Khrushchev,* pp. 237–245.

56. *Pravda,* October 16, 1964.

57. John Dornberg, *Brezhnev: The Masks of Power,* p. 179.

58. Michel Tatu, *Power in the Kremlin,* pp. 411–412.

59. *Ibid.,* pp. 410–411.

NOTES TO CHAPTER XIV

1. *Pravda,* July 14, 1973.

2. Although formally recognized by the Central Committee, no written decree has ever been published.

3. Mark Frankland, *Khrushchev* (Harmondsworth, U.K.: Penguin), p. 309.

4. John Dornberg, *Brezhnev: The Masks of Power* (New York: Basic Books, 1974), p. 183.

5. *Pravda,* October 16, 1964 carried a banner headline and pictures of Brezhnev and Kosygin taken many years earlier.

6. John Dornberg, *Brezhnev: The Masks of Power,* p. 198.

7. Backed by the Ukrainian Party organization, Nikolai Podgorny was the Party Secretary in charge of cadres under Khrushchev.

8. Michel Tatu, *Power in the Kremlin,* p. 433.

9. *Ibid.,* pp. 503–508.

10. Chapter X of this work, p. 159.

11. The difference between a consensus decision and a formal vote can usually be determined from the Russian wording of the communique reporting the results, even though the translation in all cases may be designated by the English word "unanimous." If a formal vote has been taken and the result is, indeed, unanimous, it is reported as *yedinoglasno* (literally meaning "in one voice"). If, on the other hand, decision, was reached by consensus or a formal vote that had some dissent, the result is generally reported as *yedinodushno* (literally meaning "as one soul"). For example, Gorbachev's election was reported in the Soviet press as "*yedinodushno,*" implying that there was some dissent to his appointment as General Secretary.

12. For a discussion of leadership gradations, see Harry Gelman, *The Brezhnev Politburo and the Decline of Detente* (Ithaca/London: Cornell Univ. Press, 1984), pp. 54–56.

13. Official Soviet press coverage of Suslov during the period of October 20 to March 31, 1966 is almost exclusively devoted to meetings and receptions with foreign leaders.

14. *Il Tempo,* October 28, 1964.
15. *Ibid., Il Messagero,* October 23, 1964, and *New York Herald Tribune,* October 23, 1964. Efforts to confirm the rumors were unsuccessful and diplomats in Moscow voiced skepticism about their validity.
16. Parsons, Moscow, October 31, 1964 (PRWO 1826/64).
17. John Lee Maddox, *The Medicine Man: A Sociological Study of the Character and Evolution of Shamanism* (New York: The Macmillan Co., 1923), pp. 2, 114, 91–133, and 293–294.
18. *Pravda,* October 6, 1964.
19. *Ibid.,* October 7, 1964.
20. Podgorny was "promoted" to the presidency of the USSR on December 9, 1965.
21. Suslov and Pel'she were married to sisters. Central Research, Radio Liberty, *A Biographic Directory of 100 Leading Soviet Officials,* Munich, 1982, p. 209.
22. The Party-State Control Committee was established in 1962 as part of Khrushchev's bifurcation of the Party into separate agricultural and industrial committees. It was never made clear what the Committee's functions were, but apparently it had the authority to remove both state and Party officials from their posts.
23. *Planovoye Khoziaistvo,* No. 4, April 1965.
24. For a detailed analysis of the press coverage, see: Michel Tatu, *Power in the Kremlin,* pp. 446–456.
25. *Pravda,* May 17, 1964.
26. *Izvestia,* May 21, 1964.
27. *Pravda,* May 22, 1965.
28. *Ibid.*
29. *Pravda,* June 5, 1965.
30. *Ibid.*
31. *Ibid.*
32. Michel Tatu, *Power in the Kremlin,* p. 500.
33. *Pravda,* May 9, 1965.
34. *Pravda,* March 4, 1965, April 15, 1965; *Izvestia,* March 3, 1965.
35. *Pravda,* February 21, 1965.
36. Lydia Chukovskaya, the adopted daughter of Kornei Chukovsky was the author of fiction, literary criticism and memoirs, many of which were published in *samizdat.* The novella was originally written in 1939–1940, but was not submitted for publication until 1962. The publisher's contract was abrogated in 1963, and the author brought suit against the publisher.
37. Roy Medvedev, *An End to Silence: Uncensored Opinion in the Soviet Union from Roy Medvedev's Underground Magazine Political Diary,* Ed. by Stephen Cohen (New York: W. W. Norton, 1982), pp. 158–165. The novella was published abroad in Russian and English in 1967 as *The Deserted House.*
38. *Izvestia,* April 15, 1965.
39. *Pravda,* August 29, 1965.
40. *Pravda,* October 8, 1965.
41. As cited in Michel Tatu, *Power in the Kremlin,* p. 484.
42. *Ibid.*
43. Like Milovan Djilas (Milovan Djilas, "Christ and the Commissar," in G. R. Urban,

Stalinism: Its Impact on Russia and the World (London: Maurice Temple Smith Ltd., 1982), pp. 181–183) the author is of the opinion that the term "Stalinism" is a "misnomer" in that it obscures the Leninist roots of the Soviet political system. It tends to lump under one rubric Lenin's centrist tradition and the excesses of Bolshevik despotism inherited from the Leninist past together with Stalin's personal predilection for crudeness, conspiracy, use of terror, and everything else associated with the so called "cult of personality." To avoid confusion, the author has decided to continue using the term "Stalinism," but only in its more limited framework of distinctly Stalinist characteristics of the evolving soviet system, vis., arbitrariness, one-man dominance, paranoia, use of terror, and deification of the leaders.

44. Roy Medvedev, *An End of Silence*, pp. 170–171.
45. Anatol Shub, *The New Russian Tragedy* (New York: W. W. Norton, 1969), pp. 52–53; elizabeth Teague, "Mikhail Suslov—The Power behind the Throne?" *Radio Liberty Research Bulletin*, RL 42/82, January 26, 1982, p. 2.
46. *Pravda*, April 19, 1966.
47. Podgorny briefly alluded to the "cult of personality," but only in passing. "The Party did a great deal to reinforce the socialist legal order," he said, "and eliminate the baneful influence linked with the cult of personality." *Pravda*, April 1, 1966.
48. *Pravda*, march 31, 1966.
49. Roy Medvedev, *An End of Silence*, pp. 158–159.

NOTES TO CHAPTER XV

1. For a discussion of the leadership gradations of the Brezhnev Politburo, see: Harry Gelman, *The Brezhnev Politburo and the Decline of Detente* (Ithaca/London: Cornell Univ. Press, 1984), pp. 54–56.
2. T. H. Rigby, "The Soviet Leadership: Towards a Self-Stabilizing Oligarchy?" *Soviet Studies* (U.K.), Vol. XXII (2) October 1970, p. 186.
3. It is not entirely clear if Suslov was a member of the Defense Council during the first years of the Brezhnev administration. It appears that during the first years it consisted only of First Secretary Brezhnev, Prime Minister Kosygin, President Podgorny, Defense Minister Malinovsky, and Central Committee Secretary in charge of Defense Production Ustinov. Suslov and Kirilenko apparently joined the Defense Council in 1967. Harry Gelman, *The Brezhnev Politburo and the Decline of Detente*, pp. 65–70.
4. For details on the Foreign Affairs Commissions (actually there were two such commissions) see: Robert W. Siegler, *The Standing Commissions of the Supreme Soviet* (New York: Praeger, 1982), pp. 203–211.
5. All crucial Party and government appointments in the Soviet Union require the approval of the Central Committee.
6. Arkady N. Shevchenko, *Breaking with Moscow* (New York: Alfred A. Knopf, 1985), p. 218–220.
7. Shelepin lost his position in the Secretariat in July 1967. It has generally been recognized that Shelepin's removal was prompted by Yegorychev's (Yegorychev was

a protégé of Shelepin) attack on Brezhnev and the Politburo majority for not acting more decisively during and immediately after the Arab-Israeli Six-Day War. Malcolm Mackintosh, "The Soviet Military: Influence on Foreign Policy," *Problems of Communism,* September-October 1973, p. 6; John Dornberg, *Brezhnev: The Masks of Power,* p. 214; *New York times,* June 29, 1967.

8. M. A. Suslov, "The Future Role of the Working Class in its Struggle against Imperialism for a Revolutionary Revival of the World," speech delivered at the International Scientific Conference in Moscow on November 11, 1967 in M. A. Suslov, *Marksizm-Leninizm i sovremennaia epokha,* Vol. II, pp. 136–139.

9. M. A. Suslov, "The International Solidarity of the Working Class and its Communist avant-garde: The Most Important Factor of the Communist Movement," in M. A. Suslov, *Marksizm-Leninizm i sovremennaia epokha,* Vol. II, pp. 146–151.

10. *Pravda,* May 6, 1968; M. A. Suslov, *Marksizm-Leninizm i sovremennaia epokha,* Vol. II, pp. 152–178. According to Radio Liberty Research Bulletin CRD 201/68, based on information from the *Neues Deutschland* (GDR), Suslov's long address was to be used as the principal document by the preparatory committee of the World Communist Conference.

11. As adopted at the XXII Party Congress in 1961, Khrushchev's thesis read: " . . . the fact that the socialist countries are developing as members of a single world socialist system . . . enables them to reduce the time necessary for the construction of socialism and offers them the prospect of effecting the transition to communism more or less simultaneously, within one and the same historical epoch."

12. *Ibid.*

13. *Pravda,* July 17, 1968.

14. Letter of July 14, 1968 signed in Warsaw by the USSR, the GDR, Poland, Hungary, and Bulgaria that called the situation in Czechoslovakia "absolutely unacceptable for a socialist country." An English translation of the letter is contained in Philip Windsor and Adam Roberts, *Czechoslovakia 1968: Reform and Resistance* (New York: Columbia University Press, 1969), p. 150.

15. The author has consulted the following works on the 1968 intervention in Czechoslovakia: Galia Galan, *Reform in Czechoslovakia: The Dubcek Era, 1968–1969*; Jiri Hajek, *Dix Ans Après—Prague 68–78* (Paris: Robert Laffont, 1971); Vojtech Mastny, Ed. *Crisis in World Communism* (New York: Facts on File, Inc., 1972); Stephen S. Kaplan, *Diplomacy of Power* (Washington, D.C.: The Brookings Institute, 1981), pp. 223–231; Pavel Tigrid, *Why Dubcek Fell* (London: McDonald, 1971), Jiri Valenta, *Soviet Intervention in Czechoslovakia, 1968* (Johns Hopkins Univ. Press, 1979); Philip Windsor and Adam Roberts, *Czechoslovakia 1968: Reform and Resistance* (New York: Columbia Univ. Press, 1969).

16. Pavel Tigrid, *Why Dubcek Fell,* p. 86.

17. Stephen S. Kaplan, *Diplomacy of Power,* p. 227; Jiri Valenta, *Soviet Intervention in Czechoslovakia, 1968,* pp. 25–32 and 142–143.

18. Jiri Valenta, p. 142.

19. Pavel Tigrid, p. 96.

20. *Pravda,* August 22, 1968.

21. *Ibid.*

22. Speech at the All-Union Supreme Soviet as cited in Boris Meissner, *The Brezhnev*

Doctrine, East Europe Monographs (Kansas City, Mo.: Park College, 1970), p. 21.

23. The so called "Warsaw letter" was a joint statement and warning of the Warsaw Pact nations dispatched to Czechoslovakia after the Warsaw conference. The text of the letter may be found in Philip Windsor and Adam Roberts, *Czechoslovakia 1968: Reform and Resistance,* p. 150.

24. *Pravda,* September 11, 1968, September 26, 1968; *Mezhdunarodnaia Zhizn',* November 1968. For a detailed analysis, see: Boris Meissner, *The Brezhnev Doctrine,* East Europe Monographs (Kansas City, Mo.: Park College, 1970), particularly pp. 13–14.

25. *Ibid.*

26. *Problems of Peace and Socialism* (USSR), May 1969.

27. *Ibid.*

28. *Pravda,* June 6–18, 1969. The Conference was reported in the Soviet press with unusual candor, leading some observers to conclude that the publicity given to the debate was probably a condition on which the dissenting parties agreed to participate in the Conference.

29. W. W. Kulski, "The 1969 Moscow Conference of Communist Parties," *The Russian Review,* Vol. 28 (3), October 1969, pp. 385–395.

30. Dubcek was removed in April 1969 and replaced by Dr. Gustav Husak.

31. After Nikolai A. Nekrasov's XIX century revolutionary epic poem *Who Lives Happily in Russia?*

32. *Kommunist,* No. 15, October 1969.

33. *Kommunist,* No. 18, December 1969.

34. P. Kruzhin, "A New Interpretation of Peaceful Coexistence," *Bulletin for the Study of the USSR.* Vol. XVII (4), April 1970, pp. 27–31.

35. Brezhnev's speech was not published, but a digest of it appeared in a *Pravda* editorial on January 13, 1970.

36. On July 2, 1970, Brezhnev reaffirmed that the XXIV Party Congress would take place the same year. Eleven days later, a plenary session of the Central Committee announced that the Congress would take place in March 1971.

37. *Christian Science Monitor,* March 12, 1970 and March 28, 1970. A slightly different version, that claimed that the letter had criticized both Brezhnev and Kosygin, was provided by Reuters, March 11, 1970.

38. *Politicheskii dnevnik,* Vol. I (Amsterdam: Alexander Herzen Foundation, 1972), pp. 657–658.

39. Cited in Michel Tatu, "The 'Mini Crisis' of 1970," *Interplay,* Vol. 3 (13), October 1970, p. 14.

40. Reuters, Moscow, April 6, 1970.

41. Except for Shelepin who apparently actually had a gall bladder operation and still looked drawn.

42. TASS, April 21, 1970.

43. John Dornberg, *Brezhnev, The Masks of Power,* p. 249.

44. Mohamed Heikel, *The Road to Ramadan* (New York: The New York Times Book Co., 1975), p. 94.

45. *Ibid.*

NOTES TO CHAPTER XVI

1. Milovan Djilas in G. R. Urban, *Stalinism* (London, 1982), p. 197.
2. New full members of the Politburo were Victor Grishin, F. D. Kulakov, D. A. Kunaev, and Vladimir Shcherbitsky. Kulakov, Kunayev, and Shcherbitsky were definitely Brezhnev's supporters. Kunayev was appointed without previous candidate membership.
3. Donald V. Schwartz, Ed. *Resolutions and Decisions of the CPSU, The Brezhnev Years, 1964–1981,* Vol. 5 (Toronto: Univ. of Toronto Press, 1982), p. 174.
4. For a more detailed, albeit somewhat different analysis of the origin of "developed socialism," see Alfred B. Evans, Jr., "Developed Socialism in Soviet Ideology." *Soviet Studies* (UK), Vol. XXIX (3), July 1977, pp. 409–428.
5. KPSS, *XXIV S'ezd KPSS, March 30–April 11, 1971, stenograficheskii otchet,* Vol. I (Moscow, 1972), p. 62.
6. The report of the General Secretary to the Party Congress is deemed to be the official report of the Central Committee, representing its views and decisions.
7. "Developed socialism" is the most accurate translation of the Russian term "*razvitoi sotsializm.*" Soviet sources often use this term interchangeably with "*zrelyi sotsializm* (mature socialism).
8. M. A. Suslov, *Marksizm-Leninizm i sovremennaia epokha,* Vol. I, 417.
9. While the terms "*razvitoi sotsializm*" (developed socialism), and "*zrelyi sotsializm*" (mature socialism) are used interchangeably in the Soviet Union, Suslov actually preferred the latter designation to describe the present stage of economic and social development in the Soviet Union.
10. M. A. Suslov, *Marksizm-Leninizm i sovremennaia epokha,* Vol. II, p. 269; M. A. Suslov, *Selected Speeches and Writings* (Oxford: Pergamon Press, 1980), p. 162.
11. KPSS, *Vneocherednei XXI S'ezd KPSS, January 27-February 5, 1959, stenograficheskii otchet,* Vol. I (Moscow, 1959), p. 365.
12. M. A. Suslov, *Selected Speeches and Writings,* Vol. I, pp. 269–270.
13. Vladimir Lenin, *The State and Revolution,* in Robert C. Tucker, Ed., *The Lenin Anthology* (New York: W. W. Norton, 1975), pp. 311–398.
14. *Kommunist,* No. 18 (November 1971), pp. 58–72.
15. Soviet literature on "developed or mature socialism"—the two terms being used interchangeably—is very extensive. Some of the more important examples are: Anatolii Butenko, "O Razvitom sotsialisticheskom obschchestve," *Kommunist,* No. 6 (1972); Pyotr Demichev. "Developed Socialism—Stage on the Way to Communism," *World Marxist Review,* Vol. XVI (1), January 1973; Konstantin Katushev, "The Main Direction," *Kommunist,* No. 8 (August 1973); R. Ronai and S. Karpati, "Basis and Superstructure in the Building of Full Socialism," *World Marxist Review,* Vol. XVII (1), january 1974; V. S. Simonov, "Novvye yavleniia v sotsial'noi strukture sovetskogo obshchestva." *Voprsy filosofii,* No. 7 (1972).
16. Karl Marx, *A Contribution to the Critique of Political Economy* (1859), excerpted in Robert C. Tucker, Ed. *The Marx-Engels Reader* (New York: W. W. Norton, 1978), pp. 3–6.
17. *Kommunist,* No. 14 (September 1971).

18. *Ibid.*, English translation included in M. A. Suslov, *Selected Speeches and Writings*, pp. 97–98.

19. *Pravda*, October 23, 1961.

20. For a discussion of the relationship of Soviet ideology to Soviet reality, see Alfred G. Meyer, "The Functions of Ideology in the Soviet Political System," *Soviet Studies (UK), Vol. XVII (3), January 1966; Robert V. Daniels, "The Ideological Vector," Soviet Studies, Vol. XVIII (1), July 196; Morris Bornstein, "Ideology and the Soviet Economy," Soviet Studies*, Vol. XVIII (1), July 1966, Kurt Marko, "Soviet Ideology and Sovietology," *Soviet Studies*, Vol. XIX (4), April 1968; Robert G. Wesson, "Soviet Ideology: The Necessity of Marxism," *Soviet Studies*, Vol. XX (1), July 1969; David D. Comey, "Marxist-Leninist Ideology and Soviet Policy," *Studies in Soviet Thought*, Vol. II (4), December 1962.

21. For a technical discussion of the relationship between Communist thinking and behavior, see: Frederic J. Fleron, Jr. and Rita Mae Kelly, "Personality, Behavior and Communist Ideology," *Soviet Studies*, Vol. XXI (3), January 1970.

22. *Kommunist*, No. 1 (January 1972), p. 19; M. A. Suslov, *Marksizm-Leninizm i sovremennaia epokha*, Vol. II, p. 301.

23. Nicholas Danilevsky (1822–1885), author of *Russia and Europe* (St. Petersburg, 1869), a work which, in many ways predated Oswald Spengler's *The Decline of the West* and projected Russia as a nation of the future with a destiny separate from that of Europe. Konstantin Leontiev (1831–1891), a publicist and reactionary intellectual who criticized Russia's striving to modernize her social and political institutions along Western liberal democratic lines.

24. Nicholas Ustrialov, *V bor'be za Rossiiu* (Harbin, China, 1927), *Pod znamenem revolutsii* (Harbin, 1927), and "Patriotica," *Smena vekh* (Prague, Czechoslovakia, 1921). For a comprehensive study of "national bolshevism" see Mikhail Agursky, *Ideologiia natsional-bolshevizma* (Paris: YMCA Press, 1980), also "The Soviet Legitimacy Crisis and its International Implications" in Morton A. Kaplan, Ed. *The Many Faces of Communism* (New York: The Free Press, 1978).

25. *Ibid.*, pp. 155–156.

26. For a concise and unbiased analysis of Soviet nationality policy, see Victor Zaslavsky and Robert J. Brym, *Soviet-Jewish Emigration and Soviet Nationality Policy* (London: The Macmillan Press Ltd., 1983), pp. 78–102.

27. M. A. Suslov, *Marksizm-Leninizm is sovremennaia epokha*, Vol. I., pp. 33, 53, 96–97, 204.

28. *Ibid.*, pp. 31–33.

29. The author was able to find only two instances during the period of 1940-1945 when Suslov referred specifically to the "Russian nation" and "Russia" in his speeches and writings. M. A. Suslov, *Marksizm-Leninizm i sovremennaia epokha*, Vol. I, pp. 48–49, and p. 123.

30. See Chapter VI, p. 126 of this work.

31. Roy Medvedev, *All Stalin's Men*, p. 80; John B. Dunlop, *The New Russian Nationalism* (Princeton, N.J.: Princeton Univ., Press, 1983), pp. 227–233.

32. Two months after the dismissal of Editor-in-chief Anatolii Nikonov from the *Molodaia gvardiia*, *Veche*, a *samizdat* journal became the forum of Russian nationalism, functioning in this capacity from 1971 to 1974 when it was finally suppressed by the KGB.

33. A. N. Yakovlev, "Protiv antiistorizma," *Literaturnaia gazeta,* November 15, 1972.
34. For details, see: John B. Dunlop, *The Faces of Contemporary Russian Nationalism* (Princeton, N.J.: Princeton Univ. Press, 1983), pp. 227–233.
35. V. Lenin, *Sochinenie,* Vol. XVII, 269, 428–432.
36. M. A. Suslov, *Marksizm-Leninizm i sovremennaia epokha,* Vol. III, pp. 45–58.
37. *Voprosy ekonomiki,* No. 12 (1972).
38. *Kommunist* (Lithuanian edition), No. 12 (582), December 1972.
39. *Ibid.*
40. *Sovetsakaia Kirgiziia,* December 20, 1973.
41. For a detailed examination of this controversy, see *Radio Liberty Research Bulletin,* RL 19/73.
42. *Dagens Nyheter* (Swedish newspaper), July 3, 1973.
43. Aleksandr I. Solzhenitsyn, *Arkhipelag Gulag* (Paris: YMCA Press, 1973), translated into English by Thomas A. Whitney as *The Gulag Archipelago* (New York: Harper & Row Publishers, 1974).
44. According to a December 1974 report of the Intergovernmental Committee for European Migration in Geneva, the total Jewish emigration from the USSR in 1974 was about 21,000, compared to almost 35,000 in 1973.
45. Mikhail A. Suslov. "The Great Science of Victory," address at the meeting celebrating the award of the Order of Lenin to the Institute of Marxism-Leninism, January 17, 1973, reprinted in Mikhail A. Suslov, *Marksizm-Leninizm i sovremennaia epokha,* pp. 18–23.
46. Anatol Shub, *The New Russian Tragedy* (New York: W. W. Norton, 1969), pp. 52–53.
47. "An Interview with Andrei Amalrick," *Radio Liberty Special Report,* RL 368/76, July 29, 1976.
48. *Pravda,* September 15, 1972.
49. UPI, September 14, 1972.
50. M. A. Suslov, *Marksizm-Leninizm i sovremennaia epokha,* Vol. III, p. 8.
51. M. A. Suslov, "The Great Science of Victory," in *Marksizm-Leninizm i sovremennaia epokha,* Vol. III, pp. 18–23, reprinted in English translation in M. A. Suslov, *Marxism-Leninism: The International Teaching of the Working Class* (Moscow: Progress Publishers, 1975), p. 243.
52. M. A. Suslov, "The Great Fifty Years," *Velikii Octiabr i mirovoi revolutsionnyi protsess* (Moscow: Politizdat, 1967), pp. 11–53, particularly pp. 40–53.
53. Michael J. Deane, "The Soviet Assessment of the 'Correlation of World Forces': Implications for American Foreign Policy," *Orbis,* Vol. 20 (3), Fall 1976, pp. 625–636.
54. V. V. Zagladin, Ed. *The World Communist Movement: Outline of Strategy and Tactics* (Moscow: Progress Publishers, 1973); G. Shakhnazarov, "On the Problem of the Correlation of Forces," *Kommunist,* February 1974; Sh. Sanakoyev, "The Problem of the Correlation of Forces in the Contemporary World," *Mezhdunarodnaia zhizn',* October 1974.
55. M. A. Suslov, "According to the Precepts of the Great Lenin," *Marksizm-Leninizm i sovremennaia epokha,* Vol. III, pp. 105–121.
56. M. A. Suslov, *Marzism-Leninism: The International Teaching of the Working Class,* p. 65.

57. Carl A. Linden, *The Soviet Party-State: The Politics of Ideocratic Despotism* (New York: Praeger, 1983), p. 97.
58. M. A. Suslov, *Selected Speeches and Writings*, p. 322.
59. *Ibid.*, p. 287.
60. Nathaniel Davies, "The Angola Decision of 1975: A Personal Memoir," *Foreign Affairs*, vol. 57, Fall 1978, pp. 110–117.
61. *Kommunist*, July 21, 1975, as cited in Stephen S. Kaplan, *Diplomacy of Power* (Washington, D.C.: The Brookins Institute Press, 1981), p. 195.
62. M. A. Suslov, "According to Lenin's Path to Communism," *Marksizm-Leninizm i sovremennaia epokha*, Vol. III, pp. 67–82.
63. Still known as the Congo.
64. M. A. Suslov, Address to the XX Congress of the French Communist Party (PFC), December 14, 1972, *Tass International Service Release in English 1436 GMT*, December 14, 1972.
65. *Ibid.*
66. For a well-balanced analysis of Eurocommunism and its effect on Soviet foreign policy, see: Vernon V. Asparturian, Jiri Valenta, and David P. Burke, Eds. *Eurocommunism between East and West* (Bloomington, Ind.: Indiana Univ., Press, 1980), especially Jiri Valenta's article, "Eurocommunism and the USSR," pp. 103–123.
67. Shelepin continued to pose a threat to Brezhnev, and it is conceivable that the decision to remove him was finally made when Brezhnev became ill in 1975. This view is suggested in Michael Voslensky, *Nomenklatura: The Soviet Ruling class, An Insider's Report* (Garden City, N.Y.: Doubleday, 1984), p. 260.
68. Christian Duval, "Suslov and Shcherbitsky at Odds on Brezhnev's Role in Foreign Policy," *Radio Liberty Research Bulletin*, RL 234/73, July 26, 1973, pp. 1–2.
69. *Pravda*, July 14, 1973.

NOTES TO CHAPTER XVII

1. KPSS, *XXV S'ezd KPSS, February 24-March 3, 1976, stenograficheskii otchet*, Vol. I (Moscow, 1976), pp. 18–19.
2. Georges Marchais, the Secretary General of the PCF, like Tito, declined to come to the XXV Party Congress.
3. *Ibid.*, Vol. I, pp. 369–373 and 411–415; Vol. II, pp. 61–64.
4. Erwin Weit, *At the Red Summit: Interpreter Behind the Iron Curtain* (New York: Macmillan, 1973), p. 139, as cited in Jan F. Triska, "Eurocommunism and the Decline of Proletarian Internationalism," in Vernon V. Asparturian, et al, *Eurocommunism Between East and West*, p. 73.
5. M. A. Suslov, "Our Epoch—The Triumph of Marxism-Leninism," *Marksizm-Leninizm i sovremennaia epokha*, Vol. III, pp. 166–174.
6. *Pravda*, March 18, 1976.
7. UPI, Moscow, March 18, 1976, RH/ASB/M, 2229/76.
8. *Pravda*, January 27, 1982.
9. *Pravda*, August 6, 1975.

10. Richard F. Staar, Ed. *Yearbook on International Communist Affairs, 1976*, pp. X–XIII; R. Judson Mitchel, *Ideology of a Superpower* (Stanford, Ca.: Hoover Institution Press, 1982), pp. 71–87.
11. The economic data cited in this chapter is based on *USSR: Measures of Economic Growth and Development, 1950–1980* (Washington, D.C.: Joint Economic Committee, U.S. Congress, Government Printing Office, 1982).
12. The Soviet norm for housing in the 1970s was 9 square meters of space per person.
13. Mikhail Bulgakov's *The Master and Margarita* was written in the late 1930s, but was first published only in 1966–1967 in a censured form in the journal *Moskva*. For an English translation see Mikhail Bulgakov, *The Master and Margarita* (New York: Grove Press, 1967).
14. M. A. Suslov, *Marksizm-Leninizm i sovremennaia epokha*, Vol. III, pp. 180–186.
15. *Ibid.*, pp. 261–285.
16. *Pravda*, June 17, 1977.
17. Kirilenko's decline began in the early 1970s, accelerating in the second half of the decade. Although it has been generally assumed that the decline was connected with his continued championing of the machine-building industry in the face of a more balanced program advocated by Brezhnev under the Eleventh Five-Year Plan and by Brezhnev's changing perception about his replacement, no definite explanation has been found to this day for his fall.
18. *Pravda*, April 18, 1979.
19. *Radio Liberty Research Bulletin*, RL 137/79, May, 2, 1979, pp. 3–5.
20. Martin Ebon, *The Andropov File* (New York: McGraw-Hill, 1983), p. 133.
21. Harry Gelman, *The Brezhnev Politburo and the Decline of Detente*, pp. 178–179.
22. Associated Press, October 20, 1979, 200034/79.
23. *Ibid.*
24. Roy Medvedev, *All Stalin's Men*, pp. 62–63.
25. M. A. Suslov, *Selected Speeches and Writings*, p. 361.
25. M. A. Suslov, *Selected Speeches and Writings*, p. 191.
27. *Ibid.*
28. Mikhail Agursky, "Suslov i russkii natsionalizm" (Suslov and Russian Nationalism), *Posev*, No. 6, May 1982, pp. 30–33.
29. For example, the incorporation of Georgia into the Russian empire was spurred as much by Georgian desire to protect itself from constant Turkish incursions as by Russian interests to outflank the Turks, while the first phase of the Russian incursion into Central Asia was largely engineered by ambitious generals who often disregarded orders emanating from St. Petersburg.
30. Carl A. Linden, *The Soviet Party State: The Politics of Ideocratic Despotism*, pp. 94–96.
31. John B. Dunlop, *The Faces of Contemporary Russian Nationalism*, pp. 308–311.
32. *Ibid.*
33. John B. Dunlop, *The New Russian Nationalism* (New York: Praeger, 1986), p. 13.
34. Roy Medvedev, *All Stalin's Men*, p. 80.
35. For an analysis of change in Soviet literature, see: Katerina Clark, *The Soviet Novel: History as Ritual* (Chicago: Univ. of Chicago Press, 1981), and "The Mobility of the Canon: Socialist Realism and Chingiz Aitmatov's *I dol'she veka dlitsia den'*,"

Slavic Review, Vol. 43 (4), Winter 1984, pp. 573–587.

36. Rashidov, an Uzbek, was a candidate member of the Politburo for more than twenty years, and Mukhitndinov, also an Uzbek, was a full member of the Politburo during Khrushchev's era.

37. Nikolai Valentinov, *The Early Years of Lenin* (Ann Arbor, Mich: Univ. of Michigan Press, 1969), p. 265.

38. *Pravda,* October 17, 1979.

39. M. A. Suslov, "Historical Correctness of Lenin's Ideas and Cause," *Kommunist,* No. 4, March 1980.

40. After Lenin's 1902 programmatic essay *What is to be Done?* that served as the basis for the platform of the Second Congress in 1903.

41. *Ibid.*

42. FBIS/SU (Foreign Broadcast Information Service) *Daily Report: Soviet Union,* March 2, 1979, p. R26.

43. Associated Press, Berlin, April 12, 1981.

44. *Ibid.*

45. Details of Suslov's April 23 visit to Warsaw are found in the *New York Times,* April 25, 1981, *Washington Post,* April 24, 1981, *Christian Science Monitor,* April 24 and 27, 1981, the *Manchester Guardian,* April 24, 1981, and in the Reuter and Associated Press dispatches of April 24, 1981, FF061, FF116.

46. The summary of the speech was released by Tass to the foreign press on the same day. Pertinent quotations may be found in the *Daily Telegraph* (London), October 15, 1981, and in M. A. Suslov, *Marksizm-Leninizm is sovremennaia epokha,* Vol. III, pp. 346–368.

47. Zhores A. Medvedev, *Gorbachev* (New York/London: W. W. Norton, 1986), pp. 87–89.

48. Chernenko had been a member of the Secretariat since March 1976 and candidate member of the Politburo since October 1977. He was appointed full member of the Politburo in November 1978.

49. Tikhonov had been a candidate member of the Politburo since September 1978. He was appointed full member in November 1979.

50. It should be pointed out that Shcherbitsky changed his allegiance in 1982, and apparently supported Andropov rather than Chernenko in the succession crisis after Brezhnev's death.

51. M. A. Suslov, *Marksizm-Leninizm i sovremennaia epokha,* Vol. III, pp. 222–234.

52. *KPSS, XXVI S'ezd KPSS, February 23-March 3, 1981, stenograficheskii otchet,* Vol. I (Moscow 1982).

53. *Pravda,* January 27, 1982.

54. Jonathan Steele and Eric Abraham, *Andropov in Power* (Oxford, U.K.: Martin Robertson, 1983), pp. 140–141. Variants of this story have appeared in a number of Andropov biographies: Vladimir Solovyov and Elena Klepikova. *Yuri Andropov: A Secret Passage into the Kremlin* (New York: Macmillan, 1983), pp. 224–225; Ilya Zemtsov, *Andropov* (Jerusalem, Israel: IRICS Publishers, 1983), pp. 76–78; Zhores A. Medvedev, *Andropov* (New York/London: W. W. Norton, 1983), pp. 93–96; Andrew Nagorski, "The Making of Andropov, 1982," *Harper's,* February 1983, pp. 23–26; Sidney Ploss, "Signs of Struggle," *Problems of Communism,* September-

October, 1982, pp. 43–44. Christian Schmidt-Hauer, *Gorbachev: The Path to Power* (Topsfield, Mass.: Salem House Publishers, 1986), pp. 72–74.
55. Aldous Huxley, *Grey Eminence,* p. 236.

NOTES TO EPILOGUE

1. P. Rodionov, First Deputy Director of the Institute of Marxism-Leninizm in "Loyal Son of the Party and the Soviet People," *Izvestia,* November 21, 1982.
2. *Ibid.*
3. T. H. Rigby, "Political Legitimacy, Weber and Communist Mono-organizational Systems," in T. H. Rigby and Ferenc Feher, Eds., *Political Legitimation in Communist States* (London: Macmillan, 1982), pp. 1–26.
4. Max Weber, *The Theory of Social and Economic Organization,* trans. by A. M. Henderson and Talcott Parsons (Glencoe, Illinois, 1947), pp. 328–392.
5. *New York Times,* November 5, 1987.
6. *Time,* September 9, 1985.
7. Mikhail Gorbachev, *Political Report of the CPSU Central Committee to the XXVIIth Congress of CPSU,* February 25, 1986 (Moscow: Novosti Press Agency Publishing House, 1986).
8. For a discussion of the forces of reform and counter-reform in the Soviet Union see: Stephen F. Cohen, "The Friends and Foes of Change: Reformers and Conservatism in the Soviet Union," in Stephen Cohen, Alexander Rabinowitch, and Robert Sharlet, Eds. *The Soviet Union Since Stalin* (Bloomington, Ind." Indiana University Press, 1980); Seweryn Bialer, *The Soviet Paradox* (New York: Alfred A. Knopf, 1986), especially Chapter 8, "The Politics of Reform in the Soviet Union."
9. At the time of this writing, Gorbachev has launched a massive campaign against alcoholism and absentism, initiated an experimental program for energy and civilian machine building, dismantled the industrial associations established by the economic reform of 1965, closed half-a-dozen central ministries, and created the new State Agro-Industrial Committee-*Gosagrom.* In an effort to improve the delivery of consumer goods and services, he has approved the establishment of small privately operated production and retail sales outlets. In the area of labor policy, Gorbachev has initiated the redeployment of labor in certain industries in an attempt to improve productivity. In agriculture, he has introduced two new farm incentives that are reminiscent of Lenin's reforms during the NEP. The farmers can now dispose their excess production over objectives according to their own judgment, and they have also been granted the option of settling their procurement obligations on certain basic produce through a money tax which appears to be an adaptation of Lenin's *prodnalog* (tax-in-kind). The private lot program has also been expanded to increase the production of vegetables and fruit.
10. A number of recent events attest to the emergence of a more liberal censorship policy. Anatoly Rybakov's epic novel of the Stalin years *Children of the Arbat* has now been published after many years of lying on the censor's shelves. The recent

release of the movie *Repentance*—a fictional but readily recognizable depiction of the terror and treachery during the Stalin era—also confirms the emergence of a more liberal censorship policy. There are also reports that Boris Pasternak's *Doctor Zhivago* will finally be made available to the Soviet public in 1988.

11. For a concise review of the new Soviet electoral practices, see: Werner G. Hahn, "Electoral Choice in the Soviet Bloc," *Problems of Communism*, March-April 1987, pp. 29–39.

12. Gorbachev's report to the XXVIIth Party Congress does not contain a single word about Third World socialist-oriented states and only a very general and uncommitted statement about Soviet support for national liberation.

13. Rajan Menon, Speech at the Kennan Institute, Washington, D.C., April 23, 1986.

14. Mikhail Gorbachev, Speech to the Khabarovsk party *activ* of July 31, 1986, reported in *FBIS Daily Report: Soviet Union,* August 4, 1986.

15. The most influential proponent of this view is Richard Pipes whose Fall 1984 article in *Foreign Affairs* "Can the Soviet Union Reform" continues to be the basis of the argument that Gorbachev's attempt at reform is doomed to failure.

16. A preliminary majority opinion is contained in the RAND/UCLA Center for the Study of Soviet International Behavior and the W. Averell Harriman Institute for Advanced Study of the Soviet Union, *The 27th Congress of the Communist Party of the Soviet Union: A Report from the Airlie House Conference,* December 1986.

17. The 27th Congress of the Communist Party of the Soviet Union: A Report from the Airlie House Conference, pp. 19–41.

18. Western analysts have consistently questioned the unity of the top leadership, arguing that Yegor Ligachev, Nikolai Ryzhkov, Vitaly Vorotnikov and Victor Chebrikov and Eduard Shevarnadze (appointed under Gorbachev) are men with impressive personal records who are quite independent minded in their decision-making, causing the internal dynamics of the Politburo to be less dependent on personal loyalties and more circumscribed by issues and power politics of interest groups.

19. The two most prominent specialists expressing this view are Stephen Cohen and Alexander Yanov. Cohen has voiced this view in a number of television interviews, and Yanov in a May 1987 article in the *New York Times*.

20. *New York Times,* May 24, 1987.

21. T. G. Butson, *Gorbachev,* New York: Stein and Day, 1985, and Christian Schmidt-Hauer, *Gorbachev: The Path to Power,* Toppsfield, Mass.: Salem House Publishers, 1986.

22. At the time of this writing approximately 40% of the senior *apparatchiks* and technocrats holding important positions in the Party and the government have been retired or fired. They have been replaced by younger and more flexible officials committed to the Gorbachev reform.

23. Jerry F. Hough, "Gorbachev's Strategy," *Foreign Affairs,* Spring 1986. Dr. Hough has also spoken on the same subject at the University of California, Berkeley XIth Annual Berkeley-Stanford Conference on Reforming Socialist Systems, April 3, 1987.

24. The promotion in June 1987 of Alexander Yakovlev, Victor Nikonov, and Nikolai Slyunkov to full membership in the Politburo, and of Defense Minister Dmitri Yazov to candidate membership in the Politburo in June 1987 has dramatically strengthened

Gobachev's hold on the Soviet leadership and weakened the bureaucratic old guard inherited from the Brezhnev regime.

25. Alexis de Tocqueville, *L'Ancien Regime et la Revolution* (1856).

26. Gorbachev's reform program contains elements of three different views: (1) Tat'iana Zaslavskaia's view that the main objective of the Soviet economy is to improve the performance of workers and managers by establishing better work incentives, (2) to a lesser extent, Konstanin Val'tukh's "technological" view that there is a crying need for massive investment in manufacturing and agriculture, and (3) Abel Aganbegian's official view as Chairman of the Commission for the Study of Productive Forces, that there is no need for a systemic transformation in the direction of a market economy.

27. Theodore H. Van Laue, *Why Lenin, Why Stalin?* (New York: J. B. Lippincot Company, 1964), pp. 49–51.

28. *New York Times*, November 3, 1987.

29. Mikhail Gorbachev, "In His Words," from the book *Perestroika: New Thinking for Our Country and the World*, special report in *U.S. News & World Report*, November 9, 1987.

INDEX